ARCHAEOLOGY

AN INTRODUCTION

This fully updated fifth edition of a classic classroom text is essential reading for core courses in archaeology. It explains how the subject emerged from an amateur pursuit in the eighteenth century into a serious discipline, and explores changing trends in interpretation in recent decades. The authors convey the excitement of archaeology while helping readers to evaluate new discoveries by explaining the methods and theories that lie behind them. In addition to drawing upon examples and case studies from many regions of the world and periods of the past, the book incorporates the authors' own fieldwork, research and teaching.

Archaeology: an introduction continues to include key references and guidance to help new readers find their way through the ever-expanding range of archaeological publications. The comprehensive glossary and bibliography are complemented by a support website to assist further study and wider learning.

New to the fifth edition:

- inclusion of the latest survey techniques and updated material on developments in dating, DNA analysis, isotopes and population movement
- coverage of new themes such as identity, personhood, and how different societies are defined from an anthropological point of view
- the impact of climate change and sustainability on heritage management
- increased coverage of the historical development of archaeological ideas and methods
- attractively redesigned four-colour text, and colour illustrations for the first time.

Kevin Greene is Reader in Archaeology at Newcastle University.
Tom Moore is Lecturer in Archaeology at Durham University.

What reviewers said about earlier editions:

'A most important book. Student feedback says that that this is the ideal book – easy to read and follow at the right level, and not too complex.' – Mick Aston, University of Bristol

'A first-class book, invaluable to beginners at adult education classes and on first-year university courses.' – *British Book News*

'This book scores a bull's eye.' – *Current Archaeology*

'An attractive introduction, useful to beginners in the field, whatever their background.' – *Antiquity*

'Kevin Greene has succeeded admirably in his task of providing an introduction to archaeology for sixth-formers, undergraduates, adult students, and the general reader with his clear exposition and skilful use of illustrations.' – *CBA Newsletter*

'A clear outline of the way archaeology has developed.' – *History Today*

'The content is sound, undogmatic and uncontroversial. As a general introduction to the subject and interpretation of the techniques of modern archaeology, it deserves to reach a wide audience.' – *Teaching History*

'A splendid book and a worthy introduction to the subject.' – *Times Educational Supplement*

ARCHAEOLOGY

An Introduction

Fifth edition

Kevin Greene and Tom Moore

Routledge
Taylor & Francis Group

LONDON AND NEW YORK

First published 1983
Reprinted 1986, 1988
Revised edition 1990, 1991
Reprinted 1993, 1994
Revised edition 1995
Reprinted 1996, 1997 by Routledge
Fourth edition 2002

This fifth edition first published 2010
by Routledge
2 Park Square, Milton Park, Abingdon, Oxon OX14 4RN
Simultaneously published in the USA and Canada
by Routledge
711 Third Avenue, New York, NY 10017

Routledge is an imprint of the Taylor & Francis Group, an informa business

© 2002 Kevin Greene
© 2010 Kevin Greene and Tom Moore

Designed and typeset by Fakenham Photosetting Ltd, Fakenham, Norfolk

British Library Cataloguing in Publication Data
A catalogue record for this book is available from the British Library

Library of Congress Cataloging-in-Publication Data
A catalog record for this book has been requested

ISBN13: 978-0-415-49638-4 (hbk)
ISBN13: 978-0-415-49639-1 (pbk)

Printed and bound in India by Replika Press Pvt. Ltd.

Contents

List of illustrations

List of tables

Preface

WHO IS THIS BOOK AIMED AT?

Although this is essentially a textbook, it is also aimed at general readers who would not appreciate the rather mechanical statements of aims, objectives and learning outcomes that have come to characterise much of how archaeology is taught in Britain. We have tried to provide an informative book for just about any interested reader from mid-teens upwards whose interest has been stimulated by visiting archaeological sites, or watching television programmes that show archaeological methods as well as results. It is meant to be readable, rather than exhaustively comprehensive, and, while we have attempted to draw upon a wide range of examples from around the world, both authors have made the most of their own areas of expertise in the archaeology of Britain and Europe in the first millennia BC to AD. Since many other introductory books about archaeology have been written by prehistorians, readers may notice a larger number of examples drawn from historical periods in this book.

Kevin Greene has always been just as interested in *how* archaeology works as in its outcome. His knowledge and experience of archaeology began during childhood in Devon, and developed in Cardiff through study for a degree and then a PhD in the late 1960s and early 1970s. After teaching Adult Education students in north-eastern England from 1973 to 1977 he developed an introductory undergraduate course – not just for archaeology students but also for other students taking some archaeology as part of a broader degree. This continuously evolving course was the original inspiration for a book designed to place the information imparted in lectures into a wider context, and to point students towards resources for further independent reading and study. Kevin has always found the wide reading required to keep introductory teaching (and this book) up to date tremendously stimulating, and has learned a lot from having to explain archaeological ideas to different audiences ranging from schoolchildren to academics. Furthermore, this wide range of reading and teaching has also extended the scope of his research publications – how else could a specialist on Roman economics and technology have published an article about Gordon Childe and the concept of a 'Neolithic Revolution' (Greene 1999)?

Tom Moore comes from a very different generation of archaeologists, and was still at primary school when the first edition of this book was published. After working in contract archaeology, he studied archaeology at Durham University, and then worked briefly at Newcastle University before returning to a lecturing post at Durham. His awareness of current archaeological methods has been gained from extensive fieldwork and excavation projects in Britain and France. Tom's particular interest in the transition from later prehistory to the Roman period means that he has always had to think deeply about the cultural meaning of the sites and artefacts he has investigated. He is very interested in concepts such as identity and ethnicity, and ways in which ideas about 'Celtic' and 'Roman' Britain and Gaul have been used (and abused) in creating national awareness in England and France in the recent past and present.

Thus, both Kevin and Tom are keenly aware that archaeology, its interpretation, and the presentation of its findings, are not simply a matter of neutral academic interest. 'Heritage' and the management of cultural resources are important components of the way we live today, and how we relate to our world – whether as tourists visiting Stonehenge, professional archaeologists recording sites threatened by development, or military advisers attempting to minimise the looting of sites and museums during wars. As university lecturers, we are both driven by the need to produce research publications for scrutiny by a national Research Assessment Exercise (last conducted in 2008) and the forthcoming Research Excellence Framework (to be carried out in 2012). We are both nevertheless determined to maintain the honourable tradition of communicating archaeology to students and a wider audience. We see our jobs as lecturers primarily as a way of encouraging students to learn through placing basic information in a wider context and providing plenty of signposts for them to follow during independent study. Because archaeology touches upon so many different disciplines, and introduces so many concepts that make us think about our place in the world, we believe that it provides outstanding intellectual rewards for professionals and amateurs alike.

HOW DOES THIS EDITION DIFFER FROM ITS PREDECESSORS?

Archaeology has undergone many changes since the first edition of this book appeared in 1983. The third edition (1995, taken over from Batsford by Routledge in 1996) was substantially rewritten, and acquired many new illustrations. The fourth edition (2002) was much longer, and placed archaeology into a wider context by expanding the accounts of both its historical development and its current theoretical concerns. Archaeological publication has gathered pace: Kevin's database of items relevant to introductory teaching includes 560 books published from 1900 to 1982, 1,220 published from 1983 to 1994, 1,485 from 1995 to 2001, and a further 700 from 2002 to 2008 – and many further items from the latest date-range are still being added. Guidance about further reading was enhanced in the fourth edition, and it remains an important component of the fifth.

A remarkable development since the late 1990s has been the expansion of resources available through the Internet. However, this also led to the creation of many poorly referenced and sometimes inaccurate websites on archaeology, the dangers of which many users were unaware. Kevin responded to this trend in 1997 by creating an 'electronic companion' to the third edition, using the book's chapter and section headings as a framework for organising links to relevant websites. A more sophisticated design was created for the fourth edition in 2002, but by 2008 it had become impossible to keep up with repairing broken links resulting from changed Internet addresses and disappearing pages. This level of instability is the reason why Internet addresses are not included in the printed text of this edition. A new website, hosted by Routledge rather than Kevin's university, provides a new range of educational resources to support the fifth edition.

The principal difference between the fifth edition and its predecessors is the addition of a co-author. Kevin spent two years from 2005 to 2007 as a British Academy Research Reader investigating the Roman economy, followed by a semester of university research leave to complete the publication of this research. The demands of returning to normal teaching and administrative duties in 2008 made it impossible for him to consider preparing a revised edition of the *Introduction* without assistance. Tom Moore was recruited by Routledge to carry out the process of updating each chapter and adding new reading matter and illustrations. Kevin has attempted to integrate Tom's additions seamlessly into the text, as well as introducing changes of his own. As he is almost exactly the same age as Kevin was when he wrote the first edition in 1983, Tom has injected new ideas about interpretation, and extensive experience of current fieldwork and excavation methods.

WHAT IS OUR VIEW OF ARCHAEOLOGY?

Kevin produced three editions of this book before an acute reader spotted that he had never actually defined 'archaeology'; Kristian Kristiansen noted its continuing absence from the fourth edition, but referred with approval to the concluding statement (Kristiansen 2009: 39, unfortunately introducing a spelling error). Very similar versions of this concluding phrase appear in all editions, including this one: 'A discipline that incorporates so much uncertainty and so many different academic approaches, while ignoring the conventional boundaries between the sciences and humanities, is well worth studying at school, university, or as a leisure pursuit.'

One definition of archaeology is included in the introduction to an entry that Kevin wrote for an (as yet unpublished) online encyclopedia:

The material remains of the past provide a common focus for the work of all archaeologists. While some study specific artifacts or monuments, others examine landscapes formed by human activities over long periods. Archaeology covers several million years, ranging from geological periods when species ancestral to humans are first found right up to recent historical times, including the Industrial Revolution. A distinction is frequently made between prehistory, for which no documentary sources are available, and text-aided archaeology.

Kristian Kristiansen's own definition explains how archaeological research leads not only to understanding the past, but to conservation in the present; we wholeheartedly endorse his emphasis upon the '*duality of practice*':

Archaeology is the study and preservation of the material remains of past societies and their environment, that nowadays also includes modern material culture. The objective is likewise twofold: to reconstruct past lifeworlds in order to understand and explain the historical conditions that governed people's life as it unfolded, both in their local settings and on a larger historical scale of prehistoric and historic societies; and to preserve the archaeological record in the landscape and in museums for future study and use.

(Kristiansen 2009: 4–5)

Definitions only take the reader so far. The essence of archaeology is captured very well by the moment in 1922 when Howard Carter first glimpsed the treasure of Tutankhamun by candlelight through a small hole in the wall that sealed the tomb (Winstone 1991):

As my eyes grew accustomed to the light, details of the room within emerged slowly from the mist, strange animals, statues, and gold – everywhere the glint of gold. For the moment – an eternity it must have seemed to the others standing by – I was struck dumb with amazement, and when Lord Carnarvon, unable to stand the suspense any longer, inquired anxiously, 'Can you see anything?' it was all I could do to get out the words, 'Yes, wonderful things.'

(quoted in Stiebing 1993: 83–4)

Although Carter's actual words may have been less memorable (Bahn 1996b: ix), the idea of a dark space seen from a very small point of view – with a flickering light – is a highly appropriate metaphor for the way in which most archaeologists work. We recognise first those things that are most familiar to us (animals, statues), and our eyes are attracted by superficial signs of value (glinting gold), but we find it difficult to explain them convincingly to onlookers. The importance of understanding any individual's perspective is underlined by thinking about how and why Howard Carter came to be standing at that place at that particular moment (Reeves and Taylor 1992). Foreigners had access to the archaeology of Egypt because of European political domination, and this excavation was financed by a rich member of the British aristocracy indulging in a form of cultural activity that had become socially respectable and widespread from the eighteenth century. The pursuit of the tomb of a Pharaoh, rather than the investigation (for example) of a peasant village, clearly reflected the concerns of the ruling classes. It also offered the possibility of personal fame and the acquisition of prestigious items for display in a public museum – a kind of institution that was itself a product of nineteenth-century ideas about art and education. Such factors become clearer with the benefit of 88 years' hindsight, but are not always so obvious in the work of contemporary archaeologists.

Acknowledgements

Many individuals and organisations in Britain and abroad have given help in providing illustrations; we hope that most of them have been acknowledged in the captions, but all deserve thanks for devoting time to looking out particular photographs or drawings for us or for reading parts of the text. In particular, we would like to thank the following people: Julia Greene, Claire Nesbitt, Frances Mawer, Sheila Newton, Christina Unwin, Peter Rowley-Conwy, Rob Witcher, Becky Gowland, Mike Church, Chris Gerrard, Greger Larson, Sarah Semple, Sam Turner, Ian Bailiff, Bob Johnston, Steve Trow, Simon Cox, Peter Davenport, Neil Holbrook, Vincent Guichard, Andrew Moore, John Curtis, John Creighton, Sam Lucy, Vicki Herring, Andrew Parkin, Jo Buckberry, Eberhard Sauer, Paola Moscati, A. Wadsworth.

A number of anonymous reviewers also provided some helpful comments. Finally, our grateful thanks go to Moira Taylor for all her assistance throughout, as well as to Matt Reynolds and Matthew Gibbons for their patience in seeing the volume to completion.

Referencing

This book aims not only to be an introduction to archaeology but to enable the reader to delve deeper into the debates and techniques of archaeology. We have referenced throughout the text, and provided signposts to further reading. If you are about to become, or are already, a student of archaeology you will recognise the request to 'reference your information' – it is one of the tenets of academia that you acknowledge where ideas and data come from. This also helps you explore the evidence and theories yourself so that you can construct your own opinions and arguments.

All categories of reference are listed, in alphabetical order according to their authors' names, in a consolidated bibliography at the end of the book. Three levels of information lead the reader from general to more specific publications and information sources.

1 Key references indicated beneath each heading within the text give the author, short title and year of publication of the most useful books (or occasionally chapters) on that particular subject, in preference to more specialised articles in periodicals. These should be consulted first.
2 Further reading sections, placed at the end of each chapter, are designed to lead the reader to more detailed publications or general works on related topics.
3 References within the text are given using the Harvard system (author/year/page, e.g. Evans 1990: 236) and indicate specific publications – often periodical papers – that provide examples, case studies or other forms of supporting evidence for information or statements made in the text.

Glossary and index

Many important terms are indicated in **bold** throughout the text. Some of these terms are also included in the glossary (pp. 313–21). Terms defined in the glossary are preceded by an asterisk in the index (for example '* anthropology').

Make good use of the table of contents and the index to locate topics you are interested in, and use cross-references within the text to find other pages with related information (for example 'above, p. 63').

Frontispiece   Time line and major developments in the human past

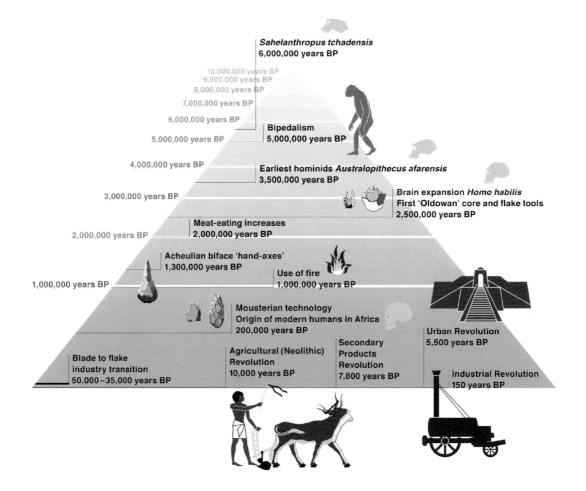

CHAPTER 1

The Idea of the Past

1

Our aim in this chapter is to show how some fundamental principles and methods emerged and combined to form the modern discipline known as archaeology. This has been the subject of several complete books, but we will attempt to map the development of archaeology in a wider intellectual context and look in more detail at some themes that are particularly important:

- Interest in landscapes and travel promoted the recognition and recording of **ancient sites**. Visits to sites, together with the habit of **collecting** ancient artefacts and works of art, eventually led to deeper investigations (with the help of excavation) of **early civilisations**.

- The study of **human origins** stimulated profound thinking about concepts of time, and forged lasting links between archaeology and the natural sciences, notably biology and geology. It also underlined the importance of being able to identify and interpret **artefacts** made by early humans.

- The word 'prehistory' was invented in the nineteenth century to describe the long period of human existence – undocumented in historical sources – revealed by newly developed archaeological methods. Later, these methods were applied to the study of other fundamental phenomena such as the **transition from hunting to farming** and the **origins of urbanism**.

These issues are not presented in a strict chronological sequence, and no clear line divides the history of archaeology from its present concerns. Many topics are discussed further in Chapter 6, which looks at more recent trends in theory and interpretation.

1.1 THE INTELLECTUAL HISTORY OF ARCHAEOLOGY

- key references: Trigger, *A history of archaeological thought* 2006; Murray, *Milestones in archaeology* 2007; Schnapp, *The discovery of the past* 1996.

It is important that the benefit of hindsight does not make us forget the constraints of the social and intellectual context in which **antiquaries** lived and worked. For example, in the early nineteenth century the Danish scholars who first organised prehistoric objects into three successive Ages (Stone, Bronze and Iron) assigned them to a very short time span. In mid-seventeenth-century Britain, Bishop Ussher had used the Bible to

calculate that the creation of the Earth took place in 4004 BC, and other estimates were not much earlier (Stiebing 1993: 32; Rowley-Conwy 2007: 6–7). Pressure from developments in geology and biology to adopt a much longer time-scale did not finally displace the biblical scheme until the 1860s. The dating of prehistory underwent major revisions after the radiocarbon dating technique was introduced and accepted in the 1950s, while techniques such as potassium-argon dating revealed that some of the earliest sites with tools made by **hominins** were much earlier than had previously been suspected (Chapter 4).

We may learn a great deal by examining how early antiquaries and archaeologists (the difference between the two will emerge later in this chapter) tackled the formidable problem of making sense of the human past without the help of the libraries, museums, travel and technical facilities available today. At the same time we should take care not to look only at the origins of ideas we still consider important, and ignore the wider setting in which they were formulated. At the most fundamental level it is possible to see the whole idea of looking for origins of things as a peculiarly Western intellectual diversion (Foucault 1970; Trigger 2006: 9–10).

We feel that it is important to place the development of archaeology within a broad intellectual, philosophical and historical framework; however, terms such as **Renaissance**, **Enlightenment** or **Romanticism** are less well known than they once were. Table 1.1 places onto a chronological scale the labels used in this chapter to indicate the cultural, political, philosophical or religious context of a particular approach to archaeology; many of these labels were only invented in the nineteenth century and are used for convenience. It is also worth remembering that in, charting the development of archaeological thought, the contribution of female archaeologists to these advances has often been underplayed because of the social context in which archaeology developed (Diaz-Andreu and Stig-Sørensen 1998; Kehoe and Emmerich 1999: 117). It is also true that this simplified account of intellectual history places Europe and America at its centre, and carries the implication that everything on the chart happened as part of a linear evolution towards the present. Although this kind of thinking can cause all sorts of problems (which are explored in Chapter 6), it may nevertheless be a useful starting point.

Table 1.1 Archaeology and the history of ideas

Intellectual or cultural phase	Date	Characteristics	Impact upon archaeology	Key names (those after '/' relevant to archaeology)
Classical	ancient Greece and Rome	philosophical and scientific outlook, particularly in Greece, embracing both the human and the natural/ physical world	collecting artistic objects, visiting sites, speculation about early human societies	Aristotle, Plato, Lucretius / Herodotus, Pausanias, Tacitus
Late Roman/ Byzantine	fourth century AD to fifteenth century AD	Christian theology emphasising lack of free will, preoccupation with truth against heresy	perpetuation of idea of Roman Empire, collecting Christian relics, pilgrimage to holy sites	St Augustine
Islam	seventh century AD onwards	conquest and conversion of much of Mediterranean Classical world, along with Persia and the East	translation into Arabic of Classical Greek literature, especially on philosophy, medicine and science	Mohammed, Avicenna, Averroes
'Dark Ages'	AD 600–1000	replacement of western Roman Empire by kingdoms of Germanic origin; continuation of scholarly Christian outlook still regarding Rome as its centre, particularly in Britain and France	interest in Roman art, architecture, and literature; relics and pilgrimage	Bede, Alcuin, Charlemagne

Medieval scholasticism	eleventh to fourteenth century AD	expanding interest in Classical intellectual heritage (especially Aristotle), scientific investigation; important background to Renaissance	rediscovery of ancient Greek philosophical and scientific writings preserved by Arab scholars	St Thomas Aquinas, Roger Bacon
Renaissance	fourteenth to sixteenth century AD	interest in humanism as well as theology, flowering of the arts (especially in Italy); broadening of horizons through European voyages of discovery	recording of Greek and Roman buildings and inscriptions, study of Roman architecture to provide models for new buildings	Erasmus, Leonardo da Vinci / Brunelleschi, Cyriac of Ancona
Reformation	sixteenth to seventeenth century AD	rejection of the authority of the Roman Church, greater emphasis on the individual; conflict between science and papal authority	growth of national awareness in Northern Europe leading to studies of local sites	Luther, Calvin, Loyola (Counter-Reformation) / Copernicus
Scientific Revolution	seventeenth century AD	rejection of Aristotle, investigation of the physical world by direct observation and experiment, particularly in astronomy; concept of scientific laws	growing curiosity about ancient sites, recording them using mathematically sound surveying methods	Descartes, Hobbes, Galileo, Isaac Newton, Francis Bacon / Aubrey
Enlightenment	eighteenth century AD	as a result of the Scientific Revolution, increasing explanation of the world in rational rather than religious terms; profound philosophical interest in the evolution of human society; emphasis upon free will and rights	expansion of scientific recording and classification of natural world (including antiquities)	Diderot, Hume, Kant / Stukeley, Winckelmann
Romanticism	late eighteenth to early nineteenth century AD	reaction against Enlightenment rationality: emotional attraction to dramatic, wild landscapes and primitive peoples	increasing national identity and interest in origins of modern nations; preference for 'Noble Savage' rather than 'brutish' image of primitive humans; interest in progress through ages	Rousseau, Schelling, Hegel
Positivism	nineteenth to twentieth century AD	continuation of Enlightenment preference for empiricism, naturalism and science rather than speculation; emergence of sociology	intellectual atmosphere receptive to developments in geology and biology leading to evolutionary theory and the study of human origins	Comte

Evolutionism (Darwinism)	nineteenth to twentieth century AD	concept of natural selection added a new scientific dimension to long-held ideas about the evolution of organisms (including humans); transformed by development of genetics in the twentieth century	extensively adopted as an analogy for explaining (and justifying) changes in societies (Social Darwinism) and for the development of archaeological objects	Lamarck, Darwin, Herbert Spencer / Pitt Rivers
Marxism (communism)	nineteenth to twentieth century AD	theory of social evolution derived from anthropology and ancient history that emphasised the economic basis of social structures, and the notion of revolutionary (rather than gradual) change	particularly important in the twentieth century when archaeologists reacted positively or negatively to developments in Russia, and highly influential in 'explaining' prehistory	Marx, Engels / Childe
nationalism	nineteenth to twentieth century AD	extension of Reformation and Romantic concepts into political action, frequently using evolutionary ideas about natural selection to include notions of racial superiority	extensive archaeological work devoted to establishing connections between modern peoples or nations and 'ancestral' sites and artefacts	Hegel, Byron / Kossinna
Modernism	late nineteenth to late twentieth century AD	culmination of the Enlightenment and positivist confidence in social progress and objective science	fundamental to much archaeological work, especially the 'New Archaeology', up to the 1980s	Hegel, Marx / Binford, David Clarke
Structuralism	early to late twentieth century AD	intellectual movement that relates superficial phenomena such as language, myths, works of art and social institutions to the underlying structure of language	particularly influential upon anthropology, and therefore upon archaeology	Saussure, Barthes, Lévi-Strauss / Hodder
Postmodernism	late twentieth century AD	breaking down of confidence in modernism and grand narratives of social evolution such as Marxism; related to post-structuralism, which denies fixed meanings, simple dichotomies and the pursuit of truths	encourages highly personal archaeological outlook that suspects that all interpretations based on supposedly objective observation are illusions reflecting prevailing power structures	Nietzsche, Lyotard, Foucault, Derrida / Christopher Tilley, Julian Thomas

1.1.1 Archaeology and antiquarianism, prehistory and history

- key references: Sweet, *Antiquaries* 2004; Pearce, *Visions of antiquity* 2007a; Rowley-Conwy, *From Genesis to prehistory* 2007; Daniel and Renfrew, *The idea of prehistory* 1988.

The concept of prehistory is perhaps the single most important contribution made by archaeology to our knowledge of humanity; furthermore, it is based almost exclusively on the interpretation of material evidence. The emergence of prehistoric archaeology in the nineteenth century, although it relied heavily upon natural sciences such as geology and biology, was a remarkable episode that changed people's ideas about themselves (Richard 1993). Indeed, research into human origins in the nineteenth century did as much as the discovery of civilisations to establish public awareness about what was distinctive about archaeology as an intellectual pursuit. Early progress in the study of ancient Greece and Rome established the value of recording sites and artefacts as well as documents and inscriptions; the term **archaeology** was already being used in Jacob Spon's publications of his research in Athens and elsewhere in the seventeenth century (Etienne and Etienne 1992: 38–41). Nevertheless, most historical scholars gave the written word priority over physical evidence, and until quite recently considered archaeology inferior to the study of texts or works of art (Trigger 2006: 498).

Archaeologists still tend to be placed in one of two categories: prehistorians or historical archaeologists. This division is not particularly helpful, but it does distinguish the latter, who study people or places within periods for which written records are available, from the former, who are concerned with any period that lacks documents. Historical archaeologists usually possess a basic framework of dates and a general idea of the society of a particular period into which to fit their findings. In contrast, those who study **prehistory**, a concept only firmly established after 1850 (Clermont and Smith 1990; Rowley-Conwy 2007), have to create some kind of framework for themselves from artefacts and sites alone, normally with the help of analogies drawn from anthropology. The methods used by both kinds of archaeologist today are very much the same, and there is considerable overlap between their ideas and interests, including those who restrict the term 'historical archaeology' to a period beginning around AD 1500 (Hicks and Beaudry 2006). Historians who studied ancient Greece, Rome, or the Bible could set out to locate physical traces on the ground of events and civilisations described in literature; this possibility was simply not available to other historians, natural scientists or collectors who tried to make sense of artefacts or graves surviving from times before the earliest existing written records in other areas, for example pre-Roman Britain.

In 1926 R.G. Collingwood, a British philosopher who combined academic philosophy with extensive involvement in archaeology, disputed the clear distinction generally drawn between history and prehistory:

> Strictly speaking, all history is prehistory, since all historical sources are mere matter, and none are ready-made history; all require to be converted into history by the thought of the historian. And on the other hand, no history is mere prehistory, because no source or group of sources is so recalcitrant to interpretation as the sources of prehistory are thought to be.
>
> (quoted in Van der Dussen 1993: 372)

Collingwood was influenced by his knowledge of the difficulties of linking the general history found in classical documents to the physical remains encountered on Roman sites (and the problems in dating them). Another challenge to the perception of prehistory is exemplified by a Bolivian Indian archaeologist who questioned the simple dichotomy between written and unwritten evidence:

> Prehistory is a Western concept according to which those societies which have not developed writing – or an equivalent system of graphic representation – have no history. This fits perfectly into the framework of evolutionist thought typical of Western cultures.
>
> (Mamani 1989: 51).

This issue will be revisited in Chapter 6; meanwhile we should recognise that prehistory as a distinctive phenomenon seen through Western eyes is not a concept accepted throughout the world (Kehoe 1991b).

1.1.2　The problem of origins and time

- key references: Rowley-Conwy, *From Genesis to prehistory* 2007; Lucas, *Archaeology of time* 2005; Murray, *Time and archaeology* 1999b; Rossi, *The dark abyss of time* 1984.

A quest for origins is only possible in an intellectual framework that has a well-developed concept of time, in particular linear time that progresses from a beginning to an end rather than going around in an endlessly repeating circle of life, death and rebirth (Gell 1992; Bintliff 1999). Recognition of the existence of a significant amount of time before historical records began was also essential before any attempt was made to understand it. Finally, people had to conceptualise using ancient objects, monuments and sites to explore prehistoric time. Many societies have developed sophisticated mythologies which, in association with religion, allow the physical environment to be fitted into an orderly system where natural features may be attributed to the work of gods. Artificial mounds, abandoned occupation sites and ancient objects were often associated with deities, fairies, ancestors or other denizens of the world of mythology, and explanations of this kind abound in surviving folklore. Many prehistoric sites in England have traditional names that reveal this background, for example the large standing stones in Yorkshire known as The Devil's Arrows.

For those early prehistorians who believed in a biblical Creation dating to 4004 BC, as calculated by Bishop Ussher, or by relating Roman and Greek historical documents back to the Old Testament (Rowley-Conwy 2007, 6–9), there was at least an upper limit to the age of any of the items that they studied. If not, an apparently insoluble range of questions was raised. Which sites and objects were in use at the same time,

and how many years had elapsed between those that looked primitive and those that seemed more advanced? Did technical improvements represent a gradual series of inventions made by a single people, or did innovations mark the arrival of successive waves of conquerors with superior skills? The first step essential to any progress was a recognition of the amount of time occupied by human development in prehistory, and this advance took place in the first half of the nineteenth century. In the view of Bruce Trigger, the liberation of archaeologists from this 'impasse of antiquarianism' had two distinct consequences. The first was the development of new dating methods in Scandinavia, and the second was the study of human origins in France and England, both of which 'added vast, hitherto unimagined, time depth to human history' (Trigger 2006: 121). We will examine dating methods in Chapter 4, and look at the more fundamental and dramatic issue of human origins later in this chapter.

Hesiod, in the eighth century BC, had talked of five ages of man, from the Golden Age to the Iron Age. Roman philosophical poetry written by Lucretius in the first century BC contained ideas about the successive importance of stone, bronze and iron as materials for the manufacture of implements (Schnapp 1996: 332–3; see also below, pages 21–4). Although this **Three-Age System** was widely accepted as a philosophical concept by AD 1800, it was not applied in a practical way to ancient objects until 1816 (Rowley-Conwy 2007: 37–8; below: 23). Some individuals, such as the British **antiquarian** Thomas Wright, argued against its validity as late as the 1870s (Rowley-Conwy 2007: 2). It is difficult now for us to appreciate the basic problem that confronted historians or philosophers in literate societies right up to the eighteenth century AD. They were able to pursue their origins through surviving historical records, but beyond the earliest documents lay a complete void, containing unverifiable traditions that merged into a mythological and religious world of ancestors and gods. Gould's thoughtful examination of the complex and varying concepts of time held by nineteenth-century geologists (1987) contains many surprises for anyone who had assumed that they rapidly adopted a 'modern' outlook. Indeed, the depth of archaeological and geological time is still grossly underestimated in the contemporary mythology of cartoons, in which prehistoric humans use stone axes or wooden clubs, wear simple animal-skin garments and have trouble with dinosaurs (**Fig. 1.1**).

Figure 1.1 In *One Million Years BC* (Hammer Films Ltd, 1968), humans competed for survival with dinosaurs, volcanoes, and other bands of equally ferocious humans. Curiously, they had developed tools, but little language – despite their thoroughly modern physiques. Ideas about human origins and early development amongst archaeologists, biologists and evolutionary psychologists remain controversial and confusing, but all agree that dinosaurs had been safely extinct for many millions of years. (*British Film Institute*)

The fundamental problem of conceptualising chronology did not change significantly between the Greek and Roman period and the eighteenth century AD (Rossi 1984). If ancient sites and artefacts were considered at all, they were linked to peoples and events known from documents. Samuel Johnson expressed a view characteristic of an English scholar of the eighteenth century: 'All that is really known of the ancient state of Britain is contained in a few pages. We can know no more than what old writers have told us' (quoted in Trigger 2006: 119).

1.2 THE EMERGENCE OF ARCHAEOLOGICAL METHODS

- key references: Stiebing, *Uncovering the past* 1993; Schnapp, *The discovery of the past* 1996; Romer and Romer, *Great excavations* 2000; Murray, *Milestones in archaeology* 2007.

1.2.1 Greece and Rome

- key references: Blundell, *The origins of civilisation in Greek and Roman thought* 1986; Hall, *Inventing the barbarian* 1989.

Greek and Roman culture and commerce grew from modest origins but eventually embraced the whole Mediterranean region as well as parts of its hinterland. Something akin to anthropology (rather than archaeology) existed in ancient Greece. Greek writers such as Herodotus, Posidonius and later Strabo wrote accounts of encounters with 'barbarian' (i.e. non-Greek) peoples such as the 'Celts' in Iron Age Europe, whom they described as heavy drinkers and head-hunters. This curiosity stemmed from their interest in the origins of their own society and political system. On a more practical level, Greek and Roman observations were useful to other travellers and colonial administrators. Such ideas were taken up again with enthusiasm during the Renaissance by Cyriac of Ancona, William Camden and John Leland (**Box 1.2**) and advanced to a stage where travel and observation developed into archaeological fieldwork.

In the Roman period Julius Caesar described life in Iron Age Gaul in the 50s BC (Riggsby 2006), and Tacitus wrote an interesting account of the Germans in the late first century AD (Rives 1999). It was not simply scientific curiosity that motivated Tacitus' description of the simple life and virtues of these barbarians, however; he wished to make a political point by contrasting them with the corruption of Roman society. His *Germania* is an early example of the **Noble Savage myth**, a philosophical and literary concept that regained popularity in the eighteenth century in the writings of Rousseau (Ellingson 2001). Unlike his Greek predecessors or Caesar, Tacitus made no attempt to gather first-hand information by travelling among the Germans. He embellished and updated Greek writings with information from army officers and civil servants from his own social circle who had held appointments on the frontiers of the Roman Empire.

Collections of antique objects were not uncommon in the past, from Babylon in the sixth century BC to the civilisations of Greece and Rome, although many were prized more for their religious or symbolic value than for their potential as sources of information about the past (Trigger 2006: 43–8). Romans collected Greek sculptures, and appreciated stages in the historical development of art and architecture. Tourists had already begun to visit ancient monuments, not only in Italy and Greece but also in Egypt. The Emperor Hadrian (AD 117–38) is a good example of a traveller and collector: during official tours of the Empire he visited ancient Greek shrines and restored or completed Greek buildings. He designed a country villa inland from Rome at Tivoli that housed a library and a collection of Greek sculpture, and incorporated gardens and lakes reminiscent of places he had visited in Egypt and Greece. Hadrian even adopted a new curly hairstyle and a beard in the manner of Greek philosophers, in contrast to the severe clean-shaven and short-haired appearance of his predecessors (**Fig. 1.2–3**). A few years after the death of Hadrian, Pausanias – a wealthy Greek traveller and geographer from Asia Minor – wrote a guide book, *Description of Greece*, that remained indispensable to anyone studying the art and architecture of ancient Greece at first hand up to the nineteenth century (Alcock, Cherry and Elsner 2001; Pretzler 2007).

The antiquarianism of the Classical world had not developed any further before it was swept away by the political and economic problems of the third and fourth centuries AD. The Western half of the Roman Empire gradually disintegrated and was invaded and settled in the fifth and sixth centuries AD by Goths, Franks and Anglo-Saxons – the descendants of Tacitus' Germans. Roman culture did survive to a certain extent under the rule of Germanic kings, and it did of course continue in the (Byzantine) eastern Roman Empire (Angold 2001). However, the Classical inheritance was modified or displaced by the growing importance of Christianity, which paid more attention to contemporary theology and the Bible than to the pagan Classical past.

1.2.2 Medieval attitudes to antiquity

- key references: Murray, *Milestones in archaeology* 2007; Bahn, *Cambridge illustrated history* 1996b: 7–13.

Figure 1.2–3   Behind the Arch of Hadrian, Athens, is the Temple of Zeus Olympius which was begun in the sixth century BC but completed by the Roman Emperor Hadrian in the early second century AD as part of his informed enthusiasm for ancient Greek culture and architecture. Hadrian adopted the beard and curly hair associated with Greek philosophers in contrast to the short straight hair and clean-shaven appearance of his predecessors. *(Stuart and Revett 1794: chapter 3 pl. 1; photograph: Kevin Greene)*

For most of its history, Christianity has been founded on total belief in the Bible; to doubt its word offended not only God, but also the political organisation of Church and State that enforced its acceptance. Thus, independent thinking was discouraged by both intellectual and social circumstances, and new ideas were likely to be treated as heresy (Kelley 2002). In particular, archaeological speculation was hampered by the account of the Creation given in the Old Testament, together with a description of the subsequent settlement of known lands by descendants of Adam and Eve. The credibility of the Bible was enhanced by the fact that it also contained episodes set in contexts with independent historical records, such as Pharaonic Egypt or the early Roman Empire. In the Islamic world things were a little different, with the historian and philosopher Ibn Khaldun (1332–1406) developing relatively complex theories on the development of civilisations (Simon 2002).

Some aspects of antiquarianism found in the medieval Church are superficially similar to those associated with Romans such as Hadrian, but on closer inspection are usually found to be motivated by religion. Tourism was common, in the form of pilgrimages to ancient shrines, as was the collecting of manuscripts and relics (Elsner and Rutherford 2005). Many travellers combined both activities; collections of relics enhanced the status of churches as centres for pilgrimage, and good libraries improved the reputation of monastic centres of learning. Since monastic libraries often contained the works of some of the more inoffensive pagan Latin and Greek authors, educated ecclesiastics could gain some knowledge of the Classical world and its culture. Indeed, early Christian monasteries in Northumbria and Ireland provided educated scholars who took part in the Carolingian Renaissance around AD 800 in northern France. Ancient Greek authors became increasingly familiar in western Europe in the twelfth century AD, thanks to the translation into Latin of important Greek manuscripts. Many of these had only survived because of their interest to Arab scholars in former parts of the Roman and Byzantine Empire that were absorbed during the rise of Islam. A medieval bishop of Winchester made a purely aesthetic collection of Roman antiquities in the twelfth century, including at least one ship-load of marble sculptures from Rome itself; his interest presumably resulted from visits to Italy, and knowledge of the works of Roman authors such as Pliny and

Vitruvius on art and architecture. Historians of the Middle Ages (such as Geoffrey of Monmouth, who died c. 1155) filled out early periods of British history with fantastic tales of mythological and real figures such as Brutus the Trojan, King Arthur and Julius Caesar (Crick 2004). Later writers tended to associate ancient monuments with Romans or Danes rather than Trojans or Druids, but a concept of the great depth of prehistoric time was still elusive. In Ireland, medieval topographical lore (the *dinnseanchas*) dating from eleventh-century AD manuscripts, but which may have their origins much earlier, allowed the identification of ancient places which were undoubtedly archaeological monuments. One such document provides a detailed account of the ceremonial complex of Tara which, in the nineteenth century, could be relatively accurately related to the standing monuments (Wardell 2005: 15–17). However, such accounts were as much about the creation of mythologies of these places and landscapes as about the recording of archaeological monuments.

1.2.3 From medieval humanism to the Renaissance

- key references: Trigger, *History of archaeological thought* 2006: 48–61; Bahn, *Cambridge illustrated history* 1996b: 21–47; Moatti, *The search for ancient Rome* 1993; Etienne and Etienne, *The search for ancient Greece* 1992; Payne, Kuttner and Smick, *Antiquity and its interpreters* 2000.

Although the western Roman Empire broke up in the fifth century AD, in the east it resisted centuries of attacks and became the Byzantine Empire. Most of its Mediterranean and Near-Eastern territory was soon lost, but the legacy of Roman rule survived in decreasing areas of Greece and Asia Minor until the capture of Constantinople by the Turks in 1453. However, the civilisation that had emerged from the ruins of the former eastern Roman Empire was very much a Greek Christian culture. Much of Greece was ruled by Italian states in the final years before the Turkish conquest, but they took little interest in its ancient

monuments. In western Europe monastic scholarship gradually drew upon a wider range of ancient Greek and Roman writers until the rediscovery of pagan philosophers such as Aristotle inspired new interest in science and the natural world during the phase known as medieval humanism. The physical heritage of ancient Rome was understandably of particular interest during the fourteenth- to fifteenth-century Italian Renaissance (a term invented by French art-historians in the nineteenth century). Scholars, artists and architects turned to pre-Christian Roman sources for largely forgotten ideas and new inspiration – for example by imitating Roman building practice in completing the new cathedral at Florence with a Classical dome rather than a Gothic spire. The monuments of the city of Rome itself were studied by Cola di Rienzo and Giovanni Dondi in the fourteenth century, and by Poggio Bracciolini and Flavio Biondo in the fifteenth, using every possible source of written evidence to elucidate the physical remains (Moatti 1993: 25–52). Nevertheless, during this period of enthusiastic recording, Roman structures were frequently demolished to provide stone for new buildings. In some ways the Renaissance attitude to the examination of the past resembled that of the Romans, for it involved travel, the study of buildings and the collection of works of art and manuscripts.

One scholar with this outlook who looked beyond Italy to Greece and even Egypt was Cyriac of Ancona (Etienne and Etienne 1992: 24–9; Bodnar and Foss 2003). Cyriac was born in 1391, well before the fall of Constantinople, which still held great symbolic significance for him as the last remnant of ancient Roman political power. He spent twenty-five years of the early fifteenth century in Greece, visiting sites and libraries for himself and publishing commentaries on his observations; unfortunately not all of these survive. Cyriac embodied some of the principal components of a modern archaeologist, notably the active recording and study of physical remains of the past, whether sites or objects, through extensive fieldwork. In addition, as a historical archaeologist Cyriac carried out his research with the help of the literary background of the culture that he investigated. On the negative side, Cyriac displayed a typically selective attitude to what he recorded, and failed to comment upon changes that had affected the condition of Athenian monuments (McNeal 1991: 52).

The Renaissance atmosphere of discovery and speculation gradually spread to the rest of Europe, including areas in the north connected only briefly with the Classical world (such as Britain) or not at all (much of Germany and Scandinavia). In these countries the same spirit of inquiry was also directed towards the non-Classical past, and the first steps began to be taken towards the methods of prehistoric archaeology. Some of this research was undertaken by individuals whose means did not permit them to travel widely in southern Europe. Thus, most advances in archaeological methods occurred in northern Europe, and the ideas fostered on the fringes of the Classical world were only applied to sites in Greece and the Near East much later.

The many voyages of discovery from Europe that began shortly before AD 1500 confirmed by direct observation that the Earth was not flat but a sphere – as mathematical astronomers claimed, and as was widely accepted in ancient Greece. European contact with North and South America revealed an extraordinary range of different societies, from hunter-gatherers to city dwellers. It became increasingly difficult to reconcile such discoveries with the authority of the Bible, with its story of the peopling of the Earth by the descendants of Noah's family who had survived the Flood. A book published in 1655 by a French Protestant theologian, Isaac de Lapeyrère, proposed that Adam was simply the 'father of the Jews, not of all men' (Schnapp 2006). His views were founded upon knowledge of the ancient civilisations of the Near East and the newly discovered inhabitants of various parts of the world. De Lapeyrère was forced to recant by the Inquisition and his book was publicly burned in Paris (Schnapp 1996: 224–31). Many must have sympathised with his views, but they could not be examined further until developments in geology and biology in the nineteenth century allowed archaeologists such as Jacques Boucher de Perthes to propose the existence of

antediluvian (i.e. before the Flood) tool-using humans by observation and fieldwork (below: 29–30). However, reports of 'savages' encountered by European traders and colonists in Africa or the Americas offered a new possibility for understanding the way of life of ancient peoples; English and French antiquarians familiar with Julius Caesar's account of his military expeditions in Britain and Gaul might well see similarities between the societies and activities of the indigenous inhabitants of North America and the 'Ancient Britons' (**Box 1.1**; Smiles 1994; Hingley 2007; Olivier 1999).

Thus, the Renaissance interest in pagan Classical literature, combined with geographical discoveries in other parts of the world, had created a favourable atmosphere for archaeological work. After the Renaissance, the religious upheaval of the Reformation encouraged sentiments of nationalism, as many countries – particularly in northern Europe – broke the long tradition of dependence on Rome. National consciousness enhanced the interest of searching for the origins of peoples such as the Celts, Germans or Slavs (Sklenár 1983: 24–8) and of nationally unifying characters in the past (Hingley 2007). Herodotus and Tacitus had written about primitive peoples who lived on the fringes of the Greek and Roman world, including Germany and Britain. These countries were now involved in Renaissance scholarship and religious Reformation, and followed the precedent set by ancient authors in investigating the primitive state of Europe; a study of Lapland published in the 1670s by John Schefferius (a Swedish professor of law) was inspired by Tacitus' *Germania*. Since primitive peoples such as the Lapps were not easily accessible for study, the alternative was the examination and description of archaeological remains – a more complicated task in northern Europe than in Mediterranean countries, where research was dominated by Classical sites recorded in documentary sources. Classification and explanation of prehistoric earthworks, tombs and artefacts offered a greater challenge because they lacked direct historical evidence. Mendyk's study of the progress of antiquarian study up to AD 1600 in Britain relates it closely to new interests and methods generated

BOX 1.1   # The past in the present: developing analogies with the New World

From the sixteenth century onwards, contact between European travellers or colonisers and the peoples of the Americas led to significant developments in concepts of the past. Artists such as John White created images of the past peoples of Europe based on drawings of indigenous peoples encountered in North America, such as that seen here (Sloan 2007). Comparisons were made between the appearance of a contemporary North American Indian and the 'painted Picts' of Britain's distant past, who had been described (but not illustrated) by Roman and early medieval writers (Pratt 2005). Stone tools brought back to Europe by travellers suggested the possible uses of those found in Europe (pp. 21–2). Parallels of this kind helped to justify interpretation of such objects as artefacts made by humans, rather than thunderbolts or other natural or mythological phenomena. The observation of peoples who were still living in a manner comparable to the prehistoric past, in contrast to more advanced Europeans, also contributed to the development of ideas about social evolution. Ethnographic observations of the comparative lack of development of indigenous peoples elsewhere in the world also encouraged concepts of racial superiority amongst Europeans when ideas derived from biological evolution became more widespread in the nineteenth century.

(Getty Images)

by the Scientific Revolution: 'During our period of study these remained under-developed ... but a start was made; experimentation, collection, and observation of material was required in the first stage, and only then could one hope to arrive at sound generalisations or theories' (Mendyk 1989: xiii).

1.2.4 Archaeology and the Enlightenment

- key references: Bahn, *Cambridge illustrated history* 1996b: 48–79; Wilson, *Encyclopedia of the Enlightenment* 1996.

The Enlightenment was the culmination of increasing separation between science and religion among many philosophers of the eighteenth century AD. This rift had been developing since medieval humanists began to use the writings of Greek philosophers such as Aristotle

in which ideas of biological and **social evolution** were already emerging (Blundell 1986: 73–97). One important shift in outlook in this new secular period was a revision of the biblical view that humans had degenerated since the expulsion of Adam and Eve from the Garden of Eden. The rapid economic and technological development that was going on in Europe encouraged an alternative idea involving progress in human material, intellectual and spiritual culture (Pluciennik 2006; Trigger 2006: 100). This was reflected in the work of philosophers such as Rousseau and Hume – rather than antiquaries – who incorporated reports of 'primitive' cultures into their attempts to define stages of social evolution. The adoption of an evolutionary frame of mind clearly encouraged both philosophers and scientists to accept the implications of new investigations into geology, biology and artefacts. Not everyone saw progress as a linear phenomenon of improvement or degeneration, however; although largely overlooked in his own time, Giambattista Vico (1668–1744) envisaged stages of human society as dynamic phases in a repeating cycle. This idea was a fundamental component of views expressed much later by Hegel and Karl Marx (Blackburn 1994: 393–4). Thus, by the early nineteenth century European scholars had finally come into possession of a range of essential concepts suitable for confronting the problem of the prehistoric origins of humanity (below: p. 26). Meanwhile many antiquaries had adopted the habit of making careful records of archaeological sites as part of a broader scientific interest in the natural environment, even though most of them could not yet be dated (Sweet 2004).

1.2.5 Antiquarian fieldwork

- key references: Mendyk, *Speculum Britanniae* 1989; Piggott, *Ancient Britons and the antiquarian imagination* 1989; Sweet, *Antiquaries* 2004.

Sixteenth century: chorography and recording

The work of antiquaries who engaged in active field archaeology in Britain illustrates the aims and concepts of research into the past undertaken after the diffusion of Renaissance thinking into northern Europe. Before the sixteenth century, historical writers occasionally referred to monuments, but with little purpose other than to display sheer wonder, or to add circumstantial detail to some actual or invented episode in their works. For example, a recognisable illustration showing Stonehenge being built by the magician Merlin appeared in a fourteenth-century British manuscript (Bahn 1996a: 9), and another was recently discovered in a French manuscript (Heck 2007; **Fig. 1.4**). The Tudor dynasty of the sixteenth century coincided with an increase in national consciousness, underlined by the Reformation and the establishment of the Church of England. John Leland (1506–52) was Keeper of the King's Libraries for Henry VIII, and on his travels recorded ancient sites such as Hadrian's Wall. William Camden (**Box 1.2**; 1551–1623; Murray 1999b: 1–14) was another royal employee who travelled extensively; his *Britannia*, published in 1586, was the first general guide to the antiquities of Britain. John Aubrey and William Stukeley were important later examples of individuals – described by their contemporaries as antiquaries, or more rarely **chorographers** (Mendyk

Figure 1.4 An image of Stonehenge discovered in a French manuscript dating from the 1440s AD. It is the first known depiction which provides observations on the form and construction techniques of Stonehenge, rather than representing it as a symbol, as in earlier images. In the words of Christopher Heck (2007): 'the drawing bridges perfectly the worlds of medieval myth and Renaissance observation'. (Mike Pitts and the Bibliothèque Municipale de Douai)

BOX 1.2

William Camden (1551–1623)

(Getty Images)

William Camden was born in London and spent much of his life at the University of Oxford and Westminster College. His book *Britannia*, published in 1586, combined observations made while travelling throughout England and Wales with information gathered by examining archives. His emphasis on the importance of the Roman occupation linked Britain to the continental centres of the Renaissance, and gave Britain a respectable position in European culture. Camden also attempted to use the unity of Britain as a Roman province for political purposes in support of forming Britain into a united kingdom in his own day (Hingley 2007). Camden's descriptions of antiquities were thorough and detailed, and sections on Roman and pre-Roman coinage and language were also included. The founding of Britain was no longer attributed to unlikely or imaginary individuals and peoples (such as Brutus the Trojan, or the Phoenicians); instead, greater reliance was placed on references contained in Classical sources, and analogies from the New World. Camden's interest in material culture, and his recognition of the part it could play in elucidating the past, was fundamentally important. His *Britannia* enjoyed great popularity, and its careful organisation allowed additions to be made for nearly two hundred years after Camden's death.

1989: x) – who paid systematic attention to field monuments in Britain from the sixteenth century onwards.

Seventeenth century: scientific antiquarianism

- key references: Trigger, *History of archaeological thought* 2006: 106–114; Murray, *Encyclopedia of archaeology* 1999a: 15–26; Tylden-Wright, *John Aubrey: a life* 1991.

John Aubrey (1626–97) lacked the depth of education of Leland or Camden, but participated in a new kind of scholarship that came to prominence in the **Scientific Revolution** of the seventeenth century. It was characterised by a desire to approach any subject from a sound basis of classification and comparison, whether astronomy, medicine, botany or antiquities. In addition to antiquities, Aubrey included natural

and artificial phenomena in accounts of his beloved Wiltshire. His great archaeological work *Monumenta Britannica* was never published, but fortunately the manuscript was donated to the Bodleian Library, Oxford, where it was examined by many later antiquaries. The first part is best known because it focused on the great prehistoric monuments of Wessex, including Stonehenge, Silbury and Avebury. Aubrey was one of the first to assign these sites to the pre-Roman Celts and their priesthood, the Druids, who were known from the writings of Tacitus and other Roman authors. On the instructions of King Charles I he made an excellent plan of the remarkable ditched enclosure at Avebury and its surviving internal stone circles, probably making use of new surveying instruments that had been developed by the seventeenth century (Welfare 1989).

To Aubrey, information was worth collecting and classifying for its own sake, rather than simply to illustrate a particular theory. A similar approach is found in the work of contemporaries in fields such as botany or the study of fossils (Hunter 1975: 95–7). Aubrey's observations and interpretations also reveal awareness of descriptions of American Indians. He did not share an idealistic Noble Savage view that might have resulted from reading the *Germania* of Tacitus: 'the inhabitants (of northern Wiltshire) almost as savage as the Beasts whose skins were their only rayment … They were 2 or 3 degrees I suppose less savage than the Americans … The Romans subdued and civilized them' (quoted in Piggott 1989: 62). Clearly, Aubrey shared Camden's view that the Roman occupation of Britain raised its status in the eyes of post-Renaissance scholarship (Hingley 2007).

Aubrey was not able to solve the conundrum of dating ancient monuments. Although he was right to place Stonehenge and Avebury into a ritual context of pre-Roman date, he attributed Iron Age hillforts to Britons, Romans or Danes with wild inconsistency (Piggott 1989: 118–20). However, Aubrey's work made a great impact upon the best-known antiquary of the eighteenth century – William Stukeley (**Fig. 1.5**).

The contemporary Welsh antiquarian Edward Lhuyd (or Llwyd) (1660–1709) was instrumental in developing awareness of the archaeology of the British Isles beyond England. His *Archaeologia Britannica* recorded archaeological monuments in Wales, Ireland, Scotland and Cornwall through systematic first-hand recording, being, for example, the first to record the impressive Neolithic monument at Newgrange in Ireland, and recording many early medieval sites in Wales (Wardell 2005: 52; Edwards 2007). Combining an expertise in linguistics with archaeology Lhuyd was influential in suggesting that these regions of the British Isles were unified by similar languages and histories, which reflected their 'Celtic' heritage (James 1999: 45–7). This suggestion was developed later by archaeologists and has led to much controversy in recent years about whether these regions really should be defined as 'Celtic' on the basis of Iron Age archaeology (James 1999; Collis 2003: 49–56).

Eighteenth century: the antiquaries
- key references: Schnapp, *The discovery of the past* 1996: 212–18; Piggott, *William Stukeley* 1985; Murray, *Encyclopedia of archaeology* 1999a: 39–50; Sweet, *Antiquaries* 2004.

Figure 1.5 A drawing by William Stukeley (1687–1765) showing him engaged in fieldwork with friends. Even in this light-hearted sketch a number of antiquities and features of the landscape are drawn and labelled; his observations and plans remain an important source of information. (Bodleian Library, Oxford: Ms Eng. Misc. b 65 fol. 43r.)

Although the eighteenth-century Enlightenment favoured Classical literature, art and architecture, it also engendered reactions against a purely rational and secular outlook. By the nineteenth century this had resulted in a Romantic movement which preferred fanciful 'Gothic' buildings incorporating medieval features, and which glorified primitive and exotic peoples. William Stukeley reflected these changes in the spirit of the age; his interpretations of sites such as Stonehenge, and their association with primitive religion, were very much in tune with the sentiments of Romanticism (Peterson 2003). These interpretations never affected the quality of his fieldwork, however.

William Stukeley (1687–1765) was trained in medicine at Cambridge but had also studied botany. The ancient monuments in the countryside captured his imagination, especially after reading the manuscript of Aubrey's *Monumenta Britannica* in 1718. Extensive fieldwork in Wessex followed in the 1720s, including accurate and thorough surveys of Avebury, Stonehenge and Silbury. He went on to travel extensively throughout Britain, making surveys and excellent sketches. His Romantic leanings are evident in a taste for dramatic landscapes such as the Lake District, and for Gothic architecture (to the extent of designing mock-ruins or 'follies'). His professional life changed direction in the 1720s, from medicine to religion.

From this point Stukeley attempted to use the results of his collected fieldwork from Wessex to establish a theological connection between the Druids and Christianity. Aubrey had made observations, sorted them into a sensible order and drawn limited conclusions from common sense and historical information; Stonehenge and its related monuments did not fit into the Roman period, so he attributed them to the pre-Roman Britons. Since the sites were apparently ritual rather than functional, Aubrey assigned them to the only known cult and priesthood attested by Classical authors, the Druids. Stukeley went on to invent a vast theological system for the Druids, supported by quite unwarranted connections with features of the monuments: 'The form of that stupendous work (Avebury) is the picture

of the Deity, more particularly of the Trinity'. He published two major books – *Stonehenge* (1740) and *Avebury* (1743) – which he intended to be part of a larger enterprise entitled *Patriarchal Christianity or a chronological history of the origin and progress of true religion, and of idolatry*.

Stukeley's basic evidence still forms an invaluable record of monuments that have suffered severe damage since his day. He recorded an avenue of stones leading from Stonehenge to the River Avon that was subsequently destroyed; it was only relocated by aerial photography in 1920 (Piggott 1985: 92) and recently excavated (Parker Pearson *et al.* 2007). A long-doubted second avenue was rediscovered in 1999 (Gillings et al. 2000). Stukeley did not just record individual sites, but placed separate earthworks in an area into a coherent pattern, such as that illustrated by Schnapp (1996: 216–17). He also made analytical observations, such as deducing that some 'Druid' burial mounds on Oakley Down, Dorset, must already have been in existence before the construction of a Roman road which cut across the ditch of one of them (Piggott 1989: pl. 27). Stukeley expressed another role for fieldwork that echoes modern **rescue archaeology**: it 'perpetuates the vestiges of this celebrated wonder & of the barrows avenues cursus &c for I foresee that it will in a few years be universally plowed over and consequently defaced' (quoted in Piggott 1989: 127). His approach to the landscape, seeing sites such as Avebury as part of a wider social landscape, also anticipated more recent approaches to landscape archaeology, such as **phenomenology** (Peterson 2003; see Chapter 6).

From a methodological point of view, field archaeology could not make substantial progress in Britain beyond the point reached by Stukeley until some new element was introduced. Accurate recording was continued and extended, but the interpretation of recorded monuments remained static because historical evidence barely stretched back beyond the Roman period. Historical events could be shuffled into a different order, or fanciful theories could be constructed to expand them, but no new source of evidence was available until the idea of excavation was adopted on a large scale in the nineteenth century, and refined in the twentieth; this development will be followed in Chapter 3.

Historians of ideas, science or archaeology can point to early antiquarian work throughout Europe. In Scandinavia, Johan Bure and Ole Worm undertook antiquarian research – with royal patronage – in the early seventeenth century (Schnapp 1996: 156–65), and similar efforts were devoted to Roman and earlier antiquities in central Europe (Sklenár 1983: 6–43). A German pioneer of the systematic investigation of Roman art and architecture in Italy, Johann Winckelmann, was a near contemporary of Stukeley (Schnapp 1996: 258–66; Murray 1999b: 51–64).

1.2.6 Antiquarianism in the Americas

- key references: Schnapp, *The discovery of the past* 1996: 142–65, 198–212; Malina and Vasícek, *Archaeology yesterday and today* 1990; Sklenár, *Archaeology in central Europe* 1983.

An indigenous archaeological tradition had also emerged in America by the nineteenth century (Trigger 2006: 177–89). It began with ethnographic accounts of the Native Americans, but gradually extended to sites and artefacts. The literate civilisations of Central and South America attracted comment as early as the sixteenth century, because their architecture, sculpture and inscriptions offered the same kind of possibilities for study as those of Greece or Italy. The King of Spain commissioned reports on the Mayan palace at Palenque in 1785–6, and Antonio del Río organised forest clearance to reveal monuments for recording – and then tore out decorated items to send back to Madrid for King Charles III, who had already financed excavations in Pompeii and established a collection of Classical archaeology (Baudez and Picasso 1992: 36–7). By the end of the eighteenth century, it was generally accepted that the native population of North America had migrated from Asia by way of the Bering Straits (Stiebing 1993: 173–5). Nevertheless, speculation about the origins of Indians was still influenced by a desire amongst European colonists to justify their conquests by proving

that the natives were inferior to themselves. Archaeological fieldworkers in North America did not find great stone cities and temples, but observed and recorded extensive ritual earthworks reminiscent of burial mounds found in northern Europe (*ibid.*: 170–80). There were attempts to attribute them to Israelites, Danes, or even Welshmen. Even the systematic fieldworkers Squier and Davis, who surveyed, excavated, classified and published 'Mound Builder' sites in the Mississippi valley in the 1840s, attributed them to a vanished non-Indian race (Meltzer 1998; **Box 1.3**). This phase in the archaeological study of North America from 1492–1840 has been called, appropriately, 'the speculative period' (Willey and Sabloff 1980: 12–27).

1.2.7 Touring, collecting and the origin of museums

- key references: Hooper-Greenhill, *Museums and the shaping of knowledge* 1992; Impey and MacGregor, *The origins of museums* 1985; Stagl, *A history of curiosity* 1995; Anderson *et al.*, *Enlightening the British* 2003.

In Western intellectual circles, the collection and study of objects ran parallel to the development of archaeological fieldwork but did not become dominant until the nineteenth century, when the expansion of agriculture, industry and (eventually) archaeological excavations began to provide sufficient quantities of pottery, metal and stone artefacts for advanced studies.

The Renaissance revived the Roman habit of visiting monuments and collecting works of art for aesthetic reasons, in contrast to the medieval Church's concentration upon shrines and relics. In particular, ownership of Classical art and architecture was linked to the focus of knowledge on rediscovered Classical literature, which emphasised education and status (Moser 2006: 11–14). The concept spread to northern Europe, and educated people of sufficient financial means began to visit the Mediterranean centres of Classical civilisation in Italy, Greece, Turkey and the Near East. Travellers purchased antiquities as souvenirs to adorn their northern residences

BOX 1.3   Discovering the archaeology of North America: the Mounds of Ohio and Illinois

Until the nineteenth century, European settlers in North America largely ignored the archaeology that they encountered, although early explorers had noted the existence of large mounds. It was only when large-scale European settlement began in areas such as the Ohio Valley that mounds and earthwork structures (such as the Serpent Mound of Ohio and this mound at Cahokia, Illinois) were encountered. These structures are now known to have been burial and ceremonial monuments dating from a range of different periods, some as early as 1000 BC; the better-known Mississippian mounds date from c. AD

(National Park Service, USA)

500–1550 (Abrams and Freter 2005). Ephraim Squier and Edwin Davis were among the first to survey and excavate the mounds systematically. North American archaeology in the nineteenth century suffered from a social evolutionary perspective that made it impossible to conceive that Native Americans could have constructed such monuments, and preferred to think that they had been built by groups from Europe such as Vikings, or lost tribes from Israel (Barnhart 2005; Trigger 2006: 159–60). This view was reinforced by the fact that the Native Americans who the colonists encountered were not settled societies like those that had originally built the mounds, but communities which had adopted nomadic ways of life in the succeeding centuries (Fagan 2007: 316–27). A more scientific approach to American archaeology in the later nineteenth century by individuals such as Joseph Henry and Cyrus Thomas refuted such ideas by demonstrating that they really had been the result of indigenous development (Alex 2000: 15–19; Trigger 2006: 163). Despite this, the earlier 'diffusionist' interpretations continue to be prominent in popular views and in pseudo-archaeology (see Box 6.2; Feder 2005).

– which were constructed and decorated, of course, in a Classical manner. The process was accelerated by agents sent to seek out further items and to arrange shipment back to their new owners' homes. An early example of an English **Grand Tour** aristocrat was Thomas Howard, Earl of Arundel (1585–1646), who first travelled (with a large entourage) to Italy in 1612; there he bought, and even dug for, antiquities. His agent, William Petty, extended the search to Greece and built up a collection (at bargain prices compared with Italy) that became a centre of great learned interest, known throughout Europe after its publication in 1628 (Penny 1985). Although Arundel's collection suffered neglect and dispersal after

the English Civil War, it had already generated similar interests amongst other noblemen and even royalty. Indeed, King Charles I stated that 'The study of antiquities is by good experience said to be very serviceable and useful to the general good of the State and Commonwealth' (Daniel 1975: 19).

Tours had other effects too; learned societies such as the Society of Dilettanti (an organisation of British antiquaries) sponsored expeditions to record Classical sites rather than simply to loot them. Individuals of lower social status and lesser wealth began to form more diverse collections (**Fig. 1.6**). John 'Gardener' Tradescant's collection was created in the first half of the seventeenth

Figure 1.6 Ole Worm's collection of natural and archaeological curiosities, formed in Denmark and illustrated in 1655. Modern museums derive from the wide scientific interests of such collectors, who embraced natural history and geology as well as displaying ethnographic and archaeological specimens. (*Museum Wormianum* (Leiden 1655); Bodleian Library, Oxford B 5.9 Art)

century and a catalogue of its contents appeared in 1656. Although largely made up of botanical specimens, it also comprised 'Mechanick artificial works in carvings, turnings, sowings and paintings' and 'warlike instruments', mainly from Polynesia, Africa and America. After his death, the material passed to Oxford University through Tradescant's friend, Elias Ashmole. A new museum was opened in Oxford in 1683 by the future king James II and it moved in the nineteenth century to the building known as the Ashmolean Museum; the original building still exists and is now the Museum of the History of Science. Thus, the Renaissance fashion for collecting contributed to the establishment of public museums attached to centres of learning

or to cities. By the eighteenth century the establishment of national museums, such as the British Museum in 1753 and the Louvre, France, in 1793, was more about national standing and colonial power than education for the masses. In the nineteenth century such institutions attempted to emphasise similarities between modern nations and the ancient civilisations whose artefacts they displayed (see Chapter 6; Anderson *et al.* 2003; Moser 2006: 2).

Museums have become the first point of contact with archaeology for many members of the public. The essential features of the early Ashmolean (collecting, scholarship and public display) are now accepted as integral parts of the cultural life of almost every modern country. The

Figure 1.7 Lord Fortrose's apartment in Naples in 1770 illustrates how the interests of northern European aristocrats extended well beyond antiquities. In addition to the classical style of the room and a collection of Greek and Roman artefacts displayed on shelves, there are books, paintings and weapons. Patronage of contemporary arts is represented by the artist (Pietro Fabris, bottom left) and a performance in progress by musicians who include the young Mozart. (Scottish National Portrait Gallery)

interest of antiquaries like Aubrey and Stukeley in prehistoric sites and objects was connected to the same phenomenon; indeed, many travelled in their own countries because they could not afford to go abroad. However, early field archaeologists naturally concentrated on sites, because the potential for using objects to distinguish between stages of development in prehistory remained extremely limited until time was conceptualised in a more scientific way.

People did not embark upon the Grand Tour purely to visit historical sites or to collect antiquities, of course. There were opportunities for many other pursuits, including art and music (**Fig. 1.7**). Tourism in the modern sense expanded dramatically in the nineteenth century with the help of improved roads and railways and regular

shipping services. It did not remain the preserve of the aristocracy, whose pioneering paths in search of more exotic destinations in Egypt and the Middle East were soon followed by less wealthy travellers. The appearance of commercial travel agents such as Thomas Cook, who organised his first tour in 1863, initiated a completely different phase of mass tourism that persists in the twenty-first century (Withey 1997).

The desire to preserve ancient ruins had its roots in the Renaissance and the Enlightenment interest in the aesthetic value of Classical ruins (Sweet 2004: 285). However, by the late nineteenth and early twentieth century preservation became more formal, and a number of countries set about creating laws to protect, and sometimes restore, historic and archaeological monuments (see

Chapter 6). For instance, Lord Curzon, Viceroy of India, did much to restore archaeological monuments in India and England (Thompson 2006: 52). Many such projects were, however, designed to enhance national identity and imperial pride in the past of these nations rather than to develop archaeological management.

1.2.8 Science and Romanticism

- key references: Bahn, *Cambridge illustrated history* 1996b: 80–115; Smiles, *The image of antiquity* 1994; Trigger, 'Romanticism, nationalism and archaeology' 1995; Gran-Aymerich, *Naissance de l'archéologie moderne* 1998; Pluciennik, *Social Evolution* 2005.

Nineteenth-century Europe experienced a spectacular rate of change. It began with an essentially rural landscape and economy in the early stages of the Industrial Revolution, and ended with mechanised factories drawing upon large urban populations completely divorced from their agrarian roots. There was also considerable political change, with the aftermath of the American and French Revolutions (1775–83, 1789) still felt at the beginning of the century, and the development of Marx's political ideas by its end (*Das Kapital* 1867–93). Science had moved on from the seventeenth and eighteenth centuries to become what we know today – a discipline based upon laboratory observation and experiment, rather than a term encompassing the pursuit of knowledge in general. Awareness of rapid change probably boosted interest in causes and effects, and assisted in the development of grand explanatory schemes. This was the context of ideas such as evolution of the natural world by **natural selection** (Darwin 1859), or human **social evolution** through stages from savagery to barbarism to civilisation (Morgan 1871, *Ancient society*, popularised by Marx and Engels). The Enlightenment and Romanticism provided a seedbed in which archaeology could grow rapidly, because scientific observation and classification had become directly linked to explanation. Furthermore, Enlightenment ideas about the value of education were actually put

into practice in the nineteenth century, and museums and art galleries were included with the schools and colleges considered essential for the 'improvement' of the general public. The scene was set for the convergence of many separate strands – fieldwork, geology, collecting of artefacts, excavation – into a discipline which is directly ancestral to the kind of archaeology practised in the twenty-first century.

1.3 THE RECOGNITION AND STUDY OF ARTEFACTS

- key references: Woolf, 'The dawn of the artifact' 1992; Pearce, 'The interpretation of ancient objects, 1770–1820' 2007b.

The history of the study of objects, like that of fieldwork, provides a useful illustration of some basic principles of archaeology. Ordinary artefacts from historical periods were only recovered by accident until excavation became an essential part of archaeology during the nineteenth century, and they attracted little interest unless they possessed aesthetic qualities. Although in the sixteenth century a number of Italian collectors accurately identified flint arrowheads or polished axes from much earlier periods as human artefacts (Schnapp 1996: 154), the concept spread slowly. It still seemed a novelty when, in the seventeenth century, de Lapeyrère proposed that stone implements were not 'thunderbolts', but tools and weapons made by peoples who had preceded the creation of Adam (Piggott 1989: 45–7). The matter was soon placed beyond doubt when similar items became available for study in ethnological collections from the South Seas and the Americas, where they could still be observed in use (**Fig. 1.8; Box 1.1**).

Concepts of successive Ages of stone, bronze and iron, suggested by actual finds, are known from Chinese literature as early as the first century BC, and Shen Kua made remarkable studies of artefacts in the eleventh century AD (Evans 1982: 13–14; Schnapp 1996: 74–9). A Greek writer of the second century AD, Pausanias, had noted the lack of any mention of iron in the poetry of

Figure 1.8 Recognition of prehistoric implements in Europe was helped by observations of similar objects, still in use, in other parts of the world. In 1699, Edward Lhuyd wrote: 'I doubt not but you have often seen of these Arrowheads they ascribe to elfs or fairies: they are just the same chip'd flints the natives of New England head their arrows with at this day; and there are also several stone hatchets found in this kingdom, not unlike those of the Americans' (quoted in Piggott 1989: 86). The artefacts on the left come from North and South America; those on the right are from northern Britain. (GNM Hancock, Newcastle upon Tyne)

Homer, and inspected ancient weapons preserved in temples, confirming that they were indeed made of bronze (Schnapp 1996: 46). John Frere published drawings of typical flint bifaces ('hand-axes') from the early Stone Age in *Archaeologia* in 1800, 'evidently weapons of war, fabricated and used by a people who had not the use of metals'. Bronze artefacts actually caused more problems than those made of stone or iron, for while early travellers could observe Stone Age communities in America and Australia, and Iron Age societies in many parts of Africa, no living Bronze Age peoples had been encountered. Bronze artefacts found in Europe were normally assigned to the Romans because they seemed too complex to have been made by 'savages', but suggestions of an earlier date found some support by the eighteenth century (Piggott 1989: 95–100; Murray 1999b: 33–4). However, as we shall see below (p. 29), Boucher de Perthes was still fighting for the acceptance of stone artefacts as the work of early humans fifty years later.

1.3.1 Scandinavia and the Three-Age System

- key references: Schnapp, *The discovery of the past* 1996: 295–303; Graslund, *The birth of prehistoric chronology* 1987; Rowley-Conwy *From Genesis to prehistory* 2007.

Why has Scandinavian archaeology, generally speaking, an advantage over foreign archaeology, if not because Scandinavian archaeologists have had an opportunity to study in their museums not isolated specimens but whole series and their development?

(Hans Hildebrand 1873, quoted in Graslund 1987: 16)

The archaeology of Scandinavia is particularly rich in finely made artefacts dating from the prehistoric to Viking periods, and many of them are found in good condition in graves. Hildebrand was right to stress these factors, for

Figure 1.9 The Oldnordisk Museum in Copenhagen was founded in 1816 and played an important role in increasing public awareness of antiquities. In this drawing (made in 1846 by Magnus Pedersen) the museum's first director, C.J. Thomsen, is inspiring great enthusiasm by showing objects to visitors. (National Museum, Copenhagen)

increased building, agriculture and excavation in the nineteenth century had provided a plentiful supply of discoveries. Fortunately, Scandinavia already had museums where objects could be preserved, studied and displayed. An Antiquities Commission was set up by the Danish government in 1807 to protect sites, promote public awareness of antiquities and establish a museum (Rowley-Conwy 2007: 33). The first curator of the resulting National Museum in Copenhagen was Christian Thomsen, who held the post from 1816 to his death in 1865 (**Fig. 1.9**).

Thomsen would have been aware of the concept of successive Ages of stone, bronze and iron not just from Greek and Roman philosophical speculation; it had been expressed particularly well by another Scandinavian antiquary, Simonsen, in 1816: 'At first the tools and weapons ... were made of stone or wood. Then the Scandinavians learnt to work copper and then to smelt it and harden it ... and then latterly to work iron. From this

point of view the development of their culture can be divided into a Stone Age, a Copper Age and an Iron Age' (quoted in Daniel 1967: 90–1). Thomsen was the first to demonstrate the validity of these hypothetical Ages by examining **closed finds** (graves, hoards, etc.) in which artefacts had been discovered. He restricted his central definition of the Three Ages to cutting-weapons and tools, and established their relative order. Some finds contained only stone tools, while a few contained stone together with bronze (but never iron). After iron weapons had been introduced, bronze continued to be used for other kinds of objects, but the Iron Age was observably the most recent period because late Iron Age artefacts were found in the same graves as Roman and medieval coins. Once this analysis had confirmed the order of stone and metal weapons and tools, Thomsen was able to see what other kinds of objects were found associated with them, as well as noting which specific burial practices and grave forms characterised different ages. Effective classification was indispensable to the advance of the study of prehistory, and the basic concept of the Three-Age System – with further subdivisions – remains a fundamental framework for understanding prehistory in much of the world.

Thomsen presented the evidence for these chronological deductions in museum displays by placing together groups of objects that had been found in association. He was keen to show them to visiting archaeologists, and also to ordinary visitors and especially farmers, who were likely to discover objects that could be added to the collections. His paper on how to deal with such artefacts when they were encountered in the field was printed in 1836, receiving wider attention after it was translated into English in 1848. The phenomenon of collecting antiquities, once a hobby of a social elite typified by the Earl of Arundel (above: p. 18), had been transformed by the nineteenth century in a remarkably democratic fashion. The popularising approach of Thomsen was reinforced by other archaeologists, such as General Pitt Rivers, and it remains essential to the survival of modern museums (below p. 299). However, unlike Pitt Rivers, Thomsen did not attempt either to study the development of the forms of individual artefacts (**typology**) or to explain the reasons for the changes that he had observed (Graslund 1987: 26–8).

Thomsen's successor as director of the Danish National Museum was another remarkable man, Jens Worsaae (1821–85). Both Thomsen's and Worsaae's recommendations for the use of systematic excavation were inspired by the need to recover still more artefacts from specific contexts that would allow Thomsen's broad classifications to be refined (Rowley-Conwy 2007: 16). In 1861 Worsaae subdivided the Stone Age into three periods according to the nature of stone artefacts. The earliest period was characterised by hand axes and large flakes, found in the gravels and caves of western Europe; these were followed by finer tools found in Denmark in kitchen middens (mounds of shells and bones left by hunter-gatherers). Finally, polished stone tools were associated with elaborate tombs that occasionally also contained the earliest metal objects. The first and third of these divisions of the Stone Age were soon named **Palaeolithic** and **Neolithic** (old and new) by Sir John Lubbock in his book *Pre-historic times* (1865), while the second was termed **Mesolithic** by Westropp in 1866 (Rowley-Conwy 1996). Worsaae used a different method to divide the Bronze Age. He identified a series of different burial practices and grave forms, and was able to place them into chronological order either by reference to artefacts found in them or by observation of excavated sites where examples of different forms had been found in a **stratigraphic** sequence. Thus, Worsaae, like Thomsen before him, relied primarily on the contexts of artefacts, rather than typological study of the artefacts themselves.

The success of the Scandinavian approach to classifying past ages in terms of materials and technology overshadowed other methods such as the Frenchman Edouard Lartet's division of early prehistory according to the prevailing mammalian fauna (reindeer, cave bear), or craniologists' attempts to recognise sequences of races according to the shapes of their skulls (Morse 1999). The focus upon objects led to the development of typology (**Fig. 1.10**).

Figure 1.10   In an explanation of his methods of studying typology, Oscar Montelius illustrated the transition of the axe head from stone to metal. The first copper axes (second and third, top row) were very similar to their stone counterparts (top left), but it was soon realised that metal could be saved by making them thinner, while increasing their effectiveness by hammering out a wider cutting edge (below). Further developments can be seen in Fig. 4.1. (Montelius 1903: 22)

1.3.2   Typology

- key references: Åström, *Oscar Montelius* 1995; O'Brien and Lyman, *Seriation, stratigraphy and index fossils* 1999; Bowden, *Pitt Rivers* 1991.

Classification was an important part of the Enlightenment approach to science; **typology** differs from classification in that artefacts are arranged into sequences according to developments and changes that may then allow them to be placed into a hypothetical chronological order. This may not seem a particularly significant distinction until it is recognised that before the nineteenth century there was a prevailing idea that the natural world was fixed at the time of the Creation. **Ray's Taxonomy**, developed in the seventeenth century, laid down the principle of fixed species. Swedish scientist Linnaeus (Linné) (1707–78) incorporated this idea into his binomial system – two-part names, such as *Homo sapiens* – which not only allowed the natural world to be classified systematically, but enabled other scientists to apply precisely the same system to their own specimens. The idea of a **Great Chain of Being** consisting of a hierarchy from God down to the simplest creatures was not a radical departure from Aristotle's Ladder of Nature defined in Greece in the fourth century BC. As long as species were regarded as fixed there was therefore no reason to look for development and change or to attempt any kind of chronology, and it required a half-century of geology and biology after 1800 before there was a shift to looking for evolution rather than stability (Turnbaugh et al. 2002).

The development of typology did not rely upon the concept of the Three-Age System or Darwin's theory of evolution. Graslund's thorough study (1987) of the original writings of Thomsen, Worsaae and other Scandinavian scholars revealed that studies of artefacts were based primarily on the contexts in which they had been discovered. These were sufficiently plentiful in Scandinavia for virtually all classes of artefacts to be placed in chronological order, and once this had been done typological studies could begin on a secure basis. Evolution provided a striking explanatory metaphor that stimulated typological studies from the 1860s onwards, despite the problem of equating biological change and technical change (Basalla 1988).

The influence of Classical archaeology on typology has been underestimated because most histories of archaeology have been written by prehistorians. The styles of Classical sculptures and Greek painted vases were also studied primarily from the objects themselves, largely because their contexts were rarely recorded. Systematic studies of Greek and Roman architectural and artistic styles began during the Renaissance, and were formalised by Johann Winckelmann in his publication of 1764 (Murray 1999b: 53–7). A parallel

phenomenon was the careful recording, classification and dating of medieval and Renaissance architecture, such as John Ruskin's studies of Venice in the 1850s. In both cases classification was inseparable from moral judgements about artistic standards and the social systems that had produced them; this consciousness of the subjective attitudes lying behind research was re-emphasised by archaeologists in the 1980s and 1990s (Chapter 6, p. 273).

Ancient coins were even more significant; Petrarch studied inscriptions and portraits in the fourteenth century, and classifications of large coin collections were published from the sixteenth century (Berghaus 1983: 19–23). Joseph von Eckhel's *Doctrina numorum veterum* (1782–98) and similar works by other authors provided comprehensive geographical and chronological classifications that must have been useful reference tools for Thomsen and his successors. It is also important to recognise that coins are artefacts, and that their study by means of stylistic sequences of portraits or other ornamentation, combined with changes in size and weight, bears many similarities to typology. Graslund rightly stressed the importance of the numismatic knowledge of Thomsen, Hildebrand and the Swede, Oscar Montelius, who all appreciated the importance of coins as dating evidence that could be used to subdivide the Scandinavian Iron Age (1987: 66). John Evans, inspired by Darwinian ideas of evolution, undertook similar work on British Iron Age coinage and successfully demonstrated the development of indigenous coinage from earlier Greek prototypes (Evans 1864; de Jersey 2008).

Augustus Henry Lane Fox (1827–1900) took the name Pitt Rivers under the terms of an inheritance in 1880 (Murray 1999b: 127–40). He collected artefacts from all over the world from the early 1850s while serving in the Grenadier Guards. He was involved in replacing muskets with rifles in the British army, and in testing various models and modifications for reliability and efficiency. Pitt Rivers applied the same approach to the study of the development of ancient objects. He liked to collect examples of the principal stages involved, and, in contrast to earlier collectors like John Tradescant, assembled artefacts '... solely with a view to instruction. For this purpose ordinary and typical specimens rather than rare objects have been selected and arranged in sequence' (Daniel 1981: 140). Pitt Rivers' concept of typology was very different from that of Montelius, for he invoked analogies with Darwinian evolution as early as the 1860s (Bowden 1991: 54). His concept of Australian weapons placed a variety of clubs, boomerangs, throwing sticks, shields and spears into sequences from simplicity to complexity, all beginning with a simple stick. This reveals the weakness of the evolutionary analogy, for a shield is only a shield when it is broad and flat, and a boomerang is not a boomerang if it does not fly; Pitt Rivers did not take sufficient account of invention.

As soon as Scandinavian prehistory had been subdivided according to groups of artefacts found together in graves and other contexts, further attention was turned to the artefacts themselves. The work of Montelius (Murray 1999b: 155–64) encompassed the whole of Europe from the 1880s, and he used his broad knowledge to fix dates for the Bronze and Iron Ages by cross-referencing north-European finds to datable objects exported from the civilisations of Egypt and the east Mediterranean (cross-dating: see below p. 149). Fellow Swedes Bernhard Salin and Nils Åberg continued typological research in the twentieth century by studying objects and ornamental styles associated with Germanic tribes of the Roman and 'Dark Age' periods. Like Montelius, they used dated finds from southern Europe to provide fixed points in the archaeological sequences of Scandinavia. Unfortunately, the introduction of radiocarbon dating in the 1960s revealed major errors in the dating of European prehistory and cast typology in a bad light, for the similarities detected between European and Near-Eastern objects turned out to be illusory (below: p. 153).

Typological studies were not restricted to Scandinavia, of course. Flinders Petrie (Murray 1999b: 221–32) produced comprehensive typologies of Egyptian pottery and stone tools from periods preceding the historically dated Pharaonic period. In the United States typology reached a peak in the study of Native American pottery by archaeologists such as James B. Griffin in the 1930s (Murray 1999b: 454); their intellectual context blended anthropology with social evolution but came under attack in the 1960s from **processualists** (Kehoe 1998: 97–112; see Chapter 6).

Nevertheless, with appropriate caution the typological technique remains fundamental to the classification and study of artefacts of virtually any kind or date found anywhere in the world.

1.4 RECOGNISING HUMAN ORIGINS

1.4.1 Evidence for human antiquity

- key references: Grayson, *The establishment of human antiquity* 1983; Thomas, *The first humans* 1995; Van Riper, *Men among the mammoths* 1993; O'Connor, *Finding time for the Old Stone Age* 2007.

Humans cannot be descended from the apes because, in some ways, they are apes themselves. Really we should ask whether humans descend from 'an' ape. Naturally, people are not descended from a present-day ape, any more than we are descended from our cousins. But palaeontology and all the disciplines of the biological sciences have taught us that humans and modern great apes had common ancestors several million years ago.

(Thomas 1995: 57)

This succinct quotation is a modern restatement of a fundamental question about human existence that has worried theologians, geologists, biologists and archaeologists for a very long time. In 1619 Lucilio Vanini was burned alive for suggesting that humans originated from apes, while the great apes were only classified as distinct (but related) species – as opposed to degenerate forms of humans – in the eighteenth century, by Linnaeus and Buffon (Thomas 1995: 19, 23–4). Pioneers of geology and fossil classification such as Ray or Cuvier were not able to contribute to this debate because neither fossil apes nor primitive

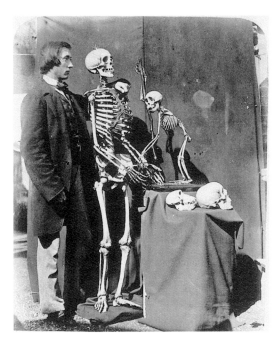

Figure 1.11 Reginald Southey photographed by Charles Dodgson between 1857 and 1859. The setting displays an interesting consciousness of the common origin of humans and primates at a time when fossil evidence had not yet been found for the development of either. It is an early example of amateur photography, taken in Oxford close to the publication date of Charles Darwin's *Origin of species* (1859). (NMPFT/Science & Society Picture Library)

Figure 1.12 In 1999 a memorial was installed in Finningham Church, Suffolk, to commemorate the powers of observation and recording shown in John Frere's publication of Stone Age artefacts found at Hoxne in the late eighteenth century (Frere 1800). From the 1850s onwards it was recognised as the first scientific account of prehistoric artefacts found in early geological strata. (Designed and cut by the Cardozo Kindersley Workshop, Cambridge)

human remains were encountered until the 1830s (*ibid.*: 26–9) – well after the existence of early humans had been predicted on the evidence of stone tools discovered alongside bones of extinct animals. Skeletal remains of humans with 'primitive' characteristics (for example, projecting brow-ridges and receding chins) that differed from anatomically modern humans were discovered with increasing frequency in Europe between 1856 and 1886, and named after the locations where they were found, Neanderthals and Cro-Magnons (Thomas 1995: 43–9). Not until the discovery of 'Java Man' by Dubois in the 1890s was there any physical evidence for a 'missing link' between apes and humans of the kind predicted by Darwin and Huxley (*ibid.*: 50–5; Bahn 1996a: 236–7); their statement that the earliest human ancestors would be found in

Africa was not supported by finds of fossil bones until the twentieth century (**Fig. 1.11**).

John Frere and Hoxne

- key references: Singer *et al.*, *The Lower Palaeolithic site at Hoxne* 1993; O'Connor, *Finding time for the Old Stone Age* 2007.

Volume 13 of the periodical *Archaeologia* (published by the Society of Antiquaries (**Box 1.4**) in 1800) included a minor item, the full significance of which did not become apparent for sixty years. Amongst an assortment of papers – on subjects ranging from a Roman fort in

BOX 1.4 The great societies: archaeology comes of age?

Informal meetings in a tavern from 1707 led to the creation of the Society of Antiquaries of London in 1717 (Pearce 2007a: 2), and a similar society began in Scotland in 1780; these societies were among the earliest formal associations of archaeological researchers in the world (Starkey et al. 2007). Societies of this kind began to publish journals recounting recent finds and concepts of the past, such as *Archaeologia* from 1770 and the *Archaeological Journal of the Royal Archaeological Institute* from 1845 (Murray 2001, 199–216). Meetings of antiquarian and archaeological societies provided a context in which influential new ideas in archaeology could be presented, such as the Danish antiquary Jens Worsaae's account of his concept of prehistory (Briggs 2007), or John Evans' magisterial analysis of Iron Age coins (de Jersey 2008). At these antiquarian societies, and their predecessors such as the Royal Society, many of the great topics of the day such as the antiquity of humans was debated and advocated (Briggs 2007). The American Institute of Archaeology (established in 1879) and several European national archaeological institutions founded archaeological schools or research centres in the countries in which they focused their research, notably in Rome, Athens and Jerusalem, whose work continues today (Murray 2001, 100; Wallace-Hadrill 2001). Research into specific periods and areas of the world was facilitated by the establishment of groups such as the Prehistoric Society (formed as a national body in 1935 by expanding the Prehistoric Society of East Anglia, which had existed since 1908) and the Society for American Archaeology (established in 1934). The histories of such societies reflect changes in the focus and direction of archaeological research over time, and before modern communications were established they provided a crucial network of communication that facilitated cross-fertilisation of ideas, allowing new information about evolution and dating to spread rapidly through the international antiquarian community (Sweet 2004: 81; Rowley-Conwy 2007). The cartoon below, by George Cruickshank in 1812, illustrates how antiquarian societies quickly became satirised in the late 18th and early 19th centuries for their odd interest in artefacts and the past (Society of Antiquaries, London).

THE ANTIQUARIAN SOCIETY.

Germany to historical documents associated with British royalty – was a short letter from John Frere (1740–1807), drawing attention to some observations made in a clay pit at Hoxne in Suffolk. He reported flint weapons found at a depth of twelve feet in a layer of gravel, overlain by a bed of sand containing bones of extinct animals and, remarkably, shells and remains of marine creatures 'which may be conjectured to have been once the bottom, or at least the shore, of the sea'. Frere was evidently conscious of the problematic implications: 'It may be conjectured that the different strata were formed by inundations happening at distant periods ... The situation in which these weapons were found may tempt us to refer them to a very remote period indeed; even beyond that of the present world' (Frere 1800: 205). Frere made no reference to the biblical Creation and Flood, and he died before an accumulation of similar finds began to suggest an alternative view of human origins (**Fig. 1.12**).

Frere's conundrum was already familiar to geologists, such as Robert Hooke and Nicolas Steno, who had been speculating about the significance of fossil animals for several centuries (Stiebing 1993: 33–4). Worries about geological time did not yet have a significant impact upon biblical views about the age of the world, but the likelihood of conflict increased as growing numbers of finds of artefacts made by humans but associated with remains of extinct animals were noted in Europe in the early nineteenth century (*ibid.*: 34–46).

Boucher de Perthes and the Somme gravels

- key reference: Schnapp, *The discovery of the past* 1996: 310–44.

By the time of Frere's death in 1807 Jacques Boucher de Perthes (1788–1868) was already becoming interested in archaeology in France; he spent several decades studying the gravel quarries of northern France (**Fig. 1.13–14**). He was impressed by the great depth and variety of the deposits of sediment and he felt that they were far too complex to result from the biblical Flood, although he did not totally reject the authority of the Old Testament. However, it was an uphill struggle to convince contemporaries that flint tools collected from the gravels were made by humans, and that they could be recognised by their artificial shaping: 'at the very mention of the words "axe" and "diluvium", I observe a smile on the face of those to whom I speak. It is the

Figure 1.13   Jacques Boucher de Perthes published many ideas about artefacts found around Amiens in northern France and their stratification. His bombastic manner diminished the credibility of his beliefs. Despite this, Perthes' central idea – that human artefacts of great age were to be found in the gravels of northern France – was confirmed when John Evans and Joseph Prestwich travelled from England to inspect his finds in 1859. (Portrait by Grèvedon, 1831; Society of Antiquaries, London)

workmen who help me, not the geologists' (quoted in Daniel 1981: 52). Because he was able to prove that these tools came from within ancient gravel beds, Boucher de Perthes concluded that humans had existed before 'the cataclysm that gave our country its present configuration', and that these humans were therefore also contemporary with a wide range of extinct animals. He did not abandon the idea of floods, but suggested that Adam and Eve resulted from a later and separate Creation, long after the flood whose results he observed had wiped out earlier humans. Whether or not people accepted this view, the Earth was seen to be becoming increasingly ancient, and humans were being drawn back into an immeasurable void.

Not all geologists treated Boucher de Perthes' work sceptically. An English geologist, Joseph

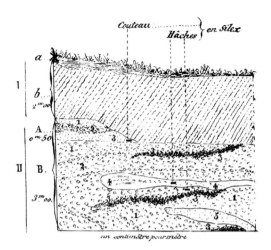

Figure 1.14 A section drawing published by Boucher de Perthes in his *Antiquités celtiques et antediluviennes* (1847) shows the geological strata in which he had found flint implements (labelled *couteau/haches en silex*) in the Somme Valley gravels. The carefully numbered and delineated layers and artefacts, with a vertical scale in metres, illustrate how geologists used this method of recording decades before it was adopted by archaeological excavators (compare with Box 3.2).

Prestwich, together with an authority on ancient implements, John Evans, travelled to France to meet him and to visit the celebrated gravel pits. In May 1859 they were rewarded with the opportunity of observing a flint axe, still firmly embedded in an ancient gravel deposit; any remaining doubts were removed (photographs were taken, too: **Fig. 1.15**; Gamble and Kruszynski 2009). Prestwich read an account of their observations to the Royal Society in London before the end of May, and a summary of his paper appeared in print in 1860. He referred to Frere's letter published in 1800, and pointed out that Frere's observations conformed with the new findings from France. Both finds were corroborated at Brixham Cave and then Kent's Cavern in Devon, where in 1858–9 flint tools had been found among the bones of Ice Age animals, firmly sealed beneath a sheet of stalagmite (Stiebing 1993: 44–5). In 1864 in France, among many important discoveries made during Edouard Lartet's excavations in rock shelters near Les Eyzies, was a piece of mammoth ivory decorated with an engraving of a mammoth

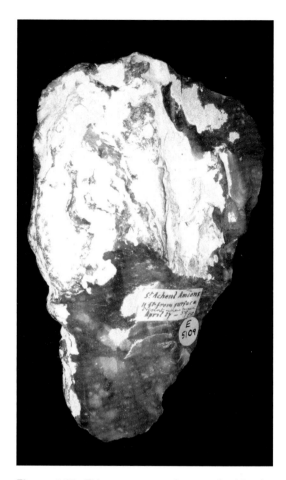

Figure 1.15 This stone was photographed in situ in the gravels of the Somme valley associated with mammoth bones in 1859, when John Evans and the geologist Joseph Prestwich visited Boucher de Perthes' excavations at St Acheul, Amiens, proving human antiquity. Evans later published hand axes similar to this example: 'That they really are implements fashioned by the hand of man, a single glance at a collection of them placed side by side . . . would, I think, be sufficient to convince even the most sceptical. There is a uniformity of shape, a correctness of outline, and a sharpness about the cutting edges and points, which cannot be due to anything but design' (Evans 1860: 288). The artefact was recently rediscovered in the collections of the Natural History Museum, London (Gamble and Kruszynski 2009.)

– clear evidence that humans were contemporary with these extinct mammals (Bahn 1996a: 120).

In 1869 Pitt Rivers (an important pioneer of typology and excavation) successfully sought and found flint implements in association with bones (elephant, hippopotamus, extinct deer etc.) at Acton, London. They occurred in a gravel terrace 25–30 m above the River Thames; however, Neolithic and Bronze Age finds from the river itself demonstrated that its present course was more than 2000 years old: 'this gives us some idea of the great length of time it must have taken to erode the whole valley' (Bowden 1991: 74). Pitt Rivers designed a particularly elegant method of proving the antiquity of early flint artefacts in Egypt by looking for them in the walls of tombs constructed around 1500 BC near Thebes. The tombs had been dug into hard gravel that included (along with other artefacts) a flint flake cut by the builders; the geologist who accompanied Pitt Rivers commented: 'It belongs to the geological delta formation, and beyond question it is older beyond calculation than the tomb which was cut into the gravel, and cut through the end of this particular flint flake' (Bowden 1991: 91).

1.4.2 Catastrophists, Uniformitarians, and the impact of Darwin

- key references: Hallam, *Great geological controversies* 1989; Good, *Sciences of the earth* 1998; Repcheck, *The man who found time* 2003; Schwartz, *Sudden origins* 1999.

Speculation about the age of the Earth took place well before the biblical story of the Creation was undermined in the mid-nineteenth century. Georges Buffon, author of a massive survey of natural history, conducted scientific tests in the mid-eighteenth century in which he heated spheres of stone and metal and then measured their rate of cooling. Since he believed that the Earth might have been formed from hot material of solar origin, he deduced that the Earth had been cooling for almost 75,000 years, and that life on the Earth would have been possible from about 40,000 years ago. Many scientists, including Georges Cuvier, reconciled fossils and geological evidence with the Bible by assuming that the creation of humans before the Flood described in the Old Testament (estimated to have taken

place in 2501 BC) was only the last of a series of creations and catastrophic destructions. The recognition of authentic associations between flint axes and the bones of extinct animals did nothing to solve the problem of dating faced by geologists and historians: how long ago did these humans and animals live? The predicament was expressed by Joseph Prestwich:

> The author does not, however, consider that the facts, as they at present stand, of necessity carry back Man in past time more than they bring forward the great extinct Mammals towards our own time, the evidence having reference only to relative and not to absolute time; and he is of the opinion that many of the later geological changes may have been sudden or of shorter duration than generally considered. In fact, from the evidence here exhibited … the author sees no reason against the conclusion that this period of Man and the extinct Mammals … was brought to a sudden end by a temporary inundation of the land.
>
> (Prestwich 1860: 58)

However, Charles Lyell (1797–1875; Wilson 1972) had published a series of books in the 1830s (entitled *Principles of Geology*) which asserted that gravel, sand and clay deposits were formed by the same processes of erosion and deposition by weather and water observable in modern times, rather than by extraordinary floods. Lyell, and subsequent historians of geology, expressed the debate in terms of **catastrophists** and **uniformitarians**. The influence of the work of the earlier James Hutton (1726–97) meant that after AD 1800 few geologists still believed that layers of gravel and sedimentary rocks were formed simply by the catastrophic Flood described in the Book of Genesis, and few were constrained by the very short time span for the Earth derived from the Old Testament (Gould 1987: 112). **Fluvialists** and catastrophists both studied and interpreted sequences of rocks and fossils, and their methods offered a solution to the problem of early human tools and weapons. If the levels observed by Frere and Boucher de Perthes really *had* been laid down by slow erosion by wind and water and gradual deposition by rivers and oceans, an immense length of time must have been involved. It could not yet be measured, but, if these processes were assumed to have operated uniformly in the present and the past, their duration could perhaps be sensed and visualised rather more easily than mysterious catastrophic floods.

Sufficient finds of human bones in early geological deposits had accumulated in many parts of Europe for Lyell to publish *The geological evidences of the antiquity of man* in 1863. Although incorporating the new evolutionary ideas of Darwin seemed revolutionary, Lyell was pushing at an open door, for concepts of biological evolution were already familiar to scientists and widely debated (for example, in France by Lamarck and Cuvier). The very gradual nature of the mechanism that Darwin proposed in *The origin of species by means of natural selection* (1859) did not just provide an appreciation of the depth of time demanded by geology. It offered an idea of progress that was almost historical in the way that it led from simple to complex organisms in a linear fashion; this concept could be adopted easily by archaeologists. Science in the nineteenth century was not divided into small, specialised compartments in the way it is today, and Darwin was well aware of the implications of recent geological thinking. Darwin and the geologists both demanded the acceptance of the same concept: the present surface of the Earth, and the plants and animals (including humans) that inhabited it, resulted from an immense period of change. At this stage Darwin had said little or nothing about the place of humans in his grand evolutionary scheme, but the impact of evolutionary thinking was evident in the work of artists who represented early humans as near-naked savages from whom modern people were clearly very different (Moser 1998).

The slow development and acceptance of a concept of human antiquity illustrates how archaeology progressed by changing prevailing explanations gradually until a **paradigm shift** (Kuhn 1962) occurred, and reminds us that new ideas normally meet resistance. We must avoid a sense of satisfaction that we may distinguish the 'right' ideas about the past simply because they accord with a modern consensus, and we must always be prepared for the emergence of new evidence about such fundamental issues as human origins. Although finds of fossils of early primates, hominins and early humans have accelerated since the middle of the nineteenth century, they are still rare, and impossible to form into a coherent pattern that will satisfy all experts in this field. DNA variability among living populations suggests that anatomically modern humans were latecomers who spread out of Africa and occupied the whole world – displacing their earlier relatives – within the last 100,000 years (Lewin 2005: 200–7).

1.5 FROM HUNTING TO FARMING

- key references: Rudebeck, *Tilling nature* 2000; Smith, *The emergence of agriculture* 1995.

The reasons behind, and the date of, the transformation of the early hunter-gatherer communities into farming societies was harder to explain. The idea had existed in purely theoretical form from the time that Greek philosophers speculated upon the origins of modern human society. Such a change was fundamental to nineteenth-century attitudes towards social evolution, and was enshrined in the writings of Karl Marx, among others (Chapter 6: 257). Little that was meaningful could be said about the *origin* of civilisation(s) until some understanding had been achieved of the earlier adoption of agriculture by settled prehistoric communities (**Fig. 1.16**).

Finds of bones and plants in Scandinavia and in Switzerland established a clear link between farming and the diagnostic polished stone tools of the so-called New Stone Age, or Neolithic period. In the 1930s such finds were combined with Marxist theory by V. Gordon Childe, who coined the term 'Neolithic Revolution' to describe the fundamental shift from hunting to farming, and many general accounts of the history of the world still employ the terms **Neolithic** and **urban revolution** as if they were historical 'events' comparable to the European Industrial

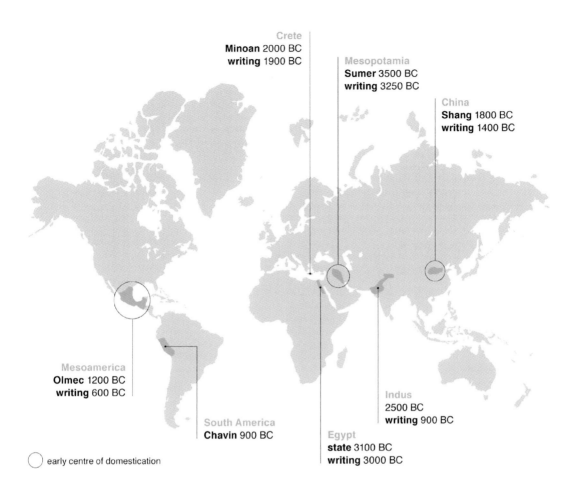

Crete
Minoan 2000 BC
writing 1900 BC

Mesopotamia
Sumer 3500 BC
writing 3250 BC

China
Shang 1800 BC
writing 1400 BC

Mesoamerica
Olmec 1200 BC
writing 600 BC

South America
Chavin 900 BC

Indus
2500 BC
writing 900 BC

Egypt
state 3100 BC
writing 3000 BC

early centre of domestication

Figure 1.16 Ideas about social evolution in the eighteenth and nineteenth centuries involved a straight-forward progression from savagery (hunting bands) through barbarism (farming communities) to civilisation (urban states). The reality revealed by archaeology is more complicated, for domestication of varying combinations of animals and plants occurred in many places independently. Civilisations with architecturally sophisticated urban centres and systems of writing also emerged independently in at least three regions (Mesoamerica, Mesopotamia, China) at different times. Nineteenth-century attempts to link them all together by means of superficially similar features, such as pyramids or pictographic writing, reflected a quest for simple linear schemes of social evolution. It required an earlier 'lost civilisation' (such as Atlantis) to be proposed as a common source for these features. However, great differences in detail and in date make such 'diffusionist' explanations very difficult, and most archaeologists are happy to acknowledge separate invention and development. (Chris Unwin, using data compiled from numerous sources)

Revolution of the eighteenth century AD (Greene 1999; **Box 1.7**).

It is one thing to discover civilisations, quite another to understand how they arose. Most parts of the world where complex societies emerged now have well-documented earlier phases during which animals and plants were domesticated. Thanks to twentieth-century scientific dating methods such as radiocarbon dating, we now know that the first signs of domestication appeared about 10,000 years ago; in the Old World, farming villages with crop cultivation and domestic animals were widespread by 5000 BC, and similar developments were beginning in the

Americas. As with civilisation, there have been attempts to trace the diffusion of agriculture back to a single source, but this is even more difficult to support in the case of farming. Completely different crops formed the basis of domestication in different parts of the world – wheat and barley in the Near East and Europe, rice in south-east Asia, and maize in Mesoamerica. The single factor most likely to have brought thousands of years of hunting and gathering to an end is climatic change; the kinds of environmental evidence upon which such an interpretation may be based are presented in Chapter 5.

1.5.1   World prehistory

- key references: Clark, *From savagery to civilisation* 1946, *World prehistory: a new outline* 1969; Fagan, *People of the Earth* 2007; Scarre, *The human past* 2005.

Developments during the twentieth century in integrating archaeological and scientific evidence with anthropological interpretation mean that **world prehistory** is now a meaningful concept. Formerly, ideas about social evolution current in Europe meant that indigenous peoples elsewhere in the world were regarded as inherently inferior, and their lands ripe for reallocation to new settlers – just as the Romans had brought 'civilisation' to Iron Age Britain (Corbey and Theunissen 1995). The grotesque figure Caliban in Shakespeare's *The Tempest* characterises Tudor attitudes to primitive peoples so well that a nineteenth-century pioneer of prehistory, Daniel Wilson, devoted an entire book to 'that imaginary intermediate being, between the true brute and man, which, if the new theory of descent from crudest animal organisms be true, was our predecessor and precursor in the inheritance of this world of humanity' (1873: xii; Trigger 1992: 58). Australia played an important role in revealing hunter-gatherer lifestyles that could serve as a model for interpreting Palaeolithic human life in Europe (Griffiths 1996). The situation was complicated by evolutionary ideas which suggested that Aborigines were an unsuccessful lower form of humanity, and made worse by the interests of

colonisers in dispossessing indigenous people. North American and African native populations had made a fundamental contribution as models for conceptualising prehistoric life in Europe in later prehistoric times. Understanding was enhanced in the nineteenth century by anthropological research in Polynesia, where Neolithic communities, relatively untouched by European intrusion, were being encountered. Social structures as well as material culture were investigated in great detail, for example by the Torres Straits Expedition of 1898 (Slobodin 1997: 19–26).

1.6   THE DISCOVERY OF CIVILISATIONS

- key references: Stiebing, *Uncovering the past* 1993: 55–226; Maisels, *The emergence of civilisation* 1993; *Early civilisations of the Old World* 1999; Whitehouse, *The first cities* 1997; Dyson, *In pursuit of ancient pasts* 2006.

It is important to remember that **civilisation** is a modern definition imposed upon the past from a Western intellectual perspective; it is used here without implying that it is intrinsically superior to other ways of living, or that it is the natural end-point of progress. The fact that the modern world is dominated by sophisticated cities and states might encourage a misleading view that the discovery of civilisations was a more important archaeological achievement than the revelation of human origins or the growth of the study of prehistory. A distinction must be drawn between the Classical civilisations that were directly ancestral to those European countries where archaeology emerged, and civilisations that were not, such as China, India or America (**Fig. 1.16**). Greece and Rome had never been forgotten, but the study of their sites and material remains developed dramatically from the Renaissance to the Enlightenment. A further group of civilisations was also well known to Europeans aware of the Bible, since the Old Testament included episodes set in Egypt and Mesopotamia; these regions were, however, relatively inaccessible to travellers and antiquaries before the nineteenth century. Other civilisations – notably the Aztec, Maya and Inca in Mesoamerica and South America – were still flourishing at the time of the Spanish conquests in the early sixteenth century AD, but their achievements were downplayed in the process of colonisation and religious conversion that followed. These American civilisations suffered such a sharp decline that even the grandest cities and temples were abandoned, so that they were in effect rediscovered in the nineteenth and twentieth centuries (Stiebing 1993: 167–97).

Archaeological study of civilisations raised new questions that continue to provide problems, particularly over definitions (Gowlett 1993: 8–9, 172–97). How may civilisations be recognised? Urban settlements and systems of writing were the most generally accepted characteristics, but how, where and when did they originate? Did civilisation begin once in a single location and spread outwards from there? Naturally, detailed investigation led to awareness of earlier phases of civilisations about which little or nothing was known – Minoan Crete, the Indus Valley, Olmec Mesoamerica. Another problem was that some written languages recorded in documents and/or inscriptions could be read by scholars (Greek, Latin, Chinese) while others could not. At least Egyptian hieroglyphs and Mesopotamian cuneiform texts, although not yet deciphered, were written in languages whose structure and vocabulary were well known from other sources, but those of Minoans or Hittites could not be assumed to relate to any known language (Pope 1999).

1.6.1 Greece and Rome

- key references: Stiebing, *Uncovering the past* 1993: 119–65; Dyson, *In pursuit of ancient pasts* 2006; Etienne and Etienne, *The search for ancient Greece* 1992; Moatti, *The search for ancient Rome* 1993; Morris, *Classical Greece* 1994.

The Classical Mediterranean civilisations of Greece and Rome received particularly close attention from the fourteenth to the eighteenth centuries AD. Their familiarity reduced the potential for Classical archaeology to introduce new techniques and concepts, compared to the study of earlier civilisations in Egypt or Mesopotamia, or prehistoric questions such as human origins. When looking at photographs of the familiar ruins of the Forum in Rome, it is easy to forget that in the eighteenth century it was still a cow pasture not yet cleared by archaeologists – little different from how it was seen by Bracciolini in 1430: 'where they assembled to enact their laws and elect their magistrates, is now enclosed for cultivation of pot-herbs, or thrown open for the reception of swine and buffaloes' (quoted in Moatti 1993: 149). However, innovations in technique that did occur included art history (pioneered by Johann Winckelmann in the eighteenth century: Dyson 2006: 2–4), architectural recording and analysis, epigraphy (the study of inscriptions), and the study of sequences of artefacts from graves or sites excavated – eventually – with careful attention to **stratification**. The archaeology of early Rome extended to study of the Etruscans, early Rome's neighbours to the north, and relations with southern Italy and Sicily, where Greek cities had been established from the eighth century BC (Stiebing 1993: 153–8). The archaeology of Greece and Rome became inextricably linked with political movements for independence and national unity, which were particularly strong during the Romantic period of the nineteenth century. Meanwhile the establishment of archaeological institutes in Greece and Italy by the nineteenth-century powers – France, Germany and Britain – reflected their desire to relate their modern empires to those of the Classical world (Dyson 2006).

The failing grip of the Ottoman Empire in the nineteenth century stimulated the exploration of Greece, which gained independence from the Turks in 1821 (Etienne and Etienne 1990: 85–93). Foreign excavators rapidly cleared the Acropolis at Athens, disengaging the remains of such buildings as the Erechtheum and the Parthenon from a harem and mosque (**Fig. 1.17**). Societies tend to select the past that they wish to emphasise; the removal of physical reminders of Turkish rule and its religion, Islam, helped the new Greek nation to emphasise European roots (McNeal 1991). Excavations by Heinrich Schliemann in Turkey and Greece and by Arthur Evans on Crete demonstrated the potential of archaeological methods for elucidating the Mycenaean and Minoan antecedents of Greek civilisation (Stiebing 1993: 130–8).

1.6.2 Egypt and Mesopotamia

- key references: Moser, *Wondrous curiosities* 2006; Siliotti, *Egypt lost and found* 1998; Vercoutter, *The search for ancient Egypt* 1992; Maisels, *The Near East* 1990; Pope, *The story of decipherment* 1999.

Interest in Egypt and Mesopotamia was not entirely separate from the investigation of Classical Greece and Rome, for the two areas had fallen under the control of Alexander the Great in the fourth century BC, and parts of both were absorbed into the Roman Empire in the first century BC. Thus, some indications of the early history and antiquities of Egypt and Mesopotamia could be gleaned from Classical writers, while even earlier references abounded in the Old Testament of the Bible. There was another reason for the expansion of interest from Egypt to other parts of the Near East during the nineteenth century. Classical archaeology had amplified written records about Greece and Rome, and hinted at the origins of their civilisations; investigations in Palestine and Mesopotamia therefore offered similar success in relation to the Bible. Thus, a wide public could take a safe interest in news of discoveries that promised to enrich and confirm one of the major formative elements of European Christian culture, in contrast to hearing of the disturbing implications of the crude stone tools that threatened to undermine the date and nature of the Creation recorded in the Book of Genesis (Moorey 1991).

Figure 1.17 Engraving of the Parthenon, Athens, published in 1787, shows Turkish houses and a mosque that were removed when Greece became independent in 1831. Stuart and Revett published five volumes of architectural studies and views of buildings between 1762 and 1830, and placed great emphasis upon accurate recording, for these books were intended for use by architects building in the neo-classical style. Fortunately for modern researchers with a wider interest in these sites, they began by sketching the actual condition of each monument. (Stuart and Revett 1787: pl. 1)

The decline of the Turkish Empire allowed progressively easier access to Egypt and Mesopotamia after AD 1800, resulting in the presence of diplomats and soldiers from France and Britain (and later Germany) around the Red Sea and Arabian Gulf – the strategic routes that connected the Mediterranean to the Indian Ocean. Many of these individuals came from the same educational and social background as the antiquaries who had studied the classics and travelled to historic sites on the Grand Tour. It is therefore not surprising to find that Claudius James Rich (agent of the East India Company at Baghdad from 1807) or Paul Émile Botta (French consul from 1842 at Mosul, the ancient Nineveh) investigated the remains of Babylon and Nineveh and other sites in Iraq near the towns where they were based (Bahn 1996a: 98–109). National prestige became embroiled in the pursuit of antiquities, and as a result sculptures and even parts of buildings were transported to the museums of London, Paris and Berlin. Napoleon's invasion of Egypt in 1798 was even more striking; although Nelson ensured that it was not a military success it was certainly an academic triumph. Two hundred scholars accompanied Napoleon's army, and they established the foundations for decades of subsequent research into Egypt's civilisation and prehistory (Vercoutter 1992: 39, 53–9; Trigger 2006: 68). Historians of archaeology sometimes overlook the fact that Napoleon's scholars were also engaged in the study of contemporary aspects of Egypt, such as its natural history; thus Drovetti, who is chiefly remembered for his acquisition and sale of antiquities, also organised the even more impressive feat of delivering a live giraffe to King Charles X in Paris (Allin 1999; **Box 1.5**). Once again we are reminded that archaeology was part of a wider cultural world.

The methods developed since the Renaissance for the study of Classical Greece and Rome, based upon a coordinated investigation of literature, art and architecture, provided a model that could be applied to the study of Egypt and the Near East (Trigger 2006: 67). Literary interest was soon given a tremendous boost, for the written languages of both regions were deciphered by the middle of the nineteenth century (Pope 1999).

An inscription on the Rosetta Stone (discovered in Egypt by a French officer in Napoleon's army in 1799) turned out to have been written in two different Egyptian scripts and also in Greek. The stone was taken to Britain after Napoleon's defeat, but attempts to use the Greek text as a key for understanding the Egyptian scripts culminated in success by Jean François Champollion, who published a grammar and dictionary of Egyptian hieroglyphics in the 1830s (Parkinson 2005). The cuneiform script of Mesopotamia was first translated at around the same time, and the early Babylonian language of the region was deciphered with the help of a gigantic inscription carved on a high cliff at Behistun in Persia, recorded by Henry Rawlinson, a soldier and diplomat in the region. It included identical texts written in Persian, Babylonian and Elamite to proclaim the authority of the Persian king Darius over his conquests, and the study was completed by 1857 (Bahn 1996a: 108–9). Rawlinson eventually became curator of the British Museum in 1876.

The implications of these translations were tremendous: in the course of the nineteenth century Egyptology and Assyriology added 3,000 years of history to two areas of particular interest in terms of biblical studies. Countless Egyptian hieroglyphic inscriptions were already known (their use had continued under Greek and Roman rule until at least the end of the fourth century AD), and buildings could now be dated according to the names of pharaohs inscribed on them. The decipherment of cuneiform writing allowed the translation of thousands of clay tablets found on excavations throughout the area; these tablets frequently provided details of palace stores and accounts, as well as historical information. Egypt and Mesopotamia thus joined Greece and Rome in having a detailed historical framework for the study of their culture and physical remains.

The increasing interest in Near-Eastern civilisations was not entirely beneficial, for it led to intensive plundering of sites for carvings and inscriptions to satisfy greater demands from museums and collectors. In Mesopotamia, even palaces and temples were largely built out of sun-dried mud-brick (**Fig 3.18**) – unlike the stone of their counterparts in Egypt. Fragile structures

BOX 1.5

Plundering and collecting: Belzoni and Lord Elgin

During the early years of archaeology, much of its activity throughout the world consisted of the unsystematic collection (or looting) of antiquities, particularly from the ancient civilisations of Greece and Egypt. Giovanni Belzoni (1778–1823), an Italian strongman, for example, collected antiquities from Egypt, such as Ramesses III's sarcophagus, which later became part of the Egyptian collections of the British Museum (Murray 2001: 155). Many classical antiquities were removed from the Ottoman Empire (which included modern Greece and Turkey) to be displayed in private collections or donated to new national museums. Most famously Lord Elgin (1766–1841), Britain's ambassador to the Ottoman Empire, had friezes from the Parthenon in Athens (the so-called 'Elgin marbles') removed and shipped to London, where they were bought by the British Museum in 1816 (Murray 2001: 467; Beard 2002). The legacy of these collectors continues today, since many of the world's most prestigious museums (for example the Metropolitan Museum in New York, the Louvre in Paris, and the British Museum) contain artefacts from many parts of the world whose provenance is either unrecorded or whose ownership is contested. In some cases entire buildings were removed, such as the Greek altar from Pergamon in Turkey re-erected

in a museum in Berlin. The opening of a new museum (seen here) in Athens in 2009 to house the Parthenon sculptures, where elements such as the Elgin marbles now held in foreign collections are represented by casts, contests the long-held argument that archaeological remains from Athens were safer, or better treated, in museums elsewhere. It adds to the much wider challenge to museums to return objects removed from other countries in the eighteenth and nineteenth centuries (see Chapter 6; Hamilakis 1999). (Getty Images)

and perishable or unimpressive artefacts were neglected for most of the rest of the nineteenth century, along with any earlier prehistoric levels underlying historical sites. Frere, Worsaae and Boucher de Perthes observed and recorded the stratigraphic contexts of prehistoric artefacts because they were the only possible source of chronological evidence (Chapter 3: 90–2); with historical records written in hieroglyphs or cuneiform, who needed strata?

Mariette's discovery of the Serapeum, at Memphis in Egypt, in 1851 (Vercoutter 1992: 101–5) may be contrasted with the way in which Schliemann approached fieldwork (below). Mariette knew about the site from an ancient Greek traveller's account and from references in

Egyptian papyri, but only discovered it thanks to a good memory and the chance observation of the head of a sphinx sticking out of the sand; four years of excavation followed. Happy accidents of this kind were the rule rather than the exception. Many sites mentioned in historical sources or the Bible were only identified because their names appeared on building inscriptions or clay tablets found during plunder for museum exhibits. One example of this kind was the site of Sippar in southern Mesopotamia (the biblical *Sepharvaim*), where Rassam excavated for the British Museum in 1881. Ironically, one of the cuneiform inscriptions that he found recorded an excavation carried out by the Babylonian king Nabonidus in the sixth century BC. Nabonidus dug beneath

Figure 1.18 Schliemann's excavations at Troy (Hissarlik, Turkey) were not a good model of archaeological technique. Only solid structures were noticed and recorded, and they were rapidly demolished to reveal earlier features. Schliemann's awareness that a succession of cities had occupied the site, and his determination to find the Homeric level, did at least force him to take note of the occurrence of artefacts in different levels. His motivation for digging is of particular interest; it was the culmination of a long programme of literary research, fieldwork and excavations on other sites, all aimed at identifying the geographical setting and physical remains of Homer's Greeks and Trojans known only from literature. (Schliemann 1880: facing p. 265)

the foundations of a temple dedicated to the Sun-god Shamash to find out who had built it, and discovered an inscription that answered his question (Schnapp 1996: 13–18).

1.6.3 The Aegean Bronze Age: Schliemann and Troy

- key references: Murray, *Encyclopedia of archaeology* 1999a: 109–26; Fitton, *Discovery of the Greek Bronze Age* 1995: 48–103; Allen, *Finding the walls of Troy* 1998; McDonald and Thomas, *Progress into the past* 1990; Runnels, *The archaeology of Heinrich Schliemann* 2007.

Heinrich Schliemann was born in Germany in 1822. His commercial skills and gift for languages allowed him to close down his business interests in 1863 to devote himself to travelling and studying the ancient Greek world until his death in 1890. Part of the enduring appeal of Schliemann's life-story lies in his rather dubious role as an outsider who took on the academic establishment and outwitted the Greek and Turkish authorities in the relentless and successful pursuit of his theories. How far this view is correct may be debated, but the persistence, discipline and intelligence that brought him commercial success and a rapid rise from shop assistant to Californian banker would have been helpful in approaching excavation. However, Schliemann was not the only archaeologist in Greece or Turkey to pay attention to the recognition and recording of stratification and finds during an excavation. In the 1870s Alexander Conze working at Samothrace and Ernst Curtius at Olympia both applied rigorous methods of excavation inspired by the work of Giuseppe Fiorelli at Pompeii in Italy (Trigger 2006: 63).

Nineteenth-century German literary scholars considered that the *Iliad* (Homer's epic poem recounting stories of the Trojan Wars) was based not on a historical reality but on accounts of mythical heroes. Schliemann held the opposite view, and, having combined study of the Homeric text with fieldwork in Greece and Turkey, he published observations about Mycenae and the location of Troy in 1869 – two years before he began to excavate the latter site. He drew wide attention to his findings through the rapid publication of his work, as well as popular reports to newspapers such as *The Times* (Fig. 1.18). His results have undergone considerable reinterpretation, initially by his co-worker Dörpfeld, who redefined the occupation level at Troy considered

to have belonged to the Homeric period only three years after Schliemann's death.

Although Schliemann's excavations and research around the Aegean were initially motivated by the desire to elucidate a specific literary text, they brought the Greek Bronze Age and its antecedents to light for the first time. He conducted his work as a conscious problem-oriented exercise, rather than simply to recover attractive finds from a known historical site; he also paid attention to the whole stratigraphic sequence at Troy, not just a single period. Clearer objectives were finally coming into the study of early civilisations. The late nineteenth century also witnessed a more systematic approach to the recording of surface remains of monuments, using improved surveying techniques, combined with the rapidly advancing technique of photography. In the early twentieth century, Gertrude Bell made the most of photography as a way

---

BOX 1.6   **Pioneer of Near Eastern archaeology: Gertrude Bell**

The role of many female pioneers has been under-played in histories of archaeology until relatively recently, despite the fact that archaeology was a discipline in which women made a significant contribution at a time when society was dominated by men. Successful women archaeologists include skilled excavators such as Kathleen Kenyon (1906–78), who excavated the Neolithic town of Jericho (Davis 2008), and the first female professor of archaeology in England, Dorothy Garrod (1892–1968). The contribution of antiquaries in Britain such as Christian MacLagan (1809–1901) is less well known (Elsdon 2004), as is the work of many others

(Cohen and Sharp Joukowsky 2004). One pioneer who is better known because of her political connections is Gertrude Bell (1868–1926), seen here investigating an Arab funerary monument in Lebanon. She was born in Washington, England, and spent a considerable part of her life travelling in western Asia during the final decades of the Ottoman Empire and the emergence of Arab countries such as Iraq. She used her knowledge of languages and her skills as a cartographer to map, survey and photograph large numbers of archaeological monuments, in addition to establishing the Iraqi Archaeological Museum in Baghdad (Asher-Greve 2004; Howell 2007). Bell also had a significant influence on many (male) pioneers in Near Eastern archaeology such as Leonard Wooley (1880–1960) and Max Mallowan (1904–78) (McCall 2001). (Mark Jackson, Gertrude Bell Archive, Newcastle University)

of recording not only ancient monuments but scenes of everyday contemporary life (**Box 1.6**).

1.6.4 Greece and the Aegean: Evans and Knossos

- key references: Dyson, *In pursuit of ancient pasts* 2006: chapter 3; Stiebing, *Uncovering the past* 1993: 134–8; Farnoux, *Knossos: unearthing a legend* 1996; Fitton, *Discovery of the Greek Bronze Age* 1995: 115–39.

One of the final stages in revealing the early civilisations of Europe and the Near East took place when Arthur Evans investigated the origins of the Mycenaean civilisation revealed by Schliemann in Greece (Bahn 1996a: 146–50). Soon after the independence of Crete in 1898 Arthur Evans excavated the Minoan palace at Knossos, where a literate civilisation had developed from around 2000 BC. Arthur Evans, like Schliemann, was following up an idea suggested by prior research. He was aware that engraved seal-stones bearing a pictographic script had been found in Crete, and that their script (now known as Linear A) was independent of those of Egypt or Turkey. It indicated that a system of writing had been developed well before the adoption of an early form of Greek by the Mycenaeans (Pope 1999: 146–58). Unlike Schliemann, Arthur Evans did not suffer opposition or ridicule; he had an impeccable academic background, and worked in the Ashmolean Museum, Oxford. At the age of eight he had accompanied his father John on the famous visit to Boucher de Perthes at Abbéville in 1859, where young Arthur actually found a flint implement.

Unlike Egypt, Mesopotamia or even Homeric Greece, the Minoan world was almost entirely unknown; the notion of a civilisation preceding that of Classical Greece was a real revelation. As at Troy, earlier levels were found below the palace at Knossos; they extended back into the prehistoric period and emphasised the depth of time that preceded the literate stages of these early civilisations. Archaeology alone provided almost everything that was known about Minoan civilisation, and this achievement paralleled the contribution made by prehistorians to the understanding of human antiquity. The excavations at Knossos were directed at the solution of a specific cultural problem, using a variety of evidence, including some small previous excavations on the site: the results were spectacularly successful (**Fig. 3.2**). Arthur Evans was helped by the fact that the Minoan palace was not overlain by extensive remains of subsequent occupation. He was able to make really detailed interpretations because it had been destroyed – probably by an earthquake – leading to its abandonment and contained the remains of most of its artefacts and furnishings.

After the discovery of Minoan Crete, the only other early European or Near-Eastern civilisation to remain unknown until the twentieth century was that of the Hittites in Turkey. Like the Mesopotamian civilisations, it was known from the Bible, but it employed a form of writing (now known as Luvian Hieroglyphic) that was even more difficult to decipher than cuneiform. Understanding was accelerated in 1906–8 by the discovery of large numbers of inscribed tablets at the large fortified city of Hattusas (Boghaz-köy), and of a bilingual Luvian and Phoenician inscription in 1947 at Karatepe (Pope 1999: 136–43).

1.6.5 India and Asia

- key references: Stiebing, *Uncovering the past* 1993: 199–225; Chakrabarti, *A history of Indian archaeology* 1988; Barnes, *The rise of civilisation in East Asia* 1999.

Despite contacts through commerce with the Roman Empire and frequent interaction with the medieval Islamic world, little was known in Europe about India or China before the sixteenth century. By this time European traders (notably from Britain and the Netherlands) were well established in the Indian Ocean, following routes and visiting ports used for centuries by Arab merchants. European trade developed into colonial rule in the eighteenth and nineteenth centuries, bringing reports by officials and soldiers about ancient cities or temples such as Ellora (north-east of Bombay), Anuradhapura (Sri Lanka) and Angkor

(Cambodia). Thus, by the nineteenth century no educated European could remain ignorant of the fact that civilisation, measured in Western terms through its cities, art, architecture and systems of writing, was not restricted to the ancient Near East and Mediterranean region. Similar observations in Central and South America made it clear that civilisation was actually a very widespread phenomenon in human history.

In the same way that discoveries around the Aegean provided a Bronze Age background for ancient Greece, fieldwork and excavation in the twentieth century in India and China eventually produced evidence of Bronze Age antecedents for their own civilisations, dating back to before 2000 and 1000 BC respectively. The Indus civilisation spread over a very wide area – larger than either Mesopotamia or Egypt – and engaged in wide-ranging trade. The impressive sites of Harappa and Mohenjo Daro (now in Pakistan) were excavated in the 1920s, and were shown to have had a much longer history than was thought, and to have had links with the Mesopotamian sites in the third millennium BC (Murray 2007: 353–7). In China, artefacts, settlements and rich burials found near Anyang revealed material evidence for the Shang Dynasty (Debaine-Francfort 1999: 51–67). The civilisations of the Indus Valley and the Shang Dynasty shared another feature with their Aegean counterpart: both made use of symbolic systems of writing, although that of the Indus has yet be deciphered.

1.6.6 Civilisations in the Americas

- key references: Lyman and O'Brien, *Measuring time with artifacts* 2006; Stiebing, *Uncovering the past* 1993: 167–98; Kennedy, *Hidden cities* 1994; Barnhart, *Ephraim George Squier and the development of American anthropology* 2005.

Spanish conquistadors and churchmen reported the existence of sophisticated urban civilisations during initial contacts in the early fifteenth century, but only recorded them in the course of their destruction. Some churchmen wrote detailed accounts of Mayan settlements, customs and religion; Diego de Landa (1524–79), first

Bishop of Yucatán, also described and sketched remains of abandoned settlements, some of which dated back to the collapse of classic Mayan civilisations in the ninth century AD. Archaeological rediscovery began in the eighteenth century, but the literate civilisation of the Maya was first presented to a wider public by John Stephens and Frederick Catherwood in the 1840s (Bourbon 1999). Stephens had published successful books about travels in the Near East and Eastern Europe before he met Catherwood, an excellent draughtsman, whose attention had already been attracted by published illustrations of Mayan buildings (**Fig. 1.19–21**). Fortunately, the accuracy of their fieldwork set an example for work elsewhere in Central and South America.

Further south, fieldwork and excavation took place from the 1850s onwards, notably by Ephraim Squier (1821–88) who, after his study of the mounds of Ohio (**Box 1.3**; Trigger 2006: 161–2), mapped the ruins of Central America and Peru (Shimada 1994; Barnhart 2005). Later the German archaeologist Max Uhle (1856–1944) conducted influential excavations in Peru and elsewhere (Murray 2007: 441–3). As in Yucatán, it became apparent that the Inca who occupied sites known from the time of the Spanish conquest stood at the end of a much longer sequence (Stiebing 1993: 186–8). All of this exploratory work falls within Willey and Sabloff's 'classificatory-descriptive period (1840–1914)' of American archaeology, and it was of course influenced by European work on both human antiquity and early civilisations (Willey and Sabloff 1980: 34–76). A drawback for South American archaeologists was that the Mayan script, unlike those of Egypt and Mesopotamia, was not deciphered until the 1960s, even though it had still been in use at the time of the Spanish conquest (Coe 1992; Pope 1999: 195–203).

The influence of Europe upon American archaeology was not entirely positive. Many early students of American antiquities, from Diego de Landa to John Stephens, were insistent that the impressive ruins were the creation of the same people who inhabited the New World at the time of the Spanish conquest, or their antecedents. For others it was inconceivable that such civilisations should have come about independently, and the concept of a lost civilisation inhabiting an island called Atlantis was invoked to link the Old and New Worlds. The idea of Atlantis began in ancient Greece with Plato's account of an island destroyed by volcanic activity, but was transformed and popularised in its modern form in *Atlantis: the antediluvian world*, written by Ignatius Donnelly in 1882. Lost civilisations that deprived indigenous peoples of the early heritage of the regions they inhabited were very helpful in justifying colonial rule in many parts of the world; this, and the underlying concept of the diffusion of culture (**diffusionism**), will be examined further in Chapter 6.

1.7 ACHIEVEMENTS OF EARLY ARCHAEOLOGY

- key references: Murray, *Milestones in archaeology* 2007; Trigger, *A history of archaeological thought* 2006; Schnapp, *The discovery of the past* 1996.

This chapter has sketched the outline of the development of archaeology as a cultural phenomenon inseparable from broader intellectual developments. It has also taken a close look at the application of archaeology to the study of artefacts, where the subject began to achieve an identity of its own. The discovery of the 'lost' civilisations, the appearance of careful excavation techniques, and the increasingly sophisticated interpretation of past societies all belong to a phase of archaeology that had scarcely begun before the nineteenth century. However, the rapid developments of the nineteenth and twentieth centuries incorporated several preoccupations already established during the Renaissance and Enlightenment. Pursuits that were considered respectable in intellectual circles happened to include collecting artefacts and recording ancient sites as part of the scientific study of natural history. The efforts of individuals, usually amateurs and often eccentrics, established the methods of fieldwork, and led to the opening of displays in museums that had to be staffed and catalogued. Natural scientists working with

archaeologists extended the perceived length of the existence of humans on Earth from a mere 6,000 years back into an immeasurable period. As a result of all these achievements, greater efforts were made to collect human artefacts, and to organise them in more sophisticated ways in order to provide evidence for technological progress and social evolution.

Early attempts to introduce some order into the past divided it into three stages of social development (savagery, barbarism, civilisation) or technological ages (Stone, Bronze, Iron). At the beginning of the twenty-first century a considerable proportion of archaeological interpretation is focused upon three rather broader topics, which are frequently described as 'revolutions'. In the twentieth century archaeology reached its heyday, developing its own theories and models of the past, independent of history and classical texts (**Box 1.7**). Considerable progress had been made by the early twentieth century in revealing the basic evidence that allowed fundamental questions to be formulated about three phenomena:

a The study of **human origins** shows how the recognition of stone artefacts led to the establishment of the existence of early prehistoric humans. Only after this nineteenth-century breakthrough did actual bones belonging to early humans begin to be recognised and classified. By the late twentieth century sufficient evidence had accumulated for a **human revolution** in which artefacts and behavioural patterns associated with 'anatomically modern' humans spread rapidly all over the world within the last 100,000 years (Mellars and Stringer 1989).

b The importance of the economic background to early civilisations placed new emphasis upon understanding how and when hunting and gathering wild animals and plants began to be supplemented by domesticating animals and growing crops, culminating in **settled farming**. Since this change took place during the final stage of the Stone Age it became known as the Neolithic (or agricultural) revolution (Childe 1935; Cowan and Watson 1992).

c The study of **civilisations** grew dramatically from the Renaissance to the nineteenth century, when archaeological excavation revealed that cities in many parts of the world were preceded by a long sequence of prehistoric developments. Observations of surviving 'prehistoric' peoples by nineteenth-century anthropologists helped to show what kinds of lifestyles and economies preceded civilisation. The emergence around 5,000 years ago of settlements comparable to modern towns – with elites of literate rulers and priests, and specialised traders and craft workers – was described as an Urban Revolution in the 1930s (Childe 1934; Whitehouse 1997). The importance of social and economic factors added depth to the study of civilisations, and stimulated improvements in excavation techniques. The archaeology of Greece and Rome developed first, followed by Near-Eastern, Asian and American civilisations; emphasis upon works of art and major monuments was gradually supplemented by studies of ordinary artefacts and settlements. Last on the scene in terms of historical archaeology came the study of medieval, post-medieval and even modern industrial periods (Hinton 1983; Crossley 1992; Palmer and Neaverson 1998), the latter very much in the twentieth century (Fig 1.24). The role of archaeology was enhanced by the growth of interest in social, economic and technological aspects of these periods, which led naturally to the study of their material culture as well as their art and architecture (Vyner 1994; Bintliff 1991b).

1.7.1 Excavation: the investigative technique of the future

● key references: Romer and Romer, *Great excavations* 2000; Lucas, *Critical approaches to fieldwork* 2001; Parslow, *Rediscovering antiquity* 1995; Ridley, *The eagle and the spade* 1992.

Interest in material remains, and in particular the concept of excavating sites for information rather than treasure, developed well after the great period of descriptive study characterised by antiquaries such as Aubrey. Although by the sixteenth century

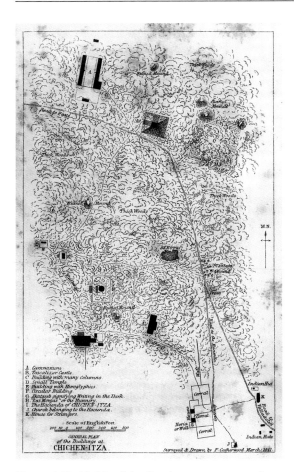

Figure 1.19–20–21 John Stephens spent several seasons travelling in Mesoamerica in the early nineteenth century and published entertaining books about his exploits. Many were illustrated by Frederick Catherwood, a gifted draughtsman and watercolour painter. Catherwood's views of buildings such the Monjas at Chichén Itzá, a ninth- to twelfth-century Mayan city in eastern Mexico, give a clear impression not only of the scale of such structures but also of their state of preservation before any conservation or excavation had been carried out. Rather neglected in comparison with illustrations such as Fig. 1.20 are measured plans made by Catherwood. At major sites such as Chichén Itzá this was a difficult task because of their size and overgrown condition. Catherwood's superb draughtsmanship is evident in engravings made from his detailed drawings and watercolours of Mayan carved decoration and inscriptions at Copán, Honduras (Fig. 1.21). Tropical vegetation and human figures were included both to provide scale and to increase the drama of these illustrations, which are an extremely valuable record of details that may have been damaged or have disappeared subsequently. Photography rapidly overtook this laborious form of recording in the second half of the nineteenth century. (Stephens 1843: opposite p. 293 and p. 290; Bodleian Library, Oxford, Stephens 1841 vol. 1: opposite p. 140; Robinson Library, University of Newcastle)

the study of ancient ruins (accompanied by attention to coins and inscriptions) was an indispensable companion to historical investigation of the past, the idea of using **systematic excavation** lay far in the future. There were of course exceptions, including Stukeley in England and Thomas Jefferson in America, who both excavated burial mounds in the eighteenth century AD – with notable success in the latter case (Stiebing 1993: 172–3). Pompeii and Herculaneum underwent substantial investigation, initially through the use of tunnels, from the early eighteenth century, and the quantity and quality of artefacts, sculptures and wall paintings recovered exerted a

BOX 1.7

V. Gordon Childe: twentieth-century archaeology begins to model the past

Despite its much earlier roots, archaeology only came of age in the twentieth century when more sophisticated explanatory models of the archaeological record began to be devised. One of the leading figures in this development was Vere Gordon Childe (1892–1957). In early works such as *The Danube in prehistory* (1929) and *Man makes himself* (1936) he sought not just to present details of the archaeological record (artefact typologies, settlement types, burials, etc.) but also to explain how societies developed and changed. Childe was instrumental in defining 'revolutions' in the past: the Neolithic Revolution marked the transition from nomadic hunting and gathering to settled farming communities, while the Urban Revolution was characterised by

the transition from agricultural villages to large communities living in cities (Greene 1999; Gathercole 2005). His theories are often considered to be part of 'culture history' in terms of archaeological thought (described more fully in Chapter 6), but they originate in Childe's lifelong Marxism (Patterson 2003); his concept of the processes of political and social evolution that formed the modern world was presented to a wide public in *What happened in history* (1942), a successful early Penguin paperback book. Childe's incorporation of archaeological data from prehistoric times into a clear theoretical explanation of the past helped archaeology to become an established discipline in its own right, rather than a subsidiary part of history, Classics or anthropology (Patterson and Orser 2004). Thus, archaeological enquiry became more than just the 'handmaiden to history' (as it was described by Noël Hume in 1964); it can tell us about a wide range of aspects of ancient societies, rather than simply reinforcing evidence from texts. A variety of visions of the past and theories which developed over the last 100 years are discussed in more detail in Chapter 6. (Edinburgh University)

strong influence upon interior design throughout Europe. Although this early work was destructive and in no way scientific, the discoveries did at least demonstrate that excavation had the potential to reveal aspects of everyday life that were only hinted at in documentary sources (Schnapp 1996: 242–7). Otherwise, archaeological exploration usually began for one of two reasons. Some structures, such as Hissarlik (Schliemann's Troy), were investigated because they were thought to relate to historical people, periods or events. Conversely, mysterious monuments – such as the

pre-Columbian North American mounds investigated by Jefferson – were dug into in the hope of revealing their nature and date (Bahn 1996a: 113–14). A third factor existed almost universally: treasure hunting, either for purely financial gain, or, on a more intellectual plane, in search of curiosities or *objets d'art* for collectors.

By the mid-nineteenth century excavations in caves had become quite common, whether in pursuit of early human remains or of artefacts associated with extinct animal species, and the finds were frequently observed and recorded

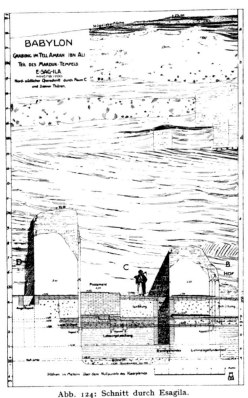

Abb. 124: Schnitt durch Esagila.

Figure 1.22–23 Babylon, on the river Euphrates in modern Iraq, was one of a number of urban sites at the time of the first phase of Mesopotamian civilisation around 3500 BC; almost 3,000 years later it was one of the capitals of the Assyrian empire. The long occupation led to a build-up of deep stratification, largely composed of the remains of buildings made from mud-brick. Clay tablets with cuneiform inscriptions occasionally provided information about the date and function of structures. **Tell** sites such as this did much to improve techniques of excavation because of both their depth and the difficulty of identifying structures. Excavation by Robert Koldewey (who had previously worked with Schliemann) was conducted with considerable skill. A 23-metre section drawn in 1900 reveals careful observation not just of brick structures but also of variations in the texture and consistency of tell material. Recording and publication of drawings of this standard did not become firmly established until well into the twentieth century. (Koldewey 1913: 207, 202; Robinson Library, Newcastle University)

with considerable care (for example by Lartet in France). Scandinavia's rich sequence of graves containing artefacts was also being excavated with excellent recording by Worsaae and others (Klindt-Jensen 1975), and the early Iron Age graves at Hallstatt in Austria were excavated and recorded in meticulous detail in the 1840s to 1860s by Johann Ramsauer (Bahn 1996a: 96–7).

The investigation of Classical civilisations did little to advance archaeological techniques until excavators such as Schliemann and Arthur Evans began to ask more sophisticated questions about

the origins or prehistory of sites such as Troy or Knossos. Advances in excavation also began to emerge from work on prehistory and ethnography by individuals such as Pitt Rivers and Petrie, who displayed a new sense of responsibility about the study of finds and publication. Some subjects – for example, human origins, prehistoric farming communities found in earlier levels in Near-Eastern tells (artificial mounds formed by the accumulation of occupation debris, especially mud-brick), or traces of civilisations preceding the Maya or Aztecs of Central

America – could *only* be studied by archaeological methods (including excavation). Without historical texts, and before the advent of radiocarbon dating, these could only be investigated by excavation – conducted with reference to stratification, and combined with typological studies of pottery and other artefacts that might provide relative dates.

Tell excavations increased awareness of deep **stratification** and (if excavated carefully) provided sequences of artefacts from successive levels such as those explored at Troy. Many of Schliemann's assistants went on from Troy to apply high standards to other sites in Greece and Turkey. Robert Koldewey, who investigated Babylon in Mesopotamia, shared this background (Daniel 1981: 122–3); he was interested both in exploring large areas of buildings on individual levels, and in excavating complete stratified sequences from the top to the bottom (**Fig. 1.22–23**). Furthermore, the majority of the structures in the Near East had been constructed from sun-dried bricks rather than stone: 'It was, therefore, in Mesopotamia that the Classical techniques were reshaped and that new techniques of stratigraphical excavation, and of the excavation of perished and semi-perished materials, were developed' (Daniel 1975: 290). Petrie built upon British traditions established by Pitt Rivers, who had conducted meticulous excavations in Britain in the 1880s and 1890s; Petrie's excavations, and those of Leonard Woolley at Ur, applied rigorous methods through the whole process of extraction, preservation, interpretation and publication (Drower 1985; Winstone 1990).

Arthur Evans' excavations at Knossos were assisted by the fact that the Minoan palace was not overlain by too many later periods of occupation, and because it had been destroyed by fire and still contained the remains of most of its artefacts and furnishings. In contrast to nineteenth-century excavators, Arthur Evans preserved and restored the crumbling gypsum masonry of the palace at Knossos while excavation proceeded. His earliest photographs show a meticulously cleaned site, and the text demonstrates close attention to the stratigraphic positions of finds, both as dating evidence and as a means of interpreting

the destruction of the palace (Arthur Evans, 1899–1900; **Fig. 3.2**). These high standards were far from universal, and – unlike Pitt Rivers – Arthur Evans did not publish *full* excavation reports. Fortunately the detailed notebooks kept by his assistant, Duncan Mackenzie, have allowed more recent archaeologists to review the evidence (Momigliano 1999).

Chapter 1 has followed archaeological concepts and techniques up to the early twentieth century; the chapters that follow will present archaeological principles and methods in detail, referring back to their historical development when necessary. The development of excavation techniques will be explored further in Chapter 3. Chapter 6 will return to concepts, and follow the development of many ideas presented in Chapter

Figure 1.24 Long after the mature development of Classical archaeology and prehistory, archaeologists developed distinctive approaches to the medieval period and – eventually – to industrial archaeology (Cossons 2000). South Wales was a centre of iron and coal production during the Industrial Revolution, and the Blaenavon Industrial Landscape was inscribed on the UNESCO World Heritage List in 2000; this water balance tower for lifting wagons was built in 1859. (CADW: Welsh Historic Monuments. Crown copyright)

1 through the twentieth century, before looking at some issues that they raise in modern archaeological practice.

A lesson to draw from this historical introduction is that archaeology is the product of ideas and information from many different sources. Fortunately, the multidisciplinary approach that made possible the study of early humans and the transition from agriculture to urbanisation has grown ever since, with the result that archaeology remains one of the few subjects available in the educational world that forms a genuine bridge between the sciences and the humanities (**Fig. 1.24**). As we will see in Chapter 6, it is a challenge for us that each generation of archaeologists rewrites the history of the discipline in its own image (Murray 2007; Murray and Evans 2008: 6); our story here might be different if we, the authors, held different theoretical perspectives on the nature of archaeology itself.

1.8 GUIDE TO FURTHER READING

Complete details of every publication mentioned in this section can be found in the consolidated bibliography. Consult the works cited as key references beneath section headings within this chapter first.

THE INTELLECTUAL HISTORY OF ARCHAEOLOGY

While Trigger presents the most detailed intellectual history and Schnapp places it into fascinating contexts, an accessible overview with comprehensive illustrations is *A short history of archaeology* 1981 by Glyn Daniel, whose earlier writings on the subject (and works by Stuart Piggott) remain stimulating and informative. Murray, *Milestones in archaeology* 2007, provides a personal overview of the key developments. Wardell, *Foundation myths* 2005, is an account of Irish archaeology, whilst Bowman and Williams, *New perspectives on Americanist archaeology* 2002,

provides perspectives on specifically American developments. Margarita Diaz-Andreu, *A world history of nineteenth century archaeology: nationalism, colonialism, and the past* 2007, charts the context of archaeology's development in the nineteenth century and provides greater discussion on the history of archaeology beyond Europe and North America. Murray and Evans, *Histories of archaeology* 2008, provides a useful collection of earlier essays by prominent historiographers of archaeology. The often neglected role of some of the early female archaeologists is explored in Cohen and Sharp Joukowsky, *Breaking ground* 2004. The Gertrude Bell archive at Newcastle University library provides an open resource to her letters and diaries.

ARCHAEOLOGY AND ANTIQUARIANISM, PREHISTORY AND HISTORY

Sweet, *Antiquaries* 2004 provides an overall account of eighteenth-century antiquarianism, while Starkey *et al.*, *Making history* 2007, a guide to the Society of Antiquaries' tricentennial exhibition, provides an illustrated introduction to many of the characters and developments. Richard, *L'invention de la préhistoire* 1992, is an extensive collection of essays, while Ferguson, *Utter antiquity* 1993, and Van Riper, *Men among the mammoths* 1993, look at prehistory in Renaissance and Victorian England. Rowley-Conwy, *From Genesis to prehistory* 2007, gives a lively account of how the concept of prehistory developed and was adopted across Britain and Scandinavia and challenges some of the claims made in other histories of archaeology. Freeman, *Victorians and the prehistoric* 2004, gives an account of the discovery of the long history of the world. A recent biography of a prehistorian who expanded the scope of prehistory in the twentieth century is Fagan, *Grahame Clark* 2001. MacGregor, *Sir John Evans* 2008, is a volume of papers examining this influential polymath. Much of the **historiography** of archaeology has focused on prehistory, but Howard Williams,

'Digging Saxon graves in Victorian Britain' 2006, and Edwards, 'Edward Lhuyd and the origins of early medieval Celtic archaeology' 2007, have recently examined approaches to early medieval archaeology. The history of archaeology can also tend towards the Anglo-American past: Schlanger and Nordbladh, *Archives, ancestors, practices* 2008, provides a balance of case studies from around the world. The *Oxford Dictionary of National Biography*, available on-line, provides good outlines of many key British figures.

THE EMERGENCE OF ARCHAEOLOGICAL METHODS

Fagan, 'Short history of archaeological methods 1870 to 1960' 2005, is a good basic introduction to the emergence of archaeological methods. Fagan, *Eyewitness to discovery* 1996, is an anthology of first-person accounts of 'the world's greatest archaeological discoveries', as is the earlier Silverberg, *Great adventures in archaeology* reprinted in 1997. For Classical archaeology see Weiss, *The Renaissance discovery of classical antiquity* 1988. Antiquarianism in Britain is best covered in Sweet, *Antiquaries* 2004, while Aubrey's and Stukeley's work appears in Ucko *et al.*, *Avebury reconsidered* 1990.

The origin of one particular museum is recounted in Wilson, *The British Museum: a history*, 2002, while essays about its founder have been edited by MacGregor, *Sir Hans Sloane: collector, scientist, antiquary* 1994 and its development examined through the lens of one of its early benefactors in Chambers, *Joseph Banks and the British Museum* 2007. Details on the controversy of cleaning the Elgin marbles are covered in Jenkins, *Cleaning and controversy* 2001. The context of the collectors and collections at the Pitt Rivers Museum, Oxford, is explored by Gosden and Larson, *Knowing things* 2007. Developments outside Britain are featured in Alexander, *The museum in America: innovators and pioneers* 1997 and Skeates, *The collecting of origins: collectors and collections of Italian prehistory* 2000. Thompson,

Ruins reused 2006, provides a basic introduction to some of the early legislation in monument protection and key figures in the development of monument preservation.

THE RECOGNITION AND STUDY OF ARTEFACTS

Romer and Romer, *Great excavations* 2000, includes an account of Scandinavia and the Three-Age System. Murray's *Encyclopedia of archaeology: Great archaeologists* 1999, and *History and discoveries* 2001, provide introductory snippets.

HUMAN ORIGINS

An excellent illustrated outline is included in Turnbaugh et al., *Understanding physical anthropology and archaeology* 2002. A biography of the discoverer of 'Java Man' in the style of a novel is Shipman, *The man who found the missing link: the extraordinary life of Eugene Dubois* 2001. For a complete overview of geology see Thompson, *Chronology of geological thinking from antiquity to 1899* 1988.

THE DISCOVERY OF CIVILISATIONS

Traill, *Schliemann of Troy: treasure and deceit* 1995, is a biography, while Moorehead, *Lost and found: the 9,000 treasures of Troy* 1997, brings Schliemann's story up to date. The life of Arthur Evans (and his father, John) are included in *Time and chance* 1943, written by his daughter Joan, while Horwitz, *The find of a lifetime* 1981, is a biography. The uses, and abuses, of the Egyptian past in the eighteenth and nineteenth century are explored in Reid, *Whose Pharaohs?* 2002. Chakrabarti, *Archaeology in the Third World* 2003, brings the story of archaeology in India up to date, examining the period from 1947 to the present.

CHAPTER 2

Discovery and Investigation

2

Archaeological prospection is a relatively new term which draws together the many non-destructive methods used to locate and characterise the surviving physical evidence of past human activity. These vary from the fundamental observation and mapping of artefact distributions and topography, to the analysis of anthropogenic chemical and geochemical signatures in the soil, and to ground-based, aerial and underwater remote sensing. The term thus embraces the more traditional methods of archaeology, such as surface collection and aerial photography, as well as those technical applications more recently adapted from the physical and chemical sciences.

(David 2001: 521)

The aim of this chapter is to introduce non-destructive methods used for discovering, investigating and recording archaeological sites and landscapes. Much can be learned about individual sites from surface observations alone, without the irreversible physical intervention of excavation (the subject of Chapter 3), which should be used as a last resort. In densely populated, intensively cultivated countries well-preserved ancient sites and landscapes still survive, but are easily damaged; indeed, many prehistoric sites in western Europe must already have been ploughed flat before the end of the Roman period. In these circumstances any approach that can 'see beneath the soil' has a particularly important role, from broad-scanning aerial photography that takes in extensive landscapes to geophysical devices that detect buried structures on individual sites.

We will present these topics in the following sequence:

1. A definition of **site** and its relationship to **landscape**.

2. **Field archaeology**: methods of observing, surveying and documenting surface traces of sites.

3. Remote sensing, including the use of **aerial photography** and **satellite images** to discover and interpret sites, whether visible on the surface or buried, and **geophysical instruments** to locate buried sites by measuring the electrical resistance, magnetism or other physical properties of the soil.

4. **Geographical Information Systems**: using computers for an integrated analysis of maps, images, sites and finds.

5. Placing sites into a wider context through **landscape archaeology**.

Chapter 1 explained how antiquaries like Cyriac of Ancona and Stukeley, or the tell-diggers of the Near East, relied on straightforward visual inspection to find ancient sites – and emphasised the fact that they frequently saw them as components of a landscape (p. 15). Standing structures or earthworks obviously attracted more attention than building materials or artefacts lying around on the surface. Some antiquaries travelled to investigate unknown areas, while others made systematic attempts to increase knowledge about regions that had already proved productive; limitations of transport continued to impose severe restrictions on fieldworkers until at least the mid-twentieth century. Early antiquaries did of course make invaluable observations about sites which in many cases have disappeared or been degraded, but their notes and drawings are usually frustratingly incomplete for modern researchers. There was a slow development from terse descriptions to schematic illustrations, and then from picturesque drawings to accurate surveys (Piggott 1979). Chance discoveries of artefacts and structures during agriculture, industry and building work – which all expanded exponentially in Europe from the late eighteenth century – made major contributions to the basic corpus of modern archaeological knowledge. Furthermore, accidental discoveries frequently provided a starting point for planned research. The pattern of discovery of artefacts and settlements in Denmark illustrates how the sources of finds and focuses of investigation changed over time, as finds made accidentally in fields and bogs during farming and drainage were gradually supplemented by objects found in graves investigated by nineteenth-century archaeologists; only in the twentieth century did finds from the excavation of settlements overtake other sources (Hedeager 1992: 14–21). Many antiquarians and early archaeologists focused on the lives of what they perceived as elites in the past, with the result that fieldwork concentrated on high-status settlements and visible funerary monuments, such as barrows. Only later was it believed that detailed recording of all forms of settlement and land-use was important in reconstructing past societies.

The scientific attitudes that developed between the Renaissance and the Enlightenment (fifteenth to eighteenth centuries) involved an increased interest in classification, which naturally required more careful observation. In addition to noticing sites visible above the ground, Camden and Stukeley made sensible observations and interpretations in the sixteenth and eighteenth centuries of buried features or structures revealed by variations in growing crops (Daniel 1967: 37, 45) while surveyors like William Roy made detailed maps of Roman remains as part of their military mapping (Hingley 2007). Stukeley also worked out the sequence of overlapping earthworks (a Roman road built across the edge of a burial mound – see Chapter 1, p. 16). Recording was revolutionised in the 1840s and 1850s by the rapid development of photography, although it was applied more to buildings and excavations than to fieldwork. British and French expeditions carried out extensive photography in Syria and Egypt (Feyler 1987); when the Crimean War began in 1854, the Society of Antiquaries of London requested the British Army to instruct its photographer 'to take and transmit photographic views of any antiquities which he may observe' (Evans 1956: 291).

2.1 SITES OR LANDSCAPES?

- key references: Drewett, *Field archaeology: an introduction* 1999; Aston, *Interpreting the landscape: landscape archaeology and local history* 1997; Thomas, 'Archaeologies of place and landscape' 2001; Dunnell, 'The notion site' 1992; Johnson, *Ideas of landscape* 2007.

According to Peter Drewett, archaeological sites 'consist essentially of activity areas and rubbish. That is where people have done things in the past and left some residue of having done something' (1999: 17). Darvill (2002) gives a very similar definition: 'any place where objects, features, or **ecofacts** manufactured or modified by human beings are found'. Dictionary definitions of **site** are less precise: 'The position of a town, building etc. especially with reference to the surrounding district or locality', according to the *New English Dictionary* in 1919 (and retained in the *Shorter NED*, 1993). It gives an idea of a centre of human activity similar to Drewett's, while 'reference to the surrounding district' is entirely compatible with modern archaeological ideas about interpreting sites in relation to wider settlement patterns, landscapes and natural environments. The definition of **landscape** is more problematic; it was adopted from the Dutch around 1600 to describe a form of painting that was not a portrait or a seascape. By the eighteenth century its meaning had transferred to a view or prospect from a particular spot (the kind of subject that such a painting would have had), and 'landscape gardening' had emerged by the early nineteenth. Surprisingly the geographical concept of a landscape as a natural tract of land and its topography only appeared at the end of the nineteenth century, largely under the influence of the Romantic movement (Johnson 2007). Since then there have been many definitions of different types of landscape, such as those that have evolved organically or those which are 'ideational landscapes'; such definitions depend on the theoretical viewpoint of the archaeologist (Ashmore and Knapp 1999; Wilkinson 2003; see Chapter 6).

The word 'landscape' is rare in the title of archaeological publications before the 1950s, when it appeared in two very different but influential books. *The making of the English landscape*, by W.G. Hoskins (1955), was not primarily archaeological and relied heavily upon documentary evidence for establishing the date and function of settlements and field systems that had shaped the modern landscape. *Ancient landscapes: studies in field archaeology*, by John Bradford (1957), made extensive use of aerial photographs to examine Roman agriculture and settlement in Italy, and raised the profile of remote sensing as a source of information for exploring historical as well as prehistoric sites in a wider context. One of the first books with landscape archaeology as its main title was by Mick Aston and Trevor Rowley (1974), *Landscape archaeology: an introduction to fieldwork techniques on post-Roman landscapes*; its subtitle underlined a conscious contrast with Hoskins' more historical approach. In recent years the concept of landscape has been widely re-examined. Some suggest that it concerns perceptions of the world as a location where lives were acted out (Johnson 2007, 2–4; Tilley 1994). Certainly it is clear that many non-Western societies have very different concepts of space and their place within it.

The relationship between concepts of site and landscape has been rather different in North America, although the early history of the discovery of ancient sites through fieldwork paralleled that carried out in Europe, the Mediterranean and the Near East (Chapter 1, p. 17). North American archaeology in the early twentieth century was preoccupied by **culture history**, and focused upon classifications of objects and chronologies of sites rather than upon societies in general or the place of sites in a landscape (Chapter 6, p. 258). However, its close links with anthropology encouraged a move towards interpreting archaeology in a broader **ecological** manner as part of a **system** in which processes of social activity and change took place (**processualism**: p. 263). The position of settlements in relation to each other and to their agricultural and material resources became an important part of **New Archaeology** in the 1960s. Archaeologists conducted increasing numbers of detailed regional studies of sites in terms of patterns of settlement and natural resources; Gordon Willey's *Prehistoric settlement patterns in the Virù Valley, Peru* (1953) is seen as a forerunner of this genre, and Flannery's *The early Mesoamerican village* (1976) is a classic mature work. Nevertheless, in 1999, 'What exactly is landscape archaeology?' was posed as a novel question by some American archaeologists, who appeared to envisage the study of sites, then settlements, and finally the landscape, as a progression that took place largely under the influence of processual archaeology (Fisher and Thurston 1999: 630). In Britain, as explained above, things had taken a different turn under the influence of local history in the 1950s.

Works on **settlement** as a specific phenomenon became numerous in the 1960s. Some were based (like Willey's Peruvian study) on fieldwork – a tradition established early around the Mediterranean and in the Near East, for example in Adams' *Land behind Bagdad: a history of settlement of the Diyala Plains* (1965). The growth of these into large-scale **field survey** projects (explained more fully below) in the 1970s and 1980s encouraged closer integration of fieldwork and environmental science in the pursuit of understanding the social and economic development of regions over extended periods of time. Such work incorporated techniques similar to those used in Britain by Aston and Rowley – whether or not the term 'landscape archaeology' was used to describe them – especially when dealing with documentary evidence from historical periods.

As computer-based mathematics expanded in 'New Geography' in the 1960s and 1970s, studies of settlement and landscape came to include spatial archaeology, which adopted models and statistical techniques to elucidate modern settlement patterns. Mathematical approaches remain useful for examining spatial information, from broad regional studies down to the positions of individual artefacts recovered from the surface of a field, and especially in determining whether scatters of sites or artefacts contain significant clusters and patterns, rather than being randomly distributed (below: p. 240). Spatial analysis had a positive impact on fieldwork: 'It is important that most of the techniques ... demand good data. ... it is to be hoped that archaeologists will be stimulated by the possibilities offered by the techniques to collect in the future more data of high standard' (Hodder and Orton 1976: 238). This hope has been fulfilled and more than justified by the development of **Geographical Information Systems (GIS)** which integrate many forms of archaeological and environmental data with maps, and allow mathematical analyses of their relationships to be carried out with a sophistication and ease never dreamed of in the 1970s (below: p. 80).

The expansion of large survey projects raised interesting problems about recording and classification which directed attention back to the question of defining a **site**. Few archaeologists would find any difficulty in recording artefacts or building materials found on the surface of the ground, or recognising and classifying physical features such as a stone wall or mound. But what combination of surface finds and surviving structures constitutes a site? When do scatters of artefacts represent 'activity areas and rubbish' of the kind described by Peter Drewett, and how may we distinguish rubbish that lies on the site of a settlement from identical finds derived from domestic waste being carried away from

a settlement and used for manuring fields? Part of the problem for archaeologists has been self-inflicted, for by 1993 the *Shorter New English Dictionary* had added a further definition of 'site': 'A place containing the remains of former human habitation; an excavation'. One solution is to abandon the term altogether; after all, only with the growth of supposedly objective twentieth-century fieldwork were functional words like 'monument', 'camp', 'village' or 'fort' replaced by the abstraction 'site' (Dunnell 1992: 22); 'Its uses are not warranted by its properties, it obscures crucial theoretical and methodological deficiencies, and it imparts a serious and unredeemable systematic error in recovery and management programs' (*ibid.*: 36–7).

A more practical solution for archaeologists involved in survey projects is to continue to use the term as a descriptive label for a place where a particular concentration of artefacts and/or features occurs, but to define it more clearly, in the manner of the **Neothermal Dalmatia Project** (NDP; **Box 2.1**):

The continuous mapping of finds densities across the countryside has produced estimates of discard rates, currently divided into 'background noise' and 'site' patterning. The finds density at which 'background noise' becomes 'site' is not only region-specific but also varies through time within a region. The definition of mean and higher-than-average levels of finds discard for each period has been attempted for NDP. ... Given the pragmatic need to classify surface remains into those areas which reflect habitation and those which do not, it is proposed here to define as residential 'sites' those scatters whose value exceeds the mean value in the relevant time period. One further concept used in interpretation of surface remains is the 'settlement focus'. The focus is taken to mean locations defined by monuments and/or high-density scatters, as well as those surface remains discovered within a 1 km radius of the centre of the focus. ... Thus, three key units of analysis – 'site', 'monument' and 'settlement focus' – provide the building blocks for an understanding of regional settlement patterns from the Neolithic to the Roman period.

(Chapman *et al.* 1996: 52–5)

Landscape archaeology (and the use of GIS) will be explored more thoroughly below; before doing that, it is necessary to explain how sites and landscapes (however defined) are discovered, recorded and investigated.

2.2 FIELD ARCHAEOLOGY

● key references: Drewett, *Field archaeology: an introduction* 1999; Bowden, *Unravelling the landscape* 1999; Carver, *Archaeological investigation* 2009: 63–112.

Discovery is pointless without **recording**, but observers (ancient or modern) only record what they see, and what they see is determined by what they consider to be significant. **Bias** is inescapable, but may be reduced by modern archaeologists if they explain their ideas and research strategies explicitly, rather than treating fieldwork as an objective recording exercise. Philosophical debate about the nature of science, and the way that it is driven by subjective factors, have promoted critical self-awareness amongst archaeologists (Chapter 6, p. 255). This encourages them to give a clearer explanation of their theoretical approach,

---

BOX 2.1   **Sampling in landscape survey**

An example of sampling applied to a field survey project is illustrated on this location map of the Neothermal Dalmatia Project (Chapman, Shiel and Batovic 1996). It consisted of a survey block and linear transects across a peninsula on the Adriatic coast of Croatia, near the modern city of Zadar. Sampling is essential to ensure that fieldwork is carried out on a representative selection of soils and environments in an area selected for study. Settlement densities are summarised in a chart. The larger the filled square, the greater the number of finds per square kilometre. Clearly, arable land was popular throughout the history of the area, and exploitation of the less favourable land expanded through time to reach a peak in Roman times. Medieval finds are more difficult to recognise, but Iška pottery shows that all five categories of land were utilised to some extent. Information about settlement and population over long periods can be obtained from field survey projects at a fraction of the cost of an excavation. (Chapman and Shiel 1993: Fig. 4, Chapman et al. 1987: Fig. 10).

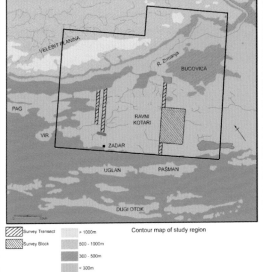

Contour map of study region

Survey Transect   > 1000m
Survey Block   500 - 1000m
                  300 - 500m
                  < 300m

Scale proportional based on
☐ 1 site per km²

	NEOLITHIC	BRONZE AGE	IRON AGE	ROMAN	IŠKA
Arable	■	■	■	■	■
Stony	▪	■	■	■	■
Terrace	·	·	■	■	■
Bottom-Land	·	·	▪	■	▪
Karst	▫	·	■	■	▫

and should allow their data to be reviewed and reinterpreted more easily by people with different ideas. In the concise (if somewhat opaque) words of Ian Hodder, introducing a publication about fieldwork at Çatalhöyük in Turkey, 'The key to this new approach is contextuality and non-fixity. … Types and terms are seen as being sensitive to context, capable of redefinition from different perspectives. Contextuality leads to multivocality, interactivity and reflexivity' (1996: 6). Fieldwork is not immune to social and professional pressures that influence archaeologists in their choice of projects with a view to career prospects, and this has interesting dimensions in relation to gender (Moser 1996).

2.2.1 Field survey

- key references: Pasquinucci and Trement, *The archaeology of the Mediterranean landscape, 4: non-destructive techniques applied to landscape archaeology* 1999; Kardulias, *Beyond the site: regional studies in the Aegean area* 1994; Barker and Lloyd, *Roman landscapes: archaeological survey in the Mediterranean region* 1991.

Much fieldwork now takes place in the context of **field survey** – a comprehensive study of an area selected either because it is threatened with damage by development or agriculture or because it has the potential to answer questions generated by wider archaeological research. Field survey projects effectively break down the conceptual division between sites and landscapes, for they investigate everything from natural vegetation and soils through settlement patterns to individual artefacts. One of the first major fieldwork projects carried out in central Italy began in the 1950s because redistribution of agricultural estates to small-scale farmers led to a sudden increase in ploughing. Fortunately, archaeologists from the British School of Archaeology in Rome realised the implications of this change, and walked over large areas of farmland recording finds and traces of sites or structures. The result was a view of the distribution of rural sites over a long period from later prehistory to the early Middle Ages. Interesting variations in the location and intensity

of sites in different periods required careful interpretation to explain the changes in terms of settlement patterns, population and methods of farming (encapsulated in the title of a general publication about the results: *The changing landscape of south Etruria* (Potter 1979)). Partly as a result of this early success, the Mediterranean region became a focus for numerous large and small projects, perhaps because of the tradition of both European and American research into Greek and Roman archaeology in this area. The most successful projects have been aimed at the analysis of long-term changes in settlement patterns, seen in the perspective of environmental factors that influenced, or were affected by, human exploitation, although the value of some of them has been questioned (Alcock and Cherry 1996). Survey projects initiated by prehistorians have had to include historical periods, not least because they tend to produce the greatest number of sites and finds. The result has been an enrichment of interpretation of prehistory by the addition of concepts, historical information and ethnographic observation from the more recent past (for example Cherry *et al.* 1991, a study of northern Keos in the Cycladic islands from earliest settlement until modern times).

Formerly, significant sites (most commonly towns) were surveyed and excavated because their plans, buildings and inscriptions were expected to reflect the political and military history of their area. Now, studies are more likely to involve extensive analysis on a regional scale, designed to elucidate the broad agricultural, economic and social developments within which individual sites operated (Greene 1986: 98–143). Notable sites that have been extensively excavated in the past may be looked at again by a programme of fieldwork aimed at understanding them in a regional context; Stonehenge was reviewed through fieldwalking and monuments survey in the 1970s and 1980s (RCHME 1979; Richards 1990), while Hodder undertook detailed local and regional fieldwork before beginning new excavations at Çatalhöyük in Turkey (1996). The same principle lies behind investigations of the rural hinterland of important ancient cities, such as Tarragona, on the coast of Spain (Carrete *et al.* 1995).

2.2.2 Fieldwalking

- key references: Wilkinson, 'Surface collection techniques in field archaeology: theory and practice' 2001; Drewett, *Field archaeology: an introduction* 1999: 42–50; Bintliff *et al.* (eds), *The future of surface artefact survey in Europe* 2000; Boismier, *Modelling the effects of tillage processes on artefact distributions in the plough zone* 1997.

Fieldwalking is the simplest procedure employed in fieldwork, and it provides many opportunities for amateurs and beginners to get involved (**Fig. 2.1**). Although it may include the recognition of sites through minor fluctuations in the form or character of the ground in areas that have had little investigation in the past, the main purpose of fieldwalking is normally the collection of artefacts

Figure 2.1 Close-spaced fieldwalking undertaken as part of the Till–Tweed archaeological landscape study in Northumberland. Following the publication of a PhD thesis about this area in 1999, Clive Waddington has directed an intensive survey of these fertile river valleys. A team using a total station follows behind recording each findspot and bagging each artefact to provide accurate spatial recording. Surface inspection of this kind is extremely economical compared with excavation, but requires careful planning and cooperation with local farmers to fit in with agricultural use of the land. (Photograph: Clive Waddington)

from the surface of ploughed fields. The area selected for examination is defined by markers laid out in lines or a grid for the guidance of teams of walkers, to ensure that the ground is inspected evenly. All finds must be recorded accurately so that they can be plotted on an overall plan to show the distribution of the results. Most areas are too large to be explored in their entirety, and are **sampled** in a way designed to allow the results to be assessed statistically and extrapolated to the whole area with some confidence (Banning 2002: 113–32). This demonstrates the need for flexibility in designing fieldwork, and the importance of relating it to modern land-use – for example, taking advantage of newly dug irrigation canals in Turkey gave an opportunity not only to recover artefacts but also to examine physical traces of sites that had been cut through (Hodder 1996: 42–4). As with aerial photography, if fieldwalking is to contribute to interpretation, data-collection is only a first step. Clusters of potsherds, flint flakes or building debris lying on the surface may suggest centres of occupation or focuses of human activity, as well as their dates; complex data of this kind may be investigated with the help of computer-based GIS (Bintliff et al. 2007; below: p. 80). A lack of obvious concentrations does not mean that no occupation existed, of course; agricultural exploitation or geological weathering of the land may affect the results in different ways, even in a small area; interesting experimental work on **post-depositional processes** has been carried out in the hope of understanding the reasons why material appears – or does not appear – on the surface where a field archaeologists may observe it (Boismier 1997).

Occasionally fieldwalking may be accompanied by something closer to excavation. Danish archaeologists have constructed a machine to sieve plough-soil from disturbed sites, rather than relying on people spotting artefacts visible on the surface alone (Steinberg 1996). **Shovel-testing** – popular in North America – involves very small shallow excavations (25–30 cm diameter, 40–50 cm depth, 15–30 m apart) to observe the character of deposits near the surface. These may reveal the extent of a site, or provide a sample of finds for precise dating of different parts of a large site (Ellis 2000: 603–4, 608–9). The latter purpose was met on the Konya plain around Çatalhöyük, Turkey, where larger collection squares (3 m × 3 m) had their vegetation removed, and surface scrapings were sieved to guarantee the recovery of small artefacts (Hodder 1996: 44–5). It is also a particularly useful technique in areas of pasture where fieldwalking is not possible, as in the large landscape survey at Shapwick in Somerset (Gerrard and Aston 2007: 266–78) (Fig. 2.2).

2.2.3 Recording and topographic/ earthwork surveying

- key references: Drewett, *Field archaeology: an introduction* 1999: 58–75; Bowden, *Unravelling the landscape: an inquisitive approach to archaeology* 1999; Bettess, *Surveying for archaeologists* 1992; Howard, *Archaeological surveying and mapping* 2007.

Aerial photographs are used extensively in recording and mapping sites, but ground-level **photography** remains important for documenting them, and can place them into a local context as well as including people engaged in fieldwork to illustrate methodology (Howell and Blanc 1995). It is important that any traces of structures, or earthworks such as ditches or field-boundaries, are planned and recorded accurately. Such plans can be used to determine the role of such features, and in some cases the sequence of earthworks and hence the chronology of a site or landscape. Detailed plans are also important in comparing monuments to establish what type of site it might be: a settlement, a ritual monument, a field system?

Such surveys have taken place since the earliest origins of archaeology (Chapter 1: pp. 13–17) and may be surveyed with a combination of modern instruments and simple equipment that has been in use for several hundred years (Fig. 2.3). A total station or electronic distance measurement system (EDM) is usually used, sometimes in conjunction with a global positioning system (GPS) that can fix a point on the ground to within a few meters (or even less given the right equipment) by tuning in

Figure 2.2 Shovel testing at Shapwick in Somerset. As part of a large study of the landscape of the medieval village of Shapwick, a survey of the surrounding areas was undertaken. As much of the region is under pasture, a technique more commonly used in North America was used: shovel testing of the topsoil provided dateable material similar to that available from fieldwalking elsewhere. (Photograph: Chris Gerrard)

to satellites put into space to improve military navigation (Bowden 1999: 43–69, 199–201; Howard 2007: Chapter 6). The human eye, informed by experience and training, remains the most sensitive instrument, however. A combination of observation, recording and interpretation can reveal new and significant information, for example the recognition of pre-Roman cord-rig field systems in northern Britain. These cultivation strips resemble medieval ridge-and-furrow fields but are much narrower; their early date can be demonstrated when Roman military earthworks overlie them, as at Greenlee Lough, Northumberland (Bowden 1999: 72). In a medieval context unsuspected early examples of landscape gardening have been revealed by detailed survey (Taylor 2000).

Survey can be undertaken at a variety of scales or levels (Bowden 1999: 73–80, 189–93):

- Level 1: **rapid survey** at a small scale to create an accurate framework over a relatively large area.
- Level 2: **landscape survey** at a medium scale to record archaeological features.
- Level 3: **detailed survey** at a large scale to provide an analytical record of sites or landscape details, using electronic methods

(a)

(b)

Figure 2.3 Survey of medieval settlements being undertaken, using Global Positioning System (GPS) in Spain (a), and using a Total Station to survey Roman sites in southern England (b). There are a number of ways of undertaking topographic survey, including using a Total Station theodolite (perhaps the most accurate) and backpack-mounted GPS (as seen here). GPS is increasingly accurate if used with a base-station. Hand-held GPS devices are sufficient for recording the general location of sites or findspots, but are seldom sufficiently accurate for detailed surveys of monuments. (Photographs: (a): Chris Gerrard; (b): Tom Moore)

for control and traditional methods for adding details. Conventional hachured plans remain most effective for illustrating details and their sequences; wedge-shaped lines illustrate the steepness and direction of slopes by variations in their thickness and length (Bowden 1999: 59 Fig. 21).

Extensive complex surface remains are almost invariably easier to interpret when the survey results have been mapped; indirect relationships between various components such as enclosures, trackways and building plots are more likely to be visible on a large-scale plan than on the ground (Fig. 2.4). A combination of field observation and analysis of plans may elucidate the sequence in which earthworks were created, altered or superseded. The order in which they were constructed

can be deduced by studying points where features overlap; as Stukeley correctly observed, the one that is cut through or overlain must be the oldest (just like **superposition** in geological or archaeological stratification – Chapter 3, p. 92). A grid of measured spot-heights can also illustrate subtle surface irregularities (**microtopography**), especially if the readings are processed by computer to enhance variations. Because data is logged in digital form the results may be displayed as a **digital terrain model** by converting the individual measurements into a continuous surface with shading to show the form of a site – perhaps at an oblique angle for clearer visibility.

Documentary evidence is an essential component of approaches to sites, but it comes in many forms, written and visual, that may only be indirectly applicable to a site; 'documents and field

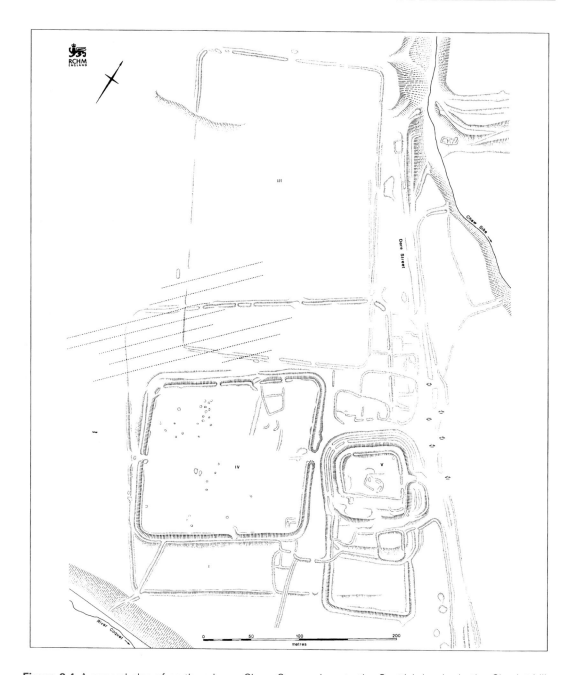

Figure 2.4 A general plan of earthworks on Chew Green, close to the Scottish border in the Cheviot hills, Northumberland, compiled by surveyors and investigators from the Royal Commission on Ancient and Historical Monuments (now part of English Heritage). There are four overlapping square or rectangular Roman military camps and forts, besides other features that probably result from more recent farming activities. The form and sequence of features is indicated by careful use of hachures and continuous lines to provide a drawing. This is simultaneously a record and an interpretation of this earthwork complex. (© NMR Crown copyright: English Heritage)

evidence run on parallel tracks, never meeting' (Bowden 1999: 93). Sequences of maps compiled at different dates, engravings of demolished stately homes and their gardens, estate records listing fields and properties, industrial archives with maps of mining concessions – these are just a few potential sources that may help in the analysis of field remains or landscapes (Bowden 1999: 31–7, 93–5). Comprehensive multiperiod fieldwork also includes standing structures, which may be buildings in ruins or still in use; architectural drawing and recording by photography requires yet more skills and understanding from archaeologists (Wood 1994; Chapter 3, p. 133–4). Results of field recording then require careful storage

and documentation if they are to be of further use for research or heritage management; ideally they will be made accessible in an archive such as a Sites and Monuments Record, also known in Britain as a Historic Environment Record (HER – see below p. 62; **Fig. 2.5**) or a national repository such as (in England) the National Monuments Record (Bowden 1999: 179–88).

2.2.4 Historic landscape and monument inventories

- key references: Baker and Baker, *An assessment of English Sites and Monuments Records* 1999; Fernie and Gilman, *Informing the future of*

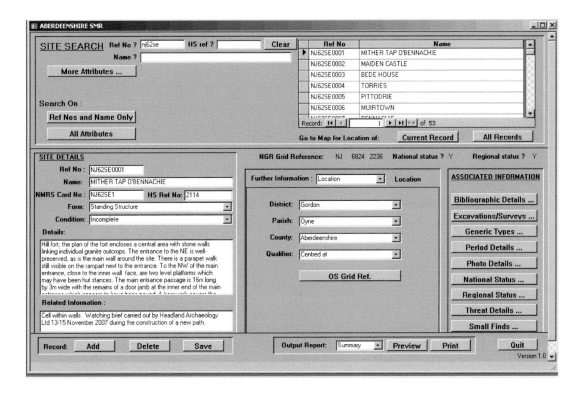

Figure 2.5 Aberdeenshire, like most British counties, has a computerised Sites and Monuments Record (or Historic Environment Record). Such records provide a basic framework of knowledge about sites, along with references to relevant publications, and form a vital resource when developers apply for planning permission. As computers have become more powerful it has become possible to incorporate maps and aerial photographs as well as text into databases of this kind and many are now being made accessible on the Internet. This is just one of several screens of information provided for each site. (Archaeology Service, Aberdeenshire Council)

the past: guidelines for SMRs 2000; Larsen, *Sites and monuments: national archaeological records* 1992.

Ideally a database of sites, with plans, photographs and sources of further information, should serve a number of different purposes. These may include further research by individuals who were not involved in collecting the data, such as academic archaeologists or planning officers considering the impact of development proposals. **Rescue archaeology** – research prompted by threats from development such as road-building – has provided a stimulus to this kind of data management, and many countries now have a policy of maintaining records of archaeological sites and monuments on a regional and/or national basis, increasingly with the help of GIS (Larsen 1992; Cooper 1995).

In the European Union, article 2 of the **Valletta Convention** (1992) requires that all signatories establish an 'inventory of its archaeological heritage and the designation of protected monuments and areas' (Willems 2007). The ways in which this is done vary considerably, but are often organised on a national and/or local basis, with varying levels and ranges of material. In England, records are organised at a national level through the **National Monuments Records** (NMR), which includes, for example, an archive of aerial photographs, and at a local level (HERs). The Record of Monuments and Places (RMP), run by the National Monuments and Historic Properties Service, is a register of archaeological sites in Ireland. In the USA, most state archaeologists also have a register of archaeological sites in addition to the National Register of Historic Places (Chapter 6: p. 295).

At a regional level, these are known in Britain as **Historic Environment Records** (HER: previously called Sites and Monuments Records) in order that information about (and protection of) archaeology should encompass areas of landscape and the environment, rather than individual sites and features of interest. In England, it also includes information about finds recorded in the **Portable Antiquities Scheme** (see below p. 77). This approach emerged from broader concepts of landscape archaeology (see below p. 82) which are also reflected in developments such as **Historic**

Landscape Characterisation. These archives form a key part of managing heritage (Cultural Resource Management), discussed further in Chapter 6.

A reliable record of the number and distribution of known sites makes it much easier to assess the implications of plans for road or building construction. If planning authorities and contractors are able to consult these records at an early stage, they may be able to adjust developments to avoid sites, or at least to take account of them so that excavation can be arranged well in advance without costly disturbances to construction schedules. The individual records about sites or structures based upon fieldwork and survey may well be crucial in providing evidence to secure legal protection in the first place.

Such records are normally stored on computers for rapid access, and the details of each site include cross-references to maps, publications and aerial photographs. This makes the data suitable for investigation by means of GIS designed to inter-relate data of different forms. Alongside the recording of monuments, some areas have also undergone Historic Landscape Characterisation (HLC), which defines areas of different types of landscape according to historical phases (**Box 2.3**). HLC is useful both as a planning and a research tool in determining the location and history of specific landscapes (Aldred and Fairclough 2003; Turner 2006). An HER is the essential starting point for anyone who wishes to study sites or finds of a particular type or period on a regional basis. Research of this kind increases our understanding of those regions and their sites, and makes it easier to draw up priorities when difficult choices have to be made about the preservation or loss of sites. Thus, besides discovering and recording sites, fieldworkers have many responsibilities, including interpretation of the results in the light of the latest research, and presentation of their conclusions in a convenient and comprehensible form for consultation by non-specialists.

2.2.5 Underwater survey

- key references: Bowens, *Underwater archaeology: the NAS guide to principles and practice*

2008; Ruppe and Barstad, *International handbook of underwater archaeology* 2002.

Fieldwork under water is not unlike that on land, for it relies both on broad-scanning methods for identifying wrecks or other underwater structures and on detailed visual inspection of smaller areas or individual locations by divers. Even aerial photography can be used for detecting anomalies in clear shallow water. Photography, recording and surveying practices on wreck sites and cargo scatters use the same general principles employed on dry land, but they are of course more time-consuming and cumbersome – not to mention dangerous. Work in deep water beyond the range of conventional divers has become increasingly possible with the help of **remotely operated vehicles** (ROVs), while the location of discoveries and reference points for detailed surveys can now be fixed by GPS (above: p. 58). Remotely operated vehicles allow visual inspection at great depth and without danger to human divers, but are very expensive to deploy; memorable images of the interior of the *Titanic*, and of passengers' possessions scattered on the seabed around it, underline the potential of combined examination by means of ROVs and video cameras. Electronic remote-sensing devices used under water are discussed further below (p. 79).

The use of seismic survey data, often created by the oil industry, has been used to map palaeo-landscapes under the sea, leading to impressive results – most notably the confirmation of the existence of 'Doggerland', an entire Mesolithic landscape now submerged under the North Sea (Gaffney *et al.* 2009). Submerged landscapes can sometimes be associated with datable finds dredged up by fishing trawlers (Gaffney *et al.* 2007).

2.3   REMOTE SENSING

- key references: Donoghue, 'Remote sensing' 2001; Scollar *et al.*, *Archaeological prospecting and remote sensing* 1990; Shennan and Donoghue, 'Remote sensing in archaeological research' 1992.

The description of **remote sensing** devices that follows begins with airborne and satellite devices, and continues with magnetometers and other geophysical devices (resistivity and magnetic susceptibility meters, and ground penetrating radar) which, although they make contact with the ground, are still 'remote' from the buried archaeological features that they are designed to detect.

2.3.1   Airborne prospection

- key references: Deuel, *Flights into yesterday: the story of aerial archaeology* 1971; Bewley *et al.*, *Archiving aerial photography and remote sensing data* 1999; Parcak, *Satellite remote sensing for archaeology* 2009.

Optical aerial photography has undoubtedly made the greatest single contribution to archaeological fieldwork and recording. Besides giving attractive bird's-eye views of surviving sites, aerial photography is overwhelmingly important in bringing to light buried sites visible through discolorations in the overlying soil or vegetation (**Box 2.2**). More recent high-altitude vertical images taken from satellites have become available since the end of the Cold War, with their resolution becoming increasingly useful for archaeological purposes. Their potential for studying the Stonehenge landscape has been demonstrated (Fowler 1996), while in areas where detailed maps are hard to come by (such as Turkey or the Middle East) they may provide an invaluable guide for fieldwork on the ground or for mapping landscape types from certain periods over large areas (Parcak 2009). At the opposite end of the scale it is possible to use model aircraft for low-altitude reconnaissance; Walker and De Vore (1995) have used this method for obtaining high-resolution vertical photographs of small areas in the United States. It is likely that the dramatic improvements underway in collection of data in digital form (see below) and by satellite imagery will continue (Parcak 2009; below: p. 68). The increasing availability of programs such as Google Earth is also allowing wider access to prospection tools. This may make the use of satellite imagery more cost-effective

BOX 2.2

Cropmark formation

Circumstances leading to the formation of anomalies visible on aerial photographs. A: Slight surface variations, which might not be apparent to an observer on the ground, are enhanced by highlights and shadows produced by low sunlight in the early morning or evening. B: Even if these surface features have been removed, subsequent disturbance of the soil by ploughing may still reveal variations in colour or texture. C: Irregularities in the depth and moisture content of the soil may lead to marked variations in the height and colour of a cereal crop during its growth or ripening.

Severe drought conditions exaggerate these effects and may also reveal much smaller features, not only in cereal crops but also in permanent pasture as in A. Note that the post hole and hearth at the left and centre of these diagrams would not show up on aerial photographs, even in extreme conditions (Sheila Newton).

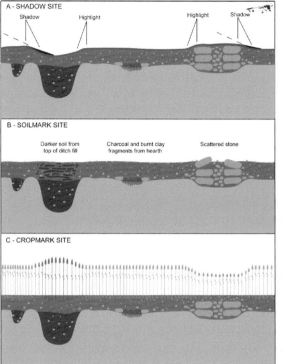

BOX 2.2

A - SHADOW SITE
Shadow   Highlight   Highlight   Shadow

B - SOILMARK SITE
Darker soil from top of ditch fill   Charcoal and burnt clay fragments from hearth   Scattered stone

C - CROPMARK SITE

BOX 2.3   # Historic Landscape Characterisation (HLC)

Historic Landscape Characterisation (HLC) interprets, maps, presents and helps us understand the landscape with particular reference to its development over time. HLC maps differ from traditional archaeological inventories, which usually represent archaeological sites as dots, lines or discrete areas on a map. Using these conventional records it can be hard to appreciate an individual monument as part of an historic landscape. HLC maps do not identify separate archaeological features. Instead, researchers consider groups of features together to identify areas whose elements are linked together by their historical development. After considering features such as fields and their boundaries, roads and tracks, vegetation and land cover and buildings or settlements, they make interpretations about the processes which led to their creation. So, like all landscape archaeology, HLC mapping involves a process of interpretation that is informed by the physical features in the landscape.

During mapping, the landscape is 'characterised' into a series of different types, resulting in a map that looks like a mosaic of irregular, interlocking shapes. HLCs usually rely on existing research to inform their interpretations of the processes that have shaped the cultural landscape and the periods when these changes took place. HLCs are normally created with geographical information systems (GIS), with the most common data sources including modern and historic maps, air photographs and satellite data. HLC maps represent the fact that the long-term development of any area has shaped the form of the features that are present, and they in turn combine to provide its distinctive historic character today.

BOX 2.3   cont.

In the UK, HLCs are now applied in a variety of practical settings, for example forestry schemes and in planning applications (see Chapter 6). Their potential for research is also being recognised. In the example, an HLC map of the territory inland of Silivri in Thrace, north-west Turkey, shows that this landscape, which at first sight appeared relatively homogenous, has a rich agricultural history linked to different episodes of change and development (Sam Turner; Turner and Crow 2010: 227 Fig. 6).

and increasingly useful for surveys in areas of the world where air photographic coverage is limited (Beck 2006; Parcak 2009).

Aerial reconnaissance must be well planned and systematic, and timed to coincide with the best conditions. In addition to knowing about sites that have already been recorded, a programme of photography should be carried out with a good understanding of the geology, farming regime and crop rotation in the survey area. Cameras and film-types used in conventional photography are very versatile, and expertise is required in selecting the optimum equipment and materials as some colour film emulsions are specially sensitive to particular colour ranges. Variations in colour or contrast can be enhanced by special developing or printing processes, or by computer scanning and filtering; infrared photography or other kinds of non-photographic digital

images may produce clearer results – multi-spectral scanning, radar and thermal imaging are discussed below (p. 68).

Aerial photography

- key references: Bewley *et al.*, *Archiving aerial photography and remote sensing data* 1999; Wilson, *Air photo interpretation for archaeologists* 2000; Riley, *Air photography and archaeology* 1987.

The visual effectiveness of aerial photographs had been appreciated since the 1850s; occasional archaeological subjects were photographed from balloons, but the First World War stimulated the practice of taking reconnaissance photographs from aeroplanes for both mapping and strategic purposes. Many pioneers of archaeological aerial photography gained their experience in this way, including Alexander Keiller (Murray, 1999) and O.G.S. Crawford, who published a manual on the subject in 1929 (Hauser 2008). The use of the technique has expanded exponentially since then, and the understanding of the conditions for its optimum application has increased. Most early aerial photographs were taken with map-making rather than archaeological research in mind; however, German photographs taken over Britain during the Second World War, and the complete coverage carried out by the RAF after the end of the war, do include vertical views of many archaeological sites. They also provide a record of the state of the British landscape in the 1940s, before the extensive removal of hedgerows and ploughing of traditional pasture, and this is now of great historical value.

Aerial photography provides a useful supplement to observations made during fieldwork on **visible sites** with traces of earthworks or walls surviving above ground. Many of the most impressive photographs taken by pioneers like Crawford and Keiller were of known sites with visible surface features, but aerial photography has been even more important in providing information and discoveries about **invisible sites** that have been levelled, and are therefore unlikely to be spotted during normal fieldwork. Even when sites are discovered by fieldwalking, after ploughing has scattered finds on the surface, their form and extent are rarely evident. Such sites are most common in areas of heavy agricultural exploitation, where different settlement patterns and field systems might have come and gone several times before the configuration of the modern landscape. Their detection by aerial photography relies on a number of phenomena that influence vegetation or the soil (**Box 2.2**):

- **Shadow sites** are best observed with the help of low sunlight which emphasises irregularities by highlighting bumps and filling hollows with deep shadow (**Fig. 2.6**). Clear sunlight cannot be guaranteed at exactly the right time of morning or evening in temperate countries, and the best shadow effects do not last long.

Figure 2.6 The ditches of Roman military earthworks at Chew Green, Northumberland, are enhanced by shadows cast by low sunlight. This extensive site lies on sloping rough moorland and is very difficult to understand on the ground because of its complexity and size: the most distinctive earthwork, in the centre of the photograph, is approximately 150 metres square. Fig. 2.4 is a plan of the same site. (© Crown copyright Tim Gates/NMR)

- **Cropmarks** are created when buried features either enhance or reduce the growth of plants (**Fig. 2.7**). Since a key factor is the availability of moisture to their roots, abnormal conditions emphasise the height and colour of crops (particularly cereals) during growth and ripening. These effects are not consistent or easily predictable, and a complex site should be photographed over many years, under different conditions, to compile a cumulative record of its features. As with shadow sites, optimum conditions do not last long. Root-crops and pasture are very insensitive, and

Figure 2.7 The fragility of archaeological sites in densely populated areas of England is illustrated at Standlake in Oxfordshire. Modern houses lie next to faint earthwork traces of a settlement and manor house of medieval date surrounded by a moat. The fields divided by a road (centre) contain cropmarks – a confusing mixture of prehistoric and Roman enclosures and structures. The dark lines are created by stronger growth of the cereal crop above ditches that hold deeper soil and moisture than the surrounding gravel subsoil. It is clear that similar traces must extend beneath the medieval earthworks and modern structures; they must also have existed in the fields from which gravel has been extracted at the bottom of the picture. (© Crown copyright; NMR SP 4003/17)

only reveal marks during extreme drought conditions.

- **Soilmarks** may be observed when land has been ploughed; human activity in the past may lead to variations in the character and colour of the topsoil. Like cropmarks, a coherent plan of subtle variations is best perceived from above. Some of the most dramatic sites discovered in this way are Roman villas photographed by Roger Agache in north-eastern France and Roman settlements and field systems with elaborate drainage channels constructed in the Fens of eastern England. The villas are visible because ploughing has brought fragments of their chalk foundations to the surface and revealed detailed plans of buildings as white lines against dark brown soil (Greene 1986: 116–18). In the Fens, drainage ditches around fields and settlements show up as thick dark features because they filled up with peat after their abandonment (Phillips 1970; Hall and Coles 1994). Unfortunately a site that shows up as a soilmark is probably being severely eroded, and may soon disappear altogether if regular ploughing continues. Some soilmarks are merely 'ghost sites', made up of soils of differing consistencies and colours derived from pits, ditches and other features that have already been destroyed by deep ploughing (Clark 1996: 110–12).

Shadow sites and buried sites may be enhanced by the reflective qualities of **frost** or light **snow** (**Fig.**

2.8), or because contrasts are enhanced by slower thawing above solid buried remains that take longer to warm up than normal soil. **Flooding** may draw attention to patches of raised ground that would have been preferred for the location of settlements, while **droughts** can reveal sites that are normally submerged, for example around Lake Titicaca high in the Andes (Erickson 1999). Such conditions are of course rare, and taking advantage of them requires careful planning.

Multispectral and thermal prospecting

- key references: Donoghue, 'Remote sensing' 2001; Shennan and Donoghue, 'Remote sensing in archaeological research' 1992; 'Thermal prospecting' in Ellis, *Archaeological method and theory* 2000: 626–30.

Remote sensing for archaeology is still in its infancy. There are important new developments in space imaging that may see vertical aerial photography replaced by high resolution satellite digital images. Airborne sensors are improving all the time and becoming much cheaper to build and deploy. Thermal and RADAR imaging sensors have also improved recently and these offer considerable potential for detecting buried structures.

(Bewley *et al.* 1999: 7)

Aerial photography relies upon energy in the form of light at wavelengths that the human eye can see. From the 1970s airborne prospecting has expanded to include devices that record a wider range of wavelengths, including multispectral

Figure 2.8 A classic Iron Age hillfort at Yarnbury Castle, Wiltshire, taken in early February 1996. The impressive ramparts and ditches are emphasised by light and shade (note the long shadows cast by trees at the bottom of the photograph, indicating very low sunlight). More significantly the reflective qualities of a thin layer of snow enhance the visibility of an oval feature (the levelled bank and ditch of a smaller, earlier fort) which is overlain by a rectangular pattern of parallel lines that represent a medieval sheep market (© Crown copyright; NMR SU 0340/149). Aerial photographs 2.6–2.8 are from the **National Monuments Record**, English Heritage's public archive. The NMR encourages the understanding and enjoyment of the historic environment by providing access to archives and information sources, as well as preserving unique archives and data for future generations.

imaging sensors, thermal imaging radiometers and imaging radar. All of these collect data in digital form that is eminently suitable for processing by computer to produce the best results (Bewley et al. 1999: 6–9). **Multispectral scanners** separate light into several narrow wave bands which may be examined separately or together in the hope that some wavelengths will reveal crop and soilmarks that do not show up on conventional photographs; results are promising in Britain and in arid areas of the Near East and United States (*ibid.*: 8; Donoghue 2001: 557–9). **Thermal prospection** is used in geology and environmental monitoring but can be useful in archaeology too. It records variations in temperature of the ground surface (not unlike the differential thawing that affects light snow cover) and can record data from large areas at low cost; readings taken before dawn and at midday may be compared to emphasise differences. Thermal imaging can detect small variations in the height of a ground surface (such as slight earthworks) and differences in the temperature of soil or vegetation that reflect anomalies beneath the surface (Bewley *et al.* 1999: 8; Ellis 2000: 626–30).

One of the most exciting recent developments in aerial prospection has been **LiDAR**. Originally designed for military and commercial use, its archaeological potential has only been widely exploited in the last ten years but is now becoming a common prospection tool (Bewley *et al.* 2005; Challis *et al.* 2008). A laser attached to a plane takes large numbers of height measurements and covers large areas, much faster and with more measurements than possible by manual topographic survey. It can detect small earthwork features invisible to the naked eye and unlikely to be detected by topographic survey. Another great advantage of LiDAR is that, unlike other aerial reconnaissance methods, it can 'see through' the leaves of deciduous trees covering a site (**Box 2.4**). As with aerial photography and other remote sensing techniques, it should be remembered that they still require interpretation, with the results (like geophysics) often representing a complex **palimpsest** of archaeological, geological and modern features (see below p. 74). Such interpretation requires both experience of the technique, and knowledge of the nature of archaeological features which might be encountered in the specific region or landscape.

Photogrammetry
- key references: Hampton, *The mapping of archaeological evidence from air photography* 1985; Johnston and Rose, *Bodmin Moor: an archaeological survey. 1: the human landscape to c.1800* 1994.

Converting photographs into plans is a complex procedure, especially if they have been taken at an oblique angle rather than vertically. It is important that they include reference points that can be identified on large-scale maps so that if necessary working plans may be drawn by hand, using geometry – and a considerable amount of patience. Computer-based techniques have been designed to overcome these problems (Scollar *et al.* 1990). Most accurate plans are produced by tracing the positions of reference features and archaeological information in digital form, either on a computer screen or on a photograph mounted on a digitising tablet. Digitising images on a screen is facilitated by viewing stereoscopic pairs of photographs that make surface features such as buildings, hedges or trees stand out in three dimensions (Ellis 2000: 464 Fig. 1). These techniques are all derived from **photogrammetry** used in map making, and may also be applied to photographs of buildings or excavated features. Conversion of optical photographic images into digital formats allows them to be used more easily with other data (for example from surveys and geophysical instruments) and incorporated into GIS.

Interpretation of aerial images
- key references: Wilson, *Air photo interpretation for archaeologists* 2000; Maxwell, *The impact of aerial reconnaissance on archaeology* 1983; Brophy and Cowley, *From the air: understanding aerial archaeology* 2005.

In the first half of the twentieth century the majority of work focused on data capture – taking and collecting aerial photographs …

BOX 2.4   Airborne topographic survey: LiDAR

The benefits of LiDAR in surveying archaeological sites can be seen in a recent survey of the late Iron Age fortified site (*oppidum*) and early Augustan settlement at Bibracte in Burgundy, eastern France. The hill is densely covered with trees, and a microtopographic survey of the site (c), using techniques described in section 2.2.3, was time-consuming and difficult. A LiDAR survey (a) was far quicker and revealed the arrangement of ramparts and terraces in much greater detail than the topographic survey, including previously unknown features. The images show the same small section of the larger survey (a). Different information can be seen on the traditional air photograph (b), the microtopographic survey (c), and the LiDAR (d). In combination, different aspects of the site are revealed by different techniques, with LiDAR increasingly recognised as the most effective method, particularly on sites which are obscured by deciduous tree cover (Centre Archéologique Européen, Bibracte).

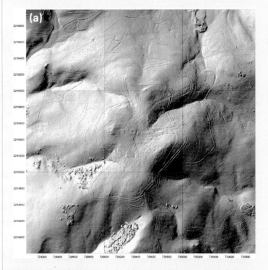

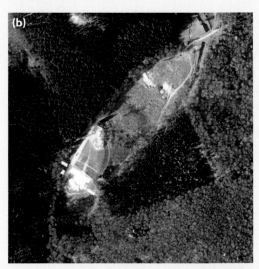

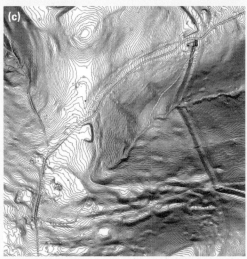

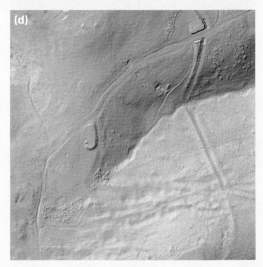

After the Second World War, and especially in the 1950s, the interpretation of information derived from aerial photographs became as important as aerial reconnaissance itself.

(Bewley *et al.* 1999: 4)

One of the first effects of aerial photography in Britain and elsewhere was to reveal cropmark and soilmark sites on heavy valley soils previously considered unsuitable for cultivation; it had been assumed that they were covered by dense forest until comparatively recent historical times. The discovery of these sites caused an upward revision of estimates of early populations and their agricultural technology (Dark 1999). However, areas where earthwork sites had already been recorded have perhaps been neglected as a result; photographers understandably concentrate on the most promising regions. Proper research programmes, such as the **National Mapping Programme** undertaken by English Heritage, are more expensive than unplanned exploration, but their results allow much firmer conclusions to be reached about site distributions, settlement patterns and other features of ancient landscapes.

It is not always easy to distinguish between archaeological features and natural geological phenomena; a thorough knowledge of archaeology is required for any attempt to classify and date sites according to their form. This problem is reduced by using a standardised method of describing traces recorded on photographs, and by using a computer data-entry system to regulate it (Lock 2003: 26–30). There is always the danger of over-simplification, however, when identifying features as belonging to certain periods based on form alone; in Britain, for instance, rectangular enclosures have often been interpreted as Roman, but upon excavation have frequently been shown to date from many other periods (Brophy and Cowley 2005). Isolated features become more coherent when seen in an overall view; for example, the relation of outlying field boundaries and trackways to a farming settlement, and new features not easily noticed on the ground, may be revealed. Such observations can be checked on the ground and recorded by the kinds of surveys described above (p. 58).

It is also important to recognise areas where sites are absent, and to decide whether they really did not exist there, or whether modern land-use does not provide circumstances that would make them visible. Land that was formerly ploughed might have been under pasture for a considerable period; in Britain, many fields used for grazing today show tell-tale traces of medieval ridge-and-furrow ploughed strips. Not only will medieval ploughing have destroyed any earthworks that preceded it, but also today's mature pasture will prevent the detection of earlier buried sites under the regular ridges except under extreme drought conditions, unless a non-photographic technique is employed (for example infrared line scanning: Palmer 1996). The use of land for modern arable farming or pasture depends on factors such as the surface geology, drainage, climate and altitude. Thus, a map of archaeological sites in any area is incomplete unless it shows how the sites were discovered (shadow, crop- or soilmark), and records the conditions likely to reveal visible traces.

The existence of tens of thousands of aerial photographs and other images from around the world leads to severe problems of storage and management. This is why the Archaeology Data Service in Britain has provided *Guides to good practice* to give advice about the preservation and use of digital resources, including aerial photography (Bewley *et al.* 1999), along with GIS, geophysics and excavation data. Ideally all of these resources may be merged into a single system to maximise the information that may be retrieved. Integrated data of this kind will become increasingly important in managing heritage as it is incorporated into Sites and Monuments Records. This has already happened in the case of the Wroxeter Hinterland project (Shropshire), where geophysical surveys help in the interpretation of aerial photographs. Features that appear on both can be related accurately to a digital terrain model and the overall plan of the Roman town and its surroundings with the help of GPS (Van Leusen 2001: 578–80). Cooperation, and access to catalogues of data, are likely to be helped by the expansion of the Internet.

2.3.2 Geophysical and geochemical surveying

- key references: Nishimura, 'Geophysical prospection in archaeology' 2001; Clark, *Seeing beneath the soil: prospecting methods in archaeology* 1996; Scollar *et al.*, *Archaeological prospecting and remote sensing* 1990; Gaffney and Gater, *Revealing the buried past: geophysics for archaeologists* 2003.

The various geophysical prospection methods reviewed here such as earth resistance, magnetometer, GPR surveys, and so forth, all detect different physical characteristics of soil. If any of these detect an anomaly, it is highly possible that an artifact or archaeological feature of some kind lies buried at that spot. Experience over the past 50 years has shown that these techniques, alone or (preferably) in combination, can provide rapid and reliable information on the location, depth and nature of buried features without the need for excavation.

(Nishimura 2001: 552)

Few archaeological sites reveal themselves in full detail on aerial photographs (or any form of survey used on its own). On some, different features show up at different times; on others, parts are invisible because they extend into areas where land-use or vegetation do not produce soilmarks or cropmarks. Geophysical surveys work on the basis of different types of response from the landscape. With many areas of the world lacking in aerial photographic evidence (because of problematic geologies or lack of recording), geophysics represents an increasingly essential part of investigating archaeological landscapes. Geophysical surveys may be additionally helpful when excavation is planned; further details may be required about details of a site that do not show up clearly from other sources. Because aerial photography, LiDAR and geophysical techniques rely on different forms of response from the ground, these techniques are increasingly used in combination in an attempt to extract the widest and most varied information from the landscape or monument.

As with aerial photography, the main purpose of geophysical instruments is to distinguish anomalies, hopefully of human origin, from the natural subsoil (**Box 2.5**). Two main classes of instrument are used in geophysical prospecting: **resistivity meters** measure the resistance of subsoil to the passage of an electrical current, and **magnetometers** detect variations in the subsoil's magnetic characteristics. Related instruments obtain useful information from the **magnetic susceptibility** of surface soil, which gives a general indication of occupation, rather than specific structures or features dug into the subsoil.

Although they remain most suitable for examining sites of which the location is already known or suspected (Bewley et al. 1996), the potential for lighter and faster instruments to reveal entire archaeological landscapes is increasingly being demonstrated (e.g. Powlesland et al. 2006; Tabor 2008). It is important that operators have an approximate idea of the likely depth and nature of the geology and subsoil, as well as the kind of anomalies that are being sought, so that the most appropriate instruments can be chosen (Conyers 2004: 7–9). Shallow pits and ditches buried beneath thick topsoil will clearly respond very differently to solid stone foundations lying only a few centimetres beneath the surface; likewise loose gravel subsoil has very different characteristics from solid bedrock. In rescue situations it may be desirable to put more effort into scanning extensive areas to find anomalies suggesting focuses of occupation debris or structures to guide exploratory excavation, through evaluation trenches for example (Chapter 3, pp. 95–6). The first archaeological uses of geophysical instruments took place in exactly these circumstances. In the USA, Hans Lundberg and Mark Malamphy were early pioneers, conducting a resistivity survey as early as 1938 in Williamsburg, Virginia (Gaffney and Gater 2003:14). At Dorchester, near Oxford, prehistoric ditches were located in 1946 by using a resistivity meter, and were excavated before destruction by gravel extraction. Magnetometers were first used in Northamptonshire in 1958 to locate Roman pottery kilns before road construction; their existence, but not position, was already known

BOX 2.5   # Geophysical survey techniques

Images A, B and C show different types of geophysical survey being undertaken on a number of different Late Iron Age sites in Burgundy, France and Gloucestershire, England. Image A shows a Bartington fluxgate gradiometer in use; this has two sensors and can be used to cover large areas relatively quickly and intensely. These instruments continue to be what Clark described as the 'workhorse of geophysics'. They are often used in advance of development or on research projects in order to assess the existence of archaeology over large areas. Image B shows an RM15 resistivity meter. Because it works in a different way to the other instruments, its results can be somewhat different and reveal other archaeological features or show them more clearly (see **Box 2.6**). Resistivity meters tend to collect data more slowly than the fluxgate gradiometers and are therefore often only used on sites where stone structures are likely to be found or where geological conditions are appropriate. Image C shows the slower but more sensitive caesium magnetometer. Recent advances in such instruments means that they are increasingly linked to GPS systems, allowing for the instant location of survey responses, and mounted on vehicles with multiple sensors allowing for more rapid survey. This makes it likely that caesium magnetometer surveys will become far more common in the near future (images (a) and (c): Tom Moore, image (b): John Creighton).

(a)

(b)

(c)

from the writings of a local early nineteenth-century antiquary. In both cases the character of the archaeological anomalies likely to be found was known in advance and determined which type of geophysical instrument was used (Clark 1996: 12–17).

A great advance in geophysical surveying occurred in the late 1960s when portable instruments became available that could record **continuous measurements**, rather than readings taken with the instrument positioned at a series of individual points. Geophysical instruments

Geophysical survey responses

The diagram shows the ability of the two principal methods of geophysical prospecting to detect buried features: resistivity and magnetometry (gradiometry). A rise in the line indicates a positive reading from a strong magnetic field, or high resistance to the passage of an electrical current, and a dip shows magnetism or resistance lower than the site's average background reading. The line gives a rough impression of the relative strengths of these results. Different instruments react to anomalies in different ways, and it should be noted that local variations in magnetism may well make significant differences to the response from a magnetometer. For both magnetic and resistivity surveys, small features such as post holes are hard to detect, although this depends on the nature of the archaeological features and how intensive the survey was. Recent intensive surveys with a caesium magnetometers demonstrated the potential, at least in certain cases, of identifying even small features such as post holes. The nature of the site, its geology, and the type of archaeological features expected to be found will determine which method is employed; if stone buildings are expected, resistivity might be more appropriate, whereas magnetometry might be more appropriate when looking for pits and ditches. The same soil profile is also used in BOX 2.2 to illustrate how these features might also show up on aerial photographs (drawn by Sheila Newton).

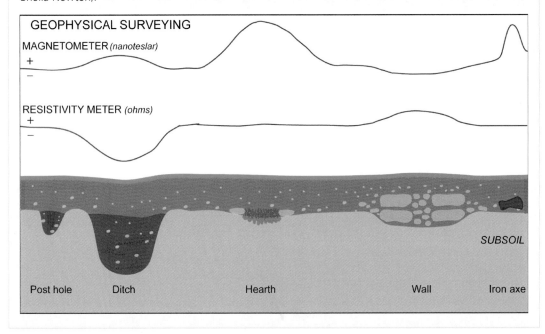

no longer require a second operator to relate readings to a survey grid laid out on the ground; they have an automatic logging system that knows the precise location of the instrument because it has been fixed with the help of a total station or GPS (above: p. 58). Early instruments produced graphs plotted on paper, but in the 1980s they were linked to portable computers that could compile and display larger site plans on their screens (Clark 1996: 19–26). Results are sometimes presented in the form of linear graphs with peaks and troughs that indicate high and low readings which suggest the positions of buried anomalies (**Fig. 2.9**) or, more commonly, as subtle greyscale images reflecting the strength of the anomaly, on a plan of the survey area.

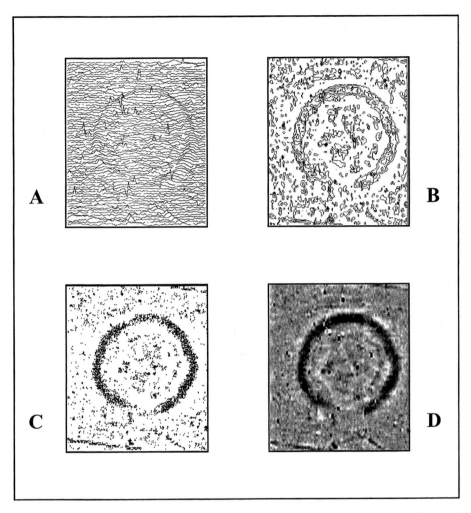

Figure 2.9 These display plots present data from a geophysical survey by fluxgate gradiometer (a form of magnet-ometer) over the site of South Side Mount Barrow, a Bronze Age burial mound in North Humberside. A and C show data recorded continuously along 70 parallel lines 1 metre apart and 60 metres long, presented in the form of line graphs whose peaks indicate areas of higher magnetism. This gives a visual impression of a circular bank (especially when seen in a 3D wire frame plot), whereas the anomaly is in fact a ditch. B and D are dot density and grey-scale images; the dark areas will immediately suggest ditches to anyone accustomed to studying aerial photo-graphs of crop marks or soil marks. In E, contour lines join areas of high readings; this plot draws more attention to linear features at the bottom of the survey area than to the others. Data derived from other geophysical techniques, aerial photographs and fieldwalking would also be scrutinised to achieve the maximum possible understanding of such a site before any excavation began. (Gaffney and Gater 1993: 213, Fig. 18.5)

The data can be filtered by computer programs that eliminate natural background variations and enhance archaeological features. Greyscale plans were improved by the introduction of laser printers, which increased the subtlety of filtered plans in a way described by Clark as 'nothing short of a revolution' (1996: 147).

Magnetic surveying
- key references: Clark, *Seeing beneath the soil: prospecting methods in archaeology* 1996: 64–117, 175–82; Nishimura, 'Geophysical prospection in archaeology' 2001: 546–7; Gaffney and Gater, *Revealing the buried past* 2003: 36–42.

Where soils and surface conditions are favourable, images of extraordinary clarity can be achieved, complementing and often extending evidence from other methods such as aerial photography. The factors of speed and the magnetic definition of a wide range of archaeological features have ensured that magnetometer survey is often the preferred method both of reconnaissance and of very detailed survey.

(David 2001: 523)

Magnetometers detect deviations from the general background of the subsoil, in this case indicated by variations in its magnetic field. Several aspects of past human occupation cause suitable anomalies. Heating at c. 700°C or above by hearths, kilns or furnaces causes the randomly aligned magnetic particles present in most soils and clays to realign along the prevailing magnetic field of the Earth, and to retain this new alignment on cooling. The alignment of magnetic particles is also affected by digging and refilling ditches and pits; solid features, such as walls or road surfaces, contain fewer magnetic minerals and therefore provide lower readings than their surroundings.

Magnetic surveying does not require probes in the ground; the instrument can be carried along a line or a grid by its operator, and when conditions are favourable it is generally preferred to resistivity for this reason. One form of instrument, the **proton magnetometer**, takes readings of the absolute magnetic field at given points on a grid. The **proton gradiometer** is less sensitive, but in many ways easier to operate; it measures the difference between two separate detector bottles at either end of a pole held vertically by the operator. Buried anomalies affect the lower bottle more than the higher, and the difference, rather than the absolute field, is recorded. More rapid and more common is the **fluxgate gradiometer**, which takes continuous, rather than spot, readings ('the workhorse – and the racehorse – of British archaeological prospecting' (Clark 1996: 69), and can be used to survey large areas quickly (**Box 2.5**). Gradiometer results are easier to interpret than magnetometer readings, which are more easily

disturbed by natural variations in the subsoil, or by the effects of wire fences, electrical storms or railways. Such technology is continually developing, with recent advances leading to equipment which can record increased amounts of data and are integrated into global positioning systems. **Caesium magnetometers** are extremely sensitive and, in appropriate conditions, can produce more detailed results of subsurface features than gradiometers, although they are currently somewhat slower and less user-friendly (Linford *et al.* 2007).

Some additional types of magnetometers are employed in the surveying of archaeological sites. Unlike normal magnetometers, they inject a signal into shallow surface deposits and record the way the response is altered by **magnetic susceptibility** (Clark 1996: 99–117, 175–82). Since susceptibility is influenced by human occupation and other activities, particularly when burning has been involved, it is particularly useful when there is a need to determine the full extent of a site, which may be achieved with the help of a relatively small number of widely-spaced measurements. On a smaller scale, susceptibility is a good indicator of intensively utilised domestic or industrial areas within sites; it provides a useful complement to the results of phosphate analysis, which reflect different kinds of activities such as waste-disposal or animal husbandry (*ibid.*: 107–9). Further development of susceptibility measurement offers the possibility of obtaining estimates of the shape and depth of magnetic anomalies.

Resistivity surveying
- key references: Clark, *Seeing beneath the soil: prospecting methods in archaeology* 1996: 27–63, 171–4; Gaffney and Gater, *Revealing the buried past* 2003: 26–35.

When an electric current is passed through the ground between electrodes, the resistance to its flow may be measured. A current will pass relatively easily through damp soil, but drier compact material such as a buried wall or a cobbled road surface creates higher resistance. Resistivity surveying is rather cumbersome, because it normally requires a number of electrode probes (usually four) to be pushed into the ground at precise intervals for each reading (**Box 2.5**). A variety of configurations has been tried to speed up the surveying procedure; for instance, instead of forming a line, probes have been fixed in a square table-like arrangement with the instrument mounted on top for single-handed surveying (Clark 1996: 45–7 Figs 35–8). An even, well-drained subsoil with features buried at a fairly constant depth is best for resistivity; otherwise, natural disturbances and variations may confuse the readings. In temperate climates, the best conditions for the moisture content of the soil occur in late summer and early autumn. Some electromagnetic instruments measure soil conductivity *without* probes, and, although less sensitive, have proved particularly successful on arid sites. Because of the laborious procedure involved, resistivity is particularly well suited to the detection of linear features such as roads, walls or ditches; their positions can be fixed by taking measurements along a straight line at 90° to their suspected position. As succinctly summarised by David (2001: 524): 'Methods of resistivity survey are still most effectively applied to the detection and definition of the two-dimensional plans of building foundations but are slower to undertake than magnetometry. ... If such profiles are surveyed in closely spaced succession across a site followed by their conversion into horizontal depth 'slices', an approximation to three-dimensional reconstruction can be achieved.'

Metal detectors
- key references: Dobinson and Denison, *Metal detecting and archaeology in England* 1995; Thomas and Stone, *Metal detecting and archaeology* 2009.

Metal detectors are not only popular with members the public who regard their use as an innocent hobby, but also with professional treasure-hunters who plunder sites for profit. The fine dividing line between these types of user accounts for the bad press metal detectors have received from archaeologists. Most types penetrate the soil only to a very limited extent, but they have been used by archaeologists to locate dispersed metal artefacts – for example a

hoard of Roman coins scattered by ploughing. A more sophisticated device (the **pulse induction meter**) gives a warning of metal objects in graves that are about to be excavated. This is not normally necessary if the site has already been surveyed by magnetometer, for when these instruments encounter iron objects they produce readings that are distinguishable from archaeological features. Some archaeologists and museum curators work in partnership with metal detector enthusiasts to make full records of any artefacts that they discover, and to provide expert assistance when important antiquities are found. This has happened near Salisbury, Wiltshire (Bronze and Iron Age metal artefacts) and at Snettisham, Norfolk (hoards of gold and silver coins and ornaments dating from the late Iron Age), where artefacts had been found both by accident during ploughing and by metal detector users. Archaeologists from the British Museum removed the topsoil, and located further hoards buried too deep for the range of metal detectors. In England, the **Treasure Act (1996)** allows for the identification of an item as 'treasure' according to the metal from which it is made. This ensures that the original finders receive the market value of their discoveries, and provides an important incentive for reporting finds (Hobbs 2003). Thus, the thrill of discovery and financial reward can be combined with full archaeological investigation (Stead 1991, 1998). The introduction of the **Portable Antiquities Scheme**, in England, enables metal detectorists to voluntarily record their finds with a local archaeologist. This has been useful in allowing for the recording of finds which previously have gone unrecorded. It is having a significant impact on modifying the distribution of certain artefacts, such as Iron Age and early medieval coins (e.g., Hutcheson 2004; Worrell 2007).

However, the laws concerning metal detecting are different throughout the world (and even within the United Kingdom e.g. Scotland). In many European countries all finds from metal detecting are the property of the state and must be reported and a licence granting permission to metal detect for archaeological finds must be sought from the authorities (e.g. France, Ireland).

In the USA it is illegal to remove artefacts from Federal land under the Antiquities Act (1906), although laws pertaining to metal detecting vary considerably from state to state.

Ground penetrating radar (GPR)

- key references: Conyers, *Ground penetrating radar for archaeology* 2004; Clark, *Seeing beneath the soil: prospecting methods in archaeology* 1996: 118–20, 183–4; Nishimura,

Figure 2.10 Ground Penetrating Radar in use in the field at Anundshögen, Västmanland, Sweden, as part of a joint UK and Swedish project run by Dr Sarah Semple, funded by the British Academy and the County Archaeology Unit, Stiftelsen Kulturmiljövård Västmanland. This survey technique, used in combination with resistivity and small scale excavation, enabled the identification of a previously unknown row of stone-packed circular features c. 3 metres in diameter, equidistantly spaced and over 180 metres in length. Small-scale excavation was used to ground-truth the features, which were revealed as sockets for large standing orthostats of wood or stone and considered to be contemporary with the use of the site as a place of burial, ceremony and political assembly from the Migration Period to the Viking Age. (Photograph: Sarah Semple)

'Geophysical prospection in archaeology' 2001: 547–51; Gaffney and Gater, *Revealing the buried past* 2003: 47–51.

Radar (GPR) has considerable potential for the examination of buried sites, particularly when major features such as burial chambers containing voids are being investigated, but a disadvantage is that it performs best on very dry deposits. Electronic signals are transmitted into the soil, and bounce back to a receiver (**Fig. 2.10**). The signals are altered by the density and position of whatever they encounter underground, and the patterns received from the ground are plotted diagrammatically. When colour is used to enhance the variations, it is possible to see not only the shapes of solid features, such as buried walls, but also the profiles of pits or ditches. GPR has been used at the Iron Age burial mound of Mine Howe, Orkney, to reveal additional possible chambers in the mound (Gaffney and Gater 2003).

Further research and development will be needed before GPR becomes a mature and predictable technique: 'If magnetic and resistivity methods remain the mainstays of routine geophysical survey, enlivened by research into three-dimensional reconstruction, it is this latter goal which has fostered the emergence of a third technique which is currently receiving much attention: ground penetrating radar or GPR' (David 2001: 524).

Seismic prospecting and geochemical examination of soil

- key references: 'Seismic refraction surveying', in Ellis, *Archaeological method and theory* 2000: 545–7; Heron, 'Geochemical prospecting' 2001; Drewett, *Field archaeology: an introduction* 1999: 55–7.

Scientific location instruments have not replaced all traditional pre-excavation techniques for examining sites. For example, if the ground is struck with a mallet it should produce a light resonance over a buried wall or thin topsoil, but a dull thud over a humus-filled ditch. Acoustic or seismic investigation is very common in geological survey and, in the form of sonar, used under water for archaeological purposes, but it has not been utilised extensively for archaeology on land. A blow from a heavy sledgehammer or a small explosion, is used to generate sound waves, and microphones placed along the surface of the ground record their reflection by buried features; this technique has been successful for discovering large ditches cut into solid subsoil (Ellis 2000: 546).

Probing or augering are also useful for testing the depth of soil, or to remove samples to gain some idea of buried stratification. The latter may be dangerous on a small complex site, for a regular series of boreholes could easily damage delicate traces of structures or fragile artefacts. Augering is more commonly used to provide soil samples for pollen analysis, or to measure variations in phosphate content that indicate areas of a site used for habitation – activities such as the disposal of excreta and organic waste, or agricultural operations such as milking, increase phosphate levels (Bethell and Maté 1989; Heron 2001: 565–8). Testing for phosphates has been used for many decades, but more recently analyses have been directed towards concentrations of other elements that reflect human activities. Lipid biomarkers also provide evidence for excreta in soils in much the same way that they can be detected in pottery to reveal foodstuffs (Heron 2001: 569–70). The potential of heavy metal soil analysis has been investigated at Shapwick, Somerset, in the hope of revealing sites occupied during periods when pottery was rare or absent and therefore unlikely to be detected during fieldwalking (Gerrard and Aston 2007), while in Greece the same technique was used (as with phosphates) to gain an impression of the intensity of occupation on sites and their surroundings (Bintliff *et al.* 1990). These approaches complement rather than replace more conventional geophysical prospection, since each one tends to reflect particular kinds of human activity, whether digging pits, burning, food processing, manuring or waste disposal.

The development of portable *x-ray fluorescence* (XRF) sensors also means that techniques used to analyse the composition of material samples, for example stone (Chapter 5, pp. 230), can now be done in the field rather than just in the laboratory.

This has been used in America to analyse, and potentially to date, rock art on the Colorado plateau in Utah. This technique has the advantage of being non-destructive and means that samples do not need to be retrieved.

Underwater location devices

- key references: Vuorela, *Scientific methods in underwater archaeology* 1994; 'Sonar', in Ellis, *Archaeological method and theory* 2000: 582–4; Bowens, *Underwater archaeology: the NAS guide to principles and practice* 2008.

Sonar scanning works in the same way as radar, but sonic (rather than electronic) signals are transmitted and received. Side-scan sonar can cover large areas because the signals are transmitted sideways to detect irregularities on the surface of the seabed. It is a routine technique used for non-archaeological seabed surveys, but is able to detect anomalies such as shipwrecks as well as natural rocks and sand banks. The *Mary Rose*, a Tudor warship subsequently excavated and lifted for display in a museum at Portsmouth, was first located with the help of this method by a marine archaeologist who knew, from documentary sources, approximately where it had sunk in 1545 (Green 1990: 50–1). Like surveying methods on land, underwater work has been simplified by the ability to relate the position of instruments taking readings to maps by means of GPS (global positioning systems) data derived from satellites.

Sub-bottom profilers transmit signals directly downwards to investigate buried features; this means that they do not cover a wide area. Archaeological anomalies such as shipwrecks or piles of cargo are clearly distinguishable from geological features by the fact that they do not have much depth. Magnetometers are also an effective aid in surveying shipwreck sites on the seabed, where metal rivets or larger objects such as cannons might have been dispersed over a large area and covered by sediments (Green 1990: 81–5). As with fieldwork on land, little can be learned about anomalies without close visual inspection by video cameras or divers (above: p. 62).

2.4 GEOGRAPHICAL INFORMATION SYSTEMS (GIS)

- key references: Wheatley and Gillings, *Spatial technology and archaeology* 2002; Gillings, 'Spatial information and archaeology' 2001; 'Geographic Information Systems', in Ellis, *Archaeological method and theory* 2000: 245–51; Chapman, *Landscape archaeology and GIS* 2006.

The extraordinary pace of development in computer technology since the 1960s has transformed the potential uses of data from remote sensing and field survey by borrowing techniques developed in geography. Computers that combine large data-storage capacity with fast mathematical processors and high-quality graphic display have in the twenty-first century become readily available. Since the 1990s, GIS software has become increasingly sophisticated and more user-friendly, with digital map data, the basis of most GIS, also now widely available in many areas of the world. GIS allows all of the techniques discussed above to be combined into a resource for assessing and analysing archaeological data, and is now a key tool in landscape archaeology.

Mark Gillings (2001: 672) favours the concept of a GIS not as a single program but as a toolbox with facilities for carrying out four principal areas of work (subsystems):

1. **Data input and preparation**: digitising maps, converting survey data and lists of finds to a standard national grid.
2. **Data storage and retrieval**: creating layers of spatial data (such as contours, land-use, archaeological site locations) derived from maps, and creating databases of their content.
3. **Data manipulation and analysis**: producing **digital terrain models** from contour data to display sites or landscapes in different ways, and combining such displays with archaeological data of various kinds.
4. **Reporting and data output**: selecting lists of data for statistical tests, printing versions of

digital elevation models with selected layers of data for publication.

In the **Upper Tisza Project**, field survey data collected from a river valley in Hungary was processed and analysed by Gillings (1997). It involved an immensely time-consuming preliminary stage in which large-scale maps of the survey area were **digitised**; the contours, natural features, geology and soil types were converted from lines and points on paper maps into a digital form understandable by the GIS. All details recovered during archaeological fieldwork (notably site categories, locations and sizes, and the find-spot, type and date of artefacts) were also digitised (subsystems 1–2). One example of the use of subsystem 3 was to map the effects on the river system of the thawing of mountain snows each spring. By fixing a specific depth of water, the map of the landscape could be transformed on the computer's screen by simulating the flooding of the river and its tributaries up to a particular contour. Sites of a specific period could be added to the map by selecting them from the database in order to test ideas about their relationship to this phenomenon. Early farming communities in the Neolithic period were found to have been located near the water's edge or on temporary islands formed by the floods, with the implication that fishing might have provided an important supplement to the farmers' diet in spring, before crops were ready for harvesting. This idea was supported by studies of fish bones from sites where suitable samples have been recovered.

This exercise *could* have been performed manually by making tracings from contour maps, shading in the flooded areas, adding Neolithic sites recorded in files of survey data, and overlaying the sheets of tracings. The advantage of a GIS approach is that questions can be asked repeatedly in slightly different ways. What if the floods were deeper? Do burial sites of the same period have the same relation to water as the settlements? Do early Bronze Age sites share the same distribution? The answers can be displayed very rapidly, and results that look significant are measurable in statistical terms (subsystem 4).

BOX 2.7 **GIS and predictive modelling: the location of Roman villas near Veii, Italy**

One of the uses of Geographic Information Systems (GIS) is to predict the location of archaeological sites. It can model past landscapes on the basis of limited existing archaeological knowledge (for example in an area where sites have been destroyed by changes in land-use), or assist in detecting new sites.

An example is the location of villas in the vicinity of the Etruscan and Roman town of Veii in Tuscany (seen here). Using GIS maps to assess the geology, slope and topographic

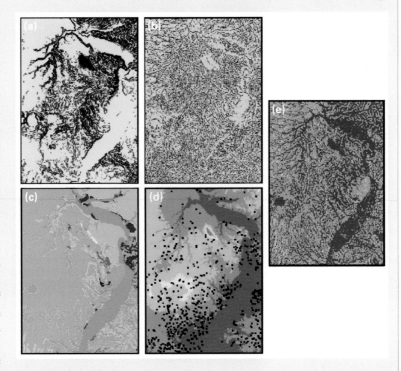

setting of known Roman villas (a–d), GIS could generate a predictive model of the likely locations of unknown villas (e). Further fieldwork could then test the reliability of the GIS model. One of the great advantages of GIS is its ability to undertake such assessments quickly whilst adjusting models as more data are added or amended (Rob Witcher and the British School at Rome; Kay and Witcher 2005).

Once maps and data have been entered into the system, they can be recalled in any combination or permutation. Some exercises could only be performed with the help of a computer; for example, if the investigator selects a specific site (such as a farmstead), it is possible to instruct the computer to display a view of the landscape from that location as it would have appeared to someone standing there, looking in any specified direction. By adding further information, perhaps by assuming that certain types of soil were still covered by mature trees while others had been cleared for fields, the view could be modified accordingly. Could a Neolithic farmer see other farmsteads, and were ritual monuments and burials positioned so that they could be seen

from settlements? Intervisibility studies of this kind, based on the creation of digital terrain models from a GIS, remain popular in work with GIS (**Box 2.7**), although the data on which such models are based must be carefully examined and such studies can be controversial (Wheatley and Gillings 2000).

Thus, GIS provide an important new dimension to field archaeology that is very widely applicable to complex problems of location and distribution. They may also slot comfortably into traditional approaches, as in the case of an attempt to locate a Roman signal station on the Yorkshire coast at Whitby through a combination of GIS and Anglo-Saxon place-name studies (Bell 1998). As with other forms of computer-based data handling, an initial investment of time and energy in recording data in an appropriate form is repaid by the flexibility that it allows at the analytical stage. Because a GIS acts as a spatially referenced database, to which further information can be linked, it is ideal for archives of monuments and landscapes and has been adopted by many national and regional records. When photographs, bibliographical references, legal information about historic monument scheduling or listing and other data involved in a Historic Environment Record (above: p. 62) are held in a GIS they can be called upon simultaneously to improve the management of heritage, whether urban or rural (Cooper 1995; Grenville 1999; see **Box 2.7**). Similarly, publication is facilitated by printing out selected graphic displays rather than drawing them by hand (subsystem 4). The actual data can be published on disks or made available over the Internet to allow other researchers not only to see the results of a project, but also to run their own analyses.

Looking forward, three trends can be identified. The first concerns the development and integration of fully 3D GIS and temporal or TGIS into everyday archaeological research. The second concerns the often uncritical and problematic relationship between GIS and archaeological theory. A number of researchers are exploring links between the rigid data models offered by the GIS and new theoretical perspectives concerning the nature of space, human perception and cognition, and the relationship between people and their environments. ... The final trend concerns the blending of GIS techniques with emerging technologies such as *Virtual Reality* (VR) modelling, *Artificial Intelligence* (AI) and the dynamic capabilities of the Internet and World Wide Web.

(Gillings 2001: 681)

2.5 LANDSCAPE ARCHAEOLOGY

- key references: Aston, *Interpreting the landscape: landscape archaeology and local history* 1997; Muir, *The new Reading the*

Figure 2.11 Wasdale Head in the Lake District National Park is a particularly remote but popular destination for people in search of nature. However, the 'natural' Cumbrian landscape is the end-product of many phases of human occupation and exploitation since hunter-gatherers re-colonised northern Britain following the last Ice Age. Volcanic rocks in nearby Great Langdale were quarried for making Neolithic stone axes; metals were extracted on a large scale in the Roman period, and with growing intensity from Tudor times to the Industrial Revolution. Meanwhile agriculture and settlement patterns have undergone many changes, and the region is probably less densely populated now than at any time since prehistory. The 'natural' and 'wild' aspects of this landscape, praised by the Romantic poets in the nineteenth century, would rapidly become overgrown today without subsidised hill-farming, along with protection by local planning authorities and conservation by charitable landowners such as the National Trust. Landscape archaeology attempts to understand how the present configuration was reached. Documentary, archaeological and environmental evidence all contribute to analysing the date and significance of visible features, such as the irregular stone walls that meander across the valley floor, the small isolated church dedicated to St Olaf, or the farm amongst the trees on the left which has a name of Scandinavian origin (Burnthwaite); was there once a Viking settlement nearby? Earlier phases of occupation and exploitation may only be revealed and understood with the help of aerial photography, fieldwalking, geophysical prospection and excavation. (photograph: Kevin Greene)

landscape: fieldwork in landscape history 2000; Ashmore and Knapp, *Archaeologies of landscape: contemporary perspectives* 1999; Johnson, *Ideas of landscape* 2007.

Traditions of field archaeology in Britain that stretch back to Aubrey and Stukeley were revived and strengthened in the twentieth century by a growing interest in local history, in particular its social and economic dimensions – undoubtedly enhanced by sentimental feelings about a countryside under visible transformation by industrialised farming practices. It incorporated research into all kinds of documents, including charters recording the extent and ownership of estates, tax registers, parish registers of births and deaths, and analyses of place-names. This kind of research led not just to studies of the physical remains of sites and buildings mentioned in documents, but also to the idea that archaeological observations about the landscape and settlements could be used to fill in gaps in the documentary record (**Fig. 2.11**). One manual summarised the objectives with particular eloquence:

> The landscape is a palimpsest onto which each generation inscribes its own impressions and removes some of the marks of earlier generations. Constructions of one age are often overlain, modified or erased by the work of another. The present patchwork nature of settlement and patterns of agriculture has evolved as a result of thousands of years of human endeavour, producing a landscape which possesses not only a beauty associated with long and slow development, but an inexhaustible store of information about many kinds of human activities in the past. The landscape archaeologist needs to develop an eye and a feeling for patterns in town and country and, even more important, to recognize anomalies in, for instance, the large isolated medieval church of the deserted medieval village; the straight stretch of stream channelled by monks in the thirteenth century; the regular eighteenth-century Parliamentary enclosure hedge lying across medieval ridge and furrow; the lumpy ground next to the church, marking the site of an old settlement; and even a fine Jacobean building in an otherwise apparently poor area, indicating a former prosperity linked to a long forgotten trade or industry. Ideally it should be possible to look at any feature in the landscape, know why it is there in that form, and understand its relation to other features.

> (Aston and Rowley 1974: 14–15)

This process may sound rather intuitive, but it is of course based on informed fieldwork and documentary research. The term retrogressive analysis is sometimes employed to describe how landscape archaeologists work back from modern features to the fragmentary remains of earlier landscapes. In a fascinating study of Roystone Grange, a hill farm in Derbyshire (where stone is readily available as a building material), the boundaries of field systems were analysed by means of aerial photography, detailed surveying and selective excavation. Features of known date were gradually eliminated, and with the help of a typology of the design and construction of enclosure walls (established by excavation), the outlines of earlier Roman and prehistoric settlements and land divisions were revealed (Hodges 2006). New techniques such as landscape characterisation have been developed to try to disentangle elements of landscape change (e.g. Rippon 2004).

The discussion of definitions of 'site' and 'landscape' at the beginning of this chapter make more sense in the light of problems in designing field survey projects and the introduction of GIS, both of which raise profound questions about the nature of archaeological knowledge. Archaeological theory (Chapter 6) is very important here, for perceptions of the way that people use and respond to landscapes have shifted markedly through different phases of archaeological thought. The concept of environmental change already formed an important part of Stone Age studies by the 1870s; Edouard Lartet divided the Upper Palaeolithic into phases according to changes in the dominant species of wild animals represented by bones found with human artefacts in France (Trigger 2006:

148–9). By the 1920s, studies of plant remains and microscopic pollen in Scandinavia had revealed a detailed 12,000-year record of climate marked by changing patterns of vegetation since the last Ice Age (Chapter 5, p. 201). If climate change is conceptualised as the principal force governing the biosphere, it is easy to take a **determinist** view of humans as passive participants who, at best, influence their environment through major social change and innovations in the exploitation of natural resources (such as the inception of settled agriculture). The systems or ecological approach of processual archaeology from the 1960s onwards was criticised for treating humans in this way. **Postprocessual** (or **interpretive**) archaeologists, who since the 1980s have been notable for the variety of their approaches rather than forming a single school of thought, are more likely to place individual humans at the centre of things, simultaneously responding to and shaping their surroundings. Their interest in landscape tends to focus upon it as a place where experiences happen at a particular moment, rather than seeing it as the setting for processes of long-term socio-economic change (Tilley 1994). Such viewpoints suggest that landscapes are as much about human perceptions as environmental processes: 'landscape is the work of the mind. Its scenery is built up as much from strata of memory as from layers of rock' (Schama 1995).

Processual archaeology's encouragement of using anthropology as a source of comparative information was extended by postprocessual archaeologists to underline how differently settlements and the landscape might be perceived in non-Western cultures. This promoted a view of monuments and landscapes in which ritual and social practices were as important (if not more important) than the practicalities of subsistence (Brück and Goodman 1998; Ingold 2000). A visit to Wessex emphasises this view, for despite several thousand years of change the landscape is still dominated by Neolithic and Bronze Age ritual monuments such as Stonehenge, Avebury and Silbury Hill, while hundreds of burial mounds are dotted along the crests of nearby hills and ridges (Richards 1990). It is very unlikely that people who invested time and energy in the construction of conspicuous monuments to death and ritual would make a clear distinction between the world of deities and ancestors and that of their everyday lives. It would be dangerous to analyse the economy of a farming settlement of this period solely by examining the potential of soils within its hypothetical territory using modern rational ideas about the efficiency of labour and the calorific value of food resources. A settlement might have been constructed in a particular location according to spiritual factors and in a position determined by monuments to ancestors, and its economy would almost certainly have involved gifts and exchanges of food and raw materials between relatives scattered over a wider region as well as donations to feasts. The Stonehenge area has been the subject of an interesting cooperation between Mike Parker Pearson, a British prehistorian, and Ramilisonina, an archaeologist from Madagascar where ritual and ancestral monuments still form part of everyday life (Parker Pearson and Ramilisonina 1998 a and b). Their interpretation of zones dedicated to the living and dead, and the symbolism of stone as a hard material associated with the process of death, is of course beyond testing or proof but provides a lesson about the kinds of factor that landscape archaeologists should bear in mind. Others, such as those involved with the project at Leskernick in Cornwall, have argued that archaeologists should be more aware of their own perceptions and processes when undertaking landscape archaeology, 'since the past is not only a creation of the present but a creation of particular sets of social relationships and values in the present' (Bender *et al.* 2007), and have thus sought to record their own thoughts and feelings as they conduct field archaeology.

Landscape archaeology is alive and well, incorporating both the collection of empirical data on the ground by fieldwork and the use of theory to disentangle it from environmental determinism or the preconceptions of modernity. It is appropriate to end this section with a sample of current interpretive thinking from Julian Thomas, who is just one of a number of British theoretical archaeologists who have devoted considerable energy to investigating how monuments and landscapes might have been experienced by people in the past.

My alternative conception of landscape is thus a network of related places, which have gradually been revealed through people's habitual activities and interactions, through the closeness and affinity that they have developed for some locations, and through the important events, festivals, calamities, and surprises which have drawn other spots to their attention, causing them to be remembered or incorporated into stories. Importantly, the series of places through which people's life histories are threaded help them to give account of their own identity. Our personal biographies are built up from located acts. So although we can say that landscapes are constructed out of the imbricated actions and experiences of people, those people are themselves constructed in and dispersed through their habituated landscape.

(Thomas 2001: 173)

2.6 CONCLUSIONS

The location and characterization of sites is best achieved using several detection methods; for instance in the right circumstances aerial photographs, magnetics, resistivity and GPR can all provide differing but highly complementary information on buried structural remains such as Roman buildings. Test pits and excavation can provide 'ground truth'. Together, such information can be imported into a GIS and subjected to a wide range of comparative analyses at any appropriate scale.

(David 2001: 525)

Archaeological fieldworkers require many skills, some of them traditional, others based on new scientific techniques. They also need to be experts in the use of documentary evidence, aerial photographs and geophysics besides understanding geology, soils and the integration of all kinds of evidence in GIS. It must be stressed that an individual site requires the application of as many of these complementary techniques as possible in order to maximise the information that may be obtained from it. The information gained from fieldwork and remote sensing has fundamental implications for the process of excavation, which is examined in Chapter 3. Our ability to investigate ancient landscapes and environments – *without* resorting to the destructive process of digging into sites – means that no excavation work should ever be carried out until a programme of fieldwork and documentary research has been completed. It is impossible to ask valid questions about an individual site without understanding its place in the historical and natural environment.

2.7 GUIDE TO FURTHER READING

Complete details of every publication mentioned in this section can be found in the consolidated bibliography. Consult the works cited as key references beneath section headings within this chapter first.

Archaeological field methods appear prominently in most general textbooks on the subject, for example Hester *et al.*, *Field methods in archaeology* 2008 and Carver, *Archaelogical investigation* 2009.

SITES OR LANDSCAPES?

Further theoretical discussion about the nature of landscapes can be found in papers edited by Ashmore and Knapp, *Archaeologies of landscape: contemporary perspectives* 1999, and Fisher and Thurston, 'Dynamic landscapes and socio-political process' 1999; an example of the problem of definition is Rhoads, 'Significant sites and non-site archaeology: a case-study from south-east Australia' 1992. David and Thomas' *Handbook of landscape archaeology* 2008 provides a range of different approaches to the subject.

FIELD ARCHAEOLOGY

Sullivan, *Surface archaeology* 1998, contains interesting case studies from the USA, while many basic problems about the survival of information are considered by Michael Schiffer in *Behavioural archaeology: first principles* 1995 and his many other works. The British fieldwork tradition is exemplified by a leading exponent, Christopher Taylor, *Fieldwork in medieval archaeology* 1974; a thoughtful paper dedicated to Taylor is Williamson, 'Questions of preservation and destruction' 1998.

FIELD SURVEY

The emergence of large-scale field survey, especially around the Mediterranean, is documented in two volumes of studies from the 1980s: Keller and Rupp, *Archaeological survey in the Mediterranean area* 1983, and Macready and Thompson, *Archaeological field survey in Britain and abroad* 1985. Excellent multiperiod examples from the eastern Mediterranean are Renfrew and Wagstaff, *An island polity: the archaeology of exploitation in Melos* 1982 (the Aegean), and Cherry *et al.*, *Landscape archaeology as long-term history: northern Keos in the Cycladic islands from earliest settlement until modern times* 1991. Meanwhile, Bintliff *et al.*, *The work of the Boeotia survey (1989–1991) in the southern approaches to the city of Thespiai* 2007, gives a good example of the role of large-scale survey in Greece. The impact of large-scale survey work in the Mediterranean is explored in Alcock and Cherry, *Side-by-side survey* 2004. In the western Mediterranean, good examples are Barker, *A Mediterranean valley: landscape archaeology and 'Annales' history in the Biferno Valley* 1995; Yntema, *In search of ancient countryside: the Amsterdam Free University survey at Oria, province of Brindisi, South Italy (1981–1983)* 1992 and Carrete *et al.*, *A Roman provincial capital and its hinterland: the survey of the territory of Tarragona, Spain, 1985–1990* 1995.

FIELDWALKING

Two volumes in an important series are relevant here: Pasquinucci and Trement, *The archaeology of the Mediterranean landscape, 4: non-destructive techniques applied to landscape archaeology* 1999, and Francovich and Patterson, *The archaeology of the Mediterranean landscape, 5: extracting meaning from ploughsoil assemblages* 2000, which contains many papers that discuss the significance of pottery collections. Banning, *Archaeological survey* 2002, provides good discussion of sampling strategies. Important questions about the meaning of finds recovered in fieldwalking are discussed in Schofield, *Interpreting artefact scatters: contributions to ploughzone archaeology* 1990. Contrasting case studies of projects involving preliminary surface collection from prehistoric Britain and historical North America are Waddington, *A landscape archaeological study of the Mesolithic-Neolithic in the Milfield Basin, Northumberland* 1999, and Fox, *Archaeology, history and Custer's Last Battle: the Little Big Horn re-examined* 1993.

RECORDING AND TOPOGRAPHIC/ EARTHWORK SURVEYING

For general background see Ritchie, *Surveying and mapping for field scientists* 1988. Further technical guidance may be obtained from Swallow and Watt, *Surveying historic buildings* 1996. The thorny problem of vocabulary to be used in classification is addressed by RCHME, *Recording archaeological field monuments: a descriptive specification* 1999. The publication of an important Irish site by Newman, *Tara: an archaeological survey* 1997, was described in the journal *Antiquity* as 'a delight to look at and use'. A good example of the high standards of Royal Commission/English Heritage survey and publication is McOmish *et al.*, *The field archaeology of the Salisbury Plain training area* 2002, with other examples, including that of Perth, by the Royal Commission for Ancient and Historic Monuments in Scotland (RCAHMS), 1994, and their well illustrated volume *In the shadow of Bennachie* 2007 on Aberdeenshire.

SITES AND MONUMENTS RECORDS AND HISTORIC ENVIRONMENT RECORDS

The general context in Britain can be explored in Hunter and Ralston, *Archaeological resource management in the UK* 2006, while Abercromby and Dyne, *Recording England's past* 1993, is a review of national and local Sites and Monuments Records in England. The development of recording and assessing the cultural landscape as a whole through schemes such as Historic Landscape Characterisation is discussed, with numerous case studies, in Fairclough and Rippon, *Europe's cultural landscape* 2002, and Rippon, *Historic landscape analysis* 2004.

UNDERWATER SURVEY

Excellent illustrations can be found in a collection of studies published by the Bayerisches Gesellschaft für UWA, *Archäologie unter Wasser, 2: Prospektionstechniken* 1998; two interesting case studies are Kingsley and Raveh, *The ancient harbour and anchorage at Dor, Israel: results of the underwater surveys 1976–1991* 1996, and, in a modern historical context, Arnold *et al.*, 'The Denbigh project: initial observations on a Civil War blockade runner and its wreck site' 1999.

REMOTE SENSING

Scollar *et al.*, *Archaeological prospecting and remote sensing* 1990, is a comprehensive source of technical information, while many papers have appeared in a new periodical, *Archaeological Prospection*, from 1994 onwards. An up-to-date well-illustrated guide is Dabas, *La prospection* 1998, while Léva, *Aerial photography and geophysical prospection in archaeology* 1990, contains many informative studies. For the general non-archaeological background, Bewley singled out Lilles and Kiefer, *Remote sensing and image interpretation* 1994, as unrivalled for its clarity and lavish illustrations.

AIRBORNE PROSPECTION

Cases employing observation methods other than aircraft include Cox, 'Satellite imagery, aerial photography and wetland archaeology' 1992, and Kennedy, 'Declassified satellite photographs and archaeology in the Middle East: case studies from Turkey' 1998.

AERIAL PHOTOGRAPHY

Much may be learned from two collections of papers that demonstrate the importance of this technique: Maxwell, *The impact of aerial reconnaissance on archaeology* 1983, and Brophy and Cowley, *From the air: understanding aerial archaeology* 2005. An excellent example of the use of aerial photography and attempts to characterise site types is Whimster, *The emerging past: air photography and the buried landscape* 1989. O.G.S. Crawford is examined in a biography of this pioneer of aerial archaeology: Hauser, *Bloody old Britain: O.G.S. Crawford and the archaeology of modern life* 2008.

GEOPHYSICAL AND GEOCHEMICAL SURVEYING

Concise background to the storage of survey data is provided by Schmidt and Wise, *Geophysics guide to good practice* 1998, while applications in the field are presented with clarity by David, *Geophysical survey in archaeological field evaluation* 1995, and Gaffney and Gater, *Revealing the buried past: geophysics for archaeologists* 2003, provides the most up-to-date basic coverage of different techniques. Further technical detail and case studies may be found in Hasek, *Methodology of geophysical research in archaeology* 1999, and Spoerry, *Geoprospection in the archaeological landscape* 1992. Up-to-date general accounts in German are Zickgraf, *Geomagnetische und geoelektrische Prospektion in der Archäologie* 1999, and Planck, *Unsichtbares sichtbar machen: geophysikalische Prospektionsmethoden in der Archäologie*

1998. Informative examples of the application of geophysics are Roosevelt, *Moundbuilders of the Amazon: geophysical archaeology on Marajo Island, Brazil* 1991, and Spoerry and Cooper, *Ramsey Abbey: an archaeological survey* 2000, while good illustrations in the context of television archaeology are contained in Taylor, *Behind the scenes at the Time Team* 1998.

GEOGRAPHICAL INFORMATION SYSTEMS (GIS)

One of the first overviews, Allen, *Interpreting space: GIS and archaeology* 1990, remains valuable, while Westcott and Brandon, *Practical applications of GIS in archaeology: a predictive modelling tool kit* 1999, is more specialised. Several collections of GIS studies have been published recently, including Lock and Stančič, *Archaeology and geographical information systems: a European perspective* 1995; Lock, *Beyond the map: archaeology and spatial technologies* 2000, and (mainly from America) Maschner, *New methods, old problems: geographic information systems in modern archaeological research* 1996. The pioneering work by Gaffney and Stančič *GIS approaches to regional analysis: a case study of the island of Hvar* 1991, is an illuminating introduction that examines a Croatian island from prehistoric to historical times, while Van West, *Modelling prehistoric agricultural productivity in Southwestern Colorado: a GIS approach* 1994, is a good example from the USA. A more recent application is that from the Perry Oaks, Heathrow, project which includes a searchable GIS on CD (Lewis *et al.* 2006). Lock, *Using computers in archaeology* 2003, provides a good general overview of computing in archaeology which covers many of these issues.

LANDSCAPE ARCHAEOLOGY

A collection of papers published in *Antiquity* over many years has been selected in Stoddart, *Landscapes from Antiquity* 2000. The development

of British approaches to landscape archaeology are succinctly analysed in Johnson, *Ideas of landscape* 2007. The British tradition may be further visually explored in Rackham, *The illustrated history of the countryside* 1994, and in two volumes of papers dedicated to Christopher Taylor: Everson and Williamson, *The archaeology of landscape* 1998, and Pattison *et al.*, *Patterns of the past* 1999. Roberts, *Landscapes of settlement: prehistory to the present* 1996, provides an overview of Britain, while a particularly interesting landscape in Wessex is explored by Fowler, *Landscape plotted and pieced: landscape history and local archaeology in Fyfield and Overton, Wiltshire* 2000 (and its summary, Fowler and Blackwell, *The land of Lettice Sweetapple: an English countryside explored* 1998). One of the most influential and thorough discussions of how to piece together a prehistoric landscape is Fleming, *The Dartmoor reaves* 2008; an informative contrast from the northern uplands is Woodside and Crow, *Hadrian's Wall: an historic landscape* 1999, while a model study of an industrial landscape is Bowden, *Furness iron: the physical remains of the iron industry and related woodland industries of Furness and southern Lakeland* 2000. Fascinating work in Scandinavia is presented in Fabech and Ringtved, *Settlement and landscape* 1999. Cooney, *Landscapes of Neolithic Ireland* 2000, reflects some of the current approaches to social landscape archaeology in Ireland. North and South America are represented in Conzen, *The making of the American landscape* 1994, and Lentz, *Imperfect balance: landscape transformations in the pre-Columbian Americas* 2000, while approaches to landscape archaeology in the Near East are introduced in Wilkinson, *Archaeological landscapes of the Near East* 2003. Interesting ethnographic and theoretical perspectives may be explored in Feld and Basso, *Senses of place* 1996, and Tilley's highly influential *A phenomenology of landscape: places, paths and monuments* 1994. Similar themes explored in Tilley, *The materiality of stone* 2004 and the application of theoretical perspectives to fieldwork in Bender *et al.*, *Stone worlds: narrative and reflexivity in landscape archaeology* 2007; there is also a website dedicated to the project.

CHAPTER 3

Excavation

Despite growing awareness of the new remote sensing techniques described in Chapter 2, excavation is still widely perceived as the main purpose of archaeology (**Fig. 3.1**). It incorporates two approaches: the exposure of **vertical sequences** of deposits that reflect the long-term occupation of a site; and the recovery of **horizontal plans** of individual features or particular periods of occupation. The most important development of the early twentieth century was improved understanding of the vertical aspect, and the use of carefully-placed **trenches** and **vertical sections** to reveal and record it. From the 1950s, large **open-area excavations** – frequently conducted in 'rescue' circumstances – inspired new ways of understanding vertical relationships while shifting the main focus from general sequences to specific actions and events.

We will present the process of excavation in the following sequence:

1 How excavation methods developed to take account of **stratification**.

2 How a particular site is **selected for study**.

3 The **background research** that precedes excavation.

4 The implementation of **excavation strategy**.

5 Problems of specific **kinds of sites** such as caves or burials, and excavating in difficult **environments**.

6 Methods by which different forms of **sites, features and structures** are excavated.

7 Systems of **recording** structures, sequences of deposits and finds.

8 The processing of site records and finds for **publication**.

3.1 THE DEVELOPMENT OF EXCAVATION TECHNIQUES

- key references: Stiebing, *Uncovering the past* 1993; Romer and Romer, *Great excavations* 2000; Parslow, *Rediscovering antiquity* 1995.

Before 1900, few sites were explored by removing distinct layers and recording objects found together within them. The exceptions were mainly investigations of caves with early prehistoric occupation, conducted by excavators with a background in geology who were familiar with the concept of superimposed layers (**strata**) containing distinctive fossils (**Fig. 3.2**). Finding artefacts made by humans together with bones of extinct animals was vital for proving the depth of prehistoric time (Chapter 1, p. 29). Historians and art-historians were more interested in finding inscriptions, documents or works of art; these could be recovered without paying attention to the contexts in which they were found. Other excavators aimed to discover objects of commercial value to satisfy the demands of collectors and museums, although some (such as Giovanni Belzoni: **Box 1.5**) became increasingly interested in revealing structures as well as finds (Mayes 2003). Impressive ruins were uncovered

BOX 3.1   # Development of excavation techniques: Mortimer Wheeler

Mortimer Wheeler's favoured method of excavation, and one imitated by many contemporary and succeeding archaeologists, consisted of a grid of unexcavated baulks separating small square trenches. These were the so-called '**box trenches**', seen here at The Tofts, part of an Iron Age fortification at Stanwick, Yorkshire, excavated in 1951–2 (image (a)). This created four permanent sections in each trench, while wooden pegs at their intersections provided reference points for planning excavated features and plotting the precise location of important finds (Wheeler 1954b: pl. VIII, facing p. 8).

Although Wheeler's box system had been a major technical advance in the 1920s, it was not always ideal. The shallow ploughsoil at Stanwick did not justify the numerous sections, whilst the baulks concealed important features. Their removal revealed the foundation of a circular timber building, which was much easier to understand in terms of a horizontal plan. This technique became known as **open-area excavation** (image (b)). Other excavations in the 1950s by younger archaeologists influenced by European methods, such as Brian Hope-Taylor at Yeavering in Northumberland, tackled complex sites by opening extensive areas and only cutting sections at critical stratigraphic points within them (Collis 2001). This is now the most common form of excavation in most parts of the world.

in Egypt, the Near East and Mesoamerica, but the best sculptures and objects were removed to museums. This process of 'digging before excavation' (Maisels 1993: 30) destroyed much evidence; objects displayed in distant museums and picturesque architectural drawings are no substitute for the information and ordinary artefacts lost through the removal of accumulated soil and debris (**Figs 3.2–3, Box 3.2**).

3.1.1 The concept of stratification

- key references: Harris, *Principles of archaeological stratigraphy* 1989; Lucas, *Critical approaches to fieldwork* 2001: 36–51.

Stratification can be defined, therefore, as any number of relatable deposits of archaeological strata (from a stake-hole to the floor of a cathedral) which are the result of 'successive operations of either nature or mankind'. **Stratigraphy**, on the other hand 'is the study of archaeological strata … with a view to arranging them in a chronological sequence'.

(Barker 1993: 21, quoting Edward Harris; our emphasis)

Modern excavators study the stratification of a site to guide the recording of individual deposits (with their associated finds) and to place them correctly in the overall sequence. Stratigraphic

Figure 3.1 Archaeology and excavation are so inextricably linked in the popular perception of the subject that large crowds turn out to see work in progress in historic cities such as York or Canterbury. Enthusiasm is so great that archaeologists taking part in a *Time Team* programme at Canterbury in August 2000 were in great demand for signing autographs as well as investigating a site. Carenza Lewis and Mick Aston can be seen here, along with programme's presenter Tony Robinson; they consistently reached audiences of between three and four million viewers through programmes which look at background research and fieldwork as well as excavation itself. (Teresa Hall)

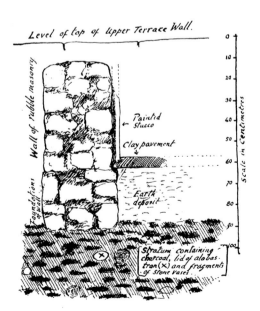

Figure 3.2 A section drawing from Arthur Evans' report on excavations at Knossos, Crete, illustrated in an unusually careful manner for such an early date. It is possible that his father, John Evans, had introduced him to geological sections such as that shown in Fig. 1.14. Arthur Evans illustrated the precise location of a vital piece of dating evidence (an imported Egyptian lid) beneath the wall and floor of part of the palace. The lid provides a *terminus post quem* for the wall foundation and earth deposit above the layer in which it was found; the wall must have been constructed later than the date of the Egyptian lid. (Evans 1899–1900: 64)

Figure 3.3 Excavation in the early twentieth century at Corbridge, a Roman military base and civilian town just south of Hadrian's Wall in Northumberland, was typical of work carried out on most historical sites at this time; there had been little or no progress in techniques since the eighteenth century. The columns of porticoes belonging to two stone granaries had been partly buried by rises in the level of the Roman main street; its stone gutter can be seen resting against them. The excavators have removed the vital deposits between the road and the granaries. These stratified layers might have revealed important details about the date and nature of changes to the buildings and their entrances. However, everything except solid masonry was simply dug out, destroying evidence that later excavators would have liked to re-examine. (Knowles and Forster 1910)

observations did take place as early as the seventeenth century in Scandinavia (Trigger 2006: 88), but before the twentieth century most excavators only observed and recorded stratification after digging down and exposing it like a natural geological section. Although published as early as 1800, John Frere's report on the context of prehistoric artefacts found at Hoxne (Chapter 1, p. 27) included the notion that, in a series of strata, those at the bottom will be older than those at the top. Geologists had already used this principle of **superposition** to arrange fossils from different strata in developmental sequences, and it was well known to early nineteenth-century investigators of human origins such as Boucher de Perthes and McEnery (Stiebing 1993: 40–6). Like geologists, early archaeologists also realised that the physical characteristics of strata, together with any accompanying bones and shells, could provide information about the environmental conditions prevailing when they were formed.

3.1.2 General Pitt Rivers

- key references: Bowden, *Pitt Rivers* 1991; Barrett *et al.*, *Landscape, monuments and society* 1991.

The progress made in the late nineteenth century is exemplified by Pitt Rivers (Augustus Henry Lane Fox) (1827–1900), whose ideas about evolution and typology have been discussed in Chapter 1 (**Fig. 3.4**). He had already played an important part in the development of the typological study of artefacts, and conducted fieldwork and surveys in England and Ireland; excavation only became Pitt Rivers' major activity after he inherited a large tract of Wessex, one of the richest archaeological areas in England. The last twenty years of his life were devoted to studying Cranborne Chase and organising educational activities, such as a museum of rural life, for his estate workers and their families.

Figure 3.4 General Pitt Rivers (1827–1900) portrayed by Frank Holl R.A. in 1882, shortly after inheriting a large estate in Hampshire and Dorset containing many archaeological sites. The prehistoric shield and the pickaxe relate to his interest in ancient weapons, which led him to conduct excavations primarily to recover artefacts for typological study, while the observant stance and notebook draw attention to his role in recording and protecting ancient monuments. (Pitt Rivers Museum, University of Oxford)

Wealth from his estates allowed Pitt Rivers to employ full-time archaeological assistants and to use his own labourers to carry out excavations on a variety of monuments, from a Neolithic burial mound (**Fig. 3.5**) to a standing medieval building. Since first undertaking excavations in Ireland in the 1860s, Pitt Rivers had devoted detailed attention to artefacts as well as structures, and the importance he attached to *all* finds, however trivial, led him to record the contexts in which they were found. His excavation technique was not revolutionary, although it was neat, methodical and accurately recorded, using skills acquired during his military career. Pitt Rivers' innovation was the production of detailed reports on his excavations, containing copious illustrations and 'relic tables' that remain valuable sources of information. This impressive series of volumes was

not designed for wide consumption, however, for they were circulated privately rather than sold. Pitt Rivers' contemporaries and successors, Schliemann, John Evans and Petrie, possessed a more advanced understanding of stratigraphy and the importance of artefacts for dating the observed layers. The working methods of modern excavators were not firmly established until Pitt Rivers' approach to recording and publication was combined with a clearer perception of the significance of stratification, the ability to recognise it during excavation, and the excavation and recording of features and deposits layer by layer.

3.1.3 Developments in the twentieth century

- key references: Lucas, *Critical approaches to fieldwork* 2001; Elliott, *Great excavations* 1995.

Three indispensable elements of excavation emerged by the beginning of the twentieth century: **horizontal** observations were combined with accurate recording, notably on German excavations of Classical cities in Turkey; vertical sequences were increasingly important, particularly on deeply stratified tell sites in the Near East (**Fig. 1.22**); systematic attention to all classes of **finds** was the newest element. American archaeology also began a 'stratigraphic revolution', although sites were still excavated in horizontal levels, rather than by layers; as in Europe and the Near East, the guiding principle was the importance of contexts and the finds they contained (Lucas 2001: 35–6). As a result, a growing number of authoritative publications of sites and catalogues of artefacts, together with accessible storage of site material in museums, allowed archaeologists such as V. Gordon Childe to make increasingly sophisticated **culture-historical** interpretations of the past (**Box 1.7**; Chapter 6, p. 260).

3.1.4 Mortimer Wheeler

- key references: Hawkes, *Mortimer Wheeler* 1982; Wheeler, *Archaeology from the earth* 1954; Collis, *Digging up the past* 2001: 9–13.

Figure 3.5 Pitt Rivers' excavation of Wor Barrow, a neolithic burial mound in Dorset, in 1893. Despite the quality of the recording, the actual excavation technique was crude (Bowden 1991: 131–4). Labourers simply moved forward against a vertical face on horizontal levels; sloping layers of the barrow's construction material are clearly visible on the sections, but no attempt was made to remove them individually. Worse still, the excavation was taken down into natural chalk well below the old ground surface, whose buried soil shows as a dark layer at wheelbarrow height in the left section. Fortunately, Pitt Rivers eventually realised his mistake when the large foundation trench of a timber mortuary structure was found underneath the barrow, but many minor features must have been dug away unnoticed. A scale model of the barrow before excavation can be seen propped up at the front of excavation. (Salisbury and South Wiltshire Museum)

With the proviso, then, that all horizontal digging must proceed from clear and comprehensible vertical sections, the question of priority is fundamentally not in doubt. Careful horizontal digging can alone, in the long run, give us the full information that we ideally want.

(Wheeler 1954a: 129)

Mortimer Wheeler (1890–1976), whose outlook and methods (like those of Pitt Rivers) explicitly reflected his military background (Chada 2002), combined horizontal and vertical excavation with stratigraphic recording of finds in his work from the 1920s. Unlike Pitt Rivers, he trained many younger assistants (such as Kathleen Kenyon) who went on to become distinguished archaeologists. Having survived the First World War, Wheeler resumed an archaeological career and

conducted excavations in Britain, France and India on sites selected for the investigation of specific research questions (interrupted by the Second World War). For example, he explored the relationship between the pre-Roman hillforts of southern England and northern France by excavating the defensive structures of several sites and comparing the styles of pottery found on them. In India, he used imported Roman coins and pottery (that could be dated by reference to sites in Europe) as a reference point for dating a sequence of Indian sites and finds. Wheeler also organised and published museum collections, wrote books and articles for the general public, and, in his later life, became a remarkably successful radio and television personality and encouraged many young people to look seriously at archaeology as a degree subject and career. His first wife, Tessa, played an underrated part in the development of Wheeler's methods, and also instigated the creation of an Institute of Archaeology in the University of London (Hawkes 1982: 122–43).

Wheeler developed a **box system** of excavation that imposed a grid of square trenches on a site, with baulks left between them as a permanent record of the stratification of all four sides of each trench. He also uncovered large open areas in a manner similar to modern practice at the Roman city at Verulamium (St Albans) and the Iron Age hillfort at Maiden Castle in Dorset (Sharples 1991). Whichever technique Wheeler used, it was designed to satisfy conflicting requirements of horizontal and vertical excavation; while stratification is essential for understanding the sequence of a site, an arbitrary grid of vertical baulks may mask important horizontal features (**Box 3.1; Fig. 3.6**). In the United States, something resembling Wheeler's box system was carried out in reverse: blocks of deposits were isolated by a grid of trenches, which revealed their stratification in advance of excavation (Lucas 2001: 49–50).

This conflict can never be resolved entirely satisfactorily, especially in urban rescue excavations constrained by limitations on time and access (Carver 1987; Rowsome 2000). Wheeler was undoubtedly aware of the problem posed by tells in the Near East, where it had become standard practice to sink deep shafts (**sondages**) to sample their successive occupations and artefacts; a shortage of space made horizontal excavation of the lower levels physically impossible. He stressed the need to excavate layers and features such as pits or walls, and the interfaces between them, as stratigraphic units, rather than removing arbitrary horizontal levels – the standard American approach of his time. Harris has compared the significance of Wheeler's approach, which included systematic numbering of layers and the finds that they contained, to the importance of ideas about strata and fossils introduced into geology by Hutton and Smith in the late eighteenth century (1989: 11).

3.1.5 From keyhole trenches to open area excavation

- key references: Barker, *Techniques of excavation* 1993; Lucas, *Critical approaches to fieldwork* 2001: 52–63; Collis, *Digging up the past* 2001: 9–20.

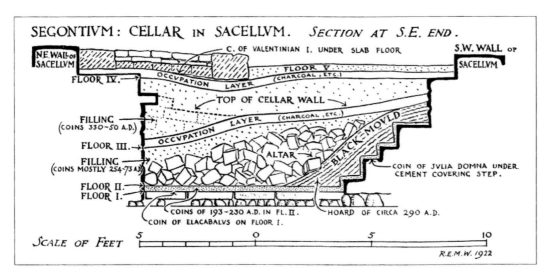

Figure 3.6 Drawing of a section through the filling of the strongroom (*sacellum*) beneath the headquarters building of the Roman fort at Segontium, Caernarvon, Wales. Because the phases of occupation of this military site were assumed to reflect the history of Roman Wales, particular emphasis was placed upon dating evidence in this drawing. Thus, for example, the layer of rubble cannot have fallen there before c. AD 290, for a coin hoard of that date was found in the soil ('black mould') beneath it. (Wheeler 1923: 55, Fig. 17)

Figure 3.7 Test pits being excavated in the centre of the Roman and medieval town of Cirencester. These small investigations are excavated in the same manner as open area excavations, but allow for a small sample of an area or site to be examined without significant destruction. In many cases, such as here, they may be used to determine the depth at which archaeological deposits occur, and their state of preservation. This is particular helpful in planning for development and may allow the building plans to be modified in order to preserve the archaeology. (Simon Cox, Cotswold Archaeology)

Keyhole excavation was carried out extensively in Roman military archaeology by Ian Richmond, who produced overall plans of many forts and fortresses in northern Britain by the judicious excavation of small narrow trenches, carefully placed to check critical details of the fairly predictable layout of their internal structures. Richmond was also an astute observer of stratification; his pioneering drawings of layers and their associated dated coins were included in a report on Wheeler's excavations in the Roman fort at Caernarvon in Wales published in 1923 (**Fig. 3.6**). An opposite extreme to the open-area approach is the procedure of digging small, widely-spaced exploratory trenches to establish the dimensions of a large site. A particularly minimal method of mapping the extent of sites which are not deeply buried is **shovel-testing**, which should perhaps be thought of as an extension of surface fieldwork, for numerous small holes are dug to locate archaeological deposits, but not actually excavated (Chapter 2, p. 58). More common is the opening of **test-pits** (usually small trenches, perhaps 2 m × 2 m) to examine the nature of the archaeology of a site and to produce stratigraphic evidence without damaging too much of the archaeology. On a larger scale, **evaluation trenches** are commonly used in commercial archaeology when large areas of the landscape need to be examined to determine the existence or nature of archaeological deposits in advance of full, open-area excavation. Evaluation trenches are usually long linear trenches (perhaps 20 m × 2 m) to allow relatively large areas to be examined. If substantial archaeological deposits are encountered they will be planned to await full excavation later (**Fig. 3.7**).

Open-area excavation methods were developed in the first half of the twentieth century on sites lying on flat alluvial land in southern Scandinavia, northern Germany and the Netherlands. This region was ideal because it contains many rural sites, ranging from Neolithic farming settlements to villages of the early medieval period, that were occupied for relatively short periods before being relocated. Their buildings were constructed entirely from wood; once excavators had learned how to recognise post holes, hearths and floors it was comparatively easy to uncover complete plans of individual buildings – or even whole settlements – because they lacked any build-up of construction and demolition layers of the kind found where stone or mud-brick was used. Since (unlike Roman forts) the plans of these settlements could not be predicted, complete uncovering was essential for understanding their form and development. A German archaeologist,

Gerhard Bersu, was invited to England in 1938 to excavate an Iron Age farmstead at Little Woodbury, Wiltshire. He demonstrated that pre-Roman Britons lived in substantial round timber houses, not (as previously thought) in cramped 'pit-dwellings' (which were actually for storing grain); their plans could only be recovered by stripping large areas (**Box 3.7**). The site was excavated in strips rather than as a continuous open area, but the contrast with the results of keyhole trenches was nevertheless dramatic (Evans 1989). North American archaeologists also employed a similar range of excavation techniques by the 1930s (Lucas 2001: 47–51). As in Europe, open-area excavation was promoted by a desire to recover plans of settlements built from wood, and it was accompanied by standardised recording methods (**Fig. 3.8**).

Wheeler (and more recent excavators) extended the concept of open-area examination to sites with a significant depth of accumulated layers; his maxim that good excavation should satisfy the demands of the vertical and horizontal aspects of a site remains fundamental. Sites excavated by a grid system of trenches, or circular mounds excavated in quadrants, normally underwent a final stage of investigation when the baulks that had preserved the vertical sections were removed. True open-area excavations dispense with baulks altogether. On shallow sites disturbed ploughsoil can be stripped off to reveal individual features; those that happen to overlap may be placed into their correct sequence by excavating cross-sections at critical points. The whole process can be extended to sites with deep stratification as long as the extent, contours, depth and consistency of each feature or layer are carefully recorded before it is removed. Sections remain important, not for producing one impressive drawing that illustrates the entire history of a site, but for presenting evidence about relationships. The focus has shifted from highly visible sections exposed as a physical entity to numerous separate sketches, measured drawings and photographs from which sequences may be reassembled. This change places greater responsibility for keeping accurate records upon excavators, but efficiency and precision may be enhanced with the help of modern digital surveying equipment such as a Total Station (Chapter 2, p. 58).

3.1.6 The future of excavation

Despite many of the changes in excavation technique, many elements such as the keyhole excavation and 'evaluation trenches' (described above) remain a key component of archaeological investigation and are frequently used in commercial archaeology and as a precursor to open-area excavation. What of the future of excavation strategies? One recent development in some regions has been the blurring of the differences between 'landscape' archaeology and excavation, with increasingly large open-area excavations uncovering huge swathes of landscape. This has been a characteristic of some of the large-scale development projects in northern Europe, particular eastern England and the Netherlands. The expansion of gravel quarries or large-scale constructions such as industrial parks has meant the stripping of large areas to allow excavation to reveal relationships between sites (e.g., Theuws and Roymans 1999; Evans 2008). In the Netherlands, for example, the shifting of houses over many generations in the Bronze Age and early Iron Age is only apparent because sufficiently large areas have been excavated (Gerritsen 2003). Elsewhere, for example in Ireland and France, investigations prior to the construction of motorways or pipelines have been conducted by excavating long continuous strips (transects) across hitherto unexplored landscapes, sometimes revealing startling new knowledge about their archaeology. (O'Sullivan and Stanley 2005; Gutherez and Odiot 2001). The implementation of excavation techniques continues to involve choosing appropriate strategies that not only take account of the nature of a landscape or a type of site, but also address specific research aims – within the available time and budget. Thus, while large-scale open-area excavation might be appropriate in advance of gravel quarrying in eastern England, small-scale test-pits would be better suited to defining the extent of a palaeo-Indian flint scatter in North America.

Figure 3.8 William Kelso's superb excavation of a house at Kingsmill Plantation, Virginia, is just one of a series of sites dating back to the first European settlements in the United States that he has investigated (Kelso 1984, 1996). The photograph illustrates how open area excavation can reveal the entire plan of a structure, in this case built partly of brick and partly of timber. There is little stratigraphic information to be gained from the thin layer of topsoil, and many isolated pits and post holes lack any stratigraphical relationship to others. Interpretation is a matter of understanding vertical relationships of layers removed from deeper contexts, such as the cellars visible in the foreground, and horizontal relationships established by relating isolated features to the overall plan. Smaller trenches, and exploratory 'test pits' dug to establish the overall extent of the site, can be seen in the background; these can be linked into a single open area to maximise the horizontal information recovered. (William M Kelso)

BOX 3.2   **Stratigraphic recording**

Recording a stratigraphic sequence using the **Harris Matrix**. The simple section (top left) and the exploded three-dimensional diagram (right) show the same stratigraphic units, often now referred to as 'contexts', and the order in which they were formed (see Fig. 3.22). It should be noted that (2) and (6) are **interfaces**, rather than physical layers. Bottom left is a Harris Matrix showing all stratigraphical relationships; in the centre, superfluous or duplicated lines have been removed to give a clear summary of the original section. This method of summarising stratigraphy can be carried out during an excavation and is useful in published excavation reports (after Harris 1989: Fig. 12).

A simple example of dating by means of stratification: the excavation of a post hole (below). Left: the post stands in its hole, with some packing stones for extra stability. The mixture of topsoil and subsoil formed during the digging and refilling of the hole give it a different texture from its surroundings. Right: a new layer has accumulated after the demolition or decay of the structure, filling the cavity left by the post (post pipe); a new topsoil has also developed.

Dating evidence The rim of a pot datable to c. AD 1300 is residual (i.e. left over from an earlier occupation); it just happened to have been in the topsoil through which the hole was dug and was accidentally incorporated into the filling. Better evidence is provided by a coin of AD 1520 whose position amongst the packing stones shows that it could not have entered the hole after the post was erected and the hole refilled; it might even have been dropped by one of the builders. Thus, the date of the potsherd is irrelevant because the coin of AD 1520 provides a better *terminus post quem* for construction: the post was certainly erected in or after 1520, but we do not know whether this event took place within days or decades of that year.

If the formation of the layer that overlies the hole and fills the post pipe could be dated by some form of reliable independent historical evidence, it would provide a *terminus ante quem* (date before which) for the end of the life of the underlying timber structure. The coin of AD 1600 can only have reached this position after the decay of the post or during demolition; again, 1600 is only a t.p.q. for the formation of the layer in which it was found. The life of the timber structure began sometime after 1520 and it had gone out of existence by the time that a new layer was formed sometime later than 1600. However, neither coin need have been new when lost and either or both of them could have been residual, like the pottery. All other forms of dating evidence from the rest of the site would have to be taken into consideration before any conclusion could be reached. Only precise stratigraphical excavation could have revealed the exact positions of the datable finds (drawn by Sheila Newton).

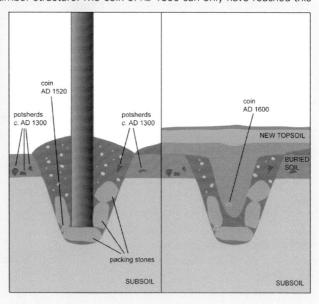

3.2 THE INTERPRETATION OF STRATIFICATION

- key references: Harris, *Principles of archaeological stratigraphy* 1989; Roskams, *Excavation* 2001: 239–66; Collis, *Digging up the past* 2001: 64–77.

As already explained, the principle of superposition holds that layers of soil (or any other material) are deposited in chronological order, with the oldest at the bottom. Stratigraphic excavation is based on this principle, whether it involves a long sequence of deposits or a unique relationship between two intersecting ditches. In the early 1970s Edward Harris developed the **Harris matrix** at Winchester, Hampshire, for coping with complex deeply stratified rescue excavations, and the method was soon adopted in London (Harris 1989: 34–9; Lucas 2001: 56–8). It brought considerable benefits to the study of stratigraphy by providing a method of summarising elaborate sequences in concise diagrams (**Box 3.2**).

Harris accepted the fundamental validity of Wheeler's ideas about stratigraphy, but demanded a more systematic approach. His term **unit of stratification**, rather than 'stratum' or 'layer', was a new element that emphasised the importance of **interfaces** between layers. For example, the sides of a silted-up ditch are simply the boundaries, or interfaces, between the filling of the ditch and the material through which it has been dug. This interface has no physical existence but nevertheless represents a specific human action (digging a ditch – a 'cut') that must be placed at the correct point in the sequence of layers. In the case of working surfaces such as floors, the interface between the floor and levels that formed above it after it went out of use may represent a long period of significant human activity, whereas the deposition of whatever overlies it might have taken a few hours or days. These units of stratification are often now referred to as '**contexts**' (see **Box 3.2** and **Fig. 3.22**). They can be distinguished from another term, '**feature**', which refers to a group of contexts. So, an enclosure ditch might be a 'feature' which is made up of a number of 'contexts', both 'cuts' and 'fills'.

Harris matrices have not replaced traditional **section drawings** in archaeological reports, as sections remain a convenient method of illustrating relationships between layers, structures or other features that are crucial to dating or interpretation. Section drawings are frequently better than photographs for showing the composition of silted-up ditches or rubbish pits; even colour photographs rarely bring out sufficient detail, and they are expensive to publish. A drawing of a section is by definition an interpretation, and it can be expressed in a variety of different styles, from baldly diagrammatic to naturalistic (Harris 1989: 69–81; Lucas 2001: 209; **Box 3.2**).

3.2.1 Dating stratification

- key reference: Harris *et al.*, *Practices of archaeological stratigraphy* 1993.

On relatively shallow archaeological sites with distinct horizontal layers, the lowest is clearly the oldest, and (following the law of superposition) the remainder accumulated in succession from the site's first occupation to the present. This law only places layers into a relative sequence, however; it says nothing about the length of time that each deposit took to accumulate, or whether there were long intervals of abandonment (**Box 3.2**). In practice, stratification rarely consists of horizontal layers, but is complicated by disturbances by human and natural activity, which is why Harris's system is so valuable. Independent evidence must be found to provide date ranges for a stratigraphic sequence. The first indication is likely to come from artefacts – this is why the precise context in which any artefact was discovered must be recorded. Unless distinctive artefacts with limited date-ranges have been found, samples of appropriate materials must be collected and submitted for scientific dating (Chapter 4).

Human activities such as digging foundation trenches, rubbish pits or wells may lead to artefacts being deposited below the contemporary living surface – and may also bring to the surface old artefacts discarded during earlier phases of occupation. Occasionally it is possible to determine how much disturbance artefacts have suffered. Flint flakes struck from a single core during tool-making at Kenniff Cave in Queensland, Australia, must have fallen to the ground during a single phase of occupation; later disturbance of this level by human and natural processes caused flakes that fitted together to be found in layers (dated by radiocarbon) separated by up to 2,500 years (Richardson 1992). Likewise, if pottery sherds which have become heavily abraded in ploughsoil or on occupation surfaces are found in an excavated context, they were redeposited at a much later date than they were in use. They do not date the context they are found in, except that it must be *later* than the date of the ceramics (see Box 3.2). The process of relating stratification to datable items or events involves two concise Latin phrases: *terminus post quem* (a fixed point from which all successive layers or features must be of later date) and the much rarer *terminus ante quem* (a dated level beneath which everything must be older). The volcanic debris deposited over Pompeii and Herculaneum in AD 79 is perhaps the best-known example of a *terminus ante quem*.

3.3 PLANNING AN EXCAVATION

- key references: Roskams, *Excavation* 2001; Collis, *Digging up the past* 2001: 21–45; Drewett, *Field archaeology* 1999: 76–186; Carver, *Archaeological investigation* 2009: 113–93.

3.3.1 Excavation, ethics and theory

- key references: Roskams, *Excavation* 2001: 30–9, 267–70; Hodder, *The archaeological process* 1999; *Towards reflexive method* 2000.

Excavation can destroy a site as thoroughly as ploughing, building construction or natural erosion; the difference is that it is initiated by people who are conscious of the significance of ancient sites. This brings responsibilities that are a combination of common sense and ethics, but have been expressed formally in the Code of Conduct of the Institute for Archaeologists (IfA), an organisation of archaeologists in Britain that attempts to set standards for professional work. This code has no official standing or legal backing, but it does illustrate the thinking of an organisation that is attempting to become the main professional body for archaeologists in Britain. It consists of five principles, each of which has an accompanying list of rules; Box 3.3 includes some of the rules that relate to excavation in particular. Similar codes exist in the USA, outlined there by the Register of Professional Archaeologists, and in Europe by the European Association of Archaeologists. In many other countries a licence is required in order to conduct an excavation; for example, in Ireland, where the project director must have appropriate qualifications and experience. Such rules do not apply in England, where a licence is only required from English Heritage if a scheduled monument (Chapter 6, pp. 295–6) is to be excavated or investigated using geophysics. However, in those countries where a licence is required, being granted a licence does not necessarily ensure that the resulting archaeology is of the highest standard.

Carrying out excavation with the greatest possible skill only meets one of many responsibilities, for no work should begin without comprehensive background research, or without plans – and funding – for the conservation of finds and publication of the results (Rule 1.4; see Box 3.3). Excavators face a fundamental ethical question: what is the justification for causing irreversible damage to structures and deposits that might have accumulated for thousands of years? Among many different answers will be claims that examination of a site will make a worthwhile contribution to knowledge, or that it will be rescued in advance of destruction by agriculture or development. A more contentious answer might involve economics, as exposing structures and creating a site museum may enhance tourism. Awareness of theoretical positions within archaeology will probably raise the profile of ethical issues surrounding excavation, particularly when politics is involved, and sites and artefacts recovered from significant periods of the past are used to promote national, religious or ethnic identities (Chapter 6, p. 259).

3.3.2 Selection of a site

- key reference: Carver, *Archeological investigation* 2010: 335–61.

BOX 3.3

Responsibilities of excavators: selection of items from the Institute for Archaeologists' code of conduct (October 2008)

Principles	Rules
1 The archaeologist shall adhere to the highest standards of ethical and responsible behaviour in the conduct of archaeological affairs.	1.2 An archaeologist shall present archaeology and its results in a responsible manner and shall avoid and discourage exaggerated, misleading or unwarranted statements about archaeological matters. 1.4 An archaeologist shall not undertake archaeological work for which he or she is not adequately qualified. He or she should ensure that adequate support, whether of advice, personnel or facilities, has been arranged.
2 The archaeologist has a responsibility for the conservation of the historic environment.	2.1 An archaeologist shall strive to conserve archaeological sites and material as a resource for study and enjoyment now and in the future and shall encourage others to do the same. Where such conservation is not possible he/she shall seek to ensure the creation and maintenance of an adequate record through appropriate forms of research, recording and dissemination of results. 2.2 Where destructive investigation is undertaken the archaeologist shall ensure that it causes minimal attrition of the archaeological heritage consistent with the stated objects of the project. 2.3 An archaeologist shall ensure that the objects of the research project are an adequate justification for the destruction of the archaeological evidence which it will entail.
3 The archaeologist shall conduct his/her work in such a way that reliable information about the past may be acquired, and shall ensure that the results be properly recorded.	3.1 The archaeologist shall keep himself/herself informed about developments in his/her field or fields of specialisation. 3.2 An archaeologist shall prepare adequately for any project he/she may undertake. 3.3 An archaeologist shall ensure that experimental design, recording, and sampling procedures, where relevant, are adequate for the project in hand. 3.4 An archaeologist shall ensure that the record resulting from his/her work is prepared in a comprehensible, readily usable and durable form. 3.5 An archaeologist shall ensure that the record, including artefacts and specimens and experimental results, is maintained in good condition while in his/her charge and shall seek to ensure that it is eventually deposited where it is likely to receive adequate curatorial care and storage conditions and to be readily available for study and examination.

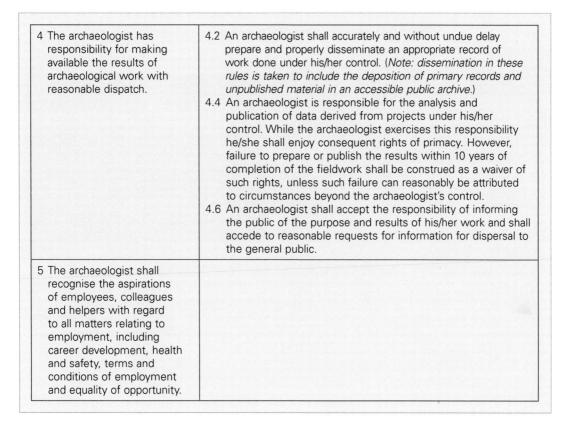

| 4 The archaeologist has responsibility for making available the results of archaeological work with reasonable dispatch. | 4.2 An archaeologist shall accurately and without undue delay prepare and properly disseminate an appropriate record of work done under his/her control. (*Note: dissemination in these rules is taken to include the deposition of primary records and unpublished material in an accessible public archive.*)

 4.4 An archaeologist is responsible for the analysis and publication of data derived from projects under his/her control. While the archaeologist exercises this responsibility he/she shall enjoy consequent rights of primacy. However, failure to prepare or publish the results within 10 years of completion of the fieldwork shall be construed as a waiver of such rights, unless such failure can reasonably be attributed to circumstances beyond the archaeologist's control.

 4.6 An archaeologist shall accept the responsibility of informing the public of the purpose and results of his/her work and shall accede to reasonable requests for information for dispersal to the general public. |
| 5 The archaeologist shall recognise the aspirations of employees, colleagues and helpers with regard to all matters relating to employment, including career development, health and safety, terms and conditions of employment and equality of opportunity. | |

One archaeological site might attract attention because it is particularly well preserved, another because it is threatened by destruction; are these good reasons for excavation? The answer depends upon whether you think that a picture of the past can be built up from a gradual accumulation of independent observations (like clues in a detective story), or whether individuals or organisations should design coherent research strategies. The 'detective story' approach characterised most work conducted up to the early twentieth century, but sufficient knowledge has been gathered in most parts of the world to make it indefensible, both ethically and intellectually, to excavate a site simply 'because it is there' (**Box 3.4**). Fieldwork techniques that reveal new archaeological sites – notably remote sensing from the air – have become very sophisticated, while geophysical surveying on the ground can provide significant information about individual sites that are already known (Chapter 2).

From the 1950s onwards increasing numbers of survey programmes looked at large areas rather than individual sites, using non-invasive field-walking and limited collection of artefacts from the surface. Such programmes provide an overall understanding of the pattern and sequence of sites (as long as representative traces actually appear on the surface) and supply a background for assessing the significance of any individual site that might be selected for research.

In densely-occupied regions such as Britain and northern Europe, the selection of sites may be determined not so much by research priorities as by pressures of development, particularly now that the main source of money for excavation comes not from the government but from **developer funding** – obligations placed upon private companies in the process of obtaining planning permission to build on archaeologically sensitive land. Do the financial resources made available in this way for rescue excavation,

Changing research priorities: the example of Roman Britain

The choice of which site to excavate has often been dictated not by considerations of which sites are likely to be destroyed, or those that are most representative of the past, but by their perceived importance by the excavators and contemporary research priorities. Richard Hingley has shown that until relatively recently archaeologists interested in the Roman period concentrated on the excavation of Roman villas and military sites at the expense of other types of site. Between 1921 and 1925 these two categories made up 25 per cent and 38 per cent of all Roman sites excavated in Britain in contrast to just 7 per cent that were ordinary rural farmsteads. Villas were not necessarily more important or more common in the Roman period, in fact non-villa settlements are the most widespread site type, but it indicates that the people conducting excavations were more interested in military and elite archaeology, probably because of their own military and upper-class backgrounds (see Chapter 6; Hingley 2000: 150–5). This pattern changed dramatically by the end of the twentieth century, partly because of the need to excavate sites in advance of destruction by development, but also because of the changing research interests of archaeologists. Excavations of non-villa farmsteads now comprised a much increased 23 per cent of all Roman sites investigated (photo: The excavation committee at the excavations of South Shields in 1875, reproduced with permission of Great North Museum, Newcastle-upon-Tyne).

finds processing and publication provide a better outcome than money raised to examine a site purely for research?

Some interesting questions are raised by considering an imaginary area that has been extensively examined by fieldwork of various kinds, and in which twenty Roman sites of a similar form have been recorded. Ten are situated on marginal land, well protected from past or present agricultural damage; of the other ten, nine lie on arable farmland, and are suffering the effects of ploughing, while the remaining one is about to be destroyed by building work. Sufficient funds are available for the complete excavation of *one* site. What should be done?

(a) The site threatened with complete destruction should be totally excavated to save a record of its information for posterity.

(b) One of the well-preserved sites should be fully excavated, because it is in better condition. It can be approached at a more leisurely pace, since it is not threatened; the quality of information should therefore be higher than in (a).

(c) Parts of several sites, including the one threatened with destruction, should be examined to provide information that allows them to be compared.

(d) None of this class of site should be excavated. The Roman period is comparatively well understood, so resources should be redirected to non-destructive fieldwork aimed at finding more sites from a different period, or investigating a completely different area about which less is known. The destruction of one site is not a cause for concern if nineteen others remain.

There are favourable arguments for each choice. It would require considerable confidence to choose (b), for no two sites are ever identical, and surface indications may be misleading – there is no guarantee that a well-preserved site will produce better information than a damaged one. If (a) or (b) is selected, how safely may results from one site be generalised to the other nineteen? Few scientists would place much confidence in results gained from 5% of a sample. Choice (c) may seem to be a good compromise, but partial excavations always leave unanswered questions; opinions will vary about whether complete knowledge of one site would be more informative than one quarter of each of four.

Whether (d) is in fact the optimum solution depends on the power of the decision-makers; a specialist on the Bronze Age would obviously prefer to direct aerial survey and fieldwork towards finding more prehistoric sites, rather than excavate a Roman site.

In many countries, government bodies or groups of researchers have attempted to provide guidance about such matters. **Research agendas** have been drawn up to help archaeologists determine where and what should be the focus of excavation. They assess the existing knowledge of the archaeology and, consulting academics, commercial archaeologists, museum specialists and other interested groups, decide on the priorities for future fieldwork. Agendas can be drawn up for countries (e.g. England: English Heritage 1998), regions (e.g. South West England: Webster 2008) or for specific periods and themes (e.g. Roman Britain: James and Millett 2001), and might take a range of forms, such as Internet documents (e.g. National Archaeological Research Agenda, Netherlands) or volumes of papers on the topic (e.g. Fabech and Ringtved 1999). Although such agendas can be in danger of perpetuating existing interests and sidelining amateur archaeologists

and the public, they raise awareness of the existing resource and highlight deficiencies in our knowledge. Not everything has to be done on a large scale, however; there is still room within archaeology for students and amateurs to initiate projects of fieldwork and excavation, and develop new research agendas. In Britain, for example, English Heritage has published its own national research agenda (English Heritage 1998), and also commented on conflicting priorities in a policy document, *Exploring our past: strategies for the archaeology of England*:

The management of the archaeological resource is based on a series of stages which form the framework for decision-making and the formulation of strategies. Three such stages can be proposed in the context of archaeological resource management and together these stages may be called the management cycle:

Stage 1
Identification, recording and the understanding of the monument or historic landscape.

Stage 2
Option 1 – curatorial management where the main aim is to arrest the natural and man-induced processes of decay through protection and management. *Option 2* – exploitative management where the archaeological resource can be used for public enjoyment through interpretation and display, or for academic interest through investigation and excavation.

Stage 3
Recording – in exceptional circumstances, when preservation is no longer possible, because the value of the archaeological resource is outweighed by some other factor, a site may be excavated to record as much as possible of its structure and form and thus in effect preserve it as a record.

Central to this cycle is the understanding of the resource which requires research and evaluation. For that reason the stages of the management cycle are preceded by the proposed framework of the academic objectives which English Heritage considers necessary in order to provide a framework for the future.

(English Heritage 1991: 34)

Endless discussion could be devoted to defining 'public enjoyment', and 'the value of the archaeological resource', but the emphasis on placing excavation within a 'framework of the academic objectives' appears reasonable. If resources are scarce, it is better that they should be distributed according to a strategic plan – but who will design the plan? Postmodern influences on archaeology have heightened awareness of the ideological aspects of such documents (Chapter 6, p. 295). Beyond ideological concerns, perhaps the most dangerous phrase in this extract lies in Stage 3, where elegant phrasing makes it sound acceptable to 'preserve' a site 'as a record'; is the process of archaeological excavation really so good that we may safely regard its results as an acceptable substitute for the site itself?

It is all very well for governments to lay down policy for sites in general, but what should be done about 'unique' sites? The great symbolic power of major sites was underlined in 2001 by the destruction by the Taliban government of gigantic Bamiyan Buddha sculptures carved into a cliff face in Afghanistan. In Britain, Stonehenge, Avebury and Silbury Hill are 'unique' prehistoric sites in Wessex, principally because they are so much bigger than other contemporary stone circles, henge monuments or mounds; the Stonehenge and Avebury landscape is inscribed in the UNESCO list of World Heritage Sites. Should more resources be directed towards understanding 'typical' sites, or do unique monuments give clearer insights into their times? It is instructive to ask the same question about sites from a historical period. Which will tell us more about medieval Kent – an architectural and archaeological analysis of Canterbury cathedral, or the study of a selection of churches from surrounding urban and rural parishes? It is clear that no answer may be made without first defining

research objectives, and that (unless dictated by a narrow-minded archbishop) these objectives would probably include relating the histories of minor churches to that of the cathedral (Blair and Pyrah 1996). In practice, by the end of the twentieth century it had become inconceivable that extensive excavation of a major monument such as Stonehenge would be permitted; indeed, the excavation of ordinary sites was being avoided through protection and management where possible. One conclusion that may be drawn from this discussion is that conscious decisions and policies should be made about all ancient sites, based on a good knowledge of their significance in a particular region or country and their relevance to research questions. At the same time, self-awareness about motivations behind research questions, and openness over deciding whether to excavate a site or not, should be second nature to a twenty-first-century archaeologist (see below, p. 138; Hodder 2000); some of the general theoretical issues involved, and the specific subject of cultural resource management (CRM), are explored in Chapter 6.

Types of archaeological investigation

The IfA has a set of *Standard and guidance* statements which defines a series of levels of investigation that an archaeological site might receive, from entirely non-intrusive examination to full-scale excavation. Four levels of work are defined:

1 **Desk-based assessment** is a programme of assessment of the known or potential archaeological resource within a specified area or site on land, inter-tidal zone or underwater. It consists of a collation of existing written, graphic, photographic and electronic information in order to identify the likely character, extent, quality and worth of the known or potential archaeological resource in a local, regional, national or international context, as appropriate.

2 **Archaeological field evaluation** is a limited programme of non-intrusive and/or intrusive fieldwork which determines the presence or absence of archaeological features, structures,

deposits, artefacts or ecofacts within a specified area or site on land, inter-tidal zone or underwater. If such archaeological remains are present, field evaluation defines their character, extent, quality and preservation, and enables an assessment of their worth in a local, regional, national or international context, as appropriate.

3 An **archaeological watching brief** is a formal programme of observations and investigation conducted during any operation carried out for non-archaeological reasons. This will be within a specified area or site on land, inter-tidal zone or underwater, where there is a possibility that archaeological deposits may be disturbed or destroyed. The programme will result in the preparation of a report and ordered archive.

4 **Archaeological excavation** is a programme of controlled, intrusive fieldwork with defined research objectives which examines, records and interprets archaeological deposits, features and structures and, as appropriate, retrieves artefacts, ecofacts and other remains within a specified area or site on land, inter-tidal zone or underwater. The records made and objects gathered during fieldwork are studied and the results of that study published in detail appropriate to the project design.

(Institute for Archaeologists, November 2008)

3.3.3 Developer-funded archaeology

• key references: *Planning Policy Guidance 16*, 1990; Roger Tym and Partners, *Review of the implementation of PPG 16 Archaeology and Planning* 1995; Darvill and Russell, *Archaeology after PPG 16* 2002; Neumann and Sanford *Cultural resources archaeology* 2001.

PPG 16 probably means little to anyone who is not engaged in professional archaeology in Britain. However, England's *Planning Policy Guidance 16: archaeology and planning* (1990), and the comparable documents for Scotland and Wales, have transformed the way in which most excavation

is conducted in Britain by embedding it in the wider processes of planning and development (**Box 3.5**). It ensures that the majority of archaeological fieldwork is funded by the developer, rather than by a university, a museum or the government. Classic open-area sites, such as Wroxeter – excavated at a leisurely pace over a number of years – belong to an era of well-funded research excavation that has come to an end. It is a long time since excavation directors were primarily academics from universities or museums, pursuing their own research projects. The professional units that grew up from the 1970s to the 1990s rely upon teams of specialists employed on short contracts, and have to meet strict budgets and deadlines. Office-bound managers cope with paperwork and accounts as well as setting the broad framework, while project officers actually carry out the excavations, using standardised recording systems that have become essential for continuity since teams have replaced individual directors.

PPG 16 was introduced in 1990 to solve the problems that arose in England when the archaeological potential of sites had not been sufficiently investigated in advance of modern development. Shakespeare's Rose Theatre in London was a high-profile example of what happened if pressure was put upon a developer only after building work had already started. Public outcry against the possible destruction of this unique site led to expensive delays and negative publicity for both the developers and English Heritage (Biddle 1989; Bowsher 1998). The new style of planning guidance reflected a broader process of carrying out Environmental Impact Assessments, which was introduced into Europe from the United States. As a result, most work by professional archaeologists is now aimed at *not* excavating sites. Ideally, desk-based assessment should be followed by archaeological field evaluation (which may involve very limited excavation), and the knowledge gained used for mitigation – working out some way in which the destruction of an archaeological site may be avoided, thus making excavation unnecessary. If there are still questions about the impact of development upon a site, an archaeological watching brief may take

Planning policy guidelines in England are based on a set of principles of when, why and how archaeological excavation should be undertaken. The statements below reflect a widespread perception of the role of archaeology in cultural resource management and can be seen reflected in the documents of both the Institute for Archaeologists and English Heritage.

3. Archaeological remains are irreplaceable. They are evidence – for prehistoric periods, the only evidence – of the past development of our civilization.

6. Archaeological remains should be seen as a finite, and non-renewable resource, in many cases highly fragile and vulnerable to damage and destruction. Appropriate management is therefore essential to ensure that they survive in good condition. In particular, care must be taken to ensure that archaeological remains are not needlessly or thoughtlessly destroyed. They can contain irreplaceable information about our past and the potential for an increase in future knowledge. They are part of our sense of national identity and are valuable both for their own sake and for their role in education, leisure and tourism.

14. Positive planning and management can help to bring about sensible solutions to the treatment of sites with archaeological remains and reduce the areas of potential conflict between development and preservation.

(PPG 16 section A: The importance of archaeology)

place to record any finds or deposits that turn up unexpectedly.

Since comprehensive excavation and publication are prohibitively expensive, most developers will alter their plans to avoid it. Some sites are 'preserved' by constructing deep piles through them to take the weight of a new building; this technique can in theory leave 95% of the archaeological site intact. It does mean, of course, that no further archaeological investigation will be possible until the new building is demolished. If a site is excavated, the system of which PPG 16 is part also has implications for the process of publication, guided by English Heritage's policy document *Management of research projects in the historic environment: Planning Policy note 3, archaeological excavation* (MoRPHE 2006). This new document replaces the earlier, highly influential, *Management of archaeological projects* (MAP2 1991), although many of the underlying principles are the same. It is necessary to compile a post-excavation assessment report that compares the outcome with what had been expected, and requires an indication of the potential of the site

archive (records, finds) for meeting the research aims of the project. Unfortunately the high quality and great quantity of data produced by a thorough modern excavation is very difficult – and expensive – to publish (below: p. 141). Despite this, the major increase in archaeological fieldwork which PPG 16 has caused is leading to a vast increase in both archaeological data (Darvill and Russell 2002) and our knowledge of many periods and regions, in some cases drastically altering existing perspectives (e.g. Bradley 2007, which has revised ideas about prehistoric Britain). Similar schemes in many other European countries are leading to comparable increases in archaeological data sets (Collis 2001: 166). In the USA, Section 106 also requires an assessment of the archaeological impact of federal projects on nationally registered sites (Neumann and Sanford 2001: 29; see Chapter 6).

PPG 16, and the system it has promoted, does have disadvantages. Limiting excavation to a threatened site may make it difficult to interpret fragmentary data if the site extends beyond the excavated zone, and the publication process may sacrifice research and discussion in the interests of speed and economy. No amount of preliminary assessment and evaluation can prevent surprises when an excavation actually takes place, of course. Work on the line of a new road in Devon uncovered a new Roman fort, which then had to be excavated. If it had been detected in advance, the planned road might well have been adjusted to avoid it and remove the need for rescue excavation – but little or nothing would have been learned about the fort (Fitzpatrick *et al.* 1999).

Because of problems with PPG 16 and PPG 15, both will be superceded from 2010 by **PPS 5 (Planning Policy Statement 5)**, produced by the Department for Communities and Local Government, subtitled *Planning for the historic environment*. The presence of 'historic environment' in the title, and the inclusion of historic buildings within its remit, reflect the increasingly integrated approach to heritage and archaeology shown by the emergence of **Historic Environment Records** in England (Chapter 2, pp. 61–2). Terms in the document such as 'heritage assets', as opposed to monuments, also emphasise a new attitude to the past, and convey the concept that 'heritage' (including archaeology) has a use and relevance in the present, and may even offer financial benefits (Chapter 6, pp. 294–5).

One of the biggest questions concerning the increasing amounts of excavation produced by much developer-funded archaeology has been whether this material is being exploited fully, both in terms of advancing research in the areas of the world affected and its impact on popular understanding of the past (Moore 2006). New guidelines are likely to emphasise the need for developer-led archaeology to provide 'advances in understanding' rather than just recording or preserving archaeological remains. This may challenge archaeologists not just to produce 'grey literature' reports but to disseminate their findings in more publicly accessible ways. It is also hoped new guidelines will answer some of the problems of pressure on archiving and storing the results of excavation (see below, p. 141). How this is to be achieved remains open to question.

3.3.4   Background research

- key reference: Roskams, *Excavation* 2001: 40–62.

> Excavation is both expensive and destructive; the increasingly refined application of geophysical and other methods, whilst not removing the need to excavate, can at least ensure that a maximum of information can be gained non-destructively and – if excavation is necessary – that this is both informed and precisely targeted.
>
> (David 2001: 525)

Excavation should not begin without prior assessment and evaluation of the kind outlined in the IfA's definitions. The more data that can be collected in advance, the easier it will be to draw up detailed plans for the excavation – and to respond to new information that is revealed as it proceeds. Much of this preparation will be conducted in libraries and archives where earlier accounts and illustrations of the site may be found. These records may also lead to material preserved in museum collections; any unpublished finds and records should be studied carefully in advance, and ideally included in the final report on new work. In countries where documentation extends far enough back into the past, archive offices may hold helpful maps and plans, such as those drawn up to record the ownership of land. These might show features of the site itself, or physical surroundings, along with forgotten but informative place-names and field-names. In England, a site or its area may even have been mentioned in an Anglo-Saxon charter, a form of land document that survives from as early as the seventh century AD. This documentary research should if possible form part of a wider programme of fieldwork investigating the local landscape (Chapter 2, p. 55).

The most important modern source of information is likely to come from aerial photographs taken over a long period under varied conditions, which may reveal surface earthworks or indicate buried features by means of cropmarks (Chapter

2: **Fig. 2.7**). Geological maps should give insights into the natural subsoil conditions that will be encountered. All visible traces must be recorded, especially on a research excavation where the original form of a monument must be restored from an accurate contour survey. If the site is not visible on the surface, detailed surveys must be undertaken to relate it to modern reference points. If sufficient resources are available, new aerial photographs may be commissioned; at the very least it should be investigated thoroughly using the most appropriate geophysical equipment (resistivity meters, magnetometers, GPR, or a combination of these: Chapter 2, p. 73–9).

There are of course thoroughly modern concerns to be addressed before excavation can begin. Known sites and monuments in many countries will be protected by legislation, and formal consent must be obtained from the government ministry responsible for antiquities as well as permission from the landowner. Assuming that all necessary financial support has been organised, numerous problems remain and require forethought – facilities and equipment; the ownership of finds, their conservation and storage, and the form and scale of publication of the completed work. Excavations – while frequently enjoyable, exciting and stimulating – are 'expensive, time-consuming, and often very stressful. Many of the problems encountered on excavations can be reduced by proper pre-planning and careful use of human and financial resources. Above all a flexible approach can save time, money and stress' (Drewett 1999: 76).

Figure 3.9 Finds-processing staff are the unsung heroes of any successful excavation project. Excavated artefacts must be systematically cleaned, labelled, catalogued and stored for further study when the report is being written. Large excavations, especially on Classical Mediterranean or urban medieval sites, produce thousands of finds from potsherds to animal bones. Here we see early Byzantine pottery being sorted at the excavations at Kilise Tepe, Turkey (Photograph: Mark Jackson, Newcastle University and Bob Miller, University of Canberra)

Staff and equipment

- key reference: Roskams, *Excavation* 2001: 63–92.

The ultimate quality of the interpretation and publication of a site depends not only on the skill of excavators but also on the quality of the recording and preservation of finds, and the ease with which information may be retrieved (Walker 1990). The number and nature of staff involved in an excavation are directly related to its size, resources and complexity; on small sites, many tasks may be performed by an individual site officer. Some basic tasks normally require specialist staff, and recording is the most important. Records come in many forms – written, drawn, photographic and (increasingly) digital – and every excavation needs staff with appropriate expertise, both archaeological and technical, to compile and maintain them. All of these categories of information are best managed by computer. A good excavation team should include someone with database skills, and the project should have robust equipment that can withstand archaeological conditions – with foolproof backup systems for the volume of data generated by electronic surveying and geophysical equipment, as well as by digital cameras.

Finds and environmental work

- key references: Roskams, *Excavation* 2001: 73–8; Ewen, *Artifacts* 2003: 19–22; Branch *et al. Environmental archaeology* 2005: chapter 2.

Finds work is defined as the process of retrieving, sorting, cleaning, marking, conserving, recording, analysing, interpreting and preparing for permanent storage all materials retained as a result of archaeological fieldwork, and disseminating the results. The term 'finds' is taken to include all artefacts, building materials, industrial residues, environmental material, biological remains (including human remains) and decay products.

(IfA *Standard and guidance* September 2001)

An excavation that produces a large quantity of finds will also require an assistant to manage their cataloguing and storage, with sufficient helpers to clean and sort pottery and other materials (**Fig. 3.9**). Lists of finds from each excavated context must be compiled, and every artefact must be labelled, bagged or boxed in such a way that it is accessible for further study when required. In some instances, choices about which materials are to be recorded and then discarded may also need to be made (Ewen 2003: 20–1). An on-site conservation laboratory is essential where delicate finds are likely to be abundant; remains of wood, leather or textiles recovered from waterlogged deposits require immediate treatment, for example (Sease 1992; Watkinson and Neal 1998). Site staff should also include someone with a good knowledge of environmental evidence, which involves the careful selection of soil samples, and the use of sieving or flotation equipment to increase the recovery of small bones and seeds (**Box 5.2**). In the words of the IfA document, 'Archaeological finds and environmental work seek to provide an understanding of societies and environments, not only at a site-specific level, but also in a local, regional, national and international context'.

3.4 EXCAVATION STRATEGY

- key references: Collis, *Digging up the past* 2001: 46–56; Drewett, *Field archaeology* 1999: 104–25; Roskams, *Excavation* 2001: 217–38; Carver, *Archaeological investigation* 2009: 113–93.

The aim of excavation is to identify, define, uncover, date, and – by understanding transformation processes – interpret each archaeological context on a site.

(Drewett 1999: 107)

There is no substitute for experience, based on an understanding of the many processes – natural and human – that are involved in the formation of an archaeological site: how ruined buildings decay, how occupation layers accumulate, how ditches silt up; this is known as **taphonomy** (Schiffer 1987; Nash and Petraglia 1987). During an excavation, individuals using hand-tools such as trowels make continuous observations and judgements about the texture, colour and significance of soils, deposits or features. In addition, they must be able to recognise all kinds of finds, from solid stone or pottery and fragile corroded metal to the faint discolourations left by organic materials that have decayed away completely. It is easy to slip unconsciously from description to interpretation when faced with a bewildering range of structures and features – this is why the neutral term **context** (or 'unit of stratification') has become increasingly popular in site recording. A ditch is a linear feature dug into the ground, but it might have been part of defences around a settlement, a boundary between land owned by different communities, or a means of improving drainage. An important theme in Ian Hodder's book *The archaeological process* (1999) is that objectivity during excavation is an illusion, emphasising the need for a site director to take account of the widest possible range of opinions (see below, p. 138). In less than a century the ideal of a site director has changed from a charismatic leader (such as Wheeler), implementing a strategy to be obeyed by site workers with almost military discipline, to a 'first amongst equals' (such as Hodder), constantly reflecting upon the views of the team, irrespective of status.

Exploratory **sondages**, larger trenches or extensive open areas may be employed in various configurations, according to the availability of resources and the nature of a site. Flexibility is important, and it depends to a large extent on the quality of the excavation's specialist staff. Interpretation of excavated structures, combined with provisional dating and other observations about the finds, should provide continuous feedback that can help to reinforce, modify or reject the chosen strategy. Computer files of site information can be analysed while the work progresses and will increase the speed with which up-to-date data are fed back into site interpretation. Viewers of **Time Team** on British television will be very familiar with the way in which decisions about site strategy are

constantly reviewed in the light of evidence that emerges from 'geophys' and exploratory trenches, along with background research into relevant archives and documents (Taylor 1998). The sites, contexts and structures described below may be excavated in a variety of ways, according to the type of information that is sought from them, but whatever strategy is chosen it should always be guided by the need for observation, recording and analysis of stratigraphic relationships. Wheeler's comments about balancing vertical sequences and horizontal plans (above: p. 94) remain valid, but the scale of excavation and configurations of trenches will also be determined by resources and time.

Safety must be monitored at all times (Drewett 1999: 82–7). Vertical sides of trenches can collapse suddenly, especially if they become waterlogged or if spoil-tips are placed too near to their edges. Heavy stones may slip and fall if excavation undermines them. Sharp-edged tools and earth-moving machinery create obvious and predictable hazards that should be avoidable through careful planning, but at least some members of the excavation team must possess sufficient knowledge of first-aid to cope with unexpected injuries. Problems are multiplied when an excavation is being mounted in areas where medical facilities are not easily accessible. It is essential that contingency plans are drawn up to cope with all easily conceivable hazards.

3.4.1 Forms of sites

Wooden settlements built on open ground, stone-built Roman forts with regular internal plans, tells formed by the accumulation of demolished mud-brick buildings, standing structures of stone or timber – all create particular technical problems for excavators. Evidence for human occupation of hunting camps and caves requires special approaches; so too do traces of ritual activities performed at temples and funeral ceremonies carried out at cemeteries. Sites where industrial processes or craft activities took place may reveal evidence ranging from sophisticated industrial furnaces for smelting metal ores or firing pottery to scatters of waste-flakes struck from flint cores during tool-making. Permanent settlements normally include diverse structures, including domestic buildings, and may also have had numerous features dug into the ground, notably pits and ditches, along with built-up contexts such as terraces, mounds, banks or rubbish dumps (middens). The natural living surface may take on a different consistency through trampling by animals or humans, and soft areas might have been consolidated with gravel or paving stones. Likewise, the interiors of structures may be floored with clay, stone or wood.

The remainder of this discussion of excavation strategy is very selective, but examines several themes. Different forms of site (temporary or permanent, domestic or ritual) have different implications for excavators, while environmental conditions (such as wetness or aridity) affect the nature of deposits and the survival of artefacts and structures. Recurrent types of contexts and features (pits, ditches) are encountered by excavators, as are structures, notably buildings constructed in a variety of materials.

Camps and caves

- key references: Smith, *Late Stone Age hunters* 1997; Bonsall and Tolan-Smith, *The human use of caves* 1997.

Early prehistoric settlements associated with hunter-gatherers were predominantly temporary, and frequently made use of natural rock-shelters or caves. Excavation is likely to focus upon identifying activity areas, and establishing whether occupation was regular or intermittent. There is always a possibility that a camp or cave was only used when specific animals and plants were available, and this should be reflected in the finds (**seasonality**; Chapter 5, p. 208). The **home base** of a hunter-gatherer group might contain semi-permanent houses and other structures, while a **field camp** associated with hunting expeditions would leave fewer traces and a different range of bones and artefacts (Smith 1997: 29, Fig. 3.1). From the point of view of excavators, the principal

problem of open sites is that seasonal occupation and insubstantial buildings did not lead to the formation of an appreciable depth of stratified deposits. They are particularly susceptible to erosion and other forms of natural disturbance; exceptionally, sites occupied at the edge of water may be covered by silt, and coastal sites were sometimes buried by blown sand. The priority of an excavator is to make exact records of the position of every fragment of bone, flint or other artefact, as an analysis of their distribution may suggest the functions of different parts of a site and imply relationships between structures and activities (Smith 1997: 30, Fig. 3.2). These objectives are best achieved by extensive open-area excavation.

The interpretation of sites as field camps or home bases, and the identification of the activities that took place on them, is based largely upon analogies with the activities of modern hunter-gatherers. This is an important arena for the development of **Middle Range Theory** for bridging the gap between fragmentary prehistoric evidence of sites and structures and modern ethno-archaeological observations (Chapter 6, p. 000). Problems of interpretation affect most sites with signs of early human occupation, including those associated with fossil hominin remains in East Africa. Opinions are divided over whether some hominins were primarily hunters or scavengers, and perceptions of key sites and their finds, such as Site FLK in the Olduvai Gorge, have changed fundamentally since the 1940s (Johanson and Shreeve 1991: 213–44).

Caves offer good potential for finding stratified deposits, but little in the way of internal structures; furthermore, their stratification is likely to result from natural weathering and sedimentation as much as from human activities. Cave excavations were very important in the nineteenth century because assemblages of tools and other artefacts could be found in association with the bones of animals and, occasionally, human burials or even cave paintings. Paintings on walls are extremely difficult to relate to the stratification of occupation, but occasionally traces of paint may be found at ground level along with charcoal from burning torches used to supply light (Clottes 1999). Animal bones found in caves are very misleading if those brought there by human hunters are not distinguished from bones introduced by carnivorous animals when humans were absent. The excavation of deep sections to reveal vertical stratification is very important in caves, but, as with hunter-gatherer camps, occupation areas both within them and around the cave mouth require extensive excavation and very precise recording if meaningful interpretations are to be attempted:

> Many repetitive tasks such as fine flint knapping or bone carving are often most comfortably carried out in a seated position and, requiring little space, may take place inside. Butchery requires space so that the operative can move around the carcass and, because it is associated with unpleasant smells, it is usually considered to be an outside activity. Stationary tasks may require warmth and need to be carried out by the fire while detailed tasks may require light and, if they are undertaken inside, will need to be located near an opening. It is inconvenient, and even dangerous, to walk on flint waste or fractured animal bone, and at a site occupied for a prolonged period such rubbish is likely to be cleared away.
>
> (Smith 1997: 31–2)

Permanent settlements

A sedentary lifestyle is a relatively recent innovation in human history. It began at different times in different parts of the world, normally when farming came to replace hunting and gathering as the predominant means of subsistence. Sites where people actually lived, as opposed to carrying out purely ritual or industrial activities, remain the most common focus for archaeological excavation. Their variety may be appreciated most easily by thinking about contrasting forms of settlements, and ways in which their characteristics would influence an excavation strategy designed to investigate them. **Rural sites** such as farms and villages in temperate regions rarely underwent sufficient changes to cause a build-up of deep stratification, particularly when constructed from wood (below: p.

129), and, unless they were restricted to using space within a defensive enclosure, obsolete buildings would probably be replaced on fresh sites rather than the same spot – resulting in a wide scatter of unrelated structures, for example the Anglo-Saxon site at Mucking in Essex (Clark 1991; Hamerow 1993). Farms and villages include all manner of subsidiary buildings, trackways, fenced or ditched enclosures, pits and middens. Open-area excavation will be essential for understanding the layout of such settlements, along with carefully placed cross-sections of any features that may provide dating evidence or indications of sequences.

Urban sites

In contrast, **urban sites** are more likely to have deep stratification, and in cases – such as London (Haynes *et al.* 2000) – where the town or city is still active today excavation is complicated by the fact that large areas are unlikely to become available for study (**Fig. 3.10**). Excavation must be very skilful to disentangle long sequences of contexts that have led to considerable disturbance – a deep well dug in the eighteenth century in Athens or Rome would have penetrated layers accumulated over thousands of years, bringing artefacts up from earlier contexts and redepositing them in later levels. Once again, this underlines the importance of recording on an excavation so that every datable find can be related to an event in the stratification. In the case of both rural and urban sites the nature of archaeological deposits will have been affected profoundly by building materials and environmental conditions. No standardised excavation strategy could be equally effective dealing both with a tell in an arid country in the Middle East, with stratification consisting primarily of mud-brick, and with a medieval port in Scandinavia where substantial remains of wooden houses survive in waterlogged levels. This underlines the importance of **environments** (below: p. 118).

Complex societies and civilisations frequently have towns and other settlements that are enclosed by **defences**, whether designed to impress visitors with their architectural splendour or for serious military purposes. An excavation strategy for a

Figure 3.10 Richard Rogers' remarkable Lloyds building in the City of London overlooks an excavation of a Roman basilica; this was a large hall attached to the forum of Londinium, capital of Roman Britain. Apart from a period of near-abandonment in early Anglo-Saxon times, London has been an administrative and commercial centre linking the British Isles with Europe and the rest of the world for nearly two thousand years. This site also illustrates the pressures of rescue excavation in an urban setting. Procedures for excavation and recording must be adjusted to take account of the timescale and nature of building work. Large modern buildings require such deep foundations and basements that, unlike most constructions in previous centuries, they remove all trace of earlier occupation. The expansion of urban development throughout the world in the second half of the twentieth century provided a last chance to examine underlying sites; resources were rarely adequate to meet this challenge. Planning legislation varies considerably in different countries, but, ideally, the costing of any major new construction should include time and money not only for archaeological investigation, but also for full study of the results for publications and archives. (Museum of London)

town of this kind would include cross-sections of its enclosing structures to detect phases of construction and modification, and to relate them

to public and domestic buildings in the interior. Towns may also contain official and religious buildings such as palaces and temples; however, in major centres in ancient Egypt or Mayan Yucatán, there was no clear dividing line between royal, official and ritual structures designed to provide a fitting architectural setting for ceremonial activities. It is easy to see that excavation of a large complex site must be designed with a high awareness of its history and culture, and that strategy must be guided by research questions, as excavation of a sequence of defences will reveal information about very different aspects of a site's history compared with open-area investigation of an industrial quarter or temple complex. Specialised forms of settlement include purpose-built military and religious sites, such as Roman forts or medieval monasteries, where background knowledge and research questions will also determine whether several small trenches will be excavated to study structural sequences, whether large areas will be opened to clarify plans and the functions of buildings, or whether both approaches will be combined. Features and structures likely to be encountered on such sites will be discussed further below (p. 127).

Industrial archaeology

Part of urban archaeology involves excavating sites of the more recent past. The redevelopment of many inner cities in the post-industrial era is leading to excavation of a range of post-medieval industrial sites in Britain and North America, such as the excavation of post-industrial Manchester (Figs 3.19 and 3.21). Excavations in urban areas and on other industrial sites can often reveal aspects of industrial processes, or the lifestyles of poorer social groups which may not have been recorded in written documents (Fig. 1.24) It may also yield evidence that challenges the textual accounts (Poirer and Feder 2001). In some instances, such as the recent discovery by the Big Trent project of a 1740s blast furnace in Trenton, New Jersey, excavation may involve knowledge of the role of technology and result in the participation of specialists in other fields, alongside the use of documentary evidence. In some instances, the hazardous and polluting nature of some of the activities in these areas, both in the past and in more recent times, may mean that archaeologists have to be conscious of particular health and safety concerns.

Cemeteries

- key references: Collis, *Digging up the past* 2001: 149–57; Parker Pearson, *The archaeology of death and burial* 1999; Lucy and Reynolds, *Burial in early medieval England and Wales* 2002.

The concept of 'time capsules' that is frequently applied to shipwrecks may be extended to **burials**, for many dead people were placed in a grave at a single moment in the past, frequently with a range of artefacts (**Fig. 3.11**). The positions of graves could be marked with anything from simple wooden memorials to structures such as the stone mausoleum of the emperor Hadrian (that can still be seen beside the Tiber in Rome, converted into a castle), or the pyramids of Egypt. In many societies, graves were placed together in cemeteries, sometimes attached to temples or churches, but the dead were not always separated from the living, and burials may be found in or around houses. Many burials were covered by earthen barrows or stone cairns, perhaps to create a visible link to ancestors who used the same piece of land; graves were often dug into the sides of these mounds in later periods, and these were frequently missed by early excavators. Collective graves to which the dead might be added over long periods of time are an alternative to cemeteries; Neolithic stone tombs with passageways leading to internal chambers (**Box 6.1**) were used for many centuries, as were family vaults in churches. The monumental character of barrows and megaliths attracted the attention of early antiquarians who 'excavated' them by digging straight into the centre of mounds and emptying chambers in the hope of finding grave goods. Ethnoarchaeological studies provide many examples which show that actual burial may be just the last of a complicated series of ceremonies and ritual practices (Humphreys and King 1981). Modern excavations should therefore examine

the area surrounding a burial where remains of ritual feasts or religious structures might be found (Niblett 1999). In Christian contexts, there may be signs of cemetery churches or facilities for pilgrims to visit notable graves (Rodwell 1989; Crummy *et al.* 1993). Excavation of the well preserved human remains in the post-medieval Spitalfields cemetery in London raised concerns that smallpox may have been preserved on some human remains, posing a potentially serious danger to the excavators (Poirer and Feder 2001).

Graves containing a single skeleton are particularly informative if the person has been buried fully clothed and accompanied by **grave goods** – a selection of personal items, or gifts to take into an afterlife – that might indicate the deceased's sex, social status and religion, and help to date the burial. Unfortunately, burials are normally more complicated; bodies were cremated in many periods, and grave goods were not always included. Worse still, acid soil may dissolve human bone and damage artefacts. If soil conditions do not favour the survival of bones it may nevertheless be possible to detect the former position of a skeleton from subtle changes in the texture of the earth, or by chemical analysis of soil samples from the grave. The exact position of human remains must be recorded, for they may be related to factors revealed by **pathology** such as injuries or disease (Chapter 5, p. 217). If grave goods are present, their position may also be significant, particularly where items of jewellery or other clothing accessories are concerned, for these may suggest the form of costume worn by the deceased person. Traces of wooden coffins should also be looked out for during excavation, while stone sarcophagi and lead coffins (popular among rich Romans) may be lifted intact from graves and opened in laboratory conditions. Excavations at the royal Anglo-Saxon cemetery at Sutton Hoo in Suffolk illustrate the complexities that may occur on a single site. Burials include both cremations and unburned bodies, humans and animals, some plain graves and others under large barrows, graves without goods, and others among the richest ever found in Britain. A complete ship had been dragged up a slope from

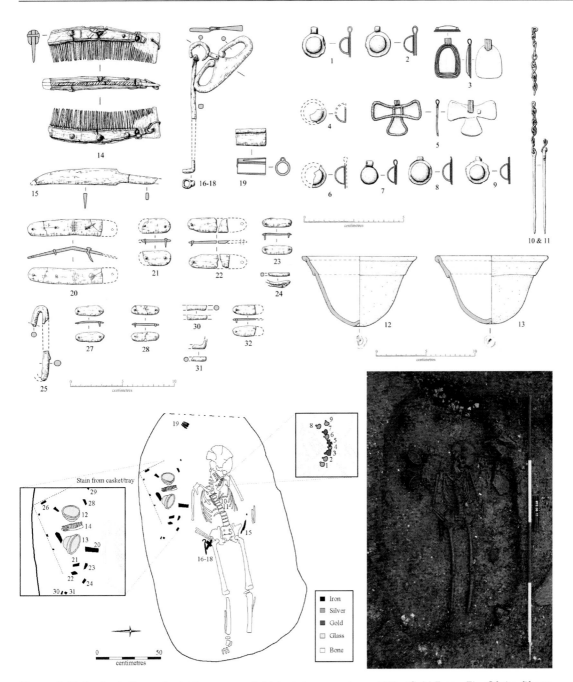

Figure 3.11 An Anglo-Saxon burial from a small, high-status cemetery at Westfield Farm, Ely. Of the fifteen graves, this example was particularly well furnished with grave goods, including the example pictured which included a gold and silver necklace and two glass cups. The excavation of such complex and delicate remains requires considerable expertise and a comprehensive understanding of the problems of lifting and conserving finds for future study and display. Further detailed work using isotope analysis (Chapter 5) and study of the grave goods suggests that the grave is from the seventh century and is potentially associated with the first monastery at Ely. (Vicki Herring and Bryan Cossan; Lucy *et al*. 2009)

the nearby River Deben and lowered into a deep trench under the most famous barrow; a wooden chamber had been constructed amidships and filled with remarkable grave goods – armour, weapons and feasting equipment that probably belonged to an early seventh-century king of East Anglia (Carver 1998).

Communal burials and cemeteries may have other benefits and challenges. Excavation of the large cemetery at Spitalfields, London, enabled a detailed analysis of the local population from the eighteenth century and comparison with local records. Recent analysis of the fourteenth-century Black Death plague cemetery at East Smithfield, London, indicates the number of people killed by the disease and the surprisingly careful and well-planned disposal of the dead at the time (Grainger *et al.* 2008). In communal burial monuments, such as the chambered tombs of the early Neolithic in northern Europe, where bones were disarticulated (separating parts of the body) and buried communally, particularly detailed excavation and recording are required, as is palaeopathological knowledge in identifying the skeletal elements (see Chapter 5); such complex recording was required at the Neolithic long barrow of Hazleton, Gloucestershire (Thomas 1999: 146–7).

Burials normally have legal implications, and the discovery of human remains in any excavated context, whether in a grave or not, may need to be reported to the police. In the USA, Native American remains have had special protection since the enactment of the Native American Graves Protection and Repatriation Act, NAGPRA, in 1990 (Thomas 1998: 602–5; Bray 1996). The disturbance of cemeteries should never be undertaken without consulting religious groups or people who consider themselves relatives of the dead. Reburial of excavated human remains and grave goods has become an important issue in many parts of the world (Hubert 1989; Box 6.10).

3.4.2 Excavation in special conditions

● key reference: Collis, *Digging up the past* 2001.

Temperate zones of the world, including Europe and large parts of the North and South American continents, have been characterised by intensive arable farming for many centuries – with predictably destructive effects on archaeological sites. Woodland is characteristic of temperate zones (or at least it was before clearance for farming), and provided raw materials for making buildings and tools; however, these organic remains decay fairly rapidly unless preserved in unusual local conditions such as **wetlands**. **Tropical areas** with extensive rainforest present enormous obstacles to fieldwork and excavation; organic materials decay rapidly, and masonry structures may be severely damaged by the penetration of roots. The rediscovery of Mayan ruins cloaked by jungle in Mesoamerica provided some of the most picturesque images of lost civilisations in the works of Catherwood and Stephens (**Figs. 1.19–21**). Clearance of rainforest for farming is normally followed by severe erosion of rich forest soils, which may either remove traces of settlements or bury them under metres of silt. Occasionally sites are preserved by **natural cataclysms** such as earthquakes or volcanic eruptions; good preservation is combined with difficult access, of course, as excavation of the ash and mud that engulfed Pompeii and Herculaneum demonstrate. Ozette, a settlement in the north-western corner of Washington State, USA, occupied between 1500 and 1700 AD, was covered by periodic mudslides, and has been described as a 'hunter-gatherer Pompeii' (Samuels 1991). Thera, a Mycenaean town on the Greek island of Akrotiri, was buried by a massive volcanic eruption in the second millennium BC and gives remarkable insights into the form of Bronze Age houses, and their decoration with elaborate wall paintings (Doumas 1983).

Organic materials, from wood to textiles or even human flesh, survive best when bacteria are unable to attack them. Bacteria need a combination of warmth, air and water: thus, excavations carried out on sites where these conditions are absent are particularly productive. Regions that are now **arid deserts** may contain sites that flourished before environmental change made permanent settlement impossible. Excellent preservation in dry conditions has of course been a major attraction of excavations in Egypt for several centuries. In addition to artefacts made from wood, textiles and basketry, excavation in Egypt of the workers' settlement at the Roman granite quarries at Mons Claudianus in the 1990s recovered all manner of organic remains that illustrated the food consumed by people living there – all of which had to be brought at least 100 km by road from the Red Sea or the Nile (Peacock and Maxfield 2001) (**Fig. 3.12**). Similar remains survive at abandoned Native American settlements in Arizona, including the famous Chaco Canyon, where timber used in constructing buildings provided samples for the first application of tree ring dating (Chapter 4, p. 164). **Permanently frozen** conditions also prevent, or at least retard, bacterial decay. The '**Ice Man**' found in 1991 on the Austrian–Italian border has become the most famous example because not only did his body survive, but also his clothes and personal possessions (Fowler 2002). Proper excavations rather than accidental discoveries offer excellent opportunities for recovering similar ranges of artefacts; well-preserved burials have been found in many parts of the former Soviet Union where the ground remains permanently frozen, and on Inca ritual sites above the snow line in the Andes. One major problem of excavating frozen sites is that they have to be thawed, and this upsets the conditions of preservation – which makes planning for conservation absolutely essential (Chapter 5, p. 237).

Wetland archaeology
- key references: Coles and Coles, *Enlarging the past* 1996; Purdy, *Enduring record: the environmental and cultural heritage of wetlands* 2001; Van de Noort and O'Sullivan, *Rethinking wetland archaeology* 2006.

For several centuries, European antiquarians relied upon reports of indigenous peoples in the Americas for analogies of the lifestyles of prehistoric people known only from stone tools (Chapter 1, p. 11). New information was added when several hundred wooden 'lake-dwellings' were revealed by a drought in Switzerland in 1853–5.

These prehistoric settlements had probably been constructed on the shore, rather than on piles in lakes as originally thought. Ferdinand Keller published an influential book about these sites in the 1860s which included illustrations of a wide range of organic structures and artefacts, as well as bones and plant remains, that complemented the stone and metal artefacts already known (Menotti 2004). In Trigger's judgement, 'the continuing study of these prehistoric remains attracted wide interest. [It] played a major role in convincing Western Europeans of the reality of cultural evolution and that ancient times could be studied using archaeological evidence alone' (2006: 135).

The growth of ecological perspectives drew attention to the potential of investigating waterlogged sites, and led to the 'classic' investigation of a Mesolithic site at **Star Carr** in Yorkshire, which has been re-examined several times since Grahame Clark's pioneering excavations in 1949 (Mellars and Dark 1998). This tradition continues in Britain, and includes major work prompted by 'rescue' archaeology, such as the Somerset Levels project (Coles and Coles 1986) or the timber platform at Flag Fen, near Peterborough

Figure 3.12 Mons Claudianus is the site of Roman quarries in a rocky landscape between the Nile and the Red Sea. Recent research and excavation has benefited from the excellent preservation of organic remains in arid conditions. In addition to the remains of plants that help in reconstructing the diet of the mining community, many artefacts made of wood, leather and fibres (including rope and basket work) extend the range of pottery and metal items that are all that survive in normal conditions. (Valerie Maxfield)

(Pryor 2005), with occasional dramatic finds like 'Seahenge', the Bronze Age timber circle in Norfolk (Pryor 2001). Recent years have seen major studies of the well-preserved archaeology in the tidal wetlands along Britain's coastline, particularly in the Severn Estuary (Fig. 3. 13; Bell *et al.* 2000) and Humber wetlands (Van de Noort 2004). Wetland archaeology also thrives in many other parts of the world, such as the north-west coast of North America and the swamps of New Zealand (Van de Noort 2006; Purdy 2001). Wet sites also enhance periods of historical archaeology. In Ireland, for example, the late prehistoric to medieval period is marked by the poverty of artefacts and absence of pottery from settlement sites. Fortunately, some were constructed on artificial islands (**crannogs**: O'Sullivan 2000; Dixon 2004) in lakes or marshland, and finds from such sites preserved in peat illustrate what is missing on land – notably a range of wooden containers and vessels that made pottery unnecessary for most storage and table purposes (Earwood 1993). Crannogs have another positive aspect; since it was difficult to recover objects accidentally dropped into water or through gaps in timber floors, crannogs also produce many finds of metal artefacts (Crone 2000).

John Coles gave the name **sensitivity analysis** to the assessment that should take place before any wetland site is examined (1984: 36–8):

1 **Site identification** (e.g. settlement, burial) and *chronological position*: the date and nature of any kind of site are fundamental to any research that is carried out.
2 **Site content**: awareness of the types of evidence likely to be encountered will determine the excavation strategy.

Figure 3.13 Like arid sites, wetland sites provide an extended range of finds and allow structures made of timber to survive for thousands of years. Fieldwork and excavation in the intertidal zone require careful planning to take advantage of unusually low tides, and they have an element of urgency because, once sites become visible (normally through coastal erosion), their decay is accelerated. This photograph shows the excavation of a rare Iron Age rectangular building preserved in the inter-tidal mud of the Gwent levels in South Wales. The building was dated by dendrochronology to 273 BC. (Bell *et al.* 2000; Martin Bell)

3 **Condition** of the site: the extent of water-logging and the nature of the deposits may vary from soft peat to hard mud.

4 **Recovery techniques** to be used: an excavator must make a hard-headed estimate of a project's resources and effectiveness in planning the tactics to be used.

5 Requirements for **post-excavation work**: 'This is probably the most crucial element in any programme, and unless it is fully debated and agreed beforehand, and arrangements made, the excavation should not proceed. Sampling and extraction of materials for analyses, specialists and their specific requirements, and relevance of such work to the project's aims, must be laid down and fully understood by all.'

6 **Conservation needs**: a very careful excavation strategy is required to limit the exposure of these finds to the air during excavation, and to ensure that adequate facilities are available for immediate treatment and long-term preservation of organic finds.

Although these six points apply to any excavation, insufficient planning is more immediately harmful to wetland sites because of the range of organic finds. Excavation trenches will be difficult to manage, and it may be necessary to erect platforms suspended above working surfaces to avoid walking on fragile remains. The complexity of structures complicates recording by planning and photography, while additional categories of find make greater demands on the cataloguing system. Publication costs are increased by the scale and quality of the discoveries.

Perhaps the single most important innovation in wetland archaeology has been the possibility of applying **dendrochronology** (tree-ring dating) to timber structures on prehistoric sites. Suitable samples may be dated back to beyond 8000 BC in some parts of Europe, and tree rings can also be used to analyse periods of construction on complex sites. This degree of precision allows parts of some prehistoric sites, such as the Iron Age timber causeway at Fiskerton, Lincolnshire (Field and Parker Pearson 2003), to be treated in almost 'historical' ways, with different parts of the structure able to be shown to have been constructed or rebuilt in specific years (Chapter 4).

Underwater archaeology

● key references: Bowens, *Underwater archaeology* 2008; Gould, *Archaeology and the social history of ships* 2000; Delgado, *Encyclopaedia of underwater and maritime archaeology* 1997; Goddio *Topography and excavation of Heracleon-Thonis and East Canopus* 2007.

As with wetland archaeology, the guiding principles and methodology of underwater archaeology are very similar to those that should be employed on dry sites (Bowens 2008). Excavation strategy is guided by the same kinds of rescue situation and research aims, and the identification of contexts and their stratigraphic sequence is equally important. However, the additional complexity of the tasks of discovery, excavation, recording and conservation forces directors of underwater projects to take a much more stringent approach to resources and safety. The **Nautical Archaeology Society**, based in Britain but with one third of its members abroad, has a very similar code of conduct to that of the IfA (above: p. 101; Bowens 2008).

Maritime archaeology is particularly troubled by indiscriminate damage to shipwreck sites by looters and souvenir hunters. This does not all have a malicious intent, for diving is a popular leisure activity made more attractive by the possibility of examining wrecks. However, commercial salvage on modern wrecks shades imperceptibly into the destruction of historical evidence from older ships by unscrupulous treasure hunters. **Shipwrecks** offer rare insights into the technology, warfare and commerce of the past, and individual ships provide a chance to study a range of artefacts that were all in use at a specific date (Redknap 1997) (**Fig. 3.14**). For this reason they are frequently described as 'time capsules'. On most dry sites on land, structures are found in the state that they reached after their useful life had ended, and artefacts were often accumulated in rubbish dumps over an extended period. In contrast, finds from the *Mary Rose*, a Tudor warship that sank in 1545, illustrate weapons, clothing and personal items that belonged to members of the crew at the moment of the ship's loss (Rule 1982; Stirland 2000). When sufficiently large numbers of ancient ships and

Figure 3.14 Underwater excavation employs techniques identical to excavation on land, but it is much more time-consuming and potentially dangerous. As with wetland archaeology, once finds are removed from conditions in which they have survived, expert conservation will be necessary to preserve them from rapid decay. In this photograph a diver is using a surveying grid to make a detailed scale drawing in the course of excavating a seventeenth-century ship (the *Swan*) that sank off the west coast of Scotland during the Civil War (Martin 1998). (Colin Martin)

their cargoes have been recorded and published carefully, each find contributes to a wider picture of ancient trade. We now have a good idea of the changing patterns of shipping and trade in the Mediterranean during the Roman period, thanks to a database of 1,259 wrecks from prehistoric times to AD 1500, compiled by Parker (1992).

Not all underwater archaeology concerns ships. The kinds of seismic or volcanic event that affect dry-land sites occasionally cause changes in sea level. The late 1990s saw the discovery, planning and underwater excavation of remarkable structures at Alexandria on the Egyptian coast – including Cleopatra's palace, and the Pharos (lighthouse) that was one of the Seven Wonders of the Ancient World (Foreman and Goddio 1999; Empereur 1998; Goddio 2007). Port Royal, a busy trading establishment on the island of Jamaica, was also engulfed by the sea after an

earthquake in 1692; excavations have revealed a port from the early years of the 'triangular trade' between Britain, Africa and the Caribbean that carried slaves across the Atlantic and brought sugar and rum back to the Britain (Pawson and Buisseret 1975). Greater changes in sea level took place during prehistory as the volume of polar ice sheets expanded or contracted. Where the sea rose relatively quickly without heavy erosion there are good chances of discovering submerged landscapes, for example on the Gwent Levels along the northern side of the Bristol Channel in South Wales (Rippon 1996; Bell *et al.* 2000).

3.4.3   Contexts and features

Banks and mounds
- key reference: Collis, *Digging up the past* 2001: 145–8.

Positive features are those that have involved the deposition of soil or other material on a surface. This might have taken place through specific acts of construction, such as making a rampart or a burial mound, or gradual accumulation, such as throwing small amounts of rubbish onto a midden over a long period. Less obviously positive features can be created by levelling uneven surfaces or laying down floors or roads (**Box 3.6**); like middens, these may reach substantial depths over a long period (**Fig. 3.15**). Other positive contexts may be created by natural processes – layers of silt washed off a road or soil from ploughed fields accumulating at the bottom of a slope, for example. Many positive features are created during the course of managing a landscape, such as cultivation ridges in fields, field-walls, hedges and other boundaries, or piles of stones heaped up at the edge of cultivated land.

Figure 3.15 The complexities of overlapping structures, features, layers and interfaces revealed by excavation are most easily sorted out with the help of single context recording (Fig. 3.22) and the construction of a Harris matrix. This relatively simple example from Usk (Gwent, Wales) includes post holes and foundation trenches from a first-century AD military building (most clearly visible top left), a V-section ditch running down the centre of the photograph, the stone foundations of a small building (centre), a cobbled area (bottom left) and a Roman road (right). Some 'events' leave distinctive physical traces – erecting posts, building foundations, surfacing the road, for example. Others only leave interfaces – the digging of the ditch is only represented by the junction between the subsoil and the material that eventually filled it up, and the use of the road took place in periods between renewals of its surface. (Photograph: Kevin Greene)

Some ancient landscapes contained dozens of substantial mounds and banks created for burials, ceremonial processions and other ritual or social purposes. The Stonehenge region in the Neolithic and Bronze Age is a well-known European example, and the Mound Builder monuments recorded by Squier and Davis in the Mississippi Valley are even more impressive (Chapter 1, p. 18).

As ramparts and mounds were frequently created by digging material from adjacent ditches (as at Wor Barrow, excavated by Pitt Rivers, **Fig. 3.5**), excavation will aim to examine both, normally by studying their relationship in section. The mound may reveal stages of construction and phases of modification, and with luck artefacts or samples suitable for scientific dating may be recovered from the ground surface upon which it was built; these will provide a *terminus post quem* for its construction. Finds from the ditch and observation of its section and filling may reveal how long it was maintained by cleaning out or recutting, and the rate at which it silted up subsequently. Linear banks or ramparts require more than a cross-section to understand their structural history. The solid earth or stone ramparts of European Iron Age hillforts were frequently reinforced by a timber framework, and/or revetted by a timber palisade or stone wall. It may require the excavation of a substantial length of rampart to reveal these features, and to recover dating evidence for their stratigraphic sequence. This is equally true of contexts that accumulated gradually, such as middens and road surfaces; a cross-section and dating evidence taken from one point are unlikely to be representative of the whole feature. Dating evidence may be misleading in all positive features, because construction material may include misleadingly old artefacts; this is why a *terminus post quem* is nothing more than a date **after** which a context containing a datable artefact was deposited, and why the *terminus post quem* is indicated by the most recent artefact.

Ditches and pits
- key reference: Collis, *Digging up the past* 2001: 131–45.

BOX 3.6

Positive features: section of Roman Ermin Street

Careful excavation of the main road between Cirencester and Swindon in England revealed many successive surfaces, including Roman Ermin Street, which the modern road overlies. The section shown here reveals phases of the road in the Roman and Medieval periods, and right up to the modern tarmac surface. The original road surface, constructed in the first century AD, overlies a buried soil of pre-Roman, Late Iron Age date. Samples taken from this buried soil may provide useful information about the nature of the local environment immediately before the road was constructed (Mudd *et al.* 1999; see Chapter 5, redrawn by Tom Moore).

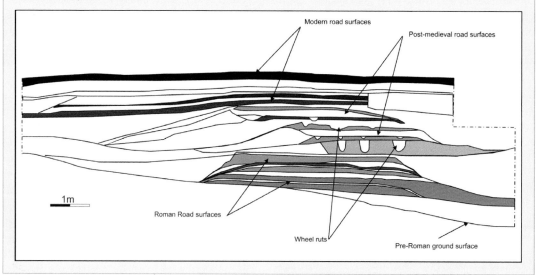

Many **negative features** were actually created during the construction of positive features, for example ditches accompanying ramparts or mounds. Many sites with suitable subsoils contain large numbers of pits dug for a bewildering number of purposes, including storage and waste disposal. Some pits might have been dug initially as quarries for building materials before being used for storage, and only have become rubbish pits at the end of their useful lives. The normal excavation method is to empty a pit in such a way that its section may be recorded, ideally on more than one axis, in order to study the way in which it was filled and to recover artefacts and environmental samples that will help elucidate its function as well as providing dating evidence (**Box 3.7**). Small ditches and pits may turn out on closer inspection to be foundation trenches and

post holes for wooden structures such as fences or buildings. Their characteristics, including size and depth, may be mapped on the plan of an area excavation in the hope that coherent outlines of structures will be visible; post holes are discussed further, below, in the context of wooden buildings. Particularly deep pits may turn out to be wells which offer the possibility of recovering complete artefacts accidentally dropped into them, along with organic materials and environmental samples if the lower parts are still waterlogged. Less deep scoops might be quarry pits or, in exceptional cases, the subsurface remains of house structures such as **Grubenhäuser** (Tipper 2004). Negative features also occur in the landscape, notably ditches dug to mark boundaries or to provide drainage or irrigation for fields.

Excavation will aim to record the sections of pits or ditches, but dating is always difficult because artefacts found in them do not tell us when they were constructed, for they only began to accumulate once the feature was no longer kept clear of debris. The latest finds from the first deposits that accumulated provide a *terminus post quem* for the filling of the feature, but are of little help in establishing its date of construction, for older material might have eroded from contexts that it had been dug through, and fallen in after abandonment.

Surfaces and working areas
- key reference: Collis, *Digging up the past* 2001: 64–77.

One of the most important things to remember when excavating is that people rarely lived on walls, down pits, in postholes or in ditches, and yet excavations are often dominated by these contexts. People lived on surfaces, and much of what they did on surfaces will leave only the slightest trace or none at all.

(Drewett 1999: 108)

BOX 3.7   Negative features: Iron Age storage pits

Negative features such as pits, such as those depicted here, from Danebury in southern England, are characteristic of many prehistoric settlements, particularly European Iron Age sites. Initially thought by many antiquarians to represent 'pit dwellings' (C. Evans 1989), careful excavation of many examples at large hillfort sites such as Danebury, Hampshire, (Cunliffe 1993) led to the discovery in some of charred remains of grain in their initial silted fills. With the help of ethnography and experimental archaeology (Reynolds 1979), their role as grain storage pits was recognised; layers of clay sealing the tops of the pits allowed grain to be stored over the winter. Excavation of pits frequently reveals human and animal remains, apparently representing ritual deposition marking the end of their use for storing food (Hill 1995).
(Ian Cartwright and Barry Cunliffe, Oxford University)

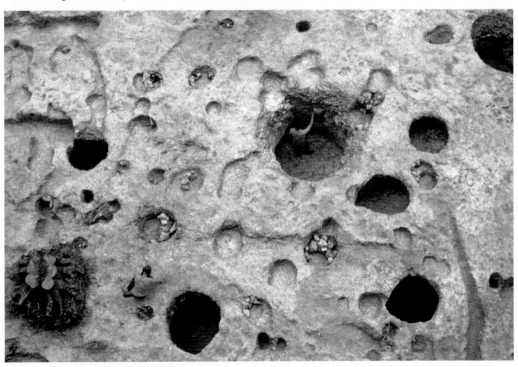

Drewett's comment about the importance of **surfaces** should be taken extremely seriously. They are central to the recording and analysis of stratigraphy, and are known as interfaces when a sequence is being worked out in order to construct a Harris matrix (above: p. 98). It is easy to conceptualise a pit or a ditch in terms of the ground through which it has been dug and the material that has filled it since it went out of use, because that is exactly what an excavator finds. What was important to the digger of the pit or ditch, however, was the size and shape of its empty internal space, whether designed to provide defence, contain water or accommodate rubbish (**Box 3.7**). It might have remained open for a considerable length of time, and this may possibly be detected by weathering of the sides, but the surface has no physical existence, since it is simply the interface between the ground and the filling of the feature. An interface cannot contain finds, and can only be dated in terms of being later than the contexts through which it has been dug, and earlier than those which subsequently filled it.

Horizontal surfaces are almost as problematic as ditch or pit interfaces, but are more likely to give some assistance to interpretation if the underlying context shows evidence of wear from use. A stone floor may be worn near a doorway, and small artefacts dropped onto it can become stuck in gaps between stones. An area discoloured by heat may indicate the position of a hearth or kiln, while unworn areas may suggest the location of partitions or fixed furnishings. Rough cobbled surfaces or soft ground provide many more opportunities for lost or discarded artefacts to become stuck in the surface and assist the interpretation of function and dating. Surfaces should be carefully cleaned and photographed, and the positions of all artefacts recorded on plans so that activity areas may be identified in the manner described above in the discussion of camps and caves. However, some caution is needed if the contexts above a surface consist only of relatively soft soil, for earthworms 'sort' the overlying material by carrying finer particles to the ground surface with the result that larger items such as stones or artefacts sink downwards

---

BOX 3.8   # Surfaces: floor levels

Surfaces are rare finds in many periods and regions. Because of later land use, such as ploughing, the surfaces upon which people lived and worked have often been destroyed, leaving only the negative archaeological features with which to interpret living areas. This is a particular problem for surfaces of prehistoric settlements which were often relatively ephemeral clay floors, easily destroyed by later ploughing, although even more substantial mosaic floors can be badly damaged by later land-use. Stone and tiled surfaces, such as that visible inside this medieval dye-vat excavated in Bristol, were common on Roman and later urban sites in Britain. Such surfaces can provide clear evidence of activities, perhaps through wear on the stone surfaces or, as in this case, signs of burning. With the help of documentary evidence, it was possible to interpret this feature as a vat in which metal containers holding water, dye and cloth were heated (Simon Cox, Cotswold Archaeology).

until they reach a firm layer that worms cannot penetrate (Drewett 1999: 108). It goes without saying that horizontal surfaces are best examined by means of open-area excavation.

3.4.4 Structures and materials

- key references: Collis, *Digging up the past* 2001: 103–48; Wright, *Ancient building technology* 2000; 2005.

Information gained from the excavation or analysis of buildings is of enormous value, from the disputed traces of Palaeolithic huts dating back to 380,000 BC at Terra Amata (Nice, France) to nineteenth-century mills and factories in the UK associated with the Industrial Revolution. Background research should include awareness of the great variety of techniques and materials used for constructing buildings so that important traces are not overlooked through ignorance. Early excavators cleared stone-built sites without any regard to the possibility that wooden structures might also have existed. In the Near East, where most buildings were constructed from perishable sun-dried mud-brick, only solid stone or fired clay structures were detected at first. Antiquarians and travellers from the Renaissance to the nineteenth century produced many excellent publications of buildings, but the possibilities for recording them have been expanded by photography and laser scanning.

Stone
- key reference: Collis, *Digging up the past* 2001: 103–13.

The use of stone for construction (**Fig. 3.16**) does not necessarily imply higher technical ability, wealth or social status than other building materials – except in obvious cases of monumental architecture such as Stonehenge or the Parthenon. Stone was used in areas where it was conveniently available; when it was not, timber, mud-brick or other building materials were employed. However, the remains of stone buildings are much easier to recognise than mud-brick or timber; as a result, incomplete perceptions of human

settlement patterns persisted in many parts of the world before aerial photography and improved excavation techniques came into general use.

Along with major earthworks and burial mounds, stone structures were easy for early archaeologists to recognise and excavate. In many cases quite reasonable conclusions were drawn from them, for many nineteenth-century excavators had an excellent understanding of architecture, especially Greek and Roman buildings. Thus, J.T. Wood explored Roman theatres and the Temple of Diana at Ephesus in Turkey in the 1860s knowing roughly what to expect from these types of buildings, and understanding how fallen columns or fragments of architectural sculpture fitted into the original structures. If less was known, narrow trenches could be dug to find buried walls, and continued alongside them to locate off-shoots or junctions, until a complete plan had been revealed. 'Islands' of unexcavated soil left inside a building by this procedure might then be cleared in the hope of recovering objects to indicate the date and function of its rooms. Unfortunately, vital stratigraphic relationships between walls, floors and occupation or destruction levels were entirely removed, making it very difficult for modern archaeologists to make sense of the remains, even by re-excavation.

A great variety of construction techniques is employed when building stone is readily available. Dry-stone walling is the simplest; uncut natural boulders or roughly quarried blocks are stacked up with care or laid in regular courses, relying on gravity and friction for their stability. Stones may also be bonded with clay or mortar to increase strength and to improve the comfort of buildings by reducing draughts and water penetration. Blocks were roughly shaped at quarries to minimise weight during transport, and trimmed and carved to precise requirements on arrival. Chippings of stone and discarded tools may be found during excavations, and these are useful for relating the stratigraphic context in which they occur to a phase of construction. Debris left by masons cutting blocks of fine imported stone into geometrical shapes for decorative wall cladding was recognised at the Roman palace at

Figure 3.16 Stone buildings are generally easier to discover and excavate than wooden structures. Complications arise when excavation takes place within a standing building that is still in use – in this case, Canterbury Cathedral in Kent (Blockley *et al.* 1997). Four Anglo-Saxon phases were found beneath the floor of the nave in 1993 including an eleventh-century cathedral that would have been amongst the largest in northern Europe. This excavation in advance of re-flooring and the insertion of a new heating system demonstrates that important research can be conducted in the context of well-planned rescue work. (Paul Bennett; Canterbury Archaeological Trust)

Fishbourne, Sussex; the excavators also found spreads of builders' mortar, and splashes of paint from the walls (Cunliffe 1998: 44, 129–30).

Stone structures may or may not have foundations set in a trench dug into the subsoil. Substantial foundations would be superfluous for a structure of modest height, or if sound bedrock lay immediately below the surface. On farmsteads in Northumberland occupied during the Roman period, traditional round timber houses were frequently rebuilt in stone. Thick dry-stone walls were erected on the surface of the ground without creating the distinctive subsoil features made by their wooden predecessors. This can create a real problem for excavators, for later agricultural clearance may easily remove all trace of stone houses. For instance a Roman farmstead was excavated on farmland at Apperley Dene, Northumberland, where the only indication of a phase of buildings that replaced a timber house was the presence of large stones pushed into a surrounding ditch (Greene 1978). At the other end of the architectural spectrum, the original design for Hadrian's Wall was so thick that it did not require foundations, but after it was reduced from c. 3 metres to c. 2.5 metres thick during construction (probably to save time and building materials), proper foundations were considered necessary for stability (Breeze and Dobson 2000: 29–32, 59–60).

When wooden roof supports decay through age it is possible to remove and replace them without disturbing stone walls; it is therefore difficult to trace the full history of a ruined building, even when the walls remain substantially intact. A long chronological span for artefacts from such a structure may be the only indication of the duration of occupation. If nothing survives apart from the foundations and a few of the lower courses, features such as blocked doorways or extended foundations may reveal some modifications. If the excavator is fortunate, further details may be revealed by fragments of masonry with clear architectural functions (vaulting, columns, pieces of arches) or with decoration that may help with dating. Stone from structures demolished at the end of one period is often reused in the next. Documents containing building accounts, or illustrations made before the building was completely ruined, should already have been located during assessment and evaluation and used to guide excavation strategy. This was the case at Norton Priory, Cheshire, where a medieval monastic complex and the secular houses that replaced it were analysed through an integrated programme of excavation and documentary research (Greene J.P. 1989).

Internal features of stone buildings, such as partitions, screens or flooring, were commonly constructed from wood, and they are difficult to detect unless parts of their structure extended below ground level. Floors of stone or beaten clay are more helpful because they were frequently laid on a foundation of rubble or other material containing architectural fragments from earlier phases, masons' chippings, and even domestic rubbish. Datable sherds of pottery or coins discovered in these layers provide a useful *terminus post quem* for the construction of the floor that covers them.

Buildings that went out of use were normally treated as quarries, especially if they contained squared facing blocks. In areas where stone is particularly scarce, even the foundations might have been removed, leaving only unusable fragments and scattered mortar. The holes left behind are known as **robber trenches**, which remove stratigraphic relationships between walls, floors and other surrounding levels in a similar manner to trenches dug by 'wall-chasing' archaeologists. However, since stone robbers did not shift more than the very minimum amount of soil

in their quest for stone, they normally followed the foundations very closely. An excavator can recover a 'negative' plan of the building by removing the filling of robber trenches. Wheeler excavated 'ghost walls' at Verulamium, St Albans, to reveal one of the city's monumental Roman gateways, of which not a single stone survived (Wheeler and Wheeler 1936: pl. 88a). On some recent excavations rough cobbled platforms turned out to be the backs of wall-faces that had collapsed outwards; these offer remarkable potential for understanding more about buildings known only from foundations – this is the only way we will ever learn about the facades and upper floors of buildings in Roman Britain, where none survive (Ling 1992). It also means that areas of apparently meaningless stonework should be checked carefully before removal.

Wood
- key references: Collis, *Digging up the past* 2001: 114–30; Brown, *Timber-framed buildings* 1997.

Unless extremely wet or dry conditions have remained constant over a long period, wood decays completely, leaving differences in the colour and texture of soil that are only detectable by careful excavation. Discoveries of ancient boats illustrate the effects of different environments on preservation. One side of the hull of a sixteenth-century warship, the *Mary Rose*, survived in excellent condition near Portsmouth because it sank on its side into deep silt that protected the timber from erosion by currents and from marine worms that eat exposed wood (Rule 1982). The world's oldest surviving ship (c. 2590 BC) was excavated on dry land in Egypt in 1954; it had been dismantled and placed in a specially constructed stone chamber beside the Great Pyramid of Cheops, where arid conditions preserved it from decay (Jenkins 1980). In complete contrast, the seventh-century Anglo-Saxon ship buried in a long trench and covered by a large mound in the royal cemetery at Sutton Hoo in Suffolk had suffered alternating wet and dry conditions in a sandy subsoil. Only one fragmentary plank from the bottom of the hull survived, but fortunately decayed timber left visible stains, and the ship's planks were revealed by meticulous excavation, and confirmed by the corroded iron rivets that once held them together (Evans 1994: frontispiece).

Although timber buildings require foundations, substantial structures can be built on the surface without leaving any traces in the subsoil. Timber-framed buildings and 'log cabins' made from interlocking timbers rely for their stability on joinery rather than earth-fast upright posts. Fortunately, problems with uneven ground and dampness usually made it wise to erect these structures on a spread of gravel or rubble make-up, or on low stone walls; even then, only indirect evidence for the actual timber building may remain. For example, despite their impressive nature, cruck-built medieval houses might leave few archaeological traces apart from the stone post-pads on which the upright timbers rested to prevent rotting.

One of the most impressive achievements of modern open-area excavation has been the discovery of a phase of late Roman timber structures built at Wroxeter in Shropshire after the Roman baths there were demolished (Barker 1998; White and Barker 1998). Earlier excavators had used narrow trenches to trace the plans of Roman masonry buildings, digging through a layer of rubble lying near the surface that they dismissed as debris left by the demolition and decay of the Roman town. However, open-area excavation by Philip Barker revealed a hitherto unsuspected final phase in the occupation of the town. The implications of his work are universal: wherever timber-framed buildings might have been erected on rubble levelling, leaving no detectable floor levels, an excavator cannot claim with complete certainty that buildings were *absent* during a phase when a site was apparently deserted. Unfortunately, this kind of excavation is virtually impossible on other Roman town sites, because, unlike Wroxeter, most have been disturbed by medieval and modern occupation, and assorted foundations, cellars, wells and pits reduce the area available for excavation (Ottaway 1992). Even intensively researched sites may still contain remains untouched by earlier excavators. The presence of gardens around a house inside the Roman fort at Birdoswald on Hadrian's Wall

protected not only the latest phases of floors and occupation of its stone structures, but also (as at Wroxeter) traces of substantial wooden buildings erected during the 'dark ages' between the end of Roman Britain and the historical Anglo-Saxon kingdom of Northumbria (Wilmott 1997).

Timber structures that *did* possess below-ground foundations are not without problems for excavators. One of the most recurrent archaeological features encountered on sites is the **post hole (Fig. 3.17)**. The simplest method of erecting a firm upright is to dig a hole, stand a post in it, and then pack the upcast from the hole firmly back around it, perhaps with the addition of some packing stones. The subsoil is rarely suitable for large posts to be rammed directly into the ground, but suitable pile-driving equipment was certainly used in the Roman period. Separate post holes might have been dug for each upright in a large complex structure, but a continuous **foundation trench** is more suitable for a regular line of posts, particularly where they need to be set close together; Roman military granaries are particularly good examples (Manning 1989). Gaps between posts were frequently filled by planks, which sometimes extended below ground level; particular care is required to detect them during excavation of foundation trenches. Some walls, fences and even large enclosures consisted of a continuous **palisade** of posts or planks set into a trench. Alternatively, horizontal **sleeper beams** may simply be laid on the ground, with upright posts mortised into them; the time and effort saved in digging post holes is offset by the need for some additional carpentry. Sleeper beams can be raised on stone footings, set into trenches or simply placed on a rubble platform; some buildings recognised at Wroxeter probably took this form (Barker 1998).

A variety of techniques of timber construction may coexist on a site, or even in a single building. Neolithic longhouses of the Linear Pottery culture in Europe, Iron Age round houses in Britain, and early medieval aisled halls in the Netherlands and north Germany frequently combined individual post holes and foundation trenches. Very similar – but unconnected – wooden buildings have been erected over wide chronological and geographical

Figure 3.17 Post holes and foundation trenches (top right) for the barracks at Jamestown, Virginia. Deep holes allowed the major structural timbers to be positioned accurately and erected firmly, while smaller holes accommodated uprights that did not carry weight but provided a framework for planking or wattle-and-daub walls. Continuous foundation trenches were more convenient for erecting close-set posts or palisades. Excavation by small trenches (such as Wheeler's boxes, Box 3.1) would not make much sense of this kind of site; the significance of individual features is only clarified by exposing complete structures. (W. Kelso)

spans. A timber hall excavated at Balbridie in Scotland was initially assumed to be early medieval because it closely resembled Anglo-Saxon structures in Northumberland; however, radiocarbon dates revealed that it was Neolithic, and more than 5,000 years old (Fairweather and Ralston 1993).

As with stone buildings, interpretation is helped by studying recent structures that are still standing, or remains of ancient structures preserved well by waterlogging or desiccation.

Excavated remains of burnt buildings are also informative, for once timber has been converted into charcoal it resists further decay. If large numbers of apparently unrelated post holes are found on sites that were occupied for long periods by structures that have left no complete or obvious plans, it may be possible to hypothesise numerous rectangular or circular structures. Sets of features that belonged together may be revealed if precise records have been kept of differences in the shape, depth and soil filling of post holes and other structural evidence. A computer database of these records would be particularly suitable for analysis in this way, and possible structures could be plotted directly onto a digitised site plan (Bradley and Small 1985).

Other building materials

- key references: Adam, *Roman building* 1994; Rosen, *Cities of clay* 1986; Brunskill, *Brick building* 1997.

The effectiveness of construction methods using perishable materials is shown by the large numbers of picturesque cob and half-timbered cottages that have survived for many centuries in the south of England; stone footings combined with an overhanging roof that throws rainwater well clear of the wall face are very effective. One of the most important ancient building materials was clay, whether applied directly to insubstantial wooden walls (**wattle and daub**), shaped into blocks and dried in the sun (**mud-brick**) (**Fig. 3.18**) or fired in kilns to make non-perishable bricks or tiles. Mud or clay walls are best suited to dry climates, and quite complex structures were already being constructed on early agricultural sites of the eighth to seventh millennium BC in the Near East, such as Çayönü in Turkey or Jarmo in Iraq. Stone footings were used as a base for packed mud walls, while stone foundations in curious 'grill plan' formations supported floors made from bundles of reeds covered in clay.

The use of hand-made bricks of sun-dried clay began around 8,000 BC in Neolithic settlements in western Asia. Hand-made bricks were used in circular houses at Jericho (Israel) in the 'pre-pottery Neolithic A' phase. Rectangular mud

Figure 3.18 Unfired mud bricks bonded together with wet clay are notoriously difficult to locate and excavate. This scrupulously cleaned section at Tepe Ali Kosh, Iran, makes it perfectly clear why early excavators of tells in the Near East failed to find any structures other than those finished in fired brick or stone. The great depth that accumulated layers of mud brick structures may reach on tell sites is illustrated by Fig. 1.22–23. (Hole *et al.* 1969: pl. 9b)

bricks, shaped in a wooden mould, were particularly suitable for rectilinear buildings, and went on to become the standard building material of the first urban civilisations of Mesopotamia, Egypt and India (Oates 1989; Schijns 2008). Mud-brick remains important for construction in these areas. Mud walls were sometimes provided with stone footings, and, where a more temperate climate made the unfired mud building technique less suitable, bundles of reeds or timber might be combined with clay walls to increase their strength; evidence from the Neolithic settlement at Nea Nikomedia in Greece provides good examples of mud and timber construction (Wardle 1996).

Mud-brick buildings have a limited life, and the ease with which they can be demolished and replaced creates a build-up of levels. A settlement occupied for many centuries may become a deeply stratified tell which is difficult to excavate because demolished structures have a similar consistency to their successors. Mud-brick decays rapidly when exposed to the elements; many pioneering excavators in the Near East found that structures crumble to dust once exposed. Sun-dried clay was also used in India and China; under the name *adobe*, it is still common in Mexico. The vast pre-Columbian city of Teotihuacán (Mexico) is famous for pyramids made from adobe with a protective facing of stone or plaster – a combination reminiscent of Mesopotamia (Millon 1967).

More durable fired bricks were in regular use in Mesopotamia by 3000 BC, but were mainly restricted to the ornate or exposed parts of ceremonial buildings. Even these are susceptible to damage by water absorbed from the ground, which, when it dries, forms salt crystals that open cracks and make bricks disintegrate. Roman brick and tile buildings still make a strong visual impression around the west Mediterranean and in Europe; indeed, most major Roman buildings of the Imperial period or later relied on brick arches and concrete vaulting rather than stone (Lancaster 2005). Internal surfaces could be concealed by attaching thin slices of marble, mosaics or painted wall plaster. Unfortunately, decorative facings were normally removed for reuse in areas where building stone is not readily available, leaving unsightly concrete cores or plain brickwork.

3.4.5 Standing buildings

- key references: Wood, *Buildings archaeology* 1994; Rodwell, *Church archaeology* 1989; Morriss, *Archaeology of buildings* 1999; Pearson and Meeson, *Vernacular buildings* 2001.

The definition of archaeological building investigation and recording (ABIR) is a programme of work intended to establish the character, history, dating, form and archaeological development of a specified building, structure, or complex and its setting, including buried components, on land, inter-tidal zone or underwater. … The purpose of ABIR is … to inform: the formulation of a strategy for the conservation, alteration, demolition, repair or management of a building, or structure, or complex and its setting; or: to seek a better understanding, compile a lasting record, analyse the findings/record, and then disseminate the results.

(IfA *Standard and guidance* 1999)

Medieval buildings modified over the centuries frequently show evidence of inserted and blocked windows, changes in roof line, extensions and rebuildings stretching over several centuries (for example St Mary's Church, Deerhurst: Rahtz 1997). In the seventeenth century, Aubrey was aware of the value of different styles of window

for dating medieval buildings, while Classical archaeologists (notably Winckelmann) deduced the sequence of Greek and Roman architectural styles from ancient texts and surviving buildings in Greece and Italy. From the Renaissance to the eighteenth century, architects examined and recorded Classical buildings because they wanted to incorporate design details into their own work, but they rarely made any efforts to preserve the originals. The Gothic Revival of the nineteenth century brought medieval buildings back into favour; many architects 'restored' existing buildings (especially churches) in a meticulously academic fashion – but destroyed original features in the process. John Ruskin was an isolated voice protesting against the way in which medieval Venice was being restored, and his remarkable drawings, paintings and photographs served a dual purpose: recording details before destruction, and providing inspiration for neo-Gothic architects. Pitt Rivers pioneered modern archaeological methods of examining buildings in his study of a medieval hunting lodge at Tollard Royal on his estate in 1889, stripping wall plaster to reveal earlier decoration and original wall faces, and excavating both within and outside the building (Bowden 1991: 122–6).

The idea of preserving representative examples of old buildings only became enshrined in planning policy in the late twentieth century, perhaps because urban renewal had damaged historic cities on an unprecedented scale – frequently removing old buildings that had survived two World Wars in Europe. At the same time many rural churches became redundant, while major cathedrals such as York and Trier underwent massive repairs (Parsons 1999). The loss of original buildings and conservation of those that remain have stimulated an approach that combines traditional architectural analysis with archaeological techniques. Analysing a standing building relies on the same principles as stratigraphy to establish its original form, to work out the sequence of later alterations, and to relate them to any available dating evidence (Harris 1989: 56–61). There may be visible indications such as the blocking of redundant doorways or the insertion of new windows; luckily, existing walls were frequently adapted to bring a building up to date with changes in function or new fashions, rather than replaced (**Fig. 3.19**). Samples of mortar compared in the laboratory may reveal different phases of construction; earthenware tiles or bricks are datable by thermoluminescence, and the exact age of structural timbers may be determined by counting tree-rings – a process known as **dendrochronology** (Chapter 4). Opportunities for detailed study of a building may be a positive outcome of accidental damage; extensive research and archaeological investigation were needed before conservation and rebuilding could be carried out after the fire at Windsor Castle in 1992 (Brindle and Kerr 1997). Some remote-sensing techniques normally associated with buried archaeological sites can be applied to standing structures, for example to detect architectural features hidden behind plaster (Brooke 1994). Laser scanning, using similar technology to that used for aerial prospection, can also be used to provide a detailed record of a building's facade (English Heritage 2007).

Spatial and functional analysis have brought a deeper understanding of the significance of changes made to the plans of buildings that were

Figure 3.19 Standing buildings may require archaeological investigation to elucidate changes that have taken place during their lifetime. This warehouse constructed at the Manchester end of the Liverpool and Manchester Railway in 1830 has been conserved and adapted to become part of a science museum. The complexities of the windows and square, stone-lined openings on the west wall were investigated by conducting an open area excavation which revealed foundations and floors where steam engines that powered lifting machinery once stood. 'Since the term [industrial archaeology] was coined there has been a search for a distinctive methodology for a separate subject. In fact it could be more helpful to regard industrial archaeology as an integral element of historical archaeology. A range of sources have contributed to the study ... They are entirely equivalent to the sources that one would use for earlier buildings or sites – the writer would draw a direct comparison with the approach taken in studying a medieval monastic site' (Greene J.P. 1995: 128). (Jean Horsfall; The Museum of Science and Industry in Manchester)

used for many centuries (Parker Pearson and Richards 1993). Medieval castles respond well to analysis using theoretical social archaeology, whether a magnificent example like Bodiam in Sussex (Johnson 2010: 192–7) or a lesser structure such as Edlingham in Northumberland, where Fairclough showed how changes in society, economics and the need for defence were reflected in ways that people of different status gained access to various parts of the building (1992). Since this approach has been developed and validated in the context of documented historical buildings, it may be used to provide analogies for the interpretation of prehistoric buildings (Foster 1989), although the results will always remain hypothetical.

3.4.6 Reconstruction

- key references: Drury, *Structural reconstruction* 1982; Davison, *Picturing the past* 1997; Barcelo et al., *Virtual reality in archaeology* 2000.

An excellent way of increasing understanding of an excavated building is to create a scale model or reconstruction drawing. Some information may be particularly helpful, notably the size and strength of foundations, pillars and walls. Fragments of architectural stonework such as window or door frames, voussoirs from arches and vaulting, and roofing slates and tiles, all may help to date the building as well as to reconstruct it; comparisons should also be made with surviving structures and relevant documentary evidence. Excavators also benefit from the detailed analysis of the excavated remains; new interpretations may be suggested, and attention drawn to parts of a site that need further investigation. If several plausible reconstructions are deduced from a single plan it is best to offer more than one interpretation in an excavation report. Computer graphics are now very sophisticated, and **virtual reality modelling** (VRM) of structures allows viewers to look around the interior, or inspect the appearance of the exterior from any angle (for example Avebury: Pollard and Gillings 1998; see also Forte and Siliotti 1997) (**Fig. 3.20**). The display for the public of an ancient site is enhanced considerably by a high-quality scale model that includes human figures and activities relevant to its function; full-scale reconstructions are even more attractive. However, Shakespeare's Globe Theatre in London provides an excellent example of the difficulties involved in relating excavated foundations to an above-ground structure, even with the help of contemporary illustrations (Wilson 1997).

3.5 RECORDS, ARCHIVES AND PUBLICATION

> Every archaeological site is itself a document. It can be read by a skilled excavator, but it is destroyed by the very process which enables us to read it. … when the site has been destroyed all that is left are the site records, the finds and some unreliable memories.
>
> (Barker 1993: 13)

3.5.1 Recording

- key references: Roskams, *Excavation* 2001: 110–216; Collis, *Digging up the past* 2001: 78–102; Westman, *MOLAS archaeological site manual* 1994; Carver, *Archaeological investigation* 2010: 197–331; Steiner, *Approaches to archaeological illustration* 2005.

Wheeler and his followers thought of archaeological sites as a succession of general layers to be revealed and placed in sequence, ideally using the box system of trenches as a ready-made reference grid; the sections exposed by baulks between trenches were drawn as a record of the stratification. These procedures were unsuitable for open-area excavations, however (**Fig. 3.21**). Conceptualising sites in terms of large numbers of separate units of stratification – as opposed to seeing each unit as a component of a more general phase – led to the introduction of **single-context recording** in the 1970s (Lucas 2001: 60). The larger the area excavated without baulks, the less likely it was that individual units would ever appear in vertical sections; as Harris explained,

Figure 3.20 The Alacami at Kadirli in south-east Turkey is a church built around AD 500, modified subsequently and converted into a mosque in the fifteenth century (Bayliss 1997). Research and excavation on the site has provided sufficient information for Bayliss to generate this remarkably realistic graphic representation of the site, which can be examined from any angle both externally and internally. The character of the stonework is based on photogrammetric recording of surviving areas, while excavated traces of mosaics have been used to generate floor coverings for the interior. Because the image is computer-generated it may be modified very easily to incorporate new evidence or interpretations. (Richard Bayliss)

this changed the balance between vertical and horizontal excavation:

> No amount of sectional drawing is of the slightest help in such a composition of these period plans, as it becomes clear that the horizontal record of stratification is far more important than the vertical ... What is needed is not a grain-by-grain plan, but a record of scaled drawings with each stratigraphic unit on a separate sheet, and which shows, at the very least, the area of the stratum and spot heights of its surface – as recorded prior to excavation. With such an archive any desired configuration of stratigraphic units can be made at any time ...
>
> (Harris 1977: 94)

The large scale of rescue excavations in the 1970s also changed the role of directors and site supervisors. Directors formerly kept an overall check on the entire excavation by writing descriptions of layers and features in site notebooks, and jotting down subjective insights that might eventually help in the interpretation of the basic plans and drawings. Each supervisor of an individual trench would maintain a similar record in one notebook. An increasing demand for objectivity and accuracy, combined with the complexity of (for example) a large open-area multiperiod urban excavation, led to the design of pre-printed forms for recording each context (**Fig. 3.22**). These allow the director to impose standardised recording methods in advance of excavation that remove control from supervisors, who no longer

Figure 3.21 A detailed view of a small open-area excavation at the 1830 warehouse, Manchester (Fig. 3.19). The features (the remains of an engine house) have been meticulously cleaned and are being planned in relation to a reference-post and strings. The archaeologist is making a detailed drawing with the help of a 1-metre-square frame subdivided by wires into 10 cm squares; this allows much detail to be added by eye. The same technique can be seen in use under water in Fig. 3.14. (Jean Horsfall; The Museum of Science and Industry in Manchester)

record observations in a rather personal way, but simply manage the procedures necessary for filling in forms. This also increasingly means that individual excavators are responsible for excavating and recording 'features' and 'contexts'.

Single Context Record forms are used to describe the position, size and characteristics of each separate excavated unit, and to record its relationships with all adjacent units. There are two principal relationships between units: **above** or cutting through another unit (and therefore later than that unit), and **beneath** or cut by another unit (and therefore earlier than that unit). Occasionally two units may be **equivalent**

(and therefore contemporary with each other) – for example, two areas of clay that once formed part of the same floor and that have been divided by a later disturbance. If the precise relationship between every unit is recorded correctly, the entire stratigraphic sequence may be converted into simplified diagrammatic form as a Harris matrix (above: p. 98). Context recording forms are designed with analysis of the site for publication in mind, so that every excavated unit is cross-referenced to all relevant photographs, plans, finds and environmental samples.

Further forms are used in the finds-shed for recording each category of excavated material, such as pottery, bones or metalwork, and for documenting individual drawings and photographs; all of these records are cross-referenced back to the individual excavated units. Recording forms should be designed in a way that allows data to be entered rapidly into a computer database. Modern database software (such as Microsoft Access) is **relational** – it allows several separate files of information to be linked and combined into a single query or report. Thus, a complete list of excavated units in which coins were found could be produced along with details of the pottery found in the same units; this would allow people writing specialist reports on pottery to check their own findings against a list of dates supplied by a numismatist. Everyone involved in preparing specialist reports would be able to locate excavated units from which significant finds came on the site's Harris matrix, which would show their position in the stratigraphic sequence. If the positions of artefacts found within excavated units have been recorded precisely it may be possible to analyse their distribution using GIS techniques (Chapter 2, p. 80). Mapping the distribution of finds such as fragments of flint, pottery or small coins may be helpful in interpreting sites where buildings were constructed without foundations, as such structures might be defined by plotting broken artefacts trampled into the ground surface around them. The significance of this kind of information may only emerge after the excavation has finished, underlining Pitt Rivers' opinion that *everything* observed should be recorded, whether it appears significant or not.

3.5.2 Postmodernism and excavation: reflexive fieldwork

- Key references: Hodder (ed) *Towards reflexive method in archaeology: the example of Çatalhöyük*, 1999; Bender *et al. Stone worlds: narrative and reflexivity in landscape archaeology*, 2007.

Gavin Lucas has argued that the practice of fieldwork has always been directly linked to interpretation and theory, and he has explained how changes in excavation technique took place in relation to prevailing theoretical concepts.

> Looking back over the developments in field archaeology since the 1880s, several major changes in perception can be identified. For Pitt Rivers and others of his time, the archaeological site was a repository of objects which, if carefully excavated and linked to types of monuments, were instrumental in the construction of evolutionary typological sequences. For Wheeler, Kidder and their contemporaries, the site became a repository of an artefactual assemblage indicative of a culture group, and, if stratified, the locus of critical information on chronological changes within this assemblage. For us, the site is a repository of behavioural patterns, structured activities revealed through close analysis of contextual association within or between assemblages. One can see how each of these views is linked to the prevailing conception of the past – as the evolution of culture, as the history of culture groups, and as cultural behaviour (however this is viewed).
>
> (Lucas 2001: 62)

Since the 1990s some field archaeologists have adopted a different approach to field archaeology and excavation as a consequence of postmodernism and postprocessualism (Chapter 6). They believe that neither excavation nor landscape survey can be divorced from the prior interpretations, feelings and personal outlooks of the practitioners themselves. Ian Hodder has tackled this issue explicitly by suggesting that

excavation is a process of 'interpretation at the trowel's edge' (1999: 92), meaning that the whole process of excavation is about making subjective decisions – how you dig, what you dig and how you interpret it. This can be at the large scale of designing research agendas (above, and Chapter 6), but it also happens whenever an archaeologist undertakes fieldwork – literally every time that they use a trowel or spade. The idea of **agency** (discussed in Chapter 6) emphasises that, because people are different, and have different ideas and feelings, they will undertake and interpret archaeology differently, not only after all the recording has been done but also during the process of excavation. Hodder argues that currently most archaeologists are reluctant to acknowledge this and attempt to see archaeology as an objective, empirical (and hence scientific) process. He has tried to develop what is called a 'reflexive' methodology to tackle this problem on his own excavations at Çatalhöyük in Turkey by encouraging the use of video diaries and discussion sessions, and including specialists on various kinds of finds in the actual excavation process. These activities encourage excavators to reflect on why they have done something in a certain way, and allow them to exchange insights with teams working on other parts of the site (Hodder 1999; 2000). Other archaeologists have also tried to incorporate the subjectivity of excavation and the excavator into recording practices more explicitly by devising types of recording sheets different to that illustrated in **Fig. 3.22** (Chadwick 2003). On the developer-funded rescue excavations conducted in advance of the construction of Terminal 5 at Heathrow airport, the recording system was designed to incorporate the views and interpretations of the individual excavators rather than simply imposing a single interpretation by the site director (Andrews *et al.* 2000). This approach contrasts starkly with the way that much fieldwork was conducted in the past, when unskilled labourers were paid to dig up the archaeology, not to interpret it.

Theoretical developments have also led to contrasting approaches to how excavations should be published. The traditional manner of presenting site plans, section drawings and

CONTEXT RECORDING SHEET

COTSWOLD ARCHAEOLOGY

SITE CODE:	Location	Grid Ref:	Type	Context No.
FFF 00	Area 1	480ᴇ / 524ɴ	Cut	1053

DEPOSIT

1. Colour
2. Composition/Particle size
3. Compaction
4. Inclusions
5. Horizon Clarity
6. Contamination risk
7. Methods and conditions
8. Other comments

CUT

1. Shape in plan
2. Corners
3. Sides
4. Base
5. Orientation
6. Other comments

Draw profile overleaf

1) Terminus of ditch

2) -

3) generally 45° straight, occ. concave

4) small flat-based slot at base (see sect. + sketch overleaf)

5) terminus of NW/SE arm of enclosure ditch

6) -

Plan No. 480/520	Section No. 66	Lgth 2m sect.	Width/Diam 2.98 m	Hgt/Dpth 1.69 m

STRATIGRAPHIC MATRIX

				1051	1052					

This context 1053

			1054							

	PHYSICAL RELATIONSHIPS		
Covered by:	Part of: Enclosure ①	Covers:	
Filled by: 1019 1020 1041-1052		Fill of:	
Cut by:	Includes:	Cuts: 1003 (NATURAL) 1054 (PIT FILL)	
Butted by:	Same as:	Butts:	

Earlier than / Contemporary with / Later than

INTERPRETATION AND DISCUSSION Internal External Structural Other

• Terminus of enclosure ditch forming NE-facing entrance into sub-rectangular enclosure (see sketch overleaf)

• filled with initial silting/slumping deposits (few finds) then subjected to deliberate backfilling (with few finds)

• no indication of re-cutting

Provisional date; ? Iron Age

△ **Special Finds** (number and type)

◇ **Environmental samples** (number)

Finds Specify anything not below

None	Pot	Bone	Glass	Metal	Wood	Leather	Flint
☐	☐	☐	☐	☐	☐	☐	☐

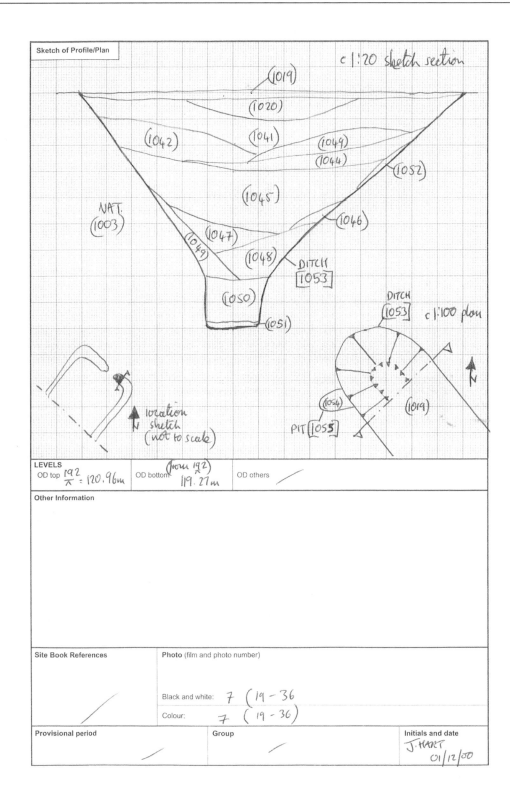

Sketch of Profile/Plan

c 1:20 sketch section

(1019)
(1020)
(1042) (1041) (1049)
(1044)
(1052)
(1045)
NAT. (1003)
(1046)
(1047)
(1049)
(1048)
DITCH 1053
(1050)
(1051)

DITCH 1053   c 1:100 plan

N

location sketch (not to scale)

(1054)
PIT 1055
(1019)

LEVELS
OD top 192/π̄ = 120.96m   OD bottom (from 192) 119.27m   OD others

Other Information

Site Book References   Photo (film and photo number)

Black and white: 7 (19 - 36

Colour: 7 (19 - 36)

Provisional period   Group   Initials and date
J. HART
01/12/00

Figure 3.22 *(page 139 & left)* A standard form for **single context recording** from Finmere, an Iron Age site in southern Britain, excavated by a commercial archaeological unit in 2000. The site has its own unique code (FFF00) to distinguish it from other projects that the organisation may also be working on, and identifies the year of excavation. This context (unit of stratification) has been given a unique code (1053) and a grid reference so that it can easily be located on plans of the site. The excavator is given suggestions about which aspects of the context to describe, in this instance a 'cut' (or interface) – in other words the event of 'cutting' the enclosure ditch. It is worth remembering that 'finds' or samples cannot derive from a context which is described as 'cut', as this type of context is recording an 'action' in the past and therefore cannot contain material. Relationships with earlier or later contexts are identified by 'fill of' or 'cuts' or 'cut by'; i.e. is the ditch 'cut' by another feature which would therefore be later? This information allows it to be incorporated into a basic 'stratigraphic matrix' which will be integrated in a larger Harris matrix (Box 3.2). Sketch section drawings and plans are drawn on the back to make the context easily identifiable later. A series of recorded dimensions follows, together with references to plans, sections or photographic records; more general observations and interpretations are entered into 'interpretation and discussion', including a provisional date. 'Finds' provides space for mentioning items recovered from the context (none in this case, as it is a 'cut') which will be fully catalogued elsewhere, and 'environmental samples' to note whether soil samples were taken for flotation processing (Box 5.2). Finally, the date of the record and the name of the recorder are added so that any discrepancies may be checked. When the form has been entered into a computer database, the context code will link it directly to other files that list photographs, plans and finds, or to details of other excavated features excavated nearby. (Simon Cox, Cotswold Archaeology)

interpretations can give a misleading air of objectivity to the practice of excavation that conceals the effects of subjectivity and emotion on the decisions made on a site. Furthermore, some archaeologists emphasise that the practice of archaeology itself is determined by the social context of its practitioners (Hodder 1999; Tilley 2008: 78). A few excavators have tried to respond by including information about these factors in the form of interviews and discussions between participants; this can be seen in the excavation report from Leskernick, Cornwall. These materials illustrate how the process of excavation and field research developed during the project (Bender *et al.* 2007), or allow different interpretations of a site to be presented, acknowledging the problematic nature of the archaeological record (e.g. Andrews *et al.* 2000). These approaches remain relatively peripheral to the way in which most field archaeology and excavation is undertaken and reported; although many archaeologists accept the validity of the theoretical motivation behind these attempts, the content of resulting reports has been criticised (Hummler 2008).

3.5.3 Publication and archiving the results

● key references: CBA, *Signposts for archaeological publication* 1991; Richards and Robinson, *Digital archives from excavation and fieldwork: a guide to good practice* 2000; Neumann and Sanford, *Cultural resources archaeology* 2001: chapter 7.

The archaeologist has responsibility for making available the results of archaeological work with reasonable dispatch.

(IfA: *Code of conduct*, Principle 4)

Publication was assisted by the invention of photogravure in 1879, which allowed photographs to be reproduced without being printed individually or redrawn as engravings (Feyler 1987: 1045). The assumption that a major excavation should be published in book form was reinforced by the magnificent printed volumes produced by Pitt Rivers at the very end of the nineteenth century. By the 1960s it was taken for granted that an excavation report would consist of an 'objective' account of the excavated features and structures, followed by descriptive catalogues of each category of finds, along with scientific reports on bones and environmental samples. However, the unparalleled size and number of rescue excavations in the 1960s and 1970s, followed by spending cuts in the 1970s and 1980s, made it impossible to continue to produce reports of this kind (**Fig. 3.23**).

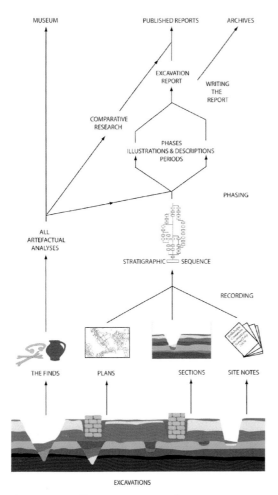

MUSEUM PUBLISHED REPORTS ARCHIVES

EXCAVATION REPORT

WRITING THE REPORT

COMPARATIVE RESEARCH

PHASES
ILLUSTRATIONS & DESCRIPTIONS
PERIODS

PHASING

ALL ARTEFACTUAL ANALYSES

STRATIGRAPHIC SEQUENCE

RECORDING

THE FINDS PLANS SECTIONS SITE NOTES

EXCAVATIONS

Figure 3.23 There are many important stages between excavation and publication. Perhaps the most important is the amalgamation of plans, section drawings and recording sheets into a stratigraphic sequence, and its interpretation in terms of periods of occupation and abandonment and phases characterised by particular activities. The finds should be processed at an early stage, for artefacts such as pottery and coins assist in dating and understanding the nature of occupation, while bones or samples of soil, plants, etc. help to elucidate environmental conditions and the economic functions of each phase. All finds, together with any information that will not appear in a published report, must be documented in full, ready for storage in a museum or archive. (Drawn by Sheila Newton, after Harris 1989: Fig. 57)

As the amount of information produced by excavation has increased, so too have expectations about its quality and detail. Now that

single context recording is well established, and computerised databases are in common use, it is possible for an excavation to be recorded almost entirely in digital form (Lock 2003: 85); this has been pioneered in rescue excavation carried out in China, by digital scanning of terracotta soldiers (Zheng and Zhang 1999). High-precision surveying equipment of the kind used in fieldwork (Chapter 2, p. 58) stores readings in electronic form which are then downloaded and processed by computer. Digital cameras are rapidly becoming important for still photography because images are available immediately, without traditional developing and printing, and can be stored on computers along with other site records. Inexpensive video cameras have become a useful additional recording method since the 1980s because they can record the actual process of excavation of important finds, contexts or structures (Hanson and Rahtz 1988). Digital images are easily incorporated in interim reports or Internet sites produced to provide rapid publicity about the results of excavations; some excavators even allow people to study the progress of work by installing webcams that send live digital pictures to Internet sites. While production of interim reports has become easier, the number of supporting techniques and sources of specialist information makes it increasingly difficult to complete a final report for publication in the conventional form of a book or substantial paper in a periodical. It is significant that the IfA's Principle 4 and its associated rules do not recommend any particular form of publication (**Fig. 3.24**).

The size and complexity of the traditional reports made them frequently unwieldy, expensive, and impossible for non-specialists to digest. How much consideration should publicly-funded archaeologists give to taxpayers? Should authors of major archaeological reports present their results in a form accessible to the public as well as to specialists – and is it possible to communicate clearly for the former without oversimplification that will irritate the latter? A number of committees formed in Britain from the 1970s onwards proposed new standards of publication, with varying emphases but with a

Figure 3.24 Publication of large, long-term excavations on complex urban sites is a major problem. The solution employed by the York Archaeological Trust for several decades has been to issue reports on specific phases, sites or categories of finds in relatively inexpensive paperback format. Each one has a volume and part number to show where it fits into the overall framework of publications planned for the whole city. The illustration shows several fascicules related to excavations at 46–54 Fishergate, a specific 'rescue' site. While a large academic library might buy all of these in order to compile a complete set, someone interested in the trading settlement of the Anglo-Saxon period need only buy one fascicule. A disadvantage is that pottery, bones and other finds will have helped shape the interpretation of the settlement, but their details are published separately. (York Archaeological Trust/Council for British Archaeology)

consistent recommendation that much material should be stored in archives, rather than published. English Heritage set out a definition of minimum requirements for the contents of a published report:

i. the research objectives as expressed in the **project design**
ii. circumstances and organisation of the work and the date at which it was undertaken
iii. identity of the individual/organisation by whom the work was undertaken
iv. summary account of the results of the project

v. summary of the content of the project archive, where it is housed and how it may be consulted.

(*MAP* 2 1991: 39)

More recent guidance by English Heritage (MoRPHE 2006) provides less explicit guidelines for 'dissemination', suggesting that publications might be aimed at a wider range of readers, not only academics and professionals.

While full publication of the results would be the ideal end result of all excavations, an archive representing the original record of the project's results is always necessary in order that future archaeologists can re-examine the nature of the archaeology and the ways in which the evidence was obtained and studied. The MoRPHE document (2006, Appendix 1) defines what an excavation archive should include:

> *Project administration documents* (e.g. landowner agreements; correspondence; project proposals)

> *The site archive* (e.g. original context sheets; photographic records; sampling records; drawing registers of plans and sections; site drawings and photographs; digital files; site notebooks; all the finds and environmental materials)

> *A site archive assessment* (an assessment of the potential of the site archive and other gathered data to support research aims and objectives)

> (MoRHPE 2006: 25–27)

The guidelines also state that the archive should be ordered, indexed and quantified as well as 'signposted appropriately to ensure future use in research'.

In addition to the paper archives, the finds from excavations need to be stored and retained, usually in a suitable museum, to enable future research on the material. Subsequent advances in techniques may mean that greater evidence can be procured from material than is possible at the time of excavations. For example, the increasing ability to analyse the residues on ceramic vessels (Chapter 5) means that pottery stored in museums may provide additional evidence. Alternatively, theoretical perspectives may change, regarding certain materials (such as coarseware pottery) as much more important for understanding a site than was the case when excavation took place. The solution to storage is not a simple one, however; the increasing number of developer-funded excavations (above: p. 106) has led to huge amounts of new material which needs to be stored. This is leading to mounting pressure on museums in many countries, such as the UK. It raises important questions as to whether all material should be stored, in case of future advances, or only certain 'important' material retained so as to save space.

The move towards unpublished archives coincided with the growing use of standardised excavation records held on computers, and is reflected in the emphasis on digital archiving made by English Heritage. Why issue site records in a possibly indigestible and expensive printed book, when they can be stored in an archive to which specialists are allowed free access? Why not publish a short summary of the principal structures and finds in a form that will be more interesting to general readers, and simply inform specialists about the existence of the archives? This solution sounds attractive, but excavations published only in summary form do not allow readers to check the details upon which the excavator's general interpretations were based. Fortunately the same developments in digital technology that have revolutionised recording also offer solutions to the problem of making archives accessible. With the advent of cheap and easily distributed media such as CD-ROM and DVD, enormous quantities of data can be virtually given away; excavation reports may increasingly become multimedia experiences, with all relevant site records, photographs, drawings and video sequences stored on a single disk (Powlesland 1997). In addition, by the twenty-first century the extraordinary growth of the Internet had transformed access to remote archives through the **Archaeological Data Service**, which includes **OASIS**, an online database of **grey literature**, and the National Monuments Record. Text, images and databases of site information are increasingly available on a global scale, together with sophisticated indexing and searching programmes that allow users to navigate their own way through the information rather than following an order laid down by the author or editor of a traditional book. Examples of such approaches to publishing can be seen in the on-line journal *Internet Archaeology*. The true implications and impact of e-publishing in archaeology are only beginning to be understood (Richards 2006).

Although the phrase 'preservation by record' was coined as a euphemism for the authorised destruction of a site, soon after 'preparation of an archive' became an acceptable alternative to a traditional excavation report, these unexpected technological developments have transformed publication – and bridged the divide between practice and theory:

> It is these materialisations – of texts and images – which guarantee the validity of archaeological interpretation, not the site itself. These materialising practices are not simply representations but materialising strategies for enabling the archaeological record to be subject to repeated investigation. They create the possibility of iterability. And, like any materialisation, they have a certain independence, a certain life of their own – indeed this is a cornerstone of post-structuralist theory in relation to texts. ... This is why we call excavation destruction – we have to, otherwise the record we make is of no value. Without these materialising practices, there would be no archaeology – they allow its discourse to develop. Indeed, the archaeologists' facts are primarily not sites or artefacts, but the textual and graphic materialisations which stand in for them – from fieldnotes to site reports, from drawings to photographs.
>
> (Lucas 2001: 213–14)

3.6 GUIDE TO FURTHER READING

Complete details of every publication mentioned in this section can be found in the consolidated bibliography. Consult the works cited as key references beneath section headings within this chapter first.

Most general manuals on archaeology, for example Hester *et al.*, *Field methods* 2008, include explanations of excavation; Carver, *Archaeological investigation* 2009 is exceptionally informative and well illustrated.

THE DEVELOPMENT OF EXCAVATION TECHNIQUES

The excellent books by Roskams, *Excavation* 2001: 7–29, and Collis, *Digging up the past* 2001: 1–20, add further detail as a background to their account of current methods. An American perspective is provided by Carmichael, *Excavation* 2003.

THE INTERPRETATION OF STRATIFICATION

Deeper understanding of how stratification is actually formed can be gained from Schiffer, *Formation processes* 1987 (and his many other publications), while Bennett and Doyle, *Unlocking the stratigraphical record* 1998, and O'Brien and Lyman, *Seriation, stratigraphy, and index fossils* 1999, explore further aspects including chronology. Roskams, *Interpreting stratigraphy* 2000, provides a range of papers containing detailed discussion of many of the problems and approaches to stratigraphy and archaeological recording.

PLANNING AN EXCAVATION

The selection of a site, excavation strategy and interpretation are most easily understood by reading well-illustrated popular syntheses of work on individual sites. The English Heritage/ Batsford series contains several, including medieval urban and rural sites (Beresford and Hurst, *Wharram Percy deserted medieval village* 1990; Hall, *Viking age York* 1994); two Iron Age hillforts (Cunliffe, *Danebury* 1993; Sharples, *Maiden Castle* 1991) and a wetland site (Pryor, *Flag Fen: prehistoric fenland centre* 1993), while Pryor's *Seahenge* 2001, gives a vivid and accessible account of discovering and understanding prehistoric sites in East Anglia. An overview of an extensively investigated historical site in the United States is Schackel *et al.*, *Annapolis pasts:*

historical archaeology in Annapolis, Maryland 1998, and finds from the site are interpreted in a fascinating way in Mullins, *Race and affluence: an archaeology of African America and consumer culture* 1999. Research agendas have been published for several periods of Britain's past (e.g. the Iron Age: Haselgrove *et al.*, *Understanding the British Iron Age: An agenda for action* 2001; Roman Britain: James and Millett, *Britons and Romans* 2001); regional agendas are more likely to be made available via the Internet. For information on changing attitudes to Hadrian's Wall see Ewin, *Hadrian's Wall* 2000. National planning policies can normally be found on government websites, and many of the guidelines published by English heritage can be downloaded as electronic documents. The Institute for Archaeologists also provides guidelines on planning and running fieldwork in electronic form.

EXCAVATION STRATEGY

Further understanding of strategy and techniques, and the way that contexts, stratification and finds are presented and interpreted, can be gained by looking at full excavation reports on sites from different periods in a variety of geographical locations and environments. Some recent publications of prehistoric sites include Bailey, *Klithi: Palaeolithic settlement and Quaternary landscapes in northwest Greece* 1997; Moore *et al.*, *Village on the Euphrates: from foraging to farming at Abu Hureyra* 2000 (Mesolithic to Neolithic), and the excellent reports in Cunliffe, *The Danebury Environs Programme* 2000. Examples of Roman sites are Fulford and Timby, *Late Iron Age and Roman Silchester* 2000; Herbert, *Tel Anafa I, i–ii. final report on ten years of excavation at a Hellenistic and Roman settlement in Northern Israel* 1994; Wilmott, *Birdoswald: excavations of a Roman fort on Hadrian's Wall and its successor settlements* 1997, and Miles, *Iron Age and Roman settlement in the Upper Thames Valley: excavations at Claydon Pike* 2007. Medieval and post-medieval sites include Astill, *A medieval industrial complex and its landscape: the metalworking, watermills and workshops of Bordesley Abbey* 1993; Driscoll

and Yeoman, *Excavations within Edinburgh castle in 1988–91* 1997, and, for very recent insights into North American transport, Hawkins and Madsen, *Excavation of the Donner-Reed wagons: historic archaeology along the Hastings cutoff* 1999.

For more specific types of sites, Pitts and Roberts, *Fairweather Eden* 1997, is an account of an open-air Palaeolithic site, while recent cave publications are Chauvet *et al.*, *Chauvet cave* 1996, and Otte and Straus, *La grotte du Bois Laiterie* 1997. A general study of permanent settlements is Billman and Feinman, *Settlement pattern studies in the Americas* 1999. Cemeteries and skeletal remains may be examined in more detail in Roberts, *Human remains in archaeology* 2009; Barber, *The Eastern cemetery of Roman London*, 2000; *The excavation of Khok Phanom Di: a prehistoric site in Central Thailand, 5 the people* 1999.

EXCAVATION IN SPECIAL CONDITIONS

Good examples of wetland archaeology are Fokkens, *Drowned landscape: the occupation of the western part of the Frisian–Drentian Plateau, 4400 BC–AD 500* 1998 and Bell *et al.*, *Prehistoric intertidal archaeology in the Welsh Severn Estuary* 2000, while particularly interesting examples of underwater archaeology are Berti, *Fortuna Maris: la nave romana di Comacchio* 1990 (an astonishingly well-preserved Roman boat from Italy), and McCann and Freed, *Deep water archaeology: a Late-Roman ship from Carthage and an ancient trade route near Skerki Bank off Northwest Sicily* 1994.

CONTEXTS AND FEATURES

Banks and mounds of various forms are included in Whittle, *Sacred mound, holy rings: Silbury Hill and the West Kennet palisade enclosures* 1997, while Stein, *Deciphering a shell midden* 1992, is a good account of a particularly common form of coastal feature. Hill, *Ritual and rubbish in the Iron Age of Wessex: a study on the formation *of a specific archaeological record* 1995, looks closely at interpreting the contents of ditches and pits. Analysis of surfaces and working areas is included in Roberts and Parfitt, *Boxgrove: a Middle Pleistocene hominid site at Eartham Quarry, Boxgrove, West Sussex* 1998.

STRUCTURES AND MATERIALS

A rich variety of materials and structural forms is to be found in books on vernacular architecture, such as Brunskill, *Houses and cottages* 1998. Examples of Roman and Egyptian stone structures are included in Johnson and Haynes, *Architecture in Roman Britain* 1996, and Hodges, *How the pyramids were built* 1993, while wooden buildings can be understood further from case studies in Yeomans, *The development of timber as a structural material* 1999, and Dixon, *Recording timber buildings* 1988. Two complicated examples of the study of standing buildings in Britain concern shops still in use on modern streets in the historic centre of Chester (Brown *et al.*, *Rows of Chester: the Chester Rows research project* 1999) and excavations within and beneath York Minster (Phillips and Heywood, *Excavations at York Minster, 1: Roman to Norman: the Roman legionary fortress and its exploitation in the early Middle Ages* 1995).

RECORDING AND PUBLISHING EXCAVATIONS

Westman, *Museum of London Archaeological Service site manual* 1994, is a good general guide; you will find most excavators in Britain use something similar to the examples provided; some commercial field archaeologists will have their own manuals, usually a version of this one. A good discussion on different ways of recording on-site and the problems with the traditional methods (incorporating some of Hodder's 'reflexive' archaeology) can be found in Chadwick, *Post-processualism, professionalisation and archaeological methodologies: towards reflective and radical practice* 2003. To explore the impact of these methodologies on Hodder's own excavations at Çatalhöyük, see: Hodder, *Çatalhöyük perspectives* 2005a. English Heritage has published on-line guidelines on *Understanding historic buildings* 2006, which outline many of the principles. The on-line archaeology journal *Internet Archaeology* provides examples of the e-publication of fieldwork as well as papers discussing the potential and problems of internet publication in archaeology. Specific guides to archaeological illustration include Collett, *An introduction to drawing archaeological pottery* 2008 and the range of guides produced by the Association of Archaeological Illustrators and Surveyors.

Finally, you can try out excavation for yourself with the help of a CD-ROM supplied with Dibble *et al.*, *Virtual dig: simulated archaeological excavation of a middle Palaeolithic site in France* 2002.

CHAPTER 4

Dating the past

4

Scientific dating techniques have caused dramatic changes in our understanding of prehistory, for example by destroying the traditional framework that related Neolithic and Bronze Age Europe to the Near East, and by adding several million years to the estimated age of tool-making hominins in East Africa. In contrast, historical archaeologists incorporate material evidence into a framework of dates and cultures established from documentary sources; this is not without problems, however, and scientific dating is important in historical periods too. Dating techniques of all kinds are most valuable when applied to objects or samples from properly recorded contexts such as stratified deposits found on excavations. The study of artefacts still requires traditional methods of classification and the use of typology for ordering them in a sequence which, ideally, can then be dated by historical or scientific means.

This chapter will look at the following aspects of archaeological dating:

- A brief review of the **historical development** of dating methods.

- The use of **texts** and **inscriptions** in historical periods.

- The arrangement of artefacts into relative sequences by means of **typology**.

- **Climatostratigraphy**, which uses environmental studies to interpret and date deep-ocean cores, ice cores, varves and pollen.

- **Dendrochronology** (tree-ring dating).

- **Absolute** methods based on radioactivity, notably radiocarbon, potassium-argon, fission track and uranium series, luminescence and Electron spin resonance (ESR).

- **Derivative** (relative) techniques, including bone diagenesis, obsidian hydration and archaeomagnetism.

4.1 BACKGROUND

- key references: Trigger, *A history of archaeological thought* 2006; Renfrew, *Before civilization* 1973; Pollard, 'Measuring the passage of time' 2008; Lucas, *The archaeology of time* 2005.

Dating the past has been a central issue in archaeology throughout its development and remains fundamentally important. Chapter 1 described how, between AD 1500 and 1800, the biblical account of the Creation, the Flood and the peopling of the world had been undermined by European voyages of discovery and the development of geology. By the 1860s Bishop Ussher's date of 4004 BC for the Creation had been largely forgotten, while Darwin's theory of evolution by natural selection had extended the geological perception of the Earth's long, slow development to plants and animals (Van Riper 1993). Enlightenment ideas about social progress were supplemented by Romantic interest in origins and change and, once **prehistory** had been conceptualised, it was rapidly subdivided into ages defined by artefact technology and social evolution. However, one major obstacle remained: even if bones and artefacts *were* carefully excavated from geological or archaeological contexts and recorded in relation to stratification, this only placed them into a relative sequence which had no meaning in terms of absolute time (Chapter 3, p. 100).

Absolute dating in calendar years remained firmly in the hands of archaeologists working on historical periods, initially the Classical civilisations of Greece and Rome, and then Egypt and the Near East as their scripts were deciphered in the early nineteenth century. In contrast, archaeological finds from Scandinavia that had been arranged neatly into three successive ages of stone, bronze and iron were completely undatable until Roman imports began to appear alongside them in the Iron Age. By the early twentieth century some progress had been made in cross-dating prehistoric finds from northern and western Europe to Egypt, often very indirectly. Similar procedures could be carried out in South America, India, China and other parts of the Far East where literate civilisations existed, but elsewhere dating only began with the first contacts between native peoples and European explorers and colonisers. Some hope of establishing absolute dates without historical documents emerged from environmental sciences in the early twentieth century when scientists began counting annual layers of lake sediments or growth of tree rings from the present into the past. Meanwhile, the new science of nuclear physics began to provide radiometric dates for the age of the Earth and the succession of geological ages. Following the development of radiocarbon dating in the 1940s the first absolute dates for prehistory began to be measured from samples of charcoal, wood, bone and other organic materials.

The radiocarbon revolution has continued for more than fifty years, gradually extending both the precision and the range of the technique. A growing number of other scientific methods have been developed for dating inorganic materials, and for extending chronology beyond the reach of radiocarbon, which is increasingly imprecise for samples more than 50,000 years old and virtually unusable by 100,000 years. It is increasingly difficult for prehistorians working in the twenty-first century to conceptualise the problems experienced by their predecessors, and approaches to interpretation before the 1960s are consistently criticised. Culture history and diffusionism may, with hindsight, seem excessively preoccupied with classification and social evolution and to have applied unsophisticated historical interpretations instead of asking fundamental questions about human behaviour (Chapter 6, p. 258). However, their exponents did not have the luxury of a global framework of independent, absolute dates; the difficulties they faced may be appreciated by looking more closely at typology and cross-dating.

4.2 TYPOLOGY AND CROSS-DATING

- key references: Graslund, *The birth of prehistoric chronology* 1987; Biers, *Art, artefacts and chronology in classical archaeology* 1992: 25–60; O'Brien and Lyman, *Seriation, stratigraphy and index fossils* 1999.

It is difficult for today's students of archaeology to imagine an era when chronometric dating methods – radiocarbon or thermoluminescence, for example – were unavailable. How, they might ask, were archaeologists working in the pre-radiocarbon era able to keep track of time; that is, how were they able to place objects and sites in proper sequence and to assess the ages of sites and objects?

(O'Brien and Lyman 1999: v)

It must be made clear at the outset that typology is, strictly speaking, not a dating method but a means of placing artefacts into some kind of order. Classification divides things up for the purposes of description, whereas typology seeks to identify and analyse changes that will allow artefacts to be placed into sequences (Fig. 4.1–2). This procedure had been carried out for living plants and animals by the eighteenth century, and geologists

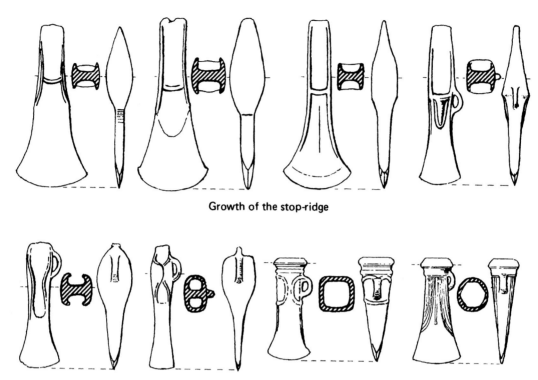

Growth of the stop-ridge

Growth of the wings

Figure 4.1 Typology. Further changes in the design of axes illustrated in Fig. 1.10 took place during the middle and later Bronze Age. Pitt Rivers outlined some technical factors in 1875 (Lane Fox 1875: 507, using the nineteenth-century term celt for these axes), but also stressed the importance of non-functional decoration: '… the bronze *celt* was furnished with a stop to prevent its being pressed too far into the handle by the blow. Others were furnished with projecting flanges to prevent them from swerving by the blow when hafted on a bent stick. Others had both stops and flanges. By degrees the flanges were bent over the stops and over the handle, and then the central portion above the stops, being no longer required, became thinner, and ultimately disappeared, the flanges closed on each other, and by this means the weapon grew into the socket celt. On this socket celt you will see that there is sometimes a semicircular ornamentation on each side. This … is a vestige of the overlapping flange of the earlier forms out of which it grew, which, like the rings on our brass cannon, are survivals of parts formerly serving for special uses.' (AVC, Newcastle University, after Smith 1920)

extended the technique to fossils. As with finds from archaeological excavations, studies of fossils were greatly assisted by observing **stratification**, which provided independent evidence for the direction of a developmental sequence from the lowest (earliest) levels to the latest (Chapter 3, p. 90–2). The adoption of an evolutionary approach to fossils influenced studies of artefacts, which were sometimes treated as if they were organisms that could interbreed. Thus, although in the nineteenth century Pitt Rivers wrote extensively about typology, his evolutionary ideas about its universal validity were too abstract to have

any chronological promise (Chapter 1, p. 25–6). An enduring problem with typology (familiar to evolutionary biologists before DNA clarified matters) is where to draw dividing lines between **types**, especially where one merges imperceptibly into another. Solutions may reveal fundamental differences in outlook – do types of artefact really exist for us to discover, or are our descriptive systems simply arbitrary impositions? 'The trap is the essentialist–materialist paradox' (O'Brien and Lyman 1999: 225).

From the 1880s, in Sweden, Montelius advanced typology towards actual dating by

Figure 4.2 A socketed bronze axe (similar to those at the end of Pitt Rivers' sequence) mounted on a modern wooden handle; leather strips hold it in place with the help of an integral loop on one side of the axe. Development of such copper alloy axes ended at this point, for the introduction of iron from c. 1000 BC provided a superior metal with radically different manufacturing techniques for making tools with sharp edges or blades. (GNM Hancock, Newcastle upon Tyne)

publishing comprehensive classifications and typologies of European artefacts; each form was arranged in a **type-series**, which normally developed from simplicity towards greater elaboration or efficiency (Fig. 4.1). He also sought **associations** between artefacts of different forms that had been buried together, such as an assortment of items deposited as grave goods in an individual burial, or a collection of objects buried in a ritual deposit or hoard. This allowed him to link different type-series together and to define phases of the past characterised by a range of artefacts at a particular stage of development (Åström 1995).

The most difficult part of Montelius' work was to **date** these prehistoric phases. The technique that he used is known as **cross-dating** (or **synchronism**) which, while entirely logical in theory, turned out to be misleading. In its strongest form, cross-dating looks for artefacts from historically-dated areas, such as Egypt or Mesopotamia, that have been imported into undated areas and found in association with local artefacts. An obvious limitation was that no historical dates extended beyond 3000 BC, so that the age of earlier artefacts could only be guessed. In 1891 Flinders Petrie identified pottery imported from Crete in Egyptian contexts dating to around 1900 BC; this date could then be applied to similar pottery found in Crete (Fig. 4.3). He subsequently recognised Egyptian artefacts dated to c. 1500 BC which had been imported into Mycenae on mainland Greece (Drower 1985: 182–5). Thus, dates derived from Egyptian historical records were extended to sites and cultures in Crete and Greece that lacked internal dating evidence. Whereas Petrie's links were based on direct associations with Egyptian material, Montelius extended cross-dating indirectly across Europe into Britain and Scandinavia by noting local artefacts associated with imports from other areas where cross-dating had been applied (Fig. 4.4).

Although these fixed points allowed phases of types in different areas to be dated, every step away from Egypt increased the possibility of a weak link in the chain. Furthermore, an independently-dated artefact imported into another area only provides a *terminus post quem* – a fixed point *after* which the context in which it was discovered was deposited (Chapter 3, p. 101). Objects imported from distant sources might have been treasured for long periods before being lost or buried with local items. Even worse, superficially similar artefacts found in different areas might have been entirely unconnected, and not contemporary at all. Confidence in Montelius' cross-dating was enhanced by a diffusionist belief that all cultural advances in Europe were inspired by earlier developments within civilisations of the Aegean and the Near East (Chapter 6, p. 260). This view survived until the 1960s, when radiocarbon dates broke the links between south-eastern Europe and the Near East and forced a

Figure 4.3 Cross-dating by pottery: Arthur Evans used imported Egyptian artefacts to date his excavation of the Palace of Knossos in Crete (Fig. 3.2). Local Cretan pottery found on his site could also be dated because similar sherds had been found in Egypt. A, B and D are from Crete and bear decoration of Evans' Latest Middle Minoan II Phase, while C was found at Kahun in Egypt. (Evans 1921: Fig. 198)

re-evaluation of ways in which major sites, such as Stonehenge or megalithic tombs, might have been the outcome of developments *within* prehistoric societies rather than a result of external influences (**Fig. 4.4**; Renfrew 1973a).

The traditional approach to classifying artefacts according to shape and placing them into some kind of order through typological observations of changes in their form remains sound. It is made much easier by modern excavation procedures in which findspots of artefacts are carefully recorded, and can be related to a stratigraphic sequence (Chapter 3, p. 100). Typologies can be used for understanding the technological and stylistic development of artefacts, as well as for dating. Some objects made from organic materials can even be dated directly using the **Accelerator Mass Spectrometry** (AMS) radiocarbon technique (below: p. 168) because it only requires small samples (**Fig. 4.5–6**). Association and cross-dating remain important in historical archaeology. Roman metalwork, pottery, glass

and coins were traded to Scandinavia, Central Europe and even India, where they still provide valuable dates when found associated with local artefacts (Tomber 2008). Apart from coins, Roman artefacts are only datable themselves because of several centuries of classification and typological study of finds from sites, such as Pompeii, that can be related to historical records.

The principle of cross-dating is also employed in scientific contexts; radiocarbon dating was tested initially on samples of known historical age from Egypt before it could be used with confidence in prehistory. Historically-dated material is even more important for creating fixed points by which relative dating methods, such as archaeomagnetism, may be converted into calendar years (below: p. 184). Occasionally natural phenomena may be used for cross-dating; in volcanic areas **tephrochronology** is possible if ash deposits from a number of sites in a region can be related to a specific eruption. If that eruption can be dated by its effect on tree rings or ice cores,

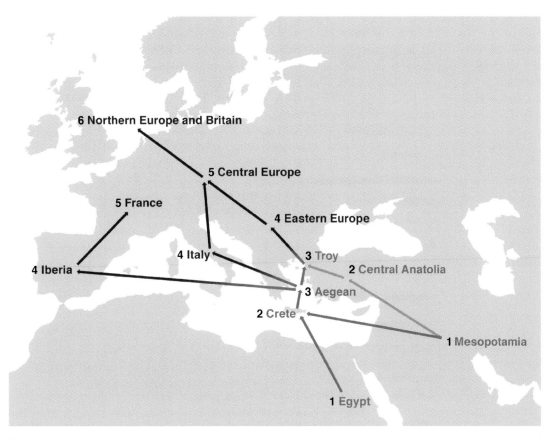

Figure 4.4 Diffusionism. Archaeologists like Oscar Montelius or Gordon Childe envisaged a spread of cultural influences and innovations from the civilisations of the Near East into prehistoric Europe. This view was based on apparent connections between the typologies of artefacts found in these regions, but by the 1970s radiocarbon dates had broken the chronological sequence of links between stages 3 and 4. A complete reconsideration of phenomena such as the use of metals and the building of megalithic tombs was required when their origins and spread could no longer be attributed simply to diffusion (**Box. 6.1**). (Chris Unwin, after Renfrew 1973a)

sites may be dated and shown to be contemporary. Furthermore, the layer of ash will provide a valuable marker in stratigraphic sequences on excavations (Branch *et al.* 2005: 166–9; see **Box 4.5**).

4.2.1 Sequence dating and seriation

- key reference: O'Brien and Lyman, *Seriation, stratigraphy and index fossils* 1999.

Sequence dating and seriation techniques both place assemblages of artefacts into relative order. Petrie used sequence dating to work back from the earliest historical phases of Egypt into pre-dynastic Neolithic times, using groups of contemporary artefacts deposited together in graves at a single time (Petrie 1899; Drower 1985: 251–4). 'Early' and 'late' artefacts, such as changing forms of pottery, were defined by typological judgements such as those used by Montelius or Pitt Rivers. Grave groups were then arranged in a sequence according to their combinations of artefacts of early or late character, in a kind of 'simultaneous typology' that considered the development of every item found in each grave. Petrie's graphs of pottery types from a sequence of fifty pre-dynastic phases showed that types did not appear and disappear abruptly, but became popular gradually before declining equally gradually (Petrie 1920: pl. L). A modern

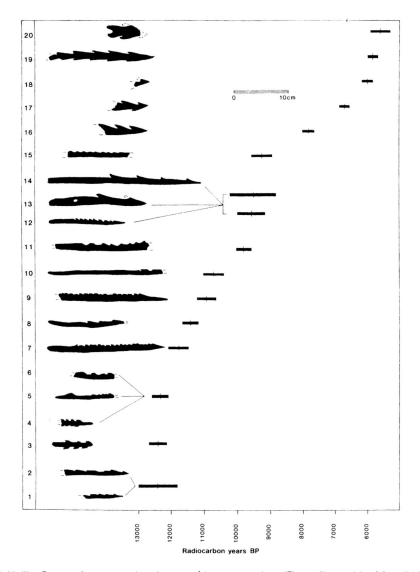

Figure 4.5 Unlike Bronze Age axes, the shapes of harpoon points (Fig. 4.6) used by Mesolithic hunters in Britain after the end of the last Ice Age show no clear typological development. However, small samples of the bone from which they were made can now be dated by the AMS radiocarbon technique, and these dates may be used to place them into chronological order. (Smith 1997: Fig. 1.2)

Figure 4.6 A Mesolithic bone harpoon point from Whitburn, Tyne and Wear; its length is 87.5 mm and, although it has not been radiocarbon dated, it was probably made more than six thousand years ago. (GNM Hancock, Newcastle upon Tyne)

analogy can be found in any car park in 2010, where there will be a few examples of the latest cars, many from the 2000s, and a much smaller number from the 1990s; even the best-selling models from the 1980s will be seen very rarely.

Seriation was developed in the USA to place in order finds from strata or other kinds of assemblages such as potsherds collected from site surfaces; O'Brien and Lyman (1999) have devoted a large part of a book to drawing distinctions between varieties of approaches. Seriation works best when assemblages contain several distinctive artefact types, such as pottery or flints, which are subject to typological change (**Box 4.1**). The artefacts are counted and converted into percentages to make them comparable. If a collection of sherds from the surface of Site 1 contains 10 per cent of pot type A and 90 per cent of type B, while Site 2 has 90 per cent of A and 10 per cent of B, it may be assumed that they are of different dates, and that, over time, type A gradually became more popular than type B or *vice versa*. If another site nearby was found to have 50 per cent of each type it would be reasonable to assume that it was dated somewhere between Sites 1 and 2. Thus, the series of sites was either 1–3–2 or 2–3–1; ideally some independent dating evidence would indicate in which direction the series ran. Seriation can, of course, be applied to much larger numbers of assemblages and they do not need to have come from the same site. Larger numbers could be arranged into the best possible sequence on the assumption that percentages of artefact types increased and declined in the orderly manner observed by Petrie in Egypt. Seriation was carried out by eye, with percentages marked on individual strips of graph paper to represent each assemblage; the strips could be shuffled to find the best sequence (O'Brien and Lyman 1999: 125; **Box. 4.1**). Returning to the modern analogy, a mixed-up set of photographs of car parks taken over several decades in one country could be arranged into order by counting the frequency of different models and changing fashions for colour and bodywork styles. Random statistical variations and differences in the character of assemblages made it rare for the results to form perfect 'battleship

curves' showing the appearance, popularity and decline of each type. Seriation is a relative dating method, like artefact typology, and its use was refined and overtaken by sequences established independently by stratigraphic excavation or, more recently, by a framework of historical and scientifically determined dates.

4.3 HISTORICAL DATING

- key references: Biers, *Art, artefacts and chronology in classical archaeology* 1992; Beaudry, *Documentary archaeology in the new world* 1987; Forsberg, *Near Eastern destruction datings* 1995; Lucas, 'Historical archaeology and time' 2006.

Prehistorians sometimes overestimate the accuracy and detail of frameworks based on historical evidence; in practice, early written sources may provide little more information than a scatter of radiocarbon dates. The extent of documentation varied considerably in 'historical' cultures, and the information that survives is determined by a variety of factors. People write about a restricted range of subjects that seem significant at the time, and their successors only preserve what is still of interest. Old documents were rarely copied accurately and were frequently edited or rewritten to introduce a new point of view. Historical writing normally has a clear purpose, either to represent an event, an individual or a regime in a good or bad light (depending on the writer's attitude), or to use history to make a particular philosophical or religious point. Thus, before any written information about the past may be exploited for archaeology it is necessary to consider several factors: the date and quality of surviving manuscripts; the distance (in time and place) of the author from the events described; the author's record of accuracy if items can be checked independently; the quality of the sources available to the writer; and any personal biases or motives that might have led the writer to present a particular version of events.

In the case of Britain the invasion of AD 43 is described by several historians, including Tacitus,

BOX 4.1   # Using seriation: Native American sites in New York State

Native American sites in New York State, USA, can be arranged into a hypothetical sequence according to finds of stone tools and pottery. The technique assumes that artefacts appear, grow in popularity, decline and disappear in an orderly manner, and that individual types do not replace each other straight away but overlap. This results in what are sometimes called 'battleship' curves of the appearance and disappearance of artefacts.

The transition from Fox Creek to Levanna projectile points is particularly clear and the direction of the sequence is supported by radiocarbon dates that place Fredenburg in the fourth century AD and Black Rock in the ninth. The technique does make a fundamental assumption about the comparability of the sites, however; might some differences in proportion of artefacts reflect differences in function, rather than their date? (Chris Unwin, after Funk 1976: 282–3)

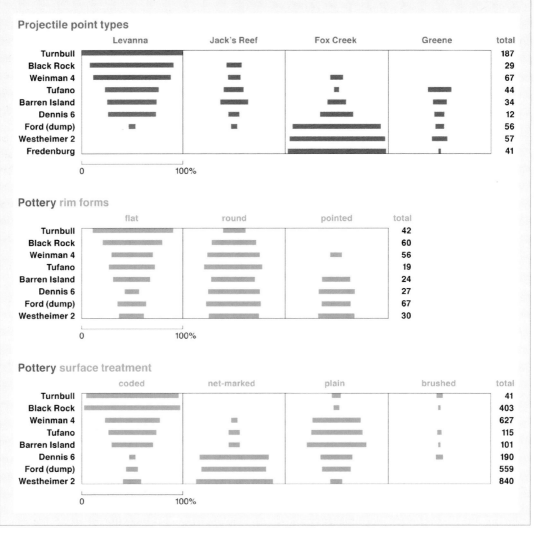

who wrote a comprehensive history of the first century AD. Tacitus also wrote a biography of Agricola (governor of Britain AD 77–84), who apparently completed the conquest of Wales and subdued northern England and Scotland for the first time. While documents such as Tacitus' *Annals* and *Agricola* were written by one person with a direct historical purpose, medieval chronicles often accumulated over many centuries in monasteries. Other forms of documents such as laws, land-charters, wills, accounts and trivial correspondence were written for short-term functions rather than posterity. This kind of material is often preserved in archive offices and is plentiful in recent periods. In addition to having a general historical outline, postmedieval archaeologists may find precise dates for sites and structures in company accounts, building designs and estate maps (Hicks and Beaudry 2006). They may well be able to read personal accounts written by or about people who lived at a site that they are studying. Rembrandt's house in Amsterdam has been painstakingly restored partly with the help of his paintings of the interior, but primarily thanks to the survival of a complete inventory of its contents drawn up when he became bankrupt and was forced to move out in 1658.

Documents may be discovered in archaeological excavations. Thousands of clay tablets with cuneiform inscriptions had been found in Mesopotamia before Rawlinson deciphered their script. Everything from the lost works of Greek poets to letters full of gossip have been recovered, written on fragments of papyrus, from the desiccated rubbish tips of Graeco–Roman cities in Egypt (Bagnall 1995). The Vindolanda tablets, a collection of letters and administrative documents written on thin sheets of wood, had been thrown away at a Roman fort in Northumberland and miraculously preserved in a waterlogged context (Bowman 2003). Inscriptions carved on stone were particularly important in Egypt, the Greek and Roman world and Mesoamerica; their content ranges from terse building dedications giving the date and builder's name to lengthy historical, religious or legal material (**Fig. 4.7**). Literate societies such as the Roman Empire produced many other forms of writing that survive on archaeological sites, such as makers' names stamped on tiles and pottery (Harris 1993). These all have the advantage of being **primary documents** that have not been copied many times over the centuries by scribes who might introduce fresh errors at every stage.

4.3.1 Applying historical dates to sites

- key reference: Biers, *Art, artefacts and chronology in classical archaeology* 1992: 61–74.

One of the most precise examples of historical dating is the burial of Pompeii and Herculaneum by the eruption of Vesuvius in August AD 79. Pliny the Younger, son of Pliny the Elder (a noted natural scientist), wrote an eye-witness account of the event in which his father was killed. The volcanic deposits that sealed these cities provide a *terminus ante quem*: everything found beneath them must be *earlier* than AD 79. Objects in use at the time of the eruption (such as pottery vessels left on a table) are particularly well dated, but because these towns had been in existence for several centuries, finds from uncertain contexts could be much older. Destruction rarely has such an obvious cause as a volcano. If a context containing burnt debris and broken artefacts is excavated on a site from a historical period, it is tempting to search the local historical framework for references to warfare or a disaster in the region, and to date the excavated context accordingly. Unfortunately, historical information is patchy, and even if an apparently relevant reference is found, there might have been other unrecorded episodes that could account for the remains. In any case, buildings, and even whole towns, do burn down accidentally (for example, parts of London in 1666). If an excavated context and the artefacts that it contains are matched with the wrong historical episode, then subsequent cross-dating will apply inaccurate dates to other sites.

Thera, a Bronze Age town on the island of Santorini in the Aegean, has been compared to Pompeii because it was buried by an enormous

Figure 4.7 This stone slab, which is just over one metre long, is a primary source for dating the construction of Hadrian's Wall. It was found in the 1750s at the site of a milecastle that formed part of the original plan for the Wall and probably once adorned its gateway. It was common for this kind of dedication slab to be carved to mark the completion of a Roman building. The inscription states: 'This work of the Emperor Caesar Trajan Hadrian Augustus (was built by) the Second Legion Augusta under Aulus Platorius Nepos, propraetorian legate'. It associates the Wall not just with Hadrian but with Nepos, governor of Britain from AD 122 to 126 and shows that the first phase of the frontier structure had been completed early in Hadrian's reign (AD 117–38). This historical dating evidence may then be used in the study of artefacts found in the milecastle. (RIB 1638 (Collingwood and Wright 1965: 520); GNM Hancock, Newcastle upon Tyne)

volcanic eruption, but there is no documentary evidence for its date (Doumas 1983). Since the 1930s, destruction had been dated to around 1500 BC by cross-dating local 'LMIA' (Late Minoan IA) pottery to Egypt. The same eruption was thought to have destroyed several Minoan palaces on Crete, providing a valuable dating horizon for the Aegean Bronze Age through destruction levels and tephrochronology (identification of volcanic ash, see Box 4.4). The analogy between Thera and Pompeii proved to be misleading, however; most scientific techniques now favour a date for the Santorini eruption before 1600 BC and do not support a correlation with events in Crete, which do not even seem to have been contemporary with each other (Forsyth 1997; Manning *et al.* 2006). Some have equated the eruption with a volcanic episode detected in Greenland ice cores at around 1645 BC, which others would claim is

also observable (and precisely dated) in tree rings at 1628 BC. However, the chemistry of the volcanic ash in Greenland does not unambiguously match that of Thera and it could be the result of an entirely different volcano (Baillie 1998c; Pearce *et al.* 2007) (Fig. 4.9). Examination of a range of radiocarbon dates using Bayesian statistics (below: p. 175) has indicated that some of these earlier suggestions, such as the 1645 BC date, do not match the radiocarbon dates and that it should be dated later, to around 1625–1600 BC (Manning *et al.* 2006). Dincauze's broader summary of the problems is still pertinent when she asks:

> Why is this so important? Why have so many excellent investigations been directed to this enigma? The entire east-Mediterranean Bronze Age chronology rides on the results, since the validity of the traditional chronology based on links with Egypt is now strongly challenged. If LMIA is earlier than 1500 BC, the entire archaeological scenario for the Bronze Age must be extensively revised and lengthened, with implications for connections in all directions.
>
> (Dincauze 2000: 134)

Whatever the true date may be, all forms of historical and scientific dating are vulnerable to the same risk: 'Any sloppily dated archaeological event, within a century or so, tends to be "sucked in" to the precisely dated tree-ring events. We all have to be on our guard against circular arguments' (Baillie 1989: 313).

Cross-dating is used extensively in the study of sites and artefacts in historical periods. Roman Germany provides a good sequence of forts established between the late first century BC and the later second century AD, resulting from advances and retreats along the Rhine and Danube. Sites of the first century AD are particularly useful, as new forts and frontier lines may be dated fairly closely with the help of Tacitus, who wrote about military events towards the end of the century. By the early twentieth century, German archaeologists had worked out detailed typologies for

BOX 4.2 **Which dating technique?**

The leading scientific dating methods are applicable to widely differing periods of the past. In the upper image, each horizontal bar indicates the range of an individual method; interrupted bars show periods where the potential is less good. Techniques with the greatest timespan are not necessarily the most useful, as examination of the lower chart reveals. The lower chart provides a summary of materials that can be examined by different scientific dating techniques; the best results will be obtained from the techniques and samples with the darkest shading. Thus, wood and other plants usually respond well to dendrochronology and radiocarbon, but no other techniques are applicable. Conversely, volcanic materials are unsuitable for either of these methods but offer many other possibilities. Archaeologists must have an understanding of these charts if they are to take the right kinds of sample for dating methods, appropriate to the period with which they are concerned; there is likely to be little point, for example, in taking radiocarbon samples if you are working on a site suspected to be hundreds of thousands of years old (Chris Unwin, after Aitken 1990, derived from various sources).

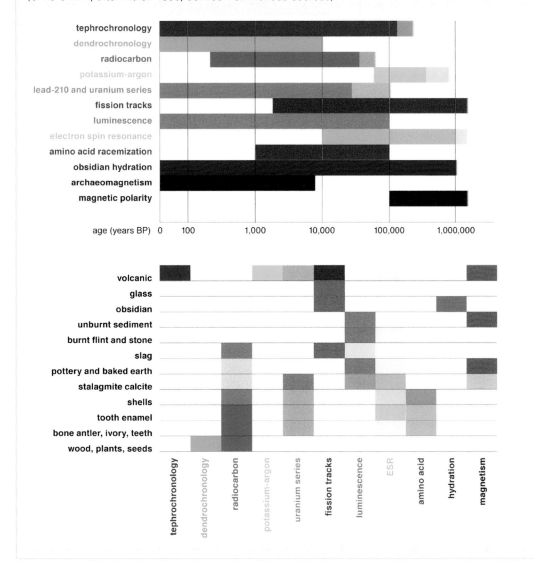

pottery and other artefacts by comparing finds from successive dated forts which could then be applied to undated sites where similar artefacts were discovered. Wheeler's use of Roman and local material for cross-dating near Pondicherry in India in 1945 was only possible because 'Arretine' tableware found there (imported from Italy) had already been classified, arranged in typological series and dated on early military sites in Germany (Wheeler 1954a: 119–25; Tomber 2008). **Coins** provide useful corroboration of typological and historical dates when found in excavated contexts in the Roman period and at other times and places where they were in sufficiently general use to be lost on sites in significant numbers (Burnett 1991).

4.4 SCIENTIFIC DATING TECHNIQUES

- key references: Brothwell and Pollard, *Handbook of archaeological sciences* 2001: 1–100; Pollard, 'Measuring the passage of time' 2008; Taylor and Aitken, *Chronometric dating* 1997; Buck and Millard, *Tools for constructing chronologies* 2004.

The transformation of archaeological dating that began around 1950 continues, but archaeologists may overlook the revolution in scientific dating that had already taken place in geology during the first half of the twentieth century. From this wider perspective, the emergence of radiocarbon dating may seem slightly less dramatic. Frederick Zeuner's book *Dating the past: an introduction to geochronology* (first published in 1946) integrated geological dating with archaeology in an exemplary manner and gives a vivid impression of the difficulties and triumphs of archaeological dating as it emerged from the nineteenth century. The text was updated and expanded several times up to 1958, by which time Zeuner was able to document the introduction of new techniques such as radiocarbon and potassium–argon dating. Zeuner began with techniques applicable to the recent past and worked back towards

measurement of the age of the Earth; in contrast, Martin Aitken's survey, *Science-based dating in archaeology* (1990), is organised according to the scientific basis of each technique. We will follow Aitken's sequence, since it was retained in a major overview edited by Taylor and Aitken in 1997.

4.4.1 Geological timescales

- key references: Dalrymple, *The age of the earth* 1991; Herz and Garrison, *Geological methods* 1998.

Nineteenth-century geologists were preoccupied with the age of the Earth and accepting the Darwinian theory of evolution made it necessary to believe that it took place over very long periods of time. Glimpses of 'deep time' could be gained by estimating the rate of erosion of geological formations; Darwin suggested it took 300 million years just to produce the modern form of the South Downs. However, an estimate of at most 100 million years for the entire age of the Earth, based on the rate of cooling of the planet, was made by the influential physicist Lord Kelvin (1824–1907), and was widely accepted (Burchfield 1975). The problem was solved by a growing understanding of radioactivity and by measurement of the rate at which uranium decayed to produce lead. From 1910 Arthur Holmes and other scientists used radiometric dating to revise the age of pre-Cambrian rocks to nearly 2,000 million years. Thus, estimates of geological time went from informed guesswork to scientific precision in little more than fifty years following the publication of Darwin's *Origin of species* in 1859. Accurate knowledge of the age of the Earth was of little direct help to archaeologists, but it emphasised the potential of scientific dating techniques. The first half of the twentieth century witnessed similar progress that began with the dating of recent geological periods in which early hominins lived, and ended with the introduction of radiocarbon dating. By 1960 absolute dates were available for important stages of recent prehistory, such as the inception of farming and the first use of metals.

4.4.2 Climatostratigraphy

- key references: Lowe, 'Quaternary geochronological frameworks' 2001; Aitken and Stokes, 'Climatostratigraphy' 1997; Imbrie, *Ice ages* 1979.

While some geologists concentrated on the age of the Earth, others studied distinctive surface traces left behind by changes in the extent of polar ice during the most recent (Quaternary) geological period. They identified a succession of Ice Ages alternating with temperate conditions (glacials and interglacials) which, if they could be dated, would reveal much about the evolution of early humans in the context of changing environmental conditions. A solution suggested during the mid-1800s, and reinforced by Milankovitch in the early twentieth century, was that glacials coincided with changes in solar radiation caused by regular (and therefore measurable) variations in the Earth's orbit (Dincauze 2000: 43, fig. 3.1). This independent dating method remained hypothetical until environmental records from ocean-bed deposits and elsewhere could be checked by absolute methods, notably potassium–argon dating, between the 1950s and 1970s (Aitken 1990: 17–23). Any environmental sequences affected by global climatic change – for example pollen, layers of ice at the polar caps or wind-blown loess soil deposits – that show the characteristic alternating peaks and troughs of glacials and interglacials can now be fine-tuned in relation to orbital changes and dated to within 10,000 years, using the SPECMAP timescale (Lowe 2001: 15–17) **(Fig. 4.8)**. This degree of precision is perfectly adequate for general geological and climatological purposes or the earlier parts of human prehistory; fortunately greater accuracy can be achieved with the help of other dating methods in more recent periods.

Seabed deposits
- key references: Aitken and Stokes, 'Climatostratigraphy' 1997: 8–13; Dincauze, *Environmental archaeology* 2000: 169–73.

Cores extracted from ocean floor deposits reveal variations in oxygen isotopes (in the shells and skeletal material of dead marine creatures) which reflect fluctuations in global temperature and the volume of the ocean. Ice ages lock up enormous amounts of water in glaciers; because of the chemistry of water and ice-formation, frozen water contains a greater number of 'lighter' oxygen isotopes (^{16}O) than sea-water, which has more ^{18}O. Thus, changes in the relative numbers of these isotopes (the oxygen isotope ratio) can be plotted, together with temperature-sensitive species of marine fauna, to reveal a pattern of climatic variations, which may be dated according to deviations in the Earth's orbit as described above. A record of 116 marine isotope stages has been defined covering the last three million years. In addition, seabed sediments contain iron particles that show changes in the Earth's magnetic field and occasional north–south reversals, which are also known from geological studies on land. These have been dated by the potassium–argon method where associated with suitable volcanic material (see below: p. 176), and dated reversals have been important in the validation of the astronomical dating of the isotopic stages (Lowe 2001: 13–15). Thanks to these integrated studies, geologists and archaeologists interested in the earliest stages of human development now possess a continuous record of global temperature and magnetism. Thus, bones or tools associated with early hominins recovered from geological deposits in East Africa are not only datable but also can be related to environmental conditions that might have triggered major changes ('climatic cycles and behavioural revolutions': Sherratt 1997b). These deep-sea cores reveal that rapid changes in climate took place in the last 100,000 years, changes which are important for archaeologists studying changes in past societies and cultures (Pettitt 2005: 344).

Ice cores
- key references: Aitken and Stokes, 'Climatostratigraphy' 1997: 13–19; Dincauze, *Environmental archaeology* 2000: 174–6.

A datable record of climatic change in relatively recent periods has been recovered from cores up to 3 km long, extracted from the ice sheets

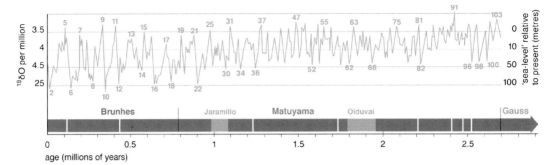

Figure 4.8 Climatostratigraphy is a multidisciplinary approach to determining the timescale of long-term environmental changes. These include reversals of the Earth's magnetic poles detectable in the magnetic properties of geological strata, sediments on land, and cores extracted from the seabed. When these reversals are associated with layers of freshly formed volcanic ash they can be dated using the potassium–argon technique. Magnetic reversals can also be correlated with fluctuations between warm and cold climatic conditions detectable in the chemistry of marine shells recovered from seabed cores (marine isotope stages). The SPECMAP temperature peaks may then be dated according to a regular cycle of deviations of the Earth's orbit and axis that affected its climate by varying the amount of solar radiation it received (see also **Box. 5.1**). (Chris Unwin, based primarily on Lowe 2001: Fig. 1.1)

of Greenland and elsewhere. Winter snowfall creates distinct annual layers that are visible for around 6,000 years in the upper parts of cores and may be counted reliably to within around fifty years. Deeper layers are too compressed to be distinguishable by eye, but analysis of fluctuations in dust, acidity and the oxygen isotope ratio still reveals an annual record going back 80,000 years. Thus, long-term patterns of climatic variation can be correlated with marine cores, while short-term fluctuations allow more precise interpretation of rapid environmental changes. Volcanoes known from historical records, such as Krakatoa (1883) or Vesuvius (AD 79), can be correlated with ice cores and provide support for their chronology by cross-dating (**Fig. 4.9**). Undocumented prehistoric eruptions may also be detected which, ideally, would provide dates for archaeological sites where **tephra** (volcanic ash) has been found – especially if the eruption can be correlated with tree rings showing abnormal growth patterns (see **Box 4.5**).

4.4.3 Varves

- key references: Hicks *et al.*, *Laminated sediments* 1994; Aitken, *Science-based dating* 1990: 35–6.

During four decades de Geer's varve chronology remained an invaluable tool the significance of which for prehistory and geochronology is all too easily overlooked today.

(Butzer 1971: 188)

Every summer the melting of glaciers causes erosion by streams and rivers and the resulting sediments are eventually deposited on lake beds. The sediments become sparser and finer as the year progresses, as the flow of water is reduced when temperatures begin to fall; winter freezing then stops erosion until the next summer. Sections cut through lake beds in glacial regions reveal a regular annual pattern of coarse and fine layers, known as **varves**. Variations in climate produced observable differences in the thickness of sediments and, like the patterns of variation in tree rings, this allows matches to be made between deposits in separate lake beds. Varves had been recognised and understood as early as the 1870s in Sweden. From 1905 onwards Baron Gerhard de Geer carried out extensive fieldwork with the aim of establishing a continuous sequence from overlapping deposits preserved in the beds of the hundreds of lakes that formed during the retreat of glaciers after the last Ice Age. Whereas tree rings can be counted back from a tree felled

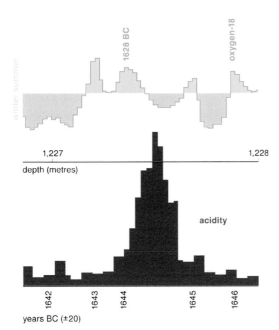

Figure 4.9 Major volcanic eruptions affect the atmosphere by emitting large quantities of acidic ash which may be detected through abnormal acidity in layers within cores taken from deep ice-sheets in Greenland. Even when the annual layers are not clearly visible, the pattern of yearly temperature variation is indicated by changes in oxygen isotope levels. Here, an eruption that left its mark around 1644±20 BC is likely to be the same event that caused damage to trees in rings dated to 1628 BC. It has been assumed that this was the explosion of Thera in the Aegean, but the evidence from the ice-core is far from incontrovertible and has been hotly debated (Hammer 2003; Keenan 2003). (Chris Unwin, after Aitken 1990: Fig. 2.10)

today, de Geer lacked a secure fixed point at the end of his sequence. A set of 3,000 varves from a lake known to have been drained in AD 1796 gave an approximate pointer and he published a sequence, covering around 12,000 years, in 1912. This sequence was finally linked to the present with the help of modern deposits from river valleys in central Sweden (Zeuner 1952: 20–45).

Varves allowed the end of the last Ice Age to be dated with confidence to around 8750 BC and introduced the first calendar dates into European prehistory. They also made it possible to date individual sites if their positions could be related to former lakes or seashores. Even more important, varves provided a means of dating

the sequence of changes in vegetation known from pollen analysis that was vitally important before radiocarbon dating was introduced in the 1950s. Finally, ice cores and varves provided an additional way of checking the reliability of radiocarbon dating in periods beyond the range of samples from precisely dated tree rings. The date of signs of abrupt climatic change in ice cores and varves around 8750 BC is underestimated by approximately 700 years by radiocarbon dating, underlining the need for radiocarbon years to be converted to calendar years with the help of a calibration curve (below: p. 172). Varves also contribute information to archaeomagnetic dating because their iron-rich clay particles contain a record of the Earth's magnetic field (below: p. 184).

4.4.4 Palynostratigraphy

- key references: Branch *et al.*, *Environmental archaeology* 2005: 159–60; Dincauze, Environmental archaeology 2000: 343–62; Dimbleby, *The palynology of archaeological sites* 1985.

Microscopic wind-blown pollen grains survive well in many soil conditions, and pollen that has accumulated in deep deposits, such as peat bogs, can provide a long-term record of changes in vegetation; suitable samples may be collected from soils exposed by excavation, or from cores extracted from bogs. Work in Scandinavia in the 1920s confirmed a pattern of climatic changes since the last Ice Age that had already been proposed from visible plant remains. These changes were also found in samples taken from varves, which meant that climatic fluctuations since the end of the Ice Age could be dated. The value of this technique for archaeology lay in the fact that broad climatic phases were likely to have been fairly uniform; thus, pollen found in samples of soil from an archaeological site anywhere in north-western Europe could be related to the established sequence. Correlations could also be made between sites in different countries that belonged to the same pollen phase without relying on dubious cross-dating of artefacts. Even individual artefacts could be dated if found in peat bogs, or if sufficient soil adhered to them for samples of pollen to be extracted. For example, a Mesolithic bone harpoon dredged from the bottom of the North Sea was placed into the period when pine was declining in favour of trees that preferred warmer conditions; this was dated by varves to around 7000 BC (Zeuner 1946: 91–2). There are problems with this method, including the problems of pollen dispersal (see p. 200), and the existence of microclimates may mean correlations are not always accurate (Branch *et al.* 2005: 160). Pollen analysis has not been used for dating sites and artefacts since radiocarbon methods became available in the 1950s. It remains, however, a very important part of environmental archaeology (see Chapter 5).

4.4.5 Dendrochronology

- key references: Kuniholm, 'Dendrochronology' 2001; Dean, 'Dendrochronology' 1997; Baillie, *A slice through time* 1995; Schweingrüber, *Trees and wood in dendrochronology* 1993; Čufar, 'Dendrochronology and past human activity' 2007.

Tree-ring dating is presented here, rather than with the absolute techniques described below, because it resembles the methods described above in that it is based on a regular biological process and is influenced by environmental conditions. It has been recognised since at least the fifteenth century that trees produce annual growth rings; their physiology was understood by the eighteenth century (Schweingrüber 1987: 256–7). It was also realised that rings could be counted to calculate the age of a tree when it was felled. Because the thickness of these rings is affected by annual climatic factors, distinctive sequences of rings may be recognised in different samples of timber and used to establish their contemporaneity (**Fig. 4.10**; **Box 4.3**). In addition to the thickness of tree rings, measurements may also include the density of the wood. This allows dendrochronology to be extended to so-called 'complacent' tree species with annual rings that vary little in width. Well-documented examples

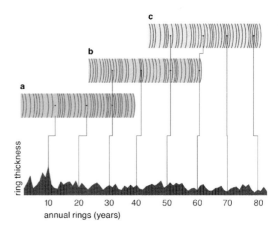

Figure 4.10 Dating by dendrochronology. A, B and C are sections from three different trees showing annual growth rings that cover a period of 83 years from the innermost ring at the left of timber A to the outermost of C. The overlapping (contemporary) portions of the timbers can be matched by observing similarities in the pattern of their rings, especially when unusually wide or narrow rings reflect particularly good or bad growing seasons for the trees. The graph records the average annual ring thickness for each year, allowing for the fact that the outer rings are always narrower than the inner because their volume of wood is spread thinly around a large trunk. Long overlapping sequences from dated timbers provide a reference graph against which individual undated samples can be compared. Thus, if this graph began in AD 1000, timber B was felled in AD 1060 and this is a *terminus post quem* for any structure into which it was incorporated. (Drawn by Chris Unwin)

of tree-ring dating begin in North America in the late eighteenth century; for example, the Reverend Cutler counted 463 rings in a tree that had grown on a Native American burial mound at Marietta in Ohio and deduced (correctly) that the mound must predate Columbus (Daniel 1981: 40–2). In 1904 A.E. Douglass began to study fluctuations in solar radiation and their effect on climate by looking at variations in tree-ring thickness in Arizona.

Douglass's work included archaeological dating in the 1920s because many samples came from structural timbers preserved in *pueblos* (prehistoric Native American sites in arid areas of Arizona and New Mexico) (Nash 2003). These samples could then be dated by cross-referencing them to the sequence of rings built up by

BOX 4.3 **Alchester: dendrochronology in action**

A Roman fort was built at Alchester, north of Oxford, in the first century AD (Sauer 2000). Stumps of the large timbers that supported the gate structure survived in wet soil conditions, and two of them were large enough for tree-ring dating to be carried out by Ian Tyers at Sheffield University's dendrochronology laboratory. The reconstruction by Deborah Miles-Williams emphasises the enormous quantities of timber that would be required every time the Roman army constructed a base. Both trees had terminal rings dating between October AD 44 and March AD 45, showing that they came from trees cut down soon after the Roman conquest of Britain (AD 43). The excavator thinks it likely that local woodland was cut down in the autumn of AD 44 in order to complete the defences before the winter. No other form of archaeological dating could provide such a precise *terminus post quem* for the construction of the fort gateway (Eberhard Sauer).

Douglass, which eventually extended back to the fourth century BC. In 1954, bristlecone pines still growing in California were found to be up to 4,000 years old, and a combination of specimens from living trees and old trunks preserved in the White Mountains now provides a continuous record going back to 6700 BC that is of vital importance for checking radiocarbon dates (below: p. 170). The discovery that some spruce tree root systems in Sweden may be more than 9,000 years old is also important in understanding past climate changes. An even more impressive achievement is the establishment of a tree-ring sequence that extends beyond 8400 BC, based on a large number of oak trees from north-western Europe (Haneca *et al.* 2009). Many of the oldest samples have been taken from ancient tree-trunks preserved in peat bogs. The sequence in Germany is approaching 10,000 BC, using pines (Kuniholm 2001: 38–9). Some rings may have distinctive markers, such as the effects of forest fires, severe frosts or volcanic eruptions, that help with cross-dating between

trees in any region, as well as providing important environmental information.

The application of tree-ring dating

Work in Arizona demonstrated the value of tree rings not simply for dating buildings, but also for studying their modification and repair; this approach has been used in many different contexts since then. Studies have been conducted in medieval buildings, such as the cathedrals at Trier in Germany and Chartres in France, to identify or date periods of construction that were not fully documented in surviving historical records. Roman forts and bridges in Germany and the Netherlands have been investigated in the same way; the precision of tree-ring dating is impossible to achieve by any other means. Once dated, such sites can be integrated into historical accounts; waterlogged timbers from the gate of a Roman fort excavated at Alchester near Oxford in 2000 came from trees felled in the autumn of AD 44, the year following the invasion of Britain (**Box 4.3**).

Unfortunately, there are many problems in the direct application of dendrochronological dating. Not all tree species are sufficiently sensitive to display distinctive variations in their ring characteristics, particularly when growing in temperate climates.

Wood only survives under exceptionally wet or dry conditions. Even when it does, large timbers must be recovered to provide sufficient rings for valid comparisons between sequences that accumulated over several decades. A precise date for a felled tree can only be established when all of the sap wood containing the outermost rings has been preserved; unfortunately this might have decayed, or have been trimmed off if the wood was used for building, in which case it is necessary to estimate how many years of growth have been lost. Timbers used in buildings were normally trimmed into regular shapes, and might also have been stored for many years before use. Worse still, roof timbers were frequently reused several times in repairs or reconstructions of wooden buildings whose foundations in contact with damp soils decayed long before the roof. Reuse is a particular problem on arid sites, where timbers do not decay easily. Despite these difficulties, tree rings are the only source of truly absolute dates, in terms of a single year. Unfortunately, they will never be universally applicable, partly because of regional and environmental variations in the growth of trees but principally because of the rarity of suitably wet or arid conditions that ensure their preservation.

The provision of samples of known age for testing the accuracy of radiocarbon dates is not the only indirect use of tree rings. Variations in ring thickness reflect climatic conditions, and there are several instances of extreme disturbances to normal growth. For example, a series of exceptionally narrow rings indicating an episode of cold, wet weather from 1159 BC, that was almost certainly the result of a volcanic eruption marked in ice cores at 1100 ± 50 BC (Baillie 1989), provides cross-dating between the two natural records. The analysis of chemicals emitted during volcanic eruptions found in individual rings may allow them to be related to specific growth declines in trees, and their chemical signatures may possibly be related to these specific volcanic eruptions (Pearson 2006).

At a more intimate level, the precision of tree-ring dates adds an exciting dimension to other finds associated with dated timbers. Star Carr, a classic settlement of Mesolithic hunter-gatherers in Britain, has benefited from the extension of tree-ring records back to the ninth millennium BC; samples that were once dated by radiocarbon with a margin of error of hundreds of years have become events that took place in a specific year (Mellars 1990; Dark 2000). This precision can be extended to other finds, such as tools and animal bones, found in the same contexts. Seahenge, a circle of timbers revealed by erosion of the coast of Norfolk in 1998, was created from timbers felled in 2050 BC, while an upturned tree-stump at its centre was felled in the following year (Pryor 2001). Such precision is impossible in the dating of contemporary stone circles. The impact is similar in historical periods. Dendrochronology is frequently used on art objects such as panel paintings and wooden sculptures made from oak, such as sixteenth and seventeenth century AD examples from the Netherlands. Again, the reuse of wooden panels may cause problems (Haneca et al. 2009: 6). Four hundred samples taken from a collection of Anglo-Scandinavian houses and workshops excavated at Coppergate in York showed that the majority were built from timber from trees felled in AD 975. This indicates planning and management of resources, rather than the piecemeal accumulation of buildings over a long period. If the final ring that was growing when a tree was cut down is preserved, it is possible to estimate the time of year at which wood was harvested; this allows detailed interpretations of human behaviour to be added to chronological information (Dean 1997).

From a discipline of limited topical and geographic scope, dendrochronology has been transformed into a global phenomenon relevant to a broad range of subjects. Firmly grounded in the principal of cross-dating – using aspects of ring morphology to identify contemporaneous rings in different trees – dendrochronology provides absolute dates accurate to the calendar year and qualitative and quantitative reconstructions of environmental variations on seasonal to century scales. … Although problems exist, they are being seriously addressed by the world dendrochronological community and progress can be expected on all fronts. The carefully controlled expansion of tree-ring science into all areas of the globe, its application to an ever broader range of past and present phenomena, and its unparalleled utility as a source of baseline data for measuring current environmental excursions and predicting future variations endow dendrochronology with a bright future.

(Dean 1997: 31, 55)

4.5 ABSOLUTE TECHNIQUES

- key references: Taylor and Aitken, *Chronometric dating* 1997; Aitken, *Science-based dating* 1990; Göksu, *Scientific dating methods* 1991; Pollard, 'Measuring the passage of time' 2008.

The proper meaning of absolute dating is that it is independent of any other chronology or dating technique, that it is based only on currently measurable quantities.

(Aitken 1990: 2)

4.5.1 Radioactive decay

- key references: Aitken, 'Principles of radioactive dating' 1991; Dincauze, *Environmental archaeology* 2000: 107–25.

Unfortunately for the study of prehistory, all of the dating techniques that emerged before 1950 required special circumstances: the survival of timber for tree rings, glacial lakes for varves, or soil conditions that favoured the preservation of pollen. However, the successful development in the early twentieth century of radiometric methods relying upon **radioactive decay** for dating geological periods offered hope that a similar technique might be found to give absolute dates for prehistoric archaeology. Many elements have different isotopes with extra neutrons besides their standard number of protons, indicated by a number showing their atomic weight (e.g. carbon-14, normally represented as ^{14}C). Isotopes of an element behave in very similar ways in chemical reactions, but may be unstable (**radioactive**) and emit radiation at a known rate. Some isotopes become stable after emitting particles, while others go through a protracted series of **progeny** (or **daughter**) **elements** before reaching a stable form (e.g. uranium to lead). The rate of radioactive decay is characterised by the **half-life** – the time taken for half of the radioactive atoms to decay; this may vary from seconds to millions of years.

4.5.2 Radiocarbon dating

- key references: Taylor, 'Radiocarbon dating' 1997; 2001; Aitken, *Science-based dating* 1990: 56–119; Pettitt, 'Radiocarbon dating' 2005; Hackens *et al.*, *^{14}C methods and applications* 1995; Taylor, 'Radioisotope dating by accelerator mass spectrometry' 1991.

Radiocarbon dating was one peaceful by-product of accelerated wartime research into atomic physics and radioactivity in the 1940s. The rate of decay of ^{14}C, which has a half-life of 5,730 ($\pm$40) years, is slow, allowing samples of carbon as old as 70,000 years to contain detectable levels of radioactive emissions, but fast enough for samples from periods since the late Stone Age to be measured with reasonable precision. What makes ^{14}C exceptionally important is that it is absorbed (in the same manner as other carbon isotopes) by all living organisms until their death (**Fig. 4.11**). In theory, all that needs to be done is to measure the radioactivity of a sample from a dead animal or plant, and to calculate the time that has elapsed since its death from the amount of ^{14}C that remains. The practicalities of age estimation are rather more complicated, and the discussion that follows will attempt to highlight the principal advantages and disadvantages of ^{14}C rather than to provide a full scientific explanation.

This simplified description does not do justice to the inspired formation and testing of hypotheses

Figure 4.11 This drawing illustrates the basis of radiocarbon dating. The arrows follow the formation of the radioactive carbon isotope (^{14}C) in the atmosphere by cosmic radiation and its incorporation into a tree through photosynthesis of carbon dioxide. It then passes to a deer that has eaten the foliage, but this animal ceases to take in fresh ^{14}C when it dies. Thus, its bones are placed at the top of a graph that shows the steady decay of the radioactive isotope as time elapses after the death of the deer. (Redrawn by Chris Unwin, after an illustration by Robert Hedges, Research Laboratory for Archaeology, Oxford University)

carried out by Willard F. Libby in Chicago in the 1940s, for which he received a Nobel Prize in 1960 (**Box 4.4**). However, the publication of his preliminary results in 1949 was only a beginning. Taylor

has divided the progress of the technique into three generations (1997: 70–3).

- The first generation (1950–70) established radiocarbon's accuracy for a period of particular significance to prehistoric archaeologists, encompassing the transition from hunting and gathering to farming, the emergence of the first civilisations and periods of later European prehistory that had previously relied upon indirect cross-dating to Egypt. Differences between conventional archaeological dates and the new radiocarbon dates stimulated discussion of both.

- The second generation (1970–80) looked more closely at variations in levels of ^{14}C in the past, and conducted comprehensive analyses of samples from tree rings of known date to provide a **calibration curve**. The results were surprising, and radiocarbon dates before 1000 BC were shown to underestimate calendar years by a progressively greater margin, so that a radiocarbon age of around 4000 BC had to be adjusted upwards by around 800 years. This was the final nail in the coffin of **diffusionism** (the idea that all European developments were inspired by innovations that began in the Near East and Egypt), as prehistoric stone structures in northern Europe turned out to be older than the Egyptian or Mycenaean models that had supposedly inspired them (Chapter 6, p. 251).

- The third generation refined the calibration curve and extended it beyond the range of tree rings by analysing samples of marine coral. It also included a major advance in accuracy and precision through the establishment of **Accelerator Mass Spectrometry (AMS)** laboratories in the 1980s (Tuniz 1998). AMS is fundamentally different because it measures the **concentration** of ^{14}C in relation to the 'normal' isotope ^{12}C, rather than its radioactivity. AMS reduces both sample size and counting times (the former from grams to milligrams, the latter from weeks to hours) and extends the range of radiocarbon dating back beyond 40,000 years (Taylor 1997: 82). This allows individual organic artefacts and bones to be dated *directly*, rather than by association with samples of other material from the contexts in which they were found. Improved precision and a greater range of calibration offer particularly exciting prospects in early prehistory, for example in dating bones associated with the disappearance of Neanderthals and the appearance of modern humans in Europe and Asia between 50,000 and 30,000 years ago (Aitken *et al.* 1993).

To Taylor's list we might now add a fourth generation: the application of Bayesian statistics to both existing and new radiocarbon dates is providing more detailed chronologies and has been called by some a new radiocarbon revolution (below: p. 175).

In essence, if a sample of ancient wood, charcoal or other organic matter is processed in a laboratory so that carbon is isolated, the amount of radioactivity that remains can be measured; the older it is, the fewer radioactive emissions of beta-particles will occur during a fixed period of observation. Ten grams of modern ^{14}C produce 150 disintegrations per minute. The age of an ancient sample of the same weight that produced only 75 counts per minute should therefore be

---

BOX 4.4   The first radiocarbon revolution: Willard Libby

The discovery of radiocarbon dating represented perhaps the greatest advance in archaeological dating in the twentieth century, creating an independent chronological framework for prehistory. Willard Libby (1908–1980), was awarded a Nobel Prize in 1960 for the development of radiocarbon dating. His book *Radiocarbon dating*, published in 1952, ensured his place as one of the most influential individuals in modern archaeology. Libby, a professor of chemistry from California, worked on carbon-14 before the Second World War and took part in the development of the Manhattan Project, which developed the atomic bomb. He realised that the half-life of the radioactive isotope carbon-14 (^{14}C) lasted thousands rather than millions of years, and that new ^{14}C was continuously formed in the atmosphere by cosmic radiation. Freshly formed isotopes were added to the carbon contained in all living plants and animals until their death. At this point a 'radioactive clock' started ticking, and the age of the sample could be estimated by measuring how much of its original radioactivity remained, and by using the known half-life of ^{14}C to

work out how many years it would have taken to fall to the observed level. After the war, Libby refined radiocarbon dating by testing samples of known age. Suitable organic material up to 5,000 years old was available from Egypt, preserved in dry conditions and dated by inscriptions. Once a correlation between radiocarbon estimations and tree rings could be established, the technique could then be applied to undated prehistoric samples. This 'first radiocarbon revolution' often had dramatic results, pushing back the suspected dates of some archaeological phenomena and leading to wholesale reassessments of parts of prehistory (Chapter 6, p. 251) (Getty Images) equal to the half-life of the isotope, around 5,730 years. The use of ^{14}C dating remains complex, and the following section looks at factors that limit its precision and application. Radiocarbon age estimations require careful examination before they can be turned into calendar dates. Some of Libby's original assumptions have been found to be incorrect, and methods of measuring ^{14}C and calculating dates have changed several times during the half-century in which the technique has been employed.

Key factors

- **Radiocarbon dating is universal**, because the radioactive isotope ^{14}C is formed continuously throughout the Earth's atmosphere by the effects of **cosmic radiation**.
- ^{14}C has a known **half-life** and **decays** at a known rate, but the original **half-life** was too low by around 3 per cent; it is now judged to be around 5,730 years, rather than 5,568.
- The rates of **formation and decay are in balance**; cosmic radiation in the past should have maintained ^{14}C in the atmosphere at a constant level. However, the level of cosmic radiation has fluctuated over time, perhaps in relation to sunspot activity and the Earth's magnetic intensity. This means that the formation of ^{14}C in the atmosphere has varied; thus, samples from organisms that absorbed abnormally larger or smaller amounts of ^{14}C will give misleadingly earlier or later dates. In addition, calibration reveals that dates from the **southern hemisphere** are around 30 years too old compared with those from the northern hemisphere; this is probably because the greater area of oceans in the southern hemisphere has affected the distribution of ^{14}C in the atmosphere.
- **All life-forms contain carbon**, and living organisms absorb carbon from the atmosphere, mainly in the form of carbon dioxide; photosynthesis by plants is one common mechanism. Animals and plants therefore maintain the same proportion of newly formed ^{14}C as the atmosphere until their death, when it begins to decay. However, different isotopes of carbon are taken into organisms at different rates (**fractionation**);

proportions of ^{13}C and ^{14}C must be checked and an adjustment made to the estimated date. Furthermore, marine organisms absorb **'old'** ^{14}C from sea water; samples taken from shells or bones of marine mammals give dates which are misleadingly early by several hundred years. Some of this old carbon has been absorbed by humans – in Scotland, for example, by people living in the Mesolithic period on Oronsay (Richards and Sheridan 2000), and in the Viking period on Orkney (Barrett *et al.* 2000), as well as by other animal species which eat large quantities of seafood.

- **A calibration curve** must be used to convert radiocarbon years into calendar years (**Fig. 4.12**). Tree rings have revealed not only short-term fluctuations in ^{14}C levels but also a long-term divergence between ^{14}C estimations and calendar years that grows increasingly wider before c. 1000 BC. Samples with a radiocarbon age of 5,000–7,000 years require upward adjustment of as much as 500–1,000 years, while uranium–thorium dating shows that coral dated to around 26,000 BC by radiocarbon is actually 30,000 years old. **Dendrochronology** provides independently dated samples of wood from annual tree rings stretching back more than 11,000 years, while earlier samples come from dead trunks preserved in semi-arid habitats and from oak trees found in bogs or river sediments in Europe. Samples from **marine corals** may extend the calibration curve back as far as 50,000 years (Fairbanks *et al.* 2005) by comparing ^{14}C with dates derived from uranium–thorium isotopes.
- A statistical estimation of error, expressed as a **standard deviation**, is attached to laboratory counts of radioactivity. Since isotope decays occur at random, a reasonably long counting period is needed to reduce this inherent error. Several counting sessions are carried out, along with measurements of laboratory standards to monitor the performance of the equipment. The standard deviation derived from the counting statistics is preceded by '±'; **Fig. 4.13** shows how the reliability of a date may be envisaged.

Table 4.1 Summary of factors involved in radiocarbon dating

Positive factors	Complications
Radiocarbon dating is universal because ^{14}C is distributed throughout the atmosphere	There is a 30-year difference between dates from the northern and southern hemispheres
^{14}C has a fixed half-life and decay rate	The half-life is now known to be 5,730 years, rather than 5,568
The formation and decay of atmospheric ^{14}C are in balance	Variations in cosmic radiation have caused ^{14}C levels to fluctuate
All life-forms contain carbon	Isotopes of carbon are taken into organisms at different rates (fractionation)
Plants and animals take in newly formed ^{14}C until their death	Marine creatures absorb old carbon from deep sea water
Dendrochronology provides an independent measure of accuracy	Radiocarbon underestimates the age of tree rings to an increasingly serious extent beyond 2000 BP (*Before Present*; for consistency the 'present' is standardised as AD 1950)
A calibration curve converts radiocarbon estimations into calendar dates	The curve contains many sections where calibration is imprecise or ambiguous
Conventional and AMS dating now provide very precise dates	The results are still subject to a statistical margin of error, indicated by the standard deviation
Excellent results may now be obtained from small samples	Good results depend on the careful selection of appropriate samples, and the quality of the archaeological context remains crucial

Table 4.2 Radiocarbon estimation from Galgenberg

Lab no.	Arch. no.	Uncalibrated determination BP	Archaeological context
GrN-12702	T14 1P	4385±35	collapsed palisade fence in W ditch

Table 4.3 Calibrated dates from Galgenberg

Uncalibrated determination BP	Corresponding historical dates BC	Estimated standard errors
4385±35	2947, 2973, 3025	59, 80, 30

4.5.3 Presenting and interpreting a radiocarbon date

- key references: Reimer, 'IntCal09' 2009; Stuiver and Van der Plicht, *INTCAL 98: calibration issue* 1998; Banning, *The archaeologist's laboratory* 2000: Pettitt, 'Radiocarbon dating' 2005: 332–4.

Health warning! Proper calibration is not easy for the non-mathematician, but doing it incorrectly, wrongly interpreting the result, or even not understanding the potential of calibration may seriously damage your archaeology. Take advice from the experts, know what calendrical band-width is necessary for correct interpretation and discuss this with the dating laboratory, preferably before taking and certainly before submitting samples. Think first, not after you get the radiocarbon date.

(Pearson 1987: 103)

Because interpretation is so complex, all radiocarbon dates included in an archaeological

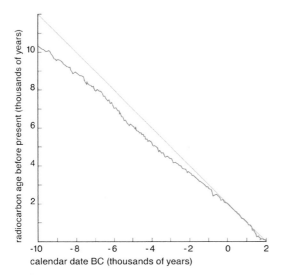

Figure 4.12 *(above left)* Tree-ring calibration curve for radiocarbon dates based on calculations published in 1998. The straight line shows what the relationship would have been if the amount of ¹⁴C in the atmosphere had remained constant so that 4,000 radiocarbon years would be equivalent to c. 2000 BC. However, beyond 500 BC there is an increasing divergence, so that a radiocarbon age of 8,000 years before present has to be increased from c. 6000 to c. 7000 BC. The process of calibration looks deceptively simple at this scale, but 'wiggles', combined with other statistical uncertainties, make calculations very complicated. Fortunately, computer programs such as OxCal are freely available for this purpose. (Chris Unwin, based on data from Stuiver and Van Der Plicht 1998)

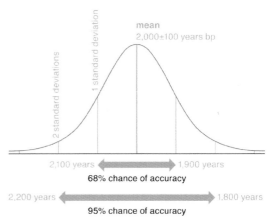

Figure 4.13 Every radiocarbon measurement has a statistical margin of error, which is quoted in terms of the mean and one standard deviation (e.g. 2000±100 BP). A normal distribution curve shows how it should be interpreted: one standard deviation either side of the mean will give a 68% probability that the age lay within a 200-year bracket (and consequently a 32% chance of it not doing so), whilst two standard deviations increase the probability of accuracy to around 95%. (Chris Unwin)

publication must be presented in a standard format. For example, a series of charcoal samples obtained from a late Neolithic site at Galgenberg, Bavaria, were quoted as shown here in Table 4.2 (Aitchison *et al.* 1991: 113; Ottaway 1999: 240).

The first column contains the code for the Groningen radiocarbon laboratory (GrN) together with a unique serial number for this particular sample, so that it could be checked with laboratory records if any problem arose. The archaeological number refers to an excavated context at the Galgenberg site, and its nature is explained in the final column. The determined age of this sample is expressed in uncalibrated form in **years** BP (the periodical *Antiquity*, where these dates were published, uses **b.p.**), complete with a small but unavoidable

counting error estimated by the laboratory (±35). The 'raw date' has been adjusted to compensate for fractionation, but it is calculated according to Libby's half-life of 5,568 years rather than the more recently determined estimate of 5,730 years; this practice is maintained to avoid confusion in comparisons with older results, but modern calibration programmes such as OxCal take account of it automatically. The standard counting error of ±35 years means that the (uncalibrated) date has a 68 per cent chance of lying between 4350 and 4420 BP, and there is a 95 per cent chance that it lies between 4315 and 4455 BP. This emphasises the importance of regarding radiocarbon age estimations as ranges of possibilities, rather than as 'dates'.

The age of this sample was calibrated with reference to a calibration curve, derived from dated tree-ring samples. Updated versions of this curve are published in the periodical *Radiocarbon*, the most recent being IntCal09 (Reimer 2009). A rapid inspection of the curve suggested that the radiocarbon estimation would be transformed into a calendar date with a range falling roughly between 2900 and 3100 BC.

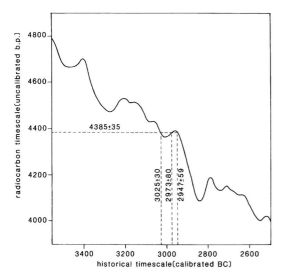

Figure 4.14 This diagram shows how a single radio-carbon age estimation (from Galgenberg, Germany) may produce three different calendar dates of varying reliability if it happens to coincide with a difficult 'wiggle' in the calibration curve. For the purposes of dating a Neolithic sample, it would normally be sufficient to know that the calibrated date lay somewhere between 2800 and 3100 BC, but a margin of error of this size would be too great for historical periods. (Chris Unwin, after Aitchison *et al.* 1991: Fig. 4)

However, closer inspection of this particular age determination revealed a common problem: a 'wiggle' in the calibration curve at around 4400 BP meant that it could represent three different 'historical' (or calendar) dates (Aitchison 1991: 113) (**Fig. 4.14**).

The tree-ring calibration curve is itself subject to statistical variations; for this reason the standard deviation should be considered as only a *minimum* estimate of uncertainty. Furthermore, precision varies according to which part of the curve is being consulted; if the line is steep, the prospects are good, but if it is flatter, the date range will be very wide. Thus, the 'date' of 3025 has the lowest of the three estimated levels of error. When all thirteen samples from Galgenberg were examined together, the main period of the whole site's occupation was estimated to lie between 2810 and 3100 BC (Ottaway 1999: 243–4). Computer programmes used for calibration (primarily OxCal or CALIB: **Fig. 4.15**) present

the probability in the form of a graph which emphasises that results are estimations of ranges, not dates in the sense understood by historians.

Thus, Galgenberg illustrates some of the problems that lie between the receipt of an age estimation from a laboratory and its interpretation in meaningful chronological terms for a site or an artefact. This is why Pearson (1987) advised archaeologists to consider the 'calendrical band-width necessary for correct interpretation' before submitting samples. In the context of later prehistoric Britain, a sample from the British Late Bronze Age and Early Iron Age that was expected to give calibrated results between 1100 and 800 BC would be very worthwhile as it would coincide with a steep slope on the calibration curve. In contrast, samples from the period between 800 and 400 BC are almost useless because this part of the curve is much flatter and does not permit refinement within a range of around four centuries; traditional forms of dating would be more precise (Bowman 1990: 55–7).

An International Radiocarbon Convention in 1985 recommended that uncalibrated age determinations should always be quoted in the form 1000 BP with the 'present' standardised as AD 1950. If dates are calibrated according to 'an agreed curve', they should be cited in the form 1000 Cal BP. In areas of the world where the AD/BC division is useful, calibrated dates can be converted to 1000 Cal BC or 1000 Cal AD (Gillespie and Gowlett 1986: 160). 'Perhaps with the benefit of hindsight it might have been preferable if radiocarbon measurements had never been expressed as "ages" or "dates"; then there could be no misunderstanding' (Bowman 1990: 49).

Radiocarbon samples

- key references: Ashmore, 'Radiocarbon dating: avoiding errors by avoiding mixed samples' 1999; Waterbolk, 'Working with radiocarbon dates' 1971; Protsch, 'Dating of bones' 1991.

Most organic materials are suitable for dating but the lower the carbon content, the larger the sample needs to be. Charcoal derived from the burning of wood is a common find on archaeological sites and samples of around 10–20 g dry weight are

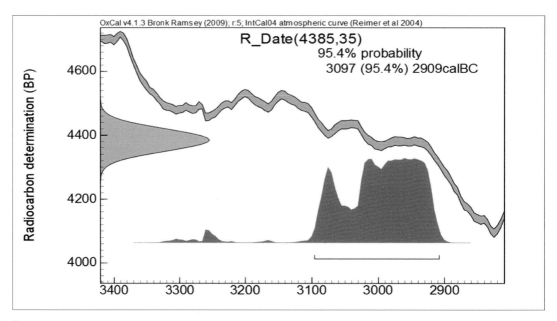

OxCal v4.1.3 Bronk Ramsey (2009); r:5; IntCal04 atmospheric curve (Reimer et al 2004)

R_Date(4385,35)
95.4% probability
3097 (95.4%) 2909calBC

Figure 4.15 This image shows the calibration plot produced by the computer program OxCAL v4.1 (released by Bronk Ramsey in 2009), for one of the dates from Galgenberg. The uncalibrated date is 4385±35 BP, with calibration indicating that there is a 95% probability that the sample dates from between 3097 and 2909 BC, demonstrating how use of the latest calibration program may refine old dates. As calibration and Bayesian statistics are introduced, such dates may be refined even further. Normally, archaeologists will rely on the 95.4% (2 sigma) date when using the radiocarbon date, whether they feel a tighter date range is more likely or not.

adequate for conventional counting, compared with around 50–100 g of peat or 100–500 g of bone; AMS requires only around one hundredth (e.g. 0.01–0.1 g) (Aitken 1990: 91). Many other materials may be tested, including cloth, flesh, pollen, shell, soil and even iron, which usually contains some carbon impurities. The collection of samples needs to be scrupulous, and their storage and handling must avoid contamination, even though they are subjected to a chemical 'laundry' process before being tested.

Archaeologists must know exactly what is being dated and, in the case of samples from excavations, their precise stratigraphic relationship to the site. The nature of charcoal and wood samples is important: twigs or nuts are ideal because they only contain ^{14}C taken in during a short growing season, whereas the central portion of a large tree will obviously give a date decades (or even centuries) earlier than its use for fuel or construction. Thought must also be given to exactly *how* samples are related to the objects or contexts that they are intended to

date; the significance of charcoal fragments from a general occupation level is a lot less clear than a sample taken directly from a wooden artefact or a human body. One of the most widely publicised examples of direct dating was the examination of the Turin Shroud; since only very small samples of linen could be provided from this unique artefact, AMS was an ideal method (Gove 1996; Taylor 1997: 84–5). They were tested in three laboratories along with a sample of ancient linen from Egypt that had been dated by AMS to 110 Cal BC–75 Cal AD. The combined result for the shroud samples was 689±16 BP and for the Egyptian linen 1,964±20 BP; when checked against the calibration curve the shroud samples gave a date of 1260–1390 Cal AD at the 95 per cent confidence level. Whatever the nature and date of the strange image painted(?) on the shroud, the linen from which it was woven grew no earlier than the thirteenth century AD, making it impossible that it was associated with Jesus, unless, of course, some undetected factors distorted the small sample selected for testing.

Even in prehistory, radiocarbon raises questions of a 'historical' nature. For example, evidence of very early human settlement linked with a hunter-gatherer economy was found on the island of Cyprus, which had previously been thought to have been settled by farming communities in the Neolithic period. However, since the relevant radiocarbon dates were too early for the conventional calibration curve, it was difficult to provide a calendar date for the earliest occupation. Evidence from varves, floating tree rings, uranium–thorium dates from coral and various other forms of dating suggest a date around 11,500–10,000 BC in calendar years (Manning 1991). Later research found that the farming communities had also arrived on the island earlier than previously thought, in the tenth millennium BC (Peltenburg 2000). Technical limitations upon radiocarbon dates are just as significant in the case of relatively recent (and in European terms, historical) periods. The question of the date of colonisation of New Zealand is a good example; estimates ranged up to 2,000 years ago, with a majority favouring a date of around 1,000 years ago. A large number of radiocarbon estimations now demonstrate that it took place as recently as the fourteenth century AD; misleading earlier dates had been given by samples from shell, bone and old wood (Anderson 1991, Higham *et al.* 1999).

4.5.4 The Bayesian radiocarbon revolution

- key references: Bayliss and Bronk Ramsey, 'Pragmatic Bayesians' 2004; Pollard, 'Measuring the passage of time' 2008: 157–9.

Radiocarbon dating has been revolutionised by the growing use of a statistical method developed more than 250 years ago by Thomas Bayes (1702–61) to refine estimations of probability. Single radiocarbon dates are relatively uninformative for constructing a chronology, whereas multiple dates help to achieve a closer approximation of the true date of the context from which samples were taken (Pollard 2008: 157). Bayesian statistics allow dates to be refined by taking account of additional information, such as other dates from the same site, or the sequence

of dates from stratified contexts: sample A must be later in date than sample B, if B was found in a context lower down the stratigraphic sequence than A (Bayliss and Bronk Ramsey 2004). Thus, the margin of statistical error attached to a radiocarbon estimation can be reduced in size in the light of other dates and evidence. It is important to stress that excavation, observation and recording must be carried out to a very high standard to ensure that the stratigraphic sequence and contexts really do show that sample A is later than B (see Chapter 3). If the interpretation of the archaeological record is incorrect, it will lead to erroneous statistical modelling of the radiocarbon dates.

Bayesian statistics have already produced interesting results by adding precision to the dating of archaeological monuments. A project that re-analysed existing radiocarbon dates from early Neolithic sites in southern Britain showed that, in many long barrows, burials only took place for a few decades, rather than over many centuries as had previously been thought (Bayliss *et al.* 2007). Bayesian analyses of radiocarbon dates have only recently begun to be undertaken on a large scale, but they are likely to lead to many similar revisions of current chronological frameworks for prehistory.

The impact of radiocarbon dating
- key references: Taylor, *Radiocarbon dating: an archaeological perspective* 1987; Taylor *et al.*, *Radiocarbon after four decades* 1992.

Radiocarbon dating has grown exponentially, and many problems and inaccuracies have been isolated and examined, some leading to major adjustments of the results. Despite many problems, radiocarbon dates now provide a framework for the prehistory of the world; for the first time its study has become more like that of historical periods and emphasis has shifted away from pure chronology towards more fundamental human behavioural factors. Without doubt, it has made the greatest single contribution to the development of archaeology since geologists and prehistorians escaped from the constraints of historical chronology in the nineteenth century.

The major stages of human development from hunting through to urbanisation are now well dated over most of the world. However, so few ^{14}C atoms remain in samples more than 40,000 years old that they are difficult to measure, even using the AMS technique; this adds still further to the existing difficulties of calibrating radiocarbon age beyond 30,000 years ago (Richards and Beck 2001). Fortunately, a related method based on an isotope of potassium allows the examination of early hominin developments beyond the range of radiocarbon.

4.5.5 Potassium–argon (^{40}K/^{40}Ar) and argon–argon dating (^{40}Ar/^{39}Ar)

- key references: Walter, 'Potassium–argon/ argon–argon dating methods' 1997; Aitken, *Science-based dating* 1990: 120–4.

Potassium–argon (K–Ar) dating has played a key role in unravelling the temporal patterns of hominin evolution as far back as the first significant discovery of East African australopithecines at Olduvai Gorge in 1959. It was in large part due to the desire to understand the age of the Olduvai hominin remains that pioneering attempts were made to date geologically early materials using the K–Ar method.

(Walter 1997: 97)

Potassium is abundant throughout the Earth's crust. Like carbon, it contains a small percentage of radioactive isotopes, notably potassium-40 (^{40}K), which decays into calcium-40 (^{40}Ca) and the gas argon. This gas escapes while volcanic rocks are being formed, but once new minerals have cooled and crystallised they trap the argon. The gas can be released in the laboratory by heating, and can then be measured; the quantity may then be related to the amount of ^{40}K and its age estimated from its half-life (1,250 million years). Since this half-life is staggeringly long in comparison with that of ^{14}C, its potential was initially limited to geological dating; archaeological applications only began in the 1950s when the controversy over the date of fossil hominins from East Africa stimulated the demand for

absolute dates beyond the range of radiocarbon. Another contrast with radiocarbon dating is that ^{14}C is based upon a **decay clock**, while ^{40}K (like other geological methods such as uranium series dating) is an **accumulation clock**. Thus, while recent samples of carbon contain high levels of its radioactive isotope because they have not yet decayed, recently formed geological deposits have very low levels of ^{40}Ar because there has been so little time for it to accumulate. As a result it is difficult to measure ^{40}Ar in samples less than 100,000 years old, although work on samples of known date, such as volcanic material from Pompeii (AD 79), is helping to provide a solution to this problem (Renne *et al.* 2001).

Improvement in the precision of K–Ar dating came with the introduction of the **argon–argon** technique, which allows smaller samples to be dated than the K–Ar method. ^{40}K is converted into ^{39}Ar in the laboratory, and instead of comparing the potassium and argon content of two separate samples, the ratio between ^{39}Ar and ^{40}Ar in a single sample is measured. A revolution began in the 1970s with **laser-fusion**, which allows extraordinarily small samples – even individual mineral grains – to be measured rapidly. The ability to measure single grains circumvents the problem of samples from eroded deposits where older grains of volcanic material have been mixed with younger ones. Further improvements in precision have extended K–Ar dating to relatively recent samples that overlap with the earliest part of the range of radiocarbon dating between 100,000 and 50,000 years ago (Walter 1997: 107, 121).

Potassium–argon is ideal for dating early hominin fossils in East Africa, as they occur in an area that was volcanically active when the fossils were deposited between one and five million years ago; pioneering results in the 1950s doubled previous estimates of their age (Walter 1997: 109–20). At Olduvai Gorge the hominin remains were shown to be 1.8 million years old, rather than the 0.6 million years suggested by radiocarbon. Layers containing bones and artefacts may be found 'sandwiched' between volcanic deposits of ash or lava that provide excellent samples of newly formed minerals for measurement. Very occasionally the association between human remains and volcanic deposits may be much more intimate, as in the case of hominin footprints around 3.6 million years old found on a layer of freshly deposited ash at Laetoli, Kenya (Leakey and Lewin 1992: 103). The laser-fusion method has been able to check and refine dates of geological stratification in Olduvai Gorge, while 'Lucy', one of the most famous hominin discoveries, from Hadar in Ethiopia, is now precisely dated to just under 3,180,000 years. Furthermore, better dates for stratification in East Africa have improved our understanding and precision of changes in the Earth's magnetic field, notably the reversals of polarity which can also be detected in cores from the seabed. Thus, climatic fluctuations revealed by oxygen isotope ratios in deep sea cores may be checked and correlated with geological deposits on land. Early stages in the evolution of human ancestors can now be placed in a secure chronological *and* environmental context. 'The future of K–Ar dating lies in its versatility. It will be intriguing to see where, how and in what form the next generation of this method will be applied' (Walter 1997: 121).

4.5.6 Uranium series dating

- key references: Latham, 'Uranium-series dating' 2001; Schwarcz, 'Uranium series dating' 1997; Aitken, *Science-based dating* 1990: 124–32.

The dating of rocks back to the Pre-Cambrian geological period by measuring the proportions of uranium to lead or uranium to helium was possible because isotopes of uranium remain radioactive for such a long period. Fortunately the decay of uranium produces a series of progeny isotopes with much shorter decay times relevant to recent geological and archaeological periods; uranium-234 is particularly useful because it decays to produce thorium-230 in the same way that potassium-40 decays to argon-40. An ideal sample material is coral, which takes in ^{234}U dissolved in sea water when it forms, but lacks (insoluble) thorium; *speleothems* (stalagmites, stalactites or flowstone formed in caves) may also be sampled. ^{230}Th begins to accumulate in these newly-formed materials at a known rate relative to the original amount of ^{234}U, and measurements can be used for dating early human activity in caves anywhere between a few hundred and 500,000 years ago. Large samples of up to 200 g are required unless **mass spectrometry** is available; mass spectrometry has revolutionised uranium series dating in the same ways that AMS enhanced radiocarbon. The precise relationship between any sample and an archaeological event or activity must always be established; human occupation levels sandwiched between layers of flowstone in a cave are ideal – for example the successive levels associated with Neanderthals and modern humans at La Chaise de Vouthon in Charente, France (Schwarcz 1997: 175–6). Uranium series dating is less satisfactory when carried out on porous material such as bones or shells, although studies of tooth enamel are more satisfactory because they can be checked against ESR dates (below: p. 182). Unlike coral or speleothems, which only take up uranium when they are formed, porous material such as bone absorbs uranium while buried in the ground. Finally, a crucially important role of uranium–thorium dating of coral has been the calibration of radiocarbon dates back towards 50,000 BC; this is possible because coral, a living organism, also contains carbon.

4.5.7 Fission-track dating

- key references: Westgate *et al.*, 'Fission-track dating' 1997; Yegingil, 'Fission-track dating' 1991; Aitken, *Science-based dating* 1990: 132–6.

The spontaneous fission of ^{238}U follows the law of radioactive decay. … Simply put, given that the spontaneous fission of ^{238}U occurs at a known rate, the age of a mineral or glass can be calculated from the amount of uranium and the number of spontaneous fission-tracks it contains.

(Westgate *et al.* 1997: 129)

This method involves counting microscopic tracks (damage trails) caused by fragments derived from the fission of uranium-238 in glassy minerals, whether of geological origin or of human manufacture. In practice the most useful samples come from zircon or obsidian, which was used extensively for making tools. However, an obsidian artefact must have been subjected to heating if it is to provide a date for an archaeological context or event; heating removes earlier fission-tracks that had accumulated since the obsidian first solidified after its volcanic formation. Obsidian tools, or obsidian waste flakes, dropped into a hearth would make ideal samples. New tracks can be counted and related to the amount of radioactive ^{238}U they contain to estimate how much time has elapsed since their last heating. Like potassium–argon dating, the fission-track method has been invaluable for checking the age of volcanic deposits associated with early hominin remains in East Africa. The two techniques test different minerals found together in the same volcanic beds, giving more confidence in each method's reliability when results agree; both methods can now analyse individual grains to avoid including older minerals that had eroded into later deposits (Westgate *et al.* 1997: 146–50).

Fission-track dating is also important in **tephrochronology** for checking the age of volcanic material found on sites or in seabed cores that can be shown by its chemical characteristics to have come from a particular volcano. This has proved very useful in establishing the contemporaneity of sites on the Indian subcontinent, where early stone artefacts have been found, thanks to ash derived from a volcano more than 3,000 km away in Malaysia (Westgate *et al.* 1997: 143–6). Likewise, layers of tephra separating deposits of loess in Alaska have been dated and these estimated ages may be checked against occasional reversals of the Earth's magnetic field, which have themselves been dated by astronomical and potassium–argon techniques (*ibid.*: 150–3).

4.5.8 Tephrochronology

- key reference: Pollard, *Measuring the passage of time* 2008: 162–3.

Pollard has suggested that tephrochronology is one of the most promising forms of archaeological dating that is being developed. Tephrochronology uses fine-grained deposits from volcanic eruptions which are scattered over wide areas. Tephra from individual volcanoes and even specific eruptions has been shown to be quite distinct; thus layers of tephra can be linked to individual events. In areas where layers of tephra are common, such as Iceland, detailed chronological sequences can be constructed with the aid of radiocarbon dating (**Box 4.5**). In addition to constructing detailed chronologies of land-use in Iceland, stratified tephra can play a significant role in relating longer geochronological sequences to sequences in ice-cores (Pollard 2008: 163). The use of tephra for archaeological dating is of course limited to areas of the world, such as Iceland, North America and New Zealand, where active volcanoes had an direct impact upon human lives.

4.5.9 Luminescence dating

- key references: Grün, 'Trapped charge dating' 2001; Aitken, 'Luminescence dating' 1997; Aitken, *Science-based dating* 1990: 141–86; Aitken, *Introduction to optical dating* 1998; English Heritage, *Luminescence dating* 2008; Wintle, 'Fifty years of luminescence dating' 2008.

The physical phenomenon of luminescence can be used to date artefacts that were made from (or include) crystalline minerals which have been subjected to strong heating. The first successful application was to pottery made from fired clay, but it is commonly used now for dating flint tools that have been burnt, for example by being dropped accidentally into a fire. Most recently it has been extended to unburned material, notably natural sediments that were exposed to sunlight for a short period and then buried, using **optical dating** (optically stimulated luminescence, abbreviated to OSL) in addition to **thermoluminescence** (TL).

Crystalline minerals have defects in their structure that 'trap' electrons displaced by radiation and by the decay of radioactive isotopes in minerals contained either in the artefacts themselves or in the soil in which they have been buried. 'Deep traps' do not release these electrons until heated above 300°C; as soon as heating

BOX 4.5

Vikings, fire and ice: the application of tephrochronology

Tephrochronology uses layers of volcanic ash, known as tephra, to date specific volcanic eruptions. Tephra is retrieved from a wide variety of locations including archaeological sites, peat bogs and lake sediment sequences. The most famous example is that which buried Pompeii under a thick layer of volcanic ash from Vesuvius in AD 79. However, most tephra layers are very thin, with the tephra only detectable with the aid of a microscope. Different volcanoes, such as those in Iceland, the Mediterranean and on the Pacific Rim, produce ash of a specific size, shape, colour and geochemistry. These characteristics are used to source the ash in the archaeological and palaeoenvironmental sites to a specific volcano or eruption that can sometimes have occurred hundreds of miles away. For example, tephra from Icelandic volcanoes has been found all over north-west Europe, with tephra from some of the largest eruptions found as far away as Russia.

When sourcing an eruption, the tephrochronologist needs to refer to a regional tephrochronology around the source volcanoes to match with the characteristics of the tephra from their site. In Iceland in particular there is a very detailed tephrochronology for most of the volcanoes and volcanic systems across the island, one that has taken over 60 years to compile. This was achieved by comparing soil sections from close to the source volcano with historical accounts of eruptions in the historic period (c. AD 870 to the present day) and dating prehistoric eruptions (pre c. AD 870) with other absolute dating techniques, such as radiocarbon or Greenland ice cores. The eruption of the volcano Hekla in AD 1341 was recorded by many contemporary accounts and tephra is widespread across much of southern Iceland. In the section of a charcoal pit (below) from Langanes, southern Iceland, tephra was used to date the use of the pit to the late fourteenth century AD, as the pit cut tephra from Hekla 1341 (providing a *terminus post quem*) and was overlain by tephra from Katla 1500 (providing a *terminus ante quem*) (Church *et al.* 2007). The eruption of a volcanic system called Veiðivötn at the time of Icelandic settlement was dated by geochemically sourcing tephra shards from the eruption in the Greenland ice cores, producing an estimated date of AD 871±2 (Grönvold *et al.* 1995). This so-called Landnám tephra (Landnám is Old Norse for 'land take') has been found all over Iceland and immediately underlies the very earliest Viking settlements of Iceland, providing a very precise *terminus post quem* for the colonisation of Iceland.

Most of the volcanic eruptions producing tephra layers before Landnám are dated by using radiocarbon dating on organic material immediately underlying the tephra layers in peat bogs. A large eruption of the volcano Hekla, known as Hekla 4, covers much of Iceland and is found as microscopic tephra in palaeoenvironmental sites across many parts of the British Isles and Scandinavia. It was dated with multiple radiocarbon dates in Irish peat bogs to 2310±20 BC (Pilcher *et al.* 1995) (photograph: Mike Church).

is over, electrons begin to accumulate again. When electrons are released, some recombine immediately with a **luminescence centre** (another type of defect) and emit light in proportion to their number. Thus, the basis of TL dating is measurement of the amount of light emitted when samples from artefacts such as potsherds or flints are reheated in the laboratory to release electrons that have accumulated since they were originally fired or burned.

The first stage in calculating a date is to measure the amount of light released and to plot its glow-curve on a graph as the sample is heated up to 500°C (the temperature at which a 'natural' glow-curve is produced). This is compared with an 'artificial' glow-curve derived from an identical sample that has been subjected to a known amount of radiation in the laboratory (**Fig. 4.16**). The relationship between the two curves gives information about the reliability of the sample, as well as revealing the amount of energy that had accumulated since it was last heated (the **palaeodose**). Pots are fired at a temperature high enough to release all the electrons trapped in the crystal lattices of minerals in their clay. Thus all of the energy released in the laboratory must have built up since the date of their firing; the older the pots, the more energy that should have accumulated. The palaeodose does not reveal the age without the **annual dose** received from radioactive minerals within the sample having first been measured; in addition, measurement of radiation from the soil that surrounded a buried artefact is crucial, especially for artefacts made of flint. The age is equivalent to the palaeodose divided by the annual dose. Thus, a palaeodose of 8.5 Gy (Grays – a standard measurement of absorbed radiation) divided by an annual dose of 5.18 Gy would give an age of 1,640 years – around AD 350 (Aitken 1990: 151).

Thermoluminescence (TL) dating is particularly valuable in situations where no suitable materials for radiocarbon dating have been found or if the age exceeds 40,000 years, beyond which radiocarbon is of rapidly diminishing usefulness. It may also assist in problem areas of the calibration curve such as the first millennium BC. TL dating is also useful in areas where volcanic

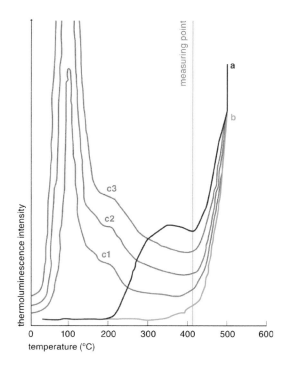

Figure 4.16 Thermoluminescence apparatus provides a graph of light released by a sample prepared from an ancient artefact as it is heated (a). A second measurement of the same sample provides a different graph for the same material *without* its ancient energy (b); the bulge in curve (a) between 300° and 400°C resulted from the electrons trapped in the sample. Curves c1–3 are further measurements taken to study the luminescence produced after the sample has been exposed to known levels of modern radiation in order study its sensitivity. When further factors about the context in which the artefact was found have been taken into account, a date may be calculated. (Drawn by Chris Unwin)

materials suitable for potassium–argon dating are absent. Fortunately, early prehistoric caves or campsites normally produce many finds of stones and flint implements burnt in fires at a sufficiently high temperature to release their trapped electrons. Flints found in deposits with relatively low surrounding radioactivity may be datable up to 500,000 or even a million years.

TL dating has been extended to specialised materials such as stalagmite, volcanic material and even the soil over which molten lava has flowed (Aitken 1990: 172). More exciting is the potential to date deposits of sand or sediment that were subjected to intense sunlight and subsequently buried. It has been established that this kind of exposure to heat and light is sufficient to remove trapped electrons ('bleaching'), which begin to accumulate again as soon as the deposit is covered (Aitken 1997: 202–9). TL has made a significant contribution to dating early human dispersal; for example, its ability to date sand deposits has been useful in dating windblown sand sealing a cave with early human remains in South Africa (Wintle 2008: 298). Quartz grains from sites in Australia have been dated to reveal the arrival of humans, which lies beyond the accurate range of radiocarbon dating more than 50,000 years ago (David 1997) (**Box 4.6**). **Optically stimulated luminescence** (OSL) has proved to be particularly suitable for examining unburned sediments; this technique uses light, rather than heat, to release only those electrons stored in 'traps' that are easily bleached, ensuring that only electrons stored since burial of the sediment are measured (Aitken 1997: 206–7). This method can be used on mineral grains (feldspar and quartz) which may be found in archaeological features such as ditch fills. However, the suitability of samples for dating depends on how the material was exposed to light and how it was deposited; it is not suitable in all geological areas (English Heritage 2008: 19–20).

New methods of obtaining and measuring luminescence signals are currently being developed and their accuracy refined, often by comparing radiocarbon and luminescence dates. OSL has been demonstrated to be extremely useful in dating brick buildings where tree-ring dating is unavailable (**Fig. 4.17**: Bailiff 2007). Bayesian statistics (above: p. 175) are also being applied to multiple luminescence dates, as well as to radiocarbon dates (Wintle 2008: 303). TL or OSL dating of artefacts may not have the precision of radiocarbon, but they do not require calibration since it relies on constant rates of radioactive emissions; uncertainty lies in the accuracy of measurement and control of the many variables that affect a sample.

While it is not possible to measure all of the necessary variables for accurate dating of objects

in museum collections, especially if their precise findspot is unknown, TL can easily detect the lack of trapped electrons in recent forgeries. In Aitken's words:

> The span of time encompassed by the various luminescence techniques is remarkable: from a few decades to approaching a million years. Extension beyond the range of calibrated radiocarbon dating is particularly to be noted and also that luminescence ages are not distorted by intensity fluctuations in cosmic radiation.
>
> (Aitken 1997: 212)

Figure 4.17 OSL is particularly useful in dating structures for which other techniques such as tree ring dating, are not possible, e.g. structures built from fired bricks. Well dated structures can also be used to confirm the accuracy of thermoluminescence dates. At Tattershall Castle, in Lincolnshire, which was known from historical sources to have been constructed between AD 1445 and 1450, was dated using OSL. The OSL dates of 1455±33 and 1453±34 matched closely the historic dates, demonstrating the relative accuracy of the method and its potential application for dating buildings of unknown date (Bailiff 2007). (Photograph: Ian Bailiff)

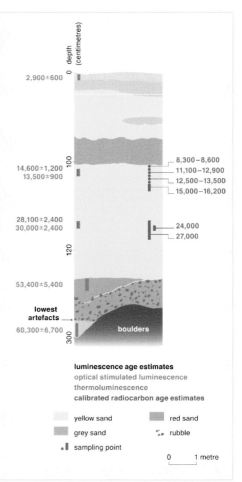

BOX 4.6

Optical stimulated luminescence: Deaf Adder Gorge, Australia

Excavation at Deaf Adder Gorge, Northern Territory, Australia, uncovered a deep profile of layers of sand overlying human artefacts. Samples were collected for radiocarbon and luminescence dating, and the correspondence between results from the two very different methods was encouraging. The deepest layers with earliest evidence of human occupation are rather early for reliable radiocarbon dating, but well within the range of luminescence, which suggests that people had arrived at this location at least 40,000 and possibly as many as 60,000 years ago (Roberts *et al.* 1994).

4.5.10 Electron spin resonance (ESR)

- key references: Grün, 'Trapped charge dating' 2001; Grün, 'Electron spin resonance dating' 1997; Aitken, *Science-based dating* 1990: 187–203.

Like thermoluminescence, ESR is a 'trapped charge' dating method, but it is applied to different kinds of samples and the method of measurement is also different. ESR does not release trapped electrons, but subjects them to electromagnetic radiation in a magnetic field, which causes electrons to resonate and absorb electromagnetic power. The strength of resonance reflects the number of electrons that have become trapped since the crystals were formed. As with TL, age is estimated by relating the amount of resonance to the radioactive content of samples, combined with any external radiation that they have received, and calculating how long it would have taken for that amount of radiation to produce the level of resonance recorded.

Tooth enamel is the best sample material, rather than the dentine of the tooth core. The dentine is porous, allowing new minerals to form after the death of the animal; this can lead to an underestimate of true age by making it possible for uranium to be transported into or out of it. Early hopes that ESR would be applicable to speleothems have not been fulfilled, but this material is very suitable for uranium-series dating. Aitken and Grün both cite convincing examples of ESR dates derived from samples of teeth from Canada, Germany and France; the dates were credible because they correlated well both with the climatic stages to which the animal species belonged and with uranium-series dates. ESR has been used in dating Border Cave in South Africa, indicating much earlier dates (around 170,000 years ago) for potential human occupation than previously suspected (Pettitt 2005: 363).

Future progress with ESR is likely to take place alongside uranium-series and other dating methods so that anomalies and errors may be detected and investigated. In contrast to potassium–argon dating, ESR is a direct method that dates teeth from animals and humans rather than the stratigraphic context in which they were found. 'This approach will overcome one of the main problems of the interpretation of dating results in palaeoanthropological contexts, namely the precise relationship between the samples that have been dated and the hominin specimen whose age is to be determined. Certainly, the best dating strategy is to analyse the human remains themselves' (Grün 1997: 243).

4.6   DERIVATIVE TECHNIQUES

Aitken (1990: 2) drew a clear distinction between **absolute** and **derivative** dating methods and this has been reinforced by Sternberg (1997: 324). Derivative methods may only be used for dating if their results can be related to a timescale or reference curve that has been established by absolute dating methods. Thus, the level of thorium-230 found in a sample of stalagmite is a product of its uranium content, and the sample's age is calculated from the known radioactive half-life of ^{230}Th; since this is not affected in any way by its environment the result can be described as **absolute**. In contrast, dating the change of one form of amino acid to another, or the absorption of water by obsidian (outlined below: p. 184), is **derivative** because the rate of alteration varies and is heavily dependent on the temperature and humidity of the context in which the sample was buried.

Fluorine, uranium and nitrogen testing (**FUN**) was one of the first scientific dating methods used in the examination of bone (Ellis 2000:

219–26; Aitken 1990: 219–20). It did not attempt to provide an estimate of age, but addressed a more fundamental problem that affects bones or artefacts of any kind: are the finds that were excavated from a single level, for example a layer containing artefacts and bones in a cave, really contemporary? Does the stratum contain older items that have eroded out of earlier contexts, or items dug up accidentally during a later phase of occupation? Bones buried in uniform conditions over the same length of time should produce identical results; if they do not, some disturbance must have taken place. FUN dating has a special place in the history of archaeological science because it revealed in the 1950s that 'Piltdown Man' – a skull that apparently linked apes to humans, excavated in Sussex in 1912 – had actually been fraudulently assembled from human and ape bones of widely differing ages. Exactly who carried out the fraud and why is a fascinating story that has been investigated several times with differing results (Russell 2003).

4.6.1   Protein and amino acid diagenesis dating

- key references: Hare *et al.*, 'Protein and amino acid diagenesis dating' 1997; Aitken, *Science-based dating* 1990: 204–14; Dincauze, *Environmental archaeology* 2000: 101–4; Berger and Protsch, 'Fluorine dating' 1991.

Bones, teeth and shells contain proteins that break down after death, and the most commonly investigated products of decomposition are amino acids. **Amino acid racemisation** dating (AAR) measures changes between the L- and D-forms of these amino acids; their ratio is an indication of age. However, the rate of change is highly dependent on temperature and burial conditions, and it is necessary to make many assumptions before any date can be suggested. Ideally, comparisons using another dating method such as ^{14}C are required before any confidence can be achieved. Shell samples have proved more reliable than bone, and ostrich eggs have been useful in dating early hominin sites in East Africa (Johnson and Miller 1997). Shell is more reliable in geological and climatic contexts than in archaeology, as samples from occupation sites might have been affected by burning or other human processes that upset the natural chemistry. Research into the essential process of calibrating and refining these techniques continues, however, despite setbacks such as the very early dating of human remains from North America that appeared to push colonisation back beyond 40,000 years, rather than the conventional 11,000 years. The specimens have been re-dated by the AMS radiocarbon technique and are now only around 5,000 years old (Hare *et al.* 1997: 272–3).

4.6.2 Obsidian hydration dating

- key references: Ambrose, 'Obsidian hydration dating' 2001; Friedman *et al.*, 'Obsidian hydration dating' 1997; Shackley, *Archaeological obsidian studies* 1998; Aitken, *Science-based dating* 1990: 214–18.

Like amino acid racemisation, this dating technique relies on a transformation that takes place over time, and, likewise, it varies according to the context in which the sample has been buried. Obsidian, a natural volcanic glass, was a popular alternative to flint for making flaked tools in many parts of the world (Fig. 5.16). As soon as a fresh surface of obsidian is exposed, for example during the process of making it into a tool, a microscopically thin **hydration rim** begins to form as a result of the absorption of water (Fig. 4.18). Unfortunately, the hydration rim forms at different rates according to the temperature and humidity of the burial context as well as the chemical composition of the obsidian. An additional problem is precise measurement of the microscopic hydration rim and the laborious (and destructive) preparation of samples cut from obsidian artefacts. In regions where radiocarbon dates are available (notably North and Central America), large numbers of measurements can be compiled to provide a calibration curve that may be used for checking the rim thicknesses of individual artefacts or assemblages found on sites with similar burial conditions. In most cases the

radiocarbon method dates the **context**, rather than the **artefact**, while obsidian hydration dates the artefact directly: 'Given the importance of association between the carbonaceous material and the obsidian, it is imperative that only bona fide associations be used to avoid constructing inaccurate rates' (Friedman *et al.* 1997: 317).

4.6.3 Archaeomagnetic dating

- key references: Sternberg, 'Magnetic properties' 2001; Sternberg, 'Archaeomagnetic dating' 1997; Aitken, *Science-based dating* 1990: 225–61; Tarling, 'Archaeomagnetism and palaeomagnetism' 1991.

The Earth's magnetic field undergoes continuous change. The position of magnetic North wanders around the North Pole and even reverses completely to the South Pole for extended periods on a geological timescale. From any reference point its position is measurable in terms of two components: movement up or down (**inclination** or 'dip') and from side to side (**declination**). The **intensity** of the magnetic field also varies over time; it is a measure of strength rather than direction. Unlike regular variations in the Earth's

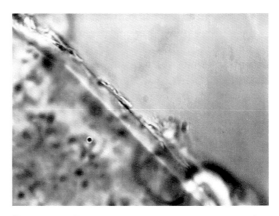

Figure 4.18 This photomicrograph shows a section through the **hydration rim** of an obsidian artefact. The interior of the specimen is on the left; the diagonal band is a layer of weathering on the surface; its depth is demarcated by a **diffusion front** that shows up as a paler line. This can be measured quite accurately, even though it is only three microns thick in this sample. (Prof. J. Michels)

orbit, changes in magnetic field do not follow a pattern that can be used as a reference scale for dating. Past variations have to be reconstructed from archaeological or geological samples dated *independently* by some other means, such as historical evidence or radiocarbon.

Records of magnetic alignment have been made by scientists in Britain since before AD 1600, but not as recently as elsewhere. The reference curve of inclination and declination has been extended back to 1000 BC in Britain; unfortunately, the Earth's magnetic field varies from region to region, so that results from Britain are not even applicable to most of France (**Fig. 4.19**). Thus, magnetic dating clearly illustrates Aitken's definition of a **derivative** method, as it is necessary to establish a separate independently-dated series of measurements for every region where the technique is required (Batt *et al.* 1998). Because the polarity of the Earth's magnetic field reverses every few hundred thousand years, it is possible to use these **geomagnetic reversals** to date geological deposits. However, because such reversals are so infrequent this is only useful for dating early

hominin species, for example at Olduvai in East Africa (Leakey and Roe 1994), where the number of reversals which have taken place in the rocks above their remains can be counted (English Heritage 2006b: 3).

Magnetic dating may be applied to archaeological samples because fine grains of iron oxide with random magnetic alignment are present in most clays and soils. The alignment of grains containing iron is lost if they are heated above 650°C, but they align with the Earth's magnetic field on cooling. This new **thermoremanent** magnetic alignment may be preserved for hundreds of thousands of years as long as heating has not been repeated. Magnetic alignment may also take place during the **deposition** of sediments, for instance in lake beds, where particles suspended in water may align with the prevailing magnetic field as they settle. This technique has been used to date sediments that formed in prehistoric ditches in Britain (English Heritage 2006b: 7). Dating according to the direction of the magnetic field is only reliable on sites where solid clay structures are found that have not moved since becoming magnetised; kilns, hearths and burnt clay walls

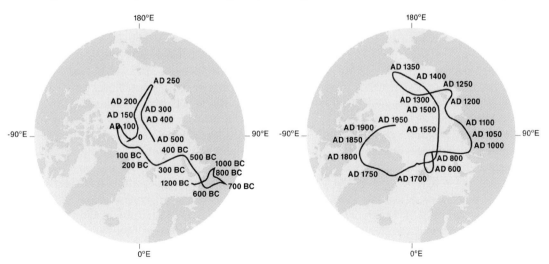

Figure 4.19 The movement of magnetic North, measured from Britain. The map shows the movement of the magnetic North pole over time since 1200 BC. These wandering lines are compiled from observations from as far back as records allow, but samples from dated deposits or structures on archaeological sites must be found to project them further back into the past. Samples from undated sites can be measured in the laboratory and dated according to where their magnetic alignments coincide with the curve established for the relevant geographical area. Difficulties do exist, for example approaching AD 1700, when the same reading also matches late Saxon measurements at the points at which the curve crosses itself. (Redrawn by Chris Unwin, based on English Heritage 2006b, Fig. 4)

or floors are ideal. Small samples are selected and their positions are carefully recorded in relation to the present magnetic field before they are removed. Their modern alignment is duplicated in a laboratory and the difference between the ancient and present alignment measured. The alignment of the ancient sample must then be related to a record of past changes in the magnetic field in the same region as the site from which it was taken. Examination of the movement of magnetic North shows that the line on the diagram crosses at many points, meaning that a sample could belong equally to more than one date. One particular date may sometimes be selected as most likely on archaeological or historical grounds. Fortifications that were possibly erected by Charles the Bald at Pont-de-l'Arche on the Seine in France produced dates around 360 BC, AD 580, AD 860 and AD 1580; of these, only AD 860 ± 20 matched a historical reference to a Viking attack in AD 865 (Dearden and Clark 1990). Even when there is no reference curve, archaeomagnetism may be used to study whether events on different sites were contemporary; measurements established that destruction by burning of Minoan sites on Crete did not happen at the same time as the eruption of Thera, which destroyed the town of Akrotiri further north in the Aegean (Sternberg 1997: 344–5).

Although archaeomagnetic dating normally requires samples that have not moved since they aligned with the Earth's magnetic field, portable fired objects such as bricks or pots that were fired in a horizontal position may be examined to determine the 'dip' angle (inclination), although the declination will have been lost. This is of limited use, but might be used to test whether objects were of the same date or indeed which way up they were fired. Magnetic intensity does not depend on a sample remaining in a particular position, but like thermoremanent magnetism it varies from area to area. An independently-dated reference series of measurements is needed before it can be used for dating; in practice, intensity varies too little for it to be useful, but it does make a valuable addition to measurements of direction, particularly at points where the reference curve crosses. Thanks to a particularly long record of magnetic measurements of intensity *and* direction,

prehistoric sites in Bulgaria can be related to a reference scale back to 6000 BC (Sternberg 1997: 336–8), while samples of known age from fired structures and sediments from near Xi'an, China, could contribute to a calibration curve (Batt *et al.* 1998). Such work underlines Sternberg's warning that, 'As a derivative dating method, the success of archaeomagnetic dating ultimately depends on the complementary success of other chronometric methods' (1997: 350).

4.7 THE AUTHENTICITY OF ARTEFACTS

- key references: Stoneham, 'Authenticity testing' 1991; Jones, *Fake? The art of deception* 1990.

When major museums buy items for their collections they become involved in expensive commercial dealings in the fine art market. The profits to be made encourage not only illicit plundering of ancient sites, but also skilful forgeries. Scientific dating techniques can provide reassurance; when what is needed is confirmation that an object is not a modern fake, rather than a precise date, full control of all the variables that affect accuracy is not necessary. Thermoluminescence and archaeomagnetism provide adequate checks on pottery and elaborate ceramic sculptures from Africa and South America that fetch high prices; samples of suitably heated clay may also be found inside cast bronze artefacts and statues if their cores have not been fully removed. It is difficult (but not completely impossible) for a forger to simulate the levels of radioactivity or magnetism that should be found in genuine items. Radiocarbon dating by the AMS technique allows very small samples to be taken from wooden, bone or other organic artefacts without affecting their appearance. Dendrochronology is helpful in the study of wooden panels used in furniture and early paintings, while paints and pigments may be examined by means of various forms of radioactive isotope dating. Other analyses can establish whether the materials and techniques used for making ancient objects existed at the time of supposed manufacture, but these are not primarily dating methods (Chapter 5, p. 227). There are ethical aspects to providing evidence of authenticity (which will reinforce high prices) if the artefacts concerned have been extracted from sites and/or exported illegally; Oxford University's laboratories withdrew this service because it might encourage further looting (Inskeep 1992).

4.8 CONCLUSIONS

Thus scientific dating is not just a boring necessity that tidies things up by providing numbers; it is vital for valid interpretation.

(Aitken 1990: 1)

Archaeological dating has been strengthened immeasurably by the growth of the extraordinarily diverse range of scientific techniques outlined above, which underline the multidisciplinary nature of archaeology (**Box 4.7**). Traditional methods have *not* been replaced, however, and the definition of stratigraphic sequences by careful observation and excavation of structures and finds is essential for understanding the development of sites and for typological studies of artefacts. Scientific dating techniques add accuracy and allow interpretation to move beyond simple hypotheses about the chronological relationships between sites, regional cultures or forms of artefacts. The transition from hunting and gathering to agriculture, and the emergence of early civilisations, may be interpreted in increasingly meaningful human terms now that we know – thanks to radiocarbon dating – when they occurred and how long the processes of transformation took. Similarly climatostratigraphy and potassium–argon, uranium series and fission-track dating have provided a framework for the study of hominin evolution and dated the point at which stone tools began to be used. The emergence of anatomically modern humans and the replacement of Neanderthals is being placed on an increasingly secure footing (Aitken, Stringer and Mellars 1993) and the recolonisation of Europe after the last Ice Age is being refined (Blockley *et al.* 2000a, b).

Scientific dating techniques play more of a supporting role in historical periods and they are particularly valuable where there is doubt over historical dates, or where gaps exist in the historical framework. It must not be forgotten that even absolute methods such as radiocarbon had to be validated first by testing samples of known historical date. Libby used finds from Egyptian pyramids up to 5,000 years old, dated by historical records of the reigns of pharaohs, to test the consistency of ^{14}C measurements beyond the record of tree rings available in the 1940s (Aitken 1990: 58, Fig. 3.2). The refinement of radiocarbon dating, combined with dendrochronology, now feeds information back into this process. Although problems remain with the eruption of Thera, detailed scientific dating of the late Bronze Age around the Aegean generally confirms the sequences built up from artefact typologies and historical records over the last century (Manning and Weninger 1992). As with other scientific approaches to archaeology, the whole procedure is founded on cooperation, and the increasing complexity of methods used to refine the accuracy of scientific dating techniques demands ever-closer collaboration between scientists, historians, prehistorians and excavators to produce results that benefit all in different ways.

Schwarcz's concluding comments about uranium series dating apply to most other scientific techniques:

As with all methods of chronometric dating, it is important to collect the best possible samples for analysis. For this reason it is desirable to have the site visited by the scientists doing the dating; even experienced archaeologists have difficulty identifying the optimal samples, or appreciating how much material of any given type may be needed for analysis. Repeated visits to a site after initial attempt at dating may be very useful ...

(Schwarcz 1997: 179)

Pollard has issued a valuable warning: 'Perhaps the greatest challenge to be overcome is the widespread perception that producing an

BOX 4.7   Dating an archaeological excavation

This hypothetical excavation trench demonstrates the methods of dating which might be applied. The relative sequence of the **stratification** can clearly be established and applied to any finds and structures associated with each level. Layer 8 contains early Stone Age animal bones which might be suitable for dating by **ESR** or **amino acid racemisation**, while some animal species may have datable evolutionary features (**biostratigraphy**) or may indicate a particular **climatic phase**. The early deposit might be related to a period when the **polarity** of the earth's magnetic field was reversed. As it is sealed by volcanic material (7) it should be datable by the **potassium–argon** method, or, if comparatively recent, by reference to eruptions that can be correlated with **ice cores** or abnormal **tree rings**. Layer 6 consists of waterlogged deposits containing well-preserved wood and other botanical material; if it dates to a period younger than the last Ice Age, the large timbers may be datable by **dendrochronology**, while **pollen** and other plants will give detailed climatic information; **radiocarbon** will be the primary technique, however. The latest dates from this level will give a valuable *terminus post quem* for layer 5, which has the first clear evidence of structures. The burning associated with hearths offers possibilities not only for radiocarbon but also **thermoluminescence** (TL) and **archaeomagnetic** dating. The **typology** of tools and pottery should also be very helpful for giving a general idea of chronology; artefacts burned at the time of their use or when discarded may be checked by TL.

The wall of a building (C) and a road with drainage ditches (D) may belong to a period when **documentary evidence** could be important. The carved block of masonry to the left of the wall looks significant from a **stylistic** or **typological** point of view, and finds of **coins** may well offer more precision than any scientific techniques. However, the period of abandonment indicated by the decay of the building, the silting up of the road ditches and the accumulation of a layer of soil (layer 3) may require radiocarbon dating on suitable organic samples, or, if those are not available, **optically stimulated luminescence** (OSL) or archaeomagnetic dating of distinct layers of sediment. Cut into layer 2 are two graves (A and B) containing skeletons, along with grave-goods such as pottery that should give clues to the age and cultural connections of the deceased people; historical records may pinpoint the period of the cemetery. Again, scientific techniques would only be needed if other sources of evidence were absent. Documentary sources may also indicate how long ago the site was abandoned and given over to the agricultural use represented by topsoil layer 1 (drawn by Chris Unwin).

archaeological date is a routine procedure' (Pollard 2008: 146). He reminds us that the use of Bayesian statistics and the increasing implementation of rigorous sampling strategies are far from straightforward. Without an understanding of error margins, the source of the material being dated and the nature of the science involved, archaeologists can all too easily misinterpret or misuse the dates which they obtain. 'Dates serve archaeology, not the other way around, and a date is only as good as the quality and integrity of the samples actually dated and their archaeological relevance' (Pettitt 2005: 332).

4.9 GUIDE TO FURTHER READING

The subject of archaeological dating is sufficiently precise for the most important works to have been included in the text; consult the works cited as key references beneath section headings within this chapter first.

Dating was a crucial part of the emergence of modern archaeology in the nineteenth century (Chapter 1) and is an important element in any excavation (Chapter 3) or fieldwork project (Chapter 2); it is also intimately related to archaeological science (Chapter 5). Thus, much may be learned by looking at discussions of chronology in excavation and fieldwork reports and in studies of archaeological objects ranging from museum catalogues and typological classifications to analyses involving laboratory science. Truncer, *Picking the lock of time* 2003, provides an interesting account of the development of chronologies in American archaeology in the early twentieth century.

Dating forms part of all general works about archaeological methods, but where specific books are concerned a good starting point is Biers, *Art, artefacts and chronology in classical archaeology* 1992. The best overview of scientific techniques remains Aitken, *Science-based dating in archaeology* 1990, which may be read selectively because it is carefully divided into introductory sections and more detailed discussions of technicalities. Authoritative essays on many forms of dating are included in Ellis, *Archaeological method and theory: an encyclopaedia* 2000; this book, along with 'Section 1: dating' in Brothwell and Pollard, *Handbook of archaeological sciences* 2001, also gives guidance about further reading. As with archaeological science, many articles about dating appear in the journals *Archaeometry* and *Journal of Archaeological Science*, as well as in non-archaeological periodicals such as *Science* and *Nature*. The tables of contents of these periodicals are available on-line, and many libraries allow access to abstracts and even complete texts of papers published in them. English Heritage has produced a number of detailed guidelines on luminescence, archaeomagnetism and dendrochronology which are particularly useful for examining sampling strategies, but which also discuss principles and case studies. A specific set of discussions about the interaction of scientific and historical dating in one of the most contentious areas of archaeology can be found in Levy and Higham, *The Bible and radiocarbon dating* 2005. Some good papers discussing problems in creating chronologies for Later European prehistory can be found in Lehoërff, *Construire le temps* 2008.

CHAPTER 5

Archaeological science

5

Archaeological science is the application of scientific techniques to archaeological problems, whose methodologies ultimately lie in a broad range of sciences including physics, chemistry, biochemistry, biology, medicine, geology, geography, and materials science.

Thinking scientifically and an awareness of scientific techniques should be part of the armoury of every archaeologist.

(QAA Benchmark Statement for Archaeology 2007)

Archaeology has always borrowed concepts and techniques from other disciplines; thus, it is not surprising to find that the impact of science on archaeology has been as dramatic as upon other aspects of modern life. The many dating methods described in Chapter 4 demonstrate the fundamental role of science, but also illustrate an interactive relationship. The 'radiocarbon revolution' originated in advances in nuclear physics, but its refinement depended heavily upon archaeological investigation of its results, while calibration of dates by means of tree rings required cooperation with environmental sciences. Radiocarbon dating now forms part of a multidisciplinary approach to understanding long-term environmental change which may help to guide twenty-first-century responses to global warming.

A question asked in earlier editions of this book – 'Is archaeology a science?' – now seems redundant. When asked by the government to provide descriptive 'benchmarks' for archaeology degrees, a team of British archaeologists stated that 'the integration of the humanities and sciences is likely to underpin most degree programmes given that this inter-disciplinarity is as much philosophical as practical/methodological.' Like individual archaeologists, 'degree programmes will be located at different points within a triangle drawn between the complementary archaeologies of the humanities, sciences, and professional practice.' (QAA 2007)

Although this chapter treats archaeological science as a separate topic, we hope to emphasise integration throughout. After some introductory thoughts about the nature of 'science' this chapter will gradually shift the focus from the environmental setting of human life to details of individual artefacts:

- **Climate**

- The **geosphere**, including geology and soils

- The **biosphere**: plants, and the use of pollen and tree rings in environmental reconstruction

- **Animals**, fish, molluscs, insects and other invertebrates

- **Humans**, including burials, pathology, diet and genetics

- **Artefacts and raw materials** including stone, metal and pottery

- **Conservation** of sites and artefacts

- **Statistics**

- **Experimental archaeology**.

5.1 THE NATURE OF SCIENCE

- key references: Pollard, 'Putting infinity up on trial' 2004; Brothwell and Pollard, *Handbook of archaeological sciences* 2001; Jones, *Archaeological theory and scientific practice* 2002; Pollard and Bray 'A bicycle made for two?' 2007; Johnson, *Archaeological theory* 2010: 35–49.

Chapter 1 outlined the growth of archaeology as a distinctive discipline; a parallel account of the history of science would be necessary for a full discussion of the relationship between them. It is easy to recognise **archaeological science** when it draws upon laboratory procedures that take place in institutions where the main activities are not archaeological. However, many museums and universities possess their own scientific laboratories which use identical methods for entirely archaeological purposes. **Scientific archaeology** is quite another matter, for, like archaeologists, natural scientists do not possess a uniform philosophical and theoretical outlook. One part of the agenda of the New Archaeology, which developed in the United States in the 1960s, was to make archaeology more scientific (Chapter 6, p. 265); however, it took a rather narrow view of science which demanded that the subject should be conducted in manner that allowed everything to be hypothesised, tested, and used to generate explanatory laws. Other approaches that emerged in the 1980s and 1990s shared the New Archaeology's links with anthropology, but rejected rigid **scientism** and directed attention towards human experience of society and the world rather than general processes that governed them (Chapter 6, p. 000). Under the influence of postmodernism and critical theory, some may view science as (at best) a discourse that it is just one of many possible ways of talking about the world, or as (at worst) an embodiment of Western capitalist ideology, designed to keep power away from oppressed and colonialised people (see Jones 2002).

These divergent attitudes may be understood (if not resolved) in a historical context. Julian Thomas, although writing about archaeologies of space and landscape rather than science, summarises the changes particularly well:

It is revealing to consider how and why these difficulties should have arisen. Contemporary western understandings of landscape are set within a distinctive conception of the world which developed during the birth of the modern era. In pre-modern Europe, no great ontological gulf was recognized between human beings and the rest of creation. All things were the products of God's handiwork, and all things could be the subjects of culture and cultivation. The categorical separation of culture from nature, and of human beings from the environment, can be identified with the growth of instrumental reason, exemplified by the Scientific Revolution and the Enlightenment. This is the hallmark of what Martin Heidegger referred to as the 'age of the world picture,' an era in which the world comes to be conceived and grasped as an image that can be apprehended by humanity. In a sense, humanity has gradually usurped God in the modern era, assuming a position at the centre of creation. But instead of the creator, Man (*sic*) has become the arbitrator of reality, so that that which exists is that which has been brought before Man. In consequence, vision has become the dominant metaphor for the acquisition of knowledge, and observational science has gained a pre-eminent position in the definition of reality and truth.

Object and subject have been split, so that Man becomes the active subject who observes a passive nature, the object of science.

(Thomas 2001: 167)

This concise summary underlines the fact that 'science', as the separate discipline that we recognise today, emerged imperceptibly in the same way that archaeology did, and for many of the same reasons. Perhaps it is a growing sensitivity to Thomas's explanation of the separation of nature from culture that leads us to begin Chapter 5 with environmental science. However, defining which areas of scientific analysis should be defined as 'Environmental Archaeology', 'Human Palaeoecology', 'Geoarchaeology' or 'Bioarchaeology' can be confusing and remains contentious (e.g. Albarella 2001). This demonstrates the increasingly multidisciplinary approaches of archaeological science and the increasingly futile attempts to study aspects of archaeology separately (Pollard and Bray 2007).

5.2   THE ENVIRONMENT

- key references: Dincauze, *Environmental archaeology* 2000; Evans and O'Connor, *Environmental archaeology* 1999; Evans, *Land and archaeology* 1999; Branch, *Environmental archaeology* 2005.

Environmental archaeology is one of the clearest demonstrations of multidisciplinarity to be found in archaeological science, and its results contribute data to an extraordinarily wide range of issues. To take one simple example, an archaeologist engaged in studies of Stone Age hunter-gatherers requires detailed knowledge of plant and animal resources, an understanding of prevailing climatic conditions, and information about human diet, diseases and life expectancy (Smith 1997). This was recognised in the early nineteenth century by pioneering prehistorians who excavated prehistoric cave sites and paid close attention to animal remains as well as to human bones and artefacts (Chapter 1, p. 30). In 1853 a drought

that lowered lake levels in Switzerland revealed Neolithic and Bronze Age settlements where remains of plants were preserved in addition to wooden and bone artefacts (Chapter 3, p. 119; Stiebing 1993: 229–31). Early research into the environmental setting of humans in the past in Scandinavia was stimulated by the diversity of modern environments and plentiful occurrence of waterlogged sites where suitable evidence was preserved. Early twentieth-century botanists defined a series of **climatic zones** characterised by changes in plant species since the last Ice Age, and these could be dated over a 12,000-year span by **varves** (Chapter 4, p. 162; Fischer and Kristiansen 1998). Awareness of this work led Grahame Clark to excavate a waterlogged Mesolithic hunter-gatherer site at Star Carr, Yorkshire, in 1949. His specific purpose was to recover a wide spectrum of botanical and zoological evidence in order to study the economy and society of its inhabitants, and to relate the site to the dated climatic phases known from Scandinavia (Trigger 2006: 353). The potential of such evidence – and the value of high-quality excavation and recording – has been reinforced by numerous reinterpretations and re-examination of Clark's work, along with further investigation of the site itself (Legge and Rowley-Conwy 1988; Mellars 2009).

The environment is a major focus for archaeological science; the historical background given above only hints at the massive expansion that has taken place; environmental archaeology now ranges from broad perspectives on global climate down to the lice and bacteria that affected the daily lives of individual people. While some sources of evidence are provided by scientists who are not directly involved in archaeology, biologists studying the distribution of plant and animal species in the past cannot ignore the impact of humans (Nicholson and O'Connor 2000). Furthermore, archaeological excavations provide stratified and dated samples of bones, shells, plants and soils; their interpretation is a joint effort between archaeologists and scientists. Studying the impact of environmental factors upon humans may also involve mapping ancient settlements and analysing economic systems through large fieldwork projects of the kind described in Chapter 2. It is not surprising to find that modern preoccupations about the environment are echoed in interpretations of the past, whether by blaming the fall of civilisations upon the failure of rainfall or holding humans responsible for catastrophic erosion caused by careless farming methods (McIntosh *et al.* 2000). 'The complexity of the natural world and, especially, of potential human responses within and to that world, defeats any hopes for easy, direct, causal connections between forms of human society or existence and the non-human world. However, no understanding of human conditions in the past can be achieved without some grasp of physical and biological contexts' (Dincauze 2000: 19).

5.3 CLIMATE

- key references: Lowe and Walker, *Reconstructing quaternary environments* 1997; Wilson *et al.*, *The great Ice Age* 2000; Burroughs, *Climate change in prehistory* 2005.

Climate is the end result of interactions between a number of 'spheres' – **atmosphere**, **geosphere**, **hydrosphere**, **cryosphere**, **biosphere** (air, rocks, water, ice, and living things). The complexity of the ways in which they produce current conditions makes it easy to see why reconstructing past climate is a difficult business, and why it is even harder to explain change (Dincauze 2000: 38–9). In addition, one fundamental external factor has affected the Earth on a planetary scale – the fluctuation of solar radiation caused by the behaviour of the Sun itself in conjunction with changes in the Earth's axis and orbit. It has already been explained how the pattern of orbital changes provides a key for dating major episodes of climatic change because it is regular and predictable; a dated succession of glaciations or 'Ice Ages' reflecting global temperature has been established through **climatostratigraphy** (Chapter 4, p. 161) (**Box 5.1**). Not only do we have astronomical dating for major Ice Age episodes, but also accurate indications of global temperatures. Evidence over a geological time scale comes

from **marine isotope stages** detected in cores extracted from deep seabed deposits, while more recent indications are derived from annual layers in ice cores. These may include layers volcanic ash, known as tephra, which may be useful in dating and relating climatic changes to volcanic eruptions (see Chapter 4; **Box 4.5**), The cores drilled from ice sheets overlap with records from **tree rings**, and the results can be correlated with historical evidence in recent centuries (Frenzel 1992).

Temperature is only part of the story, however, for glaciations affect the high latitudes very differently from the low. This is why the interaction of spheres is an important concept; it is easy to see how cold in one area could produce increases in rainfall in another which might erode soils and change the population of plants and animals that are able to live there. Global changes in climate are likely to have been critical in shaping the evolution of hominins and early humans (Willoughby 2007: 66). The dispersal of modern humans from Africa (see below: p. 223) can be directly related to changes in sea levels caused by the fluctuating climate. The peopling of Australia, for example, appears to have taken place at a period of low sea levels between 67,000 and 61,000 years ago (Burroughs 2005: 113).

As modern humans spread around the world in growing numbers, their own behaviour became increasingly important in changing plants, animals, soils – and ultimately the climate itself (Vrba *et al.* 1995). There is considerable debate on whether the arrival of humans in North America and Australia led to the mass extinction of so-called 'megafauna', such as the mammoth in North America, or whether climate change was responsible (Wilson *et al.* 2000: 230–2; Branch *et al.* 2005: 222–36). While long-term change is obviously important, short-term fluctuations also had considerable impact on human life, especially in farming communities dependent upon specialised crops and animals (Coles and Mills 1998). There is growing evidence for natural catastrophes such as meteorite impacts, earthquakes, tidal waves and volcanic eruptions (Baillie 1998a; Peiser *et al.* 1998; Koch 1998). Ice sheet cores are very interesting in this respect, for

Climate and the human past

We live in a period when **climate change** is having observable consequences on our environment. People are being affected in a variety of ways – not all of them necessarily negative. It is easy to imagine the effects of more profound changes brought about by longer-term trends in climate, especially the onset and retreat of Ice Ages. Environmental factors have been linked to changes in human settlement patterns and economies, such as the emergence of anatomically modern humans in Africa and the beginning of farming in south-western Asia (Sherratt 1997b; Burroughs 2005). The pattern of alternating ice ages and warm interludes has been established with the help of a range of geological and biological indicators (table 5.1); peaks of cold conditions are indicated by even-numbered **marine isotope stages**, and episodes of warming are indicated by odd numbers (drawn by Chris Unwin based on Lowe 2001: Fig. 1.2).

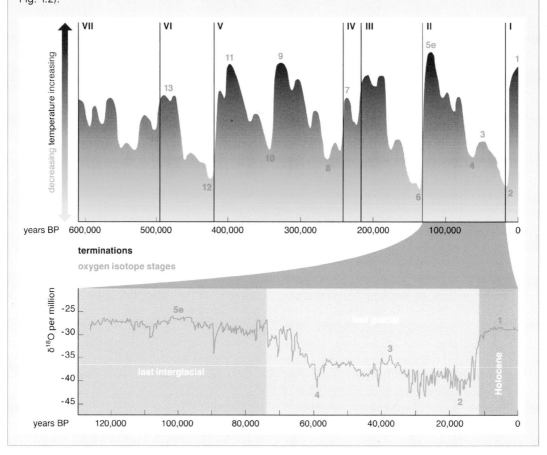

they contain clear records of volcanic eruptions, represented by layers containing high levels of dust and acidity. Volcanic ash in the upper atmosphere may cause severe disturbances to the weather by blocking solar radiation, and if these circumstances were prolonged for many years they could lead to changes in settlement patterns. The abandonment of upland settlements in northern Britain around the twelfth century BC has been attributed to this phenomenon, and supporting evidence comes from tree rings that indicate a period of around twenty years of appalling cold and wet weather from 1159 BC (Baillie 1995: 73–90). Dramatic effects in the

Table 5.1 Sources of proxy data on climates (based on Dincauze 2000: 178, table 8.2; data recoverable during archaeological investigation in CAPITALS)

Range	Indicators	Temperature	Humidity or rainfall	Chemistry of air, water or soil	Biomass	Volcanic activity	Solar activity	Atmosphere	Sea levels
beyond million years	marine cores	yes		water	yes			yes	
	GEOMORPHIC FEATURES	yes	yes			yes			yes
	sedimentary rocks		yes	soil		yes		yes	yes
,000 to million	marine cores	yes		water	yes			yes	
	ice cores	yes	yes	air	yes	yes	yes	yes	
	sedimentary rocks		yes	soil		yes		yes	yes
	lake sediments	yes	yes	water	yes	yes		yes	
	TERRESTRIAL SEDIMENTS		yes		yes			yes	
	FAUNA	yes	yes	soil	yes				
	POLLEN	yes	yes		yes				
	PALEOSOLS	yes	yes	soil		yes			
	corals			water					yes
0 to ,000	TERRESTRIAL SEDIMENTS		yes		yes	yes		yes	
	PALEOSOLS	yes	yes	soil		yes			
	POLLEN	yes	yes		yes				
	TREE RINGS	yes	yes	air	yes	yes	yes		
	FAUNA	yes	yes	soil	yes				
	lake sediments	yes	yes	water	yes	yes		yes	
	ice cores	yes	yes	air	yes	yes	yes	yes	
	corals			water					yes
	historical records	yes	yes		yes	yes	yes		yes
present 100	historical records	yes	yes		yes	yes	yes		yes
	TREE RINGS	yes	yes	air	yes	yes	yes		
	varves	yes	yes	water	yes	yes		yes	

medieval period have been attributed to a comet or meteorite strike in AD 536 (Keys 1999; Gunn 2000). Direct links between episodes of climate change and a decline in human settlement, or periods of upheaval, should be made only with caution. Climate change may have had widely varying impacts on different regions, and many societies adapted to new lifestyles (Dark 2006; Fagan 2008).

Vegetation is an important measure of regional climatic change and also has direct archaeological implications. Plants are very sensitive to temperature and moisture, and most species produce pollen. Fortunately, pollen grains resist decay well, so that cores taken from bogs or lake beds contain excellent stratified records of wind-blown pollen (below: p. 200). The general pattern of climatic change since the last Ice Age has been well known since the 1920s (**Box 5.1**) and was an important dating method before the radiocarbon method was developed. The distribution of temperature-sensitive species of animals and insects also provides detailed information about small changes in climatic conditions.

5.4 THE GEOSPHERE

It is particularly easy to appreciate the importance of interactions between atmosphere, hydrosphere, cryosphere and the **geosphere** ('the solid and viscous mineral matter of the planet, especially that manifested near the surface as rock and sediment': Dincauze 2000: 39). We are surrounded by landforms shaped by erosion by wind, water and ice, while plants (wild and domesticated) flourish or struggle according to the characteristics of surface soils formed by various forms of erosion. Human settlement patterns are also strongly influenced by terrain and soils, and climatic change can lead to silted rivers and flooding that render previously favourable locations uninhabitable. As Colin Renfrew pointed out, 'every archaeological problem starts as a problem of geoarchaeology' (1976, quoted in Pollard 1999: 7), as archaeology is bound to the broader environment in all its aspects.

5.4.1 Geology

- key references: Rapp and Hill, *Geoarchaeology: the earth-science approach to archaeological interpretation* 2006; Goldberg and Macphail, *Practical and theoretical geoarchaeology* 2006; Lewin and Foley, *Principles of human evolution* 2004, chapter 4.

The earlier the period of archaeology that is being studied, the more important geology and geomorphology are likely to be – particularly in phases related to Ice Ages. Geology and climatology also reveal major changes in sea level, and the creation of new land by sedimentation or volcanic activity. This information not only influences our concepts about the environmental context of human activities but also provides vital insights into the likelihood of finding sites and artefacts (A.G. Brown 1997). The significance of early finds of bones and flint tools in deep gravel beds was only fully appreciated when geologists had studied their formation and understood the principles of stratification. The hand-axes discovered at Hoxne, the Somme valley and elsewhere – and the bones associated

with them – did not constitute occupation sites, but had been eroded from their original resting places and redeposited in river gravels (Chapter 1, p. 29; Hosfield 1999). This makes sites such as Boxgrove, where actual living surfaces have survived with related butchered bones, hand-axes and remains of *Homo heidelbergensis*, especially important (Stringer 2006: 95–100). Geology is also a key component in the study of early hominin fossils in East Africa, where many finds have been made in layers of sediment separated by volcanic material (e.g. Isaac and Isaac 1997). It is very important to understand the stratification of these deposits, and to date them by the potassium–argon method and magnetic reversals (above: p. 185); expeditions around Lake Turkana in Kenya have actually been planned according to the location of deposits already dated in this way (Lewin and Foley 2004: chapter 4). Not all geological changes are gradual, of course, and **archaeoseismology** is a very important field of study in earthquake zones (Stiros and Jones 1996).

5.4.2 Soils

- key references: Barham and Macphail, *Archaeological sediments and soils* 1995; Holliday, *Soils in archaeological research* 2004; French, *Geoarchaeology in action* 2003: 35–58.

A knowledge of geomorphology is also vital for reconstructing the wider environment of ancient sites in terms of natural resources. Surface deposits and outcrops of rock, combined with evidence for rivers and lakes, dictate the forms of vegetation and animal life available to hunter-gatherers or early farmers. An understanding of soils adds further detail, since soils with differing colours, textures and other characteristics are formed and changed by both natural and human activities. Maps of modern soils and their present agricultural potential are published in many countries, but they are not a reliable indicator of their state in the past. Modern fieldwork projects, such as the Neothermal Dalmatia survey outlined in Chapter 2 (p. 54), collect samples of soils to study the history of land-use. Soil scientists need to examine stratified profiles, and are particularly keen to find deep deposits that have been cut through by erosion or modern construction (**Fig. 5.1**). When forests on hills are cleared for cultivation or grazing, an increase in erosion normally leads to the deposition of sediments in valleys that may cover up earlier phases of valley-floor cultivation and settlement (Evans *et al.* 1993).

Soils provide evidence of past climate through microscopic analyses of their structure (**micromorphology**: Courty 1989). The sizes and shapes of particles deposited by water during damp episodes may be distinguished from wind-blown

material that accumulated during periods of low rainfall. Soils are classified into types that provide interesting insights into human disturbance of the environment. The **podsols** characteristic of heath and moorland, which only support a thin surface layer of vegetation, are a good example. They overlie a layer of leached soil from which rain water has washed iron and humus down to the surface of the subsoil. However, when prehistoric earthworks erected on what is now moorland are excavated, the soils beneath them are frequently found to be **brownearths** typical of woodland,

Figure 5.1 One of the most important things revealed by excavation is the soil beneath, around and above excavated features. These Bronze Age stone structures were excavated at a site revealed by coastal erosion at Brean Down, Somerset (Bell 1990); deep deposits had been formed by blown sand and by soil washed down the hillside. 'Micromorphological analysis was particularly revealing of soil and sediment histories and human activity patterns, which were further examined by a combination of three-dimensional artefact recording, and chemical and magnetic susceptibility analysis. Pollen, diatoms and ostracods provide information on the environment of the marine clays and an associated peat deposit. Charred plant macrofossils revealed only limited evidence of cereal growing. Among the animal bones the usual domesticates predominated, and there were coastal and wetland birds and some fish. Around the Bronze Age structures were mineralised dog coprolites which contained the eggs of human intestinal parasites. Land molluscs reflect an exposed dry dune environment and marine molluscs reflect the rather impoverished fauna of the Severn Estuary' (Bell 1990: 264). (Martin Bell)

not poor-quality podsols. Brownearths are stable when covered by trees, but when woodland is cleared for occupation and agriculture, rainfall causes deterioration; thus, the harsh, inhospitable soil conditions characteristic of open moorlands in much of upland Britain may be a result of human interference. The process of leaching that exhausted brownearths and rendered the land uninhabitable for later farmers might have been accelerated by cold wet periods (caused by volcanic activity) that show up as groups of narrow tree rings (below: p. 205). Although modern rain forests are far from being pristine 'natural' environments (Athens and Ward 1999), the massive scale of modern clearance is leading to a similar result as the stable recycling of nutrients by trees is brought to an end, and alternations of extreme wet and dry conditions break down the structure of the soil.

Archaeological earthworks such as ramparts or burial mounds not only preserve earlier ground surfaces (**Fig. 3.5**) but also provide samples of pollen and/or molluscs (below: p. 200). Buried soils in these situations give important information about the vegetation or form of cultivation that took place immediately before they were built. Dated structures (such as the Antonine Wall in Scotland, constructed in the 130s and 140s AD) act as a *terminus ante quem* for a buried soil. Other characteristics of soils, especially a high phosphate content, can indicate areas of settlement and agriculture (above: p. 78). Samples taken systematically over a wide area may help to define the limits of a settlement without extensive excavation; measurement of the levels of trace metals offers an addition or alternative to phosphate testing (Bintliff *et al.* 1990; Aston *et al.* 1998). The acidity of a soil is a useful guide to the prospects for the survival of pollen and molluscs; if unfavourable, time need not be spent on fruitless collection and processing of inadequate samples.

Recently studies have begun to demonstrate that, through the use of DNA and of AMS radiocarbon dating, cores of soil may provide information on the types of animals which have used the land and the presence and nature of human occupation. This is often called ancient 'dirt' DNA: the extraction of DNA from material within soils rather than directly from bones or other remains. Although such studies remain in their relative infancy, a study of a Norse settlement in Greenland dating from the eleventh to the fifteenth century AD has used radiocarbon dating to date DNA from stratified soil cores to indicate the presence and absence of particular animals at certain periods, helping to establish the nature of subsistence practices for the short-lived Norse occupation of Greenland (Hebsgaard 2009).

5.5 THE BIOSPHERE

- key references: Dincauze, *Environmental archaeology* 2000: 327–493; Berglund, *Palaeoecological events during the last 15,000 years* 1996; Wilkinson and Stevens, *Environmental archaeology* 2005.

Although it takes place in conditions determined by climate and the geosphere, the evolution and expansion of human populations in the past and the present are bound up with effective exploitation of the **biosphere** ('the living organisms of the planet, occurring on and in the rocks, sediments, water, ice, and lower few hundred metres of the air': Dincauze 2000: 39). Three significant shifts have taken place in diet and food sources: the adoption of active hunting as an extension to scavenging from dead animals killed by wild predators; the use of tools and fire to prepare and process food, and (remarkably recently) the transition to farming domesticated animals and plants – a fundamental change still commonly called the Neolithic Revolution. The following sections will examine the kinds of evidence that may be used to study plants and animals, either as part of a general environmental setting or as food resources. Discussing humans in a separate section should not be taken as an indication that they are any less dependent upon general environmental factors.

5.5.1 Plants

- key references: Pearsall, *Paleoethnobotany* 1989; Gale and Cutler, *Plants in archaeology*

2000; Fritz, 'Paleoethnobotanical methods and applications' 2005; Beck, 'Plant remains' 2006.

Botanical identifications are time-consuming and expensive, but are extremely important in the interpretation of an individual site or vegetation in general. Nineteenth-century botanists concentrated on large fragments of plants, but the focus in the twentieth century moved to microscopic pollen grains. Large items such as seeds and pips remain important, however, for they not only reveal the existence of plant species but also give insights into the collection and processing of wild fruits or crops from domesticated plants. The development of flotation (**Box 5.2**), to recover charred plant remains, particularly seeds and charred grain, had a significant impact in identifying the plants which were exploited and in using these to ascertain the nature of farming economies in the past. Finds of particular species of cereal grain have implications for farming and harvesting methods, and further enlightenment about soil conditions is gained from studying seeds of weeds that grew among cereal crops. Studies of the variation of amounts of weeds versus grain found on different sites led many to argue which sites were 'producers' of wheat and which sites may be have been predominantly 'consumers' in Later Prehistoric Europe (Van der Veen 1992). Roots and tubers are important food plants in many parts of the world and their structure may be identified with the help of scanning electron micrographs (Hather 1993). The use of plants for medication, flavouring or intoxication – whether ritual or recreational – should not be overlooked in interpreting remains from sites (Sherratt 1997c; Nunn 1996; Jashemski 1999).

BOX 5.2   # Small but vital: plant and animal remains recovered by means of flotation

Much of the important information needed to reconstruct the diet and environment of people living on ancient sites is found in forms which are not readily visible during an excavation. Small shells, the bones of small animals (especially fish), charcoal and other charred plant remains (such as seeds) can be recovered

through processing soil by means of flotation equipment. Bulk samples of soils from individual archaeological contexts (see Chapter 3) are placed on an extremely fine mesh suspended in water, allowing the heavy sediment to sink while shells, bones and charred plant remains float to the surface (Wilkinson and Stevens 2005: 154–8). The practice of flotation taking place here in the 1970s at Tell Abu Hureyra, an extremely early farming settlement in Syria, was one of the first excavations to systematically use flotation to recover environmental remains providing important evidence on the earliest farming in the Levant (modern day Syria and Lebanon) (Moore *et al.* 2000: 96–102 Andrew Moore/Oxford University Press).

Plant remains visible *without* the help of a microscope survive best in predominantly wet or dry conditions; careful excavation of undisturbed deposits is required if softer parts, such as leaves or petals, are to be recovered along with more fibrous twigs and stalks. It is rare that survival will be as good as in the tomb of Tutankhamun, where bunches of flowers left by mourners were found (Hepper 1990; Vartavan 1999), but a surprisingly good source of plant remains is thatch from the roofs of medieval houses, where they may be preserved by smoke and dry conditions (Letts 1998). **Taphonomy** (the study of the formation of archaeological deposits) is vital in the recovery of all plant material; it should never be forgotten that small plants or seeds recovered from archaeological deposits might have been introduced by birds or animals, rather than humans, whether in ancient or modern times. For example, pollen evidence suggesting that flowers were placed in a Neanderthal burial at Shanidar (Iran) may indicate not reverence for the dead, but the action of a small rodent taking flower-heads into its burrow (Sommer 1999). Supposedly prehistoric grape pips from El Prado (Murcia, Spain) turned out to have radiocarbon dates in the 1960s, and were possibly dropped into excavated deposits by birds (Rivera Nunez and Walker 1991). **Anaerobic** contests, such as the waterlogged conditions found in peat bogs, ensure that plant fibres and textiles may often survive very well.

Indirect evidence of plants is also recovered in surprising ways. Impressions of grain are occasionally preserved on pottery; damp clay vessels were dried before firing, and their bases frequently picked up fragments of straw or grain from dry material that was probably spread out to prevent them from sticking. The organic matter burnt out completely during firing, leaving hollow imprints from which casts can be taken with latex or plaster. These are examined under a microscope to identify the species present. Pottery can also be examined to detect food residues absorbed into the clay during cooking; although animal fats are especially well preserved, evidence for cabbage (or turnip) was identified from epicuticular leaf wax components at the Anglo-Saxon settlement at Raunds (Northamptonshire) where

no other evidence for soft plant tissues had survived (Evershed 2001: 332–3). This kind of evidence extends the range of information about plants to food preparation and cooking.

Pollen, phytoliths and diatoms

- key references: Dimbleby, *The palynology of archaeological sites* 1985; Branch, *Environmental archaeology* 2005: 67–105; Moore *et al.*, *Pollen analysis* 1991; Dincauze, *Environmental archaeology* 2000: 343–62; Piperno, *Phytoliths: a comprehensive guide* 2006.

The most productive technique that has been applied to archaeological plant remains is undoubtedly **palynology** – the study of pollen. All hayfever sufferers know that the air is full of wind-borne pollen during the summer months. Fortunately for archaeologists, each minute grain of pollen has a tough outer shell, with a different shape for each species (**Fig. 5.2**). These shells survive well in soils in which acidity is high enough to reduce the bacterial activity that would normally cause them to decay. The loss of pollen from alkaline soils, such as those of the densely occupied and farmed chalklands of England and northern France, is unfortunate, but these soils are favourable to the survival of molluscs that also provide environmental information (below: p. 212). The toughness of pollen grains allows them to be separated from samples of soil collected on sites by straightforward laboratory methods, but they must then be identified and counted under a microscope by an experienced palynologist – a very time-consuming task. Most grains are less than 0.01 mm in diameter; their abundance makes counting a tedious procedure, but it has the advantage that statistically significant quantities are easily obtained from small samples of soil.

In addition to pollen, there are further microscopic means by which plant species may be detected. **Phytoliths** are crystalline silica bodies formed in and around cells, but are less distinct in shape than pollen grains (Dincauze 2000: 362–5). They normally play a supporting role in plant identification – for example, in a study of Polynesian farming in New Zealand (Horrocks

2000). They are particularly useful in their resistance to decay, surviving where pollen does not. **Diatoms** are microscopic unicellular algae which are commonly found in watery locations, but are also found in soils. The silica-based outer wall of these microscopic algae means they may survive in various sediments and the species identified reflect environmental conditions (Branch *et al.* 2005: 78–82).

Since pollen reflects general changes in vegetation over long periods, palynology is of considerable interest to climatologists, ecologists, botanists and geographers as well as to archaeologists. Samples of pollen taken from cores bored from deep peat bogs or lake sediments are

stratified, with the earliest part lying deepest. A deposit that has formed over thousands of years should reflect overall changes from tundra to forest or from forest to farmland, and indicate fluctuations in the prominence of individual plant species (**Fig. 5.3**). Sufficient analyses have been made to give a fairly clear picture of the major changes of vegetation since the last Ice Age, and to define a series of climatic zones that offered a valuable form of dating before the arrival of the radiocarbon technique (above: p. 163). These zones of climate and vegetation provide a general context for human activities, such as early Stone Age hunting on the open tundra, or Mesolithic hunting and gathering in forests. The application of palynology is worldwide, and its value is not restricted to prehistoric times. It can be used to examine the environment of individual sites or regions in periods before documents provide such information in sufficient detail. When a picture of background vegetation is added to other plant remains, artefacts and animal bones from an excavated settlement, there is an increased possibility of accurate interpretation of past economies and the functions of tools and weapons. However, not everything is as easy as it sounds; concepts of 'natural' environments being re-colonised by plants in an orderly manner after the last Ice Age, and visible effects of human settlers when woodland was cleared for farming, now appear simplistic. Problems begin at the level of collecting pollen samples, because every suitable findspot has its own history of vegetation combined with a myriad of distorting factors that come between actual pollen produced by local plants and the grains isolated in a laboratory sample (Branch *et al.* 2005: 70).

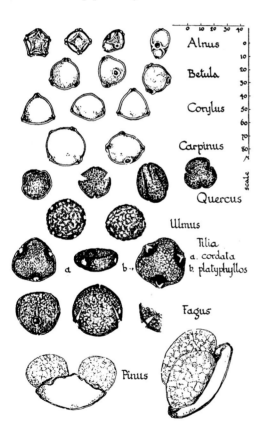

Figure 5.2 Different plant species have distinctive pollen grains whose tough outer shells can be identified by specialists using microscopes in the laboratory. This drawing shows important trees found in postglacial deposits: alder, birch, hazel, hornbeam, oak, elm, lime, beech and pine. (Zeuner 1946: Fig. 21, after Godwin)

Domestication of plants

- key references: Colledge and Conolly, *The origins and spread of domestic plants in southwest Asia and Europe* 2007; Zeder *et al.*, *Documenting domestication* 2006.

The domestication of wild plants in the early stages of settled farming is a process of profound significance that may be investigated through the remains of plants (Jones and Colledge 2001;

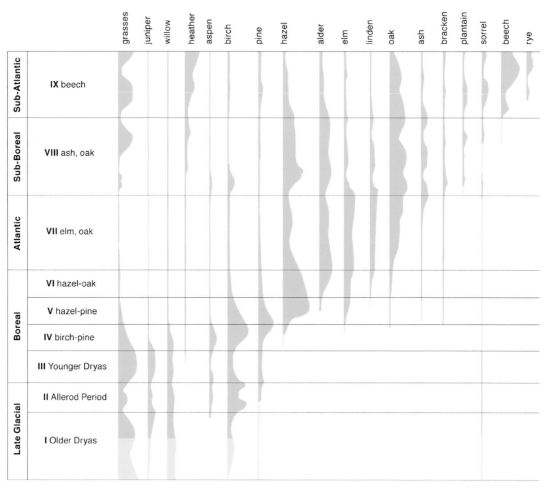

Figure 5.3 Pollen diagrams are not easy to interpret, but the method of presentation is similar to that of seriation (Box 4.1) in that the thickness of the line for each individual species reflects its relative importance. This diagram of vegetation in Jutland incorporates Iversen's results from numerous samples that revealed the recolonisation of Denmark by significant plants since the last Ice Age. The earliest period is at the bottom of the diagram, where in stages I–III, grasses and small hardy trees (birch, willow, juniper) dominated the cold landscape. From V onwards, temperate tree species appeared as warmer conditions developed, replacing open grassland. Human actions began to have marked effects in stage VIII, when forest was cleared to supply fuel and timber and to create open land for cultivation and grazing. Grasses became common again and signs of farming are evident from cereals and associated 'weeds of cultivation' such as plantain. (Drawn by Chris Unwin)

Cowan and Watson 1992). The concept of a 'fertile crescent' in the Middle East where suitable wild species existed together has underpinned many interpretations of how farming first began, but this takes a very European perspective, with cultivated cereals as the critical crop. A much wider range of species was involved in Africa, America and Asia, however, and cultivation developed independently at different times in different places. Maize was a key food source in Mesoamerica, and finds of cobs in stratified deposits show how their size gradually increased through selection in comparison with wild species (Johannessen and Hastorf 1993; Box 5.3). American food plants are of particular interest because they spread to the rest of the world after European contacts began in 1492; the European diet would be very much less varied today without potatoes, tomatoes, peanuts, peppers and pineapples (Gowlett 1993: 170–1).

DNA from ancient plant remains provides

another new avenue of research with great potential (**Box 5.3**; Zeder *et al.* 2006a). Analysis of the DNA from varieties of modern wheat grown in Europe has demonstrated that they are closely similar to each other and that they are most closely related to the wild versions of south-east Turkey, suggesting this may have been the source of the first domesticated wheat (Heun *et al.* 1997). The picture may be more complex, however, and as the science of DNA analysis develops many of its early findings may well be challenged (Allaby *et al.* 2008). As with the use of DNA in human populations, these studies are based primarily on modern animal and plant populations and suffer, as with studies of human DNA, from the relatively small number of DNA samples which derive from ancient remains.

A spectacular example of the study of cultivated plants in a historical period is the investigation of gardens at the Roman city of Pompeii in Italy, where the volcanic eruption of AD 79 sealed vineyards, orchards, vegetable plots and ornamental gardens under a thick layer of ash. Grape-pips, nuts and fruit stones were recovered, but a bonus was the discovery of cavities in the earth where the roots of trees and other large plants had decayed. It was possible to pour plaster into these holes and then excavate the root system, allowing species to be identified from their size and root pattern. One open area once thought to have been a cattle market was found to have been filled with vines and olive trees, and to have had open-air dining couches among the foliage (Jashemski 1979; Greene 1986: 94–7).

Pollen analysis offers considerable potential for identifying the arrival of Neolithic farming, which most prehistorians consider the most fundamental

---

BOX 5.3 Domestication of maize in the Americas

The domestication of wheat around 13,000 years ago in western Asia was a fundamental step from hunting and gathering towards sedentary farming, and ultimately to the rise of complex societies and urban civilisations (see Fig. 1.16). The domestication of plants was equally important in the Americas, where (until the arrival of Europeans) the main crops were maize and potatoes. Genetic analysis of maize from sites across America has indicated it was closest to a form of wild maize still found in southern Mexico, suggesting that this was the original area where domestication took place. Samples of maize from Guila Naquitz, Oaxaca, have been radiocarbon-dated to 6,300 years ago, but DNA analysis suggests that domestication may have taken place more than 8,000 years ago (Zeder 2006a; Piperno *et al.* 2007). The subsequent diffusion of domesticated maize across the Americas has been traced with the help of a variety of evidence methods, including phytoliths, charred seeds and pollen (Thompson 2006; Anthony Ranere, Temple University).

change in human subsistence and settlement. Since the Neolithic economy required the clearance of trees for pasture and arable land, as well as timber for buildings, palynologists can examine samples from a core taken from a suitable location for changes in the proportions of arboreal pollen (**AP**, from trees) and non-arboreal pollen (**NAP**, from grasses and cereals) together with 'weeds of cultivation' that thrived in the new conditions. Fine particles of charcoal may also be detected, indicating forest clearance with the help of burning. Because most pollen is deposited within a few kilometres of its source, it should provide a picture of the plant population in the immediate surroundings of an individual site, although there are always problems of sample reliability. NAP may highlight different proportions of grasses and cereals that indicate the relative importance of grazing and grain production, while pollen from plants such as legumes, flax and hemp may suggest other forms of food production and raw materials for textiles.

Pollen from excavated soils may reveal information that helps in the interpretation of a site in structural rather than environmental terms. Samples from beneath mounds or ramparts may indicate whether the land was forested or covered with scrub before its occupation. Pollen from soil that formed after the abandonment of a site may show whether the land returned to scrub and then forest, or remained open, perhaps as part of the farmland of another settlement nearby. Further questions of direct relevance to an excavator may be answered. Mounds and ramparts can be examined to see if their material was dug from the subsoil, in which case it will contain a high proportion of older fossil pollen, or whether the structures were formed by scraping up turf or topsoil from the surface. This kind of information may help in the interpretation of ditches and pits on a complex site, and clarify their relationships with earthwork features. The Roman turf rampart at North Wall, Chester, was shown by pollen analysis to have been constructed from turf gathered from wood pasture on the banks of the adjacent River Dee (Greig 1992).

Human impact upon vegetation

- key references: Dumayne-Peaty, 'Human impact on vegetation' 2001; Jones and Colledge, 'Archaeobotany' 2001.

Focus upon Neolithic farming has tended to distract attention from the effects that hunter-gatherers had already had upon woodlands. Fine-resolution pollen analysis (FRPA) suggests that they made clearings in woodland and maintained open spaces by burning in order to encourage prey animals such as deer to congregate, attracted by grass and young shoots. Thus, clearing and burning should not always be seen as a prelude to farming, although of course such locations would be an obvious choice for exploitation when the new agricultural economy began. This in turn, of course, would have had its own, sometimes devastating, impact upon wild animal populations (Grayson 2001). Environmental approaches to historical periods also have great potential, as scientific data may be compared with written records (Greene 1986: 72–6; 126–8). Considerable work has been carried out in northern England and Scotland to examine the effects of the Roman conquest of the late first century AD. This is an ideal situation for palynologists, because (unlike Neolithic farming) the Roman arrival is dated by independent historical evidence; at the same time it offers archaeologists a new source of information about the nature of the Roman occupation (Dark and Dark 1997).

Tree rings

- key references: Wimmer and Vetter, *Tree ring analysis* 1999; Schweingrüber, *Tree rings: basics* 1987; Baillie, 'Dendrochronology and environmental change' 1992.

Besides their value for dating (above: p. 164), tree rings provide a continuous annual record of climate. The correlation between modern meteorological records of temperature and precipitation and the width of individual rings seems sufficiently close to allow them to be used to make estimates of conditions in the past before such records began (Schweingrüber 1987: 170–5). At the opposite end of the scale, the pattern of tree rings in an individual trunk is influenced by the location of the tree. Minor fluctuations in the immediate locality, such as fire damage, insect attack, clearance of surrounding trees, drought or flooding, may all leave tell-tale indications in the rings (*ibid*: 176–83). A useful result of this degree of sensitivity is that timbers used in a building or a ship reflect the nature of the woodland where they grew: **dendroprovenancing**. Trees from dense forests, for example, display different ring patterns from those that grew in open spaces or hedgerows. Ring patterns characteristic of a particular area allow the origins of wood to be determined, revealing for example that the wood used to construct a Viking ship excavated in Denmark was from Ireland (Bonde and Christiansen 1993). At a larger scale, identification of wood from ships in northern Europe has been used to examine the nature of the Baltic timber trade in the Middle Ages (Haneca *et al.* 2009: 6–7).

An unexpected by-product of tree-ring dating is the detection of phases of exploitation of the landscape, reflected by the age of tree trunks preserved in river silts. During the Roman occupation of southern Germany, very large numbers of trunks from large trees up to 400 years old ended up in the Danube. It is likely that agriculture was intensified in response to the presence of Roman forts and towns, and that there was an increased demand for timber, both for building purposes and for fuel. These factors led to woodland clearance and soil erosion, resulting in an increase in the amount of sediment that was washed into rivers. This caused flooding that swept away mature trees growing some distance from the normal course of the river (Schweingrüber 1987: 186).

Several precisely dated climatic episodes are suggested by tree rings, notably the dramatic aftermaths of volcanic eruptions. A reduction in tree growth (indicated by narrow rings) in north-western Europe for three years after 1628 BC forms part of the evidence for the explosion of Thera in the Aegean in 1628 (Manning 1999: 265, Fig. 50; Friedrich *et al.* 2006). **Dendrochemical**

analysis of tree rings displaying the anomaly in growth thought to relate to this specific eruption revealed evidence of increased levels of chemicals, such as sulphur and zinc, which may suggest that the eruption was indeed the reason for this growth decline (Pearson *et al.* 2009). The complexity of environmental change is indicated by the fact that trees in nearby Turkey put on a growth spurt at this time; cooler, wetter weather that inhibited growth in one region encouraged it in another (*ibid*: 307–11). That tree rings are so closely dated provides an invitation for archaeologists to scrutinise all sorts of evidence to seek wider indications of changes caused by climatic phenomena. Baillie concluded a paper on such tree-ring events with an optimistic judgement: 'There appears to be unlimited potential for the reconstruction of various aspects of past environmental change from tree-ring records' (1992: 20).

5.5.2   Animals

- key references: Brothwell and Pollard, *Handbook of archaeological sciences* 2001: 359–440; O'Connor, *The archaeology of animal bones* 2004.

Mammals (including humans), birds, reptiles and fish are normally represented only by bones, unless special conditions such as desiccation, freezing or waterlogging have preserved soft tissues. Other kinds of invertebrate animals can be traced by shells (molluscs) or parts of their exoskeletons (crustacea, insects, arthropods). Even microscopic organisms such as parasites and bacteria can be detected in suitable samples. However, bones remain the most important source of information recovered, particularly on excavations, where they may make up a substantial proportion of finds with significant implications for recording and storage – unless the excavation has taken place where soil conditions have been unfavourable, and they have dissolved completely.

Identification of vertebrate bones
- key references: Reitz and Wing, *Zooarchaeology* 1999; Lyman, *Quantitative paleozoology* 2008; Wilson, *Ageing and sexing animal bones* 1982.

Whoever is identifying animal species must have experience of archaeological samples, and will probably need to consult reference collections of modern bones, as well as finds from other sites. Early domesticated animals differ considerably from their modern counterparts (Lepetz 1997), while closely related animals like sheep and goats are almost impossible to separate (Prummel and Frisch 1986). One measure of a site assemblage of bones is the **number of identified specimens** (NISP), which gives a record of the range of species present, but for the purposes of interpretation it is more important to estimate the actual number of animals. This is not a simple matter of counting bones; some individuals may be represented by just one bone, while others have complete skeletons. It is customary to select a bone that each animal only has one of (such as part of the jaw) to estimate the **minimum number of individuals** (MNI) of each species; such figures will only be meaningful in the context of very large collections of bones, of course (Anderson and Boyle 1997). The approximate ages of individual animals may be ascertained by examining the state of ossification of particular bone structures, the eruption of teeth in jaw bones, and the amount of wear on teeth. Sex is more difficult to establish, but statistical studies of large samples of bone dimensions may help to divide them into groups of different sizes, of which the smaller is likely to represent females, while DNA may give an authoritative answer in individual cases (O'Connor 2006).

Interpretation

- key references: Rackham, *Interpreting the past: animal bones* 1994; Lyman, *Vertebrate taphonomy* 1994; Rowley-Conwy, *Animal bones, human societies* 2000; Maltby, *Integrating zooarchaeology* 2006.

It is important to understand the nature of a collection of bones. Accompanying finds, such as datable potsherds, from excavated contexts may indicate whether they formed over a long or short period, and the condition of the bones themselves may also help explain the circumstances of the formation of archaeological deposits (**taphonomy**). Weathered, broken bones with signs of damage from rodents or scavenging animals are readily distinguishable from those that were buried immediately, and this information will of course be valuable to the excavator as well as to the bone specialist. Once reliable deposits have been identified, and the species and numbers of the animals counted, many further observations are possible. One important factor in interpreting bones from sites is the effect of human selection on the sample that survives. Hunters may well have butchered large animals where they were killed, leaving the majority of bones (especially skulls and limbs) far from their living sites (Smith 1997: 28–34; 105–7). Furthermore, bones discarded by humans are frequently moved or even destroyed by scavenging animals, such as wild hyenas or domestic dogs. Experimental work has shown that different kinds of bones have varying chances of survival (Marean *et al.* 1992).

Besides identifying species and calculating the numbers of animals represented by a collection of bones, and their sex and age, specialists may be able to glean further information from bones. Hunting techniques may be deduced from injuries, and butchery practices are sometimes revealed by ways that the bones were cut or broken to remove marrow. Bones with cut-marks caused by sharp tools during the removal of flesh not only provide evidence of butchery techniques, but in ambiguous contexts – such as Palaeolithic caves – prove that animals' bones reached the site because they were used as food by humans (Charles 1998) (**Fig. 5.4**). Other bones may represent wild animals that lived in the cave when humans were absent, or their prey. Occasionally direct evidence for hunting can be observed, such as a stone point of Neanderthal form found embedded in the vertebra of a wild ass in Syria (Boeda 1999). The recovery of very small bones is also important if a full range of resources is to be studied (Stahl 1996); romantic images of 'man the hunter' should not distract us from taking account of rabbits, badgers etc. as sources of food and fur pelts for clothing.

Where a site was a permanent habitation belonging to a period after the introduction of farming, different questions can be asked about food supply and diet, including the process and chronology of animal domestication (**Box** 5.4; **Fig.** 5.5). To what extent did the occupants still exploit wild animals along with domesticated species, and how much meat could be obtained from the animals found? The age structure of animal populations is particularly important for the analysis of animal husbandry practices. The inhabitants might have enjoyed the luxury of eating succulent young animals, or it might have been necessary to maximise the use of cows and sheep for milk and wool until they were several years old. The exploitation of domesticated animals for transport and traction has social and economic implications beyond farming, allowing a 'quantum leap' in productive capacity, tillage and carrying (Bogucki 1993: 497). Evidence that horse-riding began around 4000 BC in the Caspian region of southern Russia was found through a study of surface wear on horse teeth caused by the use of a bit, using a scanning electron microscope. Riding followed a much longer period of exploitation of horses, initially for food and then in

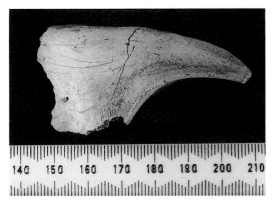

Figure 5.4 Close inspection of bones recovered from excavations reveals more than which species are present. This fragment from just above the eye-socket of a wild horse has numerous incisions made in the course of removing meat and skin with a sharp stone tool. Direct dating of bones with marks like these using the AMS radiocarbon method is very useful for demonstrating human presence in a cave where some bones could have been introduced by wild animals rather than human hunters (Charles 1998). This horse was killed more than 13,000 years ago and was found in the Trou de Chaleux, Belgium. (Ruth Charles; Institut Royal des Sciences Naturelles de Belgique)

ritual (Anthony and Brown 2000; Anthony 2007: chapter 10). Signs of rope-marks on the horns of Neolithic cattle found at Bronocice in Poland (c. 3000 BC) probably indicate that the animals had been used to pull ploughs or vehicles. This interpretation was reinforced by the discovery that many cattle bones from the site were from oxen, and that some were aged up to five or ten years – much too old for the production of beef or dairy products (Milisauskas and Kruk 1991).

Bones from large settlements or towns present additional problems; rubbish associated with houses may offer insights into diet, but care must be taken to distinguish it from waste from butchers' shops or industrial workshops where bone was used as a raw material for making artefacts. Sites occupied over a long period with good stratified collections of bones offer additional possibilities for comparisons between food supply and animal husbandry practices at different times. However, care must be taken to test the validity of any conclusions that are drawn, especially where collections of different sizes are concerned; some straightforward statistical probability tests measure the significance of any interesting observations (below: p. 240). In the Roman period, bones from dromedary camels found on fort sites in Hungary and Slovenia suggest that they were introduced from Africa as transport animals in a military context; rarer finds of Bactrian camels might represent long-distance civilian trade from Asia, however (Bartosiewicz 1996; Bartosiewicz and Dirjec 2001).

Bones found on sites reflect living populations of hunted or domesticated animals in different ways, and a sample recovered from an excavation may not be representative of the whole site. In one enlightening case in North America, the excavated bones were compared with the documented history of an eighteenth-century British fort. The number of animals represented by bones would only have been sufficient to feed the fort's occupants for a single day, but a garrison of varying strength was in occupation for eight years. The soldiers' diet consisted largely of boneless salt pork brought to the site from elsewhere (Guilday 1970). Discrepancies between bones from medieval sites and accounts of animal farming in documents also give rise to concern about the extent

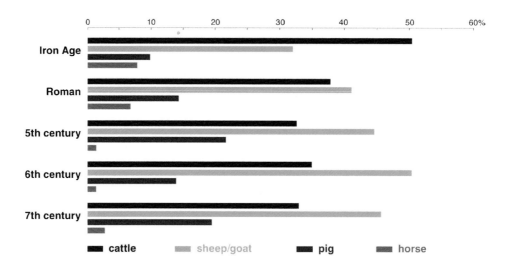

Figure 5.5 West Stow, a multi-period settlement excavated in Suffolk (West 1985), allows comparisons to be made between ratios of different animal species present in Iron Age, Roman and Anglo-Saxon levels. Pam Crabtree's bone report (1989) examined changes in the economy of the settlement; cattle were the most common species in the Iron Age, but sheep and/or goats dominated later periods. Pigs increased steadily, but remains of horses were notably rare in the Anglo-Saxon period. **Taphonomy** is important, however: do the differences reflect farming practices and diet or were there are also changes in attitudes to cleanliness and the disposal of waste? (Redrawn by Chris Unwin, after Crabtree 1989: Fig. 4)

to which excavated samples really do represent 'real' ancient populations (Albarella 1999).

Biostratigraphy and palaeoclimate

- key reference: Pals and Van Wijngaarden-Bakker, *Environmental archaeology, 3: seasonality* 1998.

In some cases the study of animal bones merges imperceptibly into dating methods. Bones of pigs and elephants are much more common in East African geological deposits than are those of hominins, and their evolutionary development is well established. Thus, fieldworkers searching for hominin fossils make a rough estimation of the age of a deposit without resorting to scientific dating methods, and this will also highlight discrepancies between scientific dates and the **biostratigraphic** date derived from the animals' evolutionary stages (Currant and Jacobi 2001). Small mammals, notably voles identifiable by the form of their teeth, are sensitive indicators of climate change and important in dating Palaeolithic sites in Britain.

Evidence of seasonality

- key references: Legge and Rowley-Conwy, *Star Carr revisited* 1988; Rocek and Bar-Yosef, *Seasonality and sedentism* 1998.

Bones found on a hunter-gatherer site that was only occupied for part of the year may give a very limited view of the inhabitants' exploitation of animals; other camps might have been associated with the same groups of people at different times according to the seasonal availability of animals, fish, molluscs and plants. Understanding the role of seasonality has been crucial in reconstructing Mesolithic societies and their relationship with exploiting the landscape. At Starr Carr, a Mesolithic hunter-gatherer site in Yorkshire, examination of teeth eruption of deer demonstrated that the majority of animals had been killed between February and June, suggesting the site was a seasonal summer camp (Legge and Rowley-Conwy 1988). Other studies have used similar evidence to argue that, in fact, there was winter use of the site, demonstrating the complexity of using such evidence

BOX 5.4   **Charting animal domestication**

From dogs, cattle and goats to reindeer and camels, the domestication of animals was just as important as that of plants. It has significantly altered human development by introducing a different way of exploiting food resources, and this has had consequences for social organisation. Domestication can be investigated with the help of new methods, notably the analysis of ancient and modern DNA (**Box 5.3**), but traditional analyses of bone remain important (Vigne *et al*. 2005). A key question in understanding domestication in the Old World is whether it took place in a single location, perhaps the Levant, or if it happened independently in different places (Zeder *et al*. 2006a; Vigne *et al*. 2005). Scientific investigation is now allowing us to construct maps that show when and where the domestication of different species took place. Analysis of mitochondrial DNA from ancient and modern pigs allows us to measure how closely domesticated pigs are related to wild boar. It reveals that domestication happened independently in several parts of western Asia and Europe, contradicting the traditional view of a single episode of domestication in the Near East (Larson *et al*. 2005; 2007).

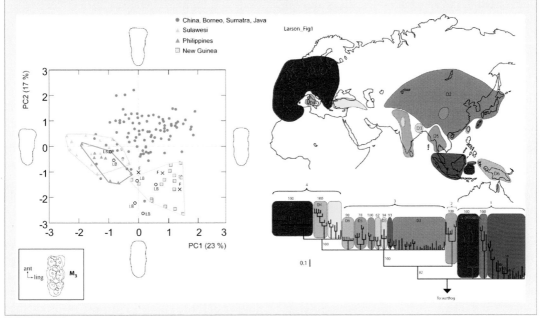

(Carter 1998). Studies of shell-middens have also provided further evidence on the seasonality of Mesolithic settlements (below: pp. 212–3). Seasonality studies can also give interesting results at sites that were occupied permanently – especially when bones from different phases can be compared (**Fig. 5.6**). Understanding whether sites were permanently or seasonally occupied, or whether they had particular animal husbandry, can have fundamental implications for reconstructing how past societies worked.

DNA and isotopes

- key references: Jones, *The molecule hunt* 2001; Brothwell and Pollard, *Handbook of archaeological sciences* 2001: 293–358; Zeder *et al*., *Documenting domestication* 2006.

Studies of DNA recovered from animal bones offer great potential for confirming difficult identifications of species or sex, and for studying the processes of domestication by examining the genetic links between wild and domesticated animals (Brown and Brown 1992: 19). For example, the nature of the domestication of cattle and pigs has important implications for how the adoption of sedentary farming in the Neolithic took place (Jones 2004: 44). Analysis of the DNA of cattle suggests that most domesticated cattle in Europe were descended from cattle imported from the Near East around 8800 cal BP, in the Early Neolithic, rather than from the indigenous wild aurochs (Edwards *et al.* 2007). Combined with other analyses, such studies can be used to chart the spread of the use of animals by different routes across the world, providing clearer evidence about how farming and animal domestication spread (see **Box** 5.4 concerning pig domestication).

Estimation of the extent to which ancient bone decays in a variety of burial environments has become a fundamental part of archaeological science, since without this understanding it is impossible to identify suitable samples for the extraction of DNA or other biomolecules (Geigl 2005). It is also important in selecting samples for scientific dating, for example by amino-acid racemisation (above: p. 183).

Studies of carbon isotopes chemically combined with calcium in bone have become an important area of research for studying ancient diet, as wild animals that eat fish, meat or plants have distinctively different ratios of isotopes. This kind of evidence from 'classic' Mesolithic sites at Star Carr and Seamer Carr in Yorkshire elucidated the role of dogs as 'companions to hunters and fishers' while the marine diet of the dogs appears to indicate that humans were also exploiting coastal resources (Clutton-Brock and Noe-Nygaard 1990; Schulting and Richards 2002, 2009); DNA and isotopes will be discussed further, below, in relation to humans. Less direct evidence of diet can be obtained from analyses of organic residues contained in pottery used for food preparation or storage (**Box** 5.5).

5.5.3 Fish

- key references: Brinkhuizen and Clason, *Fish and archaeology: studies in osteometry,*

taphonomy, seasonality and fishing methods 1986; Wheeler and Jones, *Fishes* 1989.

Sieving and flotation techniques have improved the recovery of bones from small mammals, birds, reptiles, amphibians and fish. Unlike most of these, fish bones appear on archaeological sites on dry land as a direct result of human activity. Unfortunately fish bones have a much lower chance of survival than animal bones because of their small size and cartilaginous consistency. Interesting experiments have been conducted on the survival of modern fish bones that have passed through the digestive systems of pigs, dogs and humans. Less than 10 per cent of the bones of medium-sized fish survived, with the implication that the importance of fish in the diet will be underestimated on many sites, even when small fragments have been recovered by sieving (Jones 1986). If rats were common on a site, bones that they gnawed and digested could disappear altogether.

Nevertheless, the few bones that do survive allow species to be identified. Furthermore, otoliths ('ear stones') from many species, and spines from the fins of catfish (Brewer 1987), survive rather better, allowing growth-rings visible under a microscope to be used to estimate the ages of fish, as well as their size. This information gives insights into food-gathering strategies, and the range of habitats reveals the extent of fishing, whether in local ponds and streams or far out to sea. Because they incorporate growth rings similar to those visible in mollusc shells, otoliths also reveal seasonal exploitation of fishing. Otoliths from a Mesolithic midden at Cnoc Coig in the Inner Hebrides demonstrated that most saithe (a cod-like fish) were caught in the autumn (Smith 1997: 155–7). An indirect indication of fish and other marine resources may be obtained by examining ^{12}C and ^{13}C isotopes in the bones of humans or animals, as their ratio is influenced by a diet that contains seafood (Richards and Hedges 1999; below: p. 220). There is of course considerable scope for comparing ancient fishing with information from modern anthropological data or historical periods – the Roman Empire

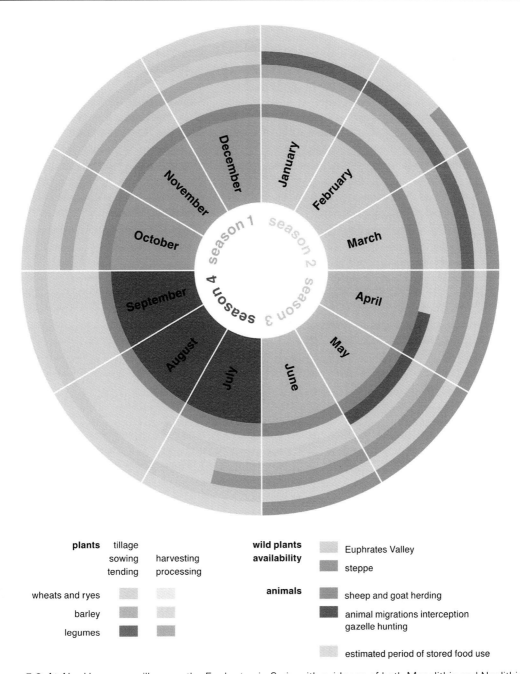

Figure 5.6 At Abu Hureyra, a village on the Euphrates in Syria with evidence of both Mesolithic and Neolithic occupation, remains of plants and animals provided evidence for resources available to the inhabitants. In the first Neolithic phase (2A), wild plants remained important alongside cultivated species for ensuring supplies throughout the year, while hunting of wild gazelles during their seasonal migration supplemented domesticated herds of sheep and goats. The site is particularly valuable for illustrating the differences between Mesolithic and Neolithic subsistence patterns; by phases 2B and 2C, domesticated cattle and pigs had become important and reliance on wild plants had disappeared. (Peter Rowley-Conwy; adapted by Chris Unwin from Moore *et al.* 2000: 499 Fig. 14.4)

Ceramics and food remains: gas chromatography

Pots excavated at Hajii Firuz Tepe in Iran were analysed in the hope of detecting 'signatures' of specific organic chemicals that might reveal their former contents. The presence of particular wavelengths on the infrared spectrum provided new evidence for wine-making in the Neolithic period (McGovern *et al.* 1995). Converting fresh fruit into dried or fermented products allows them to be stored and used after the end of the grape harvest, quite apart from the social or trading potential of wine (University of Pennsylvania Museum, based on data from McGovern *et al.* 1995: Fig. 2).

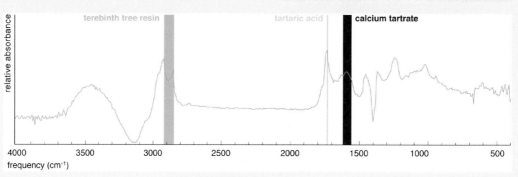

had a substantial fish products industry (McCann 1987; Rieth 1998), while medieval monasteries exploited 'farmed' fish (Aston 1988). Bones recovered from sites could not be interpreted fully without addressing this kind of evidence. Sieving for fish bones (see **Box 5.2**) is important on excavation as it can reveal periods or regions where fish appear to have been ignored as a food source, despite their availability, such as in Britain during the Iron Age (Dobney and Ervynck 2007). This potentially reflects social taboos over the exploitation of certain food sources.

5.5.4 Shells: archaeomalacology

Molluscs live in a range of different environments, both marine and terrestrial, and can represent

evidence of food exploitation or evidence for climate and land-use. The study of shells is its own sub-discipline of archaeology: archaeomalacology (Bar-Yosef Majer 2005).

Marine shells
- key references: Claassen, *Shells* 1998; Stein, *Deciphering a shell midden* 1992; Thomas and Mannino, 'The exploitation of invertebrates and invertebrate products' 2001; Milner *et al.*, *Shell middens in Atlantic Europe* 2007.

Striking evidence of marine exploitation in the past is visible in the large number and great size of mounds of discarded shells (**middens**), often several metres high, found along coastlines all over the world. The food potential of shellfish is fairly simple to calculate, but deeper insights may be gained by more detailed observations. The size and shape of common species, such as the limpet, show whether they were collected at random or whether particularly large examples were chosen at low tide; a limpet shell's shape varies according to how far below the high water mark it lived. Non-random collection would obviously imply planned exploitation, perhaps indicating a greater dependence on shellfish than other food sources. Measurement of annual growth rings may reveal whether collecting took place all year round or only seasonally (**Fig. 5.7**). Shells from a midden at Norsminde (Denmark) indicated that, while Mesolithic hunter-gatherers collected oysters predominantly in spring, Neolithic people harvested them for a more extended period well into the summer (Milner 2001). More recent indigenous Americans exploited soft-shell clams on the Atlantic coasts through a collection strategy based on intensive autumn harvesting (Lightfoot 1993). Since the 1970s, stable isotopes have also been useful in examining shell-middens from coastal locations by determining the season the shell's occupant was killed (Shackleton 1973). Shell-middens are well known from prehistoric California (Jones 2007), and isotope studies have been extended to estuarine (fresh-water) shell-middens in California, dating from c. 2000 BC–AD 500, demonstrating that shells were collected throughout the year except during the autumn, when there was, perhaps, a focus on other resources such as waterfowl (Culleton *et al.* 2009). In each case this evidence needs to be set within a wider economic and behavioural analysis of the people involved.

Shells found on settlement sites inland do not always represent food. Large examples might have been used as containers, spoons or even tools (Novella 1995). Other exotic uses, such as for jewellery, charms and even ceremonial trumpets, have been recorded by archaeologists; indeed, small shells used as beads and pendants are a distinctive component of the material culture of the first anatomically modern humans in Europe (Stiner 1999). Strontium isotope dating has demonstrated that *spondylus* shells found widely throughout Neolithic Europe were actually

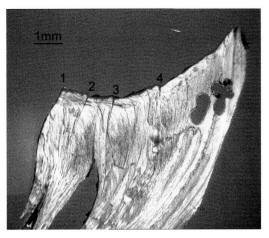

Figure 5.7 Section through the hinge of an oyster from a Mesolithic site at Krabbesholm, Denmark. Four dark annual growth lines can be seen, one on the very edge of the shell; since these are formed at the beginning of the oyster's growing season early in the year, this one must have been collected in the spring. If large numbers of shells from middens are sampled it should be possible to tell whether oysters were collected all year round or at particular seasons. (Nicky Milner)

contemporary specimens gathered around the Mediterranean coasts and distributed through some form of trade or exchange, rather than fossils collected from local geological deposits (Shackleton and Elderfield 1990). In the Roman period a high-quality transport infrastructure allowed fresh oysters to be delivered far inland, while the Mediterranean *murex* provided purple dye in industrial quantities. These examples all demonstrate the benefits of interaction between scientific techniques and archaeological interpretation.

Land molluscs

- key references: Evans, *Land snails in archaeology* 1973; Branch *et al.*, *Environmental archaeology* 2005: 106–14; Carter, 'The stratification and taphonomy of shells in calcareous soils', 1990; Bar-Yosef Mayer, *Archaeomalacology* 2005.

Snails range from large edible species to forms that are only visible and identifiable with the help of a microscope. Species recovered from ancient stratified soils or geological deposits reflect variations in the climate during successive Ice Ages and warmer periods. They mirror changes in temperature in the same way as vegetation (above: p. 202), and their distributions in the past may be compared with modern habitats in exactly the same manner. Of more direct relevance to archaeology is the fact that hundreds of small shells may be recovered from layers of soil. Samples are sorted into groups of species that prefer grassland or woodland, open or shaded localities. Thus, the snail species found in a ground surface buried beneath a structure such as a rampart or burial mound will indicate whether the structure was erected on open heath (if light-loving grassland species are dominant) or in freshly cleared forest (if species that live in dark and damp woodland conditions are more numerous). A further advantage of land snails is that they survive well on calcareous soils that do not favour the preservation of pollen. Unlike pollen, which is scattered over many miles by the wind, snails reflect a local environment. Ideally, both sources of evidence should be examined together to establish the general and immediate environment of a site. In exceptional cases, some shells might even be indicative of disease in human populations; examination of early Islamic water channels in Bahrain (eleventh–thirteenth centuries AD) produced shells of the snails which host such diseases as bilharzia (Insoll and Hutchins 2005).

5.5.5   Insects and other invertebrates

- key references: Elias, *Quaternary insects and their environments* 1994; Panagiotakopulu, *Archaeology and entomology in the Eastern Mediterranean* 2000; Branch *et al.*, *Environmental archaeology* 2005: 114–16.

Insect remains give insights into the living conditions, diet and health of humans in the past, in addition to reflecting environmental change (**Fig. 5.8**). Some fascinating pioneering analyses were done at York, where Roman and medieval deposits suitable for the preservation of the insects' shelly parts underlie much of the modern city (Hall and Kenward 1990). Insects have characteristic habitats, and therefore suggest the

Figure 5.8 The remains of insects recovered in excavation can be identified by specialists. This example is a spider beetle (*Gibbium psylloides Cz.*) about 1.3 mm in length, from the Workmen's Village, Tell-el-Amarna, Egypt (Panagiotakopulu 2001: 1237–8). Identification of pests that infested foods and stored materials shed interesting light upon the conditions of people in the past. (Eva Panagiotakopulu)

nature of vegetation and structures; others infest particular crops such as grain, suggesting storage nearby. Similar evidence has also been used to explore the wider relationship between the city and its environment (Hall and Kenward 1995). Particularly intimate interactions between pests and humans have been revealed by the discovery of remains of pubic lice in Roman and medieval Carlisle (Kenward 1999) and the common bed-bug in Pharaonic Egypt (Panagiotakopulu and Buckland 1999). Along with other mobile and sensitive creatures (such as small mammals), insects abandon habitats rapidly if the climate changes, and they provide a more precise indicator of rapid change than plants which do not have the option of moving. Beetles have been used as evidence for the improving conditions that allowed humans to reoccupy northern Europe after the end of the last Ice Age (Blockley *et al.* 2000b).

5.6   HUMANS

- key references: Brothwell and Pollard, *Handbook of archaeological sciences* 2001:

203–92; Waldron, *Shadows in the soil: human bones and archaeology* 2001; Roberts, *Human remains* 2009; Mays, *The archaeology of human bones* 1998; Katzenberg and Saunders, *Biological anthropology of the human skeleton* 2008.

Although technically part of the biosphere, the archaeological questions asked about human remains tend to be rather wider than those asked about animal bones or shells, and have had a particularly prominent place in studying the past. Given reasonably well-preserved remains, the techniques of study are sometimes very similar to those applied to animal remains but with certain distinct theoretical, technical and ethical concerns. Trying to combine the study of human remains through examination of the skeletal and scientific evidence with recent theories, which recognise that the 'body' is as much a social construct as a physical entity (Chapter 6, pp. 290–2), is one of the key challenges in studying humans (Sofaer 2006).

A number of key pieces of information may be determined from human remains:

- *Age* may be estimated from a number of osteological developments, such as the fusion of the joints and the eruption of teeth (Roberts 2009: 126). Estimating age-at-death is easier in the case of non-adults, who exhibit regular changes to their bones and teeth during the growth period (until around 18 years). Estimating the ages of older individuals is more problematic because changes are primarily degenerative and thus vary between individuals, but indicators include teeth wear patterns. It is also worth remembering that 'age' is often culturally defined, and may have meant different things to people in the past, so that an individual's numerical age may not reflect our own perceptions of social status or roles (Gowland 2006).
- *Sex* may be determined (with some difficulty) from the sizes of various parts of the skeleton, notably the pelvis and skull (Roberts 2009: 121–4). Increasingly, it may be possible to confirm sex with DNA; this has successfully been used to sex infant skeletons from Roman Britain (Brown 2000; Mays and Faerman 2001). Sex may also be supported by the character of accompanying grave goods, but archaeologists must always be wary of identifying the sex of a skeleton on grave goods alone, as frequently happened in the past. In many past societies, grave goods which might be assumed to be conferring 'male' traits (such as swords) can be found with female burials. This is why 'sex' and 'gender' should not be confused; gender is culturally specific, while sex relates to biological differences (see Chapter 6; Grauer and Stuart-Macadam 1998).
- *Stature* may be estimated from comparisons with modern people – although discrepancies of several centimetres exist between different systems of measurement, analysis may be able to determine to what extent the range of the height in a population has changed over time (Roberts 2009: 144–5).

The ability to determine age, sex or stature, as well as more detailed aspects such as diet and pathology (discussed below), will always depend on the state of preservation of the remains. Preservation can be affected by a range of factors: the means of disposal in the past (e.g. **cremation**, **inhumation**, **excarnation**), burial conditions (e.g. acidic or alkaline soils, frozen or desiccated) and treatment of the remains (e.g. mummification) (Roberts 2009: 55–71). Evidence for the earliest hominins and humans is very fragmentary, especially as the fossil bones that are so important for tracing the emergence of hominin species found in geological contexts in areas such as East Africa are normally recovered from eroded deposits, not where the individuals originally died (Klein 1999). No examinations of human remains should be conducted until ethical considerations have been taken into account (see **Box 6.10**). Ideally, evidence derived from the pathological study of human remains should be integrated with other information to develop a holistic appreciation of past societies.

5.6.1 Burials

- key references: Bahn, *Tombs, graves and mummies* 1996; Parker Pearson, *The archaeology of death and burial* 1999; Cox, *Life and death in Spitalfields 1700 to 1850* 1996; Gowland, *Social archaeology of funerary remains* 2006.

Human remains were regularly treated with respect as early as 25,000 years ago, and even at this date complete bodies were buried with 'grave goods' (Pettitt and Bader 2000). Objects placed in graves help to date burials and may indicate ritual activities or hint at the social status of the deceased. Where soil conditions are suitable, burials allow complete skeletons to be recovered for study, and this offers the possibility of establishing numerous facets about the individual buried (e.g. health, diet, lifestyle, mobility). The study of well-preserved bodies is like an excavation itself, involving x-ray examination, dissection (for mummified remains), and the study of all the materials encountered, whether fibres of clothing, skin tissues or food remains. The most famous examples of well-preserved bodies are of course Egyptian mummies (Taylor 1995), but other notable finds range from the bog bodies that are fairly common in northern Europe, for example the Iron Age Lindow Man from England (Stead 1986), to frozen bodies of medieval Inuit from Greenland (Hansen 1991) or the remarkable late Neolithic Ice Man found in the Alps (Fowler 2002). These bodies result from intentional burial, ritual murder and accidental death; each category offers different insights into ancient societies. Multiple burials, where bodies have been jumbled together in collective tombs over long periods or where cremated bones were emptied into burial chambers in irretrievable confusion, are common finds. To complicate matters further, incomplete bodies were sometimes buried after the corpse had been exposed to the elements and scavenging birds and mammals (**excarnation**). This practice is well known from indigenous peoples in North America and New Guinea, as well as on many excavated prehistoric sites in Europe (e.g. Carr and Knüsel 1997). Expert work on burials at

the Anglo-Saxon royal cemetery at Sutton Hoo, Suffolk, has demonstrated that careful excavation of soils of subtly differing colour and texture may reveal outlines of decayed flesh and bones that have been destroyed by the acidic sandy soil (Carver 1998). Burials where the body was cremated, and the surviving fragments of bone were placed into an urn or other container, are less favourable for scientific study, though in some instances sex, age, and pathological information can still be retrieved (McKinley and Bond 2001). Careful examination of all aspects of cremation sites can also produce information on the processes involved that may have significant implications for understanding the individuals' place in society or the rituals involved (McKinley 2006).

In order to draw inferences about ancient populations from burials (**palaeodemography**), archaeologists need to scrutinise evidence from human bones particularly closely (Chamberlain 2001). It is very difficult to estimate the age structure and physical well-being (or otherwise) of a population without knowing whether burials recovered from a particular culture represent the dead of all levels of society, or simply a restricted social elite. Roman gravestones frequently commemorate persons of advanced age, but memorials were only erected for individuals of high social status and wealth, whose lifestyle favoured longevity. Nevertheless, excavated remains and tombstones combine to confirm the general impression that few individuals lived to a great age, while infant mortality was high and many young women died in childbirth or as a result of it (Hedges 1983). Only very rarely do archaeologists uncover a large number of bodies that might represent a true cross-section of society – for example, a community of 486 Native Americans massacred in around AD 1325 at Crow Creek, South Dakota (Willey 1992), or citizens of Herculaneum and Pompeii, who perished during the eruption of Vesuvius in AD 79 (Bisel 1987). Even then there is always a high chance that young able-bodied individuals had already made their escape. War graves are occasionally discovered, which provide a large number of relatively young, healthy male individuals who died suddenly from injuries, unlike bodies of men from ordinary cemeteries who might have died from illnesses. Their injuries do of course give detailed insight into weapons and warfare – often in horrific detail, as in the case of victims of the Battle of Towton, Yorkshire, a major engagement in the Wars of the Roses, who were buried in a mass grave in 1461 and rediscovered in 1996 (see **Box 5.6**; Fiorato *et al.* 2007). Even more unusual are the bodies of sixteenth-century sailors who drowned when Henry VIII's flagship *Mary Rose* sank in 1545, among whom was found evidence for fractures and disease that suggested the identification of some as archers and gun-crew (Stirland 2000). These very specific observations form a small part of the larger pathological study of human remains.

5.6.2 Palaeopathology and evidence from human remains

- key references: Cox and Mays, *Human osteology in archaeology and forensic science* 2000; Roberts and Manchester, *The archaeology of disease* 2005; Roberts and Cox, *Health and disease in Britain* 2003; Roberts, *Human remains* 2009: 153–89.

Were most people in the past tall, healthy 'Noble Savages', or diseased, short-lived, stunted individuals for whom life was 'nasty, brutish, and short'? Palaeopathologists examine deformities, and evidence of disease ranging from malnutrition, arthritis and dental decay to the erosion of bone through leprosy, as well as injuries, whether healed or fatal, in much the same way that a police forensic specialist would work on a modern body (Hunter *et al.* 1996).

Disease and pollution
Palaeopathology is usually limited to identifying diseases that have left evidence on the bone, such as respiratory diseases (e.g. tuberculosis, sinusitis), although ancient DNA may provide more evidence (**Box 5.7**). Many people may have died before a disease led to any bone changes, or the remains may represent those who recovered from such illnesses or trauma (Roberts 2009:

158–9). Particular environmental and dietary stresses are also likely to affect particular sectors and genders within past populations differently; analysis of burials from Fishergate, York, for example, has illustrated the higher mortality of low-status females compared to well-fed male monks in medieval England (Sullivan 2004). The impact of pollution on past populations can also be examined. Detailed analysis of a prehistoric community of the Anasazi in eleventh–thirteenth century AD Colorado showed evidence for respiratory diseases, probably caused by smoke from sooty fires (Lambert 2002). Other studies demonstrate that variation in sinusitis relates to the environmental conditions of different archaeological populations (less, for example, in hunter-gatherers); it could also vary between people of differing gender and status depending on their roles and exposure (Roberts and Manchester 2005: 174–6; Roberts 2007). An increase in lead levels in the bones of Roman populations probably resulted from drinking water from lead piping (Roberts and Manchester 2005: 153).

Work and activities
Detailed examination of human remains has also been used to provide insights into the changing activities of people in the past, including the effects of economic change. Abu Hureyra, a village on the Euphrates in Syria, was occupied first by hunter-gatherers and then by a Neolithic farming community; this allows direct comparison between the pathology of human skeletons from each phase (Moore *et al.* 2000). Women in particular appear to have suffered new problems leading to arthritis because of spending considerable periods kneeling down to grind grain with a repetitive bending motion. However, attempting to identify particular occupations or activities for individuals in the past remains extremely contentious (Roberts 2009: 175–6). The identification of an individual from the Bronze Age site of Tell Brak in Syria as a 'juggler' (Oates *et al.* 2007) provides potentially fascinating insights into the role and disposal of an individual in the past, yet the determination remains controversial (Jurmain and Roberts 2008). Pathology may

BOX 5.6 Human remains and evidence of warfare:
Towton Moor

Archaeology rarely provides indisputable evidence of the consequences of warfare because sites of
battles rarely survive undisturbed, and damage visible on
human bones may be the result of individual injuries or acts
of violence, rather than actual warfare. One exceptional case
is the mass grave at Towton Moor in North Yorkshire, found
on the site of a known battle that took place during the
Wars of the Roses in AD 1461. The excavation uncovered a
shallow grave containing around 37 individuals, interred with
little sign of respect or normal burial practices (Fiorato *et al.*
2007: 186). Palaeopathology provided detailed information,
including evidence for the multiple wounds suffered by many
of the individuals in previous conflicts, and the examination
was able to explore the patterns of wounds associated with
particular forms of medieval fighting, as seen in this skull
(Fiorato 2007). (Photograph: Bradford University)

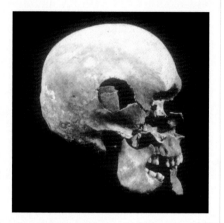

BOX 5.7 **DNA and disease: the archaeology of
tuberculosis**

Diseases in past populations have traditionally been identified
when they left visible traces on bones. Tuberculosis (TB) is
one such disease, spread through sneezing and coughing,
or by infected meat and milk. If untreated, it can spread to
bone and the lymphatic systems, leading to changes which
can be detected in bones. The image, from Bedhampton in
Hampshire, is an early medieval example of such changes. In
this individual, TB has led to the destruction of the vertebrae,
leading to collapse, and would have given a 'hunchback'
appearance to the person in life. This technique cannot,
however, recognise the presence of the illnesses in those
where it left no evidence on the actual skeleton – around 95%
of all cases. This means that current understanding of the
development and movement of TB relies on those instances
recognised through palaeopathology – a sixth-millennium BC
case from Italy being the earliest example, and one from c AD
700 representing the earliest case from the Americas. New
studies using ancient DNA are seeking to develop this picture
by looking for evidence of the presence of the TB bacterium
in human skeletons. This aims to provide a clearer picture of

how and where TB developed and how it has spread through human populations (Roberts and Buikstra
2003). This research has wider implications for modern health, with TB representing one of the most
deadly diseases, particularly in developing nations. (Photograph: Charlotte Roberts, Durham University)

provide *possibilities* for the activities of people in the past, but can rarely provide evidence of particular occupations (Waldron 1994). As with areas of archaeological science, a close eye must be kept on changing techniques and interpretations in order for archaeologists to ensure that they can interpret the available evidence in the most up-to-date way.

Facial reconstruction

Forensic study may include facial reconstruction, a technique whereby tissues, ears, nose and eyes are built according to comparative data in an attempt to recreate the actual appearance of a person whose skull survives in good condition (Prag and Neave 1999; Wilkinson 2004). Such reconstructions are valuable for modern forensic work; however, while these techniques are very popular with the producers of television programmes and designers of museum displays (Richards 1999), their use for wider archaeological research is somewhat limited.

Warfare and interpersonal violence

Human remains can provide insights into conflict in the past. The presence of battle sites in the archaeological record is rare, with only occasional examples of direct evidence of conflict, such as the spearhead in the spine of an individual from a Bronze Age ditch at Tormarton (Osgood 2005), or the mass grave at Towton Moor (**Box 5.6**). Pathological analysis can identify unhealed cuts and blunt trauma injuries (Roberts 2009: 178–81), although in some cases complex rituals after death (such as the de-fleshing and displaying of human remains) may make it difficult to distinguish trauma when alive from ritual practices after death (Roberts and Manchester 2005: 108–20). Numerous studies have attempted to chart the extent of violence in past populations, from Iron Age Britain (Redfern 2008) to the Wari Empire of first millennium AD Peru (Tung 2007). Consideration of the differences between *violence* (for example, from abuse or small-scale fighting) and all-out warfare should always be borne in mind, however, when considering the nature of *warfare* in past societies (Thorpe 2003; Parker Pearson and Thorpe 2005).

Archaeological skills are also used for more recent remains; the identities of individuals found on excavations of battles sites from the First World War have been determined through a combination of DNA matches with living relatives and archaeological evidence, such as regimental badges (Saunders 2007). Sadly, such skills are also in demand for the massacres of more recent conflicts in the Balkans, Latin America, the Middle East, and the Spanish Civil War; this raises its own set of ethical concerns and challenges for archaeologists (Ferlini 2007; Moshenka 2008; see **Box 6.10**).

Social change

When the results from many techniques are combined, pathology can provide broad insights into the changing nature of past societies (Cohen and Crane-Kramer 2007). In southern California, sites around the Santa Barbara channel dating from the eighteenth century AD back to 7200 BC were examined (Lambert and Walker 1991). A decline in tooth disease accompanied by a rise in arthritis seems to reflect a shift from the consumption of vegetables and tubers to fish and sea-mammal meat, while an increase in deaths from infectious diseases and poorer nutrition coincided with the growth of sedentary villages. Evidence for violent conflict existed at most times, represented by head injuries and embedded projectile points, but it showed a notable increase when the bow and arrow were introduced around AD 500. Evidence for social and cultural change deduced from burials and settlement sites was also related to periods of temperature change and drought known from tree-ring data.

5.6.3 Diet

- key references: Gosden and Hather, *The prehistory of food: appetites for change* 1999; Lambert and Grupe, *Prehistoric human bone: archaeology at the molecular level* 1993; Roberts, *Human remains* 2009: 169–73, 201–5.

Diet may be investigated through the analysis of carbon and nitrogen isotopes, or trace elements such as strontium, contained in bones; their ratios or levels may indicate a preponderance of seafood, maize or rice (Van der Merwe 1992; see **Box 5.9**). Isotopes have been particularly helpful in distinguishing between diets dominated by fish and other marine foods and diets based on land resources; evidence for a sudden shift from the former to the latter when farming first appeared at the beginning of the Neolithic in Britain has been a real surprise, for it had always been thought that the transition would have been gradual (Richards *et al.* 2003). Studies of ancient diet supported by isotopes are not restricted to prehistoric contexts, as recent work on the Maya of Central America in Belize shows (Powis *et al.* 1999; Whittington 1997). A detailed study of the diet of inhabitants in the city of York indicated

---

BOX 5.8

Movement and migration: Bronze Age Beaker burials

The early Bronze Age in Britain is characterised by burials associated with distinctive pottery beakers and tanged flint arrowheads (like the one shown here); similar burials have been found all around the Atlantic fringe of northwestern Europe. There has been a long debate amongst archaeologists about whether the individuals buried with beakers were migrants from elsewhere in Europe or locals who had adopted new burial rites (Brodie 1998: Parker-Pearson *et al.* 2007). Analysis of strontium isotopes is being employed in an attempt to answer this question, and has suggested that at least one individual, the so-called Amesbury Archer, originated outside Britain, possibly in central Europe. Conversely other individuals in the same area may have spent the early part of their lives in Wales (Evans *et al.* 2006b). The most recent studies of Beaker burials suggest that people buried with beakers in Yorkshire and Scotland came from close to where they were buried. This complex set of results demonstrates that V Gordon Childe's hypothesis that these people represented a single migration of itinerant metalworkers from Europe (see Chapter 6) was an oversimplification. It seems that, although there was some movement by individuals, many others simply adopted a new burial rite, and that these events took place over a period of hundreds of years (Parker-Pearson *et al.* 2007). (British Museum)

many changes in diet from the Roman to the post-medieval period. In particular, an increase in marine foods in the medieval period may have been related to Christian religious injunctions to eat fish (Müldner and Richards 2007).

Other information can also demonstrate changing diets; for example, the prevalence of dental caries reveals an increase in refined sugar and flour consumption in the Roman and post-medieval periods in Britain (Roberts and Cox 2003: 131–2). Much can still, of course, be inferred about human diet through studies of animal bones found on occupation sites (Rowley-Conwy 2000; see above: p. 206), while historical and ethnographic studies provide important comparative data about changes – or stability – in 'traditional' diets such as that of the Mediterranean region (Riley 1999).

Coprolites (solid excreta: Holden 2001) preserved in arid parts of the world – such as the south-western United States, Mexico and South America – have made a notable contribution to research into natural resources available to humans. They may also be recovered from waterlogged deposits such as those underlying much of the city of York, where early medieval specimens have been found. Coprolites contain fibrous matter that has passed through the human digestive system, including fragments of bone, skin, scales, hair, feathers and meat, as well as pieces of insect, parasites and their eggs. Coprolites may also contain the eggs of parasitic worms that once infested the digestive tract of a living human (Horne 1985). Plant fibres and seeds are also found, together with microscopic pollen and phytoliths (silica crystals formed by some plants). Even soft tissues from plants and animals can be extracted and identified by careful processing and sieving of rehydrated coprolites. Pollen, phytoliths and diatoms (above, p. 200) have been recovered from pre-1800 AD Maori coprolites in New Zealand, revealing diets and the season in which the coprolites were deposited (Horrocks *et al.* 2003). Large collections recovered from latrine deposits allow detailed surveys of the diet of the occupants of a site to be made. If deposits of different dates are recorded from a particular site or area, long-term changes of diet

may be charted and related to variations in the availability of foodstuffs.

5.6.4 Movement and migration

- key reference: Roberts, *Human remains* 2009: 205–8.

δ¹⁸O

- ■ -4 to -5
- ■ -5 to -6
- ▢ -6 to -7
- ▨ -7 to -8
- ▨ -8 to -9
- ▨ -9 to -10
- ■ > -10

0   500 kilometres

Figure 5.9 Analysis of oxygen and strontium isotopes absorbed into bones when a person was alive has become a useful method for extracting information from human remains. Oxygen isotopes and strontium can reveal information about diet, and suggest the geographical origins of individuals. If the results of analyses are plotted on a map of naturally occurring strontium levels across Europe, it may be possible to indicate where a deceased individual grew up. In many cases, more than one region may provide a match; if so, other archaeological evidence must to be used to determine which region is most likely. (Drawn by Chris Unwin)

BOX 5.9

Isola Sacra: diet and migration in Ancient Rome

In the first to third centuries AD, the city of Rome had a population of around one million people and was the centre of an extensive Empire. Historical evidence suggests there was significant migration into the city from all over the Roman Empire (Garnsey 1987). What can archaeological science tell us about the origin of these people and their diet? Analysis of the cemetery of Isola Sacra, close to Ostia (the port of Rome at the mouth of the river Tiber), has indicated the origin of the people buried there. Analysis of teeth revealed that a significant proportion of the population had migrated to the city as children, with oxygen isotope evidence suggesting that a large number came from the regions to the north and east of Rome, while one individual probably originated in North Africa. Analysis of the diet using isotopic analysis of the cemetery population suggested that these people had consumed a mixture of seafood and food derived from land. There were, however, significant differences; evidence showed that older individuals had consumed high-status foods (such as fish and olive oil), while children had a poorer diet based on plants (Prowse *et al.* 2004, 2005, 2007; the image below shows some of the second century AD 'house-tombs' from Isola Sacra: Rob Witcher, Durham University).

Many questions in archaeology are related to the origin of communities and the extent of movement and migration in the past. How many people really did move from northern Germany to Britain in the Anglo-Saxon migrations (Hamerow 1997)? Did the arrival of Beaker burials in north-west Europe represent a movement of people or the movement of an idea (see **Box 5.8**)? Analysis of the stable isotopes of strontium, oxygen and lead may help to indicate where an individual originated (Roberts 2009: 205–6). Because of chemicals in food and water the geology of an area may leave a distinctive level of strontium in the teeth of people who lived there for any length of time, while different isotopes of oxygen will be incorporated according to the local climate (Budd *et al.* 2004).

Analysis of the Roman cemeteries at Lankhills and Eagle Hotel in Winchester revealed that some of the inhabitants may have come from elsewhere in Europe, possibly Pannonia (modern Hungary) and the Mediterranean region (Evans *et al.* 2006b; Budd *et al.* 2004: 134; see Box 5.9). Studies of individuals from Machu Picchu, Peru, in the late fifteenth and early sixteenth centuries AD have examined evidence for the frequent movement of people by the state in this period. Analysis showed that the inhabitants do indeed derive from a wide range of regions (Turner *et al.* 2009).

Isotope analysis can only indicate the general area from which an individual may have come (Fig 5.9) and there may be a number of alternatives; archaeologists have to consider which is the most likely. The science behind isotope analysis is still being developed, and many technical aspects need to be resolved (Budd *et al.* 2004). DNA is also increasingly being used to tackle the nature and extent of migrations in the past (below: pp. 226–7).

5.6.5 Genetics and DNA

- key references: Jones, *The molecule hunt* 2001; Brothwell and Pollard, *Handbook of archaeological sciences* 2001: 293–358; Roberts, *Human remains* 2009: 208–13; Brown, 'Ancient DNA' 2001; Jones, 'Archaeology and the genetic revolution' 2004; Oppenheimer, *Origins of the British* 2006.

> … there are a large number of archaeological research questions waiting to be addressed through modern DNA, ancient DNA, or a combination of the two …
>
> (Jones 2004: 42)

Two lines of DNA research are presently being followed: studying both the DNA from modern populations and ancient DNA (aDNA) obtained from human and animal archaeological remains. Both have their own sets of problems and potential in answering key questions in archaeology. Work is progressing rapidly on the recovery of ancient biomolecules from bones or (when preserved) other body tissues. However, much basic chemical research remains to be done in order to understand more about how bones decay over time and may become contaminated (Gernaey *et al.* 2001). DNA in particular suffers problems of contamination, and only survives in fragments, which must be multiplied in the laboratory before any interpretation can take place (Roberts and Ingham 2008; Herrmann and Hummel 1993). The survival of DNA is affected by a range of factors: for example, it is better preserved in cold environments and rarely survives in hot climates; it is certainly not easily available from a large sample of human remains.

At a basic level, DNA may indicate the sex of a deceased individual – not always possible from skeletal remains. It also offers the possibility of studying whether bodies found in a cemetery come from related family groups; analysis of the DNA from a well-preserved burial group of fifteenth-century AD Inuit from Greenland allowed the kin relationships between the individuals to be clarified (Gilbert *et al.* 2007).

Analysis of modern DNA is having a more dramatic impact on the study of the origins of more recent populations, and is being used to explore the role of migration and movement in the past. Two types of DNA have been instrumental in this field: mitochondrial DNA (mtDNA), passed on only through the female line, preserves the DNA of the mother; mtDNA has been particularly important in the study of human evolution and dispersal from Africa (Fig. 5.10; below: pp. 224–6). The second type which has been a focus of many recent studies is Y-chromosome DNA, which is inherited only through the male line. Both types of DNA are significant because they do not recombine, only changing slowly over time through mutation, so that they preserve a record of lineage which is not available in other DNA and which can be divided into distinct **haplogroups**. Haplogroups can then be defined and are found within certain geographic populations.

Studies of Y-chromosome DNA evidence in modern populations have attempted to answer a number of questions. For example, study of British and Scandinavian populations appeared to suggest that English DNA shared characteristics

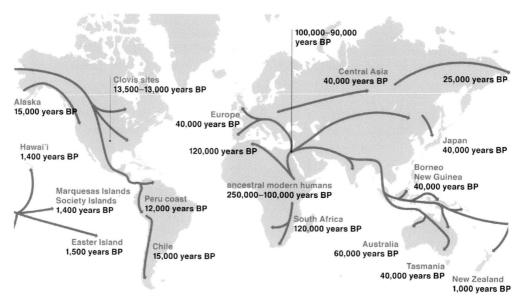

Figure 5.10 Human bioarchaeology is an area with enormous potential for research. Much work has been done already to trace people's origins through traces of lead in their teeth, or to establish the role of fish and other marine foods in people's diets. DNA studies offer further insights, including our understanding of the colonisation of the globe by humans. This map shows the process of human dispersal derived from both fossil remains and analysis of mtDNA; the latter, based on the different haplogroups, indicates that greatest genetic diversity is found in Africa, implying that humans have lived there longest. Genetic similarities can also demonstrate the origins of human ancestors: for example, America was colonised from Siberia, and New Zealand more recently from Polynesia. Allied to fossil and other archaeological evidence, a detailed map of the chronology and process of human dispersal across the globe can be recognised. (Chris Unwin, after, *inter alia*, Lewin 2005)

with northern German DNA types, potentially confirming a large contribution to the DNA record from that area, one which might be associated with Anglo-Saxon migration in the early medieval period (Weale 2002). In North America, similarities between Y-chromosome groups in Siberia and indigenous American populations helped to establish the nature of colonisation of the continent (Santos *et al.* 1999).

A key problem arises in assessing when such contributions to the DNA might have taken place. It is easy to assume that it ties in with a historical event, such as the known movement of some individuals into Britain in the fifth and sixth centuries AD, but considering the likelihood of far more interaction and movement of humans in prehistory now known from material culture (and DNA), it may have taken place far earlier. As studies of Y-chromosome data increase, they are indicating that the movement of humans around the globe, both in the distant past and

more recently, is highly complex, and earlier ideas of one 'race' of people, moving from one region to another, are likely to be far too simplistic. On a broad level, genetic information might prove useful in assessing whether episodes of change in archaeological material culture were the result of peaceful interaction and trade, or of conquest and colonisation – a major preoccupation of archaeology in the mid-twentieth century (Chapter 6, p. 259). Great difficulties are involved, however, for it will take many years before a sufficient number of samples have been studied to define recognisable groups in historical periods. While cultural change was an important focus in the twentieth century, nineteenth-century archaeology was full of racial assumptions linked to biological and social ideas derived from evolution (Chapter 6, p. 257). These ethnic ideas were linked to material culture in Nazi Germany to justify the concept of an Aryan master-race, with catastrophic effects upon supposedly inferior 'races'. Study of DNA is increasingly supporting other archaeological evidence that the concept of definable 'races', based either on material culture or genetics, is meaningless.

Human origins: the DNA evidence

- key references: Willoughby, *The evolution of modern humans* 2007; Lewin, *Human evolution* 2005; Stringer, *Homo britannicus* 2006.

The combining of DNA with other archaeological evidence is having a substantial impact on the debate on the study of human evolution (**Fig. 5.11**). There has been considerable debate about the origins of our species, *Homo sapiens sapiens*. When did modern Humans evolve and did this take place as a single evolutionary development in Africa, and did they then move out of Africa to replace earlier hominin species elsewhere in the world? Until relatively recently, opinions rested solely on the finds of fossils and stone tools. The analysis of modern, rather than ancient, DNA is revolutionising understanding of human development. Modern humans are surprisingly odd in that, unlike many other primates, they have relatively similar genes considering their geographic diversity (Stringer and McKie 1998: 113). This similarity suggests that humans only moved out of Africa relatively recently. More detailed analysis of DNA is developing this picture further and providing a much clearer view of human evolution and dispersal. Mitochondrial DNA is the easiest form to extract, but it only indicates descent through the female line (Jehaes 1998). This has led to the identification of a single female, the so-called 'mitochondrial Eve' (Berger and Hilton-Barber 2000), whose DNA we all share. This woman was not the only woman in existence at the time but was the only one whose genetic evidence did not die out (Lewin 2005: 201–2). Because it has a high rate of change, mitochondrial DNA can also be used to measure when change took place. Y-chromosome DNA, passed on only through the male line, is also now being used to chart human dispersal.

Measurement of the differences between samples of modern DNA shows that Africans have the greatest degree of variation, potentially indicating that African populations are the oldest and therefore the biological ancestors of modern humans. DNA and fossil evidence at present suggests that all modern humans originated in East Africa around 200,000 years ago (McDougall *et al.* 2005). The existence of divergences in mitochondrial DNA within different modern populations can also be used to map the spread of *Homo sapiens* and suggests that only a very small group of humans left Africa, perhaps around 70,000 years ago, moving across the Arabian Peninsula and spreading out across Eurasia (Lewin and Foley 2004: 403–8; Tishkoff *et al.* 2009). The discovery of 'Mungo Man' in New South Wales indicates that *Homo sapiens* was already moving into Australia around 60,000 years ago (Adcock *et al.* 2001). Meanwhile, the small genetic diversity of all Native Americans indicates that the indigenous populations of both continents are probably descended from a relatively small number of people who may have crossed the Bering Straits from eastern Asia to Alaska when low sea levels created a land-bridge (Schroeder *et al.* 2009). When this took place is much harder to define; it was possibly as early as 35,000 years ago (Jones 1993: 122–3; Larsen 2000), although it may have taken place much later, around 14,000 years ago (Lewin 2005: 239–43; Kemp *et al.* 2007).

DNA evidence suggests that the entire world was peopled through this process of gradual migration from a source in Africa, replacing earlier species, such as *Homo erectus*, which had previously spread out of Africa (Stringer 2002) (**Fig. 5.10**). Current genetic evidence provides little support for the theories that humans had multiple sources of origin (Willoughby 2007: 121–2) or that *Homo sapiens* interbred with any of the species already occupying the areas they entered, such as Neanderthals in Europe (Lewin 2005). It has been suggested that modern East Asians in China might have evolved from an existing *Homo erectus* population that had moved out of Africa over a million years ago (Lewin 2005: 189), but this does not correspond with the DNA evidence. Instead, DNA analysis indicates that East Asian people are genetically very close to other human populations, something that would not be the case if they had a distinct origin

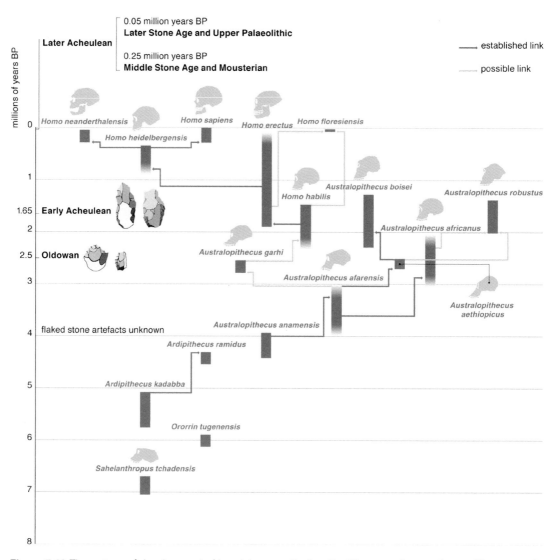

Figure 5.11 The pattern of development of hominins over the last 7 million years is complex, and is constantly being added to and redrawn. It was not (as often depicted) a single linear process; many offshoots, such as the newly discovered *Homo floresiensis*, died out, while the Neanderthals may have been driven to extinction by our own species *Homo sapiens* (Chris Unwin, redrawn after *inter alia* Lieberman 2009).

(Jin and Su 2000). There are those, however, who continue to advocate a model of multi-regional development (e.g. Wolpoff 2005).

New elements are regularly being added to the human evolutionary tree. The discovery of tiny human-like remains in Flores, Indonesia, led to the identification of a new species, *Homo floresiensis*, which existed 80,000–18,000 years ago. A combination of evidence from pathology to DNA can determine at what stage this hominin developed and where it fits on the evolutionary tree (Lieberman 2009; Fig. 5.11). Our models of human evolution and dispersal will undoubtedly change in coming years, but it seems likely that a combination of the study of human fossils, past climates, ancient artefacts and both ancient and modern DNA will provide an increasingly accurate picture of human expansion.

DNA and migrations: words of warning
All kinds of danger lurk within studies of more recent populations. Attempts have been made to

measure the contribution of male Viking DNA in the British Isles by testing people in areas (such as the Orkneys) known from historical sources to have been conquered by Vikings from Norway (Richards 2001). 'Old' surnames, which passed through the masculine line by marriage, supposedly give a different picture from mitochondrial DNA, since men are considered more likely to have moved from Scandinavia than women – but this idea is very much bound up with modern concepts about gender roles (Chapter 6, p. 288). How much interaction by sea had already taken place in prehistory? Did earlier populations with common ancestry settle both Scotland and Scandinavia after the end of the Ice Age? Anyone embarking upon the use of genetic information in studying humans, ancient or modern, should take care to examine whether they are seeking answers to nineteenth-century questions using twenty-first-century technology. A good example is the concept of Celtic identity, the idea that all British and Irish people derived from Central Europe in the Iron Age and that modern Scottish and Irish populations represent a remnant of Celtic peoples, which may be identifiable in their DNA. Many authors now suggest this is a modern myth without any biological basis and one based instead on a misreading of the archaeological evidence (James 1999; Collis 2003). This becomes even more complex with DNA evidence seeming to indicate that communities in the west of Ireland have their closest similarities to peoples of the Basque region of Spain (McEvoy 2004). Yet the possible reasons for such similarities are varied: is this because these are remnants of the expansion of humans after the last Ice Age, or is it a result of movement and migration along the Atlantic edge of Europe, from the Bronze Age to the early medieval period?

5.7 ARTEFACTS AND RAW MATERIALS

- key references: Henderson, *The science and archaeology of materials: an investigation of inorganic materials* 2000; Brothwell and Pollard, *Handbook of archaeological sciences* 2001:

441–517; Caple, *Objects, reluctant witnesses to the past* 2006; Hurcombe, *Archaeological artefacts as material culture* 2006.

Any archaeological object, whether found casually or during a controlled excavation, poses questions about its date, origin, method of manufacture and function. Some may be answered by a combination of common sense and experience, but scientific analysis offers further insights (**Fig. 5.12**). Occasionally an archaeologist will only require a straightforward 'yes' or 'no' – for example when a metal axe was found with the body of the Ice Man in the Alps (Spindler 1994). The typological form of the axe suggested a date in the early Bronze Age, but radiocarbon dates from the body indicated that he died earlier, in the late Neolithic period. Fortunately, metallurgical analysis was able to reveal very quickly that the axe was made of pure copper, which was acceptable at this date, rather than bronze, an alloy of copper and other metals that was not introduced until the early Bronze Age (*ibid.*: 87–91). Further information from the analysis will help in the investigation of additional matters, such as the likely source of the copper and the method of manufacture, while microscopic examination of wear on the cutting edge might suggest how the axe was actually used.

It is not only finished artefacts that provide interesting information. Mines and quarries illustrate methods used to extract raw materials, and industrial sites offer insights into manufacturing processes through the excavation of furnaces, kilns or workshops (Craddock 1995). Waste products, such as the slags that flowed out of metal smelting furnaces, can be subjected to the same microscopic and analytical procedures as objects (Bachmann 1982). A wide range of analytical techniques now exists for studying objects and sites ranging from fragments of stone discarded by Palaeolithic hunter-gatherers making the earliest tools in East Africa to the ruins of a nineteenth-century lead mining complex in the Pennines in northern England. In both cases, the best information comes from careful stratigraphic excavations that allow samples selected for analysis to be related to precise and meaningful contexts.

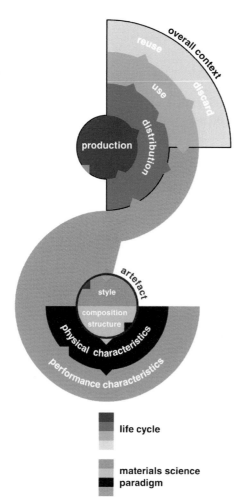

Figure 5.12 The life cycle of archaeological materials and artefacts, and the ways in which scientific analysis may be applied to them: 'The primary aim of materials studies in archaeology is to contribute to the investigation of the overall life cycle or *chaîne opératoire* of surviving artifacts (e.g., stone, ceramics, metals, glass and, when they survive, organic materials). This life cycle starts with production that includes the procurement and processing of the raw materials through to the fabrication and decoration of the artifacts. It then continues through distribution of the artifacts to their use, re-use and ultimate discard' (Tite 2001: 443). Such models can be compared with the 'biographic' approach to material culture discussed in Chapter 6 (Chris Unwin, based on Tite 2001: Fig. 56.1).

5.7.1 Methods of examination and analysis

- key references: Brothwell and Pollard, *Handbook of archaeological sciences* 2001; Ciliberto and Spoto, *Modern analytical methods in art and archaeology* 2000; Banning, *The archaeologist's laboratory* 2000.

If there is a common thread to be traced through this discussion, it is that the successful application of any technique is as much (if not more) a function of the questions that are asked as a product of reliability or accuracy in description. Both are crucial. In determining our questions, we have to ask about the limits and potentials of particular techniques. But we are also drawn into broader debates about the way that technology and social life are bound up with each other.

(Edmonds 2001: 467)

The two simplest outcomes of examination of an artefact are the identification of the materials from which it was made (and their physical properties), and accurate measurement of its constituent minerals or chemicals. However, as Edmonds emphasises (in the context of lithics), scientific analysis is of most interest when it contributes to broader archaeological interpretation. Analysis is not restricted to objects; structures such as buildings offer many possibilities for the analysis of stone, bricks and mortar.

Microscopic examination
- key references: Olsen, *Scanning electron microscopy in archaeology* 1988; Middleton and Freestone, *Recent developments in ceramic petrology* 1991; Hurcombe, *Use wear analysis: theory, experiments and results* 1992; Ellis, *Archaeological method and theory* 2000: 354–64.

Not all scientific analysis requires complex analytical methods; for several centuries geologists have used **petrography** – visual observation by microscope – for characterising stone in terms of its minerals and structure. Thin slices are cut from a specimen and polished to make microscope slides that can be examined under varying light conditions. The same approach is used in **ceramic petrology** for studying pottery and other clay objects that contain minerals of geological origin (Henderson 2000: 11–13). The Ice Man's axe required analysis to determine what it was made of, but many other aspects of metalworking may be studied by examining cross-sections under a microscope (**metallography**). Indeed, 'it should become a rule that analysis and metallography (and hardness testing) should always be combined, since a full interpretation of one is impossible without the other' (Northover 1989: 214). Because structural differences are more difficult to observe in metals than in minerals the section has to be polished and etched to enhance

the edges of crystals, and it may be necessary to use magnification to reveal subtle distinctions (**Fig. 5.13**).

Archaeologists also use microscopes for **use wear analysis** of artefacts, particularly tools, and look for patterns of wear or damage on working surfaces that suggest how a tool was used. In some cases the wear patterns can be directly related to butchered bones at the same site (Lermorini *et al.* 2006). Evidence for manufacturing techniques may also be revealed by microscopic examination; decorated metal objects were frequently ornamented by means of a range of engraving tools whose shapes may be identified. Visual examination is enhanced dramatically by **scanning electron microscopy** (SEM), which sweeps a band of electrons over a surface and projects a magnified image onto a screen (Henderson 2000: 17–20). SEM images have a depth of focus unobtainable from

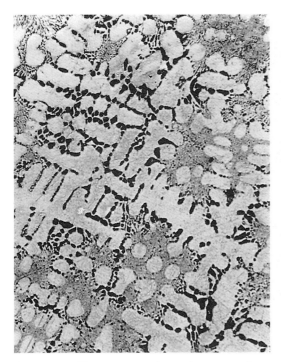 

Figure 5.13 The structure of metals seen under a microscope can reveal the processes involved in their manufacture. The cross-section on the left (c. 0.5 mm across) shows the crystalline structure of an Egyptian figurine cast from an alloy of silver and copper; in comparison, the section on the right (c. 0.5 mm across) shows considerable flattening and distortion by extensive hammering and reheating during the making of a Roman silver bowl (Vera Bird/Janet Lang; copyright British Museum).

conventional microscopes; when combined with the dramatic increase in magnification, they may reveal not only evidence of use wear on tools, but sometimes traces of tissues from animals or starches from plants that were cut by them (**Fig. 5.14**).

Analysis and characterisation

- key references: Hughes, 'Tracing to source' 1991; Ciliberto and Spoto, *Modern analytical methods in art and archaeology* 2000; Pollard and Heron, *Archaeological chemistry* 2008; Ellis, *Archaeological method and theory* 2000: 365–7.

Many forms of analysis are conducted by means of **spectrometry** (Henderson 2000: 8–11). Some techniques are destructive, and involve combusting samples in a flame to produce a spectrum of light in which individual elements will be revealed by their distinctive wavelengths. In non-destructive methods such as **neutron activation analysis** (NAA) an artefact or sample is artificially irradiated, and the subsequent pattern of decay of radiation from different elements at varying rates is measured (*ibid.*: 13). The presence or absence of significant elements may thus be detected, and the actual quantity of each measured very precisely from the amount of radiation recorded. Besides their principal elements, most raw materials and finished objects also contain **trace elements** – small quantities of impurities – which may be detected and measured down to a few parts per million by spectrographic means. Trace elements are extremely helpful in tracing the origins of raw materials, and this approach has been very useful in **characterisation** studies (Wilson and Pollard 2001). Characterisation aims to provide individual 'fingerprints' for sources of raw materials (whether stone, metal ores or clay deposits) by detecting significant trace elements; this is, however, by no means possible for all materials. The results normally require complicated statistical processing to determine whether a distinctive combination of elements found at one source genuinely differs from that found at all other sources; if so, the figures can be plotted onto graphs to illustrate differences (**Fig. 5.15**). Obviously, a large number of specimens from *known* sources needs to be analysed to establish sets of reference measurements before artefacts of unknown origin are tested.

An important consideration in the choice of analytical methods is the size and nature of the sample that is required. Traditional geological and metallurgical examination under a microscope involves the removal of a portion of an object sufficiently large to be ground flat and mounted on a microscope slide; many stone axes on display in museums show visible traces of this kind of sampling. Most spectrographic techniques based on radioactivity (such as neutron activation analysis) may be conducted on complete objects if they are small, or samples drilled from an inconspicuous part of a larger artefact. **X-ray diffraction** and **X-ray fluorescence** (and **energy dispersive spectrometry – ED-XRF**) can be non-destructive (unless it is necessary to remove a sample), but only measure the composition of the surface of an artefact. **Inductively-coupled plasma emission spectroscopy** and **particle-induced x-ray emission** (PIXE) are particularly sensitive for measuring small quantities, and can also detect variations within a sample (Henderson 2000: 10–11, 14–7, 20–21). Individual elements can be examined in more detail to establish which isotopes (elements with an abnormal number of electrons) are present and – more important – the ratios between different isotopes; the same procedure is used in AMS radiocarbon dating, where the proportion of ^{14}C in a sample relative to ^{12}C is measured. Studies of oxygen isotopes give extra assistance in identifying and distinguishing between sources of marble used in Greek and Roman architecture and sculpture, while isotopic studies of metals show some promise for the examination of ancient trade.

To produce optimum results the choice of technique requires full consultation between archaeologists and the laboratories where analyses will be carried out. Many major museums have their own laboratories, for example the Pennsylvania Museum's MASCA research centre and the British Museum in London; both

Figure 5.14 Photomicrographs taken with a scanning electron microscope (SEM) provide images with a depth of focus that allows artefact surfaces, plant remains etc., to be studied in almost three-dimensional detail. The technique has been used extensively in use wear analysis and it is proving valuable in the study of ancient textiles, both for the identification of plant and animal fibres and for detecting signs of wear resulting from manufacture or use. This image shows heavily worn fibres from woollen leg-bindings from Vindolanda, a Roman fort near Hadrian's Wall, enlarged 500 times. It is hoped that DNA studies may eventually add further precision to the identification of the plants and animals from which fibres were converted into textiles. (Dr J.-P. Wild / W.D. Cooke, Manchester Ancient Textile Unit)

conduct programmes of research involving active cooperation between museum staff and scientists (Bowman 1991). In essence, the most appropriate method of analysis will be chosen by understanding what kind of archaeological information is required to answer specific research questions, and the limitations of the analytical techniques available.

5.7.2 Stone

- key references: Edmonds, 'Lithic exploitation and use' 2001; Odell, *Lithic analysis* 2003; Kempe and Harvey, *The petrology of archaeological artefacts* 1983.

Besides the more sophisticated analytical techniques described below, traditional geological methods have much to offer the archaeologist, whether in the context of early prehistoric cultures that relied heavily on the use of stone for tools (Andrefsky 1998) or in more complex societies – such as the Roman Empire – where fine building stone was transported over long distances (Dodge 1988). Many minerals may be identified by eye or with a microscope (**petrography**), and some distinctive rocks are recognisable without the help of analysis to measure their elements. Axes made in stone from volcanic outcrops in western Britain were distributed all over England in the Neolithic period, and more than 7,500 examples were studied by petrological microscope from the 1940s onwards (Clough and Woolley 1985). However, the majority of Neolithic (and earlier) stone axes, along with other stone tools, were made from flint, which has such a uniform appearance that its source can only be traced with difficulty by spectrometry; inspection under a microscope is of no help.

The identification of building stone is very important in historical archaeology, right up to recent times; Roman villas, medieval cathedrals and nineteenth-century town halls all provide insights into the technical skills, communications and prosperity of the societies and individuals who created them. Sources of stone used in the Roman palace at Fishbourne, Sussex, demonstrate that a wide range of appropriate building stones had been identified all over southern England within a few years of the Roman conquest, and that Roman engineers were capable of selecting, quarrying and transporting specific types of stone for different parts of the building (Greene 1986: 154–6). Even more impressive is

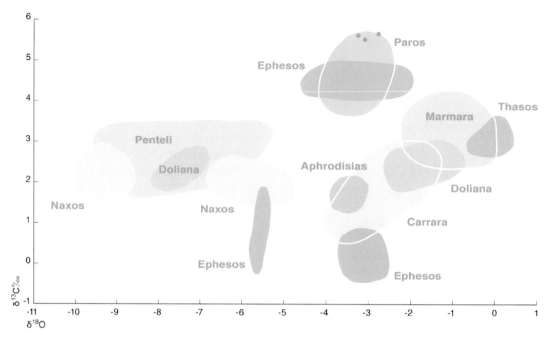

Figure 5.15 Characterisation studies aimed at locating the geological sources of stone artefacts were pioneered in the analysis of obsidian (**Fig. 5.16**). Similar studies of marble use ratios of **isotopes** of oxygen, rather than trace elements, to define the characteristics of sources of marble used in the Greek and Roman periods. White marbles are particularly difficult to distinguish from each other by eye, but unfortunately identification by analysis is not straightforward either, because results from a number of sources overlap. Nevertheless, some items may be related to a specific origin – for example, the characteristics of a statue of Minerva-Victoria in Glencairn Museum, Pennsylvania, whose isotope ratios (indicated by three points on this diagram) fell within the known range of Paros but of no other sources. (Drawn by Chris Unwin, based on Romano 1997: Fig. 2)

the quarrying of hard granite in desert conditions in Egypt between the Nile and the Red Sea, and its transport by road, river and sea for building projects in Rome (Peacock *et al.* 1994).

Although some forms of marble may be distinguished visually or under a microscope, the fine white marbles of Italy, Greece and Asia Minor have always presented difficulties. Analysis of the oxygen and carbon isotopes contained in their chemical structure now provides a method of separating them, and it allows styles of carving to be related to the areas where stone was quarried and prepared for use (Herz 1987). Isotopic analysis had to begin with samples taken from quarries known to have been in use in the past, in order to characterise each of the main sources, before their products could be identified.

Analysis of provenance and scientific dating occasionally converge. Potassium–argon dating

(Chapter 4, p. 176) has been used to identify the *origin* (rather than the date) of whetstones found on Viking-period sites; their raw material can be matched to volcanic rocks of the same type and geological age in Norway (Mitchell 1984).

The study of rock art on stone, such as that from the European Palaeolithic and from Australia (Cole and Watchman 2005), is also being advanced by the ability to use AMS radiocarbon dating (pp. 168–71) on animal fat pigments in the paint, although problems of contamination of these samples must be borne in mind (Pettitt and Bahn 2003).

Obsidian
- key references: Shackley, *Archaeological obsidian studies: method and theory* 1998; Torrence, *Production and exchange of stone tools: prehistoric obsidian in the Aegean* 1986;

Cauvin, *L'obsidienne au Proche et Moyen Orient du volcan à l'outil* 1998.

Obsidian is a volcanic glass that occurs widely in both the New and Old Worlds, and has attracted considerable attention from archaeological scientists. Like flint, it has excellent working properties for chipping, flaking and grinding into tools with sharp cutting edges (Fig. 5.16). In some parts of the world, such as New Zealand, straightforward visual inspection or microscopic examination has proved sufficient to isolate different sources. Around the Mediterranean and the American Cordillera, however, there are numerous varieties of obsidian that require more subtle differentiation. Most analyses have attempted to study patterns of prehistoric trade by identifying sources that supplied sites; this has been particularly successful in the Near East and around the Mediterranean. Distribution patterns provide insights into extensive connections between early Neolithic sites in the Near East as early as the seventh and sixth millennia BC.

This valuable information about undocumented prehistoric cultures could not have been gained without the use of scientific analysis. However, interpretation of the results in human terms remains an archaeological problem. Geology may reveal the sources of obsidian, but archaeologists must attempt to explain why any particular site should have received its raw material from one source rather than another. Analysis will not indicate whether artefacts arrived on a site as finished objects, or if blocks of raw obsidian were broken up and fashioned into tools on each site. Experienced archaeological observers may answer this question by looking for waste flakes chipped off cores during the manufacturing process. This can be done through detailed 'refitting' of **debitage** from the process (Schurmans and De Bie 2007). The nature of 'trade' is also a matter for archaeological interpretation, with the help of economic anthropology: was the raw material bartered for other goods in a commercial manner, or was there an elaborate system of gift-exchange conducted on a ceremonial basis (Ericson and Earle 1982; Bradley and Edmonds 1993)?

5.7.3 Ceramics

- key references: Whitbread, 'Ceramic petrology, clay geochemistry and ceramic production: from technology to the mind of the potter' 2001; Henderson, *The science and archaeology of materials* 2000: 109–207; Barclay, *Scientific analysis of archaeological ceramics: a handbook of resources* 2001; Knappett, 'Pottery' 2005.

Ceramic petrology
Ceramic petrology involves examination under a microscope of thin sections cut from samples of pottery in exactly the manner used to examine stone by petrography (Fig. 5.17). The best results come from pottery that includes distinctive

Figure 5.16 Obsidian, a natural volcanic glass, formed an important raw material for tool production in many parts of the world and was often traded over long distances. Since sources are rarely identifiable by eye, petrological analysis is required to study the distribution of obsidian from different sources. This flake of semi-translucent obsidian is from Greece and the flake, core and arrowheads are from Patagonia. (GNM Hancock, Newcastle upon Tyne)

Figure 5.17 A common use for the geological technique of petrology is the examination of fabrics of ceramics. This is done by cutting a section through part of a vessel and examining it under a microscope. Inclusions in the fabric can be identified and categorised, and might include fragments of distinctive rocks or minerals that can be matched with specific geological sources. Thin sections may also reveal material added to the clay by potters to improve its working properties ('temper'), such as charcoal, chaff or grog (re-used crushed pottery). Fabric samples can be catalogued to create a reference collection against which future vessels can be compared. This has allowed detailed analysis of the nature of production and exchange of different types of pottery in a number of periods and regions (Orton *et al.* 1993; Tomber and Dore 1998). (Roman rim from Silchester, Hampshire, and thin section of its fabric showing mineral grains; Alan Vince and Paul Tyers)

minerals related to the geology of the area where it was manufactured. Greek and Roman amphorae that were traded around the Mediterranean and beyond have responded particularly well to petrological study linked to their form and distribution, with the result that we now know where most types were manufactured (Whitbread 1995; Peacock and Williams 1986). As a result it is possible to study the sources and distributions of important agricultural products such as Italian wine, Spanish fish sauce or North African olive oil. Ancient documentary sources give us very little detail about trade, but amphorae are very common finds on excavations and in shipwrecks; interpretation is helped by the fact that amphorae are occasionally found still bearing handwritten inscriptions, written in black ink before their shipment, giving details of contents and origin. Petrology can also assist in defining different types of ceramics and classifying material alongside typologies; this provides a detailed record for comparison in some areas, such as Roman Britain (Tomber and Dore 1998).

Gas chromatography and ceramic residues
- key reference: Pollard *et al.*, *Analytical chemistry in archaeology* 2007: 147–59; Barnard and

Eerkens, *Theory and practice of archaeological residue analysis* 2007.

Without information on the function of ceramics from other sources, analysis of residues within pots may reveal their former contents (**Box 5.5**). Gas chromatography allows analysis of ceramic vessels to determine their original contents, which may be visible as organic residues either on their surface or within the porous fabric of a ceramic vessel. Lipids (fats) are the most commonly analysed and can reveal the residues of milk; this technique has been used to good effect to determine that secondary products from animals (milk and cheese) were exploited as early as the sixth millennium BC (Craig *et al.* 2005; see also Sherratt 1981). Such analysis can sometimes confirm typological studies; at the sixth century AD site of Sagalassos, in Turkey, cooking jars were demonstrated to have high lipid contents (Kimpe *et al.* 2004). Other substances may also be identified, such as wine, wax, oils and bitumen, including the scent once contained in Corinthian vases (Biers *et al.* 1994). In rare cases, such analysis can determine the real function of misidentified objects; so-called canopic jars of Ramesses II from the Louvre were revealed to have been used to store unguents, and were also demonstrated, by means of radiocarbon dating, to be from entirely different periods (Charrié-Duhaut *et al.* 2007).

SEM photomicrographs of cross-sections of pottery are also very informative, as they display the texture and structure of clays and glazes with remarkable clarity, displaying techniques of manufacture and decoration (Tite 1992). This, taken together with the identification of minerals by petrology, provides useful cultural information about the technology of clay preparation, potting and firing which may be interpreted with the help of ethnoarchaeological analogies (Arnold 1993).

Glass

● key references: Henderson, *The science and archaeology of materials* 2000: 24–108; Degyrse *et al.*, *Isotopes in vitreous materials* 2009.

The earliest glass was probably made from ashes of plants grown in the Middle East. The earliest known furnace from Tell el-Amarna dates to the fourteenth century BC (Henderson 2000: 40). Much of the technology involved in glass production has similarities to that involved in metalworking, and this may have been important in its origins in the third and second millennia BC in Egypt. Faience, a vitreous glaze similar to glass, developed earlier in the fifth millennium, and was probably an important development in the later emergence of glass. Colouring glass objects can be achieved by adding various oxides such as cobalt and copper. Lead was added to glass between the sixteenth and fourteenth centuries BC (*ibid.*: 27) to create a yellow colour. Glass was used in antiquity not just for the vases and bottles of the Egyptian and classical eras, but for beads in Late Prehistoric Europe, and for the window glass and mosaic tesserae of the Byzantine world (Mundell Mango and Henderson 1995). Through analysis of its chemical characteristics, different manufacturing methods can be identified and the source of glass objects discerned, leading to an understanding of the trade and exchange of glass material in prehistoric Europe (Henderson 1991) and the Middle East (Henderson 2000: 55–9). Experimental work on glass manufacturing is

further refining understanding of the manufacturing processes and trade of glass (**Box 5.11**).

5.7.4 Metals

● key references: Henderson, *The science and archaeology of materials* 2000: 208–96; LaNeice *et al.*, *Metals and mines* 2007; Craddock and Lang, *Mining and metal production through the ages* 2003.

Bronze

● key references: Killick, 'Science, speculation and the origins of extractive metallurgy' 2001; Rohl and Needham, *The circulation of metal in the British Bronze Age: the application of lead isotope analysis* 1998.

Bronze usually consists of copper alloyed with tin, and varying percentages of other metals, notably lead in some periods. Before alloys were developed, pure copper was used for making tools and objects; like gold, it occurs naturally, and can be worked to a certain extent without smelting. However, all but the simplest copper or bronze artefacts require molten metal to be poured into a mould. The form of finished artefacts, together with surface traces left by flaws in the casting and final working by the bronzesmith, usually reveals the production method. Metallographic examination under a microscope can clarify the kind of mould used (metal, stone or clay) and distinguish between cold-worked and cast objects (**Fig. 5.13**). The crystalline structure of cold-worked objects is severely distorted and flattened by hammering.

The composition of an artefact made of copper or bronze can be determined by one of the techniques of spectrometry outlined above. Programmes of analysis have been carried out since the 1930s in Europe and elsewhere, and a general pattern has emerged, although changes took place at different dates in different areas according to the availability of metal ores. Pure copper (i.e. that with only naturally occurring impurities) and copper alloyed with arsenic were soon superseded by 'true' bronze made by adding tin to the copper. This change was normally accompanied by the use of more sophisticated moulds that required less additional work after casting. In some areas (at various dates) lead was also included as a major constituent along with the tin. This required a balance to be achieved between two conflicting factors: lead made the metal easier to cast into long elaborate swords or axes with hollow sockets, but it could make it weaker in actual use. In Egypt, alloys of copper used for making axes were carefully matched to their function; axes used as weapons were primarily made from tin bronze, while tools might be copper or arsenical copper; lead bronze was only utilised for axes that were decorative rather than functional (**Fig. 5.18**).

It is theoretically possible to use trace elements to identify the areas from which artefacts came by analysing ores and products, in a manner similar to the study of obsidian. Unfortunately it was normal practice for scrap objects to be used as a source of metal in addition to quarried or mined ores. The resulting mixtures obviously confuse any attempt to pinpoint the sources of metal alloys. Lead became an important constituent of bronze, in addition to being used on its own and in other alloys such as pewter. Four different isotopes occur naturally in lead, and their ratios have been used to characterise the sources of lead

ores and those of copper that contained natural lead impurities (Stos-Gale 1995). The technique works well on ingots of metal that were lost before use, or objects that were made from fresh lead or bronze. It may even be possible to extend the technique to other artefacts that contained lead, but its usefulness will always be limited by the problem of mixing scrap metal from several sources.

Iron

- key references: Norbach, *Early iron production: archaeology, technology and experiments* 1997; Pleiner, *Iron in archaeology* 2006.

Iron differs fundamentally from copper, lead and the less common non-ferrous metals such as silver and gold in that **cast iron** did not appear until the medieval period in Europe, although it was produced somewhat earlier in China. Meteoric iron could be cold hammered and its rarity appears to have meant that its early use was restricted to exceptional items and high status objects, such as the iron dagger found in Tutankhamun's tomb dating to the fourteenth century BC. For this reason all the traces visible in pre-medieval iron objects are the result of

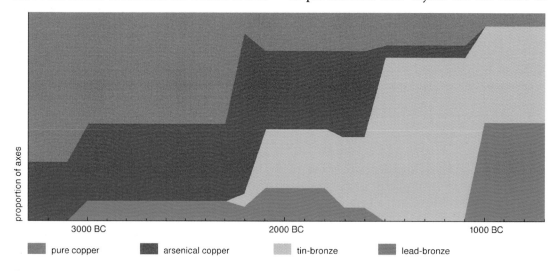

Figure 5.18 Analysis of the composition of metal alloys reveals interesting changes over time. This graph illustrates the changing proportions of Egyptian axes made from pure copper and three different alloys of copper. Axes used as weapons were primarily tin–bronze, while those used as tools might be copper or arsenical copper; decorative axes were cast in weaker lead–bronze. (Chris Unwin, after Cowell and La Niece 1991, Fig. 5.4)

laborious hammering by smiths. As with other metals, production techniques can be studied microscopically in cross-sections (Tylecote and Gilmour 1986). Treatment of the surface to harden it by quenching in water or roasting in charcoal was important in the production of iron weapons, and also leaves visible traces. However, much iron is not pure metal but contains a small percentage of carbon or phosphorus that can be measured by analysis; the make-up of alloys in finished artefacts is strongly related to working methods (Henderson 2000: 232–4). Large or complex objects were constructed from several pieces, and their joins are more easily studied in x-ray photographs than by the destructive process of cutting sections for microscopic inspection; this is also necessary for badly corroded objects. Modern ethnoarchaeological observations or experiments help to clarify the meaning of traces observed in the laboratory (Schmidt 1996; Sim 1998).

Gold, silver and lead

- key reference: Henderson, *The science and archaeology of materials* 2000: 282–5.

Metals such as gold and silver have long been prized both for their rarity and for their low melting points which allow them to be easily worked. The huge amounts of gold found with the **Chalcolithic** burial from Varna, Bulgaria, including a penis sheath, reveal that it was worked in the fifth millennium BC (Higham *et al.* 2007). Major Roman gold mines have been discovered in Wales and Spain (Annels and Burnham 1995; Burnham and Burnham 2004). Impurities in gold objects, such as the addition of copper, can be identified using ED-XRF, demonstrating the potential debasement of coins but also the choice of certain elements to change the colour, for example to rose gold in some Iron Age coins (**Box 5.10**). Analysis of Spanish coins of the late sixteenth century AD reveals the presence of gold from the New World which includes impurities found only in Peruvian and Brazilian sources (Henderson 2000: 283–4).

5.8 CONSERVATION

- key references: Brothwell and Pollard, *Handbook of archaeological sciences* 2001: 585–659; Cronyn, *Elements of archaeological conservation* 1989; Caple, *Conservation skills* 2000.

Although it is one of the most important aspects of archaeological science experienced by visitors to sites and museums, good conservation is normally invisible, and therefore easily overlooked.

5.8.1 Ancient objects

- key references: Black, *Recent advances in the conservation and analysis of artefacts* 1987; Pearson, *Conservation of marine archaeological objects* 1987; Caple, *Objects: reluctant witnesses to the past* 2006.

Whenever an ancient object is removed from the ground during an excavation, it is immediately placed at risk (**Fig. 5.19**). The environmental conditions that have protected it from total decay since its burial have been changed, particularly in the case of organic materials and objects removed from underwater, dry or frozen sites. Objects in museum collections also require constant attention, whether during storage or in public displays. It is essential that an exact identification of the composition and structure of an object is made before conservation begins. The structure may sometimes be revealed by visual inspection, using a microscope if necessary, but a particularly complex artefact (or one that has become encased in a thick layer of corrosion) may require x-ray photography to understand it. Further analysis may be necessary to find out exactly which metals or other substances are involved, for these will dictate the form of treatment to be employed.

The most important task of conservation is to neutralise decay, whether caused by the corrosion of metals or by the rotting of organic matter, and this requires a detailed knowledge of chemistry. The next stage is to stabilize the object so that

decay will not start up again; even when treated successfully, objects that are intended for display in a museum will have to be monitored to ensure that changes in temperature and humidity do not trigger further deterioration. Ethical issues are involved in conservation; a responsible archaeologist must plan the finance and facilities necessary for the preservation of finds, and no excavation is complete without at least 'first aid' facilities to minimise the onset of decay until full treatment is carried out (Watkinson and Neal 1998). The restoration of artefacts is also sensitive from an ethical point of view. A severely corroded or damaged object has little commercial value, but cleaning, stabilisation and repair not only improve its display quality for a museum, but also increase its monetary value in the antiquities trade. Since the borderline between a heavily restored genuine artefact and a fake is sometimes difficult to draw, conservators must keep detailed records and photographs of all work that they have carried out. This is also important in cases where further treatment may be required later, or where researchers need to know the original form of the object. Video recordings now provide a convenient additional medium for recording conservation work.

5.8.2   Historic buildings and archaeological sites

- key references: Sease, *A conservation manual for the field archaeologist* 1992; Williamson and Nickens, *Science and technology in historic preservation* 2000.

Newly excavated structures soon suffer from exposure, and require permanent supervision if they are to be left on display. Wind, rain, frosts, plant growth and human erosion (by visitors or vandals) soon destroy apparently sound masonry structures. Buildings that have been visible for hundreds of years are increasingly vulnerable, for ancient stonework is easily damaged by air pollution in modern urban environments. Famous monuments such as the Parthenon in Athens or Trajan's Column in Rome have been disfigured by deposits of dirt and chemical pollution in the air, while fine details of their carvings have disappeared since accurate drawings and photographs were made in the nineteenth century. These problems will only be solved by a combination of science and good environmental management; their economic importance to tourism is difficult to quantify, but should be set against the costs of

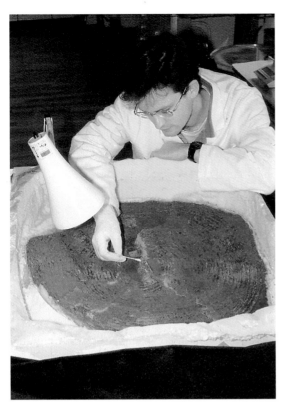

Figure 5.19 An example of the need for coordination between excavators and conservators is the find of a rare Bronze Age shield near South Cadbury, Somerset, in 1997 (Coles *et al.* 1999). It could not be removed intact because the thin sheet bronze had completely mineralised. Thus, conservators encased it in a protective wrapping along with the block of soil in which it was found and removed it for treatment in a laboratory. After x-ray examination, careful recording and stabilisation of the corrosion, the shield was ready for display in the Castle Museum, Taunton. (© South Cadbury Environs Project, University of Bristol/Wiltshire County Council Conservation Service)

conservation (Allison *et al.* 1996). Occasionally historic sites suffer catastrophic damage through earthquakes, war or accidental fires, and require intensive scientific investigation to ensure successful long-term preservation after reconstruction and repair. There is a positive side to this, however. After the destructive fire at Windsor Castle in 1992, new light was shed on the history of the castle, in particular modifications to its structure and earlier phases of decoration, by traces that had been invisible behind later walls or fittings (Brindle and Kerr 1997). Much evidence was revealed because of the care with which every part of the damaged building had to be stripped back and dried to prevent the massive quantities of water pumped in by the firefighters from causing outbreaks of rot.

Archaeological sites threatened by building development are now frequently 'preserved' by modifying the form of construction to reduce damage, rather than by salvaging information through excavation (Chapter 3, p. 108). This means that scientific knowledge about conservation has to extend to invisible deposits underground that might have been penetrated by concrete piles, as at Shakespeare's Rose Theatre in London (Bowsher 1998; Wainwright 1989). Considerable (expensive) research will be required before it is really known how foundation work affects drainage and ground-water over a long period; meanwhile organic materials and artefacts may be decaying irreversibly (Kenward and Hall 2000).

5.9 STATISTICS

- key references: Shennan, *Quantifying archaeology* 1997; Brothwell and Pollard, *Handbook of archaeological sciences* 2001: 661–747; Fletcher and Lock, *Digging numbers* 2005; Orton, *Sampling in archaeology* 2000; Aldenerfer, 'Statistics in archaeology' 2005; Baxter, *Statistics in archaeology* 2003.

Archaeology is full of statements based on intuition rather than calculation. Simple statistics are useful for checking almost any comparisons, such as claims that the dimensions of a type of artefact change over time, or that in a particular period settlement sites tended to be located on one kind of soil. **Probability testing** is appropriate in these circumstances. In the case of settlement sites, the number of sites located on each soil type could be counted, and a simple statistical test of **significance** be carried out to compare the actual totals with the numbers that would be expected if the distribution had been entirely random. Statistical tests also take account of the size of a sample, and data might have to be rejected if the sample is too small. An understanding of probability is also essential in radiocarbon dating, for the interpretation of laboratory estimates in relation to the calibration curve is no simple matter (Chapter 4, p. 171; Buck 2001). **Bayesian** statistics in particular are revolutionising radiocarbon dating (see Chapter 4, p. 175).

Correlation is another common statistical measure used by archaeologists. The relationship between sets of numerical variables may be tested by plotting them on a scatter diagram. A simple example might be to test the uniformity of the length and breadth of Anglo-Saxon timber buildings; a straight line of points on the graph would indicate that the builders shared a uniform concept of proportions, irrespective of size, whereas a dispersed scatter would indicate they were constructed without any such shared ideas. The degree of correlation may be calculated, ranging from a maximum of 1.0 (if all buildings were always exactly twice as long as they were wide) to 0.0 (if there was no relation at all). When the sample size is taken into account, correlation may also be expressed in terms of significance. Julian Richards used extensive tests of correlation and significance to investigate Anglo-Saxon burials, and discovered subtle relationships between grave goods and the sex, age or social standing of the deceased. Various factors, such as the height of pots or their decorative motifs, were found to be significant in ways that would not have been noticed without a careful numerical analysis (Richards 1987); assessing the possible meanings of such phenomena is quite another matter, of course.

Scientific analyses carried out for characterisation (above: p. 230) produce complex numerical results that need to be clarified by statistical methods. **Multivariate** procedures look for significant relationships or contrasts between elements or minerals in order to define groups that may bring some order into the data (Baxter 2001; **Fig. 5.15**). Multivariate statistics, notably **cluster analysis**, can also be used in the typological classification of artefacts or grouping of genetic data; the guiding principle is the establishment of similarity between individual samples and the extent to which they may be placed into significant groups. Modern computer software allows sophisticated tests to be carried out all too easily by archaeologists who lack an understanding of statistics; results are only as good as the evidence they are based on, and the appropriateness of the tests employed. Nevertheless, a basic awareness of statistical concepts should encourage archaeologists to collect and examine data more carefully; awareness of probability and correlation undoubtedly leads to a better understanding of **sampling** (Orton 1999). This is an important concept in planning research, whether it is related to objects or fieldwork; most modern field survey projects, such as the Dalmatian project described in Chapter 2, are designed with a clear sampling strategy in mind (Chapter 2, p. 54). In addition to applying statistics to fieldwork projects, mathematical methods can also be used for **modelling** hypothetical situations, and creating **simulations**; 'numerical models represent the real world as a set of variables linked by mathematical or logical conditions; they are iterative because they must be solved or studied by repeatedly replacing those variables with numbers until the specified conditions are met. Some mathematical models and all simulation models fall into this category' (Lake 2001: 723).

5.10 EXPERIMENTAL ARCHAEOLOGY

- key references: Coles, *Experimental archaeology* 1979; Mathieu, *Experimental archaeology* 2002; Reynolds, *Iron Age farm: the Butser experiment* 1979; Shimada, 'Experimental archaeology' 2005.

Along with the use of statistics, one by-product of increasingly scientific approaches to archaeology in the second half of the twentieth century was a trend towards designing practical experiments. While the majority have been one-off tests of specific ideas, a few – for example, the Butser Ancient Farm Project (Reynolds 1979) – have developed into long-term programmes observing a whole range of variables over several decades. The scientific ideal of an experiment is rarely fulfilled in an archaeological context, for many variables are difficult to control or measure, let alone replicate. Even when 'experiments' are in effect replications, demonstrations or simulations, they may nevertheless give valuable information about artefacts and structures. One danger inherent in experiments about the functions of artefacts is that 'efficiency', measured in terms of time and energy, is a very modern concept (Shimada 2008). An alternative approach is to study living peoples, and to incorporate additional information made available by the possibilities of discussing artefacts, structures and processes with the people involved. Anthropological observation aimed at the understanding of the nature of archaeological evidence expanded rapidly from the 1970s, and is usually known as **ethnoarchaeology** (Chapter 6, p. 269). Ethnoarchaeological studies of pre-industrial societies reveal that

BOX 5.11   Experimental archaeology: glass in Egypt

Experimental archaeology is particularly effective in providing insights into techniques for processing raw materials and manufacturing finished articles. It is possible to estimate the amount of labour required, to identify the kinds of materials needed, and to test equipment and structures (such as kilns and furnaces) used during the manufacturing process. By reconstructing ancient Egyptian glass production, archaeologist Caroline Jackson (2005) was able to ascertain the labour and material required in production, shedding wider light on the nature of production and the exchange of glass in the ancient world (Caroline Jackson and Paul Nicholson, Egypt Exploration Society).

ritual and symbolism may be more important than strictly practical considerations. Successful interpretations of important general issues – such as the prehistory of agriculture – are likely to combine archaeology with ethnoarchaeology and experiment (Anderson 1999).

5.10.1 Artefacts

- key references: Sim, *Beyond the bloom* 1998; Whittaker, *Flintknapping: making and understanding stone tools* 1994; Underwood, *Anglo-Saxon weapons and warfare* 1999.

Experimental archaeology is a useful companion to scientific analysis in the study of artefacts, for their composition and structure may suggest methods of manufacture. Ancient technology has been explored by reconstructions of metal-casting procedures, the making and firing of pottery, and various forms of stone working. If one particular manufacturing technique suggested by an archaeologist is found to be successful in practice, the experiment only confirms that it *could* have been used in the past, not that it actually was (**Box 5.10**). A single demonstration of one method of firing ancient pottery is of limited value without a series of comparative firings carried out using different fuels, kiln structures, methods of arranging the pots in the kiln. Again, it will never be proved that the method found to be most effective today was the one employed in the past, but the possibility of gross misinterpretation will be reduced if some unsatisfactory techniques are ruled out. It is of course essential to use appropriate materials and equipment known to have been available in the relevant period.

Besides experiments concerning manufacture, studies of functions and the efficiency of tools have been conducted; these may include re-enactment of ancient warfare, in addition to craft activities. Such experiments are frequently carried out in association with microscopic use wear analysis, as wear or damage to working surfaces may suggest how a tool was used; if a replica is utilised for the same purpose, it can be examined afterwards to see if the same effects are observable (e.g. Byrne *et al.* 2006).

5.10.2 Sites and structures

- key references: Stone and Planel, *The constructed past: experimental archaeology, education and the public* 1999; Bell *et al.*, *The experimental earthwork project 1960–1992* 1996; Morrison *et al.*, *The Athenian trireme: the history and reconstruction of an ancient Greek warship* 2000.

Large-scale structures such as ships, buildings and earthworks can be investigated through experiments and simulation studies, normally by means of reconstructions based on evidence derived from excavations. If possible this evidence should be supplemented with ethnoarchaeological data, or, in the case of more recent historical reconstructions, information and illustrations from archives. At the most basic level, an exercise of this kind tests whether a structure postulated by an archaeologist could actually have been built in the form suggested. Once this requirement has been satisfied, worthwhile questions include estimates of human effort involved in construction, and the quantity and sources of the necessary raw materials. If the reconstruction is found to be unworkable, the excavator can review the site evidence and look for features that were not previously thought to be significant. Other excavated traces that proved difficult to explain may be clarified; a scatter of post holes around a building, for example, could have supported scaffolding or temporary props during construction.

Since archaeologists excavate the decayed remains of structures, the study of decay processes is fundamental to their interpretation, and many experiments have been designed to explore this area. In Denmark, reconstructed timber buildings have been burnt down and then re-excavated to learn how the remains reflect the superstructure.

Work on attempting to reconstruct the Roman concrete that was able to set under water, as discussed by the writer Vitruvius, provides insights into the construction techniques used in Roman harbour construction, such as Herod's harbour at Caesarea, in Israel (Hohfelder *et al.* 2005).

Figure 5.20 A full-scale replica of a Dutch East Indiaman based on remains of the hull of the *Amsterdam*, which ran aground near Hastings on the south coast of England on its maiden voyage to Indonesia in 1749 (Marsden 1985). Ships of this kind underpinned the trading economy of the city of Amsterdam, but while many paintings and buildings from this period survive, ships do not. Several historic ships – a Greek oared trireme, Viking longboats, post-medieval sailing ships – have been reconstructed in recent decades to improve understanding of construction technology and to test their performance in use. They also make excellent displays, especially when moored beside a magnificent historic building such as the Netherlands Maritime Museum, a former naval arsenal built at a safe distance from the centre of Amsterdam in case of explosion. (Nederlands Scheepvaartmuseum, Amsterdam)

In England, an experimental earthwork project began in the early 1960s to study long-term processes of change (Ashbee and Jewell 1998); at Overton Down, Wiltshire, a bank and ditch were constructed on a chalk subsoil, and near Wareham, Dorset, a similar structure was created on sand. The earthworks were constructed to exact measurements, and objects and other organic and inorganic samples were buried at precisely recorded locations. Erosion, settlement, decay and the movement of objects by earthworms and other disturbances of the soil will continue to be monitored well into the twenty-first century by means of periodic excavations of small sections of the earthworks (Bell *et al.* 1996).

Since access to the sites is strictly limited, the effects of people on a real structure in everyday use have been excluded; furthermore, structures in the past were probably carefully maintained, and not allowed to deteriorate until they were obsolete. These problems illustrate the greatest weakness of experimental archaeology: experiments require controls, but past human activity was not necessarily rational or consistent.

Many full-sized reconstructions of ancient ships have been built and tested since the nineteenth century. Greek warships have been particularly popular because historical accounts of critical naval battles survive in Classical literature. The most recent example is the *Olympias*, an Athenian trireme constructed to test configurations of oarsmen and claims for the speed and manoeuvrability made in Greek texts (Welsh 1988). This ship raises a characteristic problem of reconstruction; many warships are illustrated in Greek paintings and carvings, and texts provide details of the size of crews, but no illustration or description gives an unambiguous account of the arrangement of the oars and rowers within the hull. Full-scale working reconstructions are not only informative about sailing and navigation; a replica of the Dutch East India Company's ship *Amsterdam*, based on remains excavated on the coast of England, also makes an attractive and educational addition to the city of Amsterdam's maritime museum (**Fig. 5.20**).

5.11   CONCLUSION

> For is it not, these days, a defining characteristic of real science that it is testable? … That archaeological science should sometimes give wrong answers, and that these can later be shown to be indeed erroneous, must be counted one of the subject's great strengths.
>
> (Renfrew 1992: 292)

The scientific methods employed in archaeological research now impinge upon most areas of the subject. Archaeologists and historians ignore scientific evidence at their peril if they wish to understand the chronological framework of the past, the natural environments where people lived, or the material resources available to ancient societies. The development of new techniques provides an opportunity for interaction between archaeology and science when disagreements arise, and a constructive re-examination of basic data and the way in which they are studied. Ethical dimensions are already inescapable: arguments about the actions of humans in the past are already applied to sensitive environmental issues, while political concerns about individual and group identity frequently make claims based on human physical evolution and genetics. Perhaps the greatest problem facing many of the new developments in archaeological

science, especially genetics, is uncritical use of their results. Problems with contamination and with sample sizes have been recognised, but we also have to ensure that valid questions are being asked – it is unlikely that science will provided an unambiguous answer to a problem, although it may appear so. As techniques are refined and become more widespread, their integration into larger research programmes will undoubtedly increase the impact of their findings. We live in interesting times.

5.12   GUIDE TO FURTHER READING

Dozens of important articles appear each year in the journals *Archaeometry* and *Journal of Archaeological Science*, and many are contained in *Antiquity* as well as in non-archaeological periodicals such as *Science* and *Nature*. The contents lists of these periodicals are available on-line, and many libraries allow access to abstracts and even complete texts of the papers published in them. Anyone interested in measuring the progress of archaeological science over several decades may compare the papers collected by Brothwell and Higgs, *Science in archaeology* (either 1963 or 1969 edition), with the contributions to Brothwell and Pollard, *Handbook of archaeological sciences* 2001. Andrews and Doonan, *Test tubes and trowels* 2003, also represent an accessible introduction. Authoritative but less technical essays on many scientific topics are included in Ellis, *Archaeological method and theory: an encyclopaedia* 2000; this book, along with Brothwell and Pollard, also gives guidance about further reading.

THE NATURE OF SCIENCE

Lambert, *Traces of the past: unravelling the secrets of archaeology through chemistry* 1997, gives a very good idea of the breadth of topics to which science may be applied, while Bayley, *Science in archaeology: an agenda for the future* 1998, reflects the experience of English Heritage's laboratories. Each year in Britain there is an

Archaeological Sciences Conference, and it is normally published – for example, Beavis and Barker, *Science and site* 1995. The application of many scientific approaches to one particular site can be found in Cunliffe and Renfrew, *Science and Stonehenge* 1997. Johnson, *Archaeological theory* 2010, includes an interesting discussion about varying approaches and attitudes to science (pp. 35–49), while Jones, *Archaeological theory and scientific practice* 2002, attempts to bridge the divide between theory and archaeological science.

THE ENVIRONMENT

More specialised studies of the broad climatic background are Roberts, *The Holocene* 1998, and Bell and Walker, *Late Quaternary environmental change* 1992. An analysis of the impact of climate on the Near East is Rosen, *Civilizing climate* 2007, while a vivid account of a much later impact of climate change, in the medieval period, is Fagan, *The Great Warming* 2008. The annual conferences of the Association of Environmental Archaeology are normally published: for example, Luff and Rowley-Conwy, *Whither environmental archaeology?* 1994; and an interesting collection of papers is contained in Reitz and Scudder, *Case studies in environmental archaeology* 1996.

THE GEOSPHERE

Herz and Garrison, *Geological methods for archaeology* 1998, is a good general guide, while Pollard, *Geoarchaeology: exploration, environments, resources* 1999, contains a variety of papers and a good introduction by the editor. Bell and Boardman, *Past and present soil erosion* 1992, and French, *Geoarchaeology in action* 2003, provide case studies from around the world.

THE BIOSPHERE

Briggs and Crowther, *Palaeobiology: a synthesis* 1993, is a thorough textbook about palaeobiology, palaeontology and evolution, while Brothwell and

Pollard, *Handbook of archaeological sciences* 2001, pp. 359–440, contains detailed studies. Harris and Thomas, *Modelling ecological change* 1991, and Huntley *et al.*, *Taphonomy and interpretation* 2000, both contain papers that underline the complexity of interactions in the biosphere and the interpretation of evidence. At the level of individual excavated sites, reports from York are particularly interesting: for example, the well-illustrated Kenwood and Hall, *Biological evidence from 16–22 Coppergate* 1995.

PLANTS

Balick and Cox, *Plants, people, and culture* 1997, is devoted to 'the science of ethnobotany', and Van Zeist, *Progress in Old World palaeoethnobotany* 1991, is a review of 20 years' work, while Hather, *Tropical archaeobotany* 1994, speaks for itself; recent case studies of the use of phytoliths are in Madella and Zurro, *Plants, people and places* 2007. Domestication of plants is a topic with an enormous published literature; a useful collection of papers has been edited by Renfrew, *New light on early farming* 1991. Studies of specific areas of the world are Van der Veen, *Exploitation of plant resources in ancient Africa* 1999, and Lie Dan Lu, *The transition from foraging to farming and the origin of agriculture in China* 1999. The increasingly important field of genetics in animal and plant domestication is covered with major studies in Zeder *et al.*, *Documenting domestication* 2006, but new studies are being added all the time in the major science journals (see Chapter 4). Insights into the human impact upon vegetation, as part of wider landscape studies, are included in Aston, *Interpreting the landscape: landscape archaeology and local history* 1997 (concentrating on medieval and later England), while the impact of Greek and Roman civilisations is included in Leveau, *Archaeology of the Mediterranean landscape, 2: environmental reconstruction in Mediterranean landscape archaeology* 1999, and in Jeskins, *Environment and the classical world* 1998. In addition to their value for dating, tree rings as indicators of environmental change are the subject of Schweingrüber, *Trees and wood in dendrochronology* 1993, and Baillie, 'Bad for trees – bad for humans?' 1998.

ANIMALS

An older book that is still very readable and relevant is Davis, *The archaeology of animals* 1987, while a comprehensive overview of animals in Britain is Yalden, *History of British mammals* 1999; the archaeology of **birds** is well served by Cohen and Serjeantson, *Bird bones* 1996, and Morales Muiz, *Archaeornithology: birds and the archaeological record* 1993. Interpretation of **assemblages of bones** from a statistical point of view can be explored in Lyman, *Quantitative palaeozoology* 2008. The general problems of understanding **finds from excavations** is explored by Bosinski, *The role of early humans in the accumulation of European Lower and Middle Palaeolithic bone assemblages* 1999, and by Wilson, *Spatial patterning among animal bones in settlement archaeology* 1996, while one important site is examined in Roberts and Parfitt, *Boxgrove: a Middle Pleistocene hominid site* 1998. An example of examining social change from an animal bones perspective is Sykes, *The Norman Conquest: a zooarchaeological perspective* 2007, while less obvious aspects are explored in Anderson and Boyle, *Ritual treatment of human and animal remains* 1996. The complexities of the important sub-topic of **fish** may be appreciated by reading Jones, 'Experiments with fish bones and otoliths: implications for the reconstruction of past diet and economy' 1990, and Barrett, 'Fish trade in Norse Orkney and Caithness: a zooarchaeological approach' 1997. The Proceedings of the 9th International Council of Archaeozoology (ICAZ) provides a set of volumes on various issues relating to animal bones and a range of case studies (e.g. Maltby, *Integrating zooarchaeology* 2006). The context of the domestication of animals and plants in the Old World Neolithic is explored in Perles, *The Early Neolithic in Greece* 2001, and Cappers and Bottema, *Dawn of farming in the Near East* 2002.

HUMANS

The best overall introductory guide is Roberts, *Human remains* 2009. For details of how to recognise and record human remains, see Bennett, *A field guide for human skeletal identification* 1993, and Ubelaker, *Human skeletal remains: excavation, analysis, interpretation* 1996. General **biological details** and their implications can be studied in Eckhardt, *Human paleobiology* 2000, and Larsen, *Bioarchaeology: interpreting behaviour from the human skeleton* 1997, while Katzenberg and Saunders, *Biological anthropology of the human skeleton* 2008, is an up-to-date collection of chapters about **interpretation**. The subject of human evolution is enormous, with the genetic evidence growing and changing rapidly. Scarre, *The human past* 2005, provides a basic introduction, with more comprehensive and accessible reviews in Lewin, *Human evolution* 2005, and Lewin and Foley, *Principles of human evolution* 2004. Stringer, *Homo britannicus* 2006, provides an easy introduction to the British evidence. Detailed publications about the fascinating analysis of **graves** in London can be found in Reeve *et al.*, *The Spitalfields project* 1993, and Molleson and Cox, *The Spitalfields project, 2: the anthropology – the middling sort* 1998.

Unusual **forms of burial** are included in Anderson and Boyle, *Ritual treatment of human and animal remains* 1996, and Turner and Scaife, *Bog bodies: new discoveries and new perspectives* 1995. The famous Alpine Ice Man is just one person examined in K Spindler *et al.*, *Human mummies: a global survey* 1996. **Pathology** is a large and complex subject, understood better with the assistance of Blau and Ubelaker, *Handbook of forensic archaeology* 2007, and Hunter, *Forensic archaeology* 2005. Further information on causes of death by **disease** is provided by Roberts and Cox, *Health and disease in Britain* 2003.

An interesting overview of the **impact of farming** is Jackes *et al.*, 'Healthy but mortal: human biology and the first farmers of western Europe' 1997, while Cohen and Crane-Kramer,

Ancient health 2007, deals with its impact in the Americas. Regional studies of diet are presented by Vaughan and Coulson, *Palaeodiet in the Aegean* 1999, and Tayles, *The excavation of Khok Phanom Di: a prehistoric site in central Thailand, 5: the people* 1999, the latter based on bone, food remains and coprolites dating to around 2000–1500 BC. Martin Jones, *Feast: why humans share food* 2007, provides a narrative overview of feasting, bringing together many different archaeological approaches. Katzenberg, 'Stable isotope analysis' 2008, discusses in detail their uses for examining human remains. **Genetics** is a rapidly developing field, but good signposts can be found in Lambert and Grupe, *Prehistoric human bone: archaeology at the molecular level* 1993, while Stone and Lurquin, *A genetic and cultural odyssey* 2005, charts genetic developments through a biography of one of its pioneers, Cavalli-Sforza. The implications for archaeology are examined in Renfrew and Boyle, *Archaeogenetics: DNA and the population prehistory of Europe* 2000; it includes correlations with languages, as does Renfrew, *America past, America present: genes and languages in the Americas and beyond* 2000. The complexities of evolutionary genetics may be approached through Berger and Hilton-Barber, *In the footsteps of Eve: the mystery of human origins* 2000, and Sykes, *The seven daughters of Eve* 2002, provides an accessible introduction to some of the most dramatic discoveries.

ARTEFACTS AND RAW MATERIALS

Insights into the **theoretical and technological context** within which scientific studies take place can be gained from Kingery, *Learning from things: method and theory of material culture studies* 1996, and Wisseman and Williams, *Ancient technologies and archaeological materials* 1994. A highly readable set of introductory papers from specialists at the British Museum is presented in Bowman, *Science and the past* 1991. Sutton and Arkush, *Archaeological laboratory methods: an*

introduction 1996, is useful, but more technical details are contained in Orna, *Archaeological chemistry: organic, inorganic and biochemical analysis* 1996, and in Pollard and Heron, *Archaeological chemistry* 1996. Examples of **microscopic examination** are Jensen, *Flint tools and plant working* 1994; Sala, *A study of microscopic polish on flint implements* 1996, and Van den Dries, *Archaeology and the application of artificial intelligence: case-studies on use-wear analysis of prehistoric flint tools* 1998. Explanations and specific studies of **analysis and characterisation** can be found in Hughes, 'Tracing to source' 1991, and in the same author's *Neutron activation and plasma emission spectrometric analysis in archaeology: techniques and applications* 1991. Their application can be seen in Herz, 'Carbon and oxygen isotope ratios: a data base for Classical Greek and Roman marble' 1987, while interesting debates about interpretation continue: for example Budd, 'Rethinking the quest for provenance' 1996, and Tite, 'In defence of lead isotope analysis' 1996.

A common **stone** raw material is thoroughly explored in Odell's *Lithic analysis* 2003, while Waddington, *Joy of flint* 2004, provides an accessible introduction. A specific study of debitage is Andrefsky, *Lithic debitage* 2001. Architectural materials are the subject of Maniatis *et al.*, *The study of marble and other stones used in antiquity* 1995. A source of decorative stone is featured in Beck and Shennan, *Amber in prehistoric Britain* 1991, while interpretation is the primary concern of Bradley and Edmonds, *Interpreting the axe trade: production and exchange in Neolithic Britain* 1993. The whole industrial cycle can be seen in Milliken and Peresani, *Lithic technology: from raw material procurement to tool production* 1998.

Further general insights into **ceramics** can be gained from Lindahl and Stilborg, *The aim of laboratory analyses of ceramics in archaeology* 1995, along with specific studies of the use of pottery in Biers and McGovern, *Organic contents of vessels: materials analysis* *and archaeological investigation* 1990; Peacock, *Pottery in the Roman world: an ethnoarchaeological approach* 1982, remains a classic work that brings together scientific study and interpretation. **Metals** can be followed up in two volumes of interesting papers edited by Young, *Metals in antiquity* 1999. Articles about how **metalworking** began in Spain in the first half of the fifth millennium BC by Ruiz-Taboada and Montero-Ruiz, 'The oldest metallurgy in western Europe' 1999, and sources of copper in Britain by Budd, 'The early development of metallurgy in the British Isles' 1992, are just two examples of the fascinating issues that may be investigated through metallurgical science. For Ancient Egypt, Nicholson and Shaw, *Ancient Egyptian materials and technology* 2000 provides an overview.

CONSERVATION

Caple, *Objects, reluctant witnesses to the past* 2006, provides a basic overview. More technical detail relating to artefacts is contained in Mills and White, *Organic chemistry of museum objects* 1994, while x-ray examination is the subject of Lang and Middleton, *Radiography of cultural material* 1997.

STATISTICS

Useful introductions to **statistics** are Fletcher and Lock, *Digging numbers: elementary statistics for archaeologists* 2005, and Aldenfelder, 'Statistics for archaeology' 2005; those who wish to get more deeply involved in their mathematical basis should try Buck and Millard, *Tools for constructing chronologies* 2004, and Baxter, *Statistics in archaeology* 2003. **Computer applications** are introduced by Lock, *Using computers in archaeology* 2003, and their use in the study of bones is explored in Anderson and Boyle, *Computing and statistics in osteoarchaeology* 1997. Each year a conference on Computer Applications and Quantitative Methods in Archaeology is held, and published subsequently by various editors; an Internet search using that title will locate them.

EXPERIMENTAL ARCHAEOLOGY

A volume of essays dedicated to one of the most notable exponents of experimental archaeology, edited by Harding, is *Experiment and design: archaeological studies in honour of John Coles* 1999. A periodical, *Journal of (Re)Construction and Experiment in Archaeology*, has been published from 2004 by EXARC.

CHAPTER 6

Making sense of the past

… theory exists, in however unsatisfactory a form, in everything that an archaeologist does regardless of region, material, period and culture… It is this pervasive, central and international aspect of archaeological theory, multiplied by its current weakness, which makes the whole issue of major importance in the further development of the discipline.

(Clarke 1973: 17–18)

- Placing interpretation and '**theory**' into a final chapter does not mean that we consider them separate from '**practice**', any more than our other chapters imply clear dividing lines between science and dating, or excavation and fieldwork.

- The first half of this final chapter presents a concise **overview of developments in archaeological theory** since the early twentieth century. These developments coincided with some fundamental changes in outlook that accompanied the end of the Second World War and the beginning of the Cold War. An optimistic and confident approach called the **New Archaeology** emerged by the 1960s, characterised by **processualism**, which attempted to make the subject more 'scientific'.

- More recent **postprocessual archaeology** is not easy to generalise about, but is very important because much general writing about archaeology – and about prehistory in particular – has been caught up in wider intellectual movements associated with **modernism** and **postmodernism**. Structuralism and post-structuralism have had profound effects upon culture in general, from art and literature to the sciences, and archaeology reflects this wider situation.

- Philosophies that have looked critically at modernism have brought positive benefits to **interpretive archaeology**, which pays greater attention to individual experiences than abstract processes and raises the profile of issues such as **gender**, **ethnicity** and approaches to material culture and the body, including **materiality** and **fragmentation**.

- The remainder of Chapter 6 examines **archaeology and the public**, especially **heritage management**, which has been heavily influenced by the changing intellectual climate of archaeological theory and contemporary social concerns.

6.1 WHERE IS ARCHAEOLOGY AT THE BEGINNING OF THE TWENTY-FIRST CENTURY?

Chapter 1 explored how archaeology (or **antiquarianism**, as its early manifestation is known) had developed in Europe through the Renaissance to the eighteenth century, into a common and relatively harmless distraction for the educated. Following great advances in geology, some aspects of archaeology (notably the study of human origins and early prehistory) developed into a 'respectable' scientific pursuit in the nineteenth century. However, what was respectable then may now seem tainted by Victorian ideology about Empire and racial supremacy. Archaeology has grown rapidly since 1900, with the result that virtually every country in the world now operates some form of state-financed protection of ancient monuments, as well as supporting the subject in universities and museums. The New Archaeology of the 1960s not only broadened interpretation, but also inspired advances in the study and recovery of archaeological evidence because it required more precise evidence about settlement patterns, site layouts and environmental conditions. Between 1950 and 2000 the ideals of the eighteenth-century Enlightenment appeared to have been achieved: democracy; public institutions for education and art; economic prosperity and literacy for the masses (in the developed world, at least). This comfortable view was increasingly undermined towards the end of the century, however, as postmodernism revealed structures of power and ideology behind these supposedly benign developments. Archaeologists themselves came under suspicion when their role in helping to explain the great story of human progress was dismissed as nothing more than story-telling aimed at supporting current political ideologies (Kehoe 1998). Aware of this, postprocessual archaeologists of the 1980s drew upon a wide range of philosophies and anthropological theory that shifted the focus from general social/ environmental processes towards individual human experience.

Archaeology has become a popular subject in schools, universities and continuing education, perhaps because it involves a variety of practical and theoretical work and a mixture of approaches from the sciences and humanities. It is also concerned with everyday objects and structures, as well as with the social elites upon whom history has tended to concentrate. Museum displays are now aimed at general visitors rather than specialists, and 'designer' displays have displaced rows of pots with terse labels. Mobility and leisure have increased to the extent that mass tourism regularly includes ancient sites and museums. Archaeology receives extensive publicity

through popular writing and journalism; it even contributes to home entertainment through television programmes shown at peak viewing times, without causing any surprise. The extraordinary popularity of archaeology from academia to popular culture makes it even more important to keep on asking questions about exactly *what* archaeologists are trying to do – and for whom.

6.1.1 Too much knowledge?

When awareness of human antiquity became widespread in the middle of the nineteenth century, the academic world was small, international, and not confined to universities and museums. John Evans, who visited Boucher de Perthes and witnessed the stratigraphic position of Palaeolithic artefacts at Amiens in 1859 (Chapter 1, p. 30), was a busy paper-mill manager who published articles and books on geology, pre-Roman coins, bronze implements and flints in his spare time (Macgregor 2008). As President of the Royal Society in London, he rubbed shoulders with most of the prominent geologists, physicists, biologists and other scientists of his day. The sort of interaction, such as that between John Evans, Charles Lyell and Charles Darwin, that lay behind this exciting phase in the development of archaeological thinking is more difficult to achieve today; multidisciplinary projects are expensive and time-consuming (Evans 2009). Few can keep up-to-date with more than one field, and specialists are increasingly reluctant to write 'overviews' or syntheses for the public. These factors have led to a fragmentation of academic archaeology into restricted periods of the past, limited geographical areas or arcane philosophies of interpretation.

Almost every discipline has undergone an 'information explosion' since 1900; librarians are particularly aware of the increase in the number and thickness of books and periodicals and of the search for alternatives to the printed page such as CD-ROMs, e-books, electronic journals and on-line databases. At the same time, the Internet has democratised information (at least for people who can afford computers); anyone can type a few keywords into a search engine and retrieve

BOX 6.1   # Archaeological theory and changing perspectives

This is the facade of a 'megalithic' chambered tomb (Cairnholy I, Dumfries and Galloway). These elaborate stone monuments are found in many parts of western Europe, Scandinavia and Germany and attracted much attention from early antiquaries. They usually contain stone-lined chambers, often with long entrance passageways. Some are architecturally sophisticated, with enormous stones or elaborate vaulting, and may bear geometric or curvilinear carving. Where the contents of the chambers survive, excavation usually reveals collective burials of large numbers of individuals.

Monumental stone architecture appeared in Egypt soon after 3000 BC and reached remarkable sophistication in monuments such as Zoser's step pyramid at Saqqara, c. 2650 BC. Tombs with stone passageways and vaulted chambers existed in the Aegean area around 1600 BC, and archaeologists adopting a 'diffusionist' interpretation assumed that these provided the inspiration for chambered tombs further north and west. In the 1960s, radiocarbon dating began to produce dates around 3000 BC for megalithic tombs – too early for the supposed prototypes in the Aegean and even earlier than the first stone architecture in Egypt; calibration according to the tree-ring curve and new dates from Brittany actually placed several before 4000 BC. 'Quite obviously, if they have their ultimate origin in the Aegean, this must have been a long time before 3000 BC. Yet there are no collective built tombs in the Aegean until after this date. The Breton dates, even without calibration, make nonsense of the diffusionist case' (Renfrew 1973a: 89–90).

Megalithic tombs, circles and alignments underwent intense mathematical analysis from the 1960s onwards to explore their astronomical significance (Ruggles 1999); this form of study coincided with the expansion of space science and computers. The scientific outlook of New Archaeology attempted to explain the megaliths in terms of identical patterns of social behaviour taking place independently in many parts of Europe. **Postprocessual** interpretations have explored how megaliths and other monuments shape, reflect and reinforce concepts of time, memory, ancestry and identity amongst communities and individuals. At the height of club-culture involving hypnotic dance music and drugs in the 1990s it was suggested that the acoustic properties of megaliths would enhance sound and cause physical sensations in people involved in ceremonies (Watson and Keating 1999). Recent advances in radiocarbon dating are leading to further transformation, refining the chronologies of these monuments even further (Chapter 4; Bayliss *et al.* 2007). Revised dating of Neolithic chambered tombs in central southern England, through the application of Bayesian statistics to radiocarbon dates, indicates that depositions took place in them for relatively short periods of time – decades rather than centuries (Bayliss *et al.* 2007; Bayliss, Whittle and Wysoki 2007). Current theories reflect the concepts of agency and individualism, which have dominated much of archaeological theory in recent years, rather than the traditional explanation of commemorating ancestors (Parker-Pearson and Ramilisonina 1998; Edmonds 1999). Studies of such monuments are also looking at their reception and understanding by later communities, including our own (Chippindale 2004; Darvill 2006).

Changing interpretations of megalithics underline the difficulty of making sense of the past. This probably helps to explain the attraction of alternative explanations linked to lost civilisations, extraterrestrial contacts or utopian New Age visions of the past. (Photograph: Mick Sharp)

information from the other side of the world. It is difficult to judge the quality of this information, however, as anyone may create web-pages about anything they like. The relative obscurity of archaeological theory and the extreme specialisation of archaeologists have undoubtedly contributed to the flourishing of writers such as Graham Hancock whose theories about familiar subjects, especially Egyptian pyramids, seize the imagination of the public and sell books by the million. Writers of this kind take particular pleasure in showing how 'experts' have not only overlooked alternative explanations, but also refuse to examine ideas that might undermine their own established positions (G Fagan 2006: **Box 6.2**). Stukeley's obsession with Druids demonstrates that supernatural or mystical interpretations of antiquities are not new (Chapter 1, p. 16), while the belief of Hancock and other writers in a lost civilisation that passed its wisdom on to ancient Egypt or the Maya repeats the theme of *Atlantis: the antediluvian world* popularised by Ignatius Donnelly from 1882. Despite brave attempts to show that conventional archaeological interpretations are actually more interesting than 'fantastic' ones (Williams 1991; Feder 2005; G Fagan 2006), books of this kind dominate the best-seller lists (**Box 6.2**). While advances in astronomy and space

exploration stimulated interest in the theories of Hancock and Erich von Däniken, the anti-technological New Age movement has been attracted to Celtic religion, American Indian ceremonies and prehistoric mother-goddesses; how should conventional archaeologists react? The nature of archaeological theory itself will be examined, before this chapter turns to the broader issues generated by this question.

6.2 ARCHAEOLOGICAL THEORY

- key references: Johnson, *Archaeological theory* 2010; Trigger, *A history of archaeological thought* 2006; Whitley, *Reader in archaeological theory* 1998; Johnson, 'The theoretical scene, 1960–2000' 2008.

Archaeology remains appallingly unaware of its own theoretical underpinnings; much if not most archaeological practice is quite uninformed about recent theoretical debates. One of the most encouraging things in recent years has been signs that this is changing.

(Johnson 1999: 182)

BOX 6.2

Are all visions of the past equal? Pseudo-archaeology

One of the greatest challenges of reflexive and postmodern approaches to archaeology is **multivocality**. If we acknowledge that more than one view or narrative account of the past is valid, and we are open to reflection about our own views, we should recognise that our models of the past are heavily influenced by Western cultural expectations. This problem can be addressed in archaeological research in a number of interesting ways (e.g. Piccini 1999), for example by incorporating the views of different people into investigations. However, when faced with '**pseudo-archaeology**', the problems become more difficult. Alternative archaeological stories by writers such as Erich von Däniken and Graham Hancock have gained a large following and enduring popularity. They tend to explain 'mysterious' archaeological sites (such as the Egyptian pyramids shown here) and artefacts in terms of extraterrestrial influences or lost civilisations which professional archaeologists deliberately ignore (Feder 2005; G Fagan 2006). Conventional archaeologists examine data and seek to interpret them, and then revise their interpretations in the light of new evidence. Pseudo-archaeologists create an overarching theory first, which they then seek to prove by amassing evidence to support it – frequently overlooking intricacies and inconsistencies and ignoring conventional archaeological research (G Fagan 2006: 27–30). Such stories are not necessarily harmless fun; attempts to 'prove' the existence of enormous stone pyramids in the Balkans (which archaeologists regard as natural geological formations) may have had a detrimental impact on the preservation of Bosnia's real archaeological heritage (Harding 2007).

Pseudo-archaeology is not necessarily deliberately dishonest. However, for some the desire to ensure that their version of the past is accepted has been so strong that they have manufactured archaeological evidence to 'prove' their beliefs. The most famous British example was the faking of a human ancestor at Piltdown in the nineteenth century (Russell 2003); it was only revealed as a fraudulent combination of a much later human skull and modern orang-utan bones in the 1950s. More recently an archaeologist in Japan was found to have repeatedly faked the discovery of Palaeolithic artefacts (G. Fagan 2006: xiii). Fagan (2006: 367) recommends that the best option for archaeologists is to 'ask hard questions, probe and expose. Critique after all is the heart of true scholarship'; we would add that archaeologists should also produce alternative explanations based on a thorough critical evaluation of the evidence. The separate teams of archaeologists who argue for an interpretation of Stonehenge either as a healing centre or as a monument commemorating the dead have both tested their views by fieldwork and excavation, and would undoubtedly abandon their current views if confronted by evidence which did not support them. (Chris Gerrard)

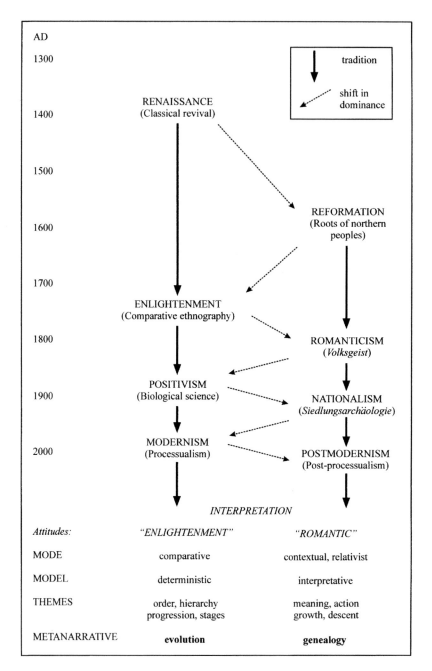

Figure 6.1 There is much to be gained from placing both the history of archaeology and contemporary theory into a broad intellectual context (see also Table 1.1). Andrew Sherratt departs from a traditional linear view of intellectual history by defining alternations between interpretations of the past characterised by 'Enlightenment' or 'Romantic' attitudes. Each of the broad movements (labelled in capitals, such as POSITIVISM) is associated with an approach to the past (in brackets beneath the label). This simplified view may help to put archaeological theory into perspective – particularly processualism and postprocessualism, which Sherratt (controversially) equates with modernism and postmodernism. (Tony Liddell, based on Sherratt 1997: 4)

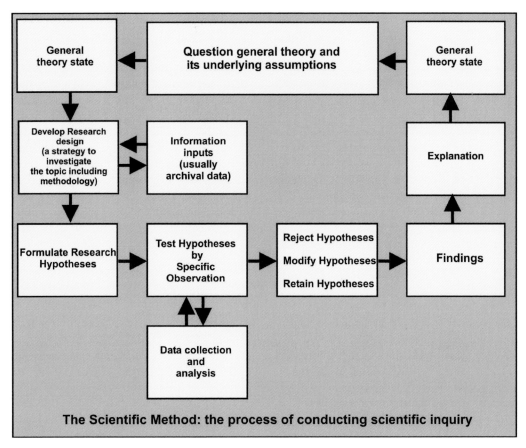

Figure 6.2 The scientific method: the process of conducting scientific inquiry by proposing a hypothesis, gathering data by which to test it, and either rejecting, accepting or modifying the hypothesis according to the results of the test. (Drawn by Tom Moore)

Two areas of knowledge are vital in the study of archaeological theory. First, it is necessary to acquire an extensive new vocabulary to participate in the subject, as much discussion is conducted at a philosophical level using scientific or socio-logical terminology that can make it seemingly inaccessible to outsiders. Second, a historical view of the development of the subject helps to place it into a wider intellectual context (**Fig. 6.1**). The words **theory**, **thought** and **ideas** overlap; Bruce Trigger's comprehensive *History of archaeological thought* grew out of a course about archaeological theory (1989: xv), while in his *Archaeological theory* (1999) Matthew Johnson waited 175 pages before defining it. Archaeological thought happens whenever archaeologists 'do archae-ology', but theory emerges when they reflect upon

what they are doing and why, and then, as a result, make decisions about the way they will proceed in the future. Most importantly, it is essential to remember that **data** (archaeological finds and apparent 'facts') do not exist independ-ently of theory and interpretation. Through our way of excavating and looking at them, we have already brought theoretical perspectives to our examination of the past (Johnson 2004: 105). In traditional scientific terms a theory was a general explanation (such as evolution by natural selection), while a hypothesis was a specific proposition put forward for testing (such as the need for animals to breathe oxygen: **Fig. 6.2**). Few archaeologists still hold the empiricist/positivist view that they can collect and examine data objectively and 'let the facts speak for themselves'.

Philosophical approaches to science underline the impossibility of establishing absolute 'truth'; scientists' investigations and interpretations are just as deeply affected by language and cultural attitudes as everyone else's. This change in outlook was crucial to the development of postprocessual archaeology (discussed below: p. 273).

All investigations of the past involve a theoretical perspective of some kind. Our social and cultural environment affects our outlook on the world, and any view of the past is inevitably influenced by perceptions of the present. The nature of a theoretical approach can often be recognised in the vocabulary used in the title of a research project or publication. Although the hypothetical examples in Table 6.1 are caricatures, they might show how the terminology may be decoded.

Awareness is a key aspect of archaeological theory, and its implications were explored in a fascinating article published in 1973 by David Clarke, a pioneer of archaeological theory in Britain. 'Archaeology: the loss of innocence' was a paper invited by the editor of *Antiquity*, Glyn Daniel, who remained sceptical about the New Archaeology but made sure that it was brought to the attention of the journal's readers. Clarke's title indicated that archaeology had crossed …

> … three significant thresholds in the transition from *consciousness* through *self-consciousness* to *critical self-consciousness* and beyond. … The era of critical self-consciousness has therefore dawned with the explicit scrutiny of the philosophical assumptions which underpinned and constrained every aspect of archaeological reasoning, knowledge and concepts.
>
> (Clarke 1973: 6, 11–12)

However, before discussing the New Archaeology it is important to look back at two approaches – social evolution and culture history – that used assorted political, philosophical, biological or anthropological ideas for interpreting the past. **Social evolution** is closely related to the ideas of Charles Darwin and Karl Marx that emerged in

the nineteenth century; **culture history** adopted historical notions of migration, diffusion, nationalism and race to explain material culture. Understanding these will greatly help in grasping the differences between processual and postprocessual archaeology which we will attempt to explain later. Before we begin, it is worth noting that the history and presence of different theoretical schools vary from country to country, sometimes without the theoretical approach being explicitly expressed (or even recognised) by archaeologists (Hegmon 2003). Here we lay out the broad development of archaeological thought which took place mainly in Britain and America; its direction in other regions was frequently quite different (Trigger 2006: 478–80).

6.2.1   Social evolution

- key references: Leonard, 'Evolutionary archaeology' 2001; Bintliff (ed.), *European social evolution* 1984; Pluciennik, *Social evolution* 2005; Johnson, *Archaeological theory* 2010: 143–63.

> … the institutions of man are as distinctively stratified as the Earth on which he lives. They succeed each other in series substantially uniform over the globe … shaped by similar human nature acting through successively changed conditions in savage, barbaric and civilized life.
>
> (Tylor 1888, quoted in Gosden 1999: 65)

There was a persistent Greek and Roman tradition of successive ages of gold, silver, bronze and iron (Blundell 1986), but these were not based on any kind of archaeological evidence, and the Greeks assumed that the ages had been characterised by degeneration rather than progress. Contact with the New World not only revealed people unknown to the Greeks and not found in the Bible, but allowed Europeans to imagine prehistory: 'The existence of really different forms of life in the present opened up the possibility of still more different ways of life in the past' (Gosden 1999: 23). Enlightenment philosophers of the eighteenth century used Classical literature and observations from the new colonies to hypothesise stages of social and economic progress, from hunting and fishing to pasturage, agriculture and commerce. Thus, any well-read antiquarian of the late eighteenth or early nineteenth century who encountered ancient objects and sites could place them into a scheme of human development that involved progress, and the same background influenced scientists and political theorists, including people who are still significant today such as Darwin and Marx.

An anthropologist, Lewis Henry Morgan, used his research into Native American kinship systems to define an elaborate series of stages of development in a very influential book, *Ancient society* (1877). He proposed that these stages were universal and could be recognised from living peoples or from historically documented societies such as Homer's Greece (Gosden 1999: 63–5). Since he considered that the evolution of social systems was also linked to economic and technical developments, Morgan's scheme was able to incorporate the Three-Age System (based upon artefacts) that had been developed in Europe in the early nineteenth century (Chapter 1, p. 22). Edward Tylor's *Primitive culture* (1871), written in England, was more overt than Morgan's *Ancient society* in seeing nineteenth-century Europe and America as the peak of achievement beneath which other peoples and societies in the world could be ranked. Herbert Spencer's Social Darwinism reinforced the enthusiasm and confidence with which nineteenth-century colonialism was conducted, for it suggested that relatively unsophisticated people could be advanced up the scale of social evolution. Conversely it might be used to justify exploiting 'savages' whose primitive state was scientific proof of lower intelligence and lack of evolutionary 'fitness'. Thus, the first Director of the Bureau of American Ethnology was able to write of American Indians in 1881 that 'The great boon to the savage tribes … has been the presence of civilization, which, under the laws of acculturation, has irresistibly improved their culture by substituting new and civilized for older and savage' (Major John Powell, quoted in Kehoe 1998: 90).

Darwin and Marx

- key references: Barton and Clark, *Rediscovering Darwin* 1997; Maschner, *Darwinian archaeologies* 1996; McGuire, *A Marxist archaeology* 1992; Saunders, *Revenge of the grand narrative* 1998; Hart and Terrell, *Darwin and archaeology* 2002; Patterson, *Marx's ghost* 2003.

The Darwinian concept of evolution by the mechanism of natural selection became widely known from the 1860s, even among those who rejected both its basis and its implications. It contributed to acceptance of the great antiquity of human ancestors by reinforcing the awareness of 'deep time' developed by geologists in the eighteenth century and by archaeologists in the nineteenth (Chapter 1, p. 31). 'Natural selection' provided a new metaphor for social theorists of the kind mentioned above who had already applied an evolutionary approach to past societies. The phrase 'survival of the fittest', commonly associated with Darwin, was actually coined by Herbert Spencer (1820–1903), who had already written extensively about economics, psychology and sociology before Darwin's work became the central element in his thinking about society after 1859. Spencer's 'Social Darwinism' is still very influential, and lies behind extreme free-market economics and proposals for solving poverty by taking money away from the poor; even Darwin eventually adopted Spencer's phrase (Gould 2000: 251–67). The science of genetics was unknown to Darwin or Spencer, and it has made the study of evolution far more sophisticated since 1900, along with behavioural studies of groups of animals that use cooperation and altruism, rather than pure aggression or competition, in their quest for survival. Johnson (1999: 137) emphasised the continuing confusion caused by merging anthropological and archaeological observations (cultural evolution) with Darwin's biological concepts; there is no reason why objects or societies should follow the same patterns as genetic inheritance.

Evolutionary biology was very significant for the New Archaeology in the 1960s because of its emphasis upon ecology (the dynamic relationship between humans, other animals, natural resources and background factors such as climate). It is also fundamental to studies of early humans and their ancestors, although this field of study emphasises **biocultural evolution**, through which early humans successfully side-stepped purely physical restrictions by means of cultural behaviour such as language, cooperative hunting and gathering and, eventually, tool-making. Intelligence, although ultimately a product of biological evolution, allowed humans to adapt to fluctuations in climate and to exploit a widening range of environments, from the edges of ice-sheets to tropical forests and deserts, by means of behaviour rather than biology.

Morgan's *Ancient society* took on wider significance when used as a source by Karl Marx, who adopted Morgan's sequence of developmental stages in society and their relationship to economics and technology:

> *Savagery* – the period in which man's appropriation of products in their natural states predominates; the products of human art are chiefly instruments that assist this appropriation. *Barbarism* – the period during which man learns to breed domestic animals and to practise agriculture and acquires methods of increasing the supply of natural products by human agency. *Civilization* – the period in which man learns a more advanced application of work to the products of nature, the period of industry proper and art.
>
> (summarised by Friedrich Engels in 1884; quoted in Daniel 1967: 139–40)

Rather than seeing these social stages as a natural state of affairs, Marx attributed them to contradictions between different classes or productive forces and (using a German philosophical tradition associated with Hegel) explained their progression not in terms of 'evolution' but by **dialectical materialism**: 'combining materialism as an embracing philosophy of nature and science, with the Hegelian notion of dialectic as a historical force, driving events onwards towards a progressive resolution of the contradictions that characterize each historical epoch' (Blackburn

1994: 104). When change occurred, it would lack the imperceptible smoothness that biologists would expect in an evolving ecosystem; indeed, the Russian Revolution of 1917 showed just how rapid and fundamental revolutionary change could be. Perhaps it is not surprising that, in the atmosphere of the early decades of the Cold War (1940s–1960s), American New Archaeologists favoured ideas of change based on evolving social systems rather than revolution. They did, however, share a belief in the underlying importance of energy and production, although the effects tended to be interpreted in a positive light as operating for the general good of society (Gosden 1999: 107, 110).

Johnson has stressed the major implications of Marxist thought for archaeology (2010: 95–9), of which the most important is the way in which a society embodies its values in **ideology**. Spencer's Social Darwinism is a crude example in which the values of nineteenth-century British ideologies of capitalism and colonialism were proclaimed as 'natural' states of affairs. Awareness of underlying ideology may lead to greater self-awareness among archaeologists, particularly those influenced by postprocessual thinking derived from the Frankfurt school of critical theory. 'One can look at ideology in the past, how for example a particular belief system legitimated the position of an élite in ancient societies. But one can also look at the present – how archaeological writing is itself ideological' (Johnson 2010: 99). However, Gosden has drawn attention to the comparative insignificance of Marx for archaeology and anthropology during the first half of the twentieth century, when he had surprisingly little impact outside Russia; this makes the thought and writing of V Gordon Childe (1892–1957), 'the only major figure in either discipline in the English-speaking world to be a self-professed Marxist', particularly interesting (Gosden 1999: 105).

6.2.2 Culture history

- key references: Trigger, *Gordon Childe* 1980; Lyman *et al.*, *The rise and fall of culture history*

1997; Morris, *Archaeology as cultural history* 2000; Johnson, *Archaeological theory* 2010: 15–21.

The culture historical approach was really just that, an approach to doing archaeology, a school of thought or paradigm, rather than an actual theory in any sense of the word. Culture history studies were the hallmark of archaeology through the nineteenth and early twentieth centuries.

(Michaels, in Fagan 1996: 162)

Links had been made between economics, technology and social progress since ancient Greece, but material culture was not incorporated into such theories in a systematic manner until the nineteenth century (Chapter 1, p. 22–4). Whether directly influenced by analogies with biological evolution or not, studies of artefacts were stimulated by the strides made in the classification of plants and animals (or their extinct fossil ancestors). By the early twentieth century many museum catalogues had been published, sites were beginning to be excavated in a stratigraphic manner, and archaeologists had studied the dating and geographical distributions of numerous artefacts. As a result it was possible to draw up maps of types of structure or artefact and to relate them to each other in chronological patterns. Meanwhile influential anthropological fieldworkers such as Franz Boas (1858–1942) included artefacts (past and present) in their studies of 'culture' – a term that embraced material objects as well as sets of beliefs, rituals or language. Archaeological culture history merged anthropology, settlement archaeology, artefact typology and early European history to produce a method for investigating prehistory. Some archaeologists, for example Nils Åberg, studied peoples (such as Goths, Franks and Saxons) involved in complex folk-movements in Europe in the late Roman and early medieval periods and matched distinctive artefacts such as decorated brooches, buckles or pottery with historical invasions or migrations into the areas where they were found. Thus, history was used for understanding

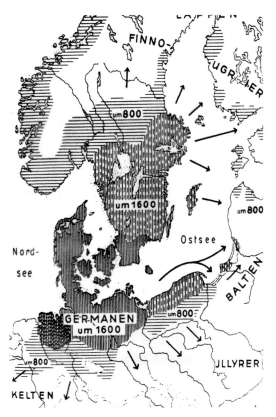

Figure 6.3 The culture–history approach to archaeology was predominant in the early twentieth century. Reinerth's map from the 1940s, influenced by the work of Kossinna, shows the movement of peoples indicated by distributions of particular types of ceramics dating from the Bronze Age. It had dangerous consequences when used by the Nazis as a prehistoric precedent for Germanic ownership of much of Europe in modern times (Arnold 1990: 466).

archaeological information and formed the basis for archaeological models applied to prehistory (**Fig. 6.3**).

Gustaf Kossinna (1858–1931) used recurrent groups of distinctive prehistoric artefacts found in Germany to define cultures. It was a small step from classifying cultures in the past in material terms to equating them with social or political units of the kind observed by ethnographers among living societies and calling them tribes or peoples (Trigger 2006: 235–40). Since most of the historical nations and linguistic groups of Europe clearly originated in an undocumented prehistoric period, nineteenth-century concepts of nationalism were projected back into earlier times (Diaz-Andreu 2007). Thus, archaeologists could record the archaeology of peoples such as the Germani described by the Roman historian Tacitus in the first century AD, and then make deductions about their earlier (unrecorded) history and origins by studying the development of their ancestral 'culture' (Fig. 6.3). An enormous assumption underlay the idea that areas where similar settlements and artefacts were found actually represented political or ethnic groups. It was a further step into the unknown to build upon that assumption and use material culture to chart the origins and growth of a modern people or state. Kossinna was a zealous patriot whose work deliberately glorified the Germans and had catastrophic consequences when it was used in Nazi Germany to document the rise of a supposed Aryan master race.

Culture history was developed to a high degree of sophistication by Childe (McNairn 1980). Like Kossinna, he organised recurrent groups of related prehistoric artefacts and settlements into 'cultures' and proposed that they represented distinct ethnic or social groupings of people. Childe, however, abandoned simplistic equations between race and culture early in his career; instead he framed all of his work within a Marxist view of social evolution. The influence of Morgan (through Marx) is exemplified in his popular book *What happened in history* (1942), where Childe employed chapter headings such as 'Palaeolithic Savagery' and 'The Higher Barbarism of the Copper Age'. Childe's great achievement was to embed the enormous amount of archaeological evidence that had emerged in Europe and the Near East – particularly for prehistory – within a grand explanatory framework. His prodigious output of publications and their impact upon a wide range of scholars beyond archaeology who shared an interest in Marxism did much to establish prehistoric archaeology as a respectable academic discipline (Harris 1994).

Although culture history continues as a general approach in many parts of the world (Trigger 2006: 490), and some archaeologists have attempted to reshape it (Morris 2000), its simplest form has been left behind in recent decades. However, the recovery of archaeological information through fieldwork and excavation, combined with the study of artefacts through typology, would be meaningless without some form of comparison that converts data into interpretations of human life in the past. Anthropology provides models of societies within which material culture operates, while history provides ideas about change and/or continuity. Prehistoric archaeology projects anthropology and history into the more distant past – but not without fundamental philosophical and theoretical problems that will be explored below.

Invasion, migration or diffusion?

● key references: Chapman and Hamerow, *Migrations and invasion in archaeological explanation* 1997; Lucassen and Lucassen, *Migration, migration history, history: old paradigms and new perspectives* 1997.

European scholars had focused their thoughts upon the civilisations of the Mediterranean and Near East ever since the medieval period because of the Bible and Graeco–Roman literature. Childe, like Montelius and others before him, made an assumption that all innovations or improvements observed in European prehistory must have originated in those areas where civilisations flourished at the earliest date (Fig. 4.4). It must be emphasised that there was no logical inconsistency in asserting that impulses towards progress should have emanated from those areas, particularly when Mesopotamia and Egypt became better known in the nineteenth century. Indeed, the whole idea of the rise and spread of civilisation had a heroic air to it that was thoroughly in tune with the Romantic ideas of the nineteenth century, in contrast to the empathy with 'natural' primitive peoples that characterised some Enlightenment philosophers (Chapter 1, p. 12). **Diffusionism** gained some support from the concept of evolution, because it provided an explanation of 'progress' through the inevitable spread of 'improvements' from advanced to less developed areas – an evolutionary concept related to the idea of the 'survival of the fittest' popularised by Herbert Spencer. This assumption became

BOX 6.3

Nationalism and archaeology

Archaeology has been used in diverse ways to emphasise different aspects of people's pasts, while the changing popularity of different periods or research themes has frequently reflected contemporary political preoccupations. Although the use of archaeology by nationalists is well known in the context of Nazi Germany, there have been many other examples. In France, Napoleon III conducted excavations at Alésia in the late nineteenth century in order to investigate the site of the last stand by Vercingetorix against the Roman conquerors in 52 BC (described by the victorious Julius Caesar in his autobiographical *Gallic Wars*). The growth of national identity in nineteenth-century France naturally focused on the leader of the Gallic resistance, and led to extensive research into the Late Iron Age culture conquered by the Romans. A statue of Vercingetorix (pictured here) was raised by Napoleon III at Alésia in 1865, with a plaque bearing a quotation from Caesar: 'United Gaul, forming a single nation, animated by a common spirit, can defy

the universe'. Since Napoleon III, Alésia and other sites like Bibracte, as well as Vercingetorix himself, have been used by a variety of French nationalists, including Marshal Pétain (leader of the collaborating Vichy government during World War II), General de Gaulle (figurehead of wartime resistance and prominent postwar president), President Mitterand (left-wing President of France in the 1980s) and Jean-Marie le Pen (leader of the right-wing Front National) to justify their visions of contemporary France (Dietler 1994, 1998). In contrast, the wider 'Celtic' past of Europe has been used to reinforce cultural unity in the European Union, which sponsored an exhibition about the Celts in Venice in 1991 (Collis 2003). Nationalism can be more complex than it first appears, however; it has been seen as both a negative and a positive force by postcolonial archaeologists, for example in the case of India (Chakrabarti 2003).

Archaeologists are also confronted and manipulated by religious fundamentalism, which may lead to the destruction of archaeological monuments such as the Bamiyan Buddhas, enormous carvings obliterated by the Taliban in Afghanistan (Chakrabarti 2003: 197–201). In the USA, a major new museum has been constructed in Cincinnati, Kentucky, to advocate the literal interpretation of the creation of the world by God described in the Old Testament, including displays that attempt to disprove evolution, geology and scientific dating methods for measuring the age of the Earth. (Photograph: Claire Nesbitt) firmly rooted in twentieth-century archaeology, whether in a rational manner among scholars like Childe, or in the 'hyper-diffusionist' views of Elliot Smith, who claimed that the influence of Egyptian pyramids and embalming techniques extended to similar phenomena found in South America at a much later date (Gosden 1999: 73–4). Hyperdiffusionist explanations advanced by anthropologists or archaeologists also gave support to popular ideas about the lost civilisation of Atlantis that supposedly passed on its wisdom to all later civilisations; indeed such ideas can still be found. Both views diminish the status of peoples encountered by European colonisers by denying that indigenous achievements had been generated independently (**Box 6.2**; Kehoe 2008: chapter 7; Chapter 1, p. 17).

The idea of diffusion illustrates the virtues of examining archaeological explanations from a theoretical standpoint. The history of technology provides many examples of invention followed by diffusion (for example, the steam locomotive running on rails) that were perfectly clear to nineteenth-century archaeologists. The problem lay in accepting diffusion as a *fact*, rather than as a theoretical proposition that might or might not be compatible with further evidence. It is not surprising that a **paradigm shift** took place in British archaeology in the 1960s that led some prehistorians to view technological and social changes as the result of independent development and internal evolution, rather than diffusion by immigrants or invaders. Most British historical archaeologists found this interpretation rather bizarre, as the supposedly invasion-free centuries of later prehistory were followed by well-documented raiding, conquest and/or colonisation by Romans, Anglo-Saxons, Vikings and Normans, from Julius Caesar in 55 BC to William the Conqueror in AD 1066.

It is interesting that, with the increasing use of DNA and isotope analysis (discussed in Chapter 5), ideas of migration and movement have re-emerged in the last ten years as prominent explanations of social change. One example is the question of whether there really was a large migration of Anglo-Saxon people into southern Britain in the fifth century AD. Recent DNA evidence has been used to argue in favour of substantial migration (Weale 2002; Härke 2004), despite the fact that much of the archaeological evidence appears ambiguous (Hills 2003). Others suggest that the DNA evidence can best be explained as migration from other areas of Europe, which happened far earlier than the Anglo-Saxon period (Oppenheimer 2006). Although these scientific advances offer exciting new information, there is a danger that archaeology could ignore some of the critical advances it has made in the last 50 years and revert to asking 'culture-historical' questions. Whilst DNA evidence is adding to earlier discussions of migrations which formed part of earlier culture-history models, we must avoid simply replacing one discredited migration with another.

Nationalism and racism

- key references: Díaz-Andreu and Champion, *Nationalism and archaeology in Europe* 1996; Kohl and Fawcett, *Nationalism, politics and the practice of archaeology* 1995; Fenton, *Ethnicity: key concepts* 2003.

Concepts of social evolution and diffusion were a mixed blessing for archaeological interpretation. Although Darwinism reinforced (rather than initiated) racist interpretations of the past, evolution and diffusion influenced the political outlook of the leading European governments. The situation in late-nineteenth-century England when Pitt Rivers was active has been summarised forcefully:

> For a society bursting with the self-congratulatory fervour of a colonial power and the potency of an industrial revolution, it took very little effort to prop this biological premise under a social construct and extend the ladder just a bit to justify the white man's inherent superiority over the 'lesser' peoples of the earth.
>
> (Johanson and Shreeve 1991: 45–6)

Pitt Rivers did not devote his extensive intellectual energy and financial resources to excavation and the typological study of artefacts for purely academic reasons. He considered that evidence for the gradual evolution of artefacts should be impressed upon museum visitors to counteract revolutionary tendencies in nineteenth-century radical politics (Bowden 1991: 141–2). John Lubbock, a close associate of Darwin, combined archaeology, anthropology and rigid evolutionary theory in his influential book *Pre-historic times* (1865), and concluded that non-European cultures were biologically inferior and that the most primitive peoples were inevitably doomed to extinction through natural selection. Thus, no moral responsibility need be felt for their decline or loss of identity through colonisation, since this was a consequence of innate biological differences (Trigger 2006: 171–4; Kehoe 1998: 57–9). Pitt Rivers was typical in believing that savages were not capable of benefiting from the civilising influence of superior races by any means other than slavery (Bradley 1983: 5–6). Political preoccupations about the present can still affect ideas about the past in some ways, and will be explored further (below: p. 294).

The reputation of Gustaf Kossinna as a pioneer of the culture-historical approach to prehistory is difficult to separate from knowledge of the way in which his studies of German origins were used. Kossinna had traced all major European developments back to origins in prehistoric Germany and attributed them to a pure Nordic 'Aryan' race (**Fig. 6.3**; Trigger 2006: 237). Pride in national origins was a feature of states that first emerged as political units in the nineteenth century, such as Greece, Germany and Italy, and embodied the spirit of Romanticism surrounding figures such as Byron and Wagner (Chapter 1, pp. 3–4). However, Kossinna's views were developed with special enthusiasm after his death (in 1931) because they gave welcome support to Nazi claims for Aryan superiority. The outcome of this enthusiasm was of course the invasion of neighbouring countries to restore Teutonic ownership and the attempt to exterminate or enslave 'inferior' races, notably Jews, Slavs and Roma. Archaeologists and physical anthropologists were employed to gather evidence for this view right up to the last months of the Second World War (Junker 1998).

6.3 TOWARDS PROCESSUAL ARCHAEOLOGY

- key references: Trigger, *A history of archaeological thought* 2006: 314–85; Kehoe, *The land of prehistory: a critical history of American archaeology* 1998: 97–114; Lamberg-Karlovsky, *Archaeological thought in America* 1991.

The development of functional and then processual approaches to archaeological data represented a replacement of the increasingly sterile preoccupation of culture-historical archaeology with ethnicity by a vital new interest in how prehistoric cultures operated and changed.

(Trigger 2006: 288)

Description, rather than exploration or explanation, was the goal of archaeology in the nineteenth and early twentieth centuries. Little or no meaningful explanation could take place until basic questions about dating had been sorted out (Chapter 4). However, once detailed sequences of artefacts and cultures had been established, and after they had been placed into a chronological framework through documentary evidence or radiocarbon dating, they could be studied in more sophisticated ways. In an ethnic approach (of which Kossinna's was an extreme example) the relationships between cultures were discussed using vocabulary derived from historical archaeology such as invasion, colonisation and trade. Alternatively, the development of cultures through time could be seen in evolutionary terms, from a biological, ecological, social, political or economic point of view. Anthropologists and archaeologists working in America in the mid-twentieth century were concerned with indigenous peoples unconnected with the Old World, some of whom still followed non-European ways of life even in the twentieth century. New World agriculture and civilisations had developed independently, but had been neglected by European archaeologists such as Childe. North America became a vigorous debating ground for new approaches to archaeological study which then influenced thinking in many other countries, especially Britain and Scandinavia.

Leslie White and Julian Steward are associated with influential styles of interpretation in America in the 1950s. White (1900–75) was familiar with the work of Marx and Engels and reintroduced the evolutionary approach associated with Lewis Henry Morgan. White was particularly interested in thermodynamics and saw technology (notably the harnessing of energy) as the driving force behind social evolution (Trigger 2006: 387–9). Steward (1902–72) was also interested in evolution, in particular through **cultural ecology** – the processes by which societies adapted to their environments. Steward placed particular emphasis on the influence exerted by environments upon core features of cultures, notably technology, subsistence and economy (Fagan 1996: 155–6). The mature publications of White (*The evolution of culture* 1959) and Steward (*Theory of culture change* 1955) appeared in the same short period as another much-cited work: *Method and theory in American archaeology* (1958) by Gordon Willey and Philip Phillips. *Method and theory* consolidated the use of the term 'processual' and included the famous phrase '(American) archaeology is anthropology or it is nothing' (*ibid.*: 2) that underlined the difference between American and European archaeology.

The adoption of evolutionary and ecological concepts had significant practical implications for archaeology. **Functionalist** views of the past demanded close attention to the excavation and recording of sites and artefacts, as excavated sites could provide evidence for economic activities such as farming, crafts and trade (Trigger 2006: 353–61). Social systems might be reflected in the disposition and form of houses, and the diversity of objects found in settlements or graves could indicate differences in status or wealth. Other aspects of sites and their surroundings could reveal the relationship between people and the natural environment; pollen analysis, soil science and the identification of seeds from food plants all gained significance for the study of ecology and adaptation. Walter Taylor's *A study of archaeology* (1948) had been extremely critical of the

excavation and recording methods of most leading American archaeologists (he described them as 'petrified puddle ducks' – Kehoe 1998: 97–105). Along with conscious improvements in data recovery, a further element that promised to help archaeology hold its head up among the physical and social sciences was the use of statistics, pioneered by Albert Spaulding. Numerical analysis could be applied to both the classification of artefacts and the distribution patterns of settlements, and offered much to people interested in using approaches such as Leslie White's thermodynamic formulae.

> A cohort of the students [Spaulding] shared with Leslie White took fire, embracing the transcendentally mechanistic worldview the two men proselytized, the world where the essence of life is harnessing energy ... and counting and statistical formulae will reveal true entities.
>
> (Kehoe 1998: 114)

Everything was in place for the emergence of the New Archaeology.

6.3.1 The New Archaeology

● key references: Kehoe, *The land of prehistory: a critical history of American archaeology* 1998: 115–49; Clarke, *Analytical archaeology* 1968; Renfrew, 'The new archaeology: prehistory as a discipline' 1988; Sabloff, *Conversations with Lew Binford: drafting the new archaeology* 1998; Watson, 'What the new archaeology has achieved' 1991; Shennan, 'Analytical archaeology' 2004.

> Explanation begins for the archaeologist when observations made of the archaeological record are linked through laws of cultural or behavioural functioning to past conditions or events.
>
> (Binford 1972: 117)

Archaeology was not unique in adopting the adjective 'new'; the 1960s also saw New Geography and New Social History (Johnson 2010: 188).

In retrospect, it clearly grew out of pre-existing archaeological and anthropological ideas and it was by no means replaced when 'postprocessualism' emerged during the 1980s. Johnson's checklist of the distinctive features of the New Archaeology (2010: 23–7) comprises seven major themes: cultural evolution; systems thinking; adaptation to an external environment; a scientific approach; culture process; explicit aims and interests; and the investigation of variability. **Systems, hypothesis-testing, laws** and **process** were recurrent keywords (see **Box 6.4**).

Systems theory (Johnson 2010: 68–88) was originally developed in the 1940s to study interactions between a society and its environment, and interpretations were frequently presented in a graphic style normally used for electrical circuits. Such diagrams could relate precise observations of archaeological and environmental evidence to each other and include **feedback loops** that might suggest how interactions caused change (e.g. Trigger 2006: 420, Fig. 8.4). Representations of this kind highlighted modifications *within* societies and discouraged 'historical' explanations that invoked diffusion, invasion or migration. Later critics saw systems thinking as an ideology of control within which individuals were subordinated to general rules (**Fig. 6.4**).

The formulation and testing of **hypotheses** (Johnson 2010: 38–42) was characteristic of a positivist scientific methodology adopted by most social sciences in the 1950s and 1960s, and it was frequently combined with the use of statistics. Traditional archaeologists and anthropologists collected data in the field, studied it in the laboratory and then drew interpretations by intuition. A New Archaeologist would use an approach known (inelegantly) as the **hypothetico-deductive-nomological** model: generate the hypothesis, look for an archaeological situation where evidence might be found for testing it, and decide after investigation whether the hypothesis was correct. Furthermore, as in experimental science, the purpose of hypothesis-testing was the establishment of generally applicable **laws**. In the words of the charismatic pioneer of the New Archaeology, Lewis Binford:

What is argued ... is that the generation of inferences regarding the fact should not be the end product of the archaeologist's work ... once a proposition has been advanced no matter by what means it was reached the next task is to deduce a series of testable hypotheses that, if verified against independent empirical data, would tend to verify the proposition. ... In our search for explanations of differences and similarities in the archaeological record, our ultimate goal is the formulation of laws of cultural dynamics.

(Binford 1972: 90, 100)

The evangelical tone of Binford's writings might have sprung from his fundamentalist religious background (Kehoe 1998: 118–21), but it was fuelled by a desire to propagate better modes of thought for a very serious purpose. Archaeology offered the possibility of providing long-term information about the past that anthropologists could never achieve, for the simple reason that they did not live long enough to observe or analyse the unfolding of a major **process**. In addition, Binford, like other exponents of the New Archaeology, was very optimistic about the range of aspects of the past that could be reconstructed from material evidence. The essential components of his approach are condensed into the following paragraph – which is also typical of his demanding written style:

Process, as I understand it, refers to the dynamic relationships (causes and effects) operative among the components of a system or between systematic components and the environment. In order to deal with process we must seek explanations for observed phenomena and it is only through explanations of our observations that we gain any knowledge of the past. ... Successful explanation and the understanding of process are synonymous and both proceed dialectically – by the formulation of hypotheses (potential laws on the relationships between two or more variables) and the testing of their validity against empirical data. Hypotheses about cause and effect must be

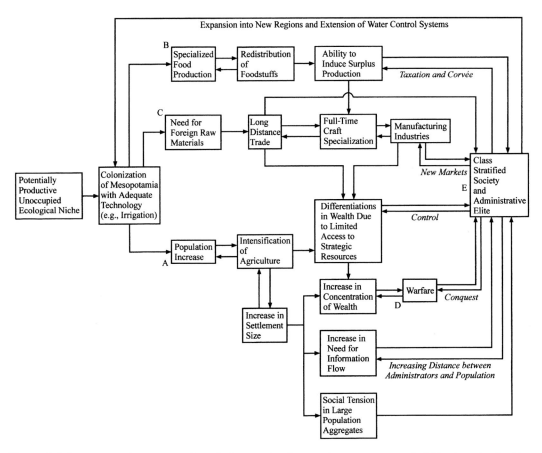

Figure 6.4 A processual representation of changes leading to the emergence of civilisations in the Near East. The words 'process' and 'system' that are so closely associated with New Archaeology, along with its tendency to downplay the role of individuals, are prominent in Charles L. Redman's explanatory text: 'This figure is not arranged chronologically from left to right but is a description of the interrelationships of the factors at work at all times throughout the process. ... it was the environmental, technological, and social systems that primarily directed the evolution of these societies. Although individuals and unique circumstances may cause minor deviations in the process of civilization, its general course was charted in a seemingly irreversible manner given the initial steps just mentioned (1978: 332–4 and Fig. 14.2). (Redrawn by Tony Liddell)

explicitly formulated and then tested. Only when this is done are we in a position to judge what facts might be relevant, only then can we objectively evaluate the implicit propositions which underlie 'plausible' historical interpretations of archaeological data.

(Binford 1972: 117)

Doubts about the two-fold assumption that laws of this kind not only existed but could be detected archaeologically prevented many 'old' archaeologists from embracing the New Archaeology. Such doubts were well founded, for Binford's extreme

positivist approach was not universally accepted by natural scientists, many of whom already doubted the existence of absolute facts or genuine objectivity. Although Binford's positivism has fallen even further out of favour as scepticism about the nature of the archaeological record and our ability to explain it has grown, his rigorous approach to data collection and explanation remains stimulating in the twenty-first century, notably in a study of the early prehistory of Europe that he published in 2000.

The New Archaeology continued Walter Taylor's demands for high-quality recording and

BOX 6.4   # Reconstructing past societies: hierarchies, heterarchies and social complexity

One of the most challenging and contentious aspects of studying the past is reconstructing and understanding how past societies worked. If we consider how many anthropologists, sociologists and philosophers attempt to understand the complexities of modern-day societies, the challenge of reconstructing a past society from its material remains alone can be appreciated. As discussion of archaeological thought makes clear, how archaeologists view past societies has been influenced not just by the ways in which they collected archaeological evidence but also by their personal political viewpoints (for example, Marxism or Darwinism) and the contemporary societies they inhabit, from aristocracies to democracies. One of the most significant questions, particularly about prehistoric societies, has been whether they were **hierarchical**, with defined social classes and elites controlling other groups, or **heterarchical**, more equally based societies where power was less stratified or where power might shift between communities of equal status (Crumley 2001).

For much of archaeology's development, antiquarians and archaeologists came from societies that were highly ranked (either by aristocracies or the class divisions of early industrialised societies). Archaeologists themselves were also usually from the upper classes of such societies. Combined with contemporary thinking that suggested a hierarchical society was the normal order of human organisation, this led them to envision past societies in a generally hierarchical way and to study and define the elites in past societies (see Box 3.4; Crumley 2001: 19). This led, amongst other things, to many analyses of cemeteries which used grave goods in burials to rank individuals in the past societies, for example the rich burials of Early Iron Age central Europe (Frankenstein and Rowlands 1978). This appeared to provide well defined social systems where one could even identify the status of an individual from the size of their tumulus and the nature of the grave goods buried with them. Such studies also usually assumed that men and warriors were naturally at the top of any social system.

In the 1960s American anthropologists, such as Marshal Sahlins and Morton Fried, in an attempt to classify societies, ranked them into different forms of increasing social complexity (below). Whilst the models differed somewhat, they emphasised the idea that societies could be placed into broader categories and that these communities evolved into ever more complex social systems. This continued to suggest that human societies developed through stages of **social evolution** (see pp. 256–8) and could readily be related to stages of human societies. For some, most of later prehistory must therefore have been dominated by some form of chiefdom societies (Renfrew 1973b; Haas 2001; Barker 2009).

Evolutionary models of social systems

Marshal Sahlins and Elman Service (1960; 1971)	Morton Fried (1967)	Suggested stages of human past
band (hunter-gatherers)	egalitarian	Early Prehistory – Mesolithic
tribe (segmentary society)	ranked	Neolithic Europe
chiefdom	stratified	Neolithic (Renfrew 1973b) and Iron Age Europe; Mississippian North America
state	state	Classical world; Maya/Aztec

(Box 6.4, cont.) The **New Archaeologists** of the 1960s and 1970s tended to classify prehistoric societies in these terms, suggesting that the size and complexity of many monuments, such as Neolithic henge monuments like Stonehenge (Renfrew 1973b), the hillforts of the European Iron Age (Cunliffe 1984), or the centralised pueblos of New Mexico (Creamer 2001), must have been constructed through the control of established elites (Earle 1998). Such approaches also believed that the territories of chiefdoms could be reconstructed through the use of the geographic tool of **Thiessen polygons**, shown in the example from Colin Renfrew (1973b), whereby sites were identified as the central places of a territory, and lines were drawn defining their territorial limits (redrawn by Tom Moore, after Renfrew 1973b).

Many archaeologists, however, have long argued that societies need not always be based on hierarchies. Anthropological studies in the twentieth century in Africa and elsewhere by the likes of Evans-Pritchard (1902–73) recognised that many societies could be organised in different ways and need not have male chieftains as their rulers (Evans-Pritchard 1940), suggesting to many that the entire concept of chiefdoms as unified social systems suitable for describing communities in Mississippian North America or prehistoric Europe is overly simplistic (e.g. Pauketat 2007; Hill 2006; cf. Haas 2001). They suggest that ranking societies on the basis of grave goods is to place Western values on objects and to make assumptions about the role of elements such as swords as markers of social status, ignoring the fact that such items may have very different roles in other societies (e.g. Bradley 1998). Study of the Mississippian mounds (**Box 1.3**) has long been argued as evidence of chiefdom communities where power resided in the hands of elites, but from the work of anthropologists it is clear that even large monuments and complex social systems can be constructed by communities where no established elite exists (Pauketat 2007).

Chris Tilley (1984) and others, from a neo-Marxist viewpoint, have also suggested that in many societies there is not always a clear correlation between expressions of power and wealth and the real nature of a society. Elsewhere, highly ranked societies may not express status and power through differences in burial or even in size of houses or settlement but through elements which are more difficult to detect archaeologically, such as the number of cattle they own. Through the ethnographic study of non-Western societies, and a more sophisticated appreciation of how our own societies work, archaeologists have increasingly reconsidered the variation and complexity of social systems; to define societies as hierarchical or heterarchical is to oversimplify and generalise the complex systems of many societies, even hunter-gatherer communities. The debate as to how to reconstruct societies continues in many areas of archaeology and represents perhaps one of the most contentious questions for the discipline. (Colin Renfrew's (1973b) reconstruction of Neolithic territories in Wiltshire using Thiessen polygons)

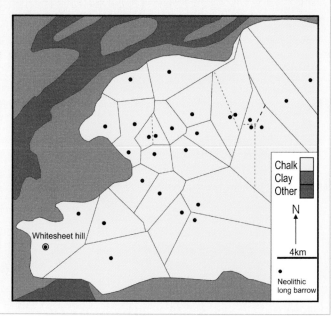

Chalk
Clay
Other

N

4km

Whitesheet hill

Neolithic
long barrow

description of archaeological information, partly through better techniques of data recovery but also through improved understanding of how sites were formed (**taphonomy**). Michael B. Schiffer was a prominent early writer on formation processes (1976; 1987); taphonomy applies not only to the understanding of artefacts and structures, but also to contexts where economic and environmental data, such as bones or plant remains, are found. Such studies may be taken further by archaeological experiments involving reconstructions of ancient buildings, or replications of crafts and food preparation methods; the residues that they leave behind can illuminate remains encountered on sites (Chapter 5, p. 240).

6.3.2 Ethnoarchaeology and Middle Range Theory

- key references: Allchin, *Living traditions: studies in the ethnoarchaeology of South Asia* 1994; Arthur and Weedman, 'Ethnoarchaeology' 2005; Hodder, *The present past* 1982; Yentsch and Beaudry, 'American material culture' 2001; LaMotta and Schiffer, 'Behavioral archaeology' 2001; Johnson, *Archaeological theory* 2010: 50–67.

… a proper understanding and use of middle range theory will allow the development of testable propositions and hypotheses that will bridge the inevitable chasm between what we believe is the explanation and what we actually observe in the archaeological record.

(Maschner, quoted in Fagan 1996: 469)

Instead of carrying out modern experiments, some archaeologists (especially prehistorians) chose to conduct the kind of fieldwork traditionally associated with anthropologists. They concentrated on making ethnographic observations of everyday life from the point of view of physical traces – structures, discarded tools and food waste – which might be recovered by excavation (**Fig. 6.5**). Ethnography carried out by archaeologists (**ethnoarchaeology**) seemed to offer a 'Rosetta Stone' for using observations of people in the present to 'translate' physical traces

Figure 6.5 Ethnoarchaeology: postgraduate students from Cambridge University observing a smith of the Tugen tribe (Barengo district, Kenya) making an iron spear. Studies of the physical traces left by such activities may help to elucidate Iron Age sites in other parts of the world, while an understanding of the social and ritual aspects of craft production may broaden our concepts of economic activities in pre-industrial, non-Western societies. Ethnoarchaeology, combined with developments in anthropological theory, did much to encourage the focus of postprocessual archaeology towards symbolism, meaning and individual behaviour rather than general social processes. (Ian Hodder)

of human behaviour in the past (Johnson 2010: 53). This logical step was taken by Lewis Binford, who conducted ethnoarchaeological investigations among the Inuit (Eskimos) in Canada (Binford 1978). He hoped to understand variations in assemblages of early Stone Age tools; did the differences detected in his research represent periods of time, groups of people, or sets of tools with different functions?

Observations of this kind contributed to the development of **Middle Range Theory** to link physical evidence with the interpretation of human behaviour. Binford's work among the Inuit had a considerable impact upon the study not just of Palaeolithic Europe but also of early hominins in East Africa. Donald Johanson witnessed at first hand Binford's intrusion into the small group of specialists who had been working in East Africa for many decades:

> … with the sweeping bravado of a Broadway veteran come to show the yokels how to act. 'It's clear from the bone distributions and the way the limbs had been busted up', Lew told me on the site. 'The Olduvai toolmaker was no mighty hunter of beasts. He was the most marginal of scavengers'. So much for romance.
>
> (Johanson and Shreeve 1991: 233, 235)

One major problem of ethnoarchaeology is shared by the whole discipline of anthropology. To what extent have the supposedly 'primitive' communities and ways of life observed by anthropologists already been transformed by centuries of interaction with Western civilisation? Detailed case studies confirm that profound changes in diet and hunting patterns had indeed taken place among indigenous peoples in North America between first contacts with Europeans and serious studies by anthropologists (Butler 2000). Furthermore, one should ask whether equating, for example, Inuit with the early humans who subsisted on the edge of the ice sheets during the last glaciation merely perpetuates nineteenth-century ideas about social evolution. Can their behaviour really be read across to even earlier humans living in East African grasslands? The answer will only be 'yes' if you believe in **essentialism** – that human behaviour has some universal underlying factors and that humans always selected foods and utilised tools in a manner that would be considered rational and efficient today.

Ethnoarchaeology was also being conducted in the late 1970s and early 1980s in several parts of Africa by Ian Hodder, a rising young British theoretician (**Fig. 6.5**; Hodder 1982b). It led to a rather different way of looking at the past, however, possibly because Hodder observed village communities of greater complexity than

the Arctic hunters studied by Binford. He was also heavily influenced by structuralist anthropology that saw material culture (including everything from ornaments to tools to buildings) as part of a symbolic language that could be 'read' as an expression of social values (**Fig. 6.6**). This played an important part in the development of postprocessual archaeology, which is outlined below.

Cognitive archaeology
- key references: Mithen, 'Archaeological theory and theories of cognitive evolution' 2001; Renfrew, 'Symbol before concept' 2001; Renfrew and Zubrow, *The ancient mind: elements of cognitive archaeology* 1994; Mithen, *The prehistory of the mind: a search for the origins of art, religion and science* 1996; Renfrew, 'Cognitive archaeology' 2005.

> British prehistory, most would now agree, is as much the story of developing concepts and beliefs as it is of developing technologies and subsistence practices and of demography. The concepts and beliefs were mediated in the structures and artefacts of the day – that is what is meant by the active role of material culture.
>
> (Renfrew 1996: 6)

One major drawback of a strictly processual view of the past is its failure to address some of the most profound aspects of human life related to thought and belief. Colin Renfrew confronted this issue in 1982 by discussing 'an archaeology of mind', and he deplored the traditional division between mind and matter: 'The gap cannot be bridged, nor can "mind" usefully be considered when taken in isolation from its "thoughts". These "thoughts", I assert, or some of them, do find effective expression in the material record' (Renfrew 1982: 27). His examples included systems of weights that indicate concepts of mass and measurement, religious objects and structures that imply ritual or ideology, deliberate designs of artefacts, and most forms of artistic depiction. A conference in 1996 linked cognition with material culture in a broader concept known as **symbolic social** storage: 'the development of devices outside the body devised either explicitly or unconsciously to hold and convey information' (Renfrew and Scarre 1998: xi). By proposing that material culture both reflected what humans were doing and at the same time helped to shape their social and mental behaviour, Renfrew incorporated an idea characteristic of postprocessual archaeology but included the feedback mechanism emphasised in processual systems thinking. The conclusion to his paper in the 1996 conference volume elegantly expressed his desire to build a bridge between processual and postprocessual thinking.

Conceptualising *all* material culture as a form of communication also breaks down the artificial dividing line between cultures that used writing (one of the criteria normally used in defining 'civilisation') and those that did not. Written language may be seen as just one particularly successful form of symbolic social storage that developed long after such phenomena began in the Palaeolithic (**Fig. 6.7**). A positive feature of philosophies of archaeology that seek meaning in psychological terms is that they are unlikely to neglect the role of individuals, whereas an excessively processual point of view could lead to a mechanical notion of human societies shaped entirely by environmental forces.

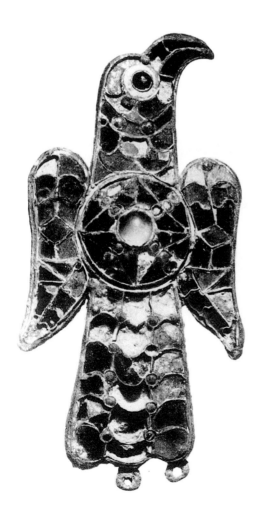

Figure 6.6 The meaningful constitution of material culture has been a recurrent theme in postprocessual archaeology since the 1980s. One study of early-medieval eagle brooches related them to Ian Hodder's approach to material culture and symbolism (Greene 1987). These distinctive jewelled eagles underwent a gradual transformation, beginning as saddle decorations for aristocratic warriors around the Black Sea, becoming imitations of Roman imperial shoulder ornaments for kings in Romania, and ending as pairs of brooches worn by women from the ruling Gothic elite in Italy and Spain. In earlier 'culture–historical' studies they had been used to provide confirmation of historical migrations and the conquest of parts of the Roman Empire by Germanic peoples, in this case the Goths, in the fourth to sixth centuries AD. Kevin proposed that eagles played an ambiguous role, projecting a familiar Roman image to subject populations in Italy and Spain, but emphasising Germanic ancestry and mythology to Goths. They also recalled the Huns from Central Asia, fierce nomadic warriors who popularised eagle symbolism amongst their Gothic allies and enemies in the fifth century AD. Thus, these superficially similar artefacts embodied varying meanings in the eyes of different people, and their symbolism operated in particular ways according to their chronological, functional and geographical context. This is similar to more recent studies of material culture in the Roman provinces which see much of the archaeological evidence as representing the fusion of identities into new, 'creolised' identities (Webster 2001), or that people and objects might have discrepant identities expressed at different times. (Brooch from Tierra de Barros, Estremadura, Spain, length 145 mm; Greene 1987: Fig. 11.6)

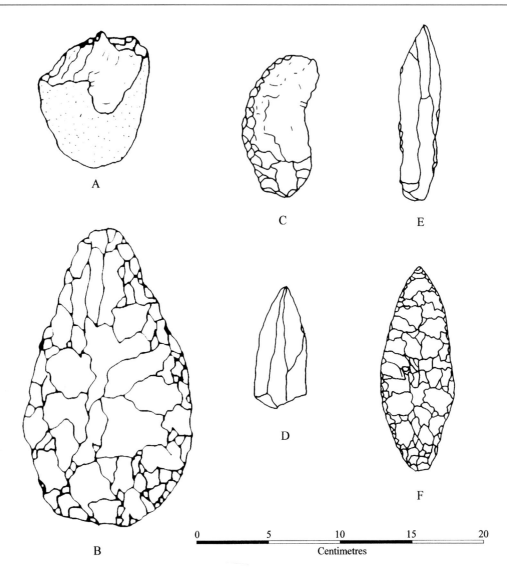

Figure 6.7 Can hominin and early human behaviour and communication be deduced from artefacts? The evolution of cognitive abilities – notably the development of language – is only indirectly reflected by this kind of evidence. Stone artefacts reveal changing conceptual approaches to tool-making. The earliest '**Oldowan**' examples from sites in East Africa are pebbles with flakes knocked off to create a sharper end (A), perhaps for hacking through animal hide and tough flesh; the flakes could be used for cutting. **Acheulian** bifaces (B) were made by removing a very large flake from a prepared core, and applying pressure to remove further flakes to produce a sharp cutting edge along both sides and at the point. Such 'hand-axes' are found not only in Africa but in other areas of the Old World colonised by *Homo erectus*. Neanderthals and other early humans extended the range of tools by striking and retouching flakes of various shapes and sizes (C, D). Anatomically modern humans seem to have been the first to strike long thin flakes from large cores and to adapt these 'blades' (or parts of them) into a wider range of specialised tools by further flaking (E). Some artefacts were extraordinarily thin and carefully flaked, to the extent that their production may have been partly for 'show' (F). Do the variety, virtuosity and rapid typological change seen in artefacts associated with 'anatomically modern humans' indicate higher cognitive and manipulative skills than were possessed by Neanderthals, or do they reflect adaptation to rapid climatic change after a long period of stability? (Drawn by Tony Liddell, from various sources at a common scale)

6.4 TOWARDS POSTPROCESSUAL ARCHAEOLOGY

... history constructs the intellectual framework that comprehends it. ... The past can no longer be understood in its own terms because now the past is to be understood in terms of the concerns of the present.

(Lechte 1994: 1)

One side-effect of the New Archaeology was a renewal of the relationship that had existed between archaeology and anthropology since the nineteenth century. Binford revitalised the study of material traces of human activity as a source for understanding human behaviour, and Hodder underlined a view that material culture was 'meaningfully constituted'. Interest amongst anthropologists in diverse modern philosophical approaches to society and culture (Gosden 1999: 119–22) spilled over into archaeology, where such thinking came to be described by the inelegant term 'postprocessualism'. David Clarke observed that 'the New Archaeology is as yet a set of questions rather than a set of answers; when the questions are answered it too will be Old Archaeology' (1973: 17); postprocessual archaeology did not wait for answers, but began to ask rather different questions.

6.4.1 Postprocessualism

- key references: Whitley, *Reader in archaeological theory* 1998; Johnson, *Archaeological theory* 2010: 102–21; Hodder and Hutson, *Reading the past: current approaches to interpretation in archaeology* 2003; Shanks, 'Culture/archaeology' 2001.

Post-processual archaeology, then, involves the breaking down of established, taken-for-granted, dichotomies and opens up study of the relationships between norm and individual, process and structure, material and ideal, object and subject. Unlike processual archaeology it does not espouse one approach or argue that archaeology should develop an agreed methodology. That is why postprocessual archaeology is simply 'post-'. It develops from a criticism of that which went before, building on, yet diverging from that path. It involves diversity and lack of consensus. It is characterized by debate and uncertainty about fundamental issues that may have been rarely questioned before in archaeology. It is more an asking of questions than a provision of answers.

(Hodder 1991: 181)

When the label 'postprocessual' emerged in the 1980s it was very loaded, for it suggested that rather than simply developing from processual New Archaeology, postprocessualism formed an intellectual alternative, or even a complete replacement. Ian Hodder's description of an indefinable movement whose only uniting characteristic was being 'post-' fitted in well with the spirit of change in the early 1980s, when the newly-elected conservative governments of Thatcher and Reagan in Britain and the USA began the job of dismantling the socialism and liberalism of the 1960s. Margaret Thatcher declared in 1987 that 'there is no such thing as society', while yuppies of the 'me generation' achieved rapid wealth as individualistic capitalism was given greater freedom. Processualism incorporated 'uniformitarian' assumptions about the way societies operate according to abstract rules, whereas postprocessual archaeology took an inside view of culture (Johnson 1999: 54, 82–3) and emphasised individuals – whether ancient people experiencing the past or modern archaeologists creating interpretations.

Eight key statements about postprocessual archaeology

Matthew Johnson attempted to capture the essentials of postprocessual archaeology in a series of statements and to explain its outlook by elaborating upon them (2010: 105–11). We now have listed each statement in Table 6.2, and related it to the philosophical approaches outlined in this chapter, while presenting some of the implications as concisely as possible in a third column.

6.4.2 Reflexive thinking

- key references: Hodder, *Towards reflexive method in archaeology: the example of Çatalhöyük* 2000; Hodder, 'Reflexive methods' 2005b.

David Clarke had anticipated deeper analysis of archaeological thinking when he called for 'the explicit scrutiny of the philosophical assumptions which underpinned and constrained every aspect of archaeological reasoning, knowledge and concepts' (1973: 11–12). Historians have long recognised the importance of placing scientific and intellectual thinking into a cultural and political context, and this attitude underlies both Chapter 1 of the present volume and this discussion of more recent archaeological theory. In the later twentieth century the role of a writer became increasingly self-conscious, and the word **reflexive** was frequently used to characterise this awareness. A reflexive approach does not mean abandoning judgement, but it does require profound thought; why do we wish to write about archaeology for beginners, rather than concentrating entirely upon producing specialised books and articles aimed only at the academic research community? Although we could provide a specific answer involving political outlook and educational philosophy, we are also well aware of the less clear-cut biographical factors, some of which are mentioned in this book's preface. Reflexive thinking does not stop there; it may lead to fundamental questions about individual identity and general concerns about the whole nature of 'Western civilisation'. We will spend some time looking at the characteristics of several philosophical '-isms' (some of which have a corresponding 'post-') because of their enormous impact since 1980. A reflexive approach has had a significant impact not only on theoretical archaeology but also on archaeological fieldwork and excavation practices over the last fifteen years (see Chapter 3).

Most theoretical publications are difficult to understand without some basic knowledge of what has been happening in wider intellectual circles since the 1950s; in other words, what characterises **the postmodern condition** – 'not really a proposition to be debated back and forth. Rather, it is a general state, the way the world is in the twenty-first century' (Johnson 2010: 202).

6.4.3 Modernity, modernism and postmodernism

- key references: Munslow, *Companion to historical studies* 2006; Lechte, *Fifty key contemporary thinkers: from structuralism to postmodernity* 1994; Miller, *Modernity: an ethnographic approach* 1994; Walsh, *The representation of the past* 1992; Taylor and Winquist, *Encyclopedia of postmodernism* 2001.

Postmodernism is a general description for the conditions of our present existence – what might better be called postmodernity. According to the French cultural critic Jean-François Lyotard postmodernism is distinguished by its denial of grand or metanarratives as deployed since the Enlightenment to explain and justify the Western conception of human progress.

(Munslow 2006: 207)

Postmodernism cannot follow in sequence after modernism, because this would be an admission of historic progress and a relapse into Grand Narrative mythology.

(Appignanesi and Garratt 1995: 114)

The 'modern' view of European history, economics and technology presents them as an upward trajectory of progress through the Renaissance to the Enlightenment, to which awareness of individual emotions and deeper rational understanding were added in the nineteenth century by Romanticism and positivist science. The nineteenth and twentieth centuries also proposed 'explanations' of the place of humans in the world. These **grand narratives** included Marx's historical account of socio-economic contradictions that would lead to revolutionary change and Darwinian evolutionary ideas applied to society by Herbert Spencer. At the same time, more subversive tendencies threatened these confident

Table 6.1 Archaeological projects and interpretations: hypothetical examples

Title	Approach	Methods and interpretations
A catalogue of Neolithic pottery from western France	**culture-historical**: material culture used to investigate the 'history' of occupation in an area	Little overt theoretical discussion will accompany the descriptive content (classification of pottery types, sequences through time, and distribution maps showing where different types are found). Comparisons with pottery from other areas of France and associations with other artefacts will be used to map cultural areas and to suggest population movements that took place when immigrant farmers displaced indigenous hunter-gatherers. The results are published in a book with a very traditional format containing many plain drawings.
Marine resources, agriculture, and the place of ceramic production in Neolithic ecosystems in western France	**processual**: material evidence and environmental data used as the focus for a rigorous scientific study	Pottery-making is placed within an economic system defined through studies of plant remains, animal bones and shells found on farming settlements. Population figures and settlement distribution will be studied statistically, and related to the agricultural potential and physical resources of the local landscape. Research hypotheses have been designed carefully and tested against the evidence. The pottery will not simply be recorded and catalogued, but integrated with many other kinds of evidence; ethnoarchaeological analogies for changes in production technology will be related to increasing social complexity. The results are published in a large monograph from a prestigious university press and followed by further volumes containing scientific data and statistical analysis.
La mer et la terre: the symbolic role of pottery-making amongst early farming communities on Europe's western coastline	**postprocessual**: sophisticated interpretations borrowed from anthropology are applied to the material evidence	A structuralist approach looks for 'binary oppositions' that show how material culture was used like a text to express people's relation to their world. The conversion of wet clay to dry pottery by the firing process is seen as a symbol of the tension between traditional Mesolithic harvesting of 'wild' resources from the sea, and new Neolithic clearance of woodland by fire to create land for raising 'domesticated' crops and animals. The results are published as an extended essay in a beautifully designed book in which old engravings are placed alongside impressionistic illustrations by a modern artist living in the study area.
Powerful men, invisible women: ideological discourses in the interpretation of Neolithic pottery in 20th-century France	**interpretive**: postmodern philosophy and anthropology provide themes for research and interpretation	The history of pottery studies reveals the dominant discourse of previous interpretations made by men in established academic positions. The new project shows how Neolithic women made pottery in differing ways using actions and rituals that reflected but simultaneously shaped and modified their everyday social experience. Excluded men gave meaning to their lives through engaging in the cyclical actions of cultivating and harvesting crops; their remains were buried in pottery containers under mounds of earth that reflected their lifeways. The project shows how the power structures of modern universities and museums had been reflected in previous studies of monumental tombs of the élite, which ignored simple memorials to ordinary people. The results are published on the Internet in the form of a debate between different researchers to which readers can contribute ideas by e-mail; photographs, documents, site-plans, etc., are available in on-line databases that may be accessed freely so that individuals may create their own interpretation rather than accepting the authority of the research team.

explanations of the world; *modernism* in the arts (as opposed to modernity in general) rejected conventions established since the Renaissance in painting, sculpture and music and delighted in abstraction.

Architecture gave modernity some of its most visible negative associations in the late twentieth century, when tower-blocks – optimistically constructed from 'new materials' in 'functional' forms suited to 'efficient' life and work – began to be demolished because of structural decay and associations with social deprivation. The fundamental crisis of modernity accelerated in the 1950s with the beginning of four decades of

Table 6.2 Influences upon and implications of Johnson's statements about postprocessual archaeology

	Johnson's statements	Possible influences	Implications
1	*We reject a positivist view of science and the theory/ data split. The data are always theory-laden.*	constructivism, hermeneutics	Postprocessualists do not reject testing entirely, but consider that it does not produce positive answers because the data and test-methods are already influenced by theoretical factors (= 2 below).
2	*Interpretation is always hermeneutic.*	phenomenology, hermeneutics, post-structuralism	We cannot interpret people or things from the past without first attaching meanings to them that arise from our own interpretation (= the **hermeneutic circle**).
3	*We reject the opposition between material and ideal.*	phenomenology	Neither the materialism of processual archaeology nor the idealism of structuralism are satisfactory on their own; people in the past experienced a constant interaction between their thoughts and their physical surroundings and material culture.
4	*We need to look at thoughts and values in the past.*	historical idealism; social anthropology	Interpretation of the human past involves *empathy* – attempting to understand the ways that people's actions were guided by ideas and cultural values.
5	*The individual is active.*	structuration	People were not passive pawns following abstract rules; individuals helped to modify rules through their everyday physical actions and social interactions.
6	*Material culture is like a text.*	semiotics, post-structuralism	Meanings are not fixed, but vary with different 'readers' (2 above); objects and structures can be used actively by people to express conformity or dissent (e.g. clothes or jewellery). Because of the possibility of multiple readings, meanings are not fixed and not fully controlled by people using material culture.
7	*We have to look at context.*	constructivism, structuralism, post-structuralism, hermeneutics	It is essential to look closely at archaeological or ethnoarchaeological contexts (in what situations objects or structures are used, and with what functions and/or social meanings) if meanings are to be understood (but see 2 and 6 above).
8	*The meanings we produce are always in the political present, and always have a political resonance. Interpreting the past is always a political act.*	Critical Theory, postcolonialism	See 1–2 above; in Johnson's own words: If scientific neutrality is argued to be a myth, then statements about the past are never cool objective judgements detached from the real world. They are always made here, in the present, with all its heady and complicated, jumbled mixture of political and moral judgements. (Johnson 2010: 110)

BOX 6.5

Phenomenology: postprocessualism and landscape archaeology

Phenomenological approaches have been particularly influential in landscape archaeology. Tilley's study of Neolithic monuments in southern England (1994) examined Neolithic perceptions of the world, focusing on what could be seen from certain locations and how movement through the landscape may have affected perceptions. These studies have been inspired by the work of anthropologists such as Keith Basso (1996) who examined how non-Western societies in North America conceive and perceive the landscapes around them. Tilley used reflexive concepts to place the feelings and perceptions of modern viewers at the heart of his study. Such models have been followed up by others who have focused on how monuments might have been created in reference to the landscape around them (Cummings *et al.* 2002; Cummings and Whittle 2003). Using such perspectives one might question, for example, what the significance is of the location of the prehistoric rock art (shown in the photo) below this prominent hill in Northumberland with

commanding views of the surrounding landscape. These approaches are by no means universally accepted however, and have been criticised by other practitioners of landscape archaeology for their neglect of practical details (Fleming 2008), as well as for broader failures: 'the current preoccupation with how prehistoric people perceived past landscapes ... leave it wilfully unclear whether the perceptions proposed are those of the investigator or the past people being studied' (Shennan 2004: 3). (Photograph: Tom Moore)

Cold-War stalemate between Soviet communism and Western capitalism. The optimism of the left, inspired by the Russian Revolution, had already been dampened by the ruthless authoritarian rule of Stalin in the 1930s, which did not end after Russia had joined the Western allies in the defeat of Hitler and fascism. Stalin's repressive system was extended to the 'liberated' countries of eastern Europe and continued in diluted forms until 1990. Meanwhile, after the Second World War, the United States – the land of freedom and democracy – began right-wing

political witch-hunts at home while fighting wars against communism in distant countries such as Korea and Vietnam from the 1950s to the 1970s. Russia and America applied scientific expertise to a ruinously expensive nuclear arms-race while attempting to achieve propaganda victories through spectacular space missions.

American military intervention in Vietnam and Russian invasions of Hungary (1956), Czechoslovakia (1968) and Afghanistan (1979) gave the clear impression that the two superpowers had become the new imperialists and colonisers. Many vigorous protest movements in the 1960s and 1970s were aroused by the contradiction between these new roles and the fact that Russia and the United States both claimed to be upholding liberty and had themselves been created by revolution against imperial or colonial rule. It is not surprising that philosophies which examined deeper structures of meaning and agendas of power underlying the ideologies of capitalism and communism were so attractive. The dramatic end of communism, symbolised by the opening of the Berlin Wall in 1989 and the dissolution of the Soviet Union in 1991, reopened many questions about the nature of Western democracy and capitalism. The phenomenon of globalisation – the spread of uniform culture throughout the world by corporations such as McDonald's or by the Internet – has been accompanied by escalation of local wars about national, religious and ethnic identity from the Balkans to Indonesia. It is hardly surprising that, in the closing decades of the twentieth century – the 'age of extremes' (Hobsbawm 1994) – a fundamental aspect of postmodernity was the abandonment of grand explanatory schemes that provided 'a "credible" purpose for action, science, or society at large' (Lechte 1994: 246). The study of history has been more directly affected by postmodernism than has archaeology, however, notably under the influence of Hayden White's argument that historians impose stories on the past, using familiar plots. 'White insists that history can never provide *the* story, rather it is *a* narrative designed by the historian as he/she organises the contents in the form of a narrative of what he/she believes the past was about' (Munslow 2006: 242). Perhaps because archaeologists are concerned with material culture – physical sites and artefacts – rather than written documents, they are less likely to see their subject entirely in terms of artificial stories created by their own imaginations. In the twenty-first century, the impact of globalisation has resonated strongly with some archaeologists, for example in their study of the Roman Empire and its reception in the modern world (Hingley 2005). Meanwhile, the impact of the terrorist atrocities of 9/11 and 7/7 has been understood by some archaeologists through

concepts of materiality and memory, reinforcing ideas of the contested nature of history and archaeology (e.g. Meskell 2005; Wallace 2004). Although the idea of a single vision of the past has become increasingly untenable, some still see the role of the archaeologist as presenting coherent narratives (Shennan 2004).

Phenomenology and hermeneutics: constructivism and Critical Theory

- key references: Tilley, *A phenomenology of landscape: places, paths and monuments* 1994; Thomas, *Time, culture and identity: an interpretive archaeology* 1996; Bond and Gilliam, *Social construction of the past* 1994; Kearney, *Modern movements in European philosophy* 1994; Pinsky and Wylie, *Critical traditions in contemporary archaeology* 1989; Gosden, 'Postcolonial archaeology' 2001; Webster and Cooper, *Roman imperialism: post-colonial perspectives* 1996.

Suspicions about modernity's confidence in discovering truth were already held by nineteenth-century philosophers such as Nietzsche and were reinforced by **phenomenology** and **hermeneutics**, which scrutinised the nature of individual consciousness and knowledge. One result was the blurring of the traditional distinction between subject and object or mind and matter that had underpinned science since Descartes. The 'de-centring' of individual humans as active subjects who perceived passive objects could be compared with the effect of seventeenth-century astronomy, when the Earth suddenly ceased to be seen as the centre of the universe and became merely one of many planets orbiting the sun. Heidegger developed a view of consciousness in which perceiving objects was an intentional and interactive process that revealed 'meaning' in terms of the observer, rather than any intrinsic characteristics of the objects themselves. The loss of a distinct subject:object relationship had serious implications for positivist science, where supposedly objective experiments were designed to measure things in order to test hypotheses. This was also impossible from a **constructivist** point of view, because each scientist had a personal/

political/cultural perspective on the world and used it to choose particular forms of science and ways to explore it. Herein lies the strongly relativist view characteristic of knowledge, which denies 'fixed' meanings that are independent of the observer and the context of observation: 'scientific knowledge is made by scientists and not determined by the world' (Craig 2000: 172; Box 6.5).

Constructivist analysis also challenges the legitimacy of particular points of view by relating them to the social setting and attitudes of those who hold them. A similar challenge comes from Critical Theory, an approach associated with a group of political thinkers frequently known as the Frankfurt school who emerged in the 1920s and 1930s. They attempted to provide a revision of Marxism from a humanist perspective by moving away from its rigid economic basis and re-emphasising the philosophy of Kant and Hegel, who scrutinised reason and knowledge and the way that they were conditioned by their historical context. 'Critical theory works dialectically, that is by searching out "contradictions" in social arrangements in which, for example, certain groups are systematically excluded from power or from the free access to information that structures rational debate' (Blackburn 1994: 146).

Archaeology and postcolonialism

- key references: Gosden, 'Postcolonial archaeology' 2001; Webster and Cooper, *Roman imperialism: post-colonial perspectives* 1996.

Power and exclusion feature prominently in postcolonial thinking, which is an even more overtly political approach to archaeology, history or anthropology because its central concern is the end of European imperialism, with particular emphasis upon the effect of colonial power on people who were oppressed (Gosden 1999: 197–203). An interest in 'otherness' promoted by critical theory, postcolonialism and other postmodern movements promotes a much more inclusive attitude to archaeology.

Traditional 'top-down' concerns with hierarchies and the archaeology of rulers and elites (Tutankhamun's tomb, Roman towns and villas,

medieval church art and architecture) can be supplemented by interest in ethnic minorities, slaves, women, gay men, lesbians and other groups whose lives were conducted outside the centres of ideological power. Neolithic henge monuments, for example, have undergone intensive study in recent decades (Box 6.1 and 6.5). A constructivist perspective would explore the reasons why particular modern individuals choose to study prehistory, and why they isolate these banked-and-ditched structures as a category of particular significance unified by the term 'henge'. What preconceptions about the nature of ancient societies do they bring to the subject? Are they simply imposing a modern idea of political power (reinforced by sacred authority) by identifying 'ritual structures' as if they were comparable to churches or temples? An ideological perspective might go further, and accuse these archaeologists of supporting the *status quo*. Does not a discourse about prehistoric communities working to build ritual monuments for their priests or leaders merely reflect – and reinforce – modern social hierarchies? Should an archaeologist not abandon this form of 'story-telling' and use a wide range of philosophical, anthropological and sociological approaches to explore 'otherness' – different possibilities for living in the past and, by implication, the present?

A classic early exposition of postcolonial scholarship was Edward Said's work on orientalism which examined how western Europe created an identity by contrasting itself with the otherness of Eastern religions and cultures (Said 1978; Gosden 2004). Whether derived from Critical Theory or from postcolonialism, insights into this kind of fundamental cultural outlook help us to be more reflexive about other people and ways of life – whether in the past or the present. Such approaches have had a significant impact on the study of other colonial encounters, especially of the Roman Empire.

Earlier approaches tended to understand Roman expansion as either a civilising process (Haverfield 1923) or one which assimilated the peoples it encountered; (Millett 1990). More recent writers view the processes by which indigenous communities and the 'Romans' themselves related to the Empire as more complex, leading to different types of identities and expressions of cultures (Hingley 2000; Webster 2001; Mattingly 2004). Postcolonial archaeology also has significant implications for modern indigenous identities, as well as for understanding recent colonial encounters.

Structuralism and semiotics, post-structuralism and deconstruction

- key references: Lechte, *Fifty key contemporary thinkers: from structuralism to postmodernity* 1994; Bapty and Yates, *Archaeology after structuralism: post-structuralism and the practice of archaeology* 1990; Tilley, *Reading material culture: structuralism, hermeneutics and post-structuralism* 1990; Nash, *Semiotics of landscape: archaeology of mind* 1997; Davis, 'The deconstruction of intentionality in archaeology' 1992; Taylor and Winquist, *Encyclopaedia of postmodernism* 2001.

An important component of postprocessual archaeology was **structuralism**, an approach developed in the study of linguistics that began in the early twentieth century. Ferdinand de Saussure held that speech is entirely dependent upon language and that language has a deep structure that consists of signs to which we attach arbitrary individual meanings to differentiate between them. Thus, meaning in speech or text emerges from the structure of *signs*, rather than from an individual or author; again, the individual is de-centred, with thoughts and speech determined by an underlying structure, rather than produced by individuals. Structuralism was extended from the field of linguistics to literature (Barthes), psychoanalysis (Lacan) and – most importantly for archaeology – anthropology (Lévi-Strauss). Structuralism 'emphasises the hidden or "unconscious" structures of language which underpin our current established discourses – social, cultural, economic' (Kearney 1994: 1). For this reason it may be compared to processualism, which shared a belief in underlying laws, and structuralism has been criticised as 'a form of intellectual modernism, a radical link with previous theoretical models and philosophical

traditions, symptomatic of post-war optimism for the global applicability of science' (Craig 2000: 484).

An important component of structuralism is **semiotics** (the study of signs), which Roland Barthes used with considerable breadth in tackling many forms of popular culture – from wrestling to fashion – in addition to language and literature. Archaeologists naturally welcomed this wider application, as well as Lévi-Strauss's structuralist anthropology, which included material culture in its analysis along with social phenomena such as kinship. The **contextual archaeology** developed by Ian Hodder as a result of his ethnoarchaeological research described above (Hodder 1982b; 1991) drew upon structuralism and semiotics. He saw material culture as a *text* that was just as complicated as spoken language and could be employed in different ways in different social contexts. The shape and decoration of pottery might act as signs that reflected not only the kinship group to which a woman potter belonged, but also some coded messages about gender relations or ritual. Likewise the form of a settlement or house was not simply a practical matter of arranging buildings and enclosures, but a physical expression of the way that a community organised and divided itself – and of course the disposition of these physical structures would silently reinforce the organisation of a community.

Lévi-Strauss also extended Saussure's concept of binary oppositions in linguistics (speech:language; signifier:signified) to anthropology when analysing culture (Lévi-Strauss 1958; Layton 1997: 88–9). Hodder used this idea of how people understood the world to write an account of European agriculture entirely in terms of the transformation of the natural into the cultural, or the wild into the domesticated, as part of a long-term social drama (1990: 18–19). Even before agriculture, households (the 'domus') had begun to domesticate the wildness of natural processes ('agrios') – such as death and fertility – through the structure and decoration of buildings and the incorporation of burials within them. 'The long-term symbolic and economic structures were manipulated within social competition for within, and between, group control and domination, production, exchange, feasting and settlement formation. A particular conjunction between structured process and climatic and environmental events at the end of the Pleistocene produced the origins of agriculture' (*ibid.*: 293).

Structuralism gave rise to a powerful reaction (**post-structuralism**) in the 1960s, involving two of the most frequently quoted writers on postmodernity: Roland Barthes and Jacques Derrida. Barthes is famous for declaring the death of the author and transferring 'meaning' to the reader rather than the writer (Thody and Course 1997: 105–15). Derrida is associated with the process of **deconstruction**: an endless peeling-away of layers of constructed meanings, rather than conducting a structuralist analysis to find a rational underlying system (Appignanesi and Garratt 1995: 77–81).

The archaeology of knowledge
- key references: Foucault, *The archaeology of knowledge* 1972; Goldstein, *Foucault and the writing of history* 1994; Munslow, *Companion to historical studies* 2006, 117.

Michel Foucault looked at the 'archaeology' of knowledge in general, rather than scrutinising texts from a post-structuralist point of view, but shared the purpose of 'de-centring' interpretation. He identified **discourses**: ways of studying or describing knowledge that characterised various periods of the past or the approaches of different disciplines, and he looked closely at the structures of power that controlled knowledge (Appignanesi and Garratt 1995: 82–7). Foucault shared the post-structuralist concern with the instability of meanings but also reinforced the critical-theorist and constructivist attitudes to **legitimation**: what gives any person or institution authority and/ or power to speak about a subject? This difficult question was a persistent theme in late twentieth-century writing about archaeology:

Taking the past seriously involves recognizing its otherness not as a matter of exoticism but as a means of undercutting and relativizing the legitimacy of the present. … Central questions to be asked here are: who produces the past

and why? For whom exactly is this production taking place? In what circumstances? Who has the right to speak and expect to have their statements considered as worthy of attention and comment?

(Shanks and Tilley 1992: 260, 263)

These questions have further implications for the role of archaeology as part of **heritage**, which is discussed below.

Postmodernism and archaeology
- key references: Bintliff, 'Post-modernism, rhetoric and scholasticism at TAG: the current state of British archaeological theory' 1991; Thomas and Tilley, 'TAG and "post-modernism": a reply to John Bintliff' 1992.

Our postmodern age is characterised generally by a self-conscious reaction against the vehicle for the Enlightenment's notion of progress, its cultural product, modernism. But the act of rejection is only found in certain spheres of intellectual activity. In others it is manifest … as modernism's self-reflexion, or a case of modernism turning to challenge its own shortcomings.

(Munslow 2006: 207)

We hope that what has emerged from the outline given above is that postmodernism is not a specific school of thought, but a persistent challenge to the assumptions of western European culture (**Fig. 6.8**). Its impact is not clear, for most recent philosophical influences upon archaeology have generated an attitude that resembles modernism challenging itself (in the manner expressed by Munslow's statement) rather than fully-fledged postmodernism. Whatever its inspiration, a relativist perspective makes it impossible to accept either the scientific basis of processual archaeology or the social evolutionary foundation of culture history. Phenomenology, involving human existence in the world and interpretation of the processes by which objects are perceived, has been very influential in interpretive archaeology. It directs attention to everyday interactions between people and their environment (whether

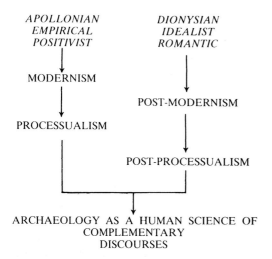

APOLLONIAN
EMPIRICAL
POSITIVIST

↓

MODERNISM

↓

PROCESSUALISM

DIONYSIAN
IDEALIST
ROMANTIC

↓

POST-MODERNISM

↓

POST-PROCESSUALISM

ARCHAEOLOGY AS A HUMAN SCIENCE OF
COMPLEMENTARY
DISCOURSES

Figure 6.8 In contrast to Fig. 6.1, John Bintliff has argued that separate traditions have merged (or should merge) into a new consensus. Differing approaches – 'complementary discourses' – can coexist in a 'tool box' to be brought out for tackling different kinds of question. Thus, a field survey project will still benefit from sampling, statistics and ecological thinking characteristic of New Archaeology, while ritual or belief might be explored more effectively with postprocessual and/or anthropological theory. Bintliff also favours the Annales approach, which distinguishes between long-term trends (scarcely perceptible in people's lifetimes), medium-term cycles, and events in which individuals are directly involved (1991b). However, archaeologists influenced by postmodernism might reject Bintliff's distinction between Apollonian and Dionysian traditions (terms coined by Nietzsche in 1872) because such definitions impose a modernist historical or evolutionary narrative. (Bintliff 1995: Fig. 2)

natural or modified by humans) and the meanings of structures and artefacts. In particular, such meanings are constantly revised through different experiences; thus, to describe a prehistoric enclosure as a 'henge monument' or a sharp heavy object as an 'axe' merely opens the questioning about how they were used and perceived in the past, and how those meanings fluctuated and changed according to the people and circumstances involved. Tim Insoll has suggested that we need to revisit many of the ways we define and understand archaeology itself, asking: '... are we trying to reconstruct a past in our own image?' (Insoll 2007b: 9). Are our archaeological

concepts merely constructs of the recent past which may in fact hinder, rather than assist, how we look at archaeological evidence? Most of the following aspects of postprocessual archaeology have attempted to address these questions.

6.5 INTERPRETIVE ARCHAEOLOGY

- key references: Hodder, *Archaeological theory today* 2001; Thomas, *Interpretive archaeology: a reader* 2000; Johnson, *Archaeological theory* 2010: 102–21; Hodder *et al.*, *Interpreting archaeology: finding meaning in the past* 1995.

The early New Archaeology shared with traditional Marxist approaches a preoccupation with subsistence and production. It developed a standpoint which might reasonably be termed 'materialist'. In that sense it was functionalist and developed a position which has been described as 'functional-processual'. The so-called 'post-processual' critique of the New Archaeology made precisely that observation and developed an alternative 'interpretive' approach, in which the key concept and desideratum was 'meaning'.

(Renfrew 2001a: 100)

The development of archaeological theory from around 1950 to 1990 could easily be presented as a neat progression from culture history to processualism and then to postprocessualism. However, postprocessualism was not a unified movement or body of thought and it underwent fundamental changes from the 1980s to the 1990s, including a move from seeing material culture in terms of symbolic structures or texts towards a greater interest in individual **agency** (Berggren 2000: 39; Gardner 2004). Furthermore, we should not make the mistake of thinking that the entire archaeological world became embroiled in debates about processualism and its theoretical successors. Indeed, much thinking from outside England and North America has been ignored, particularly when written in languages other than

English (Olivier 1999; Scarre 1999). In 1991 Felipe Criado, a Chilean archaeologist participating in a conference on Interpreting Archaeology, observed:

> Could you, Anglo–American archaeologists, realise that, from an *abroad* and *broader* perspective, the debate between processualism and postprocessualism is not any more an intellectual one and is mostly a matter of academical fighting, power within academia. This is the reason why Latin (Mediterranean as well as American) archaeologies become suspicious about postprocessualism and recent debates in English-language archaeological literature.
>
> (Felipe Criado quoted in Hodder 1995: 227)

If Ian Hodder was right to say that 'post-processual archaeology is simply "post-"' (1991: 181) he begs an obvious question in the mind of anyone taking a historical approach to the development of archaeological theory: what comes next? One answer is to side-step this question and to deny the validity of linear progressions of this kind and to refuse to polarise archaeological thought into opposing camps. A more successful means of escape employed by many archaeologists is to use the very general term **interpretive** (or **interpretative**) to describe a range of approaches to archaeology that share a commitment to being reflexive and/or display a willingness to make use of diverse twentieth-century thinkers. *Philosophy and archaeological practice: perspectives for the twenty-first century*, edited by Cornelius Holtorf and Håkan Karlsson in 2000, celebrated diversity rather than attempting to resolve an argument or define a new position. One of its ambitions was 'to decentre theoretical debates in archaeology, by moving away from oppositional struggles for theoretical hegemony to multiperspectived, multivocal, personal and individualised approaches that allow different pasts to emerge from the archaeological record' (*ibid.*: vii).

Thinkers such as Heidegger, Derrida and Giddens emphasise the role of individuals, rather than the power of abstract forces such as social evolution which had underlain most anthropological and archaeological thinking from 1800 to the 1970s. In addition to papers about theory and interpretation in general, an anthology of interpretive archaeology (Thomas 2000) included sections on social relations, gender, material culture, identity and space. By looking closely at the role of individuals in the past, the range of philosophical approaches in use by the end of the 1990s increased the importance of primary archaeological evidence such as fragments of pottery, burials or domestic structures. Once these would have been classified, labelled and possibly organised into a regional scheme of ethnic cultures and set within a 'historical' or 'evolutionary' account of the past in which their details were submerged within wider concerns. The significance and humanity of sites and artefacts are enhanced by viewing them from a perspective of individual experience: the meaning of a pot to its maker and users, the act of remembrance surrounding the disposal of the remains of a dead person. **Meaning** in this context will be a two-way process that recognises the difficulties of constructing meaning in the past and the present.

6.5.1 Agency, structuration and habitus

- key references: Giddens, *The constitution of society: outline of the theory of structuration* 1984; Dobres and Robb, *Agency in archaeology* 2000; Barrett, 'Agency, the duality of structure' 2001; Hodder and Hutson, *Reading the Past* 2003: 90–105; Gardner, *Agency uncovered* 2004; Bourdieu, *Outline of a theory of practice* 1977.

Agency is a term that expresses the role of individuals, especially in the form of 'knowledgeable agents'. When this concept is combined with a view of society that incorporates the interaction of individuals with social structures, it offers great potential for humanising the past. The following example was devised by John Barrett and Kathryn Fewster to show how Anthony Giddens' **structuration theory** might be applied to an archaeological site.

Consider the floor of an Iron Age round-house, traditionally analysed as an organised space of activity areas, or fashionably analysed as a cosmological scheme of spatial oppositions and equivalences. From the perspective of *co-presence* that floor saw the gathering of different agencies – the routine cycle of occupation, the different biographies which were brought to that place and which were then lived out from it when that place itself became a place of memory. It also demarcated different spatial experiences, not an enclosed space some 10 metres in diameter, but the co-presences of spaces traversed either from the fields and pasture of the immediate landscape or from the journey travelled many miles distant perhaps carrying with it the material manifestations of foreign and unheard-of places. These moments of co-presence addressed the absent past and distant place and looked towards different futures. These moments which were lived out sequentially through different forms of agency bound together structural conditions across time and space. Thus the intimacy touched upon here does not stand in contrast with the larger scale process, rather it is the forge at which the process was constantly reworked.

(Barrett and Fewster 2000: 31)

Barrett and Fewster also emphasise that Giddens has said nothing about material culture and that not all of his work is useful for archaeology; they do, however, go a long way towards removing the fear that modern thinking might lead to value-free relativist indecision:

But at the end of the day the way we view human beings, wherever and whenever, will inform our own politics of responsibility. We will fail to recognise this responsibility as long as we continue to objectify the lives of others into things, the material that we study. ... the study of the real conditions of human life has implications in terms of ethics, in terms of what we can contribute to the development of the social sciences and in terms of how we can write better archaeology.

(Barrett and Fewster 2000: 33)

The concept of **habitus** developed by the French sociologist Pierre Bourdieu (1930–2002) has figured prominently in these discussions. 'Habitus' is evoked by archaeologists in a variety of ways (Barrett 2005), but this complex concept is rarely defined. Essentially, it explores the ways in which people define themselves through repeated behaviour and action, carrying out the kinds of actions that they know how to perform instinctively: 'Habitus provides a way of understanding the individual's placement within "dominant" culture, incorporating and defining cultural activities and providing a context for all social actions' (Taylor and Winquist 2001: 43).

Habitus emphasises that actions are not necessarily conducted according to socially definable 'rules' (Hodder and Huston 2003: 91; Shanks 2005: 241). The concept has been used frequently in prehistoric archaeology to examine whether the use of space in houses and settlements observed in the archaeological record reflects the habitus of past peoples; for example Pollard's (1999) and Souvatzi's (2008) examinations of how space was used on Neolithic settlement sites in Britain and Greece. It is worth remembering that, because of agency, Giddens argued that individuals could reject certain modes of behaviour; thus, the concept of 'resistance' has become popular in archaeology for explaining cases where individuals or groups seem to have undertaken actions which go against perceived norms of behaviour (Hodder and Hutson 2003: 96–9).

Concepts of agency are also being explored in areas of archaeology that have long been regarded as strongly processual in their approach, such as the early Palaeolithic period. Study of this period has usually relied on scientific approaches that examine broader social change over millennia, for example climate change or human evolution and DNA; it is difficult to detect the place and role of individuals on such long timescales. However, new studies are examining elements of Palaeolithic archaeology and observing agency. The processes by which stone tools were formed were reflections of human individualism (especially when tools did not flake as required) rather than set patterns of behaviour and design to be followed in a uniform manner (Gamble and Porr 2005; Hopkinson and White 2005).

6.5.2 Archaeologies of identity

- key references: Meskell, 'Archaeologies of identity' 2001; Insoll, *The archaeology of identities* 2007; Díaz-Andreu *et al.*, *The archaeology of identity* 2005; Johnson, *Archaeological theory* 2010: 122–42; Fowler, *Archaeology of personhood* 2004.

Through its expertise at dealing with material culture and interpreting it in a contextual way, archaeology is ideally placed to add the material dimension so often lacking in other social sciences. Through looking at cultural items such as dress, spatial layout and architecture and considering them as the media through which many social relationships and interactions are negotiated, archaeology can detail how the material world both engages, and is engaged in, the articulation of social identity, both of the individual and of the group.

(Díaz-Andreu *et al.* 2005: 9)

The advent of interpretive and postprocessual approaches to the past in the last twenty years has led to a focus on the identities of people in the past. The archaeological record has been seen as the product of actions by individuals and communities, rather than as the result of general economic or environmental forces. This has led to studies of identity exploring many different perspectives, such as age, social status, ethnicity and gender. This kind of archaeology relies heavily on anthropological research which shows that expressions of identity are frequently multifaceted and may be expressed in different ways at different times. It is not easy to make direct links between the anthropological case

studies and expressions of identity detected by archaeologists. For example, does a sword placed in an Anglo-Saxon grave of the early medieval period represent an expression of the deceased individual's status, group identity, gender, age – or all or none of these? The postcolonial analyses discussed above have also led archaeologists to question the perspectives of previous research, suggesting that much of it was driven by colonialist attitudes towards people both in the past and in the present. This kind of awareness has led to deeper consideration of the place of indigenous peoples in archaeology. Status and religion have been less well explored in studies of identities, perhaps because of their importance in the models of hierarchy and social organisation that dominated processualism (Diaz-Andreu *et al.* 2005: 8). New approaches are now developing, however (Diaz-Andreu *et al.* 2005; Insoll 2005; Kryiakidis 2007), which suggest that societies were organised and ordered in more complex ways (see pp. 290–2). Gardner's study of identities in Late Roman Britain is an example of these new approaches, combining sociological theories (such as the work of Giddens) to reinterpret how people maintained and expressed new identities, such as their military or regional identity, at the time of the collapse of Late Roman Britain (Gardner 2007).

Indigenous peoples and postcolonial archaeology

- key references: Gosden, 'Postcolonial archaeology' 2001; Gosden, *Anthropology and archaeology* 1999: 190–7; Gosden, *Archaeology and colonialism* 2004; McNiven and Russell, 'Toward a postcolonial archaeology of indigenous Australia' 2008.

Archaeology has been up until now a means of domination and the colonial dispossession of our identity. If it were to be taken back by the Indians themselves it could provide us with new tools to understand our historical development and so strengthen our present demands and our projects for the future.

(Mamani Condori 1989: 58)

This observation by a Bolivian Indian archaeologist emphasises how worries over the ethics of collecting antiquities or 'tribal' art from the developing nations are closely linked to wider sensitivities about the interests of indigenous peoples. Attitudes of the developed world were made apparent during celebrations of the 500th anniversary of the 'discovery' of America by Columbus in 1992: in the words of one poster, 'Native Americans are not celebrating'.

The extreme example of Kossinna (above: p. 259) should not blind us to the prejudices contained in most research; how many archaeologists considered the feelings of Native Americans or Australians when excavating the bones of their ancestors and placing them on public exhibition in museums? Why do pictorial reconstructions of prehistoric life only show men hunting or using tools while women cook and weave? The protests of native peoples and feminists, along with the widening social background of people who have become archaeologists (Kehoe 1998: xiv), have gradually forced established archaeological institutions and museums to review their perspectives about these aspects of the past – as many had already done about nationalism and racism. Arguments about the ownership of **cultural property** in the form of antiquities and works of art take on an additional dimension in the case of human remains (Williams 2008). Western culture is curiously insensitive to the display of dead bodies – whether Egyptian mummies, Roman skeletons, or the embalmed remains of Lenin in Moscow. In North America and Australia in particular, indigenous groups have not only demanded the reburial of human remains – whatever their age – excavated by archaeologists, but have requested the return of material taken to Europe as specimens by nineteenth-century anthropologists and anatomists. Recognition of the importance of these issues by archaeologists reflects a wider attempt by Western society to deal with the colonial past (McNiven and Russell 2008: 423).

Archaeologists sometimes justify the disturbance of indigenous sites and burials on the ground that they benefit native populations today by illustrating their origins and early history. It is true that this kind of evidence may support claims for the ownership of land, but it assumes a very 'Western' view of the past, involving linear (rather than cyclical) time and a notion of death as final: 'to most Aborigines this would be meaningless sophistry. Human bones are the remains of their ancestors, the landscape itself the remains of ancestral beings and creators' (Haglund, quoted in Hubert 1989: 156). Agreements have been reached with a greater or lesser degree of goodwill or conflict; the early prehistoric Kow Swamp burials in Australia are an example of the latter (Mulvaney 1991; Bowdler 1992) and may be compared with 'Shared Principles', a cooperation agreement between a Native American group and archaeologists in North America (Kucera 1991), where the Native American Graves Protection and Repatriation Act (NAGPRA) was introduced in 1990 (Kelly and Thomas 2009: 388–9; Bray 1996). The process has been stressful for many archaeologists, forced to confront the prejudices that lurked behind their 'liberal' self-image, but the recognition of the validity of other views of the world is likely to be beneficial in the long term (**Box 6.10**: Zimmerman 1989; Kehoe 2008).

Postcolonialism also requires us to remember the role of anthropologists in the past in 'creating' the communities which they recorded. Recent studies suggest that expressions of identity and social systems which anthropologists studied in the late nineteenth and early twentieth centuries had already undergone major changes as a result of colonial encounters; this can be seen in the changing patterns of identity in North America (Gosden 2004: 87) and Melanesia (Sand *et al.* 2003). In some cases anthropologists and archaeologists have created unrepresentative, static models of indigenous peoples – a cautionary note if we are to use such models in looking at past peoples elsewhere.

Ethnicity

● key references: Jones, *Archaeology of ethnicity* 1996; Jones, 'Discourses of identity' 2007; Jenkins, *Rethinking ethnicity* 1997; Fenton, *Ethnicity: key concepts* 2003.

Examining ethnic identity in the past is far more complex than was first imagined. Ideas that distributions of pottery, or other artefact types, will mirror past peoples have been shown to be simplistic (above: p. 259). Anthropological study of African communities by Hodder (1982b) and others demonstrated that expressions of ethnic identity were far more complex than the use of (for example) a particular type of pottery. Thus, the whole question of ethnic identity has been opened up by philosophical and anthropological questions about the way in which individuals and groups define themselves (Banks 1995; Jones 1996) and by biomolecular research into DNA (Cavalli-Sforza *et al.* 1994; Chapter 5, p. 226). Interesting work in the United States has used archaeological means to explore ways in which African-American identity was expressed during periods of slavery and oppression, especially at Annapolis (Mullins 1999) or Chesapeake (Yentsch 1994). Less conventional and with a different

agenda are 'Afrocentric' interpretations of the past that propose greater black influences on history and culture that have been suppressed by the white majority (Palter 1993). Bernal stressed the non-European contribution to ancient Greek culture in a major work of scholarship with the arresting title *Black Athena: the Afroasiatic roots of classical civilization* (1987; 1991). Bernal's work stimulated much discussion and criticism (e.g. Levine 1992; Van Binsbergen 1996–7). In any case, people from ethnic minorities remain under-represented in archaeological careers in Britain and America, whether academic or in cultural resource management (Franklin 1997). Ethnic questions are not simply about minorities; they still play a powerful role in modern national and political perception, for example among 'Celtic' and 'Anglo-Saxon' people in

Figure 6.9 The death of Anne Frank in a concentration camp in 1945 is well known because of the diaries she wrote while hiding from the Nazis in a house (now a museum) in Amsterdam. Her lively diaries have helped several generations of young readers to empathise with her persecution, betrayal and untimely death. A touring exhibition from the Anne Frank Museum keeps her memory alive and supports campaigns against racism; when it visited York in 1998 the city was reminded about an episode of persecution that happened there in AD 1190. York's Jews were attacked by a mob and sought refuge in a wooden tower on this mound. They committed mass suicide as an alternative to being baptised or killed; the wooden tower was destroyed by fire and replaced in stone. This powerful image demonstrates the potential for linking sites from the past to concerns of the contemporary world. (*Yorkshire Evening Press*)

the British Isles whose identity – let alone any supposed behavioural characteristics – may be an invention of Victorian antiquarianism (James 1999; Collis 2003; Frantzen and Niles 1997). For sheer destructive power, and a significant archaeological contribution to its ideology (Arnold and Hassman 1995), nothing has equalled the doctrine of Aryan superiority that underlay the racial policies of Nazi Germany in the 1930s and 1940s (Fig. 6.9). However, colonialism based upon the supposed ethnic superiority of white Europeans, supported by 'scientific' evolutionary judgements in the nineteenth century, has had the longest-lasting effects. Colonialism was also supported by diffusionist concepts about the spread of civilisation, whether from ancient Egypt, the lost continent of Atlantis or outer space, which added a layer of prejudice by assuming that indigenous peoples were incapable of generating 'civilisation' independently (Chapter 1).

The work of a number of anthropologists, especially Barth (1969), on ethnicity, has been most influential on archaeologists by showing that ethnicity as an identity is multifaceted. Ethnic identity may change, or be expressed differently, particularly in opposition to external identities (Jones 1996); for example, the tribal identities of Africa were often only strongly formed and expressed in contrast to the colonial powers that they encountered (Jones 2007: 50). If we consider the issue in modern terms an individual might have a multitude of different identities – male, black, English, Northumbrian, African-Caribbean, western European – which are expressed in different circumstances according to which other people they are with. Some of these labels only take on an 'ethnic' identity if expressed in contrast or opposition to other 'ethnic' identities. Such concepts, together with postcolonialism (above: p. 279) have led on to the development of ideas such as the existence of 'discrepant' identities in Roman Britain. Mattingly (2004; 2006) argues that the varied archaeological record of the Roman province reflects regional and varied identities, rather than a uniform Romano-British identity, let alone a 'Roman' or 'native' (Celtic) ethnicity. Furthermore, individuals and communities could

have possessed a range of overlapping identities like those modern examples listed above (Fig. 6.6).

6.5.3 Gender

● key references: Meskell, 'Archaeologies of identity' 2001; Moser, 'Archaeological representation' 2001; Gilchrist, *Gender and archaeology* 1999; Nelson, *Handbook of gender archaeology* 2006; Gero and Conkey, *Engendering archaeology: women and prehistory* 1991.

… naming something can be a very powerful way of setting it aside and diminishing its influence. For example, 'gender archaeology' has become normalised within archaeology as a discrete subcategory of the discipline, at least partly neutralising the power and politics of a feminist approach.

(Denning 2000: 214)

Gender in archaeology, like ethnicity and indigenous rights, is an aspect of the postmodern concern with **otherness** which promotes an inclusive attitude to groups in society who face prejudice. An interest in gender is not equivalent to feminism and does not seek to promote equality by ignoring genuine differences. At first the subject looked at masculine/feminine or male/female divisions by seeing gender as a cultural concept and sex as biologically determined, but anthropological and historical studies undermine a simple binary divide between men and women; there are numerous cases of people being viewed as third or cross-genders (Gilchrist 1999: 54–78). These concepts are easier to understand now that our own society is becoming more familiar with bisexuality and transgendered individuals. Gender studies had taken on a predominantly feminist dimension because female archaeologists saw it as a perspective which males ignored. This made gender studies an ideal arena for postmodern approaches that explored power, exclusion, social practices and artistic representations of bodies or sexuality. An interest in otherness is accompanied by a rejection of **essentialism**: the idea that there is some basic enduring

Figure 6.10 The search continues for new fossils to help increase our understanding of species intermediate between apes and humans. Much of the skeleton of an australopithecine around three million years old (commonly known as Lucy) was found at Afar in Ethiopia in 1974, followed in 1978 by the discovery of fossil footprints of a similar age at Laetoli in Tanzania (Turnbaugh *et al.* 1999: 231–2). This life-sized model was created for an exhibition about human evolution in the Yorkshire Museum in 2001 to illustrate these small ape-like hominins who walked upright. However, knowledge about their behaviour is complete guesswork, and is largely based on observations of modern primates such as chimpanzees. This model may make them appear more 'human' than 'ape' by suggesting a family group consisting of a strong man protecting a woman and child. Does it also have (perhaps unconsciously) a rather conservative ideological role, suggesting that the two-parent family unit – with a dominant male – is an ancient and 'natural' way of life? Alison Jolly has commented on a similar model: 'Lucy is judged female just because she/he

was petite. ... If australopithecines lived in fission–fusion, male-bonded groups like chimps, the females may well have mated promiscuously. ... Only later, long after the evolution of both concealed ovulation and bipedality, would more monogamous bonds lead to private sex and a father's paternal obligations to his own beloved young. ... One story ... that has not, I think, been seriously proposed is that the little female was in estrus and waggling her bottom at somebody who followed after, where the first had been' (Jolly 1999: 357, 364–5). There is a clear message: every picture of the past is an artefact of the present and will embody modern concepts (Moser 1998); awareness of gender, ethnicity and politics can at least make us more thoughtful about ways in which archaeology is presented to the public. (Yorkshire Museum, York)

property of masculinity or femininity that can be looked for in different times and places on a comparative basis (**Fig. 6.10**).

> The major lesson that has been learned is that gender never stands still: boundaries and categories are transient, identity contingent, knowledge incomplete. Gender archaeology is no longer content with cross-cultural definitions of prestige, binary categories and the sexual division of labour, but seeks gender as difference, the private experiences and sensations of being a man or woman, their complementarity and competition through the lifecourse. The gendered past is a land of permeable borders, ripe for exploration.
>
> (Gilchrist 1999: 149)

Two interpretations of early Stone Age carved stone objects provide entertaining examples of unconscious masculine attitudes. Artefacts with two rounded protrusions were classified as 'breast pendants' for many years, but if rotated through 90° could equally represent penises and testicles (Kehoe 1991a). 'Venus' figurines carved around 25000 BC were supposedly given exaggerated female characteristics to symbolise fertility. However, a study of the physical proportions of modern women shows that the figurines fitted into a normal range of obesity (Duhard 1991); interpretation as 'cult figurines' had been made in comparison to an idealised (male?) perception of slim young women. The reality of life as a prehistoric woman is conveyed more clearly by the pathology of injuries caused by hard work, rather than artistic representations (Grauer and Stuart-Macadam 1998). At Abu Hureyra, Syria, the transition from hunting/gathering to farming may have led to a dramatic increase in arthritis in women's backs and feet caused by the repetitive stresses of kneeling down for long periods to grind corn.

One reaction to the male dominance of the modern world is to propose that a different kind of society existed in the past. Marija Gimbutas, an authority on European prehistory, gave progressively greater emphasis to the concept of a Great Goddess from the 1960s to the 1990s (Gimbutas 1991; see biographical notes, Chapman 1998). In the 1960s and 1970s megalithic stone monuments were seen as expressions of societies who possessed sophisticated mathematical and astronomical skills strongly associated with male practitioners today. She welcomed a shift towards emphasis on the *purpose* of their alignments with the solar and lunar calendar: 'An ideology based on belief in an unending and returning cycle is disclosed: birth, life, death, rebirth. The tombs and sanctuaries are permeated with the idea of regeneration of life powers that depend on the Cosmic Mother' (quoted in Meaden 1991: 10). Gimbutas contrasted the feminine attributes of the Goddess unfavourably with machismo in a way that echoes the 'New Age' philosophies of California, where she was based in her later years (Meskell 1995; Goodison and Morris 1998):

> ... she was Provider throughout the immense period of time which was the Neolithic and Bronze Ages, an era which for Britain, Ireland and Brittany was largely a time of tranquillity. She ruled over a classless, balanced society, until the convulsions of the Iron Age brought widespread fortifications to hilltops following invasions by male-ruling, God-dominated warrior groups – the so-called 'heroic' societies. Thus ended the serenity of the Age of the Goddess. So began the Age of Wars which has lasted to this day.
>
> (Gimbutas, quoted in Meaden 1991: 214)

The widespread archaeological evidence of trauma on Neolithic and Bronze Age human remains, caused by interpersonal violence, alongside other evidence for warfare from these periods (Christensen 2004; Osgood 2005), does not fit with such a tranquil vision, however.

General problems of sexual inequality affect archaeology in much the same way as other professions, for the same underlying reasons. Competition for careers in museums, universities or field archaeology does not favour people who have stepped off the promotions ladder to raise families; this is where feminism can stimulate changes in attitudes. Feminist approaches are challenging the ideals and approaches of archaeology as a discipline, pointing out, for example, that many of the ways in which archaeologists conduct themselves on fieldwork, including styles of dress and a stress on the physicality, are distinctively 'masculine' in their approach (Moser 2007). Whether gender archaeology has really had the impact many would have hoped for is open to debate; many general books on archaeology still neglect gender as an aspect of the past (Nelson 2006: 16).

6.5.4 Artefacts: biographies, materiality, fragmentation and personhood

- key references: Chapman, *Fragmentation in archaeology* 2000; Meskell, *Archaeologies of materiality* 2005; Taylor, 'Materiality' 2008: 297–320; Jones, 'Into the future' 2008: 89–114; Appadurai, *The social life of things* 1986; Miller, 'Artefacts and the meaning of things' 1994; Hoskins, *Biographical objects: how things tell the story of people's lives* 1998.

> ... like the body, material things are a medium through which we create ourselves and understand other people and hence an inescapable element of social reproduction.
>
> (Robb 2005: 6)

The general point is that persons require things to make and transform themselves.

... Just as persons make things, things make persons. The dualistic fashion in which we have a tendency to think of persons as active subjects and things as passive objects hinders an understanding of the manner in which material metaphors work in relation to persons and their self-knowledge and understanding of the world.

(Tilley 1999: 262)

Many archaeologists have found the model of the production and use of artefacts known as the *chaîne opératoire* (**Fig. 5.12**) insufficient for explaining the roles played by objects in human societies. Ideas developed in anthropology, notably Arjun Appadurai, *The social life of things* (1986), led archaeologists to think in terms of the **biography of objects** (Kopytoff 1986; Hoskins 1998), whether in the contemporary world or in the past. In other words, artefacts have stories, ideas and histories associated with them which relate to the humans who make, use and exchange them. Anthropological studies by Bronislaw Malinowski (1922) and Marcel Mauss (1925) demonstrated that objects which at first sight appeared to be used in trade were actually part of complex social relationships that went far beyond purely economic functions. The anthropologist Franz Boas, in the late nineteenth century, described a kind of ceremonial feast known as the **potlatch** where artefacts might be deliberately destroyed to indicate social status in terms of what a person or community could afford to destroy or give away, rather than hoard. This very different way of looking at possessions has been influential in explaining archaeological finds well beyond the regions of North America where the practice was first identified (e.g. Bradley 1982; Ratjhe 2002). These concepts have implications for social motivations behind many exchange networks: why were polished stone axes exchanged over such long distances in Europe and why were some kinds of stone more desirable than others (Bradley and Edmonds 1993; Moore 2007)? What kinds of meanings and stories were associated with objects as they passed from hand to hand? Artefact biographies are linked closely to agency: individuals act in ways which shape the artefacts (and also the landscapes) around them in different ways, but at the same time they are shaped *by* them (above: p. 283).

A further related concept is the **fragmentation** of both human and animal remains and of artefacts (Chapman 2000; Chapman and Gydarska 2007). Chapman (2000) has revealed that, in a range of societies, objects such as pots, shells or quern stones (mill stones) were broken deliberately and that the fragments were then distributed between people, as for example in the breaking and redistribution of pottery in the Balkan Neolithic. The same phenomenon has been recognised in societies in which the remains of deceased humans were divided up; some parts were taken away while others were deposited in graves or elsewhere (Fowler 2004: 40–1, 94–6). This has been argued for the interrupted-ditched enclosures of the later fifth millennium BC in eastern Germany, where apparent meeting places have a range of disposals of human remains, from intact burials to isolated bones. Human remains are sometimes associated with animal bones and artefacts, possibly reflecting the dispersed identities of these groups (Hofmann and Whittle 2008: 296–8). Thus, whenever fragmentary artefacts are discovered by excavation we must be careful to assess whether they were simply discarded as rubbish, or whether their breaking and deposition was deliberate. Complex social behaviour of this kind may reflect a variety of belief systems; the form of intentional burial that resulted is known as **structured deposition** (Hill 1995).

Recent research has moved away from empirical studies of artefacts (such as those described in Chapter 5) to explore the complex relationships between people and things (Meskell 2005: chapter 1). The concept of **materiality** has also become influential in recent archaeological studies of material culture (Meskell 2005), including not just artefacts but also architecture and landscapes (Tilley 2004; DeMarrais *et al.* 2004). Materiality is a broad term which encompasses the nature and properties of materials and how people relate to them in emotional, conceptual and tactile ways, rather than perceiving materials only in technological terms. Humans are, in turn, shaped by their experiences of objects:

> The concepts of engagement and materialization bring attention to material culture and to the activities and behaviour by means of which humans interact with and construct their social worlds. Both approaches downplay an analytical separation between mind and matter, or 'idealist' versus 'materialist' approaches.
>
> (DeMarrais *et al.* 2004: 1)

In landscape archaeology, ideas of materiality relate closely to phenomenology, which examines how people experienced and viewed landscapes (Tilley 2004). In an examination of the menhirs (standing stones) of Brittany, dating from the fifth to the third millennium BC, Chris Tilley proposed that the qualities of different types and forms of stone may have had different meanings, such as the expression of fertility and growth, for the people who erected them (Tilley 2004: 33–86).

Other anthropological ideas allow us to explore material culture to find out how social relations were arranged in the past. Concepts such as **commensality** consider whether eating was an individual or a communal activity, and what feasting may have played in past societies (Bray 2003). Do the large bronze cauldrons and flesh-hooks found widely in Late Bronze Age Europe imply feasting (Needham and Bowman 2005)? Did increasing use of large ceramic platters in the Late Roman period reflect a move towards sharing a meal, rather than serving individual portions as part of more formal dining (Hawthorne 1997)? This in turn might ask us to consider how such changes related to rearrangements of social relationships: '... the difference between eating from a communal pot and having one's own plate is quite a fundamental one' (Cool 2007: 73).

Many new ways of looking at the role and meaning of material culture in human experience are related to **personhood** (Fowler 2004). This approach lies within postprocessual archaeology, but moves on from agency by recognising that many societies conceptualise the individual person in far more complex ways than those with which we are familiar in the Western world. For example, in Melanesia, the boundaries of the person and relationships with objects are not clearly defined; even animals and objects can be 'persons' (Fowler 2004: 6, 33–4). Personhood thus has much in common with the idea of biographies of objects as both concepts emphasise the active role of material culture in forming social relationships.

Although these approaches to material and people are part of a broader postprocessual archaeology, they can by no means be attributed to a single 'school of thought'. They have not even become standard approaches to archaeology in Britain or America, let alone other parts of the world (Shennan 2004).

6.5.5 Conflict, compromise or pluralism?

- key references: Holtorf and Karlsson, *Philosophy and archaeological practice* 2000; Johnson, *Archaeological theory* 2010: 216–35.

The original claims of phenomenology, structuralism and critical theory to disclose 'deep' or 'hidden' meanings behind the play of language are being increasingly challenged from within and without. But at this point in time, it is impossible to tell whether the 'postmodern turn' represents an ephemeral fad of Parisian dilettantism, the much rumoured 'end of philosophy', the last intellectual death-rattle of post-industrial capitalism or, like the new physics, a discovery of revolutionary models of understanding.

> (Kearney 1994: 9)

On one level, we are seeking to imagine the *presents* of a very broad range of human societies and the ways in which people in those societies saw their place in the world. On another, we are drawing upon the *pasts* of contemporary societies and thus affecting our own conditions of future possibilities and contributing to the ability of people today to reflect upon themselves.

(Gardner 2004: 12)

Most of the contributors to Holtorf and Karlsson's *Philosophy and archaeological practice* (2000) consciously avoided pursuing old conflicts between processualism and postprocessualism. Instead they introduced and examined an extraordinarily wide range of philosophers and intellectual traditions with the intention of seeing how they might actually be applied in archaeological practice, rather than purely theoretical discussion. In their introduction the editors rejected a number of attempts to find a middle ground between processual and postprocessual archaeologies and the introduction of the term 'interpretive'. These represented 'a continuation of the old discussion in new guises', whereas 'diversity of theoretical positions together with continuous discussion about concrete issues is the key to keeping archaeology alive and worthwhile' (*ibid.*: 6). One contributor to the volume, John Bintliff (a vocal critic of extreme postprocessualism in the past) proposed a solution drawn from the philosophy of Ludwig Wittgenstein and the 'structural' approach to long-term history implemented by Fernand Braudel. Wittgenstein's writing was complex and austere but focused on his conclusion that most problems in philosophy were actually problems of language, which was given meaning by the way it was used, not by some underlying structure of signs. As explained by Bintliff:

> … language is embedded in human practices – it gets its meaning from the various jobs it does in furthering forms of life. Different ways of discussing the world can now include imaginary or false understandings: the point is not their relation to the reality they describe … but the job the words serve within a particular kind of discourse or 'language-game' each with its own rules of performance and each with a real-life role in the maintenance of our social and cultural life.

(Bintliff 2000: 157–8)

Thus, Wittgenstein's concepts, developed well before his death in 1951, have many resonances among the ideas about language and meaning associated with much more recent post-structuralists.

What did Bintliff draw from Wittgenstein's approach to language? Primarily that it is not necessary to solve conflict by means of compromise; different approaches to archaeology may be considered as discourses or language-games appropriate to different archaeological problems. 'It allows you quite legitimately and through a process of justified reasoning to be both a processualist *and* a post-processualist, without sacrificing your commitment to treasured standpoints associated with each position' (2000: 161). Bintliff went on to define kinds of discourse that could be used in different archaeological situations or for tackling different archaeological questions: a science discourse for measuring and describing; a biological discourse for an ecological perspective; a functionalist discourse for studying human adaptation to social structures; a culturalist discourse concentrating on language and symbols; a political discourse for discussion in the ideological language of (for example) Marxism or feminism; and a religious discourse for examining engagement with the supernatural (*ibid.*: 163–4). Lest all of these discourses should remain entirely separate, he emphasised the virtues of an approach that he has been using for many years derived from the French *Annales* school of history, particularly that of Fernand Braudel (Bintliff 1991, 2004). Braudel (1972) described actions and processes; some short-term (*événements*: such as politics or actions of individuals), many too extended to be visible in individual lifetimes (*longue durée*: geological history, long-term changes in population). 'Conjunctures' between them produce a variety of unplanned historical outcomes or events (Bintliff 1999). Bintliff suggested that 'it now seems admitted by most participants in historical and archaeological debates about interpretation of the past, that explanations have to be created using many different voices, methods, kinds of information. It would be a mistake to believe that any one discourse can offer, in advance, the dominant factor that drives a particular past event or trend – if any *one* factor is ever likely to do anyway' (Bintliff 2000: 164). Thus, diversity becomes a virtue, not a defect, and the paradox of the multiple discourses may be answered by weaving them together into a composite picture of the past according to which questions they are best at answering.

6.6 ARCHAEOLOGY AND THE PUBLIC

> Archaeology … remains significant … because it allows us to recruit past people and what they leave behind for a range of contemporary human interests, needs and desires.
>
> (Holtorf 2005: 6)

Looking at archaeological theory and the wider intellectual context in which it developed helps us to clarify our own points of view and guard against an unthinking imposition of values and preoccupations on other societies – past or present. The reaction against modernism in the late twentieth century is not limited to post-structural literary theorists or postprocessual archaeologists. Questioning underlying ideologies and supposedly 'natural' human behaviour encourages concern about environmental problems that seem to result from industrial capitalism (such as climate change), but also arouses suspicions about Romantic attractions to primitive lifestyles, whether those of modern peoples such as the Yanamamo Indians of the Amazon Forest or supposedly egalitarian and peaceful prehistoric societies. Prosperity and education have raised awareness of the rights of Western individuals to a very high degree and the social background of people who participate in archaeology is increasingly diverse. Sites are studied and preserved by professional archaeologists and civil servants rather than the leisured churchmen and indulgent landowners of the eighteenth century. Archaeology has also incorporated gender and ethnicity as major themes in response to the rise of feminism and

multiculturalism (Cheater 1999). Managing a museum now involves difficult questions about the ownership of cultural property ranging from Classical Greek sculptures to relatively modern 'tribal' artefacts from developing nations (Reid 2002). Consideration of such issues makes it impossible for students of archaeology, or its professional exponents, to exist in isolated ivory towers. There is a risk that the professionalism of archaeological practice and discipline (see p. 107 above) and the increasingly complex theoretical concepts applied to the past (as part of postprocessualism) have divorced archaeology from the general public and amateur archaeologists (Selkirk 1997). Archaeology, like any other discipline, must take account of such claims, whether they appear valid or not. As Holtorf (2005) argues, the significance of archaeology is in how we interpret it, and in how it is understood in the present. The greatest challenge for archaeologists is to convey their findings and interpretations in an accessible way while addressing the claims of different pressure groups (such as nationalists or **pseudo-archaeologists**).

6.6.1 Heritage management: controlling the present by means of the past?

- key references: MacManamon and Hatton, *Cultural resource management in contemporary society* 1999; Smith, *Uses of heritage* 2006; Fairclough *et al.*, *The heritage reader* 2008.

> You can't change the future; it grinds out the way you never want it. But the past is like clay, soft, pliable, potent. You can make of it what you want. The trouble is the present.
>
> (Sid Chaplin, *Sam in the morning* 1965: 55)

The word 'heritage' became popular in the 1980s and 'heritage management' developed as a major industry in many areas of the world, employing archaeologists who would have formerly only have been able to make their careers in universities or academic museums. Many heritage professionals (especially in the USA) prefer to apply the less emotive description **cultural resource management** (CRM) to the conservation and presentation of sites, landscapes and artefacts. The definition and identification of heritage, its management and its presentation to the public, have generated considerable critical analysis; Robert Hewison's 1987 study *The heritage industry* had the significant subtitle *Britain in a climate of decline*. Anyone with an interest in ideology will ask questions such as: Whose heritage? Who will manage it? For the benefit of whom? Does a dominant social or political elite exploit heritage to justify its modern position by claiming that it already existed in the past, in the same way that aristocrats refer back to noble ancestors? While it may be easy to spot this process at work in the past – for example, in Nazi Germany or Soviet Russia – it is harder to detect in one's own cultural environment (Brett 1996). Indeed, the term 'heritage' is sufficiently broad and vague to allow its widespread appropriation, for tourism, the marketing of old-fashioned goods, as well as by archaeologists (Schofield 2008: 17). According to many of the postprocessual concepts discussed above, 'heritage' is part of a wider process of forming identities and reflecting cultural values. Until recently, 'heritage' was dominated by Western concepts of the value of 'things' that were not shared by many non-Western peoples, who understand its role in their past and present very differently (Smith 2006).

The rise of heritage has coincided with the move towards a postindustrial society in which leisure and the service sector have replaced manufacturing. Many private industries have opened visitor attractions or museums with the dual purpose of raising their public profile and increasing income, from a global brand such as Disney (Florida and Paris) to a traditional craft industry making fishing-tackle (Alnwick, Northumberland). Some projects have been financed by property developers whose principal activities normally destroy archaeological sites; others have benefited from the injection of government funds into areas that have suffered a decline in heavy industries such as mining or ship-building. In Britain, more than £4.3 billion has been spent by the Heritage Lottery Fund

(since the establishment of a national lottery in 1995), some of it on spectacular new projects (**Fig. 6.11**). At the same time, national and local governments – committed (in theory) to reducing public expenditure through efficiency, deregulation and lower taxes – have had to establish an extensive bureaucracy to cope with legislation about ancient sites, and with guidelines about planning permission for developments affecting historic buildings or archaeological sites (see Chapter 3).

6.6.2 Archaeology and the State

- key references: Wheatley, *World Heritage Sites* 1997; Willems *et al.*, *Archaeological heritage management in the Netherlands* 1997; Brisbane and Wood, *A future for our past? An introduction to heritage studies* 1996; Tainter, 'American cultural resource management' 2004; Neumann and Sanford, *Cultural resources archaeology* 2001: chapter 2.

Many states identify and protect their archaeological monuments through some form of registration. Pitt Rivers initiated the process of guardianship of **scheduled sites** in Britain in 1882 (largely at his own expense) on behalf of His Majesty's Office of Works. In 2002, the National Heritage Act extended scheduling to include archaeological sites at sea – for example, shipwrecks and the remains of military aircraft. In North America, the US National Register of Historic Places (NHPA, based on the Historic Sites Act of 1935 and formalised in 1966) offers protection to designated buildings and archaeological sites, while the Antiquities Act (1906) and Archaeological Resource Protection Act (ARPA) of 1979 provided further protection for sites on federal land (Jameson 2008a). In both England and the USA, such protection is legally binding; destruction, or even unlicensed archaeological investigation, can be punished by legal action.

Serious questions arise in protecting archaeological monuments. Which 'sites' should be protected? Decisions on which are worthy of preservation are often based on criteria that are themselves subjective (see **Box 6.6**). Approximately 31,500 'sites' are scheduled in England, a small

Figure 6.11 Demolition in the 1970s of Victorian terraced houses at Wallsend, Tyne and Wear, gave an opportunity to excavate an entire Roman fort at the eastern end of Hadrian's Wall. Only part of the site was redeveloped at that time, however. In the 1990s the National Lottery generated a new source of money for heritage projects; a successful bid for funds allowed Tyne and Wear Museums to re-excavate the remaining part of the site and consolidate it for public display. In addition reconstructions of a length of Hadrian's Wall and a working Roman bath house were built close by. Some redundant shipyard buildings were converted into a visitor centre, while an uncompromisingly modern tower was added to provide a viewing platform. Thus, a Roman fort that was completely invisible in 1970 in a location dominated by ship-building became the centre of a new leisure attraction in 2001 – by which time most of the local shipyards had closed. Lottery funding was absolutely essential to this attempt to generate tourism in an otherwise unpromising urban environment adapting to a post-industrial age. (Segedunum Roman Fort, Baths and Museum)

fraction of more than a million that are known. The definition of a 'site' is highly problematic (see p. 52; Tainter 2004: 439); can an entire town or landscape be a 'site'? Visible features, such as enclosure ditches or walls, are usually regarded as limits of the extent of a monument, but significant archaeological remains often exist beyond such artificial boundaries. The development of archaeology shows how cultural factors have influenced decisions about which monuments are worthy of protection (**Box 6.8**). Earlier scholars thought high-status sites were more important and informative than 'ordinary' settlements, which most archaeologists would now expect to reveal just as much about past societies (see **Box 3.4**). Many heritage managers now regard excavation with some suspicion, because it is an essentially destructive process (Chapter 3). This means that it is increasingly hard to justify and to obtain permission to excavate the best-known and well-preserved sites. Others believe that the process

of excavating such monuments creates more knowledge than it destroys; this goes against the prioritisation of preservation over excavation, characteristic of English Heritage and **Valletta Convention** policy (Pitts 2009: 193).

Protection and preservation of ancient monuments is not just driven by archaeological factors; the development of the management of English archaeology by the State reveals ways in which different governments influence perceptions of a country's heritage. By the 1950s the Office of Works had been replaced by the rather more democratic-sounding Ministry of Public Building and Works. The cultivation of a positive image continued in the 1970s with the invention of the Department of the Environment, followed by the creation of the impressively named Historic Buildings and Monuments Commission, and the removal of responsibility for ancient monuments from the Department of the Environment in 1984 into the hands of English Heritage. In line

BOX 6.6   **Heritage management: state protection**

Deciding which archaeological sites should receive legal protection is not as straightforward as it might sound. English Heritage's criteria for scheduling an archaeological site provide a good example of the questions that might be posed when deciding whether to protect a monument:

- Extent of survival

- Current condition

- Rarity

- Representivity, either through diversity or because of one important attribute

- Importance of the period to which the monument dates

- Fragility

- Connection to other monuments, or group value

- Potential to contribute to our information, understanding and appreciation

- Extent of documentation enhancing the monument's significance

(English Heritage 2009)

Many of the categories are highly subjective. For example, 'importance of the period' may well change as research interests shift and new finds provoke reanalysis of individual periods (see Box 3.4). The question of 'value' in archaeological remains is likely to be culturally specific and to reflect changing archaeological and political priorities (Darvill 2005). The NHPA in the US has similar criteria for the significance of a monument, although the emphasis is on the association of a monument with historical events or people. This may reflect a categorisation that prioritises historical rather than prehistoric monuments, although it also includes a broad category 'having yielded, or likely to yield, information important in prehistory or history' – a far broader definition than that used by English Heritage (Neumann and Sanford 2001: 33).

with Conservative ideology, this organisation was independent of the government, but overall control of the purse-strings remained in the hands of the Department of the Environment. This department was rebranded first in 1992 as the Department of National Heritage, and again in 1997 by the new Labour government as the Department for Culture, Media and Sport – altogether more modern-sounding and populist without the 'h-word', and with 'environment' moved to a different department.

English Heritage (EH) had brought many changes to sites in its care open to the public: custodians wearing sweatshirts bearing EH's corporate logo, bright new ticket offices, shops containing an attractive range of souvenirs, and even cafés. Similar developments took place beyond England with the creation of Historic

Scotland and its Welsh counterpart, CADW. EH organises not only historical re-enactments at major sites but also open-air concerts and plays. The result is that it is difficult for a visitor to distinguish between a site in the care of the State and one owned by a private organisation such as the National Trust (**Box 6.7**).

EH still retains responsibility for enforcing the legal protection of sites and historic buildings and pays for a small number of excavations and research projects. However, following an ideological shift in the 1980s towards privatisation and competitive tendering (which had already happened in the USA) (Thomas 1998: 555–73; Adovasio and Carlisle 1988), much of this work is carried out indirectly by contract archaeologists and self-employed consultants. Most of the financial burden for excavation and

BOX 6.7 Tourism and heritage: Kenilworth Castle

Heritage management is often as much a matter of encouraging tourism and visitor numbers as the preservation of archaeological monuments. At Kenilworth Castle in Warwickshire, English Heritage have spent £3 million on aspects of the site related to Queen Elizabeth I and her 'favourite', Robert Dudley, Earl of Leicester. Part of this money was spent on conservation and new exhibitions in the castle's Tudor gatehouse. More than £2 million was spent on a controversial attempt to recreate the elaborate terrace and garden described in Robert Langham's contemporary account of Elizabeth's visit in 1575 (Furnivall 1907: 48–53). This project was a matter of simulation, rather than reconstruction, since no trace of the original layout was recovered by excavation to verify Langham's account, apart from the position of a fountain and some chips of the Italian marble from which the fountain was made.

Some people question whether English Heritage should spend a large amount of money (much of it from taxpayers) on this kind of simulation instead of concentrating on conserving and conducting research into the surviving structures. Should gardens remain the speciality of charitable organisations (such as the National Trust) and privately financed country houses that rely heavily on them for attracting much-needed income from visitors? Or should English Heritage also compete for visitors in this way, given the location of Kenilworth in 'Shakespeare country' near Warwick and Stratford-upon-Avon?

English Heritage's publicity declared that the Elizabethan garden was, 'once again, fit for a Queen'. In contrast, a reviewer on a garden history website regretted that the wooden features did not match the quality of Tudor craftsmanship: 'This project looks as though it belongs in an upscale garden centre near the M25' (Turner 2009). The judgements of visitors will vary, as will the opinions of historians about the reliability of Langham's description of the temporary garden and its structures and ornaments constructed in 1575. There is, however, no doubt that the new wooden aviary, obelisks and fences, the marble fountain, and the elaborate flowerbeds will require expensive maintenance for the foreseeable future. Will the costs be recovered from increased numbers of visitors to Kenilworth Castle, or will less glamorous conservation and preservation projects elsewhere suffer? (Photograph: Kevin Greene)

publication is now placed upon developers, who, as part of the process laid down in a series of Planning Policy documents (such as PPG 16, the new PPS and MORPHE in England: see Chapter 3), must commission reports on the impact of their proposals upon the environment (including archaeology). Independent consultants may bid for the contract to write 'desk-based assessments' and to carry out whatever rescue excavation for recording is required (above: p. 106). Archaeological and commercial interests collide here, for competition drives down prices and a developer has a vested interest in obtaining an impact report that plays down the harmful effects of whatever project is proposed. Fortunately, archaeology attracts considerable publicity and many developers take this opportunity to improve their public image by devoting a few thousand pounds to an excavation.

State involvement in British archaeology grew in little more than one century from informal supervision of a small number of sites (through cooperation with sympathetic landowners) to implementing planning legislation and providing a major focus for leisure and tourism. Visitors to sites are encouraged to feel that they are participating in their heritage, rather than being allowed the privilege of access to State property. Remembering that Pitt Rivers saw archaeology and museums as a means of discouraging popular desires for radical political change (above p. 262) it is only natural to ask what ideological purpose is served by the current style of presentation (Thompson 2006). Questions are being asked both in Britain and in the USA about the broader involvement of different communities within archaeology and heritage (Jameson 2008b; Marshall 2008). Have some groups and sections of the public been excluded? How can heritage and archaeology engage with all of the general public in today's diverse and mobile society?

6.6.3 Museums: from Art Gallery to 'Experience'

- key references: Hooper-Greenhill, *Museum, media, message* 1999; Denford, *Representing archaeology in museums* 1997; McManus, *Archaeological displays and the public: museology and interpretation* 1996; Jameson, *The reconstructed past* 2004.

An ancient site or historic building presented to the public will have been preserved as far as possible in its original form, but a museum is an entirely modern creation with a style of display determined by its directors and designers. Their ideas are reinforced by the selection of items for display and by the kind of information offered in labels and other documentation. Older museum displays are inseparable from art galleries when they group artefacts by period and place of origin and present them as beautiful objects to be contemplated with minimal documentation. A connoisseur of art is expected to be well informed about the significance and history of a painting and to be able to place it in context by means of a concise and inconspicuous label giving the name of the artist and perhaps where and when it was painted. Archaeological museums also once assumed that visitors only needed to know the origin, date and function of an artefact on display, but in the twentieth century they gradually attempted to provide more information through pictures of contemporary sites, explanatory diagrams and extended text commentaries and labels. Understanding was enhanced by placing objects into context with the help of models and reconstructions which might include human figures as well as objects. Many museums now include computer terminals among their displays so that visitors may explore archives of further information for themselves, while 'virtual museums' that exist only on the Internet attract thousands of people who might never visit a traditional museum (Higgins *et al.* 1997).

Archaeologists are very aware that the way the past is presented by museums and in the media (see below: p. 306) is extremely powerful in shaping a society's ideas about its own past (Smiles and Moser 2005). Much criticism has been directed at 'heritage centres' where 'The past is often mediated as a piece of theatre and transformed into something that it clearly never was' (Walsh 1991: 286). This is particularly visible at those that focus upon the recent industrial past,

---

BOX 6.8
Managing our heritage in the 21st century: climate change and archaeology

The reality and impact of climate change (especially when given the more accurate and dramatic label 'global warming') have become important for all of us. There has been a growing realisation that sacrifices in the lifestyles of Western societies are necessary, both to limit CO_2 emissions in the short term, and to move towards a sustainable economy in the longer term. Archaeologists can make a valuable contribution to discussions about the effects of climate change by examining shifts in living conditions that affected humans in the past (Chapter 5; Burroughs 2005: 283–302). Archaeologists are themselves affected by climate change because the archaeological heritage is vulnerable both to the effects of global warming and to measures aimed at coping with it (Bell 2004; English Heritage 2008b). Rising sea levels are endangering sites in many areas, for example the Mesolithic sites of California's Channel Islands (Curry 2009); elsewhere, severe storms have increased coastal erosion that is

destroying archaeological sites, notably prehistoric sites in Scotland (Chitty 2009). Warmer temperatures will also lead to shrinking glaciers, already very evident in the Swiss Alps, and the thawing of permafrost in Siberia. Although these changes will reveal long-hidden archaeological remains (such as the famous prehistoric Ice Man), many more will be destroyed without record (Curry 2009). Heritage management bodies around the world are drawing up reports to assess which threats are likely to have most impact (Collette 2007; English Heritage 2008b), but the scale and pace of these is currently far from clear.

Whilst the effects of climate change provide an additional threat to the archaeological resource, preventing them will also create a new set of threats. The pressure on governments and international bodies to reduce carbon emissions requires changes in energy sources. In Britain an increase in the number of wind farms in upland areas may damage peat bogs which have acted as a protective cover to thousands of prehistoric sites, while underwater turbines and tidal barrages may destroy shipwrecks and well-preserved waterlogged remains on the coasts of estuaries, notably that of the river Severn (**Fig. 3.13**). Some archaeologists are against such schemes because of the damage they will cause, but others argue that archaeologists, like other conservationists and environmentalists, will have to make tough choices between preserving archaeology and exploiting renewable energy sources. All aspects of cultural resource management involve difficult choices which have to take account of a range of factors, few of which only affect archaeologists (Roseff 2001). (NMR crown copyright: English Heritage)

---

such as the collection of buildings re-erected at the North of England Open Air Museum at Beamish, County Durham. A 1999 publicity leaflet stated: 'We'll take you back for a great day out. Beamish is unique. We're no ordinary museum but a living, working experience of life as it was in the Great North at the turn of the century.' The celebration of coal mining and other heavy industries emphasises cheerful communities based around terraced houses and busy local shops. It makes a poignant contrast with the realities of life in contemporary north-eastern England and evokes nostalgia

Figure 6.12 The webpage advertising *Archeon*, a theme park close to Amsterdam in the Netherlands, which contains reconstructions of buildings from prehistory to the Middle Ages excavated in various parts of the Netherlands and displays involving actors in period dress. In contrast to Pseudo-archaeology (**Box 6.2**), it focuses on the ordinary rather than the exotic: 'In Archeon you can meet the living past of the Netherlands. . . . An archaeological find is usually difficult to understand. Often, there is not much more left of a building than a foundation, part of a wall painting or a discoloration of the soil. So, what did such a building look like? Who lived there? What sort of things did those people do? In Archeon you can step right into such a building. Meet the people from days long gone and take part in their daily activities (text of 2001 leaflet).

and a sense of the loss. Yet it was the horrors of nineteenth-century industrial towns that stimulated most of the reforms of government, health and social administration that came to be valued in the twentieth century. Does a museum like Beamish simply reinforce the politics of the New Right, by idealising 'Victorian values' and glorifying a world where trade unions and socialism had not yet challenged the comfortable class-values of landowners and industrialists?

Despite such problems, museum curators stress the importance of accurate reconstructions of archaeological monuments for 'enabling visitors to make emotional connections to archaeological and historical records that help them understand and relate to the context, meaning and significance of the resource' (Jameson 2004: 13). Without such understanding and engagement of the public, wider dissemination of archaeological knowledge would be much harder (**Fig. 6.12**).

6.6.4 Heritage management and heritage practice: the case of Stonehenge

- key references: Chippindale *et al.*, *Who owns Stonehenge?* 1990; Chippindale, *Stonehenge complete* 2004; Bender, *Stonehenge: making space* 1998; Wainwright, 'The Stonehenge we deserve' 2000; Richards, *Stonehenge: the story so far* 2007; Stone, 'Stonehenge: a final solution?' 2008; Pitts, 'A year at Stonehenge' 2009.

> Beneath its weathered old surface, a superficially straightforward site is just one item in a compound of powerful ingredients: archaeology, yes, and landscape history, but, overpowering the delicacies of scholarship, a stronger and bubbling brew of issues concerning intellectual freedom, rational and intuitive knowledge, preservation, presentation and access, the place and role of religious beliefs, the State and its dissidents, the rights of dispossessed ethnic minorities, and even the concept of ownership.
>
> (Chippindale 1990: 9)

Everything that is currently known, or believed, about Stonehenge is the result of almost nine centuries of speculation, observation and excavation, guided by changing fashions and approaches. Since neither the original builders nor the purpose of the structure have any direct link to the present, its popular attraction stems more from ignorance than knowledge and provides an interesting example of the problems of cultural resource management. Critical visitors to many heritage centres and theme parks, such as Beamish in north-eastern England or Jamestown, Virginia, can 'deconstruct' the interpretations presented to them fairly easily if they disagree with them. But how should prehistoric monuments disconnected from the present be presented? Why should the public take any interest in, or feel responsible for, an accidental survival from a distant past such as Stonehenge?

In his *Stonehenge complete* (2004), Christopher Chippindale requires surprisingly little space to describe Stonehenge, but devotes most of his book to following the 'modern' history of the site from the first surviving written record (AD 1130) up to the Druidic and 'hippie' festivals of the 1970s and 1980s. Archaeological study began in the sixteenth century, accelerated in the seventeenth and eighteenth with Aubrey and Stukeley (Chapter 1, pp. 13–16), and culminated in serious excavation only after 1900. Stukeley dated Stonehenge to the pre-Roman period by means of ingenious field observations (Chippindale 2004: 74–81; Burl and Mortimer 2005). This was refined to the Bronze Age in the nineteenth century, but an age in years was only achieved in the twentieth century, first by cross-dating and finally by radiocarbon dating. Excavations between 1900 and the 1950s revealed that the site had a long sequence of phases that began, according to the current calibration of radiocarbon years, in around 3000 BC (Parker-Pearson *et al.* 2009: 26). Construction of what we recognise as Stonehenge, with its massive sarsen trilithons, started around a thousand years later and was modified several times over the next thousand years. Surprisingly, most twentieth-century excavations carried out at this major site remained unpublished until 1995, when Cleal, Montague and Walker's 500-page volume gathered together all surviving evidence accumulated since 1901 – a difficult and frustrating task (Lawson 1992). Stonehenge has recently resumed its place as a focus of attention for archaeologists putting forward and testing a range of competing theories and models (Pitts 2001, 2009; Darvill 2006; Richards 2007; Parker-Pearson *et al.* 2007). One project focused on the role of the bluestones brought to the site from Wales, suggesting that they were believed to possess healing powers which attracted people to the site (Darvill 2006; Darvill and Wainwright 2009). Another project (funded by the Arts and Humanities Research Council) is making the most serious attempt to reinterpret the monument and its wider landscape through new fieldwork. Parker-Pearson has put forward theories suggesting that Stonehenge was part of a wider landscape divided between the living (related to the timber site at nearby Durrington Walls) and the dead (Stonehenge itself), connected by the River Avon (Pitts 2001:

256–8; Parker-Pearson *et al.* 2007, 2009). Despite increasing data and new radiocarbon dates from the site, many aspects remains hotly contested and no consensus has been reached on either the chronology or the role of Stonehenge (Cunliffe and Renfrew 1997; Pitts 2009).

The preparation of Chippindale's other book about the site – *Who owns Stonehenge?* (1990) – coincided with a violent confrontation between police and people (sometimes described as 'New Age travellers') who had held a free festival each year near Stonehenge from 1974 to 1984. The police sealed off all approaches to the site over the midsummer period because English Heritage and the National Trust had banned not only the festival, but the annual rituals performed by modern Druids within the stone circles; the 'Battle of the Beanfield' between police and travellers ensued, with considerable violence and damage (Worthington 2005). The 1980s ended with Stonehenge at the time of the summer solstice 'festooned in barbed-wire, surrounded by police and patrolled by privately-employed security guards. It has looked like a concentration camp, the unacceptable face of militarism in a democracy' (*ibid.*: 33). This shocking sight inspired Barbara Bender, a prehistorian already deeply interested in landscapes, to study the political issues more closely and (almost accidentally) to become involved in preparing a low-cost exhibition about the 'ownership' of Stonehenge that would include the perspective of people now excluded from the site (Bender 1998). Her book is an excellent example of 'modernism turning to challenge its own shortcomings' and should remove any suspicion that postprocessual approaches and relativism lead to emotional detachment. Stonehenge is 'a highly contentious contemporary symbol. Among the hugely varied responses to the site and the landscape, the designated custodians see it as something to be preserved as a museum piece, an artefact, a vital part of our rooted, stable, national identity. But for a small minority it is something quite different: a living site, a spiritual centre, an integral part of an alternative life-style' (Bender 1998: 9). In the spirit of reflexiveness her book included a cartoon-strip 'intellectual autobiography' to explain the formation of her own theoretical outlook.

The two recent major research projects at Stonehenge both received funds from media organisations and were closely followed and presented through television programmes, blogs and websites (Pitts 2009), which meant that powerful interest groups (from academics to pagans) laid claim to the results almost as quickly as they were found. This leads to contrasting and conflicting views. Stonehenge illustrates the problems archaeologists encounter in dealing with a wider audience: 'audience-hungry broadcasters want simple, strong stories, and hardened journalists and cynical bloggers demand that impossible proof' (Pitts 2009: 191). The recent excavators attempted to engage with the views of modern pagans and Druids (Pitts 2009), but with limited success, as there have been further demands for the reburial of ancient remains from the area (**Box 6.10**).

Roads and tunnels: presenting Stonehenge

Since its creation in 1984, English Heritage has been working with the National Trust and the Department of Transport on the problem of the busy road that runs alongside Stonehenge and its inadequate and unsightly car-park and visitor centre. The first major plan was turned down by the local planning authority and withdrawn in 1992; the government announced in 1994 that a minister would take responsibility for Stonehenge and new proposals for dealing with the local road system were produced over the next two years – and promptly declared too expensive to implement. Plans for celebrating the year 2000 with a number of prestigious projects led English Heritage to propose a Stonehenge Millennium Park, involving commercial partners and private finance, and to apply for funds raised by the newly-created National Lottery. Newspapers were told: 'It is a grand plan and inevitably, an expensive one. But with the help of the Millennium Commission, our vision can be achieved. ... the time for action is now. For Stonehenge, it's just another millennium. For millions of visitors, it will be an opportunity that cannot be missed.' The plan was turned down in 1997. A new government was elected in that year and by 1998 new road proposals had been agreed and Culture Secretary Chris Smith (the Minister responsible) chaired a new Stonehenge Steering Group. In 2000 a World Heritage Site Management Plan was launched – some sixteen years after Stonehenge had been nominated as a UNESCO World Heritage Site (WHS) – and further road schemes were put forward between 1999 and 2006. Boring a tunnel to reroute the road that runs closest to the site was deemed too expensive by the government, while a cheaper 'cut-and-cover' tunnel was rejected by English Heritage and the National Trust because of potential damage to the archaeological landscape around the monument. Some plans flouted the agreements which the government had signed up to in the 1972 UNESCO *Convention concerning the protection of the world cultural and natural heritage* (Stone 2008). In 2007 the idea of a tunnel, and changes to the roads around Stonehenge, were finally dropped by the government because of escalating costs. Since then, a scheme to construct a new visitor centre at the site has been approved by the government; it should be completed in time for the 2012 London Olympics (although the connection with this event is not clear).

Stonehenge became public property in 1918, long after the number of visitors had begun to pose problems. By the 1980s it had been recognised that conservation and management must encompass the site's surrounding landscape and other archaeological sites and a press release about the unsuccessful 1997 Millennium Park plan envisaged 'a 6,000 acre prehistoric natural wilderness containing over 450 ancient monuments, as well as Stonehenge itself'. To us, this contradictory phrase sums up the problem: it is not possible to present a piece of land that has been used intensively by large numbers of people for at least five thousand years as a 'natural wilderness'. This was underlined in 1999 when 5,000 people took advantage of the lifting of a four-mile exclusion zone to tear down the fences that were intended to restrict admission to ticket holders (Fig. 6.13). Since 2000, greater access has been permitted to those wishing to celebrate the summer solstice, and fifteen years of photographs of riot police in newspapers have to a certain

extent been replaced by positive images of people displaying unadulterated pleasure.

Preparing the 1995 edition of this book, Kevin wrote: 'Archaeology may have achieved many things in the twentieth century, but it will not be surprising if the centenary of public management at Stonehenge has to be celebrated in visitor facilities that fall a long way short of the dignity of the site.' We see no reason to change our opinion. Despite a considerable amount of consultation, at a significant cost (c £38 million), and the dramatic new discoveries made by recent projects, few changes have taken place at Stonehenge since 2000. The saga of how to protect and present one of the world's best known archaeological monuments continues (*British Archaeology* 2009). The words of Jaquetta Hawkes (1967: 174) are often quoted: 'each generation gets the Stonehenge they deserve'. What kind of Stonehenge will be left for future generations (Stone 2008: 526)?

6.6.5 The antiquities trade

- key references: Renfrew, *Loot, legitimacy and ownership* 2000; Greenfield, *The return of cultural treasures* 1996; Tubb, *Antiquities trade or betrayed: legal, ethical and conservation issues* 1995; Schmidt and McIntosh, *Plundering Africa's past* 1996; Stone and Bajjaly, *The destruction of cultural heritage in Iraq* 2008.

Destruction of sites escalated rapidly from the eighteenth century as agriculture expanded to match the rapid population growth that accompanied the Industrial Revolution, and it accelerated throughout the twentieth century with world population growth. Although a conservation ethic began to develop in Europe and North America during the nineteenth century, most archaeologists and museums regarded sites and artefacts around the Mediterranean and in the Near East and other parts of the world as a resource to be exploited for the benefit of their own countries – in the same way that colonial governments exploited labour and raw materials in their overseas possessions. This attitude left the legacy of a vast international market for works of

Figure 6.13 'It's police vs travellers again. Welcome to the English summer' (cover of the *Guardian* media magazine *The Editor*, 25 June 1999). Stonehenge is England's most famous archaeological site, despite the impossibility of knowing its original purpose and the difficulty of explaining traces of construction phases that accumulated over several thousand years. The summer solstice has attracted Druids in flowing robes since the nineteenth century, and a large number of New Age travellers and hippies from the 1970s. The response has varied from near-total exclusion in the 1990s to a more open policy from 2000. In June 1999 fencing was torn down and the monument invaded after the police's four-mile exclusion zone was declared illegal in the High Court. Stonehenge epitomises the problems of heritage management in the face of conflicting demands. Does English Heritage 'own' Stonehenge and therefore have the right (and duty) to protect it – with riot police if necessary? Should the desire of modern pagans to celebrate the midsummer sunrise be prioritised – even if it means putting the structure at risk? (South West News Service)

art, antiquities and 'tribal' material from developing nations (Brodie 1999). Public museums have a better record today for refusing to purchase items that lack proper documentation about their origins and ownership, but private collectors are not always as scrupulous; paperwork may be forged to suggest that an item came from an old collection and can be traded legally, rather than having been a recent illegal export (Gill 1997).

Ancient sites and cemeteries all over the world are systematically plundered in the search for pots, jewellery, carvings or anything else that may be sold. This problem is most serious in developing nations, where antiquities form a valuable supplement to low incomes, along with other sought-after materials such as drugs or ivory. The treasure-hunters of Africa and South America receive pitifully small rewards in comparison with the high prices that antiquities command in London and New York. The problem is not restricted to developing nations: after the end of the Cold War in 1990, architectural sculptures, mosaics and wall-paintings stolen from eastern European churches turned up in sale-rooms. Protected sites in Britain are regularly raided by illegal metal-detector operators (Dobinson and Denison 1995). The introduction of new management schemes that attempt to bring metal-detector users into the fold of archaeology, such as the Portable Antiquities Scheme in England (see Chapter 2), shows that there are ways to tailor heritage management to everyday realities.

Political insecurity provides ideal conditions for looting sites and museums, especially during wars such as those that have affected the Middle East and the Balkans in recent decades (Chapman 1994); after the Gulf and Iraq Wars, a range of famous Mesopotamian antiquities appeared on the Western art market (see **Box 6.9**). Archaeologists working in the former colonial powers may find it difficult to denounce the antiquities trade when their museums are full of items from countries that were once overseas possessions (Barringer and Flynn 1998). The British Museum has a collection formed over more than two centuries, and many of its most famous items from other countries were removed with the permission of the people or governments who 'owned' them at the time. The Elgin marbles from the Parthenon in Athens are the most celebrated example: should modern Greece recognise legal agreements with Ottoman Turkish rulers made before Greece became an independent nation, particularly now that a new museum has been constructed to house such remains (**Box 1.5**; Cook 1997; Hitchens *et al.* 1987)? Were 'gifts' and purchases from Africa or India really made between equals, without political or military pressure? An awareness of postcolonial and postprocessual archaeology helps archaeologists and museums to confront difficult ethical issues such as these.

6.6.6 Archaeology in the media

- key references: Clack and Brittain, *Archaeology and the media* 2007; Holtorf, *Archaeology is a brand* 2007.

Archaeology has been included in British television schedules since the 1950s, when established figures such as Mortimer Wheeler and Glyn Daniel took part in a panel of experts identifying ancient objects. The launch of Channel 4's *Time Team* followed a novel game-show format (Taylor 1998) in which an archaeological puzzle was to be investigated and solved in only three days. As a result, some of the

most unlikely television celebrities of the 1990s and early 2000s in Britain were the Time Team's bearded professor of archaeology (with colourful jumpers) and a 'salt of the Earth' excavator (with funny hat and West Country accent). They regularly attracted between two and four million viewers at Sunday teatime, researching an ancient site against the clock with the help of clever geophysics and occasional hindrance from the show's presenter (comic actor Tony Robinson). The popularity of pathological studies of excavated human remains, normally culminating in a full facial reconstruction of a dead individual, was popularised by the show *Meet the Ancestors* (Richards 1999). The showpiece of each programme was the delivery of a human skull to medical specialists, who first generated a 3D computer image and then created a lifelike model of the facial features. Documentaries and dramas about forensic science used in modern murder investigations, such as the popular programme CSI, are popular on both British and American television. Such programmes parallel fly-on-the-wall 'reality' television programmes that look at the lives of individual people and echo the obsession of newspapers with the private lives of minor celebrities. Is interpretive archaeology, which looks at individual experiences rather than broader social processes, an intellectual equivalent of *Hello* magazine? Are 'media archaeologists' actually *paparazzi*, invading the privacy of deceased individuals? And why do most Western societies accept the disturbance of graves and the display of human remains in museums without raising the kinds of objection made by indigenous Australians or Native North Americans? Different attitudes to human remains provide a timely reminder that the globalisation of media will produce conflicts of interest, and that archaeologists' training should include ethical awareness (**Box 6.10**; Zimmerman *et al.* 2003).

Other archaeology programmes have tended to focus on spectacular finds, narrated as exciting adventure stories (Holtorf 2007a). Many reinforce the traditional idea that most archaeologists are male, bearded outdoor types, perpetuating a vision of archaeology which is increasingly outdated and colonial (Holtorf 2005: 42; Holtorf 2007b).

BOX 6.9 Lost treasures of Iraq: war and cultural heritage

The chaos that followed the 1991 Gulf War and the subsequent Iraq War of 2003 had a devastating effect on Iraq's cultural heritage (Russell 1998; Brodie 2008; Stone and Bajjaly 2008). While the direct consequences of war may be unavoidable, the problems were made worse by Western collectors and the antiquities trade as well as by military activity. Cultural heritage is – in theory – protected during conflict by the 1954 Hague Convention (Cole 2008: 65), but this has often been ignored. In some instances cultural heritage has been deliberately targeted in warfare, as in the former Yugoslavia in the 1990s where historic buildings (especially churches and mosques) were bound up with rival national, religious or ethnic identities. In Iraq, looting of the national museum in Baghdad led to the loss of thousands of archaeological objects, some of them extremely rare. Many ended up in the hands of antiquities collectors around the world, although a proportion were found and returned to the museum. Elsewhere military camps situated on ancient cities,

including Ur and Babel, led to damage of the archaeological remains by the digging of defensive trenches (Moussa 2008). Archaeologists face ethical dilemmas when trying to protect archaeological sites and artefacts in the midst of war, when generals and politicians will have quite different priorities (Stone and Bajjaly 2008). (Photograph: John Curtis, British Museum)

Archaeology is also seen as synonymous with 'digging' and frequently portrayed as an essentially male pursuit (Holtorf 2007a). Many films also represent archaeologists as adventurers, mostly obviously in the case of Indiana Jones, and often confuse archaeology with treasure-hunting (**Fig. 6.14**). Despite the fact these are stereotypes, they are perpetuated in a range of media, including computer games such as *Tomb Raider* (Russell 2002; Holtorf 2007a). This is unhelpful, making it difficult for members of the public to distinguish between professional archaeology and treasure-hunting or 'pseudo' archaeology (Fagan 2006; see **Box 6.2**).

Fortunately, many television programmes about archaeology give a very positive image of its ability to work with laboratory scientists and geophysical surveyors and to combine scientific information with historical and/or archaeological research to produce a rounded interpretation of life in the past – frequently enhanced by artists'

reconstructions of people and sites (Holtorf 2007b: 76). Many archaeologists, such as Francis Pryor, have embraced the challenge of effective communication with the public through a range of media (TV, press, popular books), arguing that these are essential for disseminating the important contributions that archaeology makes to human knowledge (Clack and Brittain 2007).

6.7 CONCLUSION

Archaeologists involved in the everyday realities of protecting ancient sites from building construction may not be terribly interested in philosophical questions; postprocessual archaeology certainly increased the gulf between theory and practice in the 1980s and 1990s. While there are now dozens of books about archaeological theory itself, the effects of postprocessual theory

BOX 6.10 # Archaeology and ethics: the case of human remains

Engagement with the public, media involvement, the trade in antiquities, the nature of museum displays, and how we manage heritage all raise ethical questions for archaeologists. Ethics are particularly significant when dealing with human remains (Scarre and Scarre 2006; Zimmerman 2003; Cassman *et al.* 2007; Roberts 2009: 17–37). Diverse groups of people in many countries have requested the return and reburial of human remains on the basis of beliefs and ancestral connections of the kind given legal recognition by NAGPRA in the USA (p. 286). In the USA, Australia and New Zealand, these concerns have long been recognised, but only recently has reburial been more widely demanded in Britain. Whereas many medieval and postmedieval bodies have been reburied because of specific Christian or Jewish associa-

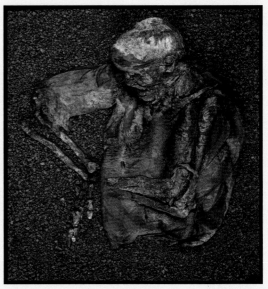

tions, few earlier remains have such direct connections (Roberts and Cox 2003). Recently, however, modern British pagans have argued that they have rights over archaeological material from prehistoric Britain. This has led to demands that excavated human bones dating from c. 3700–2000 BC (and their associated grave goods) from Avebury museum, Wiltshire, should be reburied, and that other remains, such as the Iron Age bog-body known as Lindow Man (pictured) found in Cheshire, should be 'repatriated' to their places of discovery. Ethical codes of practice have been drawn up in order to guide archaeologists in these circumstances. The Vermillion Accord was adopted by the World Archaeological Congress in 1989, and the British Association for Biological Anthropology and Osteoarchaeology has drawn up a similar guide. The Vermillion Accord states that, when dealing with human remains:

- Respect for the mortal remains of the dead shall be accorded to all, irrespective of origin, race, religion, nationality, custom and tradition.

- Respect for the wishes of the dead concerning disposition shall be accorded whenever possible, reasonable and lawful, when they are known or can be reasonably inferred.

- Respect for the wishes of the local community and of relatives or guardians of the dead shall be accorded whenever possible, reasonable and lawful.

- Respect for the scientific research value of skeletal, mummified and other human remains (including fossil hominids) shall be accorded when such value is demonstrated to exist.

- Agreement on the disposition of fossil, skeletal, mummified and other remains shall be reached by negotiation on the basis of mutual respect for the legitimate concerns of communities for the proper disposition of their ancestors, as well as the legitimate concerns of science and education.

- The express recognition that the concerns of various ethnic groups, as well as those of science are legitimate and to be respected, will permit acceptable agreements to be reached and honoured (Photograph: British Museum).

As Scarre (2006) points out, it is hard to define many of these criteria; who are the modern guardians of the ancient dead? It is impossible to prove any direct biological relationship between those buried at Avebury and people living in Britain today, and modern pagan practices and beliefs have little, if anything, in common with those of the Iron Age, when Lindow Man was ritually killed. Do the claims of the minute percentage of the population that holds 'pagan' beliefs have the same validity as those of archaeologists and broader public opinion? Advances in archaeological techniques for analysing human remains (Chapter 5) are providing an astonishing amount of new knowledge about past peoples – their origins, diets and social organisation, as well as about the origins and development of human diseases. This is a strong argument for the view that human remains should be retained to allow for future research which will inform all of us (including modern pagans) about past societies and belief systems. Ethical guidelines undoubtedly help, but questions about the 'ownership' of human remains require wide and well-informed public debate.

Figure 6.14 Channel 4's *Time Team* used fieldwork and excavation as a successful television programme formula in the 1990s (Fig. 3.1). A spin-off programme, *Extreme Archaeology*, tried to 'bring archaeology bang up to date and into the 21st century' (Mel Morpeth, cited in Holtorf 2007a: 44). This often involved doing things on projects, such as abseiling and dangling off wires over a river, which most archaeologists would never do and would be questionable as effective ways of obtaining data. Such programmes raise important questions: how far should archaeology be glamorised or exaggerated to sell it to a TV audience? The ways in which the public consume their knowledge have changed considerably since 2000 (with YouTube, Twitter and multiple digital TV channels), and archaeologists must engage with new ways of presenting themselves and their research; the extent to which the 'archaeology' might suffer remains hotly debated (Clack and Brittain 2007).(Copyright Jamie Wiggins)

– in contrast to culture history or processualism – have not been particularly visible in the ways that archaeologists carry out the basic functions of excavation and fieldwork, apart from some attempts to practise ideas about interpretation and reflexivity (see Chapter 3). When we consider the state and direction of archaeology in the twenty-first century it is worth remembering Trigger's statement that 'There is no evidence that in their interpretation of archaeological data archaeologists today are less influenced by the milieu in which they live than they were formerly' (Trigger 2006: 484).

Postprocessual and interpretive approaches to archaeology, although more reflexive and consciously aware of the external influences on archaeologists and their practices and interpretations, reflect the context and time in which they were devised. Many of the postprocessual approaches outlined above have already been criticised, with varying degrees of success (e.g. Bintliff 1993, 2004; Shennan 2004). The use of many theories and ideas remains restricted to specific regions of the world (Scarre 1999), and we should not assume that there is only one way in which archaeologists can (or should) approach artefacts, sites or landscapes. We are comfortable with the plurality of approaches now characteristic of much archaeology, and see no need for a theoretical convergence into a single dominant school of thought (Trigger 2006: 497). Indeed, one of the gains of archaeology in recent years has been the contribution of a more diverse range of voices in discussing the past and recognition of the varied ways of living which existed in the past (Habu *et al.* 2008), often referred to as **multi-vocality**. Despite the difficulties of explaining to a wider public how interpretations can be so vastly different (**Box 6.1**), diversity demonstrates archaeology's maturity as a discipline. Like philosophy and anthropology, archaeology has a wide range of schools of thought, but dialogue is always encouraged. The process of interpretation will undoubtedly develop, reacting to (and against) new philosophies and discoveries. The challenge for all those involved in archaeology, from amateur fieldwalkers to professional field practitioners and from museologists to anthropologists, is to engage with the debates over archaeology and never to feel that they have no significance for us.

The interpretation of the past from archaeological remains has come a long way since antiquarians first managed to disprove Samuel Johnson's depressing eighteenth-century contention that 'We can know no more than what old writers have told us'. Recent developments in archaeological theory, when seen as part of a broader retrospective study, encourage healthy scepticism about any school of thought that claims to be 'new', or to have discovered 'the truth'. Rapid advances in fieldwork methods and scientific techniques show that new evidence may appear at any moment from a completely unsuspected source – LiDAR, or the extraction of Neanderthal DNA, for example. A discipline that incorporates so much uncertainty and so many different academic approaches, while ignoring the conventional boundaries between the sciences and the humanities, is well worth studying at school, university, or as a leisure pursuit. If we have managed to convince any readers relatively new to the subject that archaeology offers these benefits, this book will have been a success.

6.8 GUIDE TO FURTHER READING

It is useful to have access to some background reference works before beginning serious reading about archaeological theory, as most of the concepts and thinkers that are cited originate in wider philosophical, literary, political and cultural studies. An understanding of the characteristics of modernism and postmodernism is an essential starting point. For philosophical ideas, begin with Blackburn, *Oxford dictionary of philosophy* 1994, and move on to Craig, *Routledge concise encyclopaedia of philosophy* 2000; for concise accounts of key ideas, a good starting point is Munslow, *Companion to historical studies* 2006, while the background to postprocessual archaeology is illuminated by Taylor and Winquist, *Encyclopaedia of postmodernism* 2003 .

Theoretical papers feature regularly in periodicals such as *World Archaeology*, *Antiquity*, *American Antiquity* and *Current Anthropology*, while the *Cambridge Archaeological Journal* features long review articles, especially related to cognitive archaeology. The *Journal of Material Culture* is a recent addition to the publications that bring together archaeological and anthropological approaches.

Bruce Trigger, *A history of archaeological thought* (2006), covers the entire history of the subject in great detail, while Matthew Johnson, *Archaeological theory* (2010), covers the developments of the 1990s and 2000s in a straightforward fashion. Alice Kehoe, *The land of prehistory* (1998), is refreshingly direct as well as erudite in its critical presentation of the growth of theory in the United States through the nineteenth and twentieth centuries, and provides an interesting contrast to the 'establishment view' of Willey and Sabloff (1980). Hegmon's article in *American Antiquity* in 2003 provides a challenge to American archaeology by suggesting that much of the theoretical approach is implicit rather than openly debated. The twenty-fifth anniversary of David Clarke's paper 'Archaeology: The loss of innocence' (1973) was celebrated by an interesting collection of reflections in *Antiquity* in 1998, while American New Archaeology may be studied in *Conversations with Lew Binford*, recorded by Sabloff (1998). It is a healthy sign of the maturity of the subject that several other books have been devoted to retrospective analysis of the development of archaeological theory (Wolfram 1986; Gibbon 1989; Eggert and Veit 1997).

In comparison with prehistory, classical and historical archaeology have been rather late in absorbing theoretical approaches; examples include Johnson, *An archaeology of capitalism* (1996) and a good introduction is Orser and Fagan, *Historical archaeology* (1995); global perspectives are offered in Andren, *Between artifacts and texts* (1998), and Funari *et al.*, *Historical archaeology: back from the edge* (1998); Morris, 'Classical archaeology' 2004, and *Archaeology as Cultural History* 2000, provide both a review and a theoretical stance for Roman and Greek archaeology. Interesting exercises in politically-related archaeology can be found in Leone and Potter, *Historical archaeologies of capitalism* (1999), and in Buchli, *Archaeology of socialism* (1999). Past concepts of time and its central role in archaeology are explored in Tim Murray, *Time and archaeology* (1999), and in Lucas, *The archaeology of time* (2005).

Social evolution has a wide historical and anthropological background explored in Stocking, *Victorian anthropology* 1987, and Sanderson, *Social evolutionism* 1990; comprehensive modern perspectives may be found in Bintliff, *Structure and contingency* 1999, and Pluciennik, *Social evolution* 2005, while Ruse, *Monad to man* 1996, looks at the idea of progress in the work of evolutionary scientists.

Philosophy and archaeological practice (2000), is a challenging but rewarding collection of papers about the potential of many schools of thought that have hardly been touched by archaeologists so far. Christopher Tilley, *Metaphor and material culture* (1999), is an instructive combination of theory, prehistory and anthropology, while Cerbone, *Understanding phenomenology* 2006 provides an easy introduction to the philosophy behind the archaeology. Many classic papers are included in 'readers', normally with comments by the editors; David Whitley, *Reader in archaeological theory* (1998), includes concise essays introducing each thematic group of papers. Julian Thomas, *Interpretive archaeology* (2000), has an interesting introduction and contains a good representative range of postmodern approaches. Concepts of agency are explored in Gardner, *Agency uncovered* 2004. Examining how postprocessual archaeology might deal with archaeology's place in modern concepts of the world is explored in Thomas, *Archaeology and modernity* 2004, and Insoll, *Archaeology, the conceptual challenge* 2007. Funari *et al.*, *Global archaeological theory* 2005, provides a set of papers from outside the Anglo-American focus on postprocessual approaches; Politis and Pérez Gollán, *Latin American archaeology* 2004, provides a case study of theoretical developments in one region.

POSTPROCESSUAL ARCHAEOLOGY

The development that led from processualism through ethnoarchaeology to postprocessualism is outlined in Hodder and Hutson, *Reading the past* (2003), while an entertaining collection of backlashes against such works is *Archaeological theory: who sets the agenda?* edited by Yoffee and Sherratt (1993). Andrew Sherratt's writing is always stimulating, and a collection of his papers appeared under the title *Economy and society in prehistoric Europe* in 1997, while any of Richard Bradley's books (such as *An archaeology of natural places* 2000) are readable applications of theory to interesting topics in British prehistory. Holtorf and Karlsson,

INTERPRETIVE ARCHAEOLOGY

'Interpretation' was a recurrent theme in a series of theoretical books published during the 1990s. Tilley edited a collection of papers entitled *Interpretative archaeology* in 1993. Hodder also extended the agenda as part of a team that edited the book from a 1991 conference, *Interpreting archaeology: finding meaning in the past* (1995). Thomas used the adjective in the subtitle of a book about Neolithic Britain (*Time, culture and identity: an interpretive archaeology*, 1996), while Shanks did the same thing with ancient Greece (*Art and the early Greek state: an interpretative archaeology*, 1999).

ARCHAEOLOGIES OF IDENTITY

General overviews are found in Meskell and Preucel, *A companion to social archaeology* 2004. Layton, *Who needs the past? Indigenous values and archaeology* 1989, remains an important selection of edited papers, while North America is the subject of Swiddler, *Native Americans and archaeologists* 1997. Montagu, *Man's most dangerous myth: the fallacy of race* 1997, provides a background perspective on ethnicity. Nelson, 'Gender archaeology' 2005, provides a short introduction to the development of this subject, while a broad range of approaches is presented in Nelson and Rosen-Ayalon, *In pursuit of gender* 2002. Two case-studies that apply gendered perspectives to very different kinds of archaeology are *Beads and bead makers* (Sciama and Eicher 1998), which looks at one category of material culture in detail, and Roberta Gilchrist, *Gender and material culture: the archaeology of religious women* (1993), a broad institutional and architectural study of medieval convents. An Australian collection of feminist studies has been published under the challenging title of *Redefining archaeology* (Casey *et al.* 1997), and fundamental scientific questions about sex and evolution are presented in an entertaining manner in Alison Jolly, *Lucy's legacy* (1999). The way in which images of the past reflect their contemporary social and theoretical contexts is explored in Smiles and Moser, *Envisioning the past* 2005. An interesting postprocessual focus on performance can be found in Inomata and Coben, *Archaeology of performance* 2006. Fowler, *Archaeology of Personhood* 2004 provides a comprehensive and accessible introduction to ways of exploring people's perceptions of themselves in the past. Jones, *Prehistoric Europe* 2008, provides a range of case studies relating theory to current archaeological research.

ARCHAEOLOGY AND THE PUBLIC

David Lowenthal, *The past is a foreign country* 1985, is a fundamental work about heritage, which he followed with *Possessed by the past* 1996. *Who owns the past?* 1997 (by the former editor of *Current Archaeology*, Andrew Selkirk) welcomed the impact of market economics and challenged many other discussions of heritage management. Merriman, *Public Archaeology* 2004, provides a useful range of papers, while the practical realities are described in Hunter and Ralston, *Archaeological resource management in the UK* 2006. For examples of these issues elsewhere in the world, see MacManamon, 'Managing archaeological resources' 2005, and Willems, *Archaeological heritage management in the Netherlands* 1997. There is a wealth of literature on resource management in the USA, and Neumann and Sanford, *Cultural resources archaeology* 2001, and Jameson, 'Cultural heritage in the United States: past, present and future' 2008, are good starting points; for Australia and New Zealand see Hall and McArthur, *Heritage Management* 1997. Leask and Fyall provide specific case studies in *Managing World Heritage Sites* 2006.

Cornelius Holtorf's books *From Stonehenge to Las Vegas* 2005, and *Archaeology is a brand* 2007, offer more controversial and challenging approaches to the place of archaeology in the public realm, while Holtorf and Piccini, *Contemporary archaeologies* 2009, challenges us to push the boundaries of archaeology into aspects of the contemporary world. Among older books that examine the nature and role of museums, Hudson, *Museums of influence* 1987, and Hooper-Greenhill, *Museums and the shaping of knowledge* 1992, remain informative, while Macdonald, *Politics of display: museums, science, culture* 1997, takes a very broad view. Gosden and Larson, *Knowing things: exploring the collections at the Pitt Rivers museum 1884–1945* 2007, explores the history of the development of one museum. Thompson, *Ruins reused* 2006, looks succinctly at the presentation of archaeological monuments and how ways of presenting ruins developed in Britain. The periodical *Public Archaeology*, launched in 2001, provides a forum for debate about social, political and ethical aspects of studying the past.

GLOSSARY

Terms included here are general ones that appear throughout the book; specific archaeological techniques or dating methods described at one place in the text should be looked up in the index. All terms in bold have separate entries in this glossary. Further help can be obtained from Tim Darvill's *Oxford concise dictionary of archaeology* 2002; for more detail consult Brian Fagan's *Oxford companion to archaeology* 1996 and Linda Ellis's *Archaeological method and theory* 2000.

Absolute dating: dates determined by methods whose accuracy is based on **radioactive decay** or regular natural phenomena such as **tree rings** or **varves**, or by secure historical evidence.

Aerial archaeology: reconnaissance and **remote sensing** conducted from aeroplanes, balloons or satellites.

AMS (accelerator mass spectrometry): a **radiocarbon dating** method that measures the concentration of ^{14}C **isotopes** rather than counting their **radioactive decay**.

Anaerobic: preservation conditions where there is an absence of oxygen (for example in peat bogs) that leads to a slowing of the decay process.

Anatomically modern humans: the most recent form of **hominin**, who appear to have evolved in Africa by 100,000 years ago and to have colonised the world since then, displacing earlier humans such as **Neanderthals**.

Anthropogenic: effects caused by human actions as opposed to natural biological or geological forces.

Anthropology: the study of humankind, including physical **evolution**, social systems and **material culture**.

Antiquaries, antiquarianism: the fieldworkers and collectors who studied ancient sites and artefacts before rigorous methods of excavation and interpretation were developed in the nineteenth century.

Archaeological Data Service (ADS): an online searchable database of electronic archives from projects in the UK, or run by organisations based there; see also **OASIS**.

Archaeomagnetism: magnetic properties of **artefacts** and soils caused by human activities (especially those that involved burning); these properties may be exploited for archaeomagnetic dating of hearths and kilns and for **remote sensing** (magnetometer surveys and magnetic susceptibility surveys).

Artefact: an object made or modified for use by humans.

Assemblage: a group of **artefacts** found together in a single **context** such as a grave or hoard.

Associations: **artefacts** or other items found together in the same layer or **context**.

Biosphere: the Earth's living organisms.

Bronze Age: the second of the Three Ages defined by Thomsen in the early nineteenth century, characterised by the use of **artefacts** made from copper and copper alloys.

Caesium magnetometer: a very sensitive magnetometer allowing measurement of much smaller variations in the subsoil than a gradiometer.

Calibration: correction of measurements to eliminate errors, notably in the case of the calibration curve derived from **tree rings** used to convert **radiocarbon** age estimations into calendar years.

Chalcolithic: the copper age, between the **Neolithic** and **Bronze Age**, which occurs in some areas of Europe (for example Iberia).

Characterisation: definition by scientific analysis of the distinctive minerals, elements or **isotopes** characteristic of specific sources of raw material such as quarries.

Chronology: the establishment of **relative** or **absolute dating** systems.

Chronometric dating: absolute dating based upon regular and measurable 'clocks' such as the rate of decay of radioactive **isotopes.**

Civilisation: a loose term normally associated with societies living in towns using a writing system, such as Mesopotamia, Egypt or Shang-dynasty China.

Classical archaeology: the study of Greek and Roman sites and **material culture.**

Climatostratigraphy: the use of environmental data from **seabed cores, ice cores, varves** and so on to establish and date climatic phases, notably ice ages.

Commensality: the process of eating as a group, and feasting; regarded by many archaeologists and anthropologists as a key social process in societies.

Conservation: in general, the preservation and care of ancient sites and landscapes; more specifically, laboratory techniques for stabilising objects or structures and preventing further decay.

Context: a neutral term for any deposit or structure recorded during an excavation; sometimes described as 'unit of **stratification**'.

Coprolites: solid excreta from humans or animals preserved in arid or waterlogged conditions from which fragments of foodstuffs can be extracted to study ancient diets.

Crannog: a raised settlement situated in a wetland location (usually a lake) found in Ireland, Scotland and Wales, dating from the first millennium BC to the first millennium AD.

Cremation: disposal of the dead through burning at high temperatures. Frequently, in many times and regions, the remaining burnt bones were interred in pits or vessels.

Cross-dating: the use of **artefacts** of known date to establish the age of undated contexts or **assemblages** in which they have been found; this dating may be extended to other **artefacts** found in **association** with them. It should be remembered that a dated **artefact** only provides a **terminus post quem** for the **context** in which it is found.

Cultural resource management (CRM): the protection and **conservation** of archaeological and historic sites and landscapes; cultural resources are more commonly known as 'heritage' outside North America.

Cultures: in the 'culture history' approach to archaeological interpretation that was popular in the first half of the twentieth century, recurrent associations of distinctive sites and **artefacts** that suggested a repeated pattern of human behaviour were described as **cultures.** Such patterns of **material culture** were frequently equated with tribes or other groups of people – even races.

Debitage: the waste from the production of **lithics.** Has been used to reconstruct the ways in which stone tools were made.

Dendrochronology (tree-ring dating): dating large samples of wood by matching the pattern of annual rings to a dated reference sequence; the final ring provides a **terminus post quem** for the cutting of the tree and for any structure or **artefact** made from its wood.

Diffusionism: the idea, strongly associated with the culture history approach, that all cultural and technological developments in Europe spread from the **civilisations** of the Near East and Egypt.

Digital terrain model (DTM): computer generated topography used for modelling archaeological landscapes; it is particularly effective for intervisibility studies, which reveal how many other sites can be seen from any chosen site, or for visualising past landscapes without the clutter of later features.

DNA: the material in living organisms that carries genetic information.

Domestication: systematic exploitation and selective breeding of plants and animals by means of agriculture and herding, begun by **Neolithic** communities in the Near East.

Ecofact: natural and environmental evidence that relates to human activity, as opposed to an **artefact**, which is an object made or modified by humans.

Ecology: the interaction of living organisms; in an archaeological context, the relationship between humans and their natural environment.

ED-XRF (Energy-dispersive x-ray fluorescence): the bombardment of an object with x-rays and measurement of the energy of secondary (fluorescent) x-rays. Distinctive wavelengths indicate the presence of different elements in the object. The ED-XRF technique allows more precise separation of wavelengths than other x-ray methods, permitting the measurement of smaller amounts of individual elements. It is also non-destructive, and has become a common way of analysing the composition of archaeological materials, especially metals.

Electronic distance measurement (EDM): surveying equipment using laser or infra-red beams for high-precision measurement over long distances.

Enlightenment: the eighteenth-century 'Age of Reason' in science and philosophy that followed the Scientific Revolution of the previous century.

Environmental archaeology: general term for approaches to the interaction between humans and their biological and physical environment, ranging from general climatic factors to specific foodstuffs, and from landscapes to excavated soils.

Ethnicity: the study of biological or cultural aspects of racial identity; closely related to culture history and **diffusionism** in the first half of the twentieth century. Attempts to trace the origins of modern populations through **DNA** studies have generated new interest in ethnicity.

Ethnoarchaeology: ethnographic study of contemporary peoples, with a focus on **material culture** and the **formation processes** that create archaeological deposits. See also **middle range theory.**

Ethnography: the anthropological study of contemporary cultures.

Evolution: theories of biological and social development through the selection of advantageous characteristics, associated with Darwin and Spencer in the mid-nineteenth century AD.

Excarnation: treatment of the dead through exposure to the elements and/or scavenging animals. May have taken place on designated platforms or by placing bodies in trees etc.

Experimental archaeology: simulation and/or replication of ancient activities, structures and **artefacts** to study their performance, ideally with carefully designed scientific observation and controls.

Field archaeology, fieldwork: non-intrusive methods of observing, surveying and documenting surface traces of sites without engaging in excavation.

Field survey: multi-disciplinary study of the long-term settlement history of a region and its environmental setting; closely related to **landscape archaeology.**

Fieldwalking: systematic observation of the ground surface during **fieldwork**, and especially the recovery of **artefacts** that may indicate periods of occupation.

Formation processes (taphonomy): the circumstances in which archaeological sites are created by human activities and subsequently modified by decay, erosion and other natural processes.

Gender: issues surrounding the identity and behaviour of men and women in the past and the ways in which they may be represented in archaeological terms, for example through different burial practices or the layout of settlements and buildings.

Geophysical surveying instruments: a range of equipment designed to locate and record buried sites by measuring the electrical resistance, magnetism or other physical properties of the soil. The principal forms are **resistivity** meters, magnetometers and ground penetrating radar (GPR).

GIS: (Geographical Information System(s)): a range of techniques using the graphic capabilities of powerful computers for an integrated analysis of maps, images, sites and finds. GIS has rapidly become essential in the interpretation of **fieldwork** data.

Glacials and interglacials: the succession of Ice Ages alternating with temperate conditions established from evidence of changes in the natural and physical environment; see **climatostratigraphy.**

Grave goods: a selection of personal items placed in a burial, perhaps as gifts to take into an afterlife or as an indication of the deceased's sex, social status and religion.

Grey literature: a term often used by archaeologists in Britain to describe unpublished reports from excavations and investigations produced by commercial archaeologists. Most of these are only found in archives, making access to the results of this work more difficult than to published reports; see also ADS, OASIS.

Grubenhaus: an early medieval type of building in which a rectangular pit and associated post holes provide evidence for a wooden structure which may have had a sunken or suspended floor. It is a distinctive element of Anglo-Saxon settlement sites in England.

Half-life: the time taken for half of the radioactive **isotopes** (for example **radiocarbon**) in a sample to decay. The half-life may be used to estimate the age of a sample by measuring the amount of radioactivity that remains.

Henge monument: a form of ritual enclosure, found mainly in **Neolithic** Britain, characterised by having a ditch inside its enclosing bank; burials, standing stones or settings for large timbers may be found in the interior (notably at Stonehenge).

Heritage: a term (equivalent to the American 'cultural resources') that loosely describes those aspects of the past that survive today in physical form, from landscapes to structures and **artefacts**; its management and commercial aspects such as tourism are sometimes referred to as 'the heritage industry'.

Historical archaeology: in contrast to **prehistory**, the practice of archaeology in periods when written evidence is available; subdisciplines include **Classical**, medieval and industrial archaeology.

Historiography: the study of ways of writing about the past, and their development over time under a variety of cultural and philosophical influences. Recent theoretical developments in archaeology have stressed the need to examine our own discipline more critically, and to analyse its structure and ways of thinking.

Hoard: a collection of **artefacts** buried together at the same time (and therefore **associated**), for example coins and jewellery concealed during a period of insecurity.

Hominins: the group of creatures that can be categorised as related to humans (*Homo sapiens*). Although the term is often used interchangeably with *hominid* or *human ancestor*, there are important differences between these terms. *Hominins* include all ape-like creatures, which can then be split into two groups on the basis of DNA: *Ponginae* (orang-utans) and *Homininae* (humans, human-like ancestors, chimpanzees, gorillas etc.). It is worth noting that the term 'human ancestor' is not always appropriate, as some hominins (such as *Homo floresiensis*) may not be directly related to modern humans (*Homo sapiens*).

Hunter-gatherers: people who subsist on wild animals and plants, in contrast to settled **Neolithic** farmers or pastoralists supported by **domesticated** plants and animals.

Ice cores: cylindrical samples extracted from the polar ice sheets, from which annual variations in temperature, snowfall and atmospheric chemistry may be detected.

Inhumation: the burial of a body within a grave, pit or tomb.

Institute for Archaeologists (formerly the Institute of Field Archaeologists): an organisation of professional archaeologists in the UK. Its *Registered Organisations* scheme for contract archaeology organisations aims to maintain the quality of archaeological standards. It also provides guidelines on best practice in various areas of field archaeology.

Interpretive archaeology: an assortment of theoretical approaches associated with **postprocessual archaeology** and favouring ideas about individual experience rather than general processes.

Iron Age: the third of Thomsen's **Three Ages**, characterised by iron technology.

Isotopes: atoms with different numbers of neutrons in their nuclei but similar chemical properties. *Unstable* isotopes decay to form a different element, and are fundamental to several **radiometric dating** techniques including **radiocarbon**, **potassium–argon** and uranium series. *Stable* isotopes can be used in **characterisation** studies of raw materials and for detecting variations in diet from bones.

Landscape archaeology: placing sites into a wider context using a full range of archaeological, environmental and historical information to interpret them on a regional basis on a long timescale. The techniques involved are also known as **field survey**.

LiDAR (Light Detection and Ranging): a pulsed laser beam from an aircraft scans a survey area from side to side, building up an accurate, high resolution model of the ground surface. It is particularly good at recording insubstantial earthworks, and revealing features beneath plant foliage invisible to conventional aerial photography.

Lithics: any form of stone tool, frequently made from flint.

Magnetic dating, magnetic surveying, magnetometers: see **archaeomagnetism**.

Material culture: the range of physical evidence that may be observed by archaeologists and anthropologists, from **artefacts** to structures.

Megaliths: structures built from very large stones, frequently ritual sites such as stone circles and chambered tombs. Although found throughout the world at different times, megaliths are particularly numerous in **Neolithic** and **Bronze Age** Europe.

Mesolithic: transitional stage between the **Palaeolithic** (Old Stone Age) and **Neolithic** (New Stone Age) characterised by **hunter-gatherers** who used tools made up of multiple small stone blades (microliths).

Metallurgy, metallurgical analysis: the study of metal ores, artefacts and waste products from processing (for example slag) to investigate their raw materials and technology.

Midden: deposit of waste material, commonly composed of domestic and food waste. Shell-middens left by seasonal **hunter-gatherers** are common in coastal areas in many parts of the world.

Middle Range Theory: an attempt to bridge the gap between fragmentary evidence of prehistoric sites and structures and modern **ethnoarchaeological** observations of how archaeological sites reflect human activities and behaviour.

Multivocality: literally 'many voices'. It is recognised in postprocessual archaeology that different groups and individuals have a variety of views about the past, according to their particular context and history. Thus multivocality helps to reduce the dominance of colonialist and Western interpretations. It also acknowledges that individuals in the past held many different views and underwent varying experiences.

National Mapping Programme (NMP): the plotting and mapping of oblique aerial photographs of archaeological features in England to provide a comprehensive database and **GIS** of archaeological cropmarks for research and heritage-management purposes.

National Trust: a non-governmental charitable organisation established in 1895 to preserve and protect countryside, landscapes and historic monuments in England, Wales and Northern Ireland.

Neanderthals: humans who occupied Europe and western Asia for a considerable period until they were displaced by anatomically modern humans between 100,000 and 30,000 years ago.

Neolithic: 'New Stone Age', characterised by communities farming **domesticated** plants and animals but still using stone tools, notably axes with a ground or polished rather than flaked surface. The **Mesolithic** to **Neolithic** transition is sometimes called the Neolithic Revolution or Agricultural Revolution.

New Archaeology: movement (also known as **processualism**) that emerged in the United States in the 1960s using a scientific approach to archaeological questions by designing models, suggesting hypotheses and testing them in the hope of establishing laws governing human behaviour.

Noble Savage myth: a philosophical and literary concept of the virtues of primitive life especially popular in the eighteenth century.

OASIS (Online AccesS to the Index of archaeological investigationS): an index of archaeological investigations in Scotland and England hosted by the **ADS**. Online archiving means that more excavation and project data, much of it unpublished, is accessible to a wider audience; see also **ADS, grey literature.**

Obsidian: a natural volcanic glass used for making flaked tools in many parts of the world; the obsidian hydration dating technique, in which relative age is estimated by the depth of weathering of its surface, may be applied to it.

Olduvai Gorge: an important locality in northern Tanzania where erosion of the Rift Valley has exposed many geological strata containing human remains and **artefacts**, including the earliest 'Oldowan' chipped pebble tools.

Open-area excavation: the uncovering of large continuous areas, in contrast to the box trench system developed by Mortimer Wheeler.

Palaeo-, paleo-: prefix indicating 'ancient' attached to many natural and biological sciences (e.g. palaeoenvironment, paleosols (soils), **paleodemography** (population), palaeodiet, palaeobotany (plants)).

Palaeodemography: the study of the age and sex structures of past populations, usually by examining skeletal remains from archaeological contexts.

Palaeolithic: the earliest of three subdivisions of the Stone Age, preceding the **Mesolithic** and **Neolithic**. It lasted several million years, from the first appearance of stone tools to the **Mesolithic** microlith-using **hunter-gatherers** of the most recent postglacial period, and is normally divided into Upper, Middle and Lower phases.

Palaeomagnetism: natural magnetic properties of geological rocks and sediments, whose alignment underwent periods of north–south reversal that are important in geochronology and **climatostratigraphy**. Palaeomagnetism should be distinguished from **archaeomagnetism**, which is generated by human activities, notably the heating of materials made from clay by fire.

Palimpsest: a term (adopted from the study of old manuscripts) used in archaeology to describe a landscape or a building that exhibits features and activities which accumulated over a long period. Features identifiable on an archaeological survey or geophysical plot are more likely to be a palimpsest rather than contemporary with each other.

Palynology: identification of pollen grains recovered from samples of soil from archaeological sites, peat bogs or lake beds, and the reconstruction of ancient environments and climatic phases from the species present.

Paradigm shift: a general change in outlook resulting from an accumulation of evidence undermining prevailing views. This phenomenon was identified in the sciences by Thomas Kuhn, but the term is frequently applied to wider intellectual movements.

Planning Policy Guidance (PPG) notes 15 and 16: government guidance on the role of archaeology in planning for development in England. PPG15 (1994) concerns the preservation and protection of historic buildings whilst PPG16 (1990) relates only to buried remains. Equivalent documents exist in Scotland (NPPG5) and Wales. The guidance is currently being reviewed and is likely to be replaced by Planning Policy Statement (PPS) 15.

Portable Antiquities Scheme (PAS): a voluntary scheme for the recording of archaeological objects found by metal-detector users in England and Wales. It is currently overseen by the British Museum but makes use of regional finds-liaison officers.

Positivism: approach to science and human society developed in the nineteenth century, characterised by the replacement of speculation by propositions that may be tested to establish laws; **New Archaeology** has been criticised for having an excessively positivist approach.

Postprocessual archaeology: a reaction to **processualism (New Archaeology)** avoiding **positivism** in favour of more recent anthropological approaches, such as symbolism and the role of material culture in social relationships. The term 'interpretive archaeology' is preferred by many archaeologists who have drawn upon a wider range of philosophical approaches from the 1990s onwards.

Potassium–argon dating: an **absolute** technique based on the decay of a radioactive **isotope** of potassium, especially important in dating geologically recent volcanic deposits associated with early **hominin** remains in East Africa.

Prehistory: the period – undocumented in historical sources – revealed by archaeological methods and interpreted with the help of anthropological and historical analogies.

Processualism: see **New Archaeology**.

Pseudo-archaeology: the practice of providing interpretations about the past that appear to use archaeological techniques but in reality ignore the critical and scientific approaches of archaeology. Defined and criticised in G. Fagan (2006).

Radioactive decay: the release of particles by unstable **isotopes** at a constant rate; fundamental to **radiometric dating** methods such as **radiocarbon** and **potassium–argon**.

Radiocarbon dating: the most important **radiometric** technique for dating later **prehistory** because of the short **half-life** of ^{14}C, a radioactive **isotope** of carbon that is absorbed by all living things until their death. This allows the age of organic materials such as wood or bone to be estimated and converted to calendar years with the help of a **calibration** curve established from **tree rings**.

Radiometric dating: methods measuring the decay of radioactive **isotopes**.

Register of Professional Archaeologists: a voluntary listing of archaeologists in the USA who have agreed to abide by a code of conduct and professional standards, similar to those of the **Institute for Archaeologists** in Britain.

Relative dating: relative ages (also known as derivative ages) established from methods such as obsidian hydration or **archaeomagnetism** cannot be used on their own but must be related to an **absolute** technique such as **radiocarbon**. Sequences of **contexts** established by the **stratification** of archaeological sites, or **artefacts** arranged into order by **typology**, are also relative unless fixed points can be established by **cross-dating** or **association**.

Remote sensing: the use of aerial or satellite reconnaissance and photography to discover and interpret archaeological sites and landscape features, whether visible on the surface or buried, and the use on the ground of geophysical instruments to locate buried sites.

Renaissance: a period of revival of interest in Classical Greek and Roman art, architecture and literature, especially in fifteenth-century Italy, which spread to the rest of Europe and (in combination with the Scientific Revolution) formed the basis for the Enlightenment of the eighteenth century.

Rescue archaeology: archaeological fieldwork and/or excavation prompted by threats from development such as a road-building: an important component of cultural resource (or heritage) management.

Resistivity surveying: geophysical technique based upon the extent to which buried soils and features resist the passage of an electric current.

Romanticism: a reaction (primarily in the nineteenth century) against the rationality of the Enlightenment and the effects of the Industrial Revolution, commonly expressed in admiration for wild landscapes, primitive peoples and pre-Renaissance 'Gothic' architecture.

Seabed cores: records of long-term climatic and environmental change recovered from sediments that accumulated continuously on the seabed. When correlated with reversals of the Earth's magnetic field (dated by potassium–argon), and calibrated by regular variations in the Earth's orbit, long-term changes in climate can be observed and dated (climatostratigraphy).

Sections: vertical records of stratigraphy revealed by excavation and recorded in drawings and photographs as evidence of the sequence of contexts on a site.

Site formation: see formation processes.

Social evolution, sociocultural evolution: a belief that human societies developed increasing complexity over time (found in the writings of Lewis Henry Morgan, Karl Marx and Benjamin Kidd). It was reinforced in the nineteenth century by analogies from biological evolution. Many twentieth-century anthropologists and archaeologists rejected the idea of linear social evolution because it oversimplified the complexity of the past and underestimated the sophistication of many past and present societies.

Stratification, stratigraphy: by analogy with geological strata, deposits on archaeological sites may be arranged in a sequence (with the earliest at the bottom) that may be dated with the help of any diagnostic artefacts they contain.

Structured deposition: patterns of artefacts found in archaeological contexts suggesting that they were not deposited at random but were structured by human actions, such as ritual practices governing the burial of objects as votive offerings. Anthropological studies and recent theoretical perspectives indicate that even the disposal of rubbish may reflect belief systems and 'ways-of-seeing' in the past. Structured deposition has been identified in many Neolithic and Iron Age contexts in Britain and it has frequently been related to the concept of *habitus*.

Taphonomy: see formation processes.

Taxonomy: the scientific division and classification of animals and plants, developed as part of the Enlightenment desire to understand the natural ordering of organisms, and subsequently extended to archaeological objects.

Tell: a large moundlike site common in the Near East, formed by the accumulation of occupation debris (especially mudbrick) over long periods.

Terminus ante quem, terminus post quem: reference points in the dating of a stratigraphic sequence on a site before which (*ante*) or after which (*post*) a context was formed. One famous *terminus ante quem* is the volcanic deposit that destroyed Pompeii in AD 79, sealing earlier levels beneath it; a coin, dated to AD 15 and buried in foundations, is a *terminus post quem* for a building's construction.

Thermoluminescence dating (TL): a method of determining absolute dates for fired clay or burnt stone; optically stimulated luminescence may be applied to unburned sediments that have been exposed to direct sunlight.

Thiessen polygon: a model used in geography to define territories under the influence of 'central places' (usually towns). In archaeology, lines have been drawn equidistant between Neolithic long barrows, Iron Age hillforts and Mayan cities to define hypothetical 'territories'. Models of this kind were extremely popular with exponents of New Archaeology, but they have been strongly criticised because known territorial boundaries rarely follow such simple rules.

Three-Age System: Christian Thomsen's method of organising displays in the National Museum, Copenhagen, in 1819, based on the idea of technological progression from stone to metals and validated by **associations** between artefacts made from different materials in prehistoric graves.

Total Station: a combination of a theodolite, **electronic distance measurer** (EDM) and electronic data recorder, frequently used to conduct topographic surveys or to record the precise location of excavations and geophysical surveys.

Treasure Act: passed in 1996 and affecting England, Wales and Northern Ireland. It replaced Treasure Trove. Which items should be defined as treasure is somewhat complex, but they include objects at least 300 years old (when found) which are of precious metals or consist of a hoard of coins. It allows the inclusion of archaeological finds that are associated with treasure (for example in a hoard of Bronze Age objects). It also allows for museums to have first refusal on the purchase of treasure objects, although they may not wish to do so, in which case the objects are then returned to the finder to sell (usually in agreement with the landowner).

Tree rings: layers of new wood formed annually around the circumference of tree trunks; their variations in thickness are useful for studying environmental conditions as well as for tree-ring dating (**dendrochronology**).

Typology: method of arranging classes of **artefacts** into sequences, normally according to improvements in design and efficiency (in the case of functional items such as axes) or alternatively according to changes in form or decoration (pottery, jewellery). The type-series produced in this way must first be dated independently if it is to be used for dating purposes.

Valletta Convention: a document, containing general statements about the protection of the archaeological heritage, that came into force in 2001 and that has been accepted by most countries in the European Union. It contains a number of concepts supported by national bodies such as English Heritage, including a legal framework for archaeology within the planning process, and the principle that archaeology should be preserved 'in situ' rather than being excavated.

Varves: annual deposits of silt on the beds of rivers or lakes that can be used (like **tree rings**) for **absolute dating** if related to a dated reference point.

BIBLIOGRAPHY

Abercromby, D. and Dyne, M. (eds) (1993) *Recording England's past: a review of national and local Sites and Monuments Records in England*, London: Royal Commission on the Historical Monuments of England.

Abrams, E.M. and Freter, A. (eds) (2005) *The emergence of the moundbuilders: the archaeology of tribal societies in southeastern Ohio*, Ohio City: Ohio University Press.

Adam, J.P. (1994) *Roman building: materials and techniques*, London: Routledge.

Adams, R. McC. (1965) *Land behind Bagdad: a history of settlement of the Diyala Plains*, Chicago, IL: University of Chicago Press.

Adcock, G. *et al.* (2001) 'Mitochondrial DNA sequences in ancient Australians: implications for modern human origins', *Proceedings of the National Academy of Science* 98 (2): 537–42.

Adovasio, J.M. and Carlisle, R.C. (1988) 'Some thoughts on cultural resource management archaeology in the United States', *Antiquity* 62: 72–87.

Aitchison, T., Ottaway, B. and Al-Ruzaiza, A.S. (1991) 'Summarizing a group of ^{14}C dates on the historical time scale: with a worked example from the Late Neolithic of Bavaria', *Antiquity* 65: 108–16.

Aitken, M.J. (1990) *Science-based dating in archaeology*, London: Longman.

Aitken, M.J. (1991) 'Principles of radioactive dating', in Göksu, H.Y., Oberhofer, M. and Regulla, D. (eds) *Scientific dating methods*, Dordrecht: Kluwer Academic Publishers: 3–13.

Aitken, M.J. (1997) 'Luminescence dating', in Taylor, R.E. and Aitken, M.J. *Chronometric dating in archaeology*, New York: Plenum Press: 183–216.

Aitken, M.J. (1998) *Introduction to optical dating*, Oxford: Oxford University Press.

Aitken, M.J. and Stokes, S. (1997) 'Climatostratigraphy', in Taylor, R.E. and Aitken, M.J. *Chronometric dating in archaeology*, New York: Plenum Press: 1–30.

Aitken, M.J., Stringer, M. and Mellars, P. (eds) (1993) *The origin of modern humans and the impact of chronometric dating*, Princeton: Princeton University Press.

Albarella, U. (1999) ' "The mystery of husbandry": medieval animals and the problem of integrating historical and archaeological evidence', *Antiquity* 73: 867–75.

Albarella, U. (ed.) (2001) *Environmental archaeology: meaning and purpose*, Dordrecht: Kluwer Academic Publishers.

Alcock, S. and Cherry, J. (1996) 'Survey at any price?', *Antiquity* 70: 207–11.

Alcock, S. and Cherry, J. (2004) *Side-by-side survey. Comparative regional studies in the Mediterranean world*, Oxford: Oxbow.

Alcock, S., Cherry, J. and Elsner, J. (eds) (2001) *Pausanias: travel and memory in Roman Greece*, Oxford: Oxford University Press.

Aldenerfer, M. (2005) 'Statistics in archaeology', in Maschner, H.D.G. and Chippendale, C. (eds) *Handbook of archaeological methods, 1*, Lanham, MD: Altamira Press: 501–53.

Aldred, O. and Fairclough, G. (2003) *Historic landscape characterisation: taking stock of the method*, London: English Heritage and Somerset County Council.

Alex, L.M. (2000) *Iowa's archaeological past*, Iowa: University of Iowa Press.

Alexander, E.P. (1997) *The museum in America: innovators and pioneers*, London: Sage.

Allaby, R., Fuller, D. and Brown, T. (2008) 'The genetic expectations of a protracted model for the origins of domesticated crops', *Proceedings of the National Academy of Sciences* 105 (37): 13982–6.

Allchin, B. (ed.) (1994) *Living traditions: studies in the ethnoarchaeology of South Asia*, Oxford: Oxbow Books.

Allen, K. *et al.* (eds) (1990) *Interpreting space: GIS and archaeology*, London/New York: Taylor and Francis.

Allen, S. Heuck, (1998) *Finding the walls of Troy: Frank Calvert and Heinrich Schliemann at Hisarlik*, Berkeley: California University Press.

Allin, M. (1999) *Zarafa*, London: Headline Publishing.

Allison, G. *et al.* (1996) *The value of conservation? A literature review of the economic and social value of the cultural built heritage*, London: English Heritage/Department of National Heritage/Royal Institute of Chartered Surveyors.

Ambrose, W.R. (2001) 'Obsidian hydration dating', in Brothwell, D.R. and Pollard, A.M. *Handbook of archaeological sciences*, Chichester: John Wiley and Sons: 81–92.

Anderson, A.C. (1991) 'The chronology of colonization in New Zealand', *Antiquity* 65: 767–95.

Anderson, P. (ed.) (1999) *Prehistory of agriculture*, London: UCL Institute of Archaeology Monograph 40.

Anderson, R.G.W. *et al.* (eds) (2003) *Enlightening the British: knowledge, discovery and the museum in the eighteenth century*. London: The British Museum Press.

Anderson, S. and Boyle, K. (eds) (1996) *Ritual treatment of human and animal remains*, Oxford: Oxbow Books/Osteoarchaeological Research Group.

Anderson, S. and Boyle, K. (eds) (1997) *Computing and statistics in osteoarchaeology*, Proceedings of the 2nd Osteoarchaeological Research Group meeting, Oxford: Oxbow.

Andrefsky, W. (1998) *Lithics: macroscopic approaches to analysis*, Cambridge: Cambridge University Press.

Andrefsky, W. (2001) *Lithic debitage: context, form, meaning*, Salt Lake City: University of Utah Press.

Andren, A. (1998) *Between artifacts and texts: historical archaeology in global perspective*, London/New York: Plenum.

Andrews, G., Barrett, J.C. and Lewis, J.S.C. (2000) 'Interpretation not record: the practice of archaeology', *Antiquity* 74: 525–30.

Andrews, K. and Doonan, R. (2003) *Test tubes and trowels: using science in archaeology*, Stroud: Tempus.

Angold, M. (2001) *Byzantium: the bridge from antiquity to the Middle Ages*, London: St Martin's Press.

Annels, A. and Burnham, B. (1995) *The Dolaucothi gold mines*, 3rd edn, Cardiff: University of Wales Press.

Anthony, D.W. (2007) *The horse, the wheel, and language: how Bronze Age riders from the Eurasian steppes shaped the modern world*, Princeton, NJ: Princeton University Press.

Anthony, D.W. and Brown, D.R. (2000) 'Eneolithic horse exploitation in the Eurasian steppes: diet, ritual and riding', *Antiquity* 74: 75–86.

Appadurai, A. (1986) *The social life of things*, Cambridge: Cambridge University Press.

Appignanesi, R. and Garratt, C. (1995) *Postmodernism for beginners*, Cambridge: Icon Books.

Archibald, M. and Cowell, M. (eds) (1993) *Metallurgy in numismatics 3*, London: Spink/Royal Numismatic Society.

Arnold, B. (1990) 'The past as propaganda: totalitarian archaeology in Nazi Germany', *Antiquity* 64: 464–78.

Arnold, B. (2006) 'Pseudoarchaeology and nationalism: essentializing difference', in Fagan, G. (ed.) *Archaeological fantasies*, London: Routledge: 154–79.

Arnold, B. and Hassman, H. (1995) 'Archaeology in Nazi Germany: the legacy of the Faustian bargain', in Kohl, P.L. and Fawcett, C. (eds) *Nationalism, politics and the practice of archaeology*, Cambridge: Cambridge University Press: 70–81.

Arnold, D.E. (1993) *Ecology and ceramic production in an Andean community*, Cambridge: Cambridge University Press: New Studies in Archaeology.

Arnold, J.B., Oertling, T.J. and Hall, A.W. (1999) 'The Denbigh project: initial observations on a Civil War blockade runner and its wreck site', *International Journal of Nautical Archaeology* 28: 126–44.

Arthur, J.W. and Weedman, K.J. (2005) 'Ethnoarchaeology', in Maschner, H.D.G. and Chippindale, C. (eds) *Handbook of archaeological methods*, 1, Lanham, MD: Altamira Press: 216–69.

Ashbee, P. and Jewell, P. (1998) 'The Experimental Earthworks revisited', *Antiquity* 72: 485–504.

Asher-Greve, J.M. (2004) 'Gertrude L. Bell, 1868–1926', in Cohen, G.M. and Sharp Joukwosky, M. (eds) *Breaking ground: pioneering women archaeologists*, Ann Arbor: University of Michigan Press: 142–198.

Ashmore, P.J. (1999) 'Radiocarbon dating: avoiding errors by avoiding mixed samples', *Antiquity* 73: 124–30.

Ashmore, W. and Knapp, B. (eds) (1999) *Archaeologies of landscape: contemporary perspectives*, Oxford: Blackwell.

Astill, G. (1993) *A medieval industrial complex and its landscape: the metalworking, watermills and workshops of Bordesley Abbey*, London: Council for British Archaeology Research Report 92.

Aston, M. (ed.) (1988) *Medieval fish, fisheries and fishponds in England*, Oxford: British Archaeological Reports 182.

Aston, M. (1997) *Interpreting the landscape: landscape archaeology and local history*, London: Routledge.

Aston, M., Martin, M.H. and Jackson, A.W. (1998) 'The potential for heavy metal soil analysis on low status archaeological sites at Shapwick, Somerset', *Antiquity* 72: 838–47.

Aston, M. and Rowley, T. (1974) *Landscape archaeology: an introduction to fieldwork techniques on post-Roman landscapes*, Newton Abbot: David and Charles.

Aston, M. and Taylor, T. (1998) *Atlas of archaeology*, London: Dorling Kindersley.

Åström, P. (ed.) (1995) *Oscar Montelius 150 years: proceedings of a colloquium held in the Royal Academy of Letters, History and Antiquities, Stockholm*, Stockholm: Almqvist and Wiksell.

Athens, J.S. and Ward, J.V. (1999) 'The Late Quaternary of the Western Amazon: climate, vegetation and humans', *Antiquity* 73: 287–302.

Bachmann, H.G. (1982) *The identification of slags from archaeological sites*, London: Institute of Archaeology Occasional Papers 6.

Bagnall, R.S. (1995) *Reading papyri, writing ancient history*, London: Routledge.

Bahn, P. (1996a) *Tombs, graves and mummies: great discoveries in world archaeology*, London: Weidenfeld and Nicholson.

Bahn, P. (ed.) (1996b) *The Cambridge illustrated history of archaeology*, Cambridge: Cambridge University Press.

Bahn, P. (ed.) (2000) *The atlas of world archaeology*, London: Time-Life.

Bailey, G.N. (ed.) (1997) *Klithi: Palaeolithic settlement and Quaternary landscapes in northwest Greece*, Cambridge: McDonald Institute.

Bailiff, I. (2007) 'Methodological developments in the luminescence dating of brick from English late-medieval and post-medieval buildings', *Archaeometry* 49 (4): 827–51.

Baillie, M.G. (1989) 'Do Irish bog oaks date the Shang dynasty?', *Current Archaeology* 117: 310–13.

Baillie, M.G. (1992) 'Dendrochronology and environmental change', in Pollard, A.M. (ed.) *New developments in archaeological science*, Oxford: Clarendon: 5–23.

Baillie, M.G. (1995) *A slice through time: dendrochronology and precision dating*, London: Routledge.

Baillie, M.G. (1998a) 'Bad for trees – bad for humans?', in Coles, G. and Mills, C. (eds) *Life on the edge: human settlement and marginality*, Oxford: Association for Environmental Archaeology Symposia 13/Oxbow Monograph 100: 13–19.

Baillie, M.G. (1998b) *Exodus to Arthur: catastrophic encounters with comets*, London: Batsford.

Baillie, M.G. *et al.* (1998c) 'Volcanic "mythology" and the dating problem', *Antiquity* 72: 424–32.

Baker, D. and Baker, E. (1999) *An assessment of English Sites and Monuments Records, sponsored by RCHME*, Chelmsford: Association of Local Government Archaeological Officers: Historic Environment Conservation Report 97/20.

Balick, M.J. and Cox, P.A. (1997) *Plants, people, and culture: the science of ethnobotany*, New York: Scientific American Library.

Banks, M. (1995) *Ethnicity: anthropological constructions*, London: Routledge.

Banning, E.B. (2000) *The archaeologist's laboratory: interdisciplinary contributions to archaeology*, Dordrecht: Kluwer Academic/Plenum.

Banning, E.B. (2002) *Archaeological survey*, New York: Kluwer Academic/Plenum.

Bapty, I. and Yates, I. (eds) (1990) *Archaeology after structuralism: post-structuralism and the practice of archaeology*, London: Routledge.

Bar-Yosef Majer, D.E. (2005) *Archaeomalacology: molluscs in former environments of human behaviour*. Proceedings of the 9th ICAZ conference, Durham, 2002, Oxford: Oxbow.

Barber, B. (2000) *The Eastern Cemetery of Roman London: excavations 1983-1990*, London: MoLAS.

Barcelo, J.A., Forte, M. and Sanders, D. (eds) (2000) *Virtual reality in archaeology*, Oxford: Archaeopress, British Archaeological Reports, International Series S843.

Barclay, K. (2001) *Scientific analysis of archaeological ceramics: a handbook of resources*, Oxford: Oxbow.

Barham, A.J. and Macphail, R.I. (eds) (1995) *Archaeological sediments and soils: analysis, interpretation and management*, London: Institute of Archaeology, University College/ Association of Environmental Archaeology Conference.

Barker, A.W. (2009) 'Cheifdoms', in Bentley, A. *et al.* (eds) *Handbook of archaeological theories*, Lanham, MD: Altamira Press: 515–32.

Barker, G. (1995) *A Mediterranean valley: landscape archaeology and 'Annales' history in the Biferno Valley*, London: Leicester University Press.

Barker, G. and Lloyd, J. (eds) (1991) *Roman landscapes: archaeological survey in the Mediterranean region*, Rome: British School at Rome Monograph 2.

Barker, P.A. (1993) *Techniques of archaeological excavation*, 3rd edn, London: Routledge.

Barker, P.A. *et al.* (1998) *The baths basilica at Wroxeter*, London: English Heritage.

Barnard, H. and Eerkens, J.W. (2007) *Theory and practice of archaeological residue analysis*, Oxford: British Archaeological Reports, International Series S1650.

Barnes, G.L. (1999) *The rise of civilization in East Asia: the archaeology of China, Korea and Japan*, 2nd edn, London: Thames and Hudson.

Barnhart, T.A. (2005) *Ephraim George Squier and the Development of American Anthropology*, Lincoln: University of Nebraska Press.

Barrett, J.C. (2001) 'Agency, the duality of structure, and the problem of the archaeological record', in Hodder, I. (ed.) *Archaeological theory today*, Cambridge: Polity Press: 141–64.

Barrett, J.C. (2005) 'Habitus', in Renfrew, C. and Bahn, P. (eds) *Archaeology: the key concepts*, London: Routledge: 133–7.

Barrett, J.C., Bradley, R.J. and Green, M.T. (eds) (1991) *Landscape, monuments and society: the prehistory of Cranborne Chase*, Cambridge: Cambridge University Press.

Barrett, J.C. and Fewster, K.J. (2000) 'Intimacy and structural transformation: Giddens and archaeology', in Holtorf, C. and Karlsson, H. *Philosophy and archaeological practice: perspectives for the 21st century*, Göteborg: Bricoleur Press: 25–33.

Barrett, J.H. (1997) 'Fish trade in Norse Orkney and Caithness: a zooarchaeological approach', *Antiquity* 71: 616–38.

Barrett, J.H., Beukens, R.P. and Brothwell, D.R. (2000) 'Radiocarbon dating and marine reservoir correction of Viking Age Christian burials from Orkney', *Antiquity* 74: 537–43.

Barringer, T. and Flynn, T. (eds) (1998) *Colonialism and the object: empire, material culture and the museum*, London: Routledge.

Barth, T.F. (1969) *Ethnic groups and boundaries: the social organization of culture difference*, Oslo: Universitetsforlaget.

Barton, C.M. and Clark, G.A. (eds) (1997) *Rediscovering Darwin: evolutionary theory and archaeological explanation*, Arlington, VA: Archaeological Papers of the American Anthropological Association.

Bartosiewicz, L. (1996) 'Camels in antiquity: the Hungarian connection', *Antiquity* 70: 447–53.

Bartosiewicz, L. and Dirjec, J. (2001) 'Camels in antiquity: Roman period finds from Slovenia', *Antiquity* 75: 279–85.

Basalla, G. (1988) *The evolution of technology*, Cambridge: Cambridge University Press.

Basso, K. (1996) *Wisdom sits in places: landscape and language among the western Apache*, Albuquerque: University of New Mexico Press.

Batt, C., Meng, Z. and Noël, M. (1998) 'New archaeomagnetic studies near Xi'an, China', *Archaeometry* 40: 169–75.

Baudez, C. and Picasso, S. (1992) *Lost cities of the Maya*, London: Thames and Hudson; New Horizons.

Baxter, M.J. (2001) 'Multivariate analysis in archaeology', in Brothwell, D.R. and Pollard, A.M. *Handbook of archaeological sciences*, Chichester: John Wiley and Sons: 685–94.

Baxter, M.J. (2003) *Statistics in archaeology*, Oxford: Oxford University Press.

Bayerisches Gesellschaft für UWA (1998) *Archäologie unter Wasser 2: Prospektionstechniken*, Rahden, Westfalia: Verlag Marie-Leidorf GmbH.

Bayley, J. (ed.) (1998) *Science in archaeology: an agenda for the future*, London: English Heritage.

Bayliss, A. and Bronk Ramsey, C. (2004) 'Pragmatic Bayesians: a decade of integrating radiocarbon dates into chronological models', in Buck, C.E. and Millard, A. (eds) *Tools for constructing chronologies: crossing disciplinary boundaries*, London: Springer: 25–42.

Bayliss, A. *et al.* (2007) 'Bradshaw and Bayes: towards a timetable for the Neolithic', *Cambridge Archaeological Journal* 17: 1–28.

Bayliss, A., Whittle A. and Wysocki, M. (2007) 'Talking about my generation: the date of the West Kennet Long Barrow', *Cambridge Archaeological Journal* 17: 85–101.

Bayliss, R. (1997) 'The Alacami in Kadirli: transformations of a sacred monument', *Anatolian Studies* 47: 57–87.

Beard, M. (2002) *The Parthenon*, London: Profile.

Beaudry, M. (ed.) (1987) *Documentary archaeology in the New World*, Cambridge: Cambridge University Press.

Beavis, J. and Barker, K. (eds) (1995) *Science and site (Archaeological Sciences conference, Bournemouth 1993)*, Bournemouth: Bournemouth University Conservation Studies.

Beck, A. (2006) 'Google Earth and World Wind: remote sensing for the masses?', *Antiquity* 80, 308 *Project Gallery*.

Beck, C. and Shennan, S. (1991) *Amber in prehistoric Britain*, Oxford: Oxbow Monograph 8.

Beck, W. (2006) 'Plant remains', in Balme, J. and Paterson, A. (eds) *Archaeology in practice: a student guide to archaeological analyses*, Oxford: Blackwell: 296–315.

Bell, M. (1990) *Brean Down excavations 1983–1987*, London: English Heritage Archaeological Report 15.

Bell, M. (2004) 'Archaeology and Green issues', in Bintliff, J. (ed.) *A companion to archaeology*, Oxford: Blackwell: 509–31.

Bell, M. and Boardman, J. (eds) (1992) *Past and present soil erosion*, Oxford: Oxbow Monograph 22.

Bell, M., Caseldine, A. and Neumann, H. (2000) *Prehistoric intertidal archaeology in the Welsh Severn Estuary*, Cardiff: CADW/CBA Res. Rep. 120.

Bell, M., Fowler, P.J. and Hillson, S.W. (eds) (1996) *The experimental earthwork project 1960–1992*, London: Council for British Archaeology Research Report 100.

Bell, M. and Walker, M. (1992) *Late Quaternary environmental change: physical and human perspectives*, London: Longman.

Bell, T.W. (1998) 'A Roman signal station at Whitby', *Archaeological Journal* 155: 303–22.

Bender, B. (ed.) (1993) *Landscape, politics and perspectives*, Oxford: Berg, Explorations in Anthropology.

Bender, B. (1998) *Stonehenge: making space*, Oxford: Berg.

Bender, B., Hamilton, S. and Tilley, C. (2007) *Stone worlds: narrative and reflexivity in landscape archaeology*, London: UCL Institute of Archaeology Publications; Walnut Creek, CA: Left Coast Press.

Bennett, K.A. (1993) *A field guide for human skeletal identification*, 2nd rev. edn, Springfield, IL: Charles C . Thomas.

Bennett, M. and Doyle, P. (1998) *Unlocking the stratigraphical record: advances in modern stratigraphy*, New York: John Wiley.

Beresford, M. and Hurst, J. (1990) *Wharram Percy deserted medieval village*, London: Batsford/ English Heritage.

Berger, L. and Hilton-Barber, B. (2000) *In the footsteps of Eve: the mystery of human origins*, Washington, DC: National Geographic Society.

Berger, R. and Protsch, R. (1991) 'Fluorine dating', in Göksu, H.Y., Oberhofer, M. and Regulla, D. (eds) *Scientific dating methods*, Dordrecht: Kluwer Academic Publishers: 251–70.

Berggren, K. (2000) 'The knowledge-able agent? On the paradoxes of power', in Holtorf, C. and Karlsson, H. (eds) *Philosophy and archaeological practice: perspectives for the 21st century*, Göteborg: Bricoleur Press: 39–46.

Berghaus, P. (ed.) (1983) *Der Archäologe: graphische Bildnisse aus dem Porträtarchiv Diepenbroick*, Münster: Westfälischen Museum für Kunst und Kulturgeschichte.

Berglund, B.E. *et al.* (eds) (1996) *Palaeoecological events during the last 15,000 years*, New York: John Wiley.

Bernal, M. (1987) *Black Athena: the Afroasiatic roots of Classical civilization 1: the fabrication of ancient Greece 1785–1985*, London: Free Association Books.

Bernal, M. (1991) *Black Athena: the Afroasiatic roots of classical civilization 2: the archaeological and documentary evidence*, London: Free Association Books.

Berti, F. (ed.) (1990) *Fortuna Maris: la nave romana di Comacchio*, Bologna: Nuova Alfa Editoriale.

Bethell, P. and Maté, I. (1989) 'The use of soil phosphate analysis in archaeology: a critique', in Henderson, J. (ed.) *Scientific analysis in archaeology*, Oxford: Oxford University Committee for Archaeology Monograph 19: 1–29.

Bettess, F. (1992) *Surveying for archaeologists*, 3rd edn, Durham: University of Durham.

Bewley, R. *et al.* (1996) 'New features within the henge at Avebury, Wiltshire: aerial and geophysical evidence', *Antiquity* 70: 639–46.

Bewley, R. *et al.* (ed.) (1999) *Archiving aerial photography and remote sensing data: a guide to good practice*, Oxford: Oxbow Books, Archaeology Data Service.

Bewley, R.H., Crutchley, S.P. and Shell, C.A. (2005) 'New light on an ancient landscape: LiDAR survey in the Stonehenge World Heritage Site', *Antiquity* 79: 636–67.

Biddle, M. (1989) 'The Rose reviewed: a comedy(?) of errors', *Antiquity* 63: 753–60.

Biers, W.R. (1992) *Art, artefacts and chronology in classical archaeology*, London: Routledge.

Biers, W.R., Gerhardt, K. and Braniff, R. (1994) *Lost scents: investigations of Corinthian 'plastic' vases by gas chromatography–mass spectrometry*, Philadelphia, PA: Pennsylvania University Museum: MASCA Research Papers 11.

Biers, W.R. and McGovern, P.E. (eds) (1990) *Organic contents of vessels: materials analysis and archaeological investigation*, Philadelphia, PA: Pennsylvania University Museum: MASCA Research Papers 7.

Billman, B.R. and Feinman, G.M. (eds) (1999) *Settlement pattern studies in the Americas: fifty years since Virù*, Washington, DC: Smithsonian Institution.

Binford, L.R. (1972) *An archaeological perspective*, New York: Seminar Press.

Binford, L.R. (1978) *Nunamiut ethnoarchaeology*, New York: Academic Press.

Bintliff, J.L. (ed.) (1984) *European social evolution: archaeological perspectives*, Bradford: University of Bradford Press.

Bintliff, J.L. (1991a) 'Post-modernism, rhetoric and scholasticism at TAG: the current state of British archaeological theory', *Antiquity* 65: 274–8.

Bintliff, J.L. (ed.) (1991b) *The Annales school and archaeology*, Leicester: Leicester University Press.

Bintliff, J.L. (1993) 'Why Indiana Jones is smarter than the post-processualists', *Norwegian Archaeological Review* 26 (2): 91–100.

Bintliff, J.L. (1995) ' "Whither archaeology" revisited', in Kuna, M. and Venclová, N. (eds)

Whither archaeology?, Prague: Czech Academy of Sciences: 24–35.

Bintliff, J.L. (ed.) (1999) *Structure and contingency: evolutionary processes in life and human society*, Leicester: Leicester University Press.

Bintliff, J.L. (2000) 'Archaeology and the philosophy of Wittgenstein', in Holtorf, C. and Karlsson, H. *Philosophy and archaeological practice: perspectives for the 21st century*, Göteborg: Bricoleur Press: 153–72.

Bintliff, J.L. (2004) 'Time, structure and agency: the Annales, emergent complexity and archaeology', in Bintliff, J. (ed.) *A companion to archaeology*, Oxford: Blackwell: 174–94.

Bintliff, J.L. *et al.* (1990) 'Trace metal accumulation in soils on and around ancient settlements in Greece', in Bottema, S. *et al.* (eds) *Man's role in the shaping of the eastern Mediterranean landscape*, Rotterdam: Balkema: 159–72.

Bintliff, J.L., Howard, P. and Snodgrass, A. (2007) *Testing the hinterland: the work of the Boeotia Survey (1989–1991) in the Southern Approaches to the City of Thespiai*, Oxford: Oxbow.

Bintliff, J.L., Kuna, M. and Venclová, N. (eds) (2000) *The future of surface artefact survey in Europe*, Sheffield: Sheffield Academic Press.

Bisel, S.C. (1987) 'Human bones at Herculaneum', *Rivista di Studia Pompeiana* 1: 123–30.

Black, J. (ed.) (1987) *Recent advances in the conservation and analysis of artefacts*, London: Institute of Archaeology.

Blackburn, S. (1994) *Oxford dictionary of philosophy*, Oxford: Oxford University Press.

Blair, J. and Pyrah, C. (eds) (1996) *Church archaeology: research directions for the future*, York: Council of British Archaeology Research Report 104.

Blau, S. and Ubelaker, D.H. (2008) *Handbook of forensic archaeology and anthropology*, Walnut Creek, CA: Left Coast Press.

Blockley, K., Sparks, M. and Tatton-Brown, T. (1997) *Canterbury Cathedral nave: archaeology, history and architecture*, Canterbury: Canterbury Archaeological Trust.

Blockley, S.P.E., Donahue, R.E. and Pollard, A.M. (2000a) 'Radiocarbon calibration and late glacial occupation in Northwest Europe', *Antiquity* 74: 112–21.

Blockley, S.P.E., Donahue, R.E. and Pollard, A.M. (2000b) 'Rapid human response to late glacial climate change: a reply to Housley *et al.* (2000)', *Antiquity* 74: 427–8.

Blundell, S. (1986) *The origins of civilization in Greek and Roman thought*, London: Routledge.

Bodnar, E and Foss, C. (2003) *Cyriac of Ancona: later travels*. Cambridge, MA: Harvard College.

Boeda, E. *et al.* (1999) 'A Levallois point embedded in the vertebra of a wild ass (*equus africanus*): hafting, projectiles and Mousterian hunting weapons', *Antiquity* 73: 394–402.

Bogucki, P. (1993) 'Animal traction and household economies in Neolithic Europe', *Antiquity* 67: 492–503.

Boismier, W.A. (1997) *Modelling the effects of tillage processes on artefact distributions in the plough zone*, Oxford: British Archaeological Reports 259.

Bond, G.C. and Gilliam, A. (1994) *Social construction of the past*, London: Routledge, One World Archaeology 24.

Bonde, N. and Christiansen, A.E. (1993) 'Dendrochronological dating of the Viking Age ship burials at Oseberg, Gokstad and Tune, Norway', *Antiquity* 67: 575–83.

Bonsall, C. and Tolan-Smith, C. (eds) (1997) *The human use of caves*, Oxford: British Archaeological Reports, International Series S667.

Bosinski, G. (ed.) (1999) *The role of early humans in the accumulation of European Lower and Middle Palaeolithic bone assemblages*, Mainz: RGZM, Monog.42.

Boucher de Perthes, J. (1847) *Antiquités celtiques et antédiluviennes; mémoire sur l'industrie primitive et les arts à leur origine*, Paris: Treuttel et Wurtz.

Bourbon, F. (1999) *The lost cities of the Mayas: art and discoveries of Frederick Catherwood*, Shrewsbury: Swan Hill Press.

Bourdieu, P. (1977) *Outline of a theory of practice*, Cambridge: Cambridge University Press.

Bowden, M. (1991) *Pitt Rivers: the life and archaeological work of Lt-Gen. Augustus Henry*

Lane Fox Pitt Rivers, Cambridge: Cambridge University Press.

Bowden, M. (ed.) (1999) *Unravelling the landscape: an inquisitive approach to archaeology*, Stroud: Tempus Publishing.

Bowden, M. (ed.) (2000) *Furness iron: the physical remains of the iron industry and related woodland industries of Furness and southern Lakeland*, Swindon: English Heritage.

Bowdler, S. (1992) 'Unquiet slumbers: the return of the Kow Swamp burials', *Antiquity* 66: 103–6.

Bowens, A. (ed.) (2008) *Underwater archaeology: the NAS guide to principles and practice*, 2nd edn, Hoboken, NJ: Wiley-Blackwell.

Bowman, A.K. (2003) *Life and letters on the Roman frontier: Vindolanda and its people*, 2nd edn, London: British Museum Press.

Bowman, D.L. and Williams, S. (eds) (2002) *New perspectives on the origins of Americanist archaeology*, Tuscaloosa: University of Alabama Press.

Bowman, S. (1990) *Radiocarbon dating*, London: British Museum.

Bowman, S. (ed.) (1991) *Science and the past*, London: British Museum.

Bowsher, J. (1998) *The Rose Theatre: an archaeological discovery*, London: Museum of London.

Bradford, J. (1957) *Ancient landscapes: studies in field archaeology*, London: G. Bell and Sons.

Bradley, B. and Small, C. (1985) 'Looking for circular structures in post hole distributions: quantitative analysis of two settlements from bronze age England', *Journal of Archaeological Science* 12: 285–98.

Bradley, R. (1982) 'The destruction of wealth in later prehistory', *Man* 17 (1): 108–22.

Bradley, R. (1983) 'Archaeology, evolution and the public good: the intellectual development of General Pitt Rivers', *Archaeological Journal* 140: 1–9.

Bradley, R. (1998) *The passage of arms: an archaeological analysis of prehistoric hoards*, Oxford: Oxbow.

Bradley, R. (2000a) *An archaeology of natural places*, London: Routledge.

Bradley, R. (2000b) *The good stones: a new investigation of the Clava Cairns*, Edinburgh: Society of Antiquaries of Scotland 17.

Bradley, R. (2007) *The Prehistory of Britain and Ireland*, Cambridge: Cambridge University Press.

Bradley, R. and Edmonds, M. (1993) *Interpreting the axe trade: production and exchange in neolithic Britain*, Cambridge: Cambridge University Press.

Branch, N. *et al.* (2005) *Environmental archaeology: theoretical and practical approaches*, London: Hodder Arnold.

Braudel, R. (1972) *The Mediterranean and the Mediterranean world in the age of Phillip II* (translated from French), London: Collins.

Bray, T.L. (1996) 'Repatriation, power relations and the politics of the past', *Antiquity* 70: 440–4.

Bray, T.L. (2003) *The archaeology of food and feasting in early states and empires*, New York: Kluwer Academic.

Breeze, D.J. and Dobson, B. (2000) *Hadrian's Wall*, 4th edn, London: Penguin.

Brett, D. (1996) *The construction of heritage*, Cork: Cork University Press.

Brewer, D.J. (1987) 'Seasonality in the prehistoric Faiyum based on the incremental growth structures of the Nile catfish (Pisces: *Clarias*)', *Journal of Archaeological Science* 14: 459–72.

Briggs, C.S. (2007) 'Prehistory in the Nineteenth Century', in Pearce, S. (ed.) 'Visions of antiquity: the Society of Antiquaries of London 1707–2007', *Archaeologia* 111: 227–66.

Briggs, D.E.G. and Crowther, P.R. (1993) *Palaeobiology: a synthesis*, Oxford: Blackwell.

Brindle, S. and Kerr, B. (1997) *Windsor revealed: new light on the history of the castle*, London: English Heritage.

Brinkhuizen, D.C. and Clason, A.T. (eds) (1986) *Fish and archaeology: studies in osteometry, taphonomy, seasonality and fishing methods*, Oxford: British Archaeological Reports, International Series S294.

Brisbane, M. and Wood, J. (1996) *A future for our past? An introduction to heritage studies*, London: English Heritage.

Brodie, N. (1998) 'British Bell Beakers: twenty five years of theory and practice', in Benz,

M. and Van Willingen, S. (eds) *Some new approaches to the Bell Beaker 'phenomenon': lost paradise?*, Oxford: British Archaeological Reports, International Series 690: 43–56.

Brodie, N. (1999) 'Statistics, damned statistics, and the antiquities trade', *Antiquity* 73: 447–51.

Brodie, N. (2006) 'The plunder of Iraq's archaeological heritage, 1991–2005, and the London Antiquities trade', in Brodie, N. *et al.* (eds) *Archaeology, cultural heritage, and the antiquities trade*, Gainesville: University Press of Florida: 206–26.

Brodie, N. (2008) 'The market background to the April 2003 plunder of the Iraq National Museum', in Stone, P.G. and Bajjaly, J.F. (eds) *The destruction of cultural heritage in Iraq*, Woodbridge: Boydell Press: 41–54.

Brooke, C.J. (1994) 'Ground based remote sensing of buildings and archaeological sites: 10 years research to operation', *Archaeological Prospection* 1: 105–19.

Brophy, K. and Cowley, D. (2005) *From the air: understanding aerial archaeology*, Stroud: Tempus.

Brothwell, D.R. and Higgs, E. (eds) (1969) *Science in archaeology*, London: Thames and Hudson.

Brothwell, D.R. and Pollard, A.M. (eds) (2001) *Handbook of archaeological sciences*, Chichester: John Wiley and Sons.

Brown, A. *et al.* (1999) *Rows of Chester: the Chester Rows research project*, London: English Heritage Archaeological Report 16.

Brown, A.G. (1997) *Alluvial geoarchaeology*, Cambridge: Cambridge University Press.

Brown, K.A. (2000) 'Ancient DNA applications in human osteoarchaeology: achievements, problems and potential', in Cox, M. and Mays, S. (eds) *Human osteology in archaeology and forensic science*, London: Greenwich Medical Media: 455–73.

Brown, R.J. (1997) *Timber-framed buildings of England*, new edn, London: Hale.

Brown, T.A. (2001) 'Ancient DNA', in Brothwell, D.R. and Pollard, A.M. *Handbook of archaeological sciences*, Chichester: John Wiley and Sons: 301–11.

Brown, T.A. and Brown K.A. (1992) 'Ancient DNA and the archaeologist', *Antiquity* 66: 10–23.

Brück, J. and Goodman, M. (eds) (1998) *Making places in the prehistoric world: themes in settlement archaeology*, London: UCL Press.

Brunskill, R.W. (1997) *Brick building in Britain*, London: Gollancz.

Brunskill, R.W. (1998) *Houses and cottages of Britain: origins and development of traditional buildings*, London: Gollancz.

Buchli, V. (1999) *An archaeology of socialism*, Oxford: Berg.

Buck, C.E. (2001) 'Applications of the Bayesian statistical paradigm', in Brothwell, D.R. and Pollard, A.M. *Handbook of archaeological sciences*, Chichester: John Wiley and Sons: 695–702.

Buck, C.E. and Millard, A. (2004) *Tools for constructing chronologies: crossing disciplinary boundaries*, London: Springer.

Budd, P. *et al.* (1992) 'The early development of metallurgy in the British Isles', *Antiquity* 66: 677–86.

Budd, P. *et al.* (1996) 'Rethinking the quest for provenance', *Antiquity* 70: 168–74.

Budd, P. *et al.* (2004) 'Investigating population movement by stable isotope analysis: a report from Britain', *Antiquity* 78: 127–41.

Burchfield, J.D. (1975) *Lord Kelvin and the age of the Earth*, New York: Science History Publications.

Burl, A. and Mortimer, N. (2005) *Stukeley's Stonehenge: an unpublished manuscript 1721–1724*, New Haven, CT: Yale University Press.

Burnett, A. (1991) *Interpreting the past: coins*, London: British Museum.

Burnham, B. and Burnham, H. (2004) *Dolaucothi-Pumsaint survey and excavations at a Roman gold mining complex 1987–1999*, Oxford: Oxbow.

Burroughs, W. (2005) *Climate change in prehistory: the end of the reign of the chaos*, Cambridge: Cambridge University Press.

Butler, V.L. (2000) 'Resource depression on the northwest coast of North America', *Antiquity* 74: 649–61.

Butzer, K.W. (1971) *Environmental archaeology: an ecological approach to prehistory*, Chicago, IL: Aldine Publishing Company.

Byrne, L., Ollé, A. and Vergès, J.M. (2006) 'Under the hammer: residues resulting from production and microwear on experimental stone tools', *Archaeometry* 48 (4): 549–64.

Caple, C. (2000) *Conservation skills: judgement, method and decision making*, London: Routledge.

Caple, C. (2006) *Objects: reluctant witnesses to the past*, London: Routledge.

Cappers, R. and Bottema, S. (2002) *The dawn of farming in the Near East*, Berlin: Ex Oriente.

Carmichael, D., Lafferty, R. and Molyneaux, B. Leigh (2003) *Excavations: archaeologist's toolkit 3*, Wanut Creek, CA: Altamira.

Carr, G. and Knüsel, C. (1997) 'The ritual framework of excarnation and exposure as the mortuary practice of the early and middle Iron Age of central southern Britain', in Gwilt, A. and Haselgrove, C. (eds) *Reconstructing Iron Age societies*, Oxford: Oxbow Monograph 71: 167–73.

Carrete, J.M., Keay, S. and Millett, M. (1995) *A Roman provincial capital and its hinterland: the survey of the territory of Tarragona, Spain, 1985–1990*, Ann Arbor, MI: Journal of Roman Archaeology Suppl 15.

Carter, R.J. (1998) 'Reassessment of seasonality at the early mesolithic site of Star Carr, Yorkshire based on radiographs of mandibular tooth development in red deer (*Cervus elaphus*)', *Journal of Archaeological Science* 25: 851–6.

Carter, S.P. (1990) 'The stratification and taphonomy of shells in calcareous soils: implications for land snail analysis in archaeology', *Journal of Archaeological Science* 17: 495–508.

Carver, M. (1987) *Underneath English towns: interpreting urban archaeology*, London: Batsford.

Carver, M. (1998) *Sutton Hoo: burial ground of kings?*, London: British Museum Press.

Carver, M. (2009) *Archaeological investigation*, Abingdon: Routledge.

Casey, M. *et al.* (eds) (1997) *Redefining archaeology: feminist perspectives*, Canberra: Australian National University.

Cassman, V., Odegaard, N. and Powell, J. (2007) *Human remains: guide for museums and academic institutions*, Walnut Creek, CA: Altamira Press.

Cauvin, M.C. *et al.* (eds) (1998) *L'obsidienne au Proche et Moyen Orient du volcan à l'outil*, Oxford: Archaeopress, British Archaeological Reports, International Series S738.

Cavalli-Sforza, L.L., Menozzi, P. and Piazza, A. (1994) *The history and geography of human genes*, Princeton: Princeton University Press.

CBA (1991) *Signposts for archaeological publication*, 3rd edn, London: Council for British Archaeology.

CBA (2009) *The Stonehenge saga*. London: Council for British Archaeology.

Ceram, C.W. (1957) *A picture history of archaeology*, London: Thames and Hudson.

Cerbone, D.R. (2006) *Understanding phenomenology*, Chesham: Acumen.

Chada, A. (2002) 'Visions of discipline: Sir Mortimer Wheeler and the archaeological method in India (1944–1948)', *Journal of Social Archaeology* 2 (3): 378–401.

Chadwick, A. (2003) 'Post-processualism, professionalisation and archaeological methodologies: towards reflective and radical practice', *Archaeological Dialogues* 10 (1): 97–118.

Chakrabarti, D.K. (1988) *A history of Indian archaeology: from the beginning to 1947*, New Delhi: Munshiram Manoharlal.

Chakrabarti, D.K. (2003) *Archaeology in the Third World: a history of Indian archaeology since 1947*, New Delhi: D.K. Printworld.

Challis, K. *et al.* (2008) 'Airborne lidar and historic environment records', *Antiquity* 82: 1055–64.

Chamberlain, A.T. (2001) 'Palaeodemography', in Brothwell, D.R. and Pollard, A.M. *Handbook of archaeological sciences*, Chichester: John Wiley and Sons: 260–8.

Chambers, N. (2007) *Joseph Banks and the British Museum: the world of collecting, 1770–1830*, London: Pickering and Chatto.

Chapman, H. (2006) *Landscape archaeology and GIS*, Stroud: Tempus.

Chapman, J.C. (1994) 'Destruction of a common heritage: the archaeology of war in Croatia, Bosnia and Hercegovina', *Antiquity* 68: 120–6.

Chapman, J.C. (1998) 'A biographical sketch of Marija Gimbutas', in Díaz-Andreu, M. and

Sørenson, M.L.S. (eds) *Excavating women: a history of women in European archaeology*, London: Routledge: 295–314.

Chapman, J.C. (2000) *Fragmentation in archaeology: people, places and broken objects in the prehistory of South Eastern Europe*, London: Routledge.

Chapman, J.C. and Gydarska, B. (2007) *Parts and wholes: fragmentation in prehistoric context*, Oxford: Oxbow Books.

Chapman, J.C. and Hamerow, H. (eds) (1997) *Migrations and invasion in archaeological explanation*, Oxford: British Archaeological Reports, International Series S664.

Chapman, J.C. and Shiel, R. (1993) 'Social change and land use in prehistoric Dalmatia', *Proceedings of the Prehistoric Society* 59: 61–104.

Chapman, J.C., Shiel, R. and Batovič, S. (1987) 'Settlement patterns and land use in neothermal Dalmatia, Yugoslavia: 1983–1984 seasons', *Journal of Field Archaeology* 14: 123–46.

Chapman, J.C., Shiel, R. and Batovič, S. (1996) *The changing face of Dalmatia*, London: Research Report of the Society of Antiquaries of London 54.

Charles, R. (1998) *Late Magdalenian chronology and faunal exploitation in the north-western Ardennes*, Oxford: British Archaeological Reports, International Series S737.

Charrié-Duhaut, A. *et al.* (2007) 'The canopic jars of Rameses II: real use revealed by molecular study of organic residues', *Journal of Archaeological Science* 34: 957–67.

Chauvet, J.M., Deschamps, E. Brunel and Hillaire, C. (1996) *Chauvet cave*, London: Thames and Hudson.

Cheater, A. (ed.) (1999) *The anthropology of power: empowerment and disempowerment in changing structures*, London: Routledge.

Cherry, J.F., Davis, J. and Mantzourani, E. (1991) *Landscape archaeology as long-term history: northern Keos in the Cycladic islands from earliest settlement until modern times*, Los Angeles: University of California Institute of Archaeology, Monumenta Archaeologica 16.

Childe, V.G. (1929) *The Danube in prehistory*. Oxford: Clarendon Press.

Childe, V.G. (1934) *New light on the most ancient East: the oriental prelude to European prehistory*, London: Kegan Paul, Trench, Trubner and Co.

Childe, V.G. (1935) 'Changing methods and aims in prehistory: presidential address for 1935', *Proceedings of the Prehistoric Society* 1: 1–15.

Childe, V.G. (1936) *Man makes himself*. London: Watts and Co.

Childe, V.G. (1942) *What happened in history*, Harmondsworth: Penguin.

Chippindale, C. (1988) 'The invention of words for the idea of prehistory', *Proceedings of the Prehistoric Society* 54: 303–14.

Chippindale, C. (2004) *Stonehenge complete*, rev. edn, London: Thames and Hudson.

Chippindale, C. *et al.* (1990) *Who owns Stonehenge?*, London: Batsford.

Chitty, G. (2007) 'Meeting the climate change challenge', *The Archaeologist* 66: 16–18.

Christensen, J. (2004) 'Warfare in the European Neolithic', *Acta archaeologica* 75 (2): 129–56.

Church, M.J. *et al.* (2007) 'Charcoal production during the Norse and early medieval periods in Eyjafjallahreppur, Southern Iceland', *Radiocarbon* 49: 659–72.

Ciliberto, E. and Spoto, G. (2000) *Modern analytical methods in art and archaeology*, New York: John Wiley.

Claassen, C. (1998) *Shells*, Cambridge: Cambridge University Press, Cambridge Manuals in Archaeology.

Clack, T. and Brittain, M. (2007) *Archaeology and the media*, Walnut Creek, CA: Left Coast Press.

Clark, A. (1991) *Excavations at Mucking 1: the site atlas*, London: English Heritage Archaeological Report 20.

Clark, A.J. (1996) *Seeing beneath the soil: prospecting methods in archaeology*, 2nd edn, London: Routledge.

Clark, G. (1946) *From savagery to civilization*, London: Cobbett Press.

Clark, G. (1969) *World prehistory: a new outline*, Cambridge: Cambridge University Press.

Clark, G. (1977) *World prehistory in new perspective*, Cambridge: Cambridge University Press.

Clarke, D.L. (1968) *Analytical archaeology*, London: Methuen.

Clarke, D.L. (1973) 'Archaeology: the loss of innocence', *Antiquity* 47: 6–18.

Cleal, R.M.J., Montague, R. and Walker, K.E. (1995) *Stonehenge in its landscape: twentieth century excavations*, London: English Heritage Archaeological Report 10.

Clermont, N. and Smith, P. (1990) 'Prehistoric, prehistory, prehistorian … who invented the terms?', *Antiquity* 64: 97–102.

Clottes, J. (1999) 'The Chauvet cave dates', in Harding, A.F. (ed.) *Experiment and design: archaeological studies in honour of John Coles*, Oxford: Oxbow Books: 13–19.

Clough, T.H.McK. and Woolley, A.R. (1985) 'Petrography and stone implements', *World Archaeology* 17: 90–100.

Clutton-Brock, J. and Noe-Nygaard, N. (1990) 'New osteological and C-isotope evidence on mesolithic dogs', *Journal of Archaeological Science* 17: 643–54.

Coe, M. (1992) *Breaking the Maya code*, London: Thames and Hudson.

Cohen, A. and Serjeantson, D. (1996) *Bird bones from archaeological sites*, rev. edn, London: Archetype/United Kingdom Institute for Conservation.

Cohen, G.M. and Sharp Joukowsky, M. (2004) *Breaking ground: pioneering women archaeologists*, Ann Arbor: University of Michigan Press.

Cohen, M.N. and Crane-Kramer, G.M.M. (2007) *Ancient health: skeletal indicators of agricultural and economic intensification*, Gainesville: University Press of Florida.

Cole, N. and Watchman, A. (2005) 'AMS dating of rock art in the Laura region, Cape York peninsula, Australia – protocols and results of recent research', *Antiquity* 79 (305): 661–78.

Cole, S. (2008) 'War, cultural property and the Blue Shield', in Stone, P.G. and Bajjaly, J.F. (eds) *The destruction of cultural heritage in Iraq*, Woodbridge: The Boydell Press: 65–72.

Coles, B. and Coles, J.M. (1986) *Sweet track to Glastonbury: the Somerset Levels in prehistory*, London: Thames and Hudson.

Coles, G. and Mills, C. (eds) (1998) *Life on the edge: human settlement and marginality*, Oxford: Association for Environmental Archaeology Symposia 13/Oxbow Monograph 100.

Coles, J.M. (1979) *Experimental archaeology*, London/New York: Academic Press.

Coles, J.M. (1984) *The archaeology of wetlands*, Edinburgh: Edinburgh University Press.

Coles, J.M. and Coles, B. (1996) *Enlarging the past: the contribution of wetland archaeology (1995 Rhind Lectures)*, Edinburgh: Wetland Arch. Research Project/Society of Antiquaries of Scotland Monograph 11.

Coles, J.M. *et al.* (1999) 'A Later Bronze Age shield from South Cadbury, Somerset, England', *Antiquity* 73: 33–48.

Colette, A. (ed.) (2007) *Case studies on climate change and world heritage*, Paris: UNESCO World Heritage Centre.

Colledge, S. and Conolly, J. (2007) *The origins and spread of domestic plants in Southwest Asia and Europe*, Walnut Creek, CA: Left Coast Press.

Collett, L. (2008) *An introduction to drawing archaeological pottery*, Reading: Association of Archaeological Illustrators and Surveyors.

Collingwood, R.G. and Wright, R.P. (1965) *The Roman inscriptions of Britain*, Oxford: Clarendon Press.

Collis, J. (2001) *Digging up the past: an introduction to archaeological excavation*, Stroud: Sutton Publishing.

Collis, J. (2003) *The Celts: origins, myths and reinventions*, Stroud: Tempus.

Conyers, L. (2004) *Ground-penetrating radar for archaeology*, Walnut Creek, CA: Altamira Press.

Conzen, M.P. (ed.) (1994) *The making of the American landscape*, London: Routledge.

Cook, B.F. (ed.) (1997) *The Elgin Marbles*, London: British Museum Press.

Cool, H. (2007) *Eating and drinking in Roman Britain*, Cambridge: Cambridge University Press.

Cooney, G. (2000) *Landscapes of Neolithic Ireland*, London: Routledge.

Cooper, M.A. *et al.* (ed.) (1995) *Managing archaeology*, London/New York: Routledge.

Cope, L.H. *et al.* (1997) *Metal analyses of Roman coins minted under the Empire*, London: British Museum Occasional Paper 120.

Corbey, R. and Theunissen, B. (eds) (1995) *Ape, man, apeman: changing views since 1600*, Leiden: Leiden University Department of Prehistory.

Cossons, N. (2000) *Perspectives on industrial archaeology*, London: Science Museum.

Courty, M.A. *et al.* (eds) (1989) *Soils and micromorphology in archaeology*, Cambridge: Cambridge University Press.

Cowan, C. Wesley and Watson, P.J. (1992) *Origins of agriculture: an international perspective*, Washington, DC: Smithsonian Institution Press.

Cowell, M. and La Niece, S. (1991) 'Metalwork: artifice and artistry', in Bowman, S. (ed.) *Science and the past*, London: British Museum: 74–98.

Cox, C. (1992) 'Satellite imagery, aerial photography and wetland archaeology', *World Archaeology* 24: 249–67.

Cox, M. (1996) *Life and death in Spitalfields 1700 to 1850*, London: Council for British Archaeology.

Cox, M. and Mays, S. (eds) (2000) *Human osteology in archaeology and forensic science*, London: Greenwich Medical Media.

Crabtree, P.J. (1989) *West Stow, Suffolk: early Anglo-Saxon animal husbandry*, Ipswich: Suffolk County Planning Department, East Anglian Archaeology Report No. 47.

Craddock, P.T. (1995) *Early metal mining and production*, Edinburgh: Edinburgh University Press.

Craddock, P.T. and Lang, J. (2003) *Mining and metal production through the ages*, London: The British Museum Press.

Craig, E. (ed.) (2000) *Routledge concise encyclopaedia of philosophy*, London: Routledge.

Craig, O. *et al.* (2005) 'Did the first farmers of central and eastern Europe produce dairy foods?', *Antiquity* 79: 882–94.

Crawford, O.G.S. (1929) *Air-photography for archaeologists*, London: Ordnance Survey.

Creamer, W. (2001) 'The origins of centralization: changing features of local and regional control during the Rio Grande classic period, AD 1325–1540', in Haas, J. (ed.) *From leaders to rulers*, New York: Kluwer Academic: 37–58.

Crick, J.C. (2004) 'Geoffrey of Monmouth', *Dictionary of national biography*, Oxford: Oxford University Press.

Crone, A. (2000) *The history of a Scottish Lowland crannog: excavations at Buiston, Ayrshire 1989–90*, Loanhead: Scottish Trust for Archaeological Research, Monograph 4.

Cronyn, J.M. (1989) *Elements of archaeological conservation*, London: Longman.

Crossley, D. (1992) *Post-medieval archaeology in Britain*, Leicester: Leicester University Press.

Crumley, C. (2001) 'Communication, holism and the evolution of socio-political complexity', in Haas, J. (ed.) *From leaders to rulers*, New York: Kluwer Academic: 19–36.

Crummy, N., Crummy, P. and Crossan, C. (1993) *Excavations of Roman and later cemeteries, churches and monastic sites in Colchester, 1971–88*, Colchester Archaeological Trust: Colchester Archaeological Report 9.

Čufar, K. (2007) 'Dendrochronology and past human activity – a review of advances since 2000', *Tree-Ring Research* 63 (1): 47–60.

Culleton, B.J., Kennett, D.J. and Jones, T.L. (2009) 'Oxygen isotope seasonality in a temperate estuarine shell midden: a case study from CA-ALA-17 on the San Francisco Bay, California', *Journal of Archaeological Science* 36 (7): 1354–63.

Cummings, V., Jones, A. and Watson, A. (2002) 'Divided places: phenomenology and asymmetry in the monuments of the Black Mountains, southeast Wales', *Cambridge Archaeological Journal* 12(1): 57–70.

Cummings, V. and Whittle, A. (2003) 'Tombs with a view: landscape, monuments and trees', *Antiquity* 77: 255–66.

Cunliffe, B.W. (1984) *Danebury: an Iron Age hillfort in Hampshire*. London: Council for British Archaeology.

Cunliffe, B.W. (1993) *Danebury: the anatomy of an Iron Age hillfort*, London: Batsford/English Heritage.

Cunliffe, B.W. (1998) *Fishbourne Roman Palace*, new edn, Stroud: Tempus.

Cunliffe, B.W. (2000) *The Danebury environs programme: the prehistory of a Wessex landscape*, 6 vols, Oxford: OUCA.

Cunliffe, B.W. and Renfrew, C. (eds) (1997) *Science and Stonehenge*, Oxford: Oxford University Press, Proceedings of the British Academy 92.

Cuno, J. (2008) *Who owns antiquity? Museums and the battle over our ancient heritage*, Princeton, NJ: Princeton University Press.

Currant, A. and Jacobi, R. (2001) 'A formal mammalian biostratigraphy for the Late Pleistocene of Britain', *Quaternary Science Reviews* 20: 1707–16.

Curry, A. (2009) 'Climate change: sites in peril', *Archaeology* 62 (2).

Dabas, M. *et al.* (1998) *La prospection*, Paris: Errance Collection 'Archéologiques'.

Dalla Bona, L. (1999) 'Protecting cultural resources in Ontario', in Westcott, K. and Brandon, R. (eds) *Practical applications of GIS in archaeology: a predictive modelling tool kit*, London: Taylor and Francis, GISDATA: 73–99.

Dalrymple, G.B. (1991) *The age of the earth*, Stanford, CT: Stanford University Press.

Daniel, G. (1967) *The origins and growth of archaeology*, Harmondsworth: Penguin.

Daniel, G. (1975) *150 years of archaeology*, London: Duckworth.

Daniel, G. (1981) *A short history of archaeology*, London: Thames and Hudson.

Daniel, G. and Renfrew, C. (1988) *The idea of prehistory*, Edinburgh: Edinburgh University Press.

Dark, K.R. and Dark, P. (1997) *The landscape of Roman Britain*, Stroud: Sutton Publishing.

Dark, P. (1999) *The environment of Britain in the first millennium AD*, London: Duckworth.

Dark, P. (2000) 'Revised "absolute" dating of the early Mesolithic site of Star Carr, North Yorkshire, in the light of changes in the early Holocene tree-ring chronology', *Antiquity* 74: 304–7.

Dark, P. (2006) 'Climate deterioration and land-use change in the first millennium BC: perspectives from the British palynological record', *Journal of Archaeological Science* 33: 1381–95.

Darvill, T. (2002) *Oxford concise dictionary of archaeology*, Oxford: Oxford University Press.

Darvill, T. (2005) 'Sorted for ease and whiz? Approaching value and importance in archaeological resource management', in Mathers, C., Darvill, T. and Little, B.J. (eds) *Heritage of value, archaeology of renown: reshaping archaeological assessment and significance*, Gainesville: University of Florida Press: 21–42.

Darvill, T. (2006) *Stonehenge: the biography of a landscape*, Stroud: Tempus.

Darvill, T. and Russell, B. (2002) *Archaeology after PPG16: archaeological investigations in England 1990–1999*, Bournemouth and London: Bournemouth University School of Conservation Sciences Research Report 10.

Darvill, T. and Wainwright, G. (2009) 'Stonehenge excavations 2008', *Antiquaries Journal* 89: 1–19.

Darwin, C. (1859) *The origin of species by means of natural selection*, London: John Murray.

David, A. (ed.) (1995) *Geophysical survey in archaeological field evaluation*, London: English Heritage; Ancient Monuments Laboratory.

David, A. (2001) 'Overview – the role and practice of archaeological prospection', in Brothwell, D.R. and Pollard, A.M. *Handbook of archaeological sciences*, Chichester: John Wiley and Sons: 521–7.

David, B. *et al.* (1997) 'New optical and radio-carbon dates from Ngarrabullgan Cave, a Pleistocene archaeological site in Australia: implications for the comparability of time clocks for the human colonization of Australia', *Antiquity* 71: 183–8.

David, B. and Thomas, J. (eds) (2008) *Handbook of landscape archaeology*, Walnut Creek, CA: Left Coast Press.

Davis, M. (2008) *Dame Kathleen Kenyon: digging up the Holy Land*, San Francisco, CA: Left Coast Press.

Davis, S.J.M. (1987) *The archaeology of animals*, London: Batsford.

Davis, W. (1992) 'The deconstruction of intentionality in archaeology', *Antiquity* 66: 334–47.

Davison, B. (1997) *Picturing the past, through the eyes of reconstruction artists*, London: English Heritage Gatekeeper Series.

de Geer, G. (1912) 'A geochronology of the last 12,000 years', *Proceedings of the 11th International Geological Congress (Stockholm 1912)* 1: 241–58.

de Grummond, N.T. (ed.) (1996) *An encyclopedia of the history of classical archaeology*, 2 vols, London: Greenwood Press.

de Jersey, P. (2008) 'Evans and ancient British coins', in MacGregor, A. (ed.) *Sir John Evans 1823–1908: antiquity, commerce and natural science in the age of Darwin*, Oxford: The Ashmolean Museum: 152–72.

Dean, D.R. (1992) *James Hutton and the history of geology*, Ithaca, NY: Cornell University Press.

Dean, J.S. (1997) 'Dendrochronology', in Taylor, R.E. and Aitken, M.J. *Chronometric dating in archaeology*, New York: Plenum Press: 31–64.

Dearden, B. and Clark, A. (1990) 'Pont-de-l'Arche or Pîtres? A location and archaeomagnetic dating for Charles the Bald's fortifications on the Seine', *Antiquity* 64: 567–619.

Debaine-Francfort, C. (1999) *The search for ancient China*, London: Thames and Hudson New Horizons.

Degryse, P., Henderson, J. and Hodgins, G. (2009) *Isotopes in vitreous materials*, Leuven: Leuven University Press.

Delgado, J. (ed.) (1997) *Encyclopaedia of underwater and maritime archaeology*, London: British Museum Press.

DeMarrais, E., Gosden, C. and Renfrew, C. (eds) (2004) *Rethinking materiality: the engagement of mind with the material world*, Cambridge: McDonald Institute Monograph.

Denford, G.T. (ed.) (1997) *Representing archaeology in museums*, Society of Museum Archaeologists: Museum Archaeologist Series 22.

Denning, K. (2000) 'Fuller's social epistemology: applied philosophy for archaeologists?', in Holtorf, C. and Karlsson, H. *Philosophy and archaeological practice: perspectives for the 21st century*, Göteborg: Bricoleur Press: 203–19.

Deuel, L. (1971) *Flights into yesterday: the story of aerial archaeology*, Harmondsworth: Pelican.

Díaz-Andreu, M. (2007) *A world history of nineteenth-century archaeology: nationalism, colonialism, and the past*, Oxford: Oxford University Press.

Díaz-Andreu, M. and Champion, T. (eds) (1996) *Nationalism and archaeology in Europe*, London: UCL Press.

Díaz-Andreu, M. and Stig-Sørensen, M.-L. (1998) *Excavating women: a history of women in European archaeology*, London: Routledge.

Díaz-Andreu, M. *et al.* (2005) *The archaeology of identity*, London: Routledge.

Dibble, H.L., McPherron, S.P. and Roth, B.J. (2002) *Virtual dig: simulated archaeological excavation of a middle Palaeolithic site in France*, 2nd edn, New York: McGraw-Hill.

Dietler, M. (1994) '"Our ancestors the Gauls": archaeology, ethnic nationalism, and the manipulation of ethnic identity in modern Europe', *American Anthropologist* 96: 584–605.

Dietler, M. (1998) 'A tale of three sites: the monumentalization of Celtic oppida and the politics of collective memory and identity', *World Archaeology* 30: 72–89.

Dimbleby, G.W. (1977) *Ecology and archaeology*, London: E. Arnold.

Dimbleby, G.W. (1978) *Plants and archaeology*, London: J. Baker.

Dimbleby, G.W. (1985) *The palynology of archaeological sites*, New York/London: Academic Press.

Dincauze, D.F. (2000) *Environmental archaeology: principles and practice*, Cambridge: Cambridge University Press.

Dixon, N. (2004) *The Crannogs of Scotland: an underwater archaeology*, Stroud: Tempus.

Dixon, P. (1988) *Recording timber buildings*, London: Council for British Archaeology, Practical Handbooks in Archaeology 5.

Dobinson, C. and Denison, S. (1995) *Metal detecting and archaeology in England*, London/York: English Heritage/Council for British Archaeology.

Dobney, K. and Ervynck, A. (2007) 'To fish or not to fish? Evidence for the possible avoidance of fish consumption during the Iron Age around the North Sea', in Haselgrove, C. and Moore, T.

(eds) *The later Iron Age in Britain and beyond*, Oxford: Oxbow: 403–19.

Dobres, M.A. and Robb, J. (eds) (2000) *Agency in archaeology*, London: Routledge.

Dodge, H. (1988) 'Decorative stones for architecture in the Roman empire', *Oxford Journal of Archaeology* 7: 65–80.

Donnelly, I. (1882) *Atlantis: the antediluvian world*, New York: Harper and Brothers.

Donoghue, D. (2001) 'Remote sensing', in Brothwell, D.R. and Pollard, A.M. *Handbook of archaeological sciences*, Chichester: John Wiley and Sons: 555–63.

Doumas, C. (ed.) (1983) *Thera: Pompeii of the ancient Aegean*, London: Thames and Hudson.

Drennan, R.D. (1996) *Statistics for archaeologists: a common sense approach*, New York/London: Plenum.

Drewett, P. (1999) *Field archaeology: an introduction*, London: UCL Press.

Driscoll, S.T. and Yeoman, P.A. (eds) (1997) *Excavations within Edinburgh castle in 1988–91*, Edinburgh: Society of Antiquaries of Scotland Monograph 12.

Drower, M.S. (1985) *Flinders Petrie: a life in archaeology*, London: Gollancz.

Drury, P.J. (ed.) (1982) *Structural reconstruction: approaches to the interpretation of the excavated remains of buildings*, Oxford: British Archaeological Reports 110.

Duhard, J.P. (1991) 'The shape of Pleistocene women', *Antiquity* 65: 552–61.

Dumayne-Peaty, L. (2001) 'Human impact on vegetation', in Brothwell, D.R. and Pollard, A.M. *Handbook of archaeological sciences*, Chichester: John Wiley and Sons: 379–92.

Dunnell, R.C. (1992) 'The notion site', in Rossignol, J. and Wandsnider, L. *Space, time, and archaeological landscapes*, New York: Plenum: 21–41.

Dyson, S. (2006) *In pursuit of ancient pasts: a history of classical archaeology in the nineteenth and twentieth centuries*, New Haven, CT: Yale University Press.

Earwood, C. (1993) *Domestic wooden artefacts in Britain and Ireland from Neolithic to Viking times*, Exeter: Exeter University Press.

Eckhardt, R.B. (2000) *Human paleobiology*, Cambridge: Cambridge University Press.

Edis, J., MacLeod, D. and Bewley, R. (1989) 'An archaeologist's guide to classification of cropmarks and soilmarks', *Antiquity* 63: 112–46.

Edmonds, M. (1999) *Ancestral geographies of the Neolithic: landscapes, monuments and memory*, London: Routledge.

Edmonds, M. (2001) 'Lithic exploitation and use', in Brothwell, D.R. and Pollard, A.M. *Handbook of archaeological sciences*, Chichester: John Wiley and Sons: 461–70.

Edwards, C. J. (2007) 'Mitochondrial DNA analysis shows a Near Eastern Neolithic origin for domestic cattle and no indication of domestication of European aurochs', *Proceedings of the Royal Society: Biological Science* 274 (1616): 1377–85.

Edwards, N. (2007) 'Edward Lhuyd and the origins of early medieval Celtic archaeology', *Antiquaries Journal*, 87: 165–96.

Eggert, M. and Veit, U. (eds) (1997) *Theorie in der Archäologie: zur english-sprachigen Diskussion*, Münster: Waxmann.

Eighmy, J.L. and Sternberg, R.S. (eds) (1990) *Archaeomagnetic dating*, Tucson, AZ: Arizona University Press.

Elias, S.A. (1994) *Quaternary insects and their environments*, Washington, DC: Smithsonian Institution Press.

Ellingson, T. (2001) *The myth of the Noble Savage*, Berkeley: University of California Press.

Elliott, M. (1995) *Great excavations: tales of early southwestern archaeology, 1888–1939*, Santa Fe, NM: School of American Research Press.

Ellis, L. (ed.) (2000) *Archaeological method and theory: an encyclopedia*, New York: Garland Publishing.

Elsdon, S. (2004) *Christian MacLagan: Stirling's formidable lady antiquary*, Forfar: The Pinkfoot Press.

Elsner, J. and Rutherford, I. (eds) (2005) *Pilgrimage in Graeco-Roman and early Christian antiquity: seeing the gods*, Oxford: Oxford University Press.

Empereur, J.Y. (1998) *Alexandria rediscovered*, London: British Museum Press.

Engelhardt, J. (2006) 'Archaeology', in Beckhoff, B et al. (eds) *Handbook of practical x-ray fluorescence analysis*, Berlin: Springer: 700–12.

Engels, F. (1986) [1884] *The origin of the family, private property and the state in the light of the researches of Lewis H. Morgan*, Harmondsworth: Penguin Classics.

English Heritage (1991) *Exploring our past: strategies for the archaeology of England*, London: English Heritage.

English Heritage (1992) *Managing England's heritage: setting our priorities for the 1990s*, London: English Heritage.

English Heritage (1998) *Exploring our past: research agenda*, Swindon: English Heritage.

English Heritage (2006a) *Understanding historic buildings: a guide to good recording practice*, London: English Heritage.

English Heritage (2006b) *Archaeomagnetic dating: guidelines on producing and interpreting archaeomagnetic dates*, Swindon: English Heritage.

English Heritage (2007) *3D laser scanning for heritage: advice and guidance to users on laser scanning in archaeology and architecture*, Swindon: English Heritage.

English Heritage (2008a) *Luminescence dating: guidelines on using luminescence dating in archaeology*. London: English Heritage.

English Heritage (2008b) *Climate change and the historic environment*, London: English Heritage.

Erickson, C.L. (1999) 'Neo-environmental determinism and agrarian "collapse" in Andean prehistory', *Antiquity* 73: 634–42.

Ericson, J.E. and Earle, T.K. (eds) (1982) *Contexts for prehistoric exchange*, New York: Academic Press.

Etienne, R. and Etienne, F. (1992) *The search for ancient Greece*, London: Thames and Hudson New Horizons.

Evans, A.C. (1994) *The Sutton Hoo ship burial*, London: British Museum.

Evans, A.J. (1899–1900) 'Knossos I: the palace', *Annual of the British School at Athens* 6: 3–70.

Evans, A.J. (1921) *The palace of Minos at Knossos, I: the Neolithic and early middle Minoan ages*, London: Macmillan.

Evans, C. (1989) 'Archaeology and modern times: Bersu's Woodbury 1938 and 1939', *Antiquity* 63: 436–50.

Evans, C. (2008) *Borderlands: the archaeology of Addenbrooke's environs*, Cambridge: Cambridge Archaeology Unit.

Evans, C. (2009) '1859 – marking time', *Antiquity* 83: 458–61.

Evans, J. (1860) 'On the occurrence of flint implements in undisturbed beds of gravel, sand and clay', *Archaeologia* 38: 280–307.

Evans, J. (1864) *The coins of the Ancient Britons*. London: J. Russell Smith.

Evans, J., Chenery, C. and Fitzpatrick, A. (2006) 'Bronze Age childhood migration of individuals near Stonehenge revealed by strontium and oxygen isotope tooth enamel analysis', *Archaeometry* 48 (2): 309–21.

Evans, J., Stoodley, N. and Chenery, C. (2006) 'A strontium and oxygen isotope assessment of a possible fourth-century immigrant population in a Hampshire cemetery, southern England', *Journal of Archaeological Science* 33: 265–72.

Evans, J.D. (1982) 'Introduction: on the prehistory of archaeology', in Evans, J.D., Cunliffe, B. and Renfrew, C. (eds) *Antiquity and man: essays in honour of Glyn Daniel*, London: Thames and Hudson: 12–18.

Evans, J.G. (1973) *Land snails in archaeology*, London/New York: Seminar Press.

Evans, J.G. (1999) *Land and archaeology: histories of human environment in the British Isles*, Stroud: Tempus Publishing.

Evans, J.G. et al. (1993) 'An environmental history of the upper Kennet valley, Wiltshire, for the last 10,000 years', *Proceedings of the Prehistoric Society* 59: 139–95.

Evans, J.G. and O'Connor, T. (1999) *Environmental archaeology: principles and methods*, Stroud: Sutton Publishing.

Evans, Joan (1943) *Time and chance: the story of Arthur Evans and his forebears*, London: Longman Green.

Evans, Joan (1956) *A history of the Society of Antiquaries*, Oxford: Oxford University Press.

Evans-Pritchard, E. (1940) *The Nuer: a description of the modes of livelihood and political institutions of a Nilotic people*. Oxford: Clarendon Press.

Evershed, R.P. *et al.* (2001) 'Lipids in archaeology', in Brothwell, D.R. and Pollard, A.M. *Handbook of archaeological sciences*, Chichester: John Wiley and Sons: 331–49.

Everson, P. and Williamson, T. (eds) (1998) *The archaeology of landscape: studies presented to Christopher Taylor*, Manchester: Manchester University Press.

Evin, J. *et al.* (1998) *La datation en laboratoire*, Paris: Errance Collection 'Archéologiques'.

Ewen, C. (2003) *Artifacts: archaeologist's Toolkit 4*, Walnut Creek, CA: Altamira Press.

Ewin, A. (2000) *Hadrian's Wall: a social and cultural history*, University of Lancaster: Centre for North West Regional Studies.

Fabech, C. and Ringtved, J. (eds) (1999) *Settlement and landscape: proceedings of conference in Aarhus, Denmark, May 4–7 1998*, Hojbjerg: Jutland Archaeological Society.

Fagan, B.M. (1977) *Elusive treasure: the story of early archaeologists in the Americas*, New York: Charles Scribner's.

Fagan, B.M. (1996) *Eyewitness to discovery: first-person accounts of the world's greatest archaeological discoveries*, Oxford: Oxford University Press.

Fagan, B.M. (ed.) (1996) *Oxford companion to archaeology*, Oxford: Oxford University Press.

Fagan, B.M. (2000) *Ancient lives: an introduction to archaeology*, Englewood Cliffs, NJ: Prentice Hall; London: Longman Higher Education.

Fagan, B.M. (2001) *Grahame Clark: an intellectual biography of an archaeologist*, Boulder, CO: Westview Press.

Fagan, B.M. (2005) 'Short history of archaeological methods 1870 to 1960', in Maschner, H.D.G. and Chippindale, C. (eds) *Handbook of archaeological methods, 1*, Lanham, MD: Altamira Press: 40–74.

Fagan, B.M. (2007) *People of the Earth: an introduction to world prehistory*, Upper Saddle River, NJ: Pearson Prentice Hall.

Fagan, B.M. (2008) *The great warming*, New York: Bloomsbury Press.

Fagan, G. (ed.) (2006) *Archaeological fantasies: how pseudoarchaeology misrepresents the past and misleads the public*, London: Routledge.

Fairbairn, A.S. (ed.) (2000) *Plants in Neolithic Britain and beyond*, Oxford: Oxbow Books for Neolithic Studies Group Seminar Papers 5.

Fairbanks, R.G. *et al.* (2005) 'Radiocarbon calibration curve spanning 0 to 50,000 years BP based on paired ^{230}Th/^{234}U/^{238}U and ^{14}C dates on pristine corals', *Quaternary Science Reviews* 24 (16–17): 1781–96.

Fairclough, G. (1992) 'Meaningful constructions: spatial and functional analysis of medieval buildings', *Antiquity* 66: 348–66.

Fairclough, G. and Rippon, S. (2002) *Europe's cultural landscape: archaeologists and the management of change*, Brussels: Europae Archaeologie Consilium.

Fairclough, G. *et al.* (2008) *The heritage reader*. London: Routledge.

Fairweather, A. and Ralston, I. (1993) 'The Neolithic timber hall at Balbridie, Grampian Region, Scotland: the building, the date, the plant macrofossils', *Antiquity* 67: 313–23.

Fansa, M. (ed.) (1990) *Experimentelle Archäologie in Deutschland*, Oldenburg: Archäologische Mitteilungen aus Nordwestdeutschland Beiheft 4.

Farnoux, A. (1996) *Knossos: unearthing a legend*, London: Thames and Hudson.

Farwell, D.E. and Molleson, T.I. (1993) *Poundbury, 2: the cemeteries*, Dorset: Natural History and Archaeology Society Monograph 11.

Feder, K.L. (2005) *Frauds, myths and mysteries: science and pseudo-science in archaeology*, 6th rev. edn, Mountain View, CA: McGraw-Hill.

Feld, S. and Basso, K.H. (eds) (1996) *Senses of place*, Seattle: University of Washington Press.

Fenton, S. (2003) *Ethnicity: key concepts.* Cambridge: Polity Press.

Ferguson, A.B. (1993) *Utter antiquity: perceptions of prehistory in Renaissance England*, Durham, NC: Duke University Press.

Ferlini, R. (2007) *Forensic archaeology and human rights violations*, Springfield, OH: Charles Thomas.

Fernie, K. and Gilman, P. (2000) *Informing the future of the past: guidelines for SMRs*, London: English Heritage.

Feyler, G. (1987) 'Contribution à l'histoire des origines de la photographie archéologique: 1839–1880', *Mélanges de l'école française de Rome* 99: 1019–47.

Field, N. and Parker Pearson, M. (2003) *Fiskerton: an Iron Age timber causeway with Iron Age and Roman votive offerings, the 1981 excavations*, Oxford: Oxbow.

Fiorato, V., Boylston, A. and Knusel, C. (eds) (2007) *Blood red roses: the archaeology of a mass grave from the Battle of Towton AD 1461*, 2nd edn, Oxford: Oxbow Books.

Fischer, A. and Kristiansen, K. (eds) (1998) *The birth of ecological archaeology: a history of ecological approaches to the transition to agriculture in Denmark*, Sheffield: J. R. Collis, Sheffield Archaeological Monographs 12.

Fisher, C.T. and Thurston, T.L. (eds) (1999) 'Dynamic landscapes and socio-political process: the topography of anthropogenic environments in global perspective', *Antiquity* 73: 630–88.

Fitton, J.L. (1995) *Discovery of the Greek Bronze Age*, London: British Museum Press.

Fitzpatrick, A.P. *et al.* (1999) *Prehistoric and Roman sites in East Devon: the A30 Honiton to Exeter improvement DBFO scheme, 1996–9*, Salisbury: Wessex Archaeology.

Flannery, K. (1976) *The early Mesoamerican village*, New York: Academic Press.

Fleming, A. (2008) *The Dartmoor reaves: investigating prehistoric land divisions*, 2nd edn, Oxford: Windgather Press/Oxbow.

Fleming, S.J. and Schenck, H.R. (eds) (1989) *History of technology: the role of metals*, Philadelphia, PA: Pennsylvania University Museum, MASCA Research Papers 6.

Fletcher, M. and Lock, G. (2005) *Digging numbers: elementary statistics for archaeologists*, 2nd edn, Oxford: Oxford University Committee for Archaeology Monograph 33.

Fokkens, H. (1998) *Drowned landscape: the occupation of the western part of the Frisian–Drentian plateau, 4400 BC–AD 500*, Assen: Van Gorcum.

Foreman, L. and Goddio, F. (1999) *Cleopatra's palace: in search of a legend*, New York: Random House.

Forsberg, S. (1995) *Near Eastern destruction datings as sources for Greek and Near Eastern Iron Age chronology*, Uppsala: BOREAS: Uppsala Studies in Ancient Mediterranean and Near Eastern Civilization 19.

Forsyth, P.Y. (1997) *Thera in the Bronze Age*, New York: Peter Lang, American Universities Studies IX (History) vol. 187.

Forte, M. and Siliotti, A. (1997) *Virtual archaeology: recreating ancient worlds*, New York: Harry N. Abrams.

Foster, S.M. (1989) 'Analysis of spatial patterns in buildings (access analysis) as an insight into social structure: examples from the Scottish Atlantic Iron Age', *Antiquity* 63: 40–50.

Foucault, M. (1970) *The order of things: an archaeology of the human sciences*, London: Tavistock Publications.

Foucault, M. (1972) *The archaeology of knowledge*, London: Tavistock Publications.

Fowler, B. (2002) *Iceman: uncovering the life and times of a prehistoric man found in an Alpine glacier*, 2nd edn, London: Pan.

Fowler, C. (2000) 'The individual, the subject and archaeological interpretation: reading Luce Irigaray and Judith Butler', in Holtorf, C. and Karlsson, H. *Philosophy and archaeological practice: perspectives for the 21st century*, Göteborg: Bricoleur Press 107–33.

Fowler, C. (2004) *The archaeology of personhood: an anthropological approach*, London: Routledge.

Fowler, M.J.F. (1996) 'High-resolution satellite imagery in archaeological application: a Russian satellite photograph of the Stonehenge region', *Antiquity* 70: 667–71.

Fowler, P.J. (2000) *Landscape plotted and pieced: landscape history and local archaeology in Fyfield and Overton, Wiltshire*, London: Society of Antiquaries of London Research Report 64.

Fowler, P.J. and Blackwell, I. (1998) *The land of Lettice Sweetapple: an English countryside explored*, Stroud: Tempus.

Fox, R.A. (1993) *Archaeology, history and Custer's last battle: the Little Big Horn re-examined*,

Norman, OK and London: University of Oklahoma Press.

Francovich, R. and Patterson, H. (eds) (2000) *The archaeology of the Mediterranean landscape, 5: extracting meaning from ploughsoil assemblages*, Oxford: Oxbow Books.

Frankenstein, S. and Rowlands, M. (1978) 'The internal structure and regional context of Iron Age society in South-West Germany', *Bulletin of the Institute of Archaeology* 15: 73–112.

Franklin, M. (1997) 'Why are there so few black American archaeologists?', *Antiquity* 71: 799–801.

Frantzen, A.J. and Niles, J.D. (1997) *Anglo-Saxonism and the construction of social identity*, Gainesville, FL: Florida University Press.

Freeman, M. (2004) *Victorians and the prehistoric: tracks to a lost world*, New Haven, CT: Yale University Press.

French, C. (2003) *Geoarchaeology in action*, London: Routledge.

Frenzel, B. (ed.) (1992) *European climate reconstructed from documentary data: methods and results*, European Science Foundation/ Akademie der Wissenschaft und der Litteratur, Stuttgart: Gustav Fischer.

Frere, J. (1800) 'Account of flint weapons discovered at Hoxne in Suffolk', *Archaeologia* 13: 204–5.

Fried, M. (1967) *The evolution of political society*, New York: Random House.

Friedman, I., Trembour, F.W. and Hughes, R.E. (1997) 'Obsidian hydration dating', in Taylor, R.E. and Aitken, M.J. *Chronometric dating in archaeology*, New York: Plenum Press: 297–322.

Friedrich, W. L. (2006) 'Santorini eruption radiocarbon dated to 1627–1600 B.C.', *Science* 312 (5773): 548.

Fritz, G. (2005) 'Paleoethnobotanical methods and application', in Maschner, H.D.G. and Chippindale, C. (eds) *Handbook of archaeological methods, 2*, Lanham, MD: Altamira Press: 773–834.

Fulford, M. and Timby, J. (2000) *Late Iron Age and Roman Silchester*, London: Society for Promotion of Roman Studies, Britannia Monograph Series 15.

Funari, P.P., Hall, M. and Jones, S. (eds) (1998) *Historical archaeology: back from the edge*, London: Routledge, One World Archaeology 31.

Funari, P.P., Zarankin, A. and Stovel, E. (eds) (2005) *Global archaeological theory: contextual voices and contemporary thoughts*, New York: Kluwer Academic.

Funk, R.E. (1976) *Recent contributions to Hudson Valley prehistory*, Albany, NY: SUNY Press.

Furnivall, F.J. (ed.) (1907) *Robert Laneham's letter: describing a part of the entertainment unto Queen Elizabeth at the Castle of Kenilworth in 1575*, London: Chatto and Windus.

Gaffney, C. and Gater, J. (1993) 'Development of remote sensing. Part 2: practice and methods in the application of geophysical techniques in archaeology', in Hunter, J.R. and Ralston, I. (eds) *Archaeological resource management in the UK*. Stroud: Alan Sutton: 205–14.

Gaffney, C. and Gater, J. (2003) *Revealing the buried past: geophysics for archaeologists*, Stroud: Tempus.

Gaffney, V., Fitch, S. and Smith, D. (2009) *Europe's lost world, the rediscovery of Doggerland*. York: CBA Research Reports.

Gaffney, V. and Stančič, Z. (1991) *GIS approaches to regional analysis: a case study of the island of Hvar*, Oxford: Oxbow; Ljubljana: Ljubljana University Faculty of Arts.

Gaffney, V., Thomson, K. and Fitch, S. (eds) (2007) *Mapping Doggerland: the Mesolithic landscapes of the southern North Sea*, Oxford: Archaeopress.

Gale, R. and Cutler, D. (2000) *Plants in archaeology*, Westbury: Royal Botanic Gardens.

Gamble, C. and Kruszynski, R. (2009) 'John Evans, Joseph Prestwich and the stone that shattered the time barrier', *Antiquity* 83: 461–75.

Gamble, C. and Porr, M. (2005) *The hominid individual in context: archaeological investigations of lower and middle Palaeolithic landscapes, locales and artefacts*, London: Routledge.

Gardner, A. (ed.) (2004) *Agency uncovered: archaeological perspectives on social agency, power, and being human*, London: UCL Press.

Gardner, A. (2007) *An archaeology of identity: soldiers and society in Late Roman Britain*, Walnut Creek, CA: Left Coast Press.

Garnsey, P. (1987) *The Roman Empire: economy, society and culture*, London: Duckworth.

Gathercole, P. (2005) 'Childe's revolutions', in Renfrew, C. and Bahn, P. (eds) *Archaeology: the key concepts*, London: Routledge: 35–41.

Geigl, E.-M. (2005) 'Why ancient DNA research needs taphonomy', in O'Connor, T. (ed.) *Biosphere to lithosphere: new studies in vertebrate taphonomy*. Proceedings of the 9th ICAZ conference, Durham, 2002, Oxford: Oxbow: 79–86.

Gell, A. (1992) *The anthropology of time*, Oxford: Berg.

Gernaey, A. *et al.* (2001) 'Survival and interpretation of archaeological proteins', in Brothwell, D.R. and Pollard, A.M. *Handbook of archaeological sciences*, Chichester: John Wiley and Sons: 323–9.

Gero, J.M. and Conkey, M.W. (eds) (1991) *Engendering archaeology: women and prehistory*, Oxford: Basil Blackwell.

Gerrard, C. and Aston, M. (2007) *The Shapwick project, Somerset: a rural landscape explored*, Leeds: The Society for Medieval Archaeology Monograph 25.

Gerritsen, F. (2003) *Local identities. Landscape and community in the late prehistoric Meuse–Demer–Scheldt region*, Amsterdam: Amsterdam Archaeological Studies 9.

Gersbach, E. (1998) *Ausgrabung Heute: Methoden und Techniken der Feldgrabung*, Mainz: Theiss.

Gibbon, G. (1989) *Explanation in archaeology*, Oxford: Blackwell.

Giddens, A. (1984) *The constitution of society: outline of the theory of structuration*, Cambridge: Polity Press.

Gilbert, M.T.P. *et al.* (2007) 'mtDNA from hair and nail clarifies the genetic relationship of the 15th century Qilakitsoq Inuit mummies', *American Journal of Physical Anthropology* 133: 847–53.

Gilchrist, R. (1993) *Gender and material culture: the archaeology of religious women*, London: Routledge.

Gilchrist, R. (1999) *Gender and archaeology: contesting the past*, London: Routledge.

Gill, D. (1997) 'Sotheby's, sleaze and subterfuge: inside the antiquities trade', *Antiquity* 71: 468–71.

Gillespie, R. and Gowlett, J. (1986) 'The terminology of time', in Gowlett, J. and Hedges, R. (eds) *Archaeological results from accelerator dating*, Oxford: Oxford University Committee for Archaeology Monograph 11: 157–65.

Gillings, M. (1997) 'Spatial organisation in the Tisza flood plain: dynamic landscapes and GIS', in Chapman, J.C. and Dolukhanov, P.M. (eds) *Landscapes in flux*, Oxford: Oxbow Books: 163–80.

Gillings, M. (2001) 'Spatial information and archaeology', in Brothwell, D.R. and Pollard, A.M. *Handbook of archaeological sciences*, Chichester: John Wiley and Sons: 671–83.

Gillings, M., Mattingly, D. and Van Dalen, J. (eds) (1999) *The archaeology of the Mediterranean landscape, 3: Geographical Information Systems and landscape archaeology*, Oxford: Oxbow Books.

Gillings, M., Pollard, J. and Wheatley, D. (2000) 'The Beckhampton Avenue and a "new" Neolithic enclosure near Avebury: an interim report on the 1999 excavations', *Wiltshire Archaeological and Natural History Magazine* 93: 1–8.

Gillings, M., Pollard, J. and Wheatley, D. (2001) 'Excavations at the Beckhampton Enclosure, Avenue and Cove, Avebury – an interim report on the 2000 season', *Wiltshire Archaeological and Natural History Magazine* 95: 249–58.

Gimbutas, M. (1991) *The civilization of the goddess: the world of Old Europe*, San Francisco, CA: Harper.

Goddio, F. (2007) *The topography and excavation of Heracleon-Thonis and East Canopus (1996-2006)*, Oxford. OCMA Monograph 1.

Göksu, H.Y., Oberhofer, M. and Regulla, D. (eds) (1991) *Scientific dating methods*, Dordrecht: Kluwer Academic Publishers.

Goldberg, P. and Macphail, R. (2006) *Practical and theoretical geoarchaeology*, Oxford: Blackwell.

Goldstein, J. (ed.) (1994) *Foucault and the writing of history*, Oxford: Blackwell.

Good, G.A. (ed.) (1998) *Sciences of the earth: an encyclopedia of events, people and phenomena*, 2 vols, New York and London: Garland Encyclopedias in the History of Science.

Goodfriend, G. (1992) 'The use of land snail shells in paleoenvironmental reconstruction', *Quaternary Science Review* 11: 665–85.

Goodison, L. and Morris, C. (eds) (1998) *Ancient goddesses: the myths and the evidence*, London: British Museum Press.

Gosden, C. (1999) *Anthropology and archaeology: a changing relationship*, London: Routledge.

Gosden, C. (2001) 'Postcolonial archaeology: issues of culture, identity, and knowledge', in Hodder, I. (ed.) *Archaeological theory today*, Cambridge: Polity Press: 241–61.

Gosden, C. (2004) *Archaeology and colonialism: culture contact from 5000 BC to the present*, Cambridge: Cambridge University Press.

Gosden, C. and Hather, J.G. (eds) (1999) *The prehistory of food: appetites for change*, London: Routledge, One World Archaeology 32.

Gosden, C. and Larson, F. (2007) *Knowing things: exploring the collections at the Pitt Rivers Museum 1884–1945*, Oxford: Oxford University Press.

Gould, R. (2000) *Archaeology and the social history of ships*, Cambridge: Cambridge University Press.

Gould, S.J. (1987) *Time's arrow, time's cycle: myth and metaphor in the discovery of geological time*, Harmondsworth: Penguin.

Gove, H. (1996) *Relic, icon or hoax? Carbon dating the Turin Shroud*, Bristol: Institute of Physics.

Gowland, R. (2006) 'Ageing the past: examining age identity from funerary evidence', in Gowland, R. and Knüsel, C. (eds) *Social archaeology of funerary remains*, Oxford: Oxbow: 143–54.

Gowlett, J. (1993) *Ascent to civilization: the archaeology of early man*, 2nd edn, New York: McGraw-Hill.

Grainger, I. *et al.* (2008) *The Black Death cemetery, East Smithfield, London*. London: Museum of London Monograph 43.

Gran-Aymerich, E. (1998) *Naissance de l'archéologie moderne 1798–1945*, Paris: CNRS Editions.

Graslund, B. (1987) *The birth of prehistoric chronology: dating methods and dating systems in nineteenth-century Scandinavian archaeology*, Cambridge: Cambridge University Press.

Grattan, J. and Torrence, R. (2007) *Living under the shadow: the cultural impacts of volcanic eruptions,* One World Archeology 53, Walnut Creek, CA: Left Coast Press.

Grauer, A. and Stuart-Macadam, P. (eds) (1998) *Sex and gender in palaeopathological perspective*, Cambridge: Cambridge University Press.

Grayson, D.K. (1983) *The establishment of human antiquity*, London/New York: Academic Press.

Grayson, D.K. (2001) 'The archaeological records of human impact on animal populations', *Journal of World Prehistory* 15 (1): 1–68.

Green, J. (1990) *Maritime archaeology: a technical handbook*, London: Academic Press.

Greene, J.P. (1989) *Norton Priory: the archaeology of a medieval religious house*, Cambridge: Cambridge University Press.

Greene, J.P. (1995) 'An archaeological study of the 1830 warehouse at Liverpool Road Station, Manchester', *Industrial Archaeology Review* 17 (2): 117–28.

Greene, K. (1978) 'Apperley Dene Roman fortlet: a re-examination 1974–5', *Archaeologia Aeliana* 6: 29–59.

Greene, K. (1986) *The archaeology of the Roman economy*, Berkeley: University of California Press.

Greene, K. (1987) 'Gothic material culture', in Hodder, I. (ed.) *Archaeology as long-term history*, Cambridge: Cambridge University Press: 117–31.

Greene, K. (1999) 'V. Gordon Childe and the vocabulary of revolutionary change', *Antiquity* 73: 97–109.

Greenfield, J. (1996) *The return of cultural treasures*, 2nd rev. edn, Cambridge: Cambridge University Press.

Greenhalgh, M. (1989) *The survival of Roman antiquities in the Middle Ages*, London: Duckworth.

Greig, J. (1992) 'The surroundings and possible origin of the Roman turf rampart at North Wall, Chester, as shown by pollen analysis', *Ancient Monuments Laboratory Report 64/92*, London: English Heritage.

Grenville, J. (ed.) (1999) *Managing the historic rural landscape*, London: Routledge.

Griffiths, N. and Jenner, A. (1990) *Drawing archaeological finds: a handbook*, London: Archetype, Institute of Archaeology Occasional Papers 13.

Griffiths, T. (1996) *Hunters and collectors: the antiquarian imagination in Australia*, Cambridge: Cambridge University Press.

Grönvold, K., *et al.* (1995) 'Ash layers from Iceland in the Greenland GRIP ice core correlated with oceanic and land sediments', *Earth and Planetary Science Letters* 135: 149–55.

Grün, R. (1997) 'Electron spin resonance dating', in Taylor, R.E. and Aitken, M.J. *Chronometric dating in archaeology*, New York: Plenum Press: 217–60.

Grün, R. (2001) 'Trapped charge dating (ESR, TL, OSL)', in Brothwell, D.R. and Pollard, A.M. *Handbook of archaeological sciences*, Chichester: John Wiley and Sons: 47–62.

Guilday, J.E. (1970) 'Animal remains from archaeological excavations at Fort Ligonier', *Annals of the Carnegie Museum* 42: 177–86.

Gunn, J.D. (ed.) (2000) *The years without summer: tracing AD 536 and its aftermath*, Oxford: Archaeopress, British Archaeological Reports, International Series S872.

Gutherez, X. and Odiot, T. (2001) 'L'archéologie du TGV-Mediterranée', *Nouvelles de l'archéologie* 86: 17–21.

Haas, J. (2001) 'Cultural evolution and political centralization', in Haas, J. (ed.) *From leaders to rulers*, New York: Kluwer Academic: 3–18.

Habu, J., Fawcett, C. and Matsunga, J. (eds) (2008) *Evaluating multiple narratives: beyond nationalist, colonialist, imperialist archaeologies*, New York: Springer.

Hackens, T., Konigsson, L.K. and Passnent, G. (eds) (1995) *^{14}C methods and applications*, PACT 49; Rixensart: UNESCO/Council of Europe.

Hall, C. and McArthur, S. (1997) *Heritage management in New Zealand and Australia*, 2nd edn, Sydney: Oxford University Press.

Hall, D. and Coles, J. (1994) *Fenland survey: an essay in landscape and persistence*, London: English Heritage Archaeological Report 1.

Hall, E. (1989) *Inventing the barbarian: Greek self-definition through tragedy*, Oxford: Clarendon/Oxford Classical Monographs.

Hall, R.A. (1994) *Viking age York*, London: English Heritage/Batsford.

Hall, R.A. and Kenward, H.K. (1990) *Environmental evidence from the Colonia: Tanner Row and Rougier Street*, London: Council for British Archaeology, Archaeology of York 14/6.

Hall, R.A. and Kenward, H.K. (eds) (1995) *Urban–rural connections: perspectives from environmental archaeology*, Oxford: Oxbow Monograph 47.

Hallam, A. (1989) *Great geological controversies*, 2nd edn, Oxford: Oxford University Press.

Halsall, G. (1995) *Early Medieval cemeteries: an introduction to burial archaeology in the post-Roman West (New Light on the Dark Ages 1)*, Skelmorlie: Cruithne Press.

Hambleton, E. (1999) *Animal husbandry regimes in Iron Age Britain*, Oxford: British Archaeological Reports 282.

Hamerow, H. (1993) *Excavations at Mucking 2: the Anglo-Saxon settlement*, London: English Heritage Archaeological Report 21.

Hamerow, H. (1997) 'Migration theory and the Anglo-Saxon "identity crisis" ', in Chapman, J. and Hamerow, H. (eds) *Migrations and invasions in archaeological explanation*, Oxford: British Archaeological Reports, International Series 664: 33–44.

Hamilakis, Y. (1999) 'Stories from exile: fragments from the cultural biography of the Parthenon (or "Elgin") marbles', *World Archaeology* 31 (2): 303–20.

Hamilakis, Y. (2007) *The nation and its ruins: antiquity, archaeology, and national imagination in Greece*, Oxford: Oxford University Press.

Hammer, C.U. *et al.* (2003) 'Thera eruption date 1645 B.C. confirmed by new ice core data?', in

Bietak, M. (ed.), *The synchronisation of civilisations in the eastern Mediterranean in the second millennium B.C. II*, Vienna: Austrian Academy of Sciences Press: 87–94.

Hampton, J.N. (ed.) (1985) *The mapping of archaeological evidence from air photography*, Dereham: Aerial Archaeology Publications.

Haneca, K. *et al.* (2009) 'Oaks, tree-rings and wooden cultural heritage: a review of the main characteristics and applications of oak dendrochronology in Europe', *Journal of Archaeological Science* 36: 1–11.

Hansen, J.P.H. *et al.* (eds) (1991) *The Greenland mummies*, London: British Museum.

Hanson, D.B. and Buikstra, J.E. (1987) 'Histomorphological alteration in buried human bone from the lower Illinois valley: implications for palaeodietary research', *Journal of Archaeological Science* 14: 549–64.

Hanson, W.S. and Rahtz, P.A. (1988) 'Video recording on excavations', *Antiquity* 62: 106–11.

Harding, A.F. (ed.) (1999) *Experiment and design: archaeological studies in honour of John Coles*, Oxford: Oxbow Books.

Harding, A.F. (2007) 'The great Bosnian pyramid scheme', *British Archaeology* 92, 40–45.

Hare, P.E., von Endt, D.W. and Kokis, J.E. (1997) 'Protein and amino acid diagenesis dating', in Taylor, R.E. and Aitken, M.J. *Chronometric dating in archaeology*, New York: Plenum Press: 261–96.

Härke, H. (2004) 'The debate on migration and identity in Europe', *Antiquity* 78: 453–6.

Harris, D.R. (ed.) (1994) *The archaeology of V. Gordon Childe: contemporary perspectives*, London: UCL Press.

Harris, D.R. and Thomas, K. (eds) (1991) *Modelling ecological change*, London: Institute of Archaeology.

Harris, E.C. (1977) 'Units of archaeological stratification', *Norwegian Archaeological Review* 10: 84–94.

Harris, E.C. (1989) *Principles of archaeological stratigraphy*, 2nd edn, London: Academic Press.

Harris, E.C., Brown, M.R. and Brown, G.J. (eds) (1993) *Practices of archaeological stratigraphy*, London: Academic Press.

Harris, W.V. (ed.) (1993) *The inscribed economy: production and distribution in the Roman empire in the light of* instrumentum domesticum, Ann Arbor, MI: Journal of Roman Archaeology Suppl 6.

Hart, J.P. and Terrell, J.E. (2002) *Darwin and archaeology: a handbook of key concepts*, Westport, CT: Praeger.

Hasek, V. (1999) *Methodology of geophysical research in archaeology*, Oxford: Archaeopress, British Archaeological Reports, International Series 769.

Haselgrove, C. *et al.* (2001) *Understanding the British Iron Age: an agenda for action*, Salisbury: Trust for Wessex Archaeology.

Hather, J. (ed.) (1994) *Tropical archaeobotany: applications and new developments*, London: Routledge, One World Archaeology 22.

Hather, J.G. (1993) *An archaeobotanical guide to root and tuber identification*, Oxford: Oxbow Monograph 28.

Hauser, K. (2008) *Bloody old Britain. O.G.S. Crawford and the archaeology of modern life*, London: Granta Books.

Haverfield, F. (1923) *The Romanization of Britain*, Oxford: Clarendon Press.

Hawkes, J. (1967) 'God in the machine', *Antiquity* 41: 174–80.

Hawkes, J. (1982) *Mortimer Wheeler: adventurer in archaeology*, London: Weidenfeld and Nicholson.

Hawkins, B.R. and Madsen, D.B. (1999) *Excavation of the Donner-Reed wagons: historic archaeology along the Hastings cutoff*, Salt Lake City: University of Utah Press.

Hawthorne, J. (1997) 'Post-processual economics: the role of African red slip ware vessel volume in Mediterranean demography', in Meadows, K. *et al.* (eds) *TRAC 1996: Proceedings of the sixth TRAC conference in Sheffield*. Oxford: Oxbow: 29–37.

Haynes, I., Sheldon, H. and Hannigan, L. (eds) (2000) *London under ground: the archaeology of a city*, Oxford: Oxbow.

Hays-Gilpin, K. and Whitley, D. (eds) (1998) *Reader in gender archaeology*, London: Routledge.

Hebsgaard, M.B. *et al.* (2009) ' "The Farm beneath the sand", an archaeological case study on ancient "dirt" DNA', *Antiquity* 83: 430–44.

Heck, C. (2007) 'A new medieval view of Stonehenge', *British Archaeology* 92 10–15.

Hedeager, L. (1992) *Iron-age societies: from tribe to state in northern Europe, 500 BC to AD 700*, Oxford: Blackwell.

Hedges, J.W. (1983) *Isbister: a chambered tomb in Orkney*, Oxford: British Archaeological Reports 115.

Hedges, R.E.M. and Sykes, B.C. (1992) 'Biomolecular archaeology: past, present and future', in Pollard, A.M. (ed.) *New developments in archaeological science*, Oxford: Clarendon: 267–83.

Hegmon, M. (2003) 'Setting theoretical egos aside: issues and theory in North American archaeology', *American Antiquity* 68 (2): 213–43.

Henderson, J. (1991) 'Industrial specialisation in late Iron Age Britain and Europe', *Archaeological Journal* 148: 104–48.

Henderson, J. (2000) *The science and archaeology of materials: an investigation of inorganic materials*, London: Routledge.

Henderson, J. (2001) 'Glass and glazes', in Brothwell, D.R. and Pollard, A.M. *Handbook of archaeological sciences*, Chichester: John Wiley and Sons: 471–82.

Hepper, F.N. (1990) *Pharaoh's flowers*, London: Royal Botanic Gardens /HMSO.

Herbert, S.C. (1994) *Tel Anafa I, i–ii. Final report on ten years of excavation at a Hellenistic and Roman settlement in Northern Israel*, Ann Arbor, MI: Journal of Roman Archaeology Suppl 10, Parts 1–2.

Heron, C. (2001) 'Geochemical prospecting', in Brothwell, D.R. and Pollard, A.M. *Handbook of archaeological sciences*, Chichester: John Wiley and Sons: 565–73.

Herrmann, B. and Hummel, S. (eds) (1993) *Ancient DNA: recovery and analysis of genetic material*, Berlin: Springer Verlag.

Herz, N. (1987) 'Carbon and oxygen isotopic ratios: a data base for classical Greek and Roman marble', *Archaeometry* 29: 35–44.

Herz, N. and Garrison, E. (1998) *Geological methods for archaeology*, Oxford: Oxford University Press.

Hester, T.R., Shafer, K.L. and Feder, K.L. (2008) *Field methods in archaeology*, 7th rev. edn, Walnut Creek CA: Left Coast Press.

Heun, M. *et al.* (1997) 'Site of Einkorn wheat domestication identified by DNA fingerprinting', *Science* 278 (5341): 1312–14.

Hewison, R. (1987) *The heritage industry: Britain in a climate of decline*, London: Methuen.

Hicks, D. and Beaudry, M.C. (2006) *The Cambridge companion to historical archaeology*, Cambridge: Cambridge University Press.

Hicks, S., Miller, U. and Saarnisto, M. (eds) (1994) *Laminated sediments*, PACT 41; Rixensart: UNESCO/Council of Europe.

Higgins, T. *et al.* (1997) *Imaging the past: electronic imaging and computer graphics in museums and archaeology*, London: British Museum Occasional Papers 114.

Higham, N.J. (1993) *The kingdom of Northumbria AD 350–1100*, Gloucester: Alan Sutton.

Higham, T., Anderson, A. and Jacomb, C. (1999) 'Dating the first New Zealanders: the chronology of Wairau Bar', *Antiquity* 73: 420–7.

Higham, T. *et al.* (2007) 'New perspectives on the Varna cemetery (Bulgaria): AMS dates and social implications', *Antiquity* 81: 640–54.

Hill, J.D. (1995) *Ritual and rubbish in the Iron Age of Wessex: a study on the formation of a specific archaeological record*, Oxford: Tempus Reparatum, British Archaeological Reports 242.

Hill, J.D. (2006) 'Are we any closer to understanding how later Iron Age societies worked (or did not work)?', in Haselgrove, C. (ed.) *Celtes et Gaulois, l'archéologie face à l'histoire. Les mutations de la fin de l'âge du fer. Actes de la table ronde de Cambridge, 7–8 Juillet 2005*, Glux-en-Glenne: Bibracte 12/4: 169–80.

Hills, C. (2003) *Origins of the English*, London: Duckworth.

Hines, J. *et al.* (eds) (1999) *Pace of change: studies in early medieval chronology*, Oxford: Oxbow Books: Cardiff Studies in Archaeology.

Hingley, R. (2000) *Roman officers and English gentlemen: the imperial origins of Roman archaeology*, Routledge. London.

Hingley, R. (2005) *Globalizing Roman culture: unity, diversity and empire*, London: Routledge.

Hingley, R. (2007) *The recovery of Roman Britain 1586–1906: a colony so fertile*, Oxford: Oxford University Press.

Hinton, D.A. (ed.) (1983) *25 years of medieval archaeology*, Sheffield: Department of Prehistory and Archaeology, University of Sheffield.

Hitchens, C., Browning, R. and Binns, G. (1987) *The Elgin marbles: should they be returned to Greece?*, London: Chatto and Windus.

Hobbs, R. (2003) *Treasure: finding our past*, London: British Museum.

Hobsbawm, E. (1994) *The age of extremes: the short twentieth century 1914–1991*, London: Michael Joseph.

Hodder, I. (1982a) *The present past: an introduction to anthropology for archaeologists*, London: Batsford.

Hodder, I. (1982b) *Symbols in action: ethnoarchaeological studies of material culture*, Cambridge: Cambridge University Press.

Hodder, I. (1990) *The domestication of Europe: structure and contingency in Neolithic societies*, Oxford: Blackwell.

Hodder, I. (1991) *Reading the past: current approaches to interpretation in archaeology*, 2nd edition, Cambridge: Cambridge University Press.

Hodder, I. (ed.) (1995) *Theory and practice in archaeology*, London: Routledge, Material Cultures.

Hodder, I. (ed.) (1996) *On the surface: Çatalhöyük 1993–95*, Cambridge: McDonald Institute for Archaeological Research/British Institute of Archaeology at Ankara, Çatalhöyük Project Vol. 1.

Hodder, I. (1999) *The archaeological process: an introduction*, Oxford: Blackwell.

Hodder, I. (ed.) (2001) *Archaeological theory today*, Cambridge: Polity Press.

Hodder, I. (ed.) (2005a) *Çatalhöyük perspectives: reports from the 1995–99 seasons*, Oxford: Oxbow BIAA Monograph 40.

Hodder, I. (2005b) 'Reflexive methods', in Maschner, H.D.G. and Chippindale, C. (eds) *Handbook of archaeological methods*, Lanham: AltaMira Press: 643–72

Hodder, I. and Hutson, S. (2003) *Reading the past: current approaches to interpretation in archaeology*, 3rd edn, Cambridge: Cambridge University Press.

Hodder, I. and Orton, C. (1976) *Spatial analysis in archaeology*, Cambridge: Cambridge University Press.

Hodder, I. *et al.* (eds) (1995) *Interpreting archaeology: finding meaning in the past*, new edn, London: Routledge.

Hodder, I. *et al.* (eds) (2000) *Towards reflexive method in archaeology: the example of Çatalhöyük*, Cambridge: McDonald Institute for Archaeological Research.

Hodges, P. (1993) *How the pyramids were built*, London: Aris and Philips.

Hodges, R. (2006) *Royston Grange: 6000 years of a Peakland landscape*, Stroud: Tempus.

Hofmann, D. and Whittle, A. (2008) 'Neolithic bodies', in Jones, A. (ed.) *Prehistoric Europe: theory and practice*, Oxford: Wiley-Blackwell: 287–311.

Hohlfelder, R., Brandon, C. and Oleson, J.P. (2005) 'Building a Roman *pila* in the sea – experimental archaeology at Brindisi, Italy', *International Journal of Nautical Archaeology* 34 (1): 123–37.

Holden, T.G. (2001) 'Dietary evidence from the coprolites and the intestinal contents of ancient humans', in Brothwell, D.R. and Pollard, A.M. *Handbook of archaeological sciences*, Chichester: John Wiley and Sons: 403–13.

Hole, F. et al. (1969) *Prehistory and human ecology of the Deh Luran plain*, Ann Arbor: University of Michigan Museum of Anthropology.

Holliday, V.T. (2004) *Soils in archaeological research*, Oxford: Oxford University Press.

Holtorf, C. (2005) *From Stonehenge to Las Vegas: archaeology as popular culture*, Walnut Creek, CA: Altamira Press.

Holtorf, C. (2007a) *Archaeology is a brand: the meaning of archaeology in contemporary popular culture*, Oxford: Archaeopress.

Holtorf, C. (2007b) 'An archaeological fashion show: how archaeologists dress and how they are portrayed in the media', in Clack, T. and Brittain, M. (eds) *Archaeology and the media*, Walnut Creek, CA: Left Coast Press: 69–88.

Holtorf, C. and Karlsson, H. (eds) (2000) *Philosophy and archaeological practice: perspectives for the 21st century*, Göteborg: Bricoleur Press.

Holtorf, C. and Piccini, A. (eds) (2009) *Contemporary archaeologies: excavating now*, Frankfurt am Main: Peter Lang.

Hooper-Greenhill, E. (1992) *Museums and the shaping of knowledge*, London: Routledge.

Hooper-Greenhill, E. (1999) *Museum, media, message*, new edn, London: Routledge.

Hopkinson, T. and White, M. (2005) 'The Acheulean and the handaxe: structure and agency in the Palaeolithic', in Gamble, C. and Porr, M. (2005) *The hominid individual in context: archaeological investigations of lower and middle Palaeolithic landscapes, locales and artefacts*, London: Routledge: 13–28.

Horne, P.D. (1985) 'A review of the evidence of human endoparasitism in the pre-Columbian new world through the study of coprolites', *Journal of Archaeological Science* 12: 299–310.

Horrocks, M. *et al.* (2000) 'Pollen and phytoliths in stone mounds at Pouerua, Northland, New Zealand: implications for the study of Polynesian farming', *Antiquity* 74: 863–72.

Horrocks, M. *et al.* (2003) 'Pollen, phytoliths and diatoms in prehistoric coprolites from Kohika, Bay of Plenty, New Zealand', *Journal of Archaeological Science* 30 (1): 13–20.

Horwitz, S. (1981) *The find of a lifetime: Sir Arthur Evans and the discovery of Knossos*, London: Weidenfeld and Nicholson.

Hosfield, R. (1999) *The Palaeolithic of the Hampshire basin: a regional model of hominid behaviour during the Middle Pleistocene*, Oxford: British Archaeological Reports 286.

Hoskins, J. (1998) *Biographical objects: how things tell the story of people's lives*, New York: Routledge.

Hoskins, W.G. (1955) *The making of the English landscape*, London: Hodder and Stoughton.

Howard, P. (2007) *Archaeological surveying and mapping: recording and depicting the landscape*, London: Routledge.

Howell, C.L. and Blanc, W. (1995) *A practical guide to archaeological photography*, 2nd edn, Los Angeles, CA: UCLA Institute of Archaeology Publications, Archaeological Research Tools 6.

Howell, G. (2007) *Gertrude Bell: queen of the desert, shaper of nations*. New York: Farrar, Straus and Giroux.

Hubert, J. (1989) 'A proper place for the dead: a critical review of the reburial issue', in Layton, R. *Conflict in the archaeology of living traditions*, London: Unwin Hyman, One World Archaeology 8: 131–66.

Hudson, K. (1987) *Museums of influence*, Cambridge: Cambridge University Press.

Hughes, M.J. (1991) 'Tracing to source', in Bowman, S. (ed.) *Science and the past*, London: British Museum: 99–116.

Hughes, M.J. *et al.* (eds) (1991) *Neutron activation and plasma emission spectrometric analysis in archaeology: techniques and applications*, London: British Museum Occasional Papers 82.

Hummler, M. (2008) 'New book chronicle', *Antiquity* 82: 1151–61.

Humphreys, S.C. and King, H. (eds) (1981) *Mortality and immortality: the anthropology and archaeology of death*, London/New York: Academic Press.

Hunter, J. and Cox, M. (eds) (2005) *Forensic archaeology: advances in theory and practice*, London: Routledge.

Hunter, J., Roberts, C. and Martin, A. (1996) *Studies in crime: an introduction to forensic archaeology*, London: Routledge.

Hunter, J. and Ralston, I. (eds) (2006) *Archaeological resource management in the UK*, 2nd edn, Stroud: Alan Sutton.

Hunter, M. (1975) *John Aubrey and the realm of learning*, London: Duckworth.

Huntley, J.P. and, Stallibrass, S. (eds) (2000) *Taphonomy and interpretation*, Oxford: Oxbow, Symposia of Association for Environmental Archaeology 14.

Hurcombe, L. (1992) *Use wear analysis: theory, experiments and results*, Sheffield: Sheffield Archaeological Monograph 4.

Hurcombe, L. (2006) *Archaeological artefacts as material culture*, London: Routledge.

Hutcheson, N. (2004) *Later Iron Age Norfolk: metalwork, landscape and society*. Oxford: British Archaeological Reports 361.

Imbrie, J. and Imbrie, K.P. (1979) *Ice ages: solving the mystery*, London: Macmillan.

Impey, O. and MacGregor, A. (eds) (1985) *The origins of museums: the cabinet of curiosities in sixteenth- and seventeenth-century Europe*, Oxford: Clarendon Press.

Ingold, T. (2000) *The perception of the environment: essays in livelihood, dwelling and skill*, London: Routledge.

Inomata, T. and Coben, L.S. (eds) (2006) *Archaeology of performance: theaters of power, community and politics*, Lanham, MD: Altamira.

Inskeep, R.R. (1992) 'Making an honest man of Oxford: good news for Mali', *Antiquity* 66: 114–30.

Insoll, T. (ed.) (2007a) *The archaeology of identities: a reader*, London: Routledge.

Insoll, T. (2007b) *Archaeology: the conceptual challenge*, London: Duckworth.

Insoll, T. and Hutchins, E. (2005) 'The archaeology of disease: molluscs as potential disease indicators in Bahrain', *World Archaeology* 37 (4): 579–88.

Isaac, G. and Isaac, B. (eds) (1997) *Koobi Fora 5: Plio-Pleistocene archaeology*, Oxford: Oxford University Press.

Ivanovich, M. (1991) 'Uranium series dating', in Göksu H.Y., Oberhofer M. and Regulla D. (eds) *Scientific dating methods*, Dordrecht: Kluwer Academic: 97–117.

Jackes, M., Lubell, D. and Meiklejohn, C. (1997) 'Healthy but mortal: human biology and the first farmers of western Europe', *Antiquity* 71: 639–58.

Jackson, C. (2005) 'Glassmaking in Bronze-Age Egypt', *Science* 308: 1750–2

James, P. *et al.* (1991) *Centuries of darkness*, London: Jonathan Cape.

James, S. (1999) *The Atlantic Celts: ancient people or modern invention?*, London: British Museum Press.

James, S. and Millett, M. (2001) *Britons and Romans: advancing an archaeological agenda*, York: CBA Research Report 125.

Jameson, J.H. (ed.) (2004) *The reconstructed past: reconstructions in the public interpretation of archaeology and history*, Walnut Creek, CA: Altamira Press.

Jameson, J.H. (2008a) 'Cultural heritage management in the United States: past, present and future', in Fairclough, G. *et al.* (eds) *The heritage reader*, London: Routledge: 42–61.

Jameson, J.H. (2008b) 'Presenting archaeology to the public, then and now: an introduction', in Fairclough, G. *et al.* (eds) *The heritage reader*, London: Routledge: 425–6.

Jashemski, W.F. (1979) *The gardens of Pompeii*, Rochelle: Caratzas Brothers.

Jashemski, W.F. (1999) *A Pompeian herbal: ancient and modern medicinal plants*, Austin: University of Texas Press.

Jehaes, E. (1998) *Optimisation of methods and procedures for the analysis of mtDNA sequences and their applications in molecular archaeological and historical binds*, Leuven: Leuven University Press.

Jenkins, I. (2001) *Cleaning and controversy: the Parthenon sculptures 1811-1939*, London: British Museum Occasional Paper 146.

Jenkins, N. (1980) *The boat beneath the pyramid: King Cheops' royal ship*, London: Thames and Hudson.

Jenkins, R. (1997) *Rethinking ethnicity*, London: Sage.

Jensen, H.J. (1994) *Flint tools and plant working*, Aarhus: Aarhus University Press.

Jeskins, P. (1998) *Environment and the Classical world*, Bristol: Bristol Classical Press.

Jin, L. and Su, B. (2000) 'Native or immigrant: modern human origin in East Asia', *Nature Reviews Genetics* 1: 126–33.

Johannessen, S. and Hastorf, C. (eds) (1993) *Corn and culture in the prehistoric New World*, Oxford: Westview Press.

Johanson, D. and Shreeve, J. (1991) *Lucy's child: the discovery of a human ancestor*, London: Penguin.

Johnson, B.J. and Miller, G. (1997) 'Archaeological applications of amino-acid racemisation' *Archaeometry* 39: 265–87.

Johnson, M. (1996) *An archaeology of capitalism*, Oxford: Blackwell.

Johnson, M. (1999) *Archaeological theory: an introduction*, Oxford: Blackwell.

Johnson, M. (2004) 'Archaeology and social theory', in Bintliff, J. (ed.) *A companion to archaeology*, Oxford: Blackwell: 92–109.

Johnson, M. (2007) *Ideas of landscape*, Oxford: Blackwell.

Johnson, M. (2008) 'The theoretical scene, 1960–2000', in Cunliffe, B., Gosden, C. and

Joyce, R. (eds) *The Oxford handbook of archaeology*, Oxford: Oxford University Press: 71–88.

Johnson, M. (2010) *Archaeological theory: an introduction*, 2nd edn., Oxford: Wiley-Blackwell.

Johnson, P. and Haynes, I. (eds) (1996) *Architecture in Roman Britain*, London: Council of British Archaeology Research Report 94.

Johnston, N. and Rose, P. (1994) *Bodmin Moor: an archaeological survey, 1: the human landscape to c.1800*, London: English Heritage/Royal Commission on the Historical Monuments of England/Cornwall Archaeological Unit.

Jolly, A. (1999) *Lucy's legacy: sex and intelligence in human evolution*, Cambridge, MA: Harvard University Press.

Jones, A. (2008a) 'Into the future', in Cunliffe, B., Gosden, C. and Joyce, R. (eds) *The Oxford handbook of archaeology*, Oxford: Oxford University Press: 89–114.

Jones, A. (ed.) (2008b) *Prehistoric Europe: theory and practice*, Oxford: Wiley-Blackwell.

Jones, A.K.G. (1986) 'Fish bone survival in the digestive systems of the pig, dog and man: some experiments', in Brinkhuizen, D.C. and Clason, A.T. (eds) *Fish and archaeology: studies in osteometry, taphonomy, seasonality and fishing methods*, Oxford: British Archaeological Reports, International Series S294: 53–61.

Jones, A.K.G. (1990) 'Experiments with fish bones and otoliths: implications for the reconstruction of past diet and economy', in Robinson, D.E. (ed.) *Experimentation and reconstruction in environmental archaeology*, Oxford: Oxbow: 143–6.

Jones, A.K.G. (2002) *Archaeological theory and scientific practice*, Cambridge: Cambridge University Press.

Jones, A.K.G. and O'Connor, T.P. (2001) 'Vertebrate resources', in Brothwell, D.R. and Pollard, A.M. *Handbook of archaeological sciences*, Chichester: John Wiley and Sons: 415–25.

Jones, M. (2001) *The molecule hunt: archaeology and the search for ancient DNA*, Harmondsworth: Allen Lane.

Jones, M. (2004) 'Archaeology and the genetic revolution', in Bintliff, J. (ed.) *A companion to archaeology*, Oxford: Blackwell: 39–51.

Jones, M. (2007) *Feast: why humans share food*, Oxford: Oxford University Press.

Jones, M. (ed.) (1990) *Fake? The art of deception*, London: British Museum.

Jones, M.K. and Colledge, S. (2001) 'Archaeobotany and the transition to agriculture', in Brothwell, D.R. and Pollard, A.M. *Handbook of archaeological sciences*, Chichester: John Wiley and Sons: 427–40.

Jones, S. (1993) *The language of the genes*, London: HarperCollins.

Jones, S. (1996) *The archaeology of ethnicity: a theoretical perspective*, London: Routledge.

Jones, S. (2007) 'Discourses of identity in the interpretation of the past', in Insoll, T. (ed.) *Archaeology of identities: a reader*. London: Routledge: 44–58.

Jones, S. *et al.* (eds) (1993) *The Cambridge encyclopedia of human evolution*, Cambridge: Cambridge University Press.

Jones, T. (ed.) (2007) *California prehistory: colonization, culture and complexity*, Lanham, MD: Altamira Press.

Junker, K. (1998) 'Research under dictatorship: the German Archaeological Institute 1929–1945', *Antiquity* 72: 282–92.

Jurmain, R. (1999) *Stories from the skeleton: behavioral reconstruction in human osteology*, Reading: Gordon and Breach.

Jurmain, R. and Roberts, C. (2008) 'Juggling the evidence: the purported "acrobat" from Tell Brak', *Antiquity* 82: 318.

Kardulias, P.N. (ed.) (1994) *Beyond the site: regional studies in the Aegean area*, Lanham, MD: University Press of America.

Karlsson, H. (1997) *Being and post-processual archaeological thinking: reflections upon post-processual archaeologies and anthropocentrism*, Göteborg: Göteborg University, Department of Archaeology, Gotarc Serie C. 15.

Katzenberg, M.A. (2008) 'Stable isotope analysis: a tool for studying past diet, demography and life history', in Katzenberg, M.A. and Saunders, S.R. (eds) *Biological anthropology of the human skeleton*, 2nd edn, New York: Wiley-Liss: 413–41.

Katzenberg, M.A. and Saunders, S.R. (eds) (2008) *Biological anthropology of the human skeleton*, 2nd edn, New York: Wiley-Liss.

Kay, S. and Witcher, R. (2005) 'The Tiber valley project: the role of GIS and databases in field survey data integration and analysis', *Archeologia e Calcolatori* 16: 113–27.

Kearney, R. (1994) *Modern movements in European philosophy*, 2nd edn, Manchester: Manchester University Press.

Keenan, D. J. (2003) 'Volcanic ash retrieved from the GRIP ice core is not from Thera', *Geochemistry, Geophysics, Geosystems* 4: 1097.

Kehoe, A.B. (1991a) 'No possible, probable shadow of doubt', *Antiquity* 65: 129–31.

Kehoe, A.B. (1991b) 'The invention of prehistory', *Current Anthropology* 32: 467–76.

Kehoe, A.B. (1998) *The land of prehistory: a critical history of American archaeology*, London: Routledge.

Kehoe, A.B. (2008) *Controversies in archaeology*, Walnut Creek, CA: Left Coast Press.

Kehoe, A.B. and Emmerich, M.B. (1999) *Assembling the past: studies in the professionalization of archaeology*, Albuquerque: University of New Mexico Press.

Keller, D.R. and Rupp, D.W. (eds) (1983) *Archaeological survey in the Mediterranean area*, Oxford: British Archaeological Reports, International Series S155.

Kelley, D. (2002) *The descent of ideas: the history of intellectual history*, Aldershot: Ashgate.

Kelly, R. and Thomas, D. Hurst (2009) *Archaeology*, 5th edn, Belmont CA: Wadsworth.

Kelso, W.M. (1984) *Kingsmill plantations, 1619–1800: archaeology of country life in colonial Virginia*, San Diego, CA: Academic Press, Studies in Historical Archaeology.

Kelso, W.M. (1996) *Jamestown rediscovery II*, Richmond, VA: Association for the Preservation of Virginia Antiquities.

Kemp, B.M. *et al.* (2007) 'Genetic analysis of early Holocene skeletal remains from Alaska and its implications for the settlement of the Americas', *American Journal of Physical Anthropology* 132: 605–21

Kempe, D.R.C. and Harvey, A.P. (eds) (1983) *The petrology of archaeological artefacts*, Oxford: Clarendon Press.

Kennedy, D. (1998) 'Declassified satellite photographs and archaeology in the Middle East: case studies from Turkey', *Antiquity* 72: 553–61.

Kennedy, R.G. (1994) *Hidden cities: the discovery and loss of ancient North American civilization*, New York: Free Press.

Kenward, H. (1999) 'Pubic lice (*Pthirus pubis* L.) were present in Roman and Medieval Britain', *Antiquity* 73: 911–15.

Kenward, H. and Hall, A. (2000) 'Decay of delicate organic remains in shallow urban deposits: are we at a watershed?', *Antiquity* 74: 519–25.

Keys, D. (1999) *Catastrophe: an investigation into the origins of the modern world*, London: Century.

Killick, D. (2001) 'Science, speculation and the origins of extractive metallurgy', in Brothwell, D.R. and Pollard, A.M. *Handbook of archaeological sciences*, Chichester: John Wiley and Sons: 483–92.

Kimpe, K. *et al.* (2004). 'Assessing the relationship between form and use of different kinds of pottery from the archaeological site Sagalassos (southwest Turkey) with lipid analysis', *Journal of Archaeological Science* 31(11): 1503–10.

King, C.E. and Hedges, R.E.M. (1974) 'An analysis of some 3rd century Roman coins for surface silvering and silver percentage of their alloy content', *Archaeometry* 16: 189–200.

Kingery, W.D. (ed.) (1996) *Learning from things: method and theory of material culture studies*, Washington, DC: Smithsonian Institution Press.

Kingsley, S.A. and Raveh, K. (1996) *The ancient harbour and anchorage at Dor, Israel: results of the underwater surveys 1976–1991*, Oxford: Tempus Reparatum, British Archaeological Reports, International Series 626.

Kipfer, B.A. (2000) *Encyclopedic dictionary of archaeology*, New York: Kluwer Academic/Plenum.

Klein, R.G. (1999) *The human career: human biology and cultural origins*, 2nd edn, Chicago, IL: Chicago University Press.

Klindt-Jensen, O. (1975) *A history of Scandinavian archaeology*, London: Thames and Hudson.

Knappett, C. (2005) 'Pottery', in Maschner, H.D.G. and Chippindale, C. (eds) *Handbook of Archaeological Methods, 2*, Lanham, MD: Altamira Press: 673–714.

Knowles, W. and Forster, R. (1910) *The Romano-British site at Corstopitum: an account of the excavations during 1909*, London and Newcastle upon Tyne: Andrew Reid and Co.

Koch, H.P. (1998) *Der Sintflut-Impakt: die Flutkatastrofe vor 10.000 Jahren als Folge eines Kometeneinschlags*, Frankfurt: Peter Lang.

Kohl, P.L. and Fawcett, C. (eds) (1995) *Nationalism, politics and the practice of archaeology*, Cambridge: Cambridge University Press.

Koldewey, R. (1913) *Das wieder erstehende Babylon: die bisherigen Ergebnisse der deutschen Ausgrabungen*, Leipzig: J.C. Hinrichs.

Kopytoff, I. (1986) 'The cultural biography of things: commoditization as a process', in Appadurai, A. (ed.) *The social life of things: commodities in cultural perspective*, Cambridge: Cambridge University Press: 64–94.

Kristiansen, K. (2009) 'The discipline of archaeology', in Cunliffe, B.W., Gosden, C. and Joyce, R.A. (eds) *The Oxford handbook of archaeology*, Oxford: Oxford University Press: 3–46.

Kucera, V. *et al.* (1991) '"Shared Principles": a cooperation agreement between a Native American group and archaeologists', *Antiquity* 65: 917.

Kuhn, T.S. (1962) *The structure of scientific revolutions*, Chicago, IL: Chicago University Press.

Kuniholm, P. (2001) 'Dendrochronology and other applications of tree-ring studies in archaeology', in Brothwell, D.R. and Pollard, A.M. *Handbook of archaeological sciences*, Chichester: John Wiley and Sons: 35–46.

Kyriakidis, E. (ed.) (2007) *The archaeology of ritual*, Los Angeles: Costen Institute of Archaeology, University of California.

Lake, M.W. (2001) 'Numerical modelling in archaeology', in Brothwell, D.R. and Pollard, A.M. *Handbook of archaeological sciences*, Chichester: John Wiley and Sons: 723–32.

Lamberg-Karlovsky, C.C. (ed.) (1991) *Archaeological thought in America*, Cambridge: Cambridge University Press.

Lambert, J. and Grupe, G. (eds) (1993) *Prehistoric human bone: archaeology at the molecular level*, Berlin: Springer Verlag.

Lambert, J.B. (1997) *Traces of the past: unravelling the secrets of archaeology through chemistry*, Reading, MA: Perseus Books.

Lambert, P.M. (2002) Rib lesions in a prehistoric puebloan sample from southwestern Colorado, *American Journal of Physical Anthropology* 117: 281–92.

Lambert, P.M. and Walker, P.L. (1991) 'Physical anthropological evidence for the evolution of social complexity in coastal southern California', *Antiquity* 65: 870–8.

LaMotta, V.M. and Schiffer, M.B. (2001) 'Behavioral archaeology: toward a new synthesis', in Hodder, I. (ed.) *Archaeological theory today*, Cambridge: Polity Press: 14–64.

Lancaster, L. (2005) *Concrete vaulted construction in Imperial Rome*, Cambridge: Cambridge University Press.

Lane-Fox, A. (1875) 'On the evolution of culture', *Notices and Proceedings of the Royal Institution of Great Britain* 7: 496–520.

LaNeice, S., Hook, D. and Craddock, P. (2007) *Mines and metals: studies in archaeometallurgy*, London: Archetype Publications.

Lang, J. and Middleton, A. (eds) (1997) *Radiography of cultural material*, London: Butterworth-Heinemann.

Larsen, C.S. (1997) *Bioarchaeology: interpreting behaviour from the human skeleton*, Cambridge: Cambridge University Press.

Larsen, C.S. (2000) *Skeletons in our closet: revealing our past through bioarchaeology*, Princeton: Princeton University Press.

Larsen, C.U. (ed.) (1992) *Sites and monuments: national archaeological records*, Copenhagen: National Museum of Denmark.

Larson, G. *et al.* (2005) 'Worldwide phylogeography of wild boar reveals multiple centers of pig domestication', *Science* 307 (5715): 1618–21.

Larson, G. *et al.* (2007) 'Ancient DNA, pig domestication, and the spread of the Neolithic into Europe', *Proceedings of the National Academy of Sciences of the United States of America* 104 (39): 15276–81.

Latham, A.G. (2001) 'Uranium-series dating', in Brothwell, D.R. and Pollard, A.M. *Handbook of archaeological sciences*, Chichester: John Wiley and Sons: 63–72.

Latour, B. (1987) *Science in action: how to follow scientists and engineers through society*, Cambridge, MA: Harvard University Press.

Lawson, A.J. (1992) 'Stonehenge: creating a definitive account', *Antiquity* 66: 934–41.

Layton, R. (1997) *An introduction to theory in anthropology*, Cambridge: Cambridge University Press.

Layton, R. (ed.) (1989) *Who needs the past? Indigenous values and archaeology*, London: Unwin Hyman, One World Archaeology 5.

Leakey, M. and Roe, D. (1994) *Olduvai Gorge, 5: excavations in Beds III, IV and the Masek Beds, 1968–71*, Cambridge: Cambridge University Press.

Leakey, R. and Lewin, R (1992) *Origins reconsidered: in search of what makes us human*, London: Little Brown.

Leask, A. and Fyall, A. (2006) *Managing world heritage sites, London*: Butter-worth-Heinemann.

Lechte, J. (1994) *Fifty key contemporary thinkers: from structuralism to postmodernity*, London: Routledge.

Legge, A.J. and Rowley-Conwy, P.A. (1988) *Star Carr revisited: a re-analysis of the large mammals*, University of London: Department of Extra-Mural Studies.

Lehoërff, A. (ed.) (2008) *Construire le temps: histoire et méthodes des chronologies et calendriers des derniers millénaires avant notre ère en Europe occidentale*, Glux-en-Glenne: Collection Bibracte 16.

Lemorini, C. *et al.* (2006) 'Use-wear analysis of an Amudian laminar assemblage from the Acheuleo-Yabrudian of Qesem Cave, Israel', *Journal of Archaeological Science* 33 (7): 921–34.

Lentz, D.L. (ed.) (2000) *Imperfect balance: landscape transformations in the precolumbian Americas*, New York: Columbia University Press.

Leonard, R.D. (2001) 'Evolutionary archaeology', in Hodder, I. (ed.) *Archaeological theory today*, Cambridge: Polity Press: 65–97.

Leone, M.P. and Potter, P.B. (eds) (1999) *Historical archaeologies of capitalism*, New York: Kluwer Academic/Plenum.

Lepetz, S. (1997) 'L'amélioration des espèces animales doméstiques à la période romaine en France de Nord', in Garcia, D. and Meeks, D. (eds) *Techniques et économie antiques et médiévales: colloque d'Aix-en-Provençe (mai 1996)*, Paris: Errance: 157–65.

Lerche, G. (ed.) (1994) *Ploughing implements and tillage practices in Denmark from the Viking period to about 1800: experimentally substantiated*, Herning: Poul Kristensen, Royal Danish Academy of Science and Letters.

Letts, J.B. (1998) *Smoke-blackened thatch: a unique source of late medieval plant remains from southern England*, London: English Heritage.

Léva, C. (ed.) (1990) *Aerial photography and geophysical prospection in archaeology*, Brussels: CIRA.

Leveau, P. *et al.* (eds) (1999) *The archaeology of the Mediterranean landscape, 2: environmental reconstruction in Mediterranean landscape archaeology*, Oxford: Oxbow Books.

Lévi-Strauss, C. (1958) *Structural anthropology*, New York: Basic Books (1963); London: Allen Lane (1973).

Levine, M.M. (1992) 'The use and abuse of "Black Athena" ', *American Historical Review* 97: 440–64.

Levy, T. and Higham, T. (2005) (eds) *The bible and radiocarbon dating: archaeology, text and science*, London: Equinox.

Lewin, R. (2005) *Human evolution: an illustrated introduction*, 5th edn, Oxford: Blackwell Science.

Lewin, R, and Foley, R. (2004) *Principles of human evolution*, Oxford: Blackwell Science.

Lewis, J. *et al.* (2006) *Landscape evolution in the Middle Thames valley: Heathrow Terminal 5 Excavations, 1, Perry Oaks (Framework Archaeology Monograph 1)*, Oxford: BAA, Oxford and Wessex Archaeology.

Lie Dan Lu, T. (1999) *The transition from foraging to farming and the origin of agriculture in China*, Oxford: British Archaeological Reports, International Series S774.

Lieberman, D.E. (2009) '*Homo floresiensis* from head to toe', *Nature* 459: 41–2.

Lightfoot, K.G. *et al.* (1993) 'Prehistoric shellfish-harvesting strategies: implications from the growth patterns of soft-shell clams (*Mya arenaria*)', *Antiquity* 67: 358–69.

Lilles, T.M. and Kiefer, R.W. (1994) *Remote sensing and image interpretation*, 3rd edn, Chichester: John Wiley and Sons.

Lindahl, A. and Stilborg, O. (eds) (1995) *The aim of laboratory analyses of ceramics in archaeology*, Stockholm: Almqvist and Wiksell, Konferenser 34.

Linford, N. *et al.* (2007) 'Recent results from the English Heritage caesium magnetometer system in comparison with recent fluxgate gradiometers', *Archaeological Prospection* 14: 151–66.

Ling, R. (1992) 'A collapsed building facade at Cassington, Derbyshire', *Britannia* 23: 233–6.

Lock, G. (ed.) (2000) *Beyond the map: archaeology and spatial technologies*, Amsterdam: IOS Press.

Lock, G. (2003) *Using computers in archaeology: towards virtual pasts*, London: Routledge.

Lock, G. and Brown, K. (eds) (2000) *On the theory and practice of archaeological computing*, Oxford: Oxford University Committee for Archaeology Monograph 51.

Lock, G. and Stančič, Z. (1995) *Archaeology and Geographical Information Systems: a European perspective*, London: Taylor and Francis.

Lowe, J.J. (2001) 'Quaternary geochronological frameworks', in Brothwell, D.R. and Pollard, A.M. *Handbook of archaeological sciences*, Chichester: John Wiley and Sons: 9–21.

Lowe, J.J. and Walker, M.J.C. (1997) *Reconstructing quaternary environments*, 2nd edn, London: Longman.

Lowenthal, D. (1985) *The past is a foreign country*, Cambridge: Cambridge University Press.

Lowenthal, D. (1996) *Possessed by the past: the heritage crusade and the spoils of history*, London: Viking; New York: Free Press.

Lubbock, J. (1865) *Pre-historic times*, London: Williams and Norgate.

Lucas, G. (2001) *Critical approaches to fieldwork: contemporary and historical archaeological practice*, London: Routledge.

Lucas, G. (2005) *The archaeology of time*, London: Routledge.

Lucas, G. (2006) 'Historical archaeology and time', in Hicks, D. and Beaudry, M.C. *The Cambridge companion to historical archaeology*, Cambridge: Cambridge University Press: 34–47.

Lucassen, J. and Lucassen, L. (eds) (1997) *Migration, migration history, history: old paradigms and new perspectives*, Frankfurt: Peter Lang Verlag.

Lucy, S. and Reynolds, A. (eds) (2002) *Burial in Early Medieval England and Wales*, London: Society for Medieval Archaeology Monograph 17.

Lucy, S. *et al.* (2009) 'The burial of a princess? The later seventh-century cemetery at Westfield Farm, Ely', *Antiquaries Journal*, 89: 81–141.

Luedtke, B.E. (1992) *An archaeologist's guide to chert and flint*, Los Angeles: UCLA Institute of Archaeology, Archaeological Research Tools 7.

Luff, R. and Rowley-Conwy, P. (eds) (1994) *Whither environmental archaeology?*, Oxford: Oxbow Monograph 38, papers from Association of Environmental Archaeology Conference, Selwyn College, Cambridge.

Lutyck, C. (ed.) (1992) *The adventure of archaeology*, Washington, DC: National Geographic Society.

Lyell, C. (1830–3) *Principles of geology*, London: John Murray.

Lyell, C. (1863) *The geological evidence of the antiquity of man*, London: John Murray.

Lyman, R. (1994) *Vertebrate taphonomy*, Cambridge: Cambridge University Press.

Lyman, R.L. (2008) *Quantitive palaeozooarchaeology*, Cambridge: Cambridge University Press.

Lyman, R.L. and O'Brien, M.J. (2006) *Measuring time with artifacts: a history of methods in American archaeology*, Lincoln: University of Nebraska Press.

Lyman, R.L., O'Brien, M.J. and Dunnell, R.C. (1997) *The rise and fall of culture history*, New York: Plenum Press.

McCall, H. (2001) *The life of Max Mallowan: archaeology and Agatha Christie*. London: British Museum.

McCann, A.M. *et al.* (1987) *The Roman port and fishery of Cosa: a centre of ancient trade*, Princeton, NJ: Princeton University Press.

McCann, A.M. and Freed, J. (1994) *Deep water archaeology: a Late-Roman ship from Carthage and an ancient trade route near Skerki Bank off Northwest Sicily*, Ann Arbor, MI: Journal of Roman Archaeology Supplement 13.

Macdonald, S. (ed.) (1997) *Politics of display: museums, science, culture*, London: Routledge.

McDonald, W.A. and Thomas, C.G. (1990) *Progress into the past: the rediscovery of Mycenean civilization*, 2nd edn, Bloomington: Indiana University Press.

McDougall, I., Brown, F. and Fleagle, J. (2005) 'Stratigraphic placement and age of modern humans from Kibish, Ethiopia', *Nature* 433: 733–6.

McEvoy, B. *et al.* (2004) 'The longue durée of genetic ancestry: multiple genetic marker systems and Celtic origins on the Atlantic facade of Europe', *American Journal of Human Genetics* 72 (4): 693–702.

McGovern, P., Fleming, S. and Katz, S. (eds) (1995) *The origins and ancient history of wine*, Langhorne, PA: Gordon and Breach.

MacGregor, A. (ed.) (1994) *Sir Hans Sloane: collector, scientist, antiquary: founding father of the British Museum*, London: British Museum Press.

MacGregor, A. (2000) 'An aerial relic of O.G.S. Crawford', *Antiquity* 74: 87–100.

MacGregor, A. (ed.) (2008) *Sir John Evans 1823–1908: antiquity, commerce and natural science in the age of Darwin*, Oxford: The Ashmolean Museum.

McGuire, R.H. (1992) *A Marxist archaeology*, London: Academic Press.

McIntosh, R.J., Tainter, J.A. and McIntosh, S. Keech, (2000) *The way the wind blows: climate, history and human action*, New York: Columbia University Press.

McKinley, J.I. (2006) 'Cremation … the cheap option?', in Gowland, R. and Knüsel, C. (eds) *Social archaeology of funerary remains*, Oxford: Oxbow: 81–8.

McKinley, J.I. and Bond, J.M. (2001) 'Cremated bone', in Brothwell, D.R. and Pollard, A.M. *Handbook of archaeological sciences*, Chichester: John Wiley and Sons: 281–92.

MacManamon, F.P. (2005) 'Managing archaeological resources', in Maschner, H.D.G. and Chippindale, C. (eds) *Handbook of archaeological methods, 2*, Lanham, MD: Altamira Press: 1227–69.

MacManamon, F.P. and Hatton, A. (eds) (1999) *Cultural resource management in contemporary society: perspectives on managing and presenting the past*, London: Routledge, One World Archaeology 33.

McManus, P.M. (ed.) (1996) *Archaeological displays and the public: museology and interpretation*, London: Institute of Archaeology.

McNairn, B. (1980) *The method and theory of V. Gordon Childe: economic, social and cultural interpretations of prehistory*, Edinburgh: Edinburgh University Press.

McNeal, R.A. (1991) 'Archaeology and the destruction of the later Athenian acropolis', *Antiquity* 65: 49–63.

McNiven, I.J. and Russell, L. (2008) 'Towards a postcolonial archaeology of indigenous Australia', in Bentley, R.A., Maschner, H. and Chippindale, C. (eds) *Handbook of archaeological theories*, Lanham, MD: Altamira Press: 423–46.

McOmish, D., Field, D. and Brown, G. (2002) *The field archaeology of the Salisbury Plain training area*, Swindon: English Heritage.

Macready, S. and Thompson, F.H. (eds) (1985) *Archaeological field survey in Britain and abroad*, London: Society of Antiquaries.

Madella, M. and Zurro, D. (2007) *Plants, people and places: recent studies in phytolith analysis*, Oxford: Oxbow Books.

Maisels, C.K. (1990) *The Near East: archaeology in the 'Cradle of civilization'*, London: Routledge.

Maisels, C.K. (1993) *The emergence of civilization from hunting and gathering to agriculture, cities and the state of the Near East*, London: Routledge.

Maisels, C.K. (1999) *Early civilizations of the Old World: the formative histories of Egypt, the Levant, Mesopotamia, India and China*, London: Routledge.

Malina, J. and Vasíček, Z. (1990) *Archaeology yesterday and today: the development of archaeology in the sciences and humanities*, Cambridge: Cambridge University Press.

Malinowski, B. (1922) *Argonauts of the western Pacific: an account of native enterprise and adventure in the archipelagos of Melanesian New Guinea*, London: Routledge and Kegan Paul.

Maltby, M. (2006) *Integrating zooarchaeology. Proceedings of the 9th conference of the International Council of Archaeozoology, Durham, 2002*, Oxford: Oxbow.

Mamani Condori, C. (1989) 'History and prehistory in Bolivia: what about the Indians?', in Layton, R. *Conflict in the archaeology of living traditions*, London: Unwin Hyman, One World Archaeology 8: 46–59.

Maniatis, Y., Herz, N. and Basiakos, Y. (eds) (1995) *The study of marble and other stones used in antiquity*, London: Archetype/United Kingdom Institute for Conservation.

Manning, S.W. (1991) 'Approximate calendar date for the first human settlement of Cyprus?', *Antiquity* 65: 870–8.

Manning, S.W. (1999) *A test of time: the volcano of Thera and the chronology and history of the Aegean and East Mediterranean in the mid-2nd millennium BC*, Oxford: Oxbow Books.

Manning, S.W. *et al.* (2006) 'Chronology for the Aegean Late Bronze Age 1700–1400 BC', *Science* 312 (5773): 565–9.

Manning, S.W. and Weninger, B. (1992) 'A light in the dark: archaeological wiggle matching and the absolute chronology of the close of the Aegean Late Bronze Age', *Antiquity* 66: 636–63.

Manning, W.H. (1989) *Usk: the fortress excavations 1972–1974*, Cardiff: University of Wales Press.

MAP2 (1991) *The management of archaeological projects*, London: English Heritage.

Marean, C.W. *et al.* (1992) 'Captive hyena bone choice and destruction, the schlepp effect and Olduvai archaeofauna', *Journal of Archaeological Science* 19: 101–21.

Marsden, P. (1985) *The wreck of the Amsterdam*, London: Hutchinson.

Marshall, Y. (2008) 'Community archaeology', in Cunliffe, B., Gosden, C. and Joyce, R. (eds) *The Oxford handbook of archaeology*, Oxford: Oxford University Press: 1078–102.

Martin, C. (1998) *Scotland's historic shipwrecks*, London: Batsford/Historic Scotland.

Maschner, H.D.G. (ed.) (1996a) *Darwinian archaeologies*, New York: Plenum Press.

Maschner, H.D.G. (ed.) (1996b) *New methods, old problems: geographic information systems in modern archaeological research*, Carbondale: Center for Archaeological Investigations, Southern Illinois University.

Maschner, H.D.G. and Chippindale, C. (2005) *Handbook of archaeological methods*, 2 vols, Lanham, MD: Altamira Press.

Mathieu, J. (ed.) (2002) *Experimental archaeology: replicating past objects, behaviours and processes*, Oxford: British Archaeological Report, International Series 1036.

Mattingly, D. (2004) 'Being Roman: expressing identity in a provincial setting', *Journal of Roman Archaeology* 17: 5–25.

Mattingly, D. (2006) *An imperial possession: Britain in the Roman Empire*, London: Penguin.

Mauss, M. (1990) [1925] *The Gift: forms and functions of exchange in archaic societies*. London: Routledge

Maxwell, G.S. (ed.) (1983) *The impact of aerial reconnaissance on archaeology*, London: Council for British Archaeology Research Report 49.

Mayes, S. (2003) *The great Belzoni: the circus strongman and explorer who discovered Egypt's ancient treasures*, London: Tauris Parke.

Mayne, A. and Murray, T. (eds) (2001) *The archaeology of urban landscapes: explorations in slumland*, Cambridge: Cambridge University Press.

Mays, S. (1998) *The archaeology of human bones*, London: Routledge.

Mays, S. and Faerman, M. (2001) 'Sex identification in some putative infanticide remains from Roman Britain using ancient DNA', *Journal of Archaeological Science* 28: 555–9.

Meaden, T. (1991) *The goddess of the stones: the language of the megaliths*, London: Souvenir Press.

Mehrer, M. and Wescott, K. (2006) *GIS and archaeological site location modeling*, London: CRC Press.

Mellars, P. (1990) 'A major "plateau" in the radio-carbon time-scale at c. 9650 BP: the evidence from Star Carr (North Yorkshire)', *Antiquity* 64: 836–41.

Mellars, P. (2009) 'Moonshine over Star Carr: post-processualism, Mesolithic myths and archaeological realities', *Antiquity* 83: 502–17.

Mellars, P. and Dark, P. (1998) *Star Carr in context*, Cambridge: McDonald Institute.

Mellars, P. and Stringer, C. (eds) (1989) *The human revolution: behavioural and biological perspectives on the origins of modern humans*, Edinburgh: Edinburgh University Press.

Meltzer, D.J. (ed.) (1998) Squier, E.G. and Davis, E.H. [1848] *Ancient monuments of the Mississippi Valley*, Washington, DC: Smithsonian Institution Press.

Mendyk, S. (1989) *'Speculum Britanniae': regional study, antiquarianism, and science in Britain to 1700*, Toronto: University of Toronto Press.

Menotti, F. (ed.) (2004) *Living on the lake in Prehistoric Europe: 150 years of lake-dwelling research*, London: Routledge.

Merriman, N. (2004) *Public archaeology*, London: Routledge.

Meskell, L. (1995) 'Goddesses, Gimbutas and 'New Age' archaeology', *Antiquity* 69: 74–86.

Meskell, L. (2001) 'Archaeologies of identity', in Hodder, I. (ed.) *Archaeological theory today*, Cambridge: Polity Press: 187–213.

Meskell, L. (2005) *Archaeologies of materiality*, Oxford: Blackwell.

Meskell, L. and Preucel, R.W. (eds) (2004) *A companion to social archaeology*, Oxford: Blackwell.

Middleton, A. and Freestone, I. (eds) (1991) *Recent developments in ceramic petrology*, London: British Museum Occasional Papers 81.

Mignon, M.R. (1993) *Dictionary of concepts in archaeology*, London: Greenwood, Reference Sources for the Social Sciences and Humanities 13.

Miles, D. *et al.* (2007) *Iron Age and Roman settlement in the Upper Thames Valley: excavations at Claydon Pike and other sites within the Cotswold Water Park*, Oxford: Oxbow.

Milisauskas, S. and Kruk, J. (1991) 'Utilization of cattle for traction during the Neolithic in southeastern Poland', *Antiquity* 65: 562–6.

Miller, D. (1994a) 'Artefacts and the meaning of things', in Ingold, T. (ed.) *Companion encyclopedia of anthropology*, London: Routledge: 396–419.

Miller, D. (1994b) *Modernity: an ethnographic approach*, Oxford: Berg.

Milliken, S. and Peresani, M. (eds) (1998) *Lithic technology: from raw material procurement to tool production*, Forli: ABACO Edizioni.

Millon, R. (1967) 'Teotihuacan', *Scientific American* 216 (6): 38–48.

Mills, J.S. and White, R. (1994) *Organic chemistry of museum objects*, 2nd edn, London: Butterworth-Heinemann.

Milner, N. (2001) 'At the cutting edge: using thin sectioning to determine season of death of the European oyster, *Ostrea edulis*', *Journal of Archaeological Science* 28: 861–73.

Milner, N., Craig, O. and Bailey, G. (eds) (2007) *Shell middens in Atlantic Europe*, Oxford: Oxbow.

Mitchell, J.G. *et al.* (1984) 'Potassium-argon ages of schist honestones from the Viking age sites at Kaupang, Aggersborg, and Hedeby', *Journal of Archaeological Science* 11: 171–6.

Mithen, S. (1996) *The prehistory of the mind: a search for the origins of art, religion and science*, London: Thames and Hudson.

Mithen, S. (2001) 'Archaeological theory and theories of cognitive evolution', in Hodder, I. (ed.) *Archaeological theory today*, Cambridge: Polity Press: 98–121.

Moatti, C. (1993) *The search for ancient Rome*, London: Thames and Hudson New Horizons.

Molleson, T. and Cox, M. (1998) *Spitalfields Project, 2: the anthropology – the middling sort*, London: Council for British Archaeology.

Momigliano, N. (1999) *Duncan Mackenzie: a cautious canny Highlander and the palace of Minos at Knossos*, London: Institute of Classical Studies.

Montagu, A. (1997) *Man's most dangerous myth: the fallacy of race*, 6th edn, London: Sage.

Montelius, O. (1903) *Die typologische Methode: die ältere Kulturperioden im Orient und in Europa*, Stockholm: Selbstverlag.

Moore, A.T.M., Hillman, G.C. and Legge, A.J. (2000) *Village on the Euphrates: from foraging to farming at Abu Hureyra*, Oxford: Oxford University Press.

Moore, P.D., Webb, J.A. and Collinson, M.E. (1991) *Pollen analysis*, Oxford: Blackwell Scientific.

Moore, T. (2007) Perceiving communities: exchange, landscapes and social networks in the Later Iron Age of western Britain, *Oxford Journal of Archaeology* 26 (1): 79–102.

Moorehead, C. (1997) *Lost and found: the 9,000 treasures of Troy – Heinrich Schliemann and the gold that got away*, Harmondsworth: Penguin Books.

Moorey, P.R.S. (1991) *A century of Biblical archaeology*, London: Lutterworth Press.

Morales Muñiz, A. (ed.) (1993) *Archaeornithology: birds and the archaeological record*, Madrid: Archaeofauna 2.

Morgan, L.H. (1877) *Ancient society, or researches in the lines of human progress from savagery through barbarism to civilization*, New York: Henry Holt.

MoRPHE (2006) *The management of research projects in the historic environment*, Swindon: English Heritage.

Morris, I. (ed.) (1994) *Classical Greece: ancient histories and modern archaeologies*, Cambridge: Cambridge University Press.

Morris, I. (2000) *Archaeology as cultural history*, Oxford: Blackwell.

Morris, I. (2004) 'Classical archaeology', in Bintliff, J. (ed.) *A companion to archaeology*, Oxford: Blackwell: 253–71.

Morrison, J.S., Coates, J.F. and Rankov, N.B. (2000) *The Athenian trireme: the history and reconstruction of an ancient Greek warship*, 2nd edn, Cambridge: Cambridge University Press.

Morriss, R.K. (1999) *The archaeology of buildings*, Stroud: Tempus.

Morse, M.A. (1999) 'Craniology and the adoption of the Three Age System in Britain', *Proceedings of the Prehistoric Society* 65: 1–16.

Moser, S. (1996) 'Science, stratigraphy and the deep sequence: excavation vs regional survey and the question of gendered practice in archaeology', *Antiquity* 70: 813–23.

Moser, S. (1998) *Ancestral images: the iconography of human origins*, Stroud: Sutton; Ithaca, NY: Cornell University Press.

Moser, S. (2001) 'Archaeological representation: the visual conventions for constructing knowledge about the past', in Hodder, I. (ed.) *Archaeological theory today*, Cambridge: Polity Press: 262–83.

Moser, S. (2006) *Wondrous curiosities: ancient Egypt at the British Museum*, Chicago, IL: Chicago University Press.

Moser, S. (2007) 'On disciplinary culture: archaeology as fieldwork and its gendered associations', *Journal of Archaeological Method and Theory* 14 (3): 235–63.

Moshenka, G. (2008) 'Ethics and ethical critique in the archaeology of modern conflict', *Norwegian Archaeological Review* 41 (2): 159–75.

Moussa, M. (2008) 'The damages sustained to the ancient city of Babel as a consequence of the military presence of Coalition forces in 2003', in Stone, P.G. and Bajjaly, J.F. (eds) *The destruction of cultural heritage in Iraq*, Woodbridge: The Boydell Press: 143–50.

Mudd, A., Williams, R. and Lupton, A. (1999) *Excavations alongside Roman Ermin Street, Gloucestershire and Wiltshire: the archaeology of the A419/A417 Swindon to Gloucester road scheme Vol. 2*. Oxford: Oxford Archaeological Unit.

Muir, R. (2000) *The new Reading the landscape: fieldwork in landscape history*, Exeter: Exeter University Press.

Müldner, G. and Richards, M.P. (2007) 1500 years of human diet in York: the evidence from stable isotopes, *American Journal of Physical Anthropology* 133: 682–97.

Mullins, P.R. (1999) *Race and affluence: an archaeology of African America and consumer culture*, New York: Kluwer Academic/Plenum.

Mulvaney, D.J. (1991) 'Past regained, future lost: the Kow Swamp Pleistocene burials', *Antiquity* 65: 12–21.

Mundell Mango, M. and Henderson, J. (1995) 'Glass at medieval Constantinople: preliminary scientific evidence', in Mango, C. and Dagron, G. *Constantinople and its hinterland: papers from the twenty-seventh spring symposium of Byzantine Studies, Oxford, April 1993,* Aldershot: Ashgate: 333–58.

Munslow, A. (2006) *Routledge companion to historical studies,* 2nd edn, London: Routledge.

Murray, L.J.A. (1999) *Zest for life: the story of Alexander Keiller,* Swindon: Morven Press.

Murray, T. (ed.) (1999a) *Encyclopedia of archaeology: the great archaeologists,* 2 vols, Oxford: ABC-CLIO.

Murray, T. (ed.) (1999b) *Time and archaeology,* London: Routledge.

Murray, T. (ed.) (2001) *Encyclopedia of archaeology: history and discoveries,* 3 vols, Oxford: ABC-CLIO.

Murray, T. (2007) *Milestones in archaeology,* Santa Barbara, CA: ABC-CLIO.

Murray, T. and Evans, C. (eds) (2008) *Histories of archaeology: a reader in the history of archaeology,* Oxford: Oxford University Press.

Nash, D.T. and Petraglia, M.D. (eds) (1987) *Natural formation processes and the archaeological record,* Oxford: British Archaeological Reports, International Series S352.

Nash, G. (ed.) (1997) *Semiotics of landscape: archaeology of mind,* Oxford: British Archaeological Reports, International Series S661.

Nash, S.E. (ed.) (2000) *It's about time: a history of archaeological dating in North America,* Salt Lake City: University of Utah Press.

Nash, S.E. (2003) 'Not so talkative tree rings: why did archaeologists wait for an astronomer to establish tree-ring dating?', in Truncer, J. (ed.) *Picking the lock of time: developing chronology in American archaeology,* Gainesville: University of Florida Press: 140–58.

Needham, S. and Bowman, S. (2005) 'Flesh-hooks, technological complexity and the Atlantic Bronze Age feasting complex', *European Journal of Archaeology* 8 (2): 93–136.

Needham, S.P. and Macklin, M.G. (eds) (1992) *Alluvial archaeology in Britain,* Oxford: Oxbow Monograph 27.

Nelson, S. Milledge (2005) 'Gender archaeology', in Renfrew, C. and Bahn, P. (eds) *Archaeology: the key concepts,* London: Routledge: 127–33.

Nelson, S. Milledge (ed.) (2006) *Handbook of gender in archaeology,* Lanham, MD: Altamira Press.

Nelson, S. Milledge and Rosen-Ayalon, M. (eds) (2002) *In pursuit of gender: worldwide archaeological approaches,* Walnut Creek, CA: Altamira Press.

Neumann, T.W. and Sanford, R. (2001) *Cultural resources in archaeology: an introduction,* Walnut Creek, CA: Altamira Press.

Newman, C. (1997) *Tara: an archaeological survey,* Dublin: Royal Irish Academy/Discovery Programme Monograph 2.

Niblett, R. (1999) *Excavation of a ceremonial site at Folly Lane, Verulamium,* London: Britannia Monograph 14, Roman Society.

Nicholson, P.T. and Shaw, I. (eds) (2000) *Ancient Egyptian materials and technology,* Cambridge: Cambridge University Press.

Nicholson, R.A. and O'Connor, T.P. (eds) (2000) *People as an agent of environmental change,* Oxford: Oxbow Books, Symposia of Association for Environmental Archaeology 16.

Nishimura, Y. (2001) 'Geophysical prospection in archaeology', in Brothwell, D.R. and Pollard, A.M. *Handbook of archaeological sciences,* Chichester: John Wiley and Sons: 543–53.

Noel Hume, I. (1964) 'Handmaiden to history', *North Carolina Historical Review* 41 (2): 215–25.

Norbach, L.C. (ed.) (1997) *Early iron production: archaeology, technology and experiments,* Lejre: Historical–Archaeological Experimental Centre, Technical Report 3.

Northover, J.P. (1989) 'Non-ferrous metallurgy in British archaeology', in Henderson, J. (ed.) *Scientific analysis in archaeology,* Oxford: Oxford University Committee for Archaeology Monograph 19: 213–36.

Novella, R.A. (1995) *Classification and interpretation of marine artifacts from Western Mexico,* Oxford: British Archaeological Reports, International Series S622.

Nunn, J.F. (1996) *Ancient Egyptian medicine,* London: British Museum Press.

O'Brien, M.J. and Lyman, R. Lee, (1999) *Seriation, stratigraphy, and index fossils: the backbone of archaeological dating*, Dordrecht: Kluwer Academic/Plenum.

O'Connor, A. (2007) *Finding time for the Old Stone Age: a history of palaeolithic archaeology and quaternary geology in Britain 1860–1960*, Oxford: Oxford University Press.

O'Connor, T.P. (2004) *The archaeology of animal bones*, Stroud: Sutton Publishing.

O'Connor, T.P. (2006) 'Vertebrate demography by numbers: age, sex, and zooarchaeological practice', in Ruscillo, D. (ed.) *Recent advances in ageing and sexing animal bones. Proceedings of the 9th conference of ICAZ, Durham, 2002*, Oxford: Oxbow: 1–8.

O'Sullivan, A. (2000) *Crannogs: lake dwellings of early Ireland*, Dublin: Town House.

O'Sullivan, J. and Stanley, M. (eds) (2005) *Recent archaeological discoveries on national road schemes 2004*, Dublin: NRA.

Oates, D.J. (1989) 'Innovations in mud-brick: decorative and structural techniques in ancient Mesopotamia', *World Archaeology* 21: 388–406.

Oates, J., Molleson, T. and Sołtysiak, A. (2007) 'Equids and an acrobat: closure rituals at Tell Brak', *Antiquity* 82: 390–400.

Oddy, W.A. (ed.) (1992) *The art of the conservator*, London: British Museum.

Odell, G.H. (2003) *Lithic analysis: manuals in archaeological method, theory and technique*, London: Springer.

Olivier, L. (1999) 'The origins of French archaeology', *Antiquity* 73 (1): 76–83.

Olsen, S.L. (ed.) (1988) *Scanning electron microscopy in archaeology*, Oxford: British Archaeological Reports, International Series S452.

Oppenheimer, S. (2006) *The origins of the British*, London: Constable and Robinson.

Orna, M.V. (ed.) (1996) *Archaeological chemistry: organic, inorganic and biochemical analysis*, Washington, DC: American Chemical Society.

Orser, C.E. and Fagan, B.M. (eds) (1995) *Historical archaeology*, New York: Harper Collins College Publishers.

Orton, C. (1999) *Sampling in archaeology*, Cambridge: Cambridge University Press.

Orton, C., Tyers, P. and Vince, A. (1993) *Pottery in archaeology*, Cambridge: Cambridge University Press.

Osgood, R. (2005) 'The dead of Tormarton – Middle Bronze Age combat victims?', in Parker Pearson, M. and Thorpe, I.J.N. (eds) *Warfare, violence and slavery in prehistory. Proceedings of a Prehistoric Society conference at Sheffield University*, Oxford: Archaeopress: 139–44.

Ottaway, B.S. (1999) *A changing place: the Galgenberg in Lower Bavaria from the fifth to the first millennium BC*, Oxford: British Archaeological Reports, International Series S752.

Ottaway, P. (1992) *Archaeology in British towns from the emperor Claudius to the Black Death*, London: Routledge.

Otte, M. and Straus, L.G. (eds) (1997) *La Grotte du Bois Laiterie*, Liège: University of Liège, ERAUL 80.

Palmer, M. and Neaverson, P. (1998) *Industrial archaeology: principles and practice*, London: Routledge.

Palmer, R. (1984) *Danebury: an aerial photographic interpretation of its environs*, London: HMSO, Royal Commission on the Historical Monuments of England Suppl Series 6.

Palmer, R. (1996) 'A further case for the preservation of earthwork ridge-and-furrow', *Antiquity* 70: 436–40.

Pals, J.P. and Wijngaarden-Bakker, L. Van (eds) (1998) *Environmental archaeology 3: seasonality*, Oxford: Association for Environmental Archaeology/Oxbow Books.

Palter, R. (1993) '"Black Athena", Afro-centrism, and the history of science', *History of Science* 31: 227–87.

Panagiotakopulu, E. (2000) *Archaeology and entomology in the Eastern Mediterranean*, Oxford: British Archaeological Reports, International Series S836.

Panagiotakopulu, E. (2001) 'New records for ancient pests: archaeoentomology in Egypt', *Journal of Archaeological Science* 28: 1235–46.

Panagiotakopulu, E. and Buckland, P.C. (1999) '*Cimex lectularius L.*, the common bed bug from Pharaonic Egypt', *Antiquity* 73: 908–11.

Parcak, S. (2009) *Satellite remote sensing for archaeology*, London: Routledge.

Parker, A.J. (1992) *Ancient shipwrecks of the Mediterranean and the Roman provinces*,

Oxford: British Archaeological Reports, International Series S580.

Parker Pearson, M. (1999) *The archaeology of death and burial*, Stroud: Sutton Publishing.

Parker Pearson, M. and Ramilisonina (1998a) 'Stonehenge for the ancestors: the stones pass on the message', *Antiquity* 72: 308–26.

Parker Pearson, M. and Ramilisonina (1998b) 'Stonehenge for the ancestors: part two', *Antiquity* 72: 855–6.

Parker Pearson, M. and Richards, R. (eds) (1993) *Architecture and order: approaches to social space*, London: Routledge, Material Cultures.

Parker Pearson, M. and Thorpe, I.N.J. (2005) *Warfare, violence and slavery in prehistory: proceedings of a Prehistoric Society conference at Sheffield University*, Oxford: British Archaeological Reports, International Series 1374.

Parker Pearson, M. *et al.* (2007) 'The age of Stonehenge', *Antiquity* 81: 617–39.

Parker Pearson, M. *et al.* (2009) 'Who was buried at Stonehenge?' *Antiquity* 83: 23–39.

Parkinson, R. (2005) *The Rosetta stone*, London: British Museum.

Parry, G. (2007) 'The discovery of Britain', in Starkey, D. *et al.* (eds) *Making history*, London: Royal Academy: 15–50.

Parslow, C.C. (1995) *Rediscovering antiquity: Karl Weber and the excavation of Herculaneum, Pompeii, and Stabiae*, Cambridge: Cambridge University Press.

Parsons, D. (1999) *Churches and chapels: investigating places of worship*, 2nd rev. edn, London: Council for British Archaeology Practical Handbook 8.

Pasquinucci, M. and Trement, F. (eds) (1999) *The archaeology of the Mediterranean landscape, 4: non-destructive techniques applied to landscape archaeology*, Oxford: Oxbow Books.

Patterson, T.C. (2003) *Marx's ghost: conversations with archaeologists*, Oxford: Berg.

Patterson, T.C. and Orser, C.E. (2004) *Foundations of social archaeology: selected writings of V. Gordon Childe*, Walnut Creek, CA: Altamira Press.

Pattison, P., Field, D. and Ainsworth, S. (eds) (1999) *Patterns of the past: essays in landscape archaeology for Christopher Taylor*, Oxford: Oxbow Books.

Pauketat, T. (2007) *Chiefdoms and other archaeological delusions*, Lanham, MD: Altamira Press.

Pawson, M. and Buisseret, D. (1975) *Port Royal, Jamaica*, Oxford: Clarendon Press.

Payne, A., Kuttner, A. and Smick, R. (eds) (2000) *Antiquity and its interpreters*, Cambridge: Cambridge University Press.

Payton, R. (ed.) (1992) *Retrieval of objects from archaeological sites*, Denbigh: Archetype.

Peacock, D.P.S. (1982) *Pottery in the Roman world: an ethnoarchaeological approach*, London: Longman.

Peacock, D.P.S. *et al.* (1994) 'Mons Claudianus and the problem of the "granito del foro": a geological and geochemical approach', *Antiquity* 68: 209–30.

Peacock, D.P.S. and Maxfield, V.A. (2001) *Survey and excavations at Mons Claudianus 1987–1993, 2: the excavations, part 1*, Cairo: Institut Français d'Archéologie Orientale.

Peacock, D.P.S. and Williams, D.F. (1986) *Amphorae and the Roman economy: an introductory guide*, London: Longman.

Pearce, N. *et al.* (2007) 'Reinterpretation of Greenland ice-core data recognises the presence of the late Holocene Aniakchak tephra (Alaska), not the Minoan tephra (Santorini) at 1645 BC, in Bietak, M. and Czerny, E. (eds) *The synchronization of civilizations in the eastern Mediterranean in the second millennium BC III*, Vienna: OAW: 139–48.

Pearce, S. (ed.) (2007a) 'Visions of antiquity: the Society of Antiquaries of London 1707–2007', *Archaeologia* 111.

Pearce, S. (2007b) 'The interpretation of ancient objects, 1770–1820', in Pearce, S. (ed.) 'Visions of antiquity: the Society of Antiquaries of London 1707–2007', *Archaeologia* 111: 147–72.

Pearsall, D.M. (1989) *Paleoethnobotany: a handbook of procedures*, London: Academic Press.

Pearson, C. (ed.) (1987) *Conservation of marine archaeological objects*, London: Butterworth.

Pearson, C.L. (2006) *Volcanic eruptions, tree rings and multielemental chemistry*, Oxford: British

Archaeological Reports, International Series 1556.

Pearson, C.L. *et al.* (2009) 'Dendrochemical analysis of a tree-ring growth anomaly associated with the Late Bronze Age eruption of Thera', *Journal of Archaeological Science* 36: 1206–14.

Pearson, G.W. (1987) 'How to cope with calibration', *Antiquity* 61: 98–103.

Pearson, S. and Meeson, B. (2001) *Vernacular buildings in a changing world: understanding, recording and conservation*, London: Council for British Archaeological Research Report 126.

Peiser, B.J., Palmer, T. and Bailey, M.E. (eds) (1998) *Natural catastrophes during Bronze Age civilizations: archaeological, geological, astronomical and cultural perspectives*, Oxford: British Archaeological Reports, International Series S728.

Peltenburg, E. *et al.* (2000) 'Agro-pastoralist colonization of Cyprus in the 10th millennium BP: initial assessments', *Antiquity* 74: 844–53.

Penny, N. (1985) *Thomas Howard, Earl of Arundel*, Oxford: Ashmolean Museum.

Perlès, C. (2001) *The Early Neolithic in Greece*, Cambridge: Cambridge University Press.

Peterson, R. (2003) 'William Stukeley: an eighteenth century phenomenologist?', *Antiquity* 77: 394–400.

Petrie, W.F. (1899) 'Sequences in prehistoric remains', *Journal of the Royal Anthropological Institute* 29: 295–301.

Petrie, W.F. (1920) *Prehistoric Egypt*, London: British School of Archaeology in Egypt.

Pettitt, P.B. (2005) 'Radiocarbon dating', in Maschner, H.D.G. and Chippindale, C. *Handbook of archaeological methods, 1*, Lanham, MD: Altamira Press: 309–36.

Pettitt, P.B. and Bader, N.O. (2000) 'Direct AMS radiocarbon dates for the Sungir mid Upper Palaeolithic burials', *Antiquity* 74: 269–70.

Pettitt, P.B. and Bahn, P. (2003) 'Current problems in dating palaeolithic cave art: Candamo and Chauvet', *Antiquity* 77 (295): 134–41.

Phillips, C.W. (ed.) (1970) *The Fenland in Roman times*, London: Royal Geographical Society Research Series 5.

Phillips, D. and Heywood, B. (ed. Carver, M.) (1995) *Excavations at York Minster I: Roman to Norman: the Roman legionary fortress and its exploitation in the early middle ages*, 2 vols, London: HMSO.

Piccini, A. (1999) 'Welsh Celts or Celtic Wales? The production and consumption of a (not so) different Iron Age', in Bevan, B. (ed.) *Northern exposure*, Leicester: Leicester University Press: 51–63.

Piggott, S. (1979) *Antiquity depicted: aspects of archaeological illustration*, London: Thames and Hudson.

Piggott, S. (1985) *William Stukeley, an 18th century antiquary*, London: Thames and Hudson.

Piggott, S. (1989) *Ancient Britons and the antiquarian imagination: ideas from the Renaissance to the Regency*, London: Thames and Hudson.

Pilcher, J.R., Hall, V.A. and McCormac, F.G. (1995) 'Dates of Holocene Icelandic volcanic eruptions from tephra layers in Irish peats', *The Holocene* 5: 103–10.

Pinsky, V. and Wylie, A. (eds) (1989) *Critical traditions in contemporary archaeology*, Cambridge: Cambridge University Press.

Piperno, D.R. (2006) *Phytoliths: a comprehensive guide for archaeologists and palaeoecologists*, Lanham, MD: Altamira Press.

Piperno, D.R. *et al.* (2007) 'Late Pleistocene and Holocene environmental history of the Iguala Valley, Central Balsas watershed of Mexico', *Proceedings of the National Academy of Sciences* 104 (29): 11874–81.

Pitts, M. (2001) *Hengeworld*, 2nd edn, London: Arrow.

Pitts, M. (2009) 'A year at Stonehenge', *Antiquity* 83: 184–94.

Pitts, M. and Roberts, M. (1997) *Fairweather Eden: life in Britain half a million years ago as revealed by the excavations at Boxgrove*, London: Century.

Planck, D. (ed.) (1998) *Unsichtbares sichtbar machen: geophysikalische Prospektionsmethoden in der Archäologie*, Frankfurt: Konrad Theiss.

Pleiner, R. (2006) *Iron in archaeology: early European blacksmiths*, Prague: Archeologický Ústav.

Pluciennik, M. (2005) *Social evolution*, London: Duckworth.

Pluciennik, M. (2006) 'From primitive to civilised: social evolution in Victorian anthropology and archaeology', in Pearson, R. (ed.) *The Victorians and the ancient world: archaeology and classicism in nineteenth-century culture*, Cambridge: Cambridge Scholar Press: 1–24.

Poirer, D.A. and Feder, K.L. (eds) (2001) *Dangerous places: health, safety and archaeology*, Westport, CT: Greenwood.

Politis, G.P. and Pérez Gollán, A. (2004) 'Latin American archaeology: from colonialism to globalization', in Meskell, L. and Preucel, R.W. (eds) *A companion to social archaeology*, Oxford: Blackwell: 353–73.

Pollard, A.M. (ed.) (1992) *New developments in archaeological science: a joint symposium of the Royal Society and the British Academy, February 1991*, Oxford: Oxford University Press, Proceedings of the British Academy 77.

Pollard, A.M. (ed.) (1999) *Geoarchaeology: exploration, environments, resources*, London: Geological Society.

Pollard, A.M. (2004) 'Putting infinity up on trial: a consideration of the role of scientific thinking in future archaeologies', in Bintliff, J. (ed.) *A companion to archaeology*, Oxford: Blackwell: 380–96.

Pollard, A.M. (2008) 'Measuring the passage of time: achievements and challenges in archaeological dating', in Cunliffe, B., Gosden, C. and Joyce, R. (eds) *The Oxford handbook of archaeology*, Oxford: Oxford University Press: 145–68.

Pollard, A.M. *et al.* (2007) Analytical chemistry in archaeology, Cambridge: Cambridge University Press.

Pollard, A.M. and Bray, P. (2007) 'A bicycle made for two? The integration of scientific techniques into archaeological interpretation', *Annual Review of Anthropology* 36: 245–59.

Pollard, A.M. and Heron, M. (eds) (2008) *Archaeological chemistry*, 2nd edn, Cambridge: Royal Society of Chemistry.

Pollard, J. (1999) 'These places have their moments: thoughts on settlement practices in the British Neolithic', in Brück, J. and Goodman, M. (eds) *Making places in the prehistoric world: themes in settlement archaeology*, London: UCL Press: 76–93.

Pollard, J. and Gillings, M. (1998) 'Romancing the stones: towards an elemental and virtual Avebury', *Archaeological Dialogues* 5: 143–64.

Pope, M. (1999) *The story of decipherment from Egyptian hieroglyphs to Mayan script*, rev. edn, London: Thames and Hudson.

Potter, T.W. (1979) *The changing landscape of south Etruria*, London: Paul Elek.

Powis, T.G. *et al.* (1999) 'A reconstruction of Middle Preclassic Maya subsistence economy at Cahal Pech, Belize', *Antiquity* 73: 364–76.

Powlesland, D. (1997) 'Publishing in the round: a role for CD-ROM in the publication of archaeological field-work results', *Antiquity* 71: 1062–6.

Powlesland, D. *et al.* (2006) 'Beneath the sand: remote sensing, archaeology, aggregates and sustainability: a case study from Heslerton, the Vale of Pickering, North Yorkshire, UK', *Archaeological Prospection* 13: 291–9.

PPG16 (1990) *Planning Policy Guidance 16: archaeology and planning*, London: Department of the Environment/Department of National Heritage.

Prag, A.J.W. and Neave, R. (1999) *Making faces: using forensic and archaeological evidence*, new edn, London: British Museum Press.

Pratt, S. (2005) 'The American time machine: Indians and the visualisation of ancient Europe', in Smiles, S. and Moser, S. *Envisioning the past*, Oxford: Blackwell: 51–71.

Prestwich, J. (1860) 'On the occurrence of flint implements, associated with the remains of extinct mammalia, in beds of a late geological period', *Proceedings of the Royal Society London* 10: 50–9.

Pretzler, M. (2007) *Pausanias: travel writing in Ancient Greece*, London: Duckworth.

Protsch, R. (1991) 'Dating of bones in archaeology and anthropology', in Göksu, H.Y., Oberhofer, M. and Regulla, D. (eds) *Scientific dating methods*, Dordrecht: Kluwer Academic Publishers: 271–300.

Prowse, T. *et al.* (2004) 'Isotopic paleodiet studies of skeletons from Imperial Roman-age cemetery of Isola Sacra, Rome,

Italy', *Journal of Archaeological Sciences* 31: 259–72.

Prowse, T. *et al.* (2005) Isotopic evidence for age related variation in diet from Isola Sacra, Italy, *American Journal of Physical Anthropology* 128: 2–13.

Prowse, T. *et al.* (2007) Isotopic evidence for age related immigration to Imperial Rome, *American Journal of Physical Anthropology* 132: 510–19.

Prummel, W. and Frisch, H.J. (1986) 'A guide for the distinction of species, sex and body side in bones of sheep and goat', *Journal of Archaeological Science* 13: 567–78.

Pryor, F. (1993) *Flag Fen: prehistoric fenland centre*, London: English Heritage/Batsford.

Pryor, F. (2001) *Seahenge: a quest for life and death in Bronze Age Britain*, London: HarperCollins.

Pryor, F. (2005) *Flag Fen: life and death of a prehistoric landscape*. Stroud: Tempus.

Purdy, B. (2001) *Enduring records: the environmental and cultural heritage of wetlands*, Oxford: Oxbow.

Rackham, J. (1994) *Interpreting the past: animal bones*, London: British Museum.

Rackham, O. (1994) *The illustrated history of the countryside*, London: Weidenfeld and Nicholson.

Rahtz, P. *et al.* (1997) *St Mary's Church, Deerhurst, Gloucestershire: fieldwork, excavations and structural analysis 1971–84*, Woodbridge: Boydell Press, Report of the Research Committee of the Society of Antiquaries of London 55.

Randsborg, K. (ed.) (1996) *Absolute chronologies: archaeological Europe 2500–500 BC*, Copenhagen: Munksgaard, Acta Archaeologica 67.

Rapp, G. and Hill, C.L. (2006) *Geoarchaeology: the earth-science approach to archaeological interpretation*, 2nd edn, New Haven, CT: Yale University Press.

Rapp, G. and Mulholland, S. (eds) (1992) *Phytolith systematics: emerging issues*, New York: Plenum Press, Advances in Archaeology and Museum Science 1.

Rathje, W.L. (2002) 'The nouveau elite potlatch: one scenario for the monumental rise of early

civilizations', in Masson, M. and Freidel, D. (eds) *Ancient Maya political economies*, Walnut Creek, CA: Altamira Press: 31–40.

RCAHMS (1994) *South-East Perth: an archaeological landscape*, Royal Commission on the Ancient and Historical Monuments of Scotland, Edinburgh: HMSO.

RCAHMS (2007) *In the shadow of Bennachie: a field archaeology of Donside, Aberdeenshire*, Edinburgh: RCAHMS/Society of Antiquaries of Scotland.

RCHME (1979) *Stonehenge and its environs: monuments and land use*, Royal Commission on the Historical Monuments of England, Edinburgh: Edinburgh University Press.

RCHME (1999) *Recording archaeological field monuments: a descriptive specification*, Royal Commission on the Historical Monuments of England, London: HMSO.

Redfern, R. (2008) New evidence for Iron Age secondary burial practice and bone modification from Gussage All Saints and Maiden Castle, Dorset, England, *Oxford Journal of Archaeology* 27 (3): 281–301.

Redknap, M. (ed.) (1997) *Artefacts from wrecks: dated assemblages from the late Middle Ages to the Industrial Revolution*, Oxford: Oxbow Monograph 84 for the Nautical Archaeology Society and Society for Post-Medieval Archaeology.

Redman, C.L. (1978) 'Mesopotamian urban ecology: the systemic context of the emergence of urbanism', in Redman, C.L. *Social archaeology: beyond subsistence and dating*, New York: Academic Press: 329–47.

Reeve, J. *et al.* (1993) *The Spitalfields project*, 2 vols, London: Council for British Archaeology Research Report 86.

Reeves, N. and Taylor, J. (1992) *Howard Carter before Tutankhamun*, London: British Museum.

Reid, D.M. (2002) *Whose pharaohs? Archaeology, museums, and Egyptian national identity from Napoleon to World War I*, Berkeley: University of California Press.

Reimer, P.J. *et al.* (2009) 'IntCal09 and Marine09 radiocarbon age calibration curves, 0–50,000 years cal BP', *Radiocarbon* 51(4): 1111–50.

Reimer, P. *et al.* (2009) 'IntCal09 and Marine09 radiocarbon age calibration curves, 0–50,000 years cal BP', *Radiocarbon* 51(4): 1111–50.

Reitz, E.J., Scarry, C.M. and Scudder, S.J. (eds) (1996) *Case studies in environmental archaeology*, New York: Plenum Press, Interdisciplinary Contributions to Archaeology.

Reitz, E.J. and Wing, E.A. (1999) *Zooarchaeology*, Cambridge: Cambridge University Press.

Renfrew, C. (1973a) *Before civilization; the radiocarbon revolution and prehistoric Europe*, London: Jonathan Cape.

Renfrew, C. (1973b) 'Monuments, mobilization and social organization in Neolithic Wessex', in Renfrew, C. (ed.) *The explanation of culture change models in prehistory*, London: Duckworth: 539–58.

Renfrew, C. (1982) *Towards an archaeology of mind*, Cambridge: Cambridge University Press.

Renfrew, C. (1988) 'The New Archaeology: prehistory as a discipline', in Daniel, G. and Renfrew, C. *The idea of prehistory*, Edinburgh: Edinburgh University Press: 157–213.

Renfrew, C. (1992) 'The identity and future of archaeological science', in Pollard, A.M. (ed.) *New developments in archaeological science*, Oxford: Clarendon Press: 285–93.

Renfrew, C. (1996) 'Kings, tree rings and the Old World', *Nature* 5 (381): 733–4.

Renfrew, C. (2000) *Loot, legitimacy and ownership*, London: Duckworth, Debates in Archaeology.

Renfrew, C. (ed.) (2000) *America past, America present: genes and languages in the Americas and beyond*, Cambridge: McDonald Institute, Papers in the Prehistory of Languages.

Renfrew, C. (2001a) 'Commodification and institution in group-oriented and individualizing societies', in Runciman, W.G. (ed.) *The origin of human social institutions*. Proceedings of the British Academy 100, Oxford: Oxford University Press: 93–117.

Renfrew, C. (2001b) 'Symbol before concept: material engagement and the early development of society', in Hodder, I. (ed.) *Archaeological theory today*, Cambridge: Polity Press: 122–40.

Renfrew, C. (2005) 'Cognitive archaeology', in Renfrew, C. and Bahn, P. (eds) *Archaeology: the key concepts*, London: Routledge: 41–5.

Renfrew, C. and Bahn, P. (eds) (2005) *Archaeology: the key concepts*, London: Routledge.

Renfrew, C. and Boyle, K. (eds) (2000) *Archaeogenetics: DNA and the population prehistory of Europe*, Cambridge: McDonald Institute for Archaeological Research.

Renfrew, C. and Scarre, C. (eds) (1998) *Cognition and material culture: the archaeology of symbolic storage*, Cambridge: McDonald Institute for Archaeological Research.

Renfrew, C. and Wagstaff, J.M. (eds) (1982) *An island polity: the archaeology of exploitation in Melos*, Cambridge: Cambridge University Press.

Renfrew, C. and Zubrow, E. (eds) (1994) *The ancient mind: elements of cognitive archaeology*, Cambridge: Cambridge University Press, New Directions in Archaeology.

Renfrew, J. (ed.) (1991) *New light on early farming: recent developments in palaeoethnobotany*, Edinburgh: Edinburgh University Press.

Renne, P.R. *et al.* (2001) 'Ar-40/Ar-39 dating into the historical realm: calibration against Pliny the Younger', *Science* 277: 1279–80.

Repcheck, J. (2003) *The man who found time: James Hutton and the discovery of the earth's antiquity*, New York: Basic Books.

Reynolds, P.J. (1979) *Iron Age farm: the Butser experiment*, London: British Museum Press.

Rhoads, J.W. (1992) 'Significant sites and non-site archaeology: a case-study from south-east Australia', *World Archaeology* 24: 198–217.

Richard, J.D., Richards, J.C. and Horsler, V (2007) *Stonehenge: the story so far*, Swindon: English Heritage.

Richard, N. (ed.) (1992) *L'invention de la préhistoire: anthologie*, Paris: Presse Pocket, Agora, Les Classiques, 86.

Richard, N. (ed.) (1993) 'Histoire de la préhistoire', *Bulletin de la société préhistorique française* 90: 10–112.

Richards, D.A. and Beck, J.W. (2001) 'Dramatic shifts in atmospheric radiocarbon during the last glacial period', *Antiquity* 75: 482–5

Richards, J. (1990) *The Stonehenge environs project*, London: HBMC Archaeological Report 16.

Richards, J. (1999) *Meet the ancestors*, London: BBC Books.

Richards, J. (2001) *Blood of the Vikings*, London: Hodder and Stoughton.

Richards, J. (2007) *Stonehenge: the story so far*, Swindon: English Heritage.

Richards, J. and Robinson, D. (eds) (2000) *Digital archives from excavation and fieldwork: a guide to good practice*, Oxford: Archaeological Data Service/Oxbow Books.

Richards, J.D. (1987) *The significance of form and decoration of Anglo-Saxon cremation urns*, Oxford: British Archaeological Reports 166.

Richards, J.D. (2006) 'Electronic publication in archaeology', in Evans, T. and Daly, P. (eds) *Digital archaeology: bridging method and theory*, London: Routledge: 213–25.

Richards, M.P., Schulting, R.J. and Hedges, R.E.M. (2003) 'Sharp shift in diet at onset of Neolithic', *Nature* 425: 366.

Richards, M.P. and Sheridan, J.A. (2000) 'New AMS dates on human bone from Mesolithic Oronsay', *Antiquity* 74: 313–15.

Richardson, N. (1992) 'Conjoin sets and stratigraphic integrity in a sandstone shelter: Kenniff Cave (Queensland, Australia)', *Antiquity* 66: 408–18.

Ridley, R.T. (1992) *The eagle and the spade: archaeology in Rome during the Napoleonic era*, Cambridge: Cambridge University Press.

Rieth, E. (ed.) (1998) *Mediterrannée antique: pêche, navigation, commerce*, Paris: Editions de CTHS.

Riggsby, A. (2006) *Caesar in Gaul and Rome: war in words*. Austin: University of Texas Press.

Riley, D.N. (1987) *Air photography and archaeology*, London: Duckworth.

Riley, F.R. (1999) *The role of the traditional Mediterranean diet in the development of Minoan Crete*, Oxford: British Archaeological Reports, International Series S810.

Rippon, S. (1996) *Gwent Levels: the evolution of a wetland landscape*, London: Council for British Archaeology.

Rippon, S. (2004) *Historic landscape analysis*. CBA Practical Handbook 16, York: Council for British Archaeology.

Ritchie, W. *et al.* (1988) *Surveying and mapping for field scientists*, London: Longman.

Rivera Nunez, D. and Walker, M.J. (1991) 'Grape remains and direct radiocarbon dating: a disconcerting experience from El Prado, Murcia, Spain', *Antiquity* 65: 905–8.

Rives, J. (1999) *Tacitus: Germania*, Oxford: Oxford University Press.

Robb, J. (2005) 'Agency', in Renfrew, C. and Bahn, P. (eds) *Archaeology: the key concepts*, London: Routledge: 3–7.

Roberts, B. (1996) *Landscapes of settlement: prehistory to the present*, London: Routledge.

Roberts, C.A. (2007) 'A bioarchaeology study of maxillary sinusitis', *American Journal of Physical Anthropology* 133: 792–807.

Roberts, C.A. (2009) *Human remains in archaeology: a handbook*, York: Council for British Archaeology.

Roberts, C.A. and Buikstra, J. (2003) *The bioarchaeology of tuberculosis*, Gainesville: University of Florida Press.

Roberts, C.A. and Cox, M. (2003) *Health and disease in Britain*, Gloucester: Sutton.

Roberts, C.A. and Ingham, S. (2008) 'Using ancient DNA analysis in palaeopathology: a critical analysis of published papers with recommendations for future work', *International Journal of Osteoarchaeology* 18: 600–13.

Roberts, C.A. and Manchester, K. (2005) *The archaeology of disease*, 3rd edn, Ithaca, NY: Cornell University Press.

Roberts, M. and Parfitt, S. (1998) *Boxgrove: a Middle Pleistocene hominid site at Eartham Quarry, Boxgrove, West Sussex*, London: English Heritage.

Roberts, N. (1998) *The Holocene: an environmental history*, 2nd edn, Oxford: Blackwell.

Roberts, R.G. *et al.* (1994) 'The human colonisation of Australia: optical dates of 53,000 and 60,000 years bracket human arrival at Deaf Adder Gorge', *Quaternary Geochronology* 13: 575–84.

Rocek, T.R. and Bar-Yosef, O. (1998) *Seasonality and sedentism: archaeological perspectives from old and new world sites*, Cambridge, MA: Peabody Museum of Archaeology and Ethnology, Harvard University.

Rodwell, W. (1989) *Church archaeology*, London: Batsford/English Heritage.

Roger Tym and Partners and Pagoda Associates (1995) *Review of the implementation of PPG16 Archaeology and Planning*, London: English Heritage.

Rogers, A. and Rowley, T. (eds) (1974) *Landscapes and documents*, London: Bedford Square Press.

Rohl, B. and Needham, S. (1998) *The circulation of metal in the British Bronze Age: the application of lead isotope analysis*, London: British Museum Occasional Paper 102.

Romano, I.B. (1997) 'No longer the "Pitcairn Nike": a Minerva-Victoria from Cyrene', *Expedition* 39:3: 15–26

Romer, J. and Romer, E. (2000) *Great excavations: John Romer's history of archaeology*, London: Cassell.

Roosevelt, A.C. (1991) *Moundbuilders of the Amazon: geophysical archaeology on Marajo Island, Brazil*, London: Academic Press.

Roseff, R. (2001) 'The responsibility of archaeologists to nature conservation', in Albarella, U. (ed.) *Environmental archaeology: meaning and purpose*, Dordrecht: Kluwer Academic Publishers: 89–96.

Rosen, A.M. (1986) *Cities of clay: the geoarchaeology of tells*, Chicago, IL: Chicago University Press.

Rosen, A.M. (2007) *Civilizing climate: social responses to climate change in the ancient Near East*, Lanham, MD: Altamira Press.

Roskams, S. (ed.) (2000) *Interpreting stratigraphy: site evaluation, recording procedures and stratigraphic analysis*, Oxford: Archaeopress.

Roskams, S. (2001) *Excavation*, Cambridge: Cambridge University Press, Cambridge Manuals in Archaeology.

Ross, S. *et al.* (eds) (1991) *Computing for archaeologists*, Oxford: Oxford University Committee for Archaeology Monograph 18.

Rossi, P. (1984) *The dark abyss of time; the history of the earth and the history of nations from Hooke to Vico*, Chicago, IL: Chicago University Press.

Rowley-Conwy, P. (1996) 'Why didn't Westropp's "Mesolithic" catch on in 1872?', *Antiquity* 70: 940–4.

Rowley-Conwy, P. (ed.) (2000) *Animal bones, human societies*, Oxford: Oxbow Books.

Rowley-Conwy, P. (2007) *From Genesis to prehistory: the archaeological three age system and its contested reception in Denmark, Britain and Ireland*, Oxford: Oxford University Press.

Rowsome, P. (2000) *Heart of the city: Roman, medieval and modern London revealed by archaeology at 1 Poultry*, London: English Heritage/Museum of London.

Rudebeck, E. (2000) *Tilling nature: harvesting culture: exploring images of the human being in the transition to agriculture*, Stockholm: Almqvist and Wiksell International: Acta Archaeologica Lundensia.

Ruggles, C. (1999) *Astronomy in prehistoric Britain and Ireland*, New Haven, CT: Yale University Press.

Ruiz-Taboada, A. and Montero-Ruiz, I. (1999) 'The oldest metallurgy in western Europe', *Antiquity* 73: 897–903.

Rule, M. (1982) *The Mary Rose: the excavation and raising of Henry VIII's flagship*, London: Conway Press.

Runnels, C. (2007) *The archaeology of Heinrich Schliemann*, Boston, MA: Archaeological Institute of America.

Ruppe, C. and Barstad, J. (eds) (2002) *International handbook of underwater archaeology*, Berlin: Springer.

Ruse, M. (1996) *Monad to man: the concept of progress in evolutionary biology*, Cambridge, MA: Harvard University Press.

Russell, J.M. (1998) *The final sack of Nineveh: the discovery, documentation, and destruction of King Sennacherib's throne room at Nineveh, Iraq*, New Haven, CT: Yale University Press.

Russell, M. (2002) *Digging holes in popular culture: archaeology and science fiction*, Oxford: Oxbow.

Russell, M. (2003) *Piltdown Man: The secret life of Charles Dawson and the world's greatest archaeological hoax*, Stroud: Tempus.

Sabloff, P.L.W. (1998) *Conversations with Lew Binford: drafting the New Archaeology*, Norman: University of Oklahoma Press.

Sahlins, M. and Service, E. (eds) (1960) *Evolution and culture*, Ann Arbor: University of Michigan Press.

Said, E. (1995) [1978] *Orientalism*, London: Routledge and Kegan Paul.

Sala, I. Levi (1996) *A study of microscopic polish on flint implements*, Oxford: British Archaeological Reports, International Series S629.

Samuels, S.R. (ed.) (1991) *Ozette archaeological project research report 1: house structure and floor midden*, Pullman: Washington State University, Department of Anthropology.

Sand, C., Bole, J. and Ouetcho, A. (2003) 'Prehistory and its perception in a Melanesian archipelago: the New Caledonia example', *Antiquity* 77: 505–19.

Sanderson, S.K. (1990) *Social evolutionism: a critical history*, Oxford: Blackwell.

Santos, F. *et al.* (1999) 'The central Siberian origins for Native American Y-chromosomes', *American Journal of Human Genetics* 64 (2): 619–28.

Sauer, E. (2000) 'Alchester, a Claudian "vexillation fortress" near the western boundary of the Catuvellauni: new light on the Roman invasion of Britain', *Archaeological Journal* 157: 1–78.

Saunders, N.J. (2002) 'Excavating memories: archaeology and the Great War, 1914–2001', *Antiquity* 76: 101–8.

Saunders, N.J. (2007) *Killing time: archaeology and the First World War*, Stroud: Sutton.

Saunders, T. (ed.) (1998) *Revenge of the grand narrative: Marxist perspective in archaeology*, Aldershot: Avebury, Worldwide Archaeology Series.

Scarre, C. (1999) 'Archaeological theory in France and Britain', *Antiquity* 73: 155–61.

Scarre, C. (2005) *The human past: world prehistory and the development of human societies*, London: Thames and Hudson.

Scarre, C. and Scarre, G. (eds) (2006) *The ethics of archaeology: philosophical perspectives on archaeological practice*, Cambridge: Cambridge University Press.

Scarre, G. (2006) 'Can archaeology harm the dead?', in Scarre, C. and Scarre, G. (eds) *The ethics of archaeology: philosophical perspectives on archaeological practice*, Cambridge: Cambridge University Press: 181–98.

Schackel, P., Mullins, P. and Warner, M. (eds) (1998) *Annapolis pasts: historical archaeology in Annapolis, Maryland*, Knoxville: University Tennessee Press.

Schama, S. (1995) *Landscape and memory*, New York: Knopf.

Schiffer, M.B. (1976) *Behavioral archaeology*, New York: Academic Press.

Schiffer, M.B. (1987) *Formation processes of the archaeological record*, Albuquerque: University of New Mexico Press.

Schiffer, M.B. (1995) *Behavioral archaeology: first principles*, Salt Lake City: University of Utah Press.

Schijns, W. (2008) *Vernacular mud brick architecture in the Dakhleh Oasis, Egypt*, Oxford: Oxbow Books, Dakhleh Oasis Project Monograph 10.

Schlanger, N. and Nordbladh, J. (eds) (2008) *Archives, ancestors, practices: archaeology in the light of its history*, New York: Berghahn Books.

Schliemann, H. (1880) *Ilios: the city and country of the Trojans*, London: John Murray.

Schmidt, A. and Wise, A. (1998) *Archaeological geophysics: a guide to good practice*, Oxford: Oxbow Books, Archaeology Data Service.

Schmidt, P.R. (ed.) (1996) *The culture and technology of African iron production*, Gainesville: Florida University Press.

Schmidt, P.R. and McIntosh, R.J. (eds) (1996) *Plundering Africa's past*, London: James Currey; Bloomington (IN): Indiana University Press.

Schnapp, A. (1996) *The discovery of the past: the origins of archaeology*, London: British Museum Publications.

Schnapp, A. (2006) 'The pre-adamites: an abortive attempt to invent pre-history in the seventeenth century?', in Ligota, C. and Quantin, J.-L. (eds) *History of scholarship: a selection of papers from the Seminar on the History of Scholarship held annually at the Warburg Institute*, Oxford: Oxford University Press: 399–412.

Schofield, J. (ed.) (1990) *Interpreting artefact scatters: contributions to ploughzone archaeology*, Oxford: Oxbow Books.

Schofield, J. (2008) 'Heritage management, theory and practice', in Fairclough, G. *et al.* (eds) *The heritage reader*, London: Routledge: 15–30.

Schroeder, K.B. *et al.* (2009) 'Haplotypic background of a private allele at high frequency in the Americas', *Molecular Biology and Evolution* 26 (5): 995–1016.

Schulting, R. and Richard, M. (2002) 'Dogs, ducks, deer and diet: new stable isotope evidence on early Mesolithic dogs from the Vale of Pickering, northeast England', *Journal of Archaeological Science* 25: 191–202.

Schulting, R. and Richard, M. (2009) 'Dogs, divers, deer and diet: stable isotope results from Star Carr and a response to Dark', *Journal of Archaeological Science* 36: 498–503.

Schurmans, U. and De Bie, M. (2007) *Fitting rocks: lithic refitting examined*, Oxford: British Archaeological Report 1596.

Schwarcz, H.P. (1997) 'Uranium series dating', in Taylor, R.E. and Aitken, M.J. *Chronometric dating in archaeology*, New York: Plenum Press: 159–82.

Schwartz, J.H. (1999) *Sudden origins: fossils, genes and the emergence of species*, Chichester: John Wiley.

Schweingrüber, F.H. (1987) *Tree rings: basics and applications of dendrochronology*, Dordrecht: Reidel.

Schweingrüber, F.H. (1993) *Trees and wood in dendrochronology: morphological, anatomical, and tree-ring analytical characteristics*, Berlin: Springer Verlag.

Sciama, L. and Eicher, J.B. (eds) (1998) *Beads and bead makers: gender, material culture and meaning*, Oxford: Berg.

Scollar, I. *et al.* (eds) (1990) *Archaeological prospecting and remote sensing*, Cambridge: Cambridge University Press.

Sease, C. (1992) *A conservation manual for the field archaeologist*, 2nd edn, Los Angeles, CA: UCLA Institute of Archaeology.

Selkirk, A. (1997) *Who owns the past? A grass roots critique of heritage policy*, London: Adam Smith Institute.

Service, E. (1971) *Primitive social organisation: an evolutionary perspective*, 2nd edn, New York: Random House.

Shackleton, J. and Elderfield, H. (1990) 'Strontium isotope dating of the source of Neolithic European Spondylus shell artefacts', *Antiquity* 64: 312–15.

Shackleton, N.J. (1973) 'Oxygen isotope analysis as a means of determining season of occupation of prehistoric midden sites', *Archaeometry* 15: 133–41.

Shackley, M.S. (ed.) (1998) *Archaeological obsidian studies: method and theory*, New York and London: Plenum Press, Advances in Archaeological and Museum Science 3.

Shanks, M. (1999) *Art and the early Greek state: an interpretative archaeology*, Cambridge: Cambridge University Press, New Studies in Archaeology.

Shanks, M. (2001) 'Culture/archaeology: the dispersion of a discipline and its subjects', in Hodder, I. (ed.) *Archaeological theory today*, Cambridge: Polity Press: 284–305.

Shanks, M. (2005) 'Theory of social practice', in Renfrew, C. and Bahn, P. (eds) *Archaeology: the key concepts*, London: Routledge: 240–2.

Shanks, M. and Tilley, C. (1987) *Social theory and archaeology*, Cambridge: Polity Press.

Shanks, M. and Tilley, C. (1992) *Re-constructing archaeology: theory and practice*, 2nd edn, London: Routledge.

Sharples, N.M. (1991) *Maiden Castle*, London: Batsford/English Heritage.

Shaw, I. and Jameson, R. (eds) (1999) *A dictionary of archaeology*, Oxford: Blackwell.

Shennan, I. and Donoghue, D. (1992) 'Remote sensing in archaeological research', in Pollard, A.M. (ed.) *New developments in archaeological science*, Oxford: Clarendon Press: 223–32.

Shennan, S. (1997) *Quantifying archaeology*, 2nd rev. edn, Edinburgh: Edinburgh University Press.

Shennan, S. (2004) 'Analytical archaeology', in Bintliff, J. (ed.) *A companion to archaeology*, Oxford: Blackwell: 3–20.

Sherratt, A. (1980) *The Cambridge encyclopedia of archaeology*, Cambridge: Cambridge University Press.

Sherratt, A. (1981) 'Plough and pastoralism: aspects of the secondary products revolution', in Hodder, I., Isaac, G. and Hammond, N. (eds) *Pattern of the past: studies in honour* of David Clarke, Cambridge: Cambridge University Press: 261–305.

Sherratt, A. (1997a) *Economy and society in prehistoric Europe: changing perspectives*, Edinburgh: Edinburgh University Press.

Sherratt, A. (1997b) 'Climatic cycles and behavioural revolutions: the emergence of modern humans and the beginning of farming', *Antiquity* 71: 271–87.

Sherratt, A. (1997c) 'Sacred and profane substances: the ritual use of narcotics in later neolithic Europe', in Sherratt, A., *Economy and society in prehistoric Europe: changing perspectives*, Edinburgh: Edinburgh University Press: 403–30.

Shimada, I. (1994) *Pampa Grande and the Mochica Culture*, Austin: University of Texas Press.

Shimada, I. (2005) 'Experimental archaeology', in Maschner, H.D.G. and Chippindale, C. (eds) *Handbook of archaeological methods, 2*, Lanham, MD: Altamira Press: 603–42.

Shipman, P. (2001) *The man who found the missing link: the extraordinary life of Eugene Dubois*, London: Weidenfeld and Nicolson.

Siliotti, A. (1998) *Egypt lost and found: explorers and travellers on the Nile*, London: Thames and Hudson.

Silverberg, R. (1997) *Great adventures in archaeology*, Lincoln: Nebraska University Press.

Sim, D. (1998) *Beyond the bloom*, Oxford: British Archaeological Reports, International Series S725.

Simon, R. (2002) *Ibn Khaldūn: history as science and the patrimonial empire*, translated by Klára Pogátsa, Budapest: Akadémiai Kiadó.

Simpson, M.G. (1996) *Making representations: museums in the post-colonial era*, London and New York: Routledge.

Sims-Williams, P. (1998) 'Genetics, linguistics, and prehistory: thinking big and thinking straight', *Antiquity* 72: 505–27.

Singer, R., Gladfelter, B.G. and Wymer, J.J. (1993) *The Lower Palaeolithic site at Hoxne, England*, Chicago, IL: Chicago University Press.

Skeates, R. (2000a) *Debating the archaeological heritage*, London: Duckworth.

Skeates, R. (2000b) *The collecting of origins: collectors and collections of Italian prehistory and the cultural transformation of value (1550–1999)*, Oxford: British Archaeological Reports, International Series S868.

Sklenár, K. (1983) *Archaeology in central Europe: the first 500 years*, Leicester: Leicester University Press.

Sloan, K. (2007) *A New World: England's first view of America*, Chapel Hill: University of North Carolina Press.

Slobodin, R. (1997) *Rivers*, Stroud: Sutton Publishing.

Smiles, S. (1994) *The image of antiquity: Ancient Britain and the Romantic imagination*, New Haven, CT: Yale University Press.

Smiles, S. and Moser, S. (2005) *Envisioning the past*, Oxford: Blackwell.

Smith, B.D. (1995) *The emergence of agriculture*, Oxford: W.H. Freeman.

Smith, C. (1997) *Late Stone Age hunters of the British Isles*, London: Routledge.

Smith, L. (2006) *Uses of heritage*, London: Routledge.

Smith, M.E. and Masson, M.A. (1999) *The ancient civilizations of Mesoamerica: a reader*, Oxford: Blackwell.

Smith, R.A. (1920) *A guide to the antiquities of the Bronze Age*, 2nd edn, London: British Museum.

Sofaer, J.R. (2006) *The body as material culture*, Cambridge: Cambridge University Press.

Sommer, J.D. (1999) 'The Shanidar "flower burial": a reevaluation of Neanderthal burial ritual', *Cambridge Archaeological Journal* 9: 127–9.

Souvatzi, S.G. (2008) *A social archaeology of households in Neolithic Greece: An anthropological approach*, Cambridge: Cambridge University Press, Studies in Archaeology.

Spencer, F. (1990) *Piltdown: a scientific forgery*, London: Natural History Museum.

Spindler, K. (1994) *The man in the ice*, London: Weidenfeld and Nicholson.

Spindler, K. *et al.* (eds) (1996) *Human mummies: a global survey of their status and the techniques of conservation*, The Man in the Ice, vol. 3, Vienna and New York: Springer-Verlag.

Spoerry, P. (ed.) (1992) *Geoprospection in the archaeological landscape*, Oxford: Oxbow Monograph 18.

Spoerry, P. and Cooper, S. (2000) *Ramsey Abbey: an archaeological survey*, Fulbourn: Cambridge County Council.

Stagl, J. (1995) *A history of curiosity: the theory of travel, 1550-1800*, Chur: Harwood Studies in Anthropology and History 13.

Stahl, P. (1996) 'The recovery and interpretation of microvertebrate bone assemblages from archaeological contexts', *Journal of Archaeological Method and Theory* 3: 31–75.

Starkey, D. *et al.* (2007) *Making history: antiquaries in Britain 1707-2007*, London: Royal Academy.

Stead, I.M. (1991) 'The Snettisham Treasure: excavations in 1990', *Antiquity* 65: 447–65.

Stead, I.M. (1998) *The Salisbury hoard*, Stroud: Tempus.

Stead, I.M. *et al.* (eds) (1986) *Lindow man: the body in the bog*, London: British Museum.

Stein, J.K. (ed.) (1992) *Deciphering a shell midden*, London: Academic Press.

Steinberg, J.M. (1996) 'Ploughzone sampling in Denmark: isolating and interpreting site signatures from disturbed contexts', *Antiquity* 70: 368–92.

Steiner, M. (2005) *Approaches to archaeological illustration: a handbook*, York: Council for British Archaeology.

Stephens, J.L. (1841) *Incidents of travel in Central America, Chiapas, and Yucatan*, 2 vols, New York: Harper and Brothers.

Stephens, J.L. (1843) *Incidents of travel in Yucatan*, 2 vols, London: John Murray.

Sternberg, R.S. (1997) 'Archaeomagnetic dating', in Taylor, R.E. and Aitken, M.J. *Chronometric dating in archaeology*, New York: Plenum Press: 323–56.

Sternberg, R.S. (2001) 'Magnetic properties and archaeomagnetism', in Brothwell, D.R. and Pollard, A.M. *Handbook of archaeological sciences*, Chichester: John Wiley and Sons: 73–9.

Steward, J. (1955) *Theory of culture change*, Urbana: University of Illinois Press.

Stiebing, W.H. (1993) *Uncovering the past*, Oxford: Oxford University Press.

Stiner, M.C. (1999) 'Palaeolithic mollusc exploitation at Riparo Mochi (Balzi Rossi, Italy): food and ornaments from the Aurignacian through Epigravettian', *Antiquity* 73: 735–54.

Stirland A.J. (2000) *Raising the dead: the skeletal crew of King Henry VIII's great ship, the 'Mary Rose'*, Chichester: John Wiley.

Stiros, S. and Jones, R.E. (1996) *Archaeoseismology*, Oxford: Oxbow, British School at Athens/Fitch Laboratory Occasional Paper 7.

Stocking, G.W. (1974) *A Franz Boas reader: the shaping of American anthropology, 1883-1911*, New York: Basic Books.

Stocking, G.W. (1987) *Victorian anthropology*, New York: Free Press.

Stoddart, S. (ed.) (2000) *Landscapes from antiquity*, Cambridge: Antiquity Papers 1.

Stone, L. and Lurquin, P. (2005) *A genetic and cultural odyssey*, New York: Columbia University Press.

Stone, P.G. (2008) 'Stonehenge – a final solution?', in Fairclough, G. *et al.* (eds) *The heritage reader*, London: Routledge: 524–35.

Stone, P.G. and Bajjaly, J.F. (eds) (2008) *The destruction of cultural heritage in Iraq*, Woodbridge: Boydell Press.

Stone, P.G. and Planel, P. (eds) (1999) *The constructed past: experimental archaeology, education and the public*, London: Routledge, One World Archaeology 36.

Stoneham, D. (1991) 'Authenticity testing', in Göksu, H.Y., Oberhofer, M. and Regulla, D. (eds) *Scientific dating methods*, Dordrecht: Kluwer Academic Publishers: 175–92.

Stos-Gale, Z.A. (1995) 'Isotope archaeology – a review', in Beavis, J. and Barker, K. (eds) *Science and site*, Bournemouth: Bournemouth University Conservation Sciences Department: 12–28.

Stove, G.C. and Addyman, P.V. (1989) 'Ground probing impulse radar: an experiment in archaeological remote sensing at York', *Antiquity* 63: 337–42.

Stringer, C. (2002) 'Modern human origins: progress and prospects', *Philosophical Transactions of the Royal Society* 357: 563–79.

Stringer, C. (2006) *Homo britannicus*, London: Allen Lane.

Stringer, C. and McKie, R. (1998) *African exodus*, London: Jonathan Cape.

Stuart, J. and Revett, N. (1787) *The antiquities of Athens*, 2, London: J. Haberkorn.

Stuart, J. and Revett, N. (1794) *The antiquities of Athens*, 3, London: J. Haberkorn.

Stuiver, M. and Van Der Plicht, J. (eds) (1998) *INTCAL 98: calibration issue, Radiocarbon* 40 (3).

Sullivan, A. (2004) 'Reconstructing relationships among mortality, status, and gender at the Medieval Gilbertine Priory of St. Andrew, Fishergate, York', *American Journal of Physical Anthropology* 124: 330–45.

Sullivan, A.P. (1998) *Surface archaeology*, Albuquerque: University of New Mexico Press.

Sutton, M. and Arkush, B. (1996) *Archaeological laboratory methods: an introduction*, Dubuque, IA: Kendall Hunt.

Swallow, P. and Watt, D. (1996) *Surveying historic buildings*, Shaftesbury: Donhead Publishing.

Sweet, R. (2004) *Antiquaries: the discovery of the past in eighteenth-century Britain*, London: Hambledon & London.

Swiddler, N. *et al.* (eds) (1997) *Native Americans and archaeologists: stepping stones to common ground*, Walnut Creek, CA/London: Altamira, for American Archaeology Society/Sage.

Sykes, B. (2002) *The seven daughters of Eve*, London: Corgi.

Sykes, N. (2007) *The Norman conquest: a zooarchaeological perspective*, Oxford: British Archaeological Report, International Series 1656.

Tabor, R. (2008) *Cadbury Castle: the hillfort and landscapes*, Stroud: Tempus.

Tainter, J.A. (2004) 'Persistent dilemmas in American cultural resource management', in Bintliff, J. (ed.) *A companion to archaeology*, Oxford: Blackwell: 435–53.

Tarling, D.H. (1991) 'Archaeomagnetism and palaeomagnetism', in Göksu, H.Y., Oberhofer, M. and Regulla, D. (eds) *Scientific dating methods*, Dordrecht: Kluwer Academic Publishers: 217–50.

Tayles, N.G. (1999) *The excavation of Khok Phanom Di: a prehistoric site in Central Thailand, 5: the people*, London: Society of Antiquaries of London.

Taylor, C. (1974) *Fieldwork in medieval archaeology*, London: Batsford.

Taylor, C. (2000) 'Medieval ornamental landscapes', *Landscapes* 1: 38–55.

Taylor, J.H. (1995) *Unwrapping a mummy*, London: British Museum Press, Egyptian Bookshelf.

Taylor, R.E. (1987) *Radiocarbon dating: an archaeological perspective*, London: Academic Press.

Taylor, R.E. (1991) 'Radioisotope dating by Accelerator Mass Spectrometry: archaeological and paleoanthropological perspectives', in Göksu, H.Y., Oberhofer, M. and Regulla, D. (eds) *Scientific dating methods*, Dordrecht: Kluwer Academic Publishers: 37–54.

Taylor, R.E. (1997) 'Radiocarbon dating', in Taylor, R.E. and Aitken, M.J. *Chronometric dating in archaeology*, New York: Plenum Press: 65–96.

Taylor, R.E. (2001) 'Radiocarbon dating', in Brothwell, D.R. and Pollard, A.M. *Handbook of archaeological sciences*, Chichester: John Wiley and Sons: 23–34.

Taylor, R.E. and Aitken, M.J. (eds) (1997) *Chronometric dating in archaeology*, New York: Plenum Press, Advances in Archaeological and Museum Science.

Taylor, R.E., Long, A. and Kra, R.S. (eds) (1992) *Radiocarbon after four decades: an interdisciplinary perspective*, California Conference, 1990, Berlin: Springer Verlag.

Taylor, T. (1998) *Behind the scenes at the Time Team*, London: Macmillan.

Taylor, T. (2008) 'Materiality', in Bentley, R.A., Maschner, H. and Chippindale, C. (eds) *Handbook of archaeological theories*, Lanham, MD: Altamira Press: 297–320.

Taylor, V. and Winquist, C.E. (2001) *Encyclopedia of postmodernism*, London: Routledge.

Taylor, W. (1948) *A study of archaeology: memoir*, Menasha, WI: American Anthropological Association.

Theuws, F. and Roymans, N. (eds) (1999) *Land and ancestors: cultural dynamic in the urnfield period and the middle ages in the southern Netherlands*, Amsterdam: Amsterdam University Press.

Thody, P. and Course, A. (1997) *Barthes for beginners*, Cambridge: Icon Books.

Thomas, H. (1995) *The first humans: the search for our origins*, London: Thames and Hudson, New Horizons.

Thomas, J. (1996) *Time, culture and identity: an interpretive archaeology*, London: Routledge, Material Cultures.

Thomas, J. (1999) *Understanding the Neolithic.* London: Routledge.

Thomas, J. (ed.) (2000) *Interpretive archaeology: a reader*, Leicester: Leicester University Press.

Thomas, J. (2001) 'Archaeologies of place and landscape', in Hodder, I. (ed.) *Archaeological theory today*, Cambridge: Polity Press: 165–86.

Thomas, J. (2004) *Archaeology and modernity.* London: Routledge.

Thomas, J. and Tilley, C. (and reply by Bintliff, J.) (1992) 'TAG and "post-modernism": a reply to John Bintliff', *Antiquity* 66: 106–14.

Thomas, K.D. and Mannino, M.A. (2001) 'The exploitation of invertebrates and invertebrate products', in Brothwell, D.R. and Pollard, A.M. *Handbook of archaeological sciences*, Chichester: John Wiley and Sons: 427–40.

Thomas, R. (2000) *Herodotus in context: ethnography, science and the art of persuasion*, Cambridge: Cambridge University Press.

Thomas, S. and Stone, P.G. (eds) (2009) *Metal detecting and archaeology*, London: Boydell.

Thompson, M. (2006) *Ruins reused: changing attitudes to ruins since the late eighteenth century*, King's Lynn: Heritage Marketing and Publication.

Thompson, R. (2006) 'Documenting the presence of maize in central and south America through phytolith analysis of food residues', in Zeder, M. *et al.* (eds) *Documenting domestication: new genetic and archaeological paradigms*, Berkeley: University of California Press: 82–98.

Thompson, S.J. (1988) *Chronology of geological thinking from antiquity to 1899*, London: Scarecrow Press.

Thorpe, I.N.J. (2003) Anthropology, archaeology and origins of warfare, *World Archaeology* 35 (1): 145–65.

Tilley, C. (1984) 'Ideology and the legitimation of power in the middle Neolithic of Sweden', in Miller, D. and Tilley, C. (eds) *Ideology, power and prehistory*, Cambridge: Cambridge University Press: 111–46.

Tilley, C. (1990) *Reading material culture: structuralism, hermeneutics and post-structuralism*, Oxford: Basil Blackwell.

Tilley, C. (ed.) (1993) *Interpretative archaeology*, Oxford: Berg.

Tilley, C. (1994) *A phenomenology of landscape: places, paths and monuments*, Oxford: Berg.

Tilley, C. (1999) *Metaphor and material culture*, Oxford: Blackwell.

Tilley, C. (2004) *The materiality of stone: explorations in landscape phenomenology*, Oxford: Berg.

Tilley, C. (2008) 'Excavation as theatre', in Fairclough, G. *et al.* (eds) *The heritage reader*, London: Routledge: 75–81.

Tipper, J. (2004) *The Grubenhäus in Anglo-Saxon England: an analysis and interpretation of the evidence from a distinctive building type*, Yedingham: Landscape Research Centre.

Tishkoff, S. *et al.* (2009) 'The genetic structure and history of Africans and African Americans', *Science* 324 (5930): 1035–44.

Tite, M.S. (1991) 'Archaeological science – past achievements and future prospects', *Archaeometry* 32: 139–51.

Tite, M.S. (1992) 'The impact of electron microscopy on ceramic studies', in Pollard, A.M. (ed.) *New developments in archaeological science*, Oxford: Clarendon: 111–31.

Tite, M.S. (1996) 'In defence of lead isotope analysis', *Antiquity* 70: 959–62.

Tite, M.S. (2001) 'Overview – materials study in archaeology', in Brothwell, D.R. and Pollard, A.M. *Handbook of archaeological sciences*, Chichester: John Wiley and Sons: 443–8.

Tomber, R. (2008) *Indo-Roman trade: from pots to people*, London: Duckworth.

Tomber, R. and Dore, J. (1998) *The National Roman Fabric Reference Collection: a handbook* London: MoLAS Monograph.

Torrence, R. (1986) *Production and exchange of stone tools: prehistoric obsidian in the Aegean*, Cambridge: Cambridge University Press.

Traill, D.A. (1995) *Schliemann of Troy: treasure and deceit*, London: John Murray.

Trigger, B.G. (1980) *Gordon Childe: revolutions in archaeology*, London: Thames and Hudson.

Trigger, B.G. (1992) 'Daniel Wilson and the Scottish Enlightenment', *Proceedings of the Society of Antiquaries of Scotland* 122: 55–75.

Trigger, B.G. (1995) 'Romanticism, nationalism, and archaeology', in Kohl, P.L. and Fawcett, C. (eds) *Nationalism, politics and the practice of archaeology*, Cambridge: Cambridge University Press: 263–79.

Trigger, B.G. (1998) *Sociocultural evolution: calculation and contingency*, Oxford: Blackwell.

Trigger, B.G. (2006) *A history of archaeological thought*, 2nd edn, Cambridge: Cambridge University Press.

Truncer, J. (2003) (ed.) *Picking the lock of time: developing chronology in American archaeology*, Gainesville: University of Florida Press.

Tubb, K.W. (ed.) (1995) *Antiquities trade or betrayed: legal, ethical and conservation issues*, London: Archetype Publications/ United Kingdom Institute for Conservation Archaeology Section.

Tung, T.A. (2007) 'Trauma and violence in the Wari empire of the Peruvian Andes: warfare, raids, and ritual fights', *American Journal of Physical Anthropology* 133: 941–56.

Tuniz, C. *et al.* (1998) *Accelerator mass spectrometry: ultrasensitive analysis for global science*, Boca Raton, FL: CRC Press Report S737.

Turnbaugh, W.A., *et al.* (2002) *Understanding physical anthropology and archaeology*, 8th edn, Belmont, CA: West/Wadsworth Publishing.

Turner, B.L. *et al.* (2009) 'Insights into immigration and social class at Machu Picchu, Peru based on oxygen, strontium, and lead isotopic analysis', *Journal of Archaeological Science* 36: 317–32.

Turner, R.C. and Scaife, R.G. (eds) (1995) *Bog bodies: new discoveries and new perspectives*, London: British Museum Press.

Turner, S. (2006) 'Historic landscape characterisation: a landscape archaeology for research, management and planning', *Landscape Research* 31 (4): 385–98.

Turner, S. and Crow, J. (2010) 'Unlocking historic landscapes in the Eastern Mediterranean: two pilot studies using Historic Landscape Characterisation', *Antiquity* 84: 216–29.

Tylden-Wright, D. (1991) *John Aubrey: a life*, London: HarperCollins.

Tylecote, R.F. and Gilmour, B.J.J. (1986) *The metallography of early ferrous edge tools and edged weapons*, Oxford: British Archaeological Reports 155.

Tylor, E.B. (1871) *Primitive culture*, London: John Murray.

Tylor, E.B. (1888) 'On a method of investigating the development of institutions, applied to laws of marriage and descent', *Journal of the Anthropological Institute* 8: 245–72.

Ubelaker, D. (1996) *Human skeletal remains: excavation, analysis, interpretation*, 2nd edn, Washington, DC: Taraxacum.

Ucko, P.J., Hunter, M. and Clark, A. (1990) *Avebury reconsidered: from the 1660s to the 1990s*, London: Unwin Hyman/Institute of Archaeology.

Underwood, R. (1999) *Anglo-Saxon weapons and warfare*, Stroud: Tempus.

Uzzell, D. and Ballantyne, R. (eds) (1998) *Contemporary issues in heritage and environmental interpretation*, London: HMSO.

Van Binsbergen, W.M.J. (ed.) (1996–7) *Black Athena: ten years after*, Hoofddorp: Dutch Archaeological and Historical Society, *Talanta* 28–9, special issue.

Van den Dries, M.H. (1998) *Archaeology and the application of artificial intelligence: case-studies on use-wear analysis of prehistoric flint tools*, Leiden: Leiden University Archaeological Studies 1.

Van der Dussen, J. (ed.) (1993) *R.G. Collingwood: the idea of history: revised edition with lectures 1926–1928*, Oxford: Clarendon.

Van der Merwe, N.J. (1992) 'Light stable isotopes and the reconstruction of prehistoric diets', in Pollard, A.M. (ed.) *New developments in archaeological science*, Oxford: Clarendon: 247–64.

Van de Noort, R. (2004) *The Humber wetlands: the archaeology of a dynamic landscape*, Bollington: Windgather Press.

Van de Noort, R. and O'Sullivan, A. (2006) *Rethinking wetland archaeology*, London: Duckworth.

Van der Veen, M. (1992) *Crop husbandry regimes: an archaeobotanical study of farming in northern England 1000 BC–AD 500*, Sheffield: Collis, Sheffield Archaeological Monograph 3.

Van der Veen, M. (ed.) (1999) *Exploitation of plant resources in ancient Africa*, Dordrecht: Kluwer/Plenum.

Van Leusen, M. (2001) 'Archaeological data integration', in Brothwell, D.R. and Pollard, A.M. *Handbook of archaeological sciences*, Chichester: John Wiley and Sons: 575–83.

Van Riper, A.B. (1993) *Men among the mammoths: Victorian science and the discovery of human prehistory*, Chicago, IL: Chicago University Press.

Van West, C.R. (1994) *Modelling prehistoric agricultural productivity in Southwestern Colorado: a GIS approach*, Pullman, WA: Department of Anthropology, Washington State University; Cortez, CO: Crow Canyon Archaeological Center, Reports of Investigations 67.

Van Zeist, W. *et al.* (eds) (1991) *Progress in Old World palaeoethnobotany: a retrospective*, Rotterdam: Balkema.

Vartavan, C. de (1999) *Hidden fields of Tutankhamun: from identification to interpretation of newly discovered plant material from the Pharaoh's grave*, London: Triade Exploration.

Vaughan, S.J. and Coulson, W.D.E. (eds) (1999) *Palaeodiet in the Aegean*, Oxford: Oxbow Books/Wiener Laboratory Monograph.

Vercoutter, J. (1992) *The search for ancient Egypt*, London: Thames and Hudson New Horizons.

Vigne, J.-D., Peters, J. and Helmer, D. (2005) *First steps of animal domestication: new archaeozoological approaches. Proceedings of the 9th ICAZ, Durham, 2002*, Oxford: Oxbow Books.

Von den Driesch, A. (1995) *Guide to the measurement of animal bones from archaeological sites*, 4th rev. reprint, Cambridge, MA: Harvard University Press.

Vrba, E. *et al.* (eds) (1995) *Paleoclimate and evolution, with emphasis on human origins*, New Haven, CT: Yale University Press.

Vuorela, I. (ed.) (1994) *Scientific methods in underwater archaeology*, PACT 47; Rixensart: UNESCO/Council of Europe.

Vyner, B.E. (ed.) (1994) *Building on the past: papers celebrating 150 years of the Royal Archaeological Institute*, London: Royal Archaeological Institute.

Waddington, C. (1999) *A landscape archaeological study of the Mesolithic–Neolithic in the Milfield Basin, Northumberland*, Oxford: British Archaeological Reports 290.

Waddington, C. (2004) *The joy of flint: an introduction to stone tools and guide to the Museum of Antiquities collections*, Newcastle upon Tyne: Museum of Antiquities, University of Newcastle.

Wainwright, G.J. (1989) 'Saving the Rose', *Antiquity* 63: 430–5.

Wainwright, G.J. (1990) *The henge monuments*, London: Thames and Hudson.

Wainwright, G.J. (1996) 'Stonehenge saved?', *Antiquity* 70: 9–12.

Wainwright, G.J. (2000) 'The Stonehenge we deserve', *Antiquity* 74: 334–42.

Waldron, T. (1994) *Counting the dead: the epidemiology of skeletal populations*, Chichester: John Wiley and Sons.

Waldron, T. (2001) *Shadows in the soil: human bones and archaeology*, Stroud: Tempus.

Walker, D.R. (1976–8) *The metrology of the Roman silver coinage I–III*, Oxford: British Archaeological Reports, International Series S5, S22 and S40.

Walker, J.W. and De Vore, S.L. (1995) *Low altitude large-scale reconnaissance: the method of obtaining high resolution vertical photographs for small areas*, rev. edn, Denver, CO: National Park Service.

Walker, K. (1990) *Guidelines for the preparation of excavation archives for long-term storage*, United Kingdom Institute for Conservation: Archaeology Section.

Wallace, J. (2004) *Digging the dirt: the archaeological imagination*, London: Duckworth.

Wallace-Hadrill, A. (2001) *The British School in Rome: one hundred years*, London: British Academy.

Walsh, K. (1991) 'The post-modern threat to the past', in Bapty, I. and Yates, I. *Archaeology after structuralism: post-structuralism and the practice of archaeology*, London: Routledge: 278–93.

Walsh, K. (1992) *The representation of the past: museums and heritage in the post-modern world*, London: Routledge.

Walter, R.C. (1997) 'Potassium–argon/argon–argon dating methods', in Taylor, R.E. and Aitken, M.J. *Chronometric dating in archaeology*, New York: Plenum Press: 97–126.

Wardell, J. (2005) *Foundation myths: the beginning of Irish archaeology*, Bray: Wordwell.

Wardle, K. (ed.) (1996) *Nea Nikomedeia I: the excavation of an early Neolithic village in northern Greece 1961–1964: the excavation and ceramic assemblage*, London: British School at Athens, Supplement Vol. 25.

Waterbolk, H.T. (1971) 'Working with radiocarbon dates', *Proceedings of the Prehistoric Society* 37: 15–33.

Waters, M.R. (1992) *Principles of geoarchaeology: a North American perspective*, Tucson, AZ: Arizona University Press.

Watkinson, D. and Neal, V. (1998) *First aid for finds*, new edn, Hertford, CT: Rescue.

Watson, A. and Keating, D. (1999) 'Architecture and sound: an acoustic analysis of megalithic monuments in prehistoric Britain', *Antiquity* 73: 325–36.

Watson, R.A. (1991) 'What the new archaeology has achieved', *Current Anthropology* 32: 275–91.

Weale, M. *et al.* (2002) 'Y chromosome evidence for Anglo-Saxon mass migration', *Molecular Biology and Evolution* 19: 1008–21.

Webster, C. (2008) *The archaeology of South West England: South West Archaeological Research Framework: resource assessment and Research Agenda*, Taunton: Somerset County Council.

Webster, J. (2001) 'Creolizing the Roman provinces', *American Journal of Archaeology* 105: 209–25.

Webster, J. and Cooper, N. (eds) (1996) *Roman imperialism: post-colonial perspectives*, Leicester: School of Archaeological Studies, University of Leicester Monograph 3.

Weiss, R. (1988) *The Renaissance discovery of classical antiquity*, Oxford: Blackwell.

Welfare, H.G. (1989) 'John Aubrey: the first archaeological surveyor?', in Bowden, M., Mackay, D. and Topping, P. (eds) *From Cornwall to Caithness: some aspects of British field archaeology*, Oxford: British Archaeological Reports 209: 17–28.

Welsh, F. (1988) *Building the trireme*, London: Constable.

West, S.E. (1985) *West Stow; the Anglo-Saxon village*, 2 vols, Norwich: University of East Anglia, East Anglian Archaeology Report 24.

Westcott, K. and Brandon, R. (eds) (1999) *Practical applications of GIS in archaeology: a predictive modelling tool kit*, London: Taylor and Francis, GISDATA.

Westgate, J., Sandhu, A. and Shane, P. (1997) 'Fission-track dating', in Taylor, R.E. and Aitken, M.J. *Chronometric dating in archaeology*, New York: Plenum Press: 127–58.

Westman, A. (ed.) (1994) *MoLAS archaeological site manual*, 3rd edn, London: Museum of London.

Wheatley, D.W. and Gillings, M. (2000) 'Vision, perception and GIS: developing enriched approaches to the study of archaeological visibility', in Lock, G. (ed.) *Beyond the map: archaeology and spatial technologies*, Amsterdam: IOS Press: 1–27.

Wheatley, D.W. and Gillings, M. (2002) *Spatial technology and archaeology: a guide to the archaeological applications of GIS*, London: Taylor and Francis.

Wheatley, G. (1997) *World heritage sites*, London: English Heritage.

Wheeler, A. and Jones, A. (1989) *Fishes*, Cambridge: Cambridge University Press, Cambridge Manuals in Archaeology.

Wheeler, R.E.M. (1923) *Segontium and the Roman occupation of Wales*, London: Honourable Society of Cymmrodorion.

Wheeler, R.E.M. (1954a) *Archaeology from the earth*, Harmondsworth: Penguin.

Wheeler, R.E.M. (1954b) *The Stanwick fortifications*, Oxford: Report of Research Committee of Society of Antiquaries of London 17.

Wheeler, R.E.M. and Wheeler, T.V. (1936) *Verulamium: a Belgic and two Roman cities,*

Oxford: Research Report of the Society of Antiquaries of London 11.

Whimster, R. (1989) *The emerging past: air photography and the buried landscape*, London: RCHME.

Whitbread, I.K. (1995) *Greek transport amphorae*, Athens: British School at Athens, Fitch Laboratory Occasional Paper 4.

Whitbread, I.K. (2001) 'Ceramic petrology, clay geochemistry and ceramic production – from technology to the mind of the potter', in Brothwell, D.R. and Pollard, A.M. *Handbook of archaeological sciences*, Chichester: John Wiley and Sons: 449–59.

White, L. (1959*) The evolution of culture*, New York: McGraw-Hill.

White, R. and Barker, P. (1998) *Wroxeter: life and death of a Roman city*, Stroud: Tempus.

Whitehouse, R. (1997) *The first cities*, Oxford: Phaidon.

Whitley, D. (ed.) (1998) *Reader in archaeological theory: post-processual and cognitive approaches*, London: Routledge.

Whittaker, J.C. (1994) *Flintknapping: making and understanding stone tools*, Austin: University of Texas Press.

Whittington, S.L. (ed.) (1997) *Bones of the Maya*, Washington, DC: Smithsonian Institution Press.

Whittle, A. (1997) *Sacred mound, holy rings: Silbury Hill and the West Kennet palisade enclosures: a later Neolithic complex in north Wiltshire*, Oxford: Oxbow Monograph 73.

Whittle, A., Pollard, J. and Grigson, C. (1999) *The harmony of symbols: the Windmill Hill causewayed enclosure, Wiltshire*, Oxford: Oxbow Books.

Wiber, M.G. (1997) *Erect men, undulating women: the visual imagery of gender, race and 'progress' in reconstructive illustrations of human evolution*, Waterloo, Ontario: Wilfrid Laurier University Press.

Wilkinson, C. (2004) *Forensic facial reconstruction*, Cambridge: Cambridge University Press.

Wilkinson, K. and Stevens, C. (2005) *Environmental archaeology: approaches, techniques and applications*, Stroud: Tempus.

Wilkinson, T.J. (2001) 'Surface collection techniques in field archaeology: theory and practice', in Brothwell, D.R. and Pollard, A.M. *Handbook of archaeological sciences*, Chichester: John Wiley and Sons: 529–41.

Wilkinson, T.J. (2003) *Archaeological landscapes of the Near East*, Tucson: University of Arizona Press.

Willems, W.J.H. (2007) 'The work of making Malta: the council of Europe's archaeology and planning committee 1988–1996', *European Journal of Archaeology* 10 (1): 57–71.

Willems, W.J.H., Kars, H. and Hallewas, D.P. (eds) (1997) *Archaeological heritage management in the Netherlands: fifty years of state service for archaeological investigations*, Amersfoort: ROB.

Willey, G. (1953) *Prehistoric settlement patterns in the Virù Valley, Peru*, Washington, DC: US Government Printing Office, United States Bureau of American Ethnology 155.

Willey, G. and Philips, P. (1958) *Method and theory in American archaeology*, Chicago, IL: University of Chicago Press.

Willey, G.R. and Sabloff, J.A. (1980) *A history of American archaeology*, 2nd edn, San Francisco, CA: Freeman.

Willey, P. (1992) *Prehistoric warfare on the Great Plains: skeletal analysis of the Crow Creek massacre victims*, Hamden, CT: Garland.

Williams, H. (2006) 'Digging Saxon graves in Victorian Britain', in Pearson, R. (ed.) *The Victorians and the ancient world: archaeology and classicism in nineteenth-century culture*, Cambridge: Cambridge Scholar Press: 61–80.

Williams, J. (2008) 'Indigenous voices, archaeology, and the issue of repatriation', in Cunliffe, B., Gosden, C. and Joyce, R. (eds) *The Oxford handbook of archaeology*, Oxford: Oxford University Press: 1001–28.

Williams, S. (1991) *Fantastic archaeology: the wild side of North American prehistory*, Washington, DC: Smithsonian Institute Press.

Williamson, R.A. and Nickens, P.R. (eds) (2000) *Science and technology in historic preservation*, Dordrecht: Kluwer Academic, Advances in Archaeological and Museum Science 4.

Williamson, T. (1998) 'Questions of preservation and destruction', in Everson, P. and Williamson, T. (eds) *The archaeology of landscape: studies presented to Christopher Taylor*, Manchester: Manchester University Press: 1–24.

Willoughby, P.R. (2007) *The evolution of modern humans in Africa: a comprehensive guide*, Lanham, MD: Altamira.

Wilmott, T. (1997) *Birdoswald: excavations of a Roman fort on Hadrian's Wall and its successor settlements*, London: English Heritage Archaeological Report 14.

Wilson, B. (1996) *Spatial patterning among animal bones in settlement archaeology*, Oxford: British Archaeological Reports 251.

Wilson, B. *et al.* (eds) (1982) *Ageing and sexing animal bones from archaeological sites*, Oxford: British Archaeological Reports 109.

Wilson, D. (1873) *Caliban: the missing link*, London: Macmillan.

Wilson, D.M. (2002) *The British Museum: a history*, London: British Museum Press.

Wilson, D.R. (ed.) (1975) *Aerial reconnaissance for archaeology*, London: Council of British Archaeology Research Report 12.

Wilson, D.R. (2000) *Air photo interpretation for archaeologists*, revised reprint, Stroud: Tempus.

Wilson, E.J. (1996) *Encyclopedia of the Enlightenment* (ed. Reill, P.H.), New York: Facts on File.

Wilson, J. (1997) 'The great globe itself: Sam Wanamaker's "Shakespeare's Globe"', *Antiquity* 71: 744–50.

Wilson, L. and Pollard, A.M. (2001) 'The provenance hypothesis', in Brothwell, D.R. and Pollard, A.M. *Handbook of archaeological sciences*, Chichester: John Wiley and Sons: 507–17.

Wilson, L.G. (1972) *Charles Lyell: the years to 1841: the revolution in geology*, New Haven, CT, and London: Yale University Press.

Wilson, R.C.L., Drury, S.A. and Chapman, J.L. (2000) *The great Ice Age: climate change and life*, London: Routledge.

Wimmer, R. and Vetter, R.E. (eds) (1999) *Tree ring analysis: biological, methodological and environmental aspects*, Oxford: CABI Publishing/Oxford University Press.

Winstone, H.V.F. (1990) *Woolley of Ur*, London: Secker and Warburg.

Winstone, H.V.F. (1991) *Howard Carter and the discovery of the tomb of Tutankhamun*, London: Constable.

Wintle, A.G. (2008) 'Fifty years of luminescence dating', *Archaeometry* 50 (2): 276–312.

Wisseman, S. and Williams, W. (eds) (1994) *Ancient technologies and archaeological materials*, Langhorne, PA: Gordon and Breach.

Withey, L. (1997) *Grand tours and Cook's Tours: a history of leisure travel, 1750 to 1915*, Somers Point, NJ: William Morrow.

Wolfram, S. (1986) *Zur Theoriediskussion in der prähistorischen Archäologie Grossbritanniens: ein Forschungsgeschichte*, Oxford: British Archaeological Reports, International Series S306.

Wolpoff, M.H. (2005) 'Multiregional evolution', in Renfrew, C. and Bahn, P. (eds) *Archaeology: the key concepts*, London: Routledge: 176–81.

Wood, J. (ed.) (1994) *Buildings archaeology: applications in practice*, Oxford: Oxbow Monograph 43.

Woodside, R. and Crow, J. (1999) *Hadrian's Wall: an historic landscape*, London: National Trust.

Woodward, A. and Leach, P. (1991) *The Uley shrines: excavation of a ritual complex on West Hill, Uley, Gloucestershire, 1977–9*, London: English Heritage Archaeological Report 17.

Woolf, D.R. (1992) 'The dawn of the artifact: the antiquarian impulse in England, 1500–1730', *Studies in Medievalism* 4: 5–35.

Worrell, S. (2007) 'Detecting the later Iron Age: a view from the portable antiquities scheme', in Haselgrove, C. and Moore, T. (eds) *The later Iron Age in Britain and beyond*. Oxford: Oxbow: 371–88.

Worthington, A. (2005) *The battle of the beanfield*, Teignmouth: Enabler Publications.

Wright, G.H.R. (2000) *Ancient building technology, 1, historical background*, Leiden: E.J. Brill.

Wright, G.H.R. (2005) *Ancient building technology, 2, materials*, Leiden: E.J. Brill.

Wright, H.E. Jr *et al.* (1993) *Global climates since the last glacial maximum*, Minneapolis: University of Minnesota Press.

Yalden, D.W. (1999) *History of British mammals*, London: Academic Press.

Yegingil, Z. (1991) 'Fission track dating and its application', in Göksu, H.Y., Oberhofer, M. and Regulla, D. (eds) *Scientific dating methods*, Dordrecht: Kluwer Academic Publishers: 77–96.

Yentsch, A.E. (1994) *A Chesapeake family and their slaves: a study in historical archaeology*, Cambridge: Cambridge University Press.

Yentsch, A.E. and Beaudry, M.C. (2001) 'American material culture in mind, thought, and deed', in Hodder, I. (ed.) *Archaeological theory today*, Cambridge: Polity Press: 214–40.

Yeomans, D.T. (ed.) (1999) *The development of timber as a structural material*, Guildford: Ashgate.

Yntema, D.G. (1992) *In search of ancient countryside: the Amsterdam Free University Survey at Oria, province of Brindisi, South Italy (1981–1983)*, Amsterdam: Thesis Publishers, Scrinium 6.

Yoffee, N. and Sherratt, A. (eds) (1993) *Archaeological theory: who sets the agenda?*, Cambridge: Cambridge University Press, New Directions in Archaeology.

Young, D. (1992) *The discovery of evolution*, Cambridge: Cambridge University Press/ Natural History Museum Publications.

Young, S.M.M. *et al.* (eds) (1999) *Metals in antiquity*, Oxford: British Archaeological Reports, International Series S792.

Zeder, M. *et al.* (2006a) *Documenting domestication: new genetic and archaeological paradigms*, Berkeley: University of California.

Zeder, M. *et al.* (2006b) 'Documenting domestication: the intersection of genetics and archaeology', *Trends in Genetics* 22 (3): 139–55.

Zeuner, F.E. (1946, 1952) *Dating the past: an introduction to geochronology*, London: Methuen.

Zheng, J.Y. and Zhang, Z.L. (1999) 'Virtual recovery of excavated relics', *IEEE Computer Graphics and Applications* 19: 6–11.

Zickgraf, B. (1999) *Geomagnetische und geoelektrische Prospektion in der Archäologie: Systematik – Geschichte – Anwendung*, Rahden, Westfalia: Verlag Marie-Leidorf GmbH.

Zimmerman, L.J. (1989) 'Made radical by my own: an archaeologist learns to accept reburial', in Layton, R. *Conflict in the archaeology of living traditions*, London: Unwin Hyman, One World Archaeology 8: 60–7.

Zimmerman, L.J., Vitelli, K.D. and Hollowell-Zimmer, J. (eds) (2003) *Ethical issues in archaeology*, Walnut Creek, CA: Altamira Press.

Zohary, D. and Hopf, M. (1993) *Domestication of plants in the Old World: the origin and spread of cultivated plants in West Asia, Europe and the Nile Valley*, Oxford: Clarendon Press.

INDEX

Important terms that are also included in the glossary (pp. 313–21) are preceded by an asterisk (for example '* anthropology').

9/11 278

Aborigines, Australian 34, 286
* absolute dating *see* dating
Abu Hureyra, Syria 199, 211, 217, 290
* accelerator mass spectrometry (AMS) *see* radiocarbon dating
Acheulian stone tools 30, 272
* aerial archaeology 63–71; multispectral, radar, thermal 68–9; *see also* LiDAR
aerial photography 16, 61–71, 83, 87, 109–10; cropmarks 52, 64–7, 71, 109; shadow sites 64–8; soilmarks 67–8, 71
Africa: early prehistoric finds 27, 32, 113, 161, 176–8, 181, 183, 185, 193–4, 196, 215, 223–7, 270, 272, 289; ethnoarchaeology 22, 34, 268, 270, 287–8
agency 138, 252, 282–5, 291–2, 311; *see also* structuration
Agricola see Tacitus
agriculture, farming 32–4, 49, 53, 56, 65, 71, 79, 80, 82–4, 187, 198–211, 234, 242, 245–6, 257–8, 263–4, 275, 280–1; Agricultural (or Neolithic) Revolution 32, 46, 198; transition from hunting-gathering to farming 32–4, 43, 46, 114, 168, 187, 194, 198, 203, 210, 220, 290; *see also* animal husbandry, domestication, landnám
Akrotiri *see* Thera
Alchester, Oxfordshire 165

Alésia, France 261
alloys *see* metals
amateur archaeologists 43, 57, 105, 294, 310
America *see* civilisations
American Institute of Archaeology 28
Americans, Native 17–18, 118, 156, 216–7, 225, 257, 286; *see also* civilisations, American
amino acid racemization dating 183–4, 188, 210
* AMS (accelerator mass spectrometry) *see* radiocarbon dating
Amsterdam see ships
* anaerobic conditions *see* excavation
analysis *see* scientific analysis
* anatomically modern humans 27, 32, 43, 187, 194, 213, 272; *see also* Cro-Magnons
Anglo-Saxons 8, 222, 224, 262, 287
Anglo-Saxon archaeology 81, 114, 116–7, 128–31, 200, 208, 240, 285; *see also* Sutton Hoo
animals: extinct 7, 27–31, 46, 193, 259; animal husbandry 76, 207–9; *see also* domestication; apes, bones, camels, cattle, goats, horses, insects, oxen, pigs, sheep
Annales approach 282, 293
Anne Frank museum, Amsterdam 287
* anthropology 4–5, 8, 26, 31, 34, 44, 46, 53, 84, 191, 210, 233, 2418, 250–65; 267–70, 273, 275–7, 279–80, 282–3, 285–8, 291–2, 310–11; *see also* ethnoarchaeology, ethnography, social evolution, sociology
* antiquaries, antiquarianism 1, 5–20, 28, 35–7, 40, 44, 49–52, 116, 119, 125, 127, 251, 257, 267, 288, 310; chorography 13; *see also* Aubrey, Camden, Leland, Lhuyd, Society of Antiquaries, Stukeley